# DEVELOPING DEMOCRATIC
## HUMAN RELATIONS

Developing
# *Democratic Human Relations*

Through Health Education, Physical
Education and Recreation

FIRST YEARBOOK

AMERICAN ASSOCIATION FOR HEALTH,
PHYSICAL EDUCATION AND RECREATION

COPYRIGHT 1951

AMERICAN ASSOCIATION FOR HEALTH, PHYSICAL
EDUCATION AND RECREATION

A DEPARTMENT OF THE NATIONAL EDUCATION ASSOCIATION
OF THE UNITED STATES

1201 Sixteenth Street, Northwest
Washington 6, D. C.

Price $4.25

# Yearbook Planning Committee

First Yearbook of the
## AMERICAN ASSOCIATION FOR HEALTH, PHYSICAL EDUCATION AND RECREATION

*Editor and General Chairman:*

HILDA CLUTE KOZMAN, Formerly Oakland Public Schools, Oakland, California. Writer and Editor.

*Editorial Committee:*

RUTH ABERNATHY, University of California, Los Angeles, California

BEN MILLER, American Youth Hostels, New York, New York

DELBERT OBERTEUFFER, The Ohio State University, Columbus, Ohio

PATTRIC RUTH O'KEEFE, Kansas City Public Schools, Kansas City, Missouri

STERLING S. WINANS, Recreation Commission, Sacramento, California

*Planning Committee:*

CLIFFORD L. BROWNELL, Teachers College, Columbia University, New York, New York

ROSALIND CASSIDY, University of California, Los Angeles, California

ELWOOD C. DAVIS, University of Southern California, Los Angeles, California

MARTHA DEANE, University of California, Los Angeles, California

HARRY D. EDGREN, George Williams College, Chicago, Illinois

LESLIE W. IRWIN, Boston University, Boston, Massachusetts

RUTH EVANS, Public Schools, Springfield, Massachusetts

ESTHER FRENCH, Illinois State Normal University, Normal, Illinois

ELIZABETH HALSEY, University of Iowa, Iowa City, Iowa

HELEN HAZELTON, Purdue University, Lafayette, Indiana

VERNE S. LANDRETH, Department of Education, Sacramento, California

MABEL LEE, University of Nebraska, Lincoln, Nebraska

BEN MILLER, American Youth Hostels, New York, New York

CARL L. NORDLY, University of Minnesota, Minneapolis, Minnesota

[ v ]

DELBERT OBERTEUFFER, The Ohio State University, Columbus, Ohio

PATTRIC RUTH O'KEEFE, Kansas City Public Schools, Kansas City, Missouri

JACKSON SHARMAN, University of Alabama, University, Alabama

FRANK STAFFORD, Office of Education, Washington, D. C.

WILLIAM K. STREIT, Cincinnati Public Schools, Cincinnati, Ohio

CARL A. TROESTER, JR., American Association for Health, Physical Education and Recreation, Washington, D. C.

RUTH WEYTHMAN, Western Washington College of Education, Bellingham, Washington

JESSE FEIRING WILLIAMS, M.D., Emeritus Professor, Teachers College, Columbia University, New York, New York

CHARLES C. WILSON, M.D., Yale University, New Haven, Connecticut

# *Contents*

# *Introduction*

The mission of this yearbook is to turn the full attention of professional workers in the fields of health education, physical education and recreation to the problem of developing democratic human relations. The subject was selected by the Yearbook Planning Committees and approved by the Association's Board of Directors as being the most crucial task facing all educators and leaders of youth today. The thoughtful reader may well conclude that this volume is only an initial statement on the problem. Little is known about how to help children and youth in becoming democratic persons through experiences in the three related fields. This yearbook is, then, a way of pointing up the need for experimentation and research to find better ways to educate for democratic living.

One of the functions of an introduction is to orient the reader. This involves explaining the relationships of the chapters in the development of the subject. The diagram on the following page will serve to make clear how this volume is organized.

It will be noted from the diagram that in programs for developing democratic human relations at each age level there are chapters devoted to Concepts and Attitudes To Be Developed, Methods and Evaluation. The reader should anticipate that there will be repetition of points in these chapters. The repetition was not eliminated by the editors because of the desirability of making each section as complete a whole as the authors' materials permitted.

The reader should also anticipate that over forty writers will not think alike about the problem of developing democratic relations with others. Consistency of statement should not be demanded to the degree expected in the case of a single author or even with two or three collaborators.

## SCHEMATIC VIEW OF CHAPTERS IN THIS YEARBOOK

**BASIC POINT OF VIEW**

1. People in Today's World
2. Democratic Behavior
3. The Related Fields of Health Education, Physical Education and Recreation
4. Democratic Leadership

**PROGRAMS FOR CHILDREN**

5. The Child's World
6. Concepts and Attitudes to be Developed
7. Methods
8. Evaluation

**PROGRAMS FOR ADOLESCENTS**

9. The Adolescent's World
10. Concepts and Attitudes to be Developed
11. Methods
12. Evaluation

**PROGRAMS FOR OLDER YOUTH**

13. The Period of Later Adolescence
14. Concepts and Attitudes to be Developed
15. Methods
16. Evaluation

**PROGRAMS FOR ADULTS**

17. The Adult's World Today
18. Concepts and Attitudes to be Developed
19. Methods
20. Evaluation

# Basic Point of View

DELBERT OBERTEUFFER, *Coordinator*
*Professor of Physical Education*
*The Ohio State University*

## 1. PEOPLE IN TODAY'S WORLD

ETHEL J. ALPENFELS
*Associate Professor of Education*
*New York University*

HILDA CLUTE KOZMAN
*Teacher of Physical Education*
*Oakland Public Schools, 1918-1940*
*Oakland, California*
*Writer and Editor*

## 2. DEMOCRATIC BEHAVIOR

GORDON HEARN
*Assistant Professor of Social Welfare*
*University of California*
*Berkeley, California*

## 3. THE RELATED FIELDS OF HEALTH EDUCATION, PHYSICAL EDUCATION AND RECREATION

CHARLES C. WILSON, M.D.
*Professor of Education and Public Health*
*Yale University*

JESSE FEIRING WILLIAMS, M.D.
*Emeritus Professor of Physical Education*
*Columbia University*

GEORGE HJELTE
*General Manager, Department of Recreation and Parks*
*Los Angeles, California*

## 4. DEMOCRATIC LEADERSHIP

ROSALIND CASSIDY
*Professor of Physical Education*
*University of California*
*Los Angeles, California*

*The keynote of democracy as a way of life may be expressed, it seems to me, as the necessity for the participation of every human being in formation of values that regulate the living of men together; which is necessary from the standpoint of both the general social welfare and the full development of human beings as individuals.*—JOHN DEWEY, **Problems of Men**

## CHAPTER ONE

# *People in Today's World*

ETHEL J. ALPENFELS
HILDA CLUTE KOZMAN

T HE problem with which this yearbook is concerned is identical with the problem faced by people everywhere in the world today. Put in terms of this volume, the problem resolves itself into two parts: (a) What *are* democratic human relations? (b) *How* may they be developed? Phrased in terms of the world scene, the questions become: (a) What relationships must be developed among the nations of the world, in order for people to live at peace with one another with an adequate degree of security and fulfillment in living? (b) How may these relationships be achieved?

It is the thesis of this book and of all those who believe in the democratic way of life that solutions to the troubles of the world today can be reached only by people who have a clear understanding of what democratic relations are and possess skills to develop such relations. Those who look forward to a brave new world do well to recall that Shakespeare's full statement was, "O brave new world, that has such people in't!" It will not be technological know-how which will create a world in which all people live at peace with an adequate degree of human dignity; nor will it be the atomic bomb or other more devastating weapons of destruction which will destroy the chances, for a long time to come, of moving toward a better life for all. It will be how leaders behave, how those empowered to use the tools for living or for destruction actually use their power and what mandates for its use they receive from the people as a whole. The central problem facing people in today's world is, as it has always been, a problem of relationships. The problem now has elements in it particular to our times.

It is the function of this chapter to examine the broader problem,

[ 3 ]

to look at people in today's world, in an effort to understand the elements or factors which prescribe the kinds of relationships that need to be developed. The task here is to make plain the crucial importance of the problem with which this yearbook is concerned. All the remaining chapters are devoted to determining what democratic relations are and how they may be developed. An analysis of democratic behavior is undertaken and the fields of health education, physical education and recreation are described as media for educating for democracy. Principles for leadership in the three fields are considered as derived from the needs of people in today's world, from our democratic beliefs, and our scientific knowledge of the nature of the human being and how he grows and learns. From the basic point of view established, detailed answers are sought—in programs for children, adolescents, older youth and adults—to the question of democratic relations and how they may be developed.

There are myriads of facts and opinions having their impact upon our ideas of how people live today. These facts and opinions are derived from personal experience, newspapers, magazines and books, the radio, television, the visiting lecturer and the local authority. It is not easy to sort out and classify all the data we have and thereby try to see what they mean. From time to time, various persons attempt this and come up with their interpretations of events. These are sure to clash with the interpretations of others. One will affirm our civilization is going into a decline, another will be as equally convinced that the powers of "good" and "progress," as we conceive of them in the democratic philosophy, cannot fail. Of this, Johnson in *Incredible Tale* says, ". . . if it [democracy] cannot fail, no thought is necessary; if it is bound to fail, thought is useless. The assumption that the country can fail, but need not do so, is the only one that justifies an American in taking thought for the future." [1]

The effort here to organize facts and opinions about people in today's world is premised neither on the surety of doom and chaos nor on a certainty of survival and orderly change. It is based upon these convictions: we must understand what people need to enable

[1] Johnson, Gerald W. *Incredible Tale.* New York: Harper and Brothers, 1950, p. 290.

them to live together peacefully and productively in today's world; we must understand also the conditions in today's world under which people are striving to meet their needs; then, we must bring to bear upon the situation our democratic faith in human beings and in their rights and responsibilities to share in designing their own destinies. We will thus not only hope for desired outcomes, but will do the work needed to help achieve them. Margaret Mead used a New England yankee expression for the title of one of her books which fits the case, "Trust God—and keep your powder dry." The ammunition which we may use as educators and leaders of youth is the subject of this book.

## The Needs of Human Beings

What do people want out of life? What does little Jennie Jones of Middletown want? What does Ivan Ivanovitch want? Or the people of Paris, London, New York, Tokyo and Cape Town? We have to know some answers to these questions to understand people in today's world. Whether we look for these answers to psychology and biological science or to developed insight into the wishes, desires and wants of people, the conclusion is reached that every human being has basic needs he seeks to satisfy continually from the time he is a babe in arms until the day of his death. It may be concluded likewise that the basic needs of all human beings are alike, though their expressions of need have an infinite variety.

Mumford has said that the needs of mankind are of two types: needs for survival and needs for fulfilment.[2] He points out that separating needs into these categories for purposes of analysis does violence to their interrelatedness, ilustrating this fact by saying that individuals have a need to love and be loved but lovers must eat.

If we think of the needs for survival, such as for air, water, food and shelter, and at the same time think of the human infant able to do no more to satisfy his needs than to cry and thus make his wants known, it is not difficult to see how other needs, social in nature, arise. To be fed, to be sheltered, the human infant depends upon the cooperation of others. The child seeks approval of adults and reassurance that they will take care of him. The need for

[2] Mumford, Lewis. *The Condition of Man.* New York: Harcourt, Brace and Co., 1944, p. 413.

parental care is both a survival need and a social need. The same may be said of the need for sexual experiences.

Needs for companionship and love seem to be planted deeply in the human breast. Man has sought to satisfy these needs in larger social groupings than the family circle. Needs for survival were also instrumental. They led to cooperative efforts to wrest a living from the environment and ultimately to designing the social patterns in which the cooperative efforts would be made. The first patterns were simple as we know. They bear little resemblance to the complex social organizations in today's world, organizations so involved that people sometimes forget that their purpose and intent are to meet better the needs of all through the efforts of all.

Life to be good for humankind has to make sense, has to have meaning, value, and purpose. The needs for fulfilment are met through seeking this meaning, assigning value and striving to achieve purposes that seem significant. Mumford says of the ascending scale of needs "from bare physical life to social stimulus and personal growth" that the "most important needs from the standpoint of life-fulfilment are those that foster spiritual activity and promote spiritual growth; the needs for order, continuity, meaning, value, purpose and design—needs out of which language and poesy and music and science and art and religion have grown. The deepest, the most organic, of these higher needs is that for love: here all the stronger because it is rooted in survival." [3]

For life fulfilment human beings need to be free from too much fear. To be constantly afraid engenders hate, suspicion, distrust, servility, resentment—not love. The child afraid of its parents seeks a scapegoat in some weaker person or animal on which to vent his stored up aggression or he may become a docile, passive, dependent tool for others to exploit and use. A people afraid, afraid of not having enough to eat, afraid of being the prey of more powerful neighbors, afraid of being different, afraid of those who govern them, will sooner or later erupt into action to meet their need to be free of the fear.

To be free of fear means to live with a degree of security that makes it possible for an individual or for a people or nation to work

[3] *Ibid.*

out his or their destiny with tangible chances of success. When people cannot cope with a situation they may submit to it, they may try to escape it or they may try to change it. When it becomes intolerable, they either flee elsewhere or revolt. We have today thousands of displaced persons who have escaped situations intolerable to them. We have revolt, the cumulative resentments of centuries, among the peoples of Asia and Africa. We have in Europe people, sickened and disillusioned with war as a means of solving problems, attempting to change situations by peaceful evolutions rather than by violent revolutions.

As we become concerned with people, whether as individuals or in the aggregate, one fact holds our attention. All of us want to belong. Whether we are six, sixteen or sixty years old; whether we are Italian, Korean, American or Zulu, meeting the need to belong is basic to our well-being. Meeting the need means being accepted by others, being liked, being considered important as a person or as a nation; it means recognition by others and achieving a place of our own in group life. It means security in being accepted, being liked for ourselves, being a part of the social whole.

With some understandings of the needs of human beings, the next step is to try to understand the world in which they are attempting to meet their needs today. This is a large task, not to be done by any cursory survey of happenings and events in our time. Rather is it necessary to identify the major forces influencing people's lives today. All analyses of events reveal: people live in a changing world, in an interdependent world, in a diversified world.

## People Live in a Changing World

As the anthropologist studies people he learns that they grow and change and that cultures, too, are constantly changing. In the time of Queen Elizabeth, in the last half of the 1500's, it seemed as though England would go on to produce some of the greatest musicians of the world. But England turned her eyes toward exploration and colonial expansion and Germany, a backward nation in this respect, went on to win the world's acclaim for musical genius. Less than fifty years ago it was said, "The Japanese are like butterflies, fluttering from flower to flower, unable to withstand the drives of Western Civilization." In the past three decades we have seen the Japanese engage in two wars overseas; World War II illustrated how they could withstand the drives of our technological culture. Their genes have not changed, but their culture has. Culture changes first along material lines, in clothes and weapons and tools; second it changes in the area of major culture drives and values.

The element in change which is particular to our times is the rapidity with which it occurs. People everywhere in the world have felt the impact as old ways of living have been altered. People of the Western World, largely instrumental in bringing about the changes, have been sharply affected. Within the lifetime of those now adult a new environment for living has been developed. A changed and still changing economy is a major feature of the new environment. Change has never been uniformly accepted and social conflicts have resulted; social values have become confused.

## Life Has a New Environment

Modern technology has given life a new setting. Ways of living have been changed by the automobile, the radio and television, labor-saving devices, mass production of innumerable articles from textiles and wearing apparel to gadgets of every description. In all countries becoming industrialized there has been a shift from rural to urban living, bringing changes in family life, in the work people do, and in their recreation. The shift from farms to industrial jobs brought the growth of cities, cities which face perennial problems in housing, delinquency and crime, health and sanitation. "The worker" came into existence, thought of not as a human being but as a hand to tend machines. The automobile and the state of being an employee combined, in the United States particularly, to create greater geographical mobility. Every industrial city today has its scores of people without roots in community life, abiding there just so long as the jobs hold out, ready to follow rumors of better jobs elsewhere.

Human experience is a shared experience. In our great cities with their depersonalizing of contacts this truth is often forgotten. People live next door for years without ever coming to know one another. The employee often does not know his boss. People get into trouble, fall sick, get well or die, and those about them know nothing of these tribulations. There are social agencies to take care of these things. We hire people to look out for the orphaned, the widowed, the disabled and handicapped. We no longer tend to extend a helping hand, to be neighborly. One reason is that we may be told to mind our own business. Another is that just as we get around to it, the neighbors move away.

Any number of other phenomena might be listed as examples of the marked changes that took place through industrialization, such as what happened to women, the rise of labor unions, the development of mass communication media for propagandizing and for education. The changes have been far-reaching and the pace so fast that people have not been able to understand what the changes mean and to direct political organization toward a fuller sharing by all in the fruits of industrial development.

## A Changing Economy

From the eighteenth century until the last quarter of the nineteenth was an era of industrial expansion. Machines meant an increased food supply. This, coupled with progress in medicine and hygiene, brought about increasing populations all over the world. Expanding industry could count on expanding markets. Colonization of nonindustrialized people went on apace to assure these markets and the sources of raw materials.

The era of expansion in land, in population, and to a great extent in industry came to a close at the opening of the twentieth century. World frontiers for further colonization were gone just as surely as the American western frontier had become a thing of the past. Since the beginning of the century most populations have shown a tendency toward stabilization at the numbers they have attained. There are said to be two factors accounting for this last phenomenon: intelligent people prefer to raise two or three children well to raising a dozen badly (and the chances in a money economy that the children may fare badly are increased); and secondly, urban living has proved a poor setting for family life, if the measure used as evidence is the declining birthrate in cities, declining increasingly as cities grow in size. The era of expansion for industry ceased, because of the other two changes and because a large part of the industrial system of the Western World had already been mechanized. Expansion must come largely in the development of new industries or in nonindustrialized countries.

If industrialization had not been based upon the exploitation of natural resources and human beings, it could not have gone forward as rapidly as it did. Industrialists of the time took great risks, often met failure but expected no quarter for themselves and gave none to others; further opportunities to make good abounded. Colonial peoples were usually left in grinding poverty and ignorance while the profits of their labors went to the industrialists. The resources of the countries of the Western World were wasted and little thought was given to the welfare of the worker in the competitive struggle for markets.

Since the beginning of the century we have been living in a situation for which thinking in terms of expansion is inappropriate and misleading. There is no "west" in the United States to which the disgruntled and unsuccessful may move. There are no "backward" peoples left to exploit. Hegemony was established over them by one or another industrial nation and is now being thrown off as these people seek independent status. The world now has to conserve its resources in land, mines, forests and water. As populations become stabilized, markets will no longer expand. They will tend to shrink in some countries as others become industrialized. The only way now for markets to expand is to raise the standard of living by increasing the purchasing power of people everywhere.

Chronic unemployment of millions has been a feature of an industrial society, save in wartime. The machine has shortened the work day and work week and brought increased leisure. Still the attrition in the number needed to do the world's work goes on and will go further with more and better machines. Great disparity in the distribution of national incomes has resulted from industrialization. The physical environment of the bulk of populations was improved with the cheap manufacture of many articles through mass production. But in every country from a third to a half of the people reaped little beyond uncertainty about their jobs and frustration in the jobs they filled.

All these developments existed at the beginning of the century but few saw them. The Western World went on behaving as though expansion were unlimited in the face of evidence to the contrary. The struggle for world markets became more intense. The nations that fared badly or got a late start felt themselves to be the "have-nots." One nation in particular, Germany, superimposed this "have-not" concept upon an atavistic nationalist philosophy and its people were persuaded that meeting their needs satisfactorily meant wars of aggression against other peoples directed by "supermen."

Here, again, there are other features of change that might be listed such as the growth of monopolies and cartels, the growth in power of labor unions and the increase in government intervention between the two warring parties. There might also be listed the periodic depressions of the economy with the breakdown that occurred during the thirties. These happenings were not unique to the United States. They were experienced by all industrial countries in various ways and in varying degrees.

It is not the province of this discourse to say what the solutions to the situation of the world today might be. It is free, however, to say that the solutions will be directed by the values the people have; they will be according to what people believe to be of most worth.

## Confused Values

Those who predict the possible decline of the Western World do not base the possibility on the fact that the era of expansion is over, but on the fact that the aftermath of rapid change has been confusion over values. Mumford states that people have forgotten the primacy of their needs for fulfilment in concentrating on embellishing the means of survival, their material living.[4]

The undermining of orthodox religion by the findings of science had a part in this confusion. The prestige of science, because of its very real achievements, had an effect. Scientific deduction became the fashion; philosophical syntheses came into disrepute. Human beings had been devalued in the industrial revolution which meant that life itself was devalued. How else account for the general apathy at the time of the Nazis' ruthless extermination of millions or of the desire to swiftly forget these acts afterwards?

[4] *Ibid.*, p. 413-23.

In its neglect of the ends for living and its absorption in means, the Western World was slow to understand the threat to its neglected basic values in fascism and German national socialism. When the threat was finally realized, the challenge was met. There has thereby been time gained to clarify democratic beliefs, time gained for the democracies to set their own houses in order, time gained to prepare for the inevitable next attack. These things we have been doing at a significant pace since World War II. The democracies have been freed of complacency and come to see that all is not right, that the world is not the best of all possible worlds in which to live for large numbers of people. There are sincere efforts going on to clarify the meaning of democracy and to seek solutions to social problems within national boundaries and upon the world stage.

## People Live in an Interdependent World

Yesterday what people did in our town mattered only there. Today, we know that no longer is any one part of the world an island independent of other parts. Today, the actions of individuals as far away as Tasmania affect us.

One of the greatest misconceptions which grew out of Charles Darwin's *Origin of Species* was that "survival of the fittest" meant survival only through destruction of the weak. Survival of all living things also means cooperation. It is true in animal life.[5] It is particularly true of man. Those nations which have built great civilizations have done so through the combined action of individuals and groups directed toward common goals.

Interdependence is not, then, a new factor in the life of man. He became dependent upon others and others upon him the moment he recognized the existence of his social needs for nurturing, for belonging, for recognition and acceptance. Interdependence is an augmented factor today because of the development of interlocking economics and the swiftness of air transport and travel, bringing all peoples into quicker, more immediate interactive relations. The threat of the atomic bomb did not create this interdependence. It only brought heightened awareness of interdependence as an irrefutable fact.

[5] Allee, Clyde. *Social Life of Animals.* New York: W. W. Norton and Co., 1938.

Americans have learned the hard way to accept interdependence as a social fact. It is certainly accepted today by the majority who altered their former isolationism to assume a share of responsibility for world affairs. Efforts to keep out of European wars proved futile. Realization of inevitable involvement was the first big step toward understanding interdependence. It was so great a step that after World War II Americans were willing to pour millions of dollars into rehabilitating devastated countries, not only out of humanitarian concern but also with awareness that John Donne spoke truly when he said, "Never send to know for whom the bell tolls; it tolls for thee." Without peace and prosperity in Western Europe, peace and prosperity for the United States was seen as impossible. The ambitions and actions of Soviet Russia sharpened this awareness. The Russians' possession of the atomic bomb brought it to a peak.

It would seem there is one more step to take for full understanding of interdependence, that is, acceptance of the fact that our peace and prosperity are dependent upon the solutions to social and economic problems the peoples of Asia and Africa accept. If they do not find solutions that will meet their needs for life-fulfilment, there will be no peace or prosperity anywhere in the world. Trygve Lie states:

The days of dependency or inferior status are fast coming to an end in Asia. Its peoples are the inheritors of some of the world's greatest cultures; they are building their own new worlds on the foundations of the old. Their influence in the affairs of the United Nations is growing. Given time, and the necessary development of their economic resources, their influence will be more nearly commensurate with their population than it is today. The idea that all this vast diversity of ancient peoples stirring to new life and power could ever become the mere reflection of any form of society in other parts of the world is unrealistic.

In Africa the movement forward is slower. . . . The effects of the Trusteeship System will certainly give new impetus to the economic, social and educational advancement of the peoples of these Territories and to their progress towards self-government or independence.[6]

In our relations with these peoples, fear of the Soviet Union should not guide our policies. We must not confuse these peoples

[6] Lie, Trygve. "A Year of Progress." *United Nations Bulletin*, August 15, 1949, p. 163-64. Introduction to the Fourth Annual Report of the United Nations, June 7, 1949.

by making their oppressors our allies against Russia or by refusing them help because they work out political and economic forms different from our own. Mr. Lie implies both the futility and danger in such a line of action.

## People Live in a Diversified World

The real test of our quality as a world leader in the United Nations will be our capacity to understand other peoples and take their aspirations, and not ours alone, into consideration in our blueprints for the future. In plotting a strategy of ideas we do not face an insuperable task. All that we need to do is to translate into practice the ideals we have been preaching for many years—ideals of anti-colonialism, international cooperation, racial equality, greater rights for labor. In the war of ideas which, far more effectively than the atomic or hydrogen bomb, will determine the shape of the world, we have nothing to fear if we but keep faith with the best that is in ourselves. This may seem a lightweight weapon to those who place their main reliance on armaments. Yet in other seedtimes of history, the courage to see fellow-beings with compassion and to translate compassion into practical policy has served to bring light and order out of seeming chaos.[7]

To understand other peoples requires accepting them as human beings who differ from us in some respects but who have the same basic life needs as we have. We should guard against false ideas about them, try to understand them and the cultures they are building. We have to refrain from assigning superiority or inferiority on the basis of differences. We have to refrain from stereotyping national groups; it is not true that "all Mexicans are shiftless," "orientals are incapable of self-government," "Jews are radical," "the Japanese are sly and untrustworthy." The last stereotype has already undergone change since the success of the MacArthur occupation in Japan. There is no evidence to show that such assigned characteristics are common to all members of these groups. Where traits are identifiable in common they are acquired not innate. They arise out of participation in a common environment. As the environment changes, individuals change.

A recent statement on race by a group of scientists has bearing

[7] Dean, Vera Micheles. "A Strategy for a War of Ideas," *Nation* 171:185-7; August 26, 1950, p. 187.

on this matter of differences. Representatives from eight countries under the auspices of Unesco met in Paris. These scientists first defined race precisely: "a race is one of a group of populations which make up mankind. These populations have a few inherited physical or physiological differences—but no others—and the differences are relatively slight when compared to the whole human constitutions." [8] Then, this group reached the following seven conclusions about race.

Race, as the term is commonly used, is less a biological fact than a social myth. The myth has been used in recent years to justify the snuffing out of large numbers of human lives. And today it is still used to keep millions of persons from normal development and civilization from the full benefit of cooperation from productive minds.

No large modern national or religious group, scientifically speaking, is a race. Nor are people who speak any single language, who live in any one geographical area or who share in a specific cultural community necessarily a race.

Racial discrimination has no scientific foundation in biological fact.

All human beings can be educated and can adapt themselves. These traits, more than all others, have permitted mankind's mental development.

Scientific tests have shown that the mental characters among all human racial groups are essentially similar. Given similar cultural opportunities, the average achievement of people from groups with different traits or customs is about the same.

The range of mental capacity in all races is much the same. There is no proof that the groups of mankind differ in intelligence, temperament or other mental traits.

Extensive study produces no evidence that race mixture produces biologically bad results. There is no biological justification for prohibiting intermarriage of persons from different groups.[9]

The scientists finished by declaring:

Biological studies lend support to the ethic of universal brotherhood. . . . Man is born a social being who can reach his full development only through interaction with his fellows. The denial at any point of this social bond between men and man brings with it disintegration. In this

---

[8] "Science Panel Sees Mankind as a Unity." *United Nations Reporter*. New York: American Association for the United Nations, September 10, 1950, p. 3.
[9] *Ibid.*

sense, every man is his brother's keeper. For every man is a piece of the continent, a part of the main, because he is involved in mankind.[10]

As we well know, acceptance of people who are different has not only an international aspect, but is a problem Americans are facing in their national life. We have made some progress in eliminating prejudice and discrimination against minority groups, but there is still much to be done before all Americans regardless of national origin, color or religion will be fully accepted as equal though different.

Our people still need further education regarding the facts in the case to understand that many traits arbitrarily assigned as indigenous to all members of a minority group are not the result of biological determinants, but the product of cultural and social conditions which can be alleviated and changed. Poor housing, slum conditions, economic insecurity, segregation, lack of educational opportunity are factors which are controllable. Active contact and joint participation among all groups may promote understanding and willingness to accept the individual for what he is and does.

Krogman summarized the education all Americans should be provided in a "Decalogue of Race" written some years ago:

1. Thou shalt not bow down before the false god of "racial superiority";

2. Thou shalt not vaunt thyself that only thy race is "pure";

3. Thou shalt not preach that races or peoples are at different levels of physical development;

4. Thou shalt not claim that racial differences are of fundamental biological import;

5. Thou shalt not establish racial groups as fixed or unchangeable;

6. Thou shalt not hold that "racial personality traits" are innate and inherited;

7. Thou shalt not, to the detriment of thy neighbor, assert that cultural achievements are based on racial characteristics;

8. Thou shalt not demean thy brother because his appearance differs from thine;

9. Thou shalt not, because a man is of a different religion, insist that he belongs to a different race;

[10] *Ibid.*

10. Thou *shalt* faithfully and sincerely observe the foregoing admonitions and then, indeed, wilt thou love thy neighbor as thyself.[11]

The world is infinitely enriched by differing cultures and by individual differences. It will be the richer as individuals, peoples and nations are granted the right to be different without assignment of inferiority or superiority to the differences. What is required, along with granting this right, is the creation of a framework of unity through the fully shared cooperative action of equals to achieve common social goals, in our own national life and in the world at large.

## Will People Live in a Democratic World?

Are people becoming increasingly important in today's world? They have always been important in our professional creed as teachers and leaders of children and youth. They have always been important in our democratic beliefs in the inherent dignity of man, the right of opportunity for all, individual responsibility and the potentiality of each one as a human being. Yet it has taken mankind a long time to reach an understanding that people are important and the understanding is only partial even now. There is still a long distance to go before the concepts of the importance of human life and individual dignity will receive full recognition. When they do, no person will be exploited to serve the ends of some other person or persons, no child will be rejected as less smart or less capable than other boys and girls, no black or brown man will suffer because of color of skin, no worker will be treated as a cog of the machine he operates, no woman will be made to feel that the roles of wife and mother or her ways of earning a living are less valued than the roles men play in society.

Franklin Delano Roosevelt said, "Today we are faced with the preeminent fact that if civilization is to survive, we must cultivate the science of human relationships—the ability of peoples of all kinds to live together and work together in the same world, at peace."

In spite of its world-wide dimensions, the problem of human relations is not an abstract and remote one. It affects every one. It is being worked out, toward or away from solution, in the life of

[11] Krogman, Wilton M. "Physical Anthropology and Race Relations: A Biosocial Evaluation." *Scientific Monthly* 66:317-27; April, 1948.

every individual. The problem may be seen as each one of us is contributing to solving or not solving it. It may be seen as it affects the life of ten-year-old Mary Smith who lives with her parents and five brothers and sisters in one of a thousand identical homes of a Government housing project, whose father is dependent upon economic conditions for a job, whose conceptions of life and how one behaves toward others are being formed out of her parents' attitudes, out of the standards of the boys and girls on her block, out of the programs she sees and hears at the movies, on the radio and television, and finally, out of the influences acting upon her by other social institutions, particularly the church and the school.

The problem may be seen as it affects the lives of the people of Asia, of Indo-China, India, the Philippines, China, seeking to cast off feudalistic practices, to have a share in governing themselves, to have enough to eat to sustain life. It may be seen as it affects the peoples of Western Europe, struggling to create new patterns of government which will better serve them. It may be seen as it affects us in the United States, caught in the dilemma of professing values by which to live and not living by them completely enough. It may be seen as applied to the Soviet Union, though we are loathe to believe it. It is hard for us, in the face of Russian recalcitrance, propaganda and aggression, to think of this people as basically desiring and striving to meet the same needs that other peoples are struggling to meet.

Since man began to invent forms for ordering his social life, philosophers have pondered upon the relation of man to man, particularly of the one to the many, the individual's role in the social whole and the responsibility of the whole for the individual. Many answers have been given and the adaptable human being has functioned in many different kinds of roles assigned him in different societies. Until recently, mankind had little guidance beyond personal experience for judging the worth of different social patterns. Since personal experience is shaped by the social environment in which we happen to grow up, the values and standards of our own society are all we have had by which to judge the suitability for meeting human needs of cultures other than our own. Today, however, there are other and more objective standards. We have the findings from the biological sciences and psychology to guide us. We now know what social setting a child needs to grow toward full maturity as a human being.

Science, however, does not tell us whether it is "good" or "bad" to foster the growth of individuals to the limits of their capacities. It only tells us the means whereby this end may be attained. It is an act of faith to say we believe it is *best* for the individual to develop fully as a self-directing, self-responsible cooperative person. Upon this belief democracy rests its case.

In this century, our democratic belief met its first great challenge with the rise of fascism and national socialism in Italy and Germany. The world was becoming dominated by ideas of totalitarian rule by supermen, of the state as an entity outside of and apart from the individuals composing it, of the limiting of individual responsibility to obeying orders of some leader superimposed upon them, of the use of force and aggression to solve problems, of racial superiority and the elimination of millions of unfortunate members of "inferior" races.

The democracies were forced to fight for a world in which they might continue to try to move toward realization of democratic beliefs. They won the struggle but the end is not yet. Totalitarian ideas of the nazi and fascist brand are not dead; they only await opportune times, times when people are so distressed and deprived and confused that they will welcome any demagogue who holds out a promise of bettering their condition.

Today, in communism, lies another threat to the desire to go on perfecting democracy. The threat this time is more insidious, because in the communist ideology the relation of the one to the many is equalitarian as it is ideally in democracy. When full communism is achieved, the state is supposed to melt away and full democratic participation of all in what little governing needs to be done, in the fruits of common labor, in all aspects of living, is to be the result. It has not worked out this way in Soviet Russia where the Politburo rules with an iron hand, nevertheless, this is communist theory.

Much has been written about the differences between communism and democracy, but in the final analysis the basic difference rests on one divergence in viewpoint: communism avers the ends justify the means; democracy affirms the ends design the means, that means must be consistent with ends in order to lead toward achieving those ends. In concrete terms, we affirm that the way for people to participate in all aspects of the common life is for them to participate here and now, not at some later time when the ways in which they may participate have been worked out by some "elite." The basic difference between communism and democracy is as simple as that. Adherents to democracy do well to keep this in mind and not be fooled into being for or against any line of action merely to be on the other side from the communists.

Because of the industrial power of the United States and the responsibility for leadership that power brings, Americans more than other peoples today are challenged to clarify their basic social values for themselves and to tell the rest of the world, not only in words but in consistent action, where they stand. The values are inherent in American life. They have never been denied. The time has come to ask ourselves: Do we really believe in the worth and dignity of every human being? Do we really believe it is every individual's right and responsibility to share fully in the common social, political and economic life? Do we really believe that people are themselves the best judges of ways to satisfy their needs in relation to others with the same requirements? Do we really believe in the effectiveness of cooperative action on the basis of decisions cooperatively derived? If we believe in these values fully and firmly enough to act consistently in our relations with others at home and abroad, democracy will survive. If we are not sure, if we vacillate, if we become opportunists, the outcomes will be different for both ourselves and the world.

It is the purpose of this yearbook to try to describe what characterizes the democratic person in his relationships with others. It is the purpose of this yearbook to take the next step and attempt to determine how democratic persons may be developed through experiences in health education, physical education and recreation. If this chapter has helped to heighten awareness of the crucial importance of the task of developing democratic human relations, it has served its function.

# Bibliography

ADAMS, JAMES TRUSLOW. *The American.* New York: Charles Scribner's Sons, 1943.

ALLEE, CLYDE. *Social Life of Animals.* New York: W. W. Norton and Co., 1938.

ANSHEN, RUTH M., editor. *The Family: Its Function and Destiny.* New York: Harper and Brothers, 1949.

BENEDICT, RUTH. *Patterns of Culture.* Boston: Houghton Mifflin Co., 1934.

BROGAN, DENIS W. *The American Character.* New York: Alfred A. Knopf, 1944.

BROWN, JAMES F. *Psychology and the Social Order.* New York: McGraw-Hill Book Co., 1936.

CASSIDY, ROSALIND. "Contributions of Physical Education to Democratic Citizenship." *Journal of the American Association for Health, Physical Education and Recreation* 21:218-19, April 1950.

CHANDLER, ALBERT. *The Clash of Political Ideas.* New York: Appleton-Century-Crofts, Inc., 1940.

COMMAGER, HENRY S. *The American Mind.* New Haven: Yale University Press, 1950.

DAVIS, W. ALLISON, and HAVIGHURST, ROBERT J. *Father of the Man.* Boston: Houghton Mifflin Co., 1947.

DEAN, VERA MICHELES. "A Strategy for a War of Ideas." *Nation* 171: 185-87; August 26, 1950.

FRANK, LAWRENCE K. *Society as the Patient.* New Brunswick: Rutgers University Press, 1948.

FROMM, ERICH. *Escape from Freedom.* New York: Farrar and Rinehart, 1941.

HORNEY, KAREN. *The Neurotic Personality of Our Time.* New York: W. W. Norton and Co., 1937.

HOYT, ELIZABETH. "Freedom from Want: A World Goal." *Public Affairs Pamphlets* No. 80. New York: Public Affairs Committee, 1943.

JOHNSON, GERALD W. *Incredible Tale.* New York: Harper and Brothers, 1950.

KROGMAN, WILTON M. "Physical Anthropology and Race Relations: A Biosocial Evaluation." *Scientific Monthly* 66: 317-21; April 1948.

LIE, TRYGVE. "A Year of Progress." *United Nations Bulletin,* August 15, 1949, p. 163-64. Introduction to the Fourth Annual Report of the United Nations, June 7, 1949.

LIEBMAN, JOSHUA. *Peace of Mind.* New York: Simon and Schuster, 1946.

LILIENTHAL, DAVID E. *This I Do Believe.* New York: W. W. Norton and Co., 1949.

MACLEISH, ARCHIBALD. "The Conquest of America." *Atlantic* 184: 17-22; August 1949.

MEAD, MARGARET. *And Keep Your Powder Dry.* New York: William Morrow and Co., 1942.

MENNINGER, WILLIAM C. *Psychiatry in a Troubled World.* New York: Macmillan Co., 1948.

MOON, BUCKLIN. *The High Cost of Prejudice.* New York: Julian Messner, 1947.

MUMFORD, LEWIS. *The Condition of Man.* New York: Harcourt, Brace and Co., 1944.

MUMFORD, LEWIS. *The Culture of Cities.* New York: Harcourt, Brace and Co., 1938.

MUMFORD, LEWIS. *Faith for Living.* New York: Harcourt, Brace and Co., 1940.

PLANT, JAMES S. *Personality and the Cultural Pattern*. New York: Commonwealth Fund, 1937.

ROSE, ARNOLD, and ROSE, CAROLINE. *America Divided—Minority Group Relations in the United States*. New York: Alfred A. Knopf, 1948.

SPITZ, DAVID. *Patterns of Anti-Democratic Thought*. New York: Macmillan Co., 1949.

UNITED NATIONS REPORTER. "Science Panel Sees Mankind as a Unity." *United Nations Reporter* 22: 3; September 10, 1950.

WARNER, W. LLOYD. *Democracy in Jonesville*. New York: Harper and Brothers, 1949.

WARNER, W. LLOYD; HAVIGHURST, ROBERT J.; and LOEB, MARTIN B. *Who Shall Be Educated?* New York: Harper and Brothers, 1944.

# CHAPTER TWO

# Democratic Behavior

GORDON HEARN

I F ASKED to say what democratic behavior is, many Americans would probably express their ideas in some such phrases as these: "It is treating others as equals," "It means live and let live," "It is doing to others as you would be done by," "It means granting to others the same rights that one wants for one's self," "It is taking turns." Some insightful persons may even offer, "It means sharing responsibility with others for what happens—in the home, at work, in school, in the community, in the nation and world."

These phrases express some of our democratic conceptions of how people ought to behave toward one another. They describe behavior much needed on the part of large numbers of individuals, if people in today's world are to arrive at peaceful, orderly control of their own, yet interdependent, destinies. But in a book devoted to considering developing democratic human relations through experiences in particular fields of education, these socially derived descriptions are not enough to explain the end product for which to strive, namely, democratic behavior. It is necessary to delve deeper to be sure of understanding what behavior itself is and how in relations with others different types of behavior patterns are developed.

The present chapter attempts to perform the service of helping to deepen understanding of democratic behavior. To do this, the first step seems to be to see what are the principles governing individual development and the motivations underlying all behavior. With these discussions as base, the second step seems to be to analyze segments of behavior involving two individuals; this has been called the process of interpersonal interaction. Then, it is needful to consider the developmental process through which each human being moves toward maturity. The final phase of analysis is examining the types of interaction among individuals fostered in groups with differing organizational patterns. From these discussions it should be possible to derive a description of democratic behavior which will provide more explicit direction than generalized statements for those engaged in helping children and youth to develop democratic relations with others.

## The Dynamics of Individual Behavior

The purpose of the first part of the chapter is to aid understanding of individual behavior as a basis for understanding group behavior. On the foundations of what we can postulate as true of individual responses, we can later distinguish a type of group behavior best suited to individuals living in a democratic society.

### *Principles Governing Individual Development*

We cannot understand behavior without a clear conception of the fundamental principles governing the growth and development of the human being. At the present writing there seem to be three major principles to consider: the unity of the organism, the interacting unity of individual and environment and the concept of individual differences in growth and development. These principles are now well known and accepted by most educators, so that only a brief discussion of them is called for by way of emphasizing that they are basic to understanding behavior.

*The organism is a unified whole.* We can all recall having seen a cat crouched, poised ready to pounce upon its prey. We have seen a swimmer balanced on the edge of the pool ready to plunge at the sound of the gun or a man in the act of putting the shot. One thing must have impressed us: the organism was acting as a whole. Every part of the organism was participating. Every functional system, the visceral, the glandular, the respiratory and circulatory systems, the central and autonomic nervous systems, were in a state of readiness and were contributing, each in its own way, to the consummation of the intended action. On the point of the unity of the organism there is almost universal agreement among scientists. The physiologists tell us that a change in one part of the organism is accompanied by a compensatory change in all of the others. The psychologists tell us that thinking, feeling and doing are interrelated, inseparable parts of every act. Any explanations of behavior today must take into account and be consistent with this first principle.

*Individual and environment are an interacting unity.* In explaining behavior, it is useful to distinguish between the individual and his environment. It seems natural to think of certain things as being within us and certain things as being outside and around us. We get into some difficulty, however, with this distinction. The air around us, for instance, seems to be clearly of the environment. But what shall we say about that part of the same body of air that passes down our windpipe into the lungs? What shall we say about the oxygen carried in the red blood cells? What part of it is of the individual and what part of it is of his environment? Because of this kind of difficulty, many psychologists no longer try to make such a distinction. Murphy says, for instance, "The life process is merely focused in the organism; it includes a field extending beyond the body. Organization embraces the entire organism-environment relation, of which the organism is the nodal point but not the complete functioning system." [1] Just as we now regard the organism as a functional unit, we also regard the organism and its environment as a functional unity. Any change in the organism changes the environment as does also the environment effect changes in the organism.

This interacting unity of individual and environment means for teachers and leaders of children and youth that the behavior of any boy or girl must be seen in relation to the influences acting upon the individual to which he is responding in the situation in which the behavior is observed. The implications are far-reaching for knowing and creating the kinds of situations in which boys and girls are encouraged and helped to respond in ways revealing that democratic relations with others are being developed.

*Each individual is different.* Each individual develops a unique "self" through interaction with his environment. Out of his experi-

---

[1] Murphy, Gardner. *Personality—A Biosocial Approach to Origins and Structure.* New York: Harper and Brothers, 1947, p. 40.

ences and his responses to them he develops attitudes which lead him to respond in certain ways in subsequent experiences. But behavior is not completely the result of external forces impinging upon the individual. If this were true, we could expect in a given situation that the responses of all concerned would be the same. This never happens. Each individual's response is different. Interaction means he is not only acted upon; he also acts, and acts in ways peculiar to him. His particular assortment of genes, inherited from his forebears, give him a unique endowment, influencing his physical development and appearance, his health, his thinking and temperament. So it is that out of the elements in the unique inheritance of each individual interacting with the elements in the experiences each has, personality is developed. No two individuals develop the same personality, because some elements in heredity and experience are always different. Moreover, internal and external factors are always in different interacting relationships.

The concept of individual differences means that leaders of young people must study to understand the particular configuration of influences operating to produce the behavior of each boy or girl. Undesirable responses may be changed by changes in the forces operating. But to know how this might be done means understanding the configuration of causes for the behavior. And the configuration will be different in each case.

## The Motivations Behind Behavior

Questions regarding why we behave as we do and regarding how we ought to behave have occupied the thoughts of mankind in every generation. Lacking objective scientific findings about these vexing matters, philosophy and religion were looked to for the answers. The answers remained matters of belief in the superiority of one or another tenet or ethic. Today, with the development of modern sciences, though we still turn to philosophy and religion for answers to the ought to be, we have an ever increasing number of facts out of which to formulate our conceptions of what is. We do not have all the facts by any means, but we do have far more than ever before, so that we have more assurance of reaching a sounder idea about why we behave as we do.

*The individual is motivated by basic needs.* Biologists, physiologists, psychologists, anthropologists have proffered many theories to explain what lies at the basis of behavior. They have experimented, analyzed and surveyed. One by one, widely divergent ideas have been modified, discarded, replaced by other ideas. As research has moved ahead and the evidence piled up, a common approach and a generally accepted explanation of behavior has developed. Today, behavior is seen as the expression of the individual's efforts to meet basic needs. Various need theories are current in psychology. Freud, for instance, talks about the "Id" which is one of the three classes of impulses which he believes constitute the human personality. The "Id" includes the sum total of basic animal impulses, appetites, drives, whose satisfactions in some form and degree are essential to survival.

Many have tried to list and classify the various needs that motivate people. Henry A. Murray probably has done the most exhaustive and systematic job.[2] Gardner Murphy would probably accept Murray's list of needs, but would point out that there are two main classes of needs, the viscerogenic, like Freud's "Id" impulses, and the psychogenic.[3] The psychogenic needs, seen as secondary needs, can be reclassified into dependence and independence needs. For example, a baby is born with needs such as for air, water, food, defecation-urination, rest, exercise, sex, harm avoidance. Very soon after birth, if not immediately, the child perceives that he is dependent upon others for the satisfactions of the basic visceral needs. Consequently he begins to develop certain secondary social or dependence needs. He has a need for nurturance, to be cared for; a need for succorance, to care for the one who cares for him; a need for affiliation. In general, he has a need to establish a dependence relation that will guarantee the satisfaction of his basic needs. But dependence upon another implies that the other has power over him. If one person controls the means of satisfying another's needs, that person also has the power to deny or limit the other's need satisfaction. Thus at the same time that the child is developing a dependence relationship he is also striving to develop an independence relationship. He develops needs, for instance, for auton-

[2] Murray, Henry A. *Explorations in Personality*. New York: Oxford University Press, 1938.
[3] Murphy, Gardner, *loc. cit.*

omy, for recognition, aggression, which are manifestations of the
need to escape or be free, in part, from his dependency relationship. Later we shall discuss a high order of needs which may develop as individuals try to live amicably with one another. These we
shall call interdependence needs.

Having simply enumerated a series of needs and called them the
source of motivation for behavior does not explain behavior or the
process involved in a behavioral act. Kurt Lewin has tackled this
problem. His explanation is somewhat as follows. A person exists
as part of his life space.

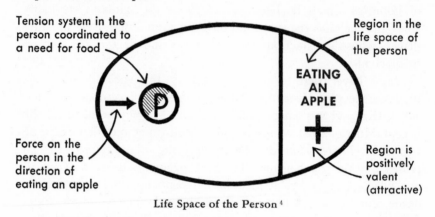

Life Space of the Person [4]

The figure represents the life space of this person at a given
moment in time. In this over-simplified example, which could never
exist, the person has a need system for food in a state of tension;
he is hungry. At the same time, the person perceives a region in his
life space (eating an apple); he sees something good to eat. This
region has valence (attractiveness), says Lewin, which exerts a
psychological force on the individual to move from where he is
now into the region of eating the apple. The strength of the force
and, therefore, the speed with which he will move will depend upon
the valence of the region (attractiveness of the apple) and the
strength of his need at the moment (how hungry he is). Sometimes
a person has a need to avoid a region; the region has negative
valence (it is repulsive or dangerous).

[4] Reprinted by permission from *Manual of Child Psychology* by L. Carmichael, published by John
Wiley and Sons, Inc., 1946.

Always, there are many different needs in varying states of tension at one and the same time. Often there are many objects in the environment, with varying degrees of attractiveness or repulsion, all of which exert psychological pressures on the organism in many different directions at the same time. In such a case it is the resultant of all these forces (the forces cancelling one another) which determines the direction and nature of behavior in the next moment of time. Lewin reminds us, too, that the life space of the individual is constantly changing as need tensions increase or are satisfied, as environmental conditions continually change.

Lewin believes he has experimental proof of his theory of psychological forces in some of the early experiments done under his direction by Zegarnik.[5] She gave her subjects a series of simple tasks to accomplish. She allowed some of the subjects to complete the tasks, others were interrupted before the series had been completed. Later, those who finished had dismissed the tasks from their minds; those who did not, remembered what the tasks were. Lewin explains that she created in her subjects a need to complete the tasks. There was a need system in tension which was dissipated when the tasks were completed. In the case of the uncompleted tasks the need system remained in tension, causing the tasks to remain on the subjects' minds and consequently to be remembered.

*The individual seeks to maintain inner balance.* So far we have postulated the existence of certain basic visceral needs, often expressed in the form of a variety of secondary needs as the energy source of human behavior. It follows that behavior of the organism is the action it undertakes to lower the general tension level coordinated to these needs. Since some needs will be increasing while others are being satisfied, the process of need-satisfaction is endless, as is behavior. It can be observed so long as there is life in the organism. This suggests a biological principle credited to Walter B. Cannon which he calls homeostasis, by which he means the principle of inner constancy or the maintenance of stability.[6] Cannon describes the tendency in the organism to adjust to each successive situation

[5] Zeigarnik, Bluma. "Über das Behalten von erledigten und unerledigten Handlungen," *Psychologische Forschung*. 9:1-85; 1927.

[6] Cannon, Walter B. *The Wisdom of the Body.* New York: W. W. Norton and Co., 1932.

in such a way as to maintain an inner constancy or stability, or, in Lewin's terms, to lower the general tension level.

Psychologists have added to our understanding of the tendency in the organism to seek inner balance or equilibrium. They tell us that when needs are felt, purposes are formed to meet them and the individual's behavior is thus directed by purpose. With the achievement of the purpose and need-fulfilment, equilibrium is restored. If the direct road to fulfilment is blocked by others, the individual takes devious paths to meet the need—rationalization, substitution, fantasy, projections, aggression. The point to be remembered is that the individual must find some way to release tensions and restore equilibrium. It is an important point for understanding behavior.

*The individual has an urge to explore, to learn.* Following Cannon's principle of homeostasis to its logical conclusion, it would seem that the ideal state for man, for which all ought to be striving, would be a vegetative state in which our basic needs would be met as they arose. The baby in its mother's womb would have achieved this ideal state, for instance, or a person amid sufficient abundance to satisfy all his needs would be in this ideal state and presumably would never move. How then can we account for a Ulysses or other humans like him who become dissatisfied as more and more of their basic needs are met? Murphy acknowledges the central importance of the homeostatic principle for personality study but suggests that "there must be as much digression from homeostasis as there is return to it, as much exploration as there is homecoming, as much extravagance as there is thrift." [7] In fact, Murphy affirms "homeostasis is a useful concept, not merely in showing the safety-maintaining system of the body, but in suggesting that against a background of relatively constant factors there are factors which permit a wide 'variability,' 'trial and error' in the execution of activities in contact with the outer world." [8] This seems to be substantiated by experience and yet we are left without an answer to the questions of why it is so.

Some will find their answers in a teleological point of view. They

[7] Murphy, Gardner, *op. cit.*, p. 32.
[8] *Ibid.*

will hold that there is some all-pervasive purpose in the universe to which all living things are attracted. This they would claim accounts for man's restless quest for something higher, in the face of the homeostatic principle. This would be their basis also for a belief in the inevitability of continuous progress.

To many, however, particularly those with a scientific frame of mind, such a teleological concept is unsatisfactory. It sounds like magic and is, therefore, rejected by the scientist. To refute it he may counter with one further proposal. It grows out of the commonly observed fact that man is not comfortable while confronted by the unknown. There seems to be a basic need in all of us to understand the unknown. Whenever we encounter any area which is unfamiliar to us we seem to move through a three-phase process in our attempt to understand or know it. First, we look at the area and try to see it as a whole. Second, we try to differentiate the parts that comprise this undifferentiated whole. Finally, we try to integrate the parts, to see the differentiated whole, the relationship of whose parts we now understand.

For example, let us look at the swimmer whom we mentioned earlier. He has mastered the crawl and the breast stroke, let us say, and recently he has become intrigued and challenged by the backstroke. He has never tried, nor has he ever seen it demonstrated, but he has heard of it. First of all, he may seek out a backstroker so that he may observe the stroke. His first objective, unconscious of course, will be to see the backstroke as a whole. He will get the general image in his mind, of a swimmer on his back rotating his arms behind his head and kicking in a manner not unlike the flutter-kick. He will probably try it at the first opportunity and do rather poorly which may only increase his determination to master this new skill. His next objective, to this end, will be to analyze the components of the stroke. He will study closely the path followed by the arm in rotation. He will analyze the kick, as to its rate and principle of propulsion. He will try to master the turn employed by the backstroker because he will have noticed that it is unlike any other turn he has ever used. Finally, he will try to understand the relation of arm motion to kick motion, and to integrate the pace of each so that they work with, rather than against one another.

Let us try to analyze this person's behavior conceptually. Following our assumption about needs as the motivating force in behavior, we would say that this swimmer has a need to master the skills of swimming. This need might arise from many other needs which are more basic. He may have a need for exercise. He may have a need for approval from a sex object which can be met partially by mastery in swimming. He may have a need for self-esteem which can be satisfied by mastering the strokes he hears about. According to the homeostatic principle, he would swim fairly often as a way of reducing the tension level in various of his need systems and thus maintain a constancy or inner balance. But at the same time his curiosity about the hinterlands of his experience might lead him to the discovery of a swimming stroke he has not previously known or mastered. Thus is created a new need or an increase in the tension level in this area and thus the inner constancy is thrown out of balance. This imbalance demands correction which demand, in turn, accounts for his subsequent behavior.

Lewin calls the process of differentiating or dividing up an undifferentiated region "cognitive structuring," and Tolman calls it the "making of cognitive maps." [9] The reader will understand what they mean if he can conceive of a map in the mind. Part of the map is very clear and highly detailed. This is the part of a person's world that is familiar to him. Other parts will be vague and unclear. These are the parts of his world that are relatively unknown to him. If we, the observers, could also know the details of the person's cognitive map at the moment and know what needs were in tension and to what degree, we then could predict how he would behave, where he would move in his perceived world.

Another thing that can happen in this process of differentiating an undifferentiated region is that one can and does often encounter regions that are contradictory to or in conflict with other regions already in the life space. For instance, the swimmer may have been taught to breathe once in every complete stroke and has always done this. In one particular race he is beaten by a swimmer who breathes every third stroke and in conversations after the race the defeated swimmer becomes convinced that the limited breathing

[9] Tolman, Edward C. "The Psychology of Social Learning." *Journal of Social Issues*. Supplement Series Number 3, December, 1949.

pattern has constituted the margin of difference in the race. The path that once led to victory, to need satisfaction in his cognitive map, no longer leads there. As a consequence, there is created a need to learn the new method.

At this point three important concepts regarding the motivations underlying behavior have been presented: (a) the individual is motivated by certain basic needs which create tensions that are resolved with need-fulfilment; (b) the organism strives constantly to release tensions and restore inner balance; (c) the human being has an insatiable curiosity, a desire to learn, to explore the unknown, this last accounting for continuous digressions from equilibrium and return to it as need-tensions are created and resolved.

## The Process of Interpersonal Interaction

Our focus in this second section is still upon the individual, upon that part of the individual's behavior in which he is trying to satisfy his needs through another person. We shall therefore be concerned with the process of interpersonal interaction. We seek a framework within which we may interpret how and why people behave as they do with respect to one another. How shall we explain the behavior we have observed, for instance, between a parent and a child, between the director of a recreation center and a volunteer crafts instructor, a home-owner and the plumber who has been called in to mend a leak, an office secretary and her boss, two department heads within the same agency? How shall we describe the interaction between such groups as unions and management, Negroes and whites, adults and adolescents?

In the first place, we must recognize that it is difficult if not impossible to generalize about interpersonal relations. Each relation must be analyzed and described with respect to the unique characteristics of the two interactors as well as in the light of the purposes of the interaction and the situation in which the interaction is taking place.

Fortunately, we have an analytic system for just such a purpose. Douglas McGregor, now president of Antioch College, and Irving Knickerbocker, his administrative assistant, have developed an analytical scheme which they used effectively to analyze interpersonal interaction in an industry during the time they were associated with the Industrial Relations Section at the Massachusetts Institute of Technology.[10]

They found that in any interpersonal interaction it is possible to identify with respect to a given situation a person, or subgroup A, who is trying to get a certain desired behavior from person or subgroup B. The reason A is trying to get this desired behavior from B is that A senses that this behavioral response by B will satisfy one or another of A's needs.

A might be a parent who, in a particular situation, is trying to get B, this child, to clean up his room. Keeping one's room neat in our culture is one evidence of the "well brought up" child. If this parent has a need to be seen by his peers as a competent parent, this behavior from B will satisfy the need to some extent. In another situation, A might be a camp counselor trying to get permission from B, the camp director, to remain away from camp longer than is usually permitted on a "day-off." In this case, the counselor, A, may have asked for the extended time in order to be able to attend a party in town which, of course, could be the means of satisfying a variety of A's needs.

But how does A get the desired behavior from B? In order to answer this question it is helpful to recall Lewin's notion of need constellations. He says, it will be remembered, that at any moment in time the individual has a certain constellation of needs demanding different amounts of satisfaction. This is true both of A and B. It is also necessary to realize that in every situation A controls some of the means by which B can satisfy his needs at that moment while at the same time B controls some of the means by which A can satisfy his needs. This is the essential characteristic of all interdependent relations. In the first example, A, the parent, controls the means by which the child may satisfy his needs for food, shelter, affection, to name but a few. At the same time the child, B, controls the means by which A, the parent, can satisfy his succorance need, or his need for acceptance and recognition by his peers as a parent who can maintain a harmonious relationship with his child.

McGregor and Knickerbocker suggest that in any interdependent

[10] McGregor, Douglas, and others. "The Consultant Role and Organizational Leadership: Improving Human Relations in Industry." *Journal of Social Issues.* 4:6-23; Summer, 1948.

relationship such as this there are two ways in which A can get a certain desired behavior from B. One method is to *augment,* that is for A to supplement in some way the means by which B can satisfy one or another of his needs. A, the parent, might say to the child, for instance, "If you keep your room clean for the next month, I'll help you to get the bicycle you want." Here A is promising to augment B's means of getting an object which will satisfy some of his many needs. The other method is to *reduce.* He might say to the child instead, "If your room is not cleaned you are not going to the movie on Saturday." In this case A is threatening to take away some of the means by which B satisfies his needs. Any time that A induces B to behave in a certain way it is by the use of one or the other of these two methods, augmentation or reduction.

There is an important difference between the two examples cited above of the parent-child and of the counselor-camp director. The parent-child is an example of a situation in which A has the balance of power, where A controls more of B's means of need satisfaction than B controls of A's. The counselor-director is an example of a situation in which B probably holds the balance of power. There is still a third type of interpersonal interaction—one in which the balance of power between A and B is relatively equal. The United Mine Workers and the mine operators is a good case in point.

It is important to distinguish these three situations because the methods to which A usually resorts in each case are very different. While considering these different methods, it will be helpful to speculate as to which methods create the kind of interpersonal interaction that will insure the attainment of our ideal of democratic behavior.

## Type I—*When "A" Has the Balance of Power*

In this kind of situation observation seems to indicate that A more often resorts to reduction than to augmentation probably because it is the easier method. When A holds the balance of power the terms that govern the interpersonal relationship are usually determined by A, again probably because it is easier and also because A is essentially concerned with satisfying his own needs. The later consequences of the use of reduction are usually unfortunate, however, because they lead to an increase in B's need tension, and consequently, to greater frustration which we know often leads to hostility and aggression and to a general deterioration of the interpersonal relations. The child will react much more positively to the parent with the prospect of getting a bicycle for cleaning his room than with the prospect of missing his regular Saturday movie for failing to do so, although each method might elicit the immediate desired behavior.

This is not to suggest, however, that A in dealing with B should use augmentation exclusively. An over-indulgent parent, for instance, who caters to the child's every desire and whim, will, by such action, keep the child in a state of over-dependence and immaturity. Along with a liberal amount of augmentation of needs there must be some reduction or prospect of reduction if maximum growth toward maturity is to result. It was noted earlier in our discussion of Murray's need theory that the limiting of need satisfaction by the one controlling the means, or even the threat of such limitation, led to the development of independence needs. In the terminology we have been using in this section, reduction or threat of reduction, leads to the development of egoistic needs. Reduction, then, is the basis of the struggle for independence. Although we recognize that excessive independence is as unsatisfactory as excessive dependence, we also recognize the fact that the person who has achieved a high measure of maturity is the one who does have both and who has achieved a proper balance between his dependence and independence needs. It follows, therefore, that whenever A has the balance of power over B and where A is concerned with B's welfare, wishing to contribute toward his development, he will do well to use sufficient augmentation to give B a feeling of being accepted and having basic security, but will set limits on the extent of his augmentation of B's means so that B will be left to struggle somewhat for more complete need satisfaction.

## Type II—*When "B" Has the Balance of Power*

It is very obvious that the situation, here, is quite different. A, because he controls so little of the means of B's need satisfaction cannot resort effectively to reduction but is obliged to rely almost entirely upon augmentation. The camp counselor, for instance, might do everything in his power to do a competent job which would contribute in part to the total camp's reputation. He might, also, in many situations, do more than is expected of him. In both ways he would be augmenting the means by which B, the camp director, satisfies some of his needs and thus would tend to make himself more valuable to the director. In this situation it would have the effect of making it more difficult for B to refuse A's request for extended time off. In a situation like this the Counselor, A, can play upon B's social conscience because it is in this area that the counselor has the greatest measure of control over the director's means. The camp director wants to be regarded as fair and decent in his relationships and A controls to a great extent, in this situation, whether he will retain this reputation. Again, in this situation, it appears that the method of augmentation, or concern for the satisfaction of the other person's needs, is most desirable, indeed, apparently the only effective course. If we take this same example of the counselor-director relationship but now focus on the camp director, that is, if we regard the situation as one in which the camp director is A, who in this case is trying to get a certain desired behavior, let us say more competence, from the counselor, B, we have a situation of the first type. If, too, we apply the same formula as we did in the child-parent case, the most appropriate behavior for the camp director would be to augment the counselor's means of need satisfaction in various ways. What we would have, then, is a situation in which each is trying to augment the means of need satisfaction of the other. This probably comes close to defining democratic behavior in interpersonal relations.

## Type III—*When the Balance of Power Between "A" and "B" Is Relatively Equal*

We turn to the third type of situation and find that it is one that frequently exists, between husband and wife, for instance, or between labor and management; between the Western Democracies, on the one hand and Soviet Russia and her satellites on the other.

In these examples, each will want a certain desired behavior from the other and each will control, about equally, the means by which the other can satisfy his needs. If A, in the effort to get a certain desired behavior from B, as in the case of the United States striving to get Russia to agree to some proposal for atomic control, chooses to use reduction such as threat of economic sanctions, she will likely receive similar treatment in return from Russia. On the other hand, if A chooses to use augmentation, she runs the danger of upsetting the balance of power in favor of B. The United States hesitates to make Russia economically and industrially strong for fear Russia may turn her new found strength against her benefactor. For this reason such interpersonal relations as these are often characterized by persistent unresolved conflicts. Only in rare instances are these conflicts resolved.

The situations in which conflicts are resolved are those in which A and B have chosen, for one reason or another, to work together for a bigger goal which can satisfy the needs of both. There were numerous examples of this phenomenon during the war when individuals or groups, who had never been able to work together, put aside their private conflicting goals and began cooperating in the attainment of some bigger objective. There are several examples in the industrial world of labor-management profit- and policy-sharing plans, through which profits and morale of both labor and management have increased as they found a way of working together for higher productivity. The Scanlon Plan now operating in scores of industrial concerns is a case in point. The cooperative method of working for larger objectives through which the means of need satisfaction of both parties can be augmented would also seem to be a part of what we mean by democratic behavior.

It will be noted in all of these situations that the kind of behavior that has led to the most satisfactory interpersonal behavior has been that in which each party has tried to augment the means of need satisfaction of the other. Augmentation, wherever possible, always seems more appropriate than reduction. This of course is not a new idea. This is the essence of the Golden Rule. Man has believed in it, though seldom practiced it, since the earliest times. It has been central to most of the great religions of the world.

## The Developmental Process

Having considered the process of interpersonal interaction, the process, by which one person satisfies his needs through another, we turn now to consider the nature of the developmental process,— how the individual develops from infancy through maturity and how his behavior patterns change in each stage of development. Before embarking upon this analysis, however, we pause momentarily to consider what we mean by maturity. What is the nature of this state we call maturity toward which we want to help all individuals to move?

First of all, it seems clear that maturity is not a finite state. It is not a quality possessed only by some and not by all, but rather a quality possessed by all in some measure. Surely the newborn babe possesses the seed of his own maturity which can begin immediately and continue to grow until the process is terminated at life's end. Furthermore, the same individual will probably manifest various levels of maturity at different times depending upon the circumstances in which he finds himself and his current state of well-being.

But what is maturity? Murray, as we have already noted, would probably say that the degree of maturity at a given moment for a given individual is revealed in the extent to which the individual has achieved a satisfactory balance between his dependence and his independence needs. He would say that the mature person is the one who recognizes his areas of dependence and independence and can accept both, whereas the immature person is either one who is overly dependent or one who is overly independent. It would seem then that a mature person is one who has learned the meaning of inter-dependence, mutuality and cooperation, and who had learned to behave accordingly.

Freud would probably describe a person's maturity level in terms of the extent to which he had developed his ego sufficiently to control the counter demands of his "Id" and his "Super-ego" impulses.

From Cannon's homeostatic point of view maturity would be defined in terms of the person's ability to maintain an internal consistency amid the complexity of influences impinging upon him.

If, however, we accept Murphy's modification of the homeostatic principle, maturity would have to be stated in terms of the capacity to maintain an inner balance while at the same time endeavoring to differentiate the unknown regions of one's experience, that is, to distinguish new regions in the life space, and incorporate these into one's cognitive map while maintaining the total balance of the organism.

As an example let us say that an individual had made a fairly satisfactory adjustment to the pre-atomic world. He was able to satisfy most of his needs. That world had meaning to him and he saw his function in it. Then, with Hiroshima, the impact of the atomic era broke upon him. He can be regarded as mature if he is able to face the staggering implications of this new age and effect the changes in his philosophy, his beliefs and his actions which are indicated.

So much for the concept maturity. We turn now to a consideration of the normal course by which the individual moves toward maturity. The process of development from infancy to old age is described.[11] An average picture is presented, a norm for the various stages of the life cycle. When such a norm is proposed it is always necessary to point out that individuals vary around the norm, and that variability in itself is natural, not to be feared unless deviation assumes extreme proportions. Parents have been known to become very anxious, for instance, when they found their child deviating a few pounds one way or another from the point posed as normal for his age.

## Infancy (Birth to two years)

The beginning of the life cycle is a period of rapid physical growth. The child's needs in this period stem almost entirely from primitive animal drives—in Freudian terms he is all "Id" impulses. He is dependent for the satisfaction of those needs solely upon his mother or a mother substitute. The way and the extent to which his needs are satisfied determine in large part whether he will develop a general feeling of acceptance and security or of rejection and

[11] For the material in this section on the developmental process the author has drawn heavily from the following sources:

Harsh, Charles M., and Schrickel, Harry G. *Personality, Development and Assessment*. New York: Ronald Press, 1950.

Wilson, Gertrude, and Ryland, Gladys. *Social Group Work Practice*. Boston: Houghton Mifflin Co., 1949.

insecurity. The difference is important for its later consequences. If he feels accepted and secure, he will, toward the end of this period, be able to accept some degree of limitation and frustration of his needs.

Psychosexually, he will be in the narcissistic stage of development—self-centered, loving himself or his mother whom he sees as an extension of himself. He will be exploring the world about him largely through the exercise of the sense of touch. As a way of satisfying a seemingly insatiable need for exercise, he will be almost endlessly in motion during his waking hours.

Probably, the prospects of the child displaying any democratic behavior are almost nil at this stage. However, the development of a feeling of security and of being accepted is a necessary prerequisite for the establishment of the healthy interpersonal relationships which in turn will be the foundation of his future democratic participation in groups.

## Preschool (2 to 6 years)

Rapid physical growth continues although it becomes progressively slower. The child still has abundant energy which is released principally through the exercise of the large muscles.

The physical dependency observed in the infant continues in part, although normally the child learns how to care for his own physical needs. His limited world becomes enlarged somewhat to include other children and adults. He loves to play and the patterns of his play show both imitation and imagination. Although he likes to play in the presence of others, his play patterns are solitary rather than cooperative, for the most part. Several children of this age will play with various play objects in a parallel rather than an interdependent fashion. For instance, each will play in a sandbox, with a toy, if there are sufficient toys to go around. If there are not, the children will compete for the toy rather than share it. Each wants what he wants when he wants it.

Efforts by adults to teach children of this age to share are premature. They are as futile and potentially harmful as are efforts to train children to walk or to read before they are constitutionally able. The few cases of "well-behaved" four- or five-year-olds that one may have observed, probably learned that sharing was one of the many incomprehensible demands adults make of them and the price they must pay for obtaining what they want from the adult. If a child shares at this age we can be reasonably sure that he does not do it voluntarily but rather out of necessity.

It follows, therefore, that democratic behavior which implies interdependent pursuit of common goals cannot and does not exist at this age. The groundwork for such behavior must continue to be built, however. It is of extreme importance, to this end, that the child develop a positive feeling toward the children and adults with whom he associates. He can and should be encouraged to make responsible decisions that are within his range of ability. A brief episode was observed in a department store which illustrates what is possible in this regard with preschool children. A mother and her three-year-old daughter were buying socks. The mother selected three pairs which apparently she decided were suitable for the little girl's outfits and were satisfactorily priced. She laid the three pairs of socks, a red pair and two blue pairs, on the edge of the counter and said to the little girl, "You may have the pair that you like best." The girl chose one of the blue pairs, perhaps because its pattern appealed to her. She had made a decision which was within the range of ability at that age. Her mother respected her decision. This is valuable preparation for later democratic behavior.

## Elementary School Age (6 to 12 years)

Actually there are two periods, the first often called the latency period and the second the prepubescent period. In the former the child's physical growth is somewhat slower. He still needs abundant nourishment and sleep. He is continuing to develop greater coordination particularly of the finer muscles. Perhaps because his coordination is improving, he loves to test the limits of his newly acquired powers. Play patterns among children in the early phases of the period are characterized by informal contests with others designed to demonstrate skill supremacy.

Psychosexually children of this age are in the homosexual stage of development, that is, the love object is one of the same sex. Boys play with boys scorning girls and girls act similarly.

It is a period in which the intimate circle of friends assumes great importance for the child. This group is beginning to replace the parents as the chief source of the child's attitudes, preferences and habits. His struggle for independence and emancipation from adults begins in this stage. In this emancipation process the group is important in providing him with the security and acceptance he must have to undertake the struggle for freedom. The child's group life in this early stage, as one would expect, is patterned after the family in many respects because this is the only group experience he has known. It is to be noted also that although his loyalty to the group as a whole is strong, it does not result in complete interdependent behavior. Typically, relationships within a group are loose and transient and often are in the form of pair relations. Each child at a given moment has his special friend within the general structure of the play group and his relationships for the time are confined to this friend. Later he may change and devote his entire attention to another playmate.

He will likely have a strong sense of justice, for this is characteristic of the period. Games must have rules and he will argue endlessly about any apparent infringements of the rules, although he will frequently "rewrite" the rules to suit his convenience.

His interest span which was very short as a preschool child is becoming longer now. He can conceive longer-term goals and will participate in longer-term projects. Because he is growing in his capacity to think, he responds to activities which demand reasoning and activities which are imaginative and creative.

Sharing *is* possible at this age and can and should be encouraged. Concern for the interests of others has some meaning for him now so that there is the basis for the earliest forms of democratic behavior. It should be realized, however, that his earliest experiences with democratic organization should not be of the more formal types of organization that are characteristic of older children and adults. A most frequent error made with children of six to ten is to try to induce them to participate in meetings patterned after their elders. Boys and girls of this age have little interest in such activities. Electing officers seldom if ever arises from the group's interest because it has no meaning to them. It is true that they derive temporary satisfaction out of the prestige which accompanies election to an office. It will probably be short-lived because the other children will soon forget that the election was held. The idea of committees will have some limited meaning, although they have to be organized around short-term projects rather than on a permanent basis. It must be remembered that their time-perspective of the future is still relatively short.

The later prepubescent period is characterized by a continuation of several of the trends noted in the earlier period, the development of finer motor coordination, greater physical resistance, loyalty to the gang, the struggle for independence and the ability to cooperate. But the period also marks the beginning of some new characteristics. For instance, because he is beginning to move out of the homosexual phase he will now be ambivalent about the opposite sex. Although the boy may still tend to reject any kind of identification with the society of girls, he will be curious about them and will want to experiment with and to probe the mysteries of the sex.

This age group shows an acceleration in the rate of growth combined with some unevenness of growth. Growth tends to be confined to the arms and legs making for clumsiness and awkwardness of appearance. The need to compete and to demonstrate physical superiority will assume major proportions at this age and it will be channelled into team effort. Very often, and this is a tendency which should be controlled, boys and girls will give of themselves beyond the limits of their strength and endurance.

## Adolescence (13 to 17-18 years)

The onset of puberty ushers in a period which is very stressful for many boys and girls. Many parents recognize this period as the one in which their children experience the greatest degree of stress and the period in which the parents' role is the most difficult.

There are important physical changes. The focus of growth shifts to the trunk. The heart and lungs increase in size, although not proportionately in strength. This is the period, too, when the secondary sex characteristics emerge. The differentiation in bodily contours between boys and girls which began in prepubescence becomes more marked in adolescents. Boys become more angular while girls become more curvaceous. All these physical changes tend to throw the basic metabolism out of balance, one of the embarrassing manifestations being the appearance of acne and boils. Neuromuscular controls are also erratic and undependable. It becomes clear why the adolescent is so highly susceptible to emotional stress. Lewin explains the stress in this way.[12] Until adolescence is reached the child has become more and more familiar with his body. He has learned to depend upon it. It has become a dependable point of reference. Suddenly, in adolescence his body functioning begins to change in unusual ways. It will no longer do for him some of the things it has done in the past. It is no longer dependable. It is as if the firm ground beneath his feet began to move. This loss of a familiar frame of reference leads some adolescents to doubt the reality of everything. This might be a reason for the spells of despondency which many adolescents undergo.

Another significant factor of physical development in adolescence is the fact that the growth rate of boys and girls of this age is quite different. At the age of twelve the girl is approximately two years more physically mature than the boy and this difference continues, although at a diminishing rate, until about seventeen when the two are again at about the same stage of development. This can and does create some social problems for the adolescent. During the adolescent period, if his psychosexual development is normal, he will move from the homosexual into the heterosexual phase and although this is normal and necessary if he is going to achieve maturity it, too, creates stresses. Again the balance is upset for in the earlier period he has probably achieved a fairly satisfactory balance between his "Id" impulses and his "Super-ego," but now the ego is called upon to perform superhuman feats to control the new and potent impulses that are emerging.

But not all of the stress of adolescence has a physical origin. Much of it is culturally and socially based. The adolescent in our culture has the position of a marginal man. In his struggle to be independent of adult control and with the appearance of the physical attributes of impending adulthood, the adolescent rejects childhood and seeks admittance into the adult world. He is thwarted in his efforts, how-

[12] Lewin, Kurt. "Field Theory and Experiments in Social Psychology: Concepts and Methods." *American Journal of Sociology.* 44:873-84; May 1939.

ever, for we are not ready as yet to admit him to our world. We say to him, "Some day when you are ready, but not yet." We keep him, as it were, in suspension for several years. Because adolescents do not wish to be regarded as children and are not yet recognized as adults, they do the most obvious and sensible thing under the circumstances: they form a world of their own. It is a phenomenon which can be observed universally in our culture. They develop their own dress, their own language, their own customs and their own secrets. Also, as an added insurance against adult encroachment, they change their customs so rapidly that adults are kept in a continuous state of bewilderment.

While adolescents seek admittance into the adult world they often demonstrate by their behavior their inability to assume the responsibilities of adulthood. They are undependable. At one time they will demonstrate in their behavior a degree of maturity that is truly surprising, but very likely in the next moment they will regress to some child-like behavior pattern.

Because of his frequent undependability and unpredictability, we are reluctant to give the adolescent freedom, finding him unable and unwilling to assume the responsibility that must accompany this freedom. Sometimes adults err in giving adolescents too much, but more often in giving them too little freedom. Because of their own insecurity or perhaps their unwillingness to relinquish the satisfaction enjoyed from children's dependence upon them and because of an underestimation of the ability of the adolescent to struggle through difficult situations, adults often tend to overprotect him. They make decisions which he could, with a struggle and perhaps some minor misfortune, make for himself.

We need to allow the adolescent some opportunity to experiment with freedom and to realize through experience the consequences of irresponsible actions and decisions. Adults can, by the continued imposition of unnecessary restrictions and the prolongation of the parent-child relationship, drive the adolescent to a point where he will either be forever dependent and thus forever immature or he will use his hard won freedom in an irresponsible way.

Group life is of tremendous importance for the adolescent. In a friendly group he can work out his fears and his confusions; in it he can get the support he needs while in this period of conflict with adults. We should remember, of course, that adolescent groups need expert adult leadership. The relationship that an adult has to establish is a difficult one because of adolescents' tendency to reject adults generally. It will require a mature person with infinite patience and faith in young people, a person who can allow adolescents to grow through struggle at the same time being ready to enter and protect them from serious consequences.

## Young Adulthood (18 to 30 years)

When the age of young adulthood is reached at approximately eighteen, the young man and woman will have reached physical maturity. During this period each will probably have completed general education. Each will make a choice of vocation and will acquire the specialized training for that vocation.

The earliest years of this period will find young people at the point of highest sexual potency while at the same time being required in our culture to delay marriage for several years. As a result strong new stresses will be placed upon the ego, as was the case in early adolescence.

Young adulthood is the period in which young people have to make more important decisions, have to meet more new problems and have to take more crucial action steps than at any period in their development up to this point. They will choose whether or not to marry. The women will choose between a career, marriage or some combination of both. For those who marry there will be the crucial choice of a compatible life partner. There will be the problems of finding satisfying work, building a home and raising a family. To all of this there may be added the complicating necessity of getting further vocational or professional training.

People in young adulthood are often impetuous and impatient. They are at the peak of physical vitality; and when their exuberance, their high hopes and their ideals encounter the more realistic expectations and the tempered ideals of their elders there is often considerable friction and stress.

With marriage and the establishment of a home and family, emancipation from parental control ought to be complete. Actually, however, for many young people parental domination continues. They may never, in adolescence, have developed sufficient capacity for independent action. In some cases the difficulties of establishing themselves may make them financially dependent. In other cases, however, the difficulty may be the responsibility of the parents who are reluctant to see the dependence relationship come to an end.

We have said that young adulthood is a period fraught with many problems and one in which decisions of serious consequence must be made. It is a period, again, where group life can be very important. They will need their close circle of friends with whom they can share their fears, their frustrations, their enthusiasms and their plans. They will need the support of their friends in achieving independence. The capacity for democratic behavior must be demonstrated in this period if it is ever to appear as a permanent characteristic of the behavior of the individual. It is of utmost importance that at this point in their development young people should have developed a capacity for exercising, and have the opportunity to exercise democratic self-determination. This is important for many reasons, not the least of which is the hope that some measure of their youthful idealism will become woven into the fabric of our culture.

## Adulthood (30 to 60 years)

By the time the individual has arrived at the period in the life-cycle which we have called adulthood, he will probably be established in some vocation although perhaps still unclear as to the specific kinds of services and activities for which he is best fitted. He will be struggling to feed, clothe, and educate his family. Greater and greater responsibilities will be placed upon many persons in their vocation or profession and in the community. This added responsibility will have the effect of making some people more conservative, even reactionary in some respects. Their ideals which were crystal clear in adolescence and young adulthood may become clouded and their high resolves may tend to be compromised in the struggle with reality.

Some adults will find it difficult to assume the adult authority role, particularly, if, as adolescents, they had to struggle long and hard for their independence. As parents they will find it difficult to fill the parent role toward their own children who, as adolescents are struggling for their own independence. Typically, such parents will succumb to one of two hazards. They may be overly permissive as a reaction to the strictness of their own parents or they may be overly strict as they make their own children the displaced object of the aggression that has resulted from their own earlier frustration.

Physically and sexually the energies of the adults will be waning throughout the period. Consequently, they will have, continually, to adjust their play and work pace. This, however, will be difficult because the tendency will be for more and more responsibility and demands to be placed upon them as they grow in experience and maturity.

## Old Age (60 and over)

Many persons will reach and live well beyond the age of sixty. If they do, they will face some special problems due to the fact that in our culture we do not prepare people for old age. They will be retired, the world of ideas and activities will move beyond them and they may be ignored. Very likely they will have to be cared for in their last years. All of this may give them the feeling of being a burden, of being superfluous and unwanted. If they do develop such feelings, they may make things unpleasant for themselves and others. They may tend to become hypercritical of current trends in community life and politics and of the behavior of young people.

Some method needs to be found so that they may continue longer in their professions at a restricted pace consonant with their waning energies. Some means must be found by which they may continue to render important service. If this can be accomplished through new social, economic and recreational outlets, it may be possible to tap the rich resources they possess by virtue of their long experience and by virtue of the fact that they are sufficiently removed from the main stream of life to gain perspective and judgment. It may be possible to make the closing years of life, which might for some become the most tedious and unpleasant, the richest and most satisfying.

Through this section, as we have been charting the course of human development through the life cycle, we have tried to indicate the special contribution which each life period can make toward developing in the individual the capacity for democratic behavior. In the section which follows this will again be our focus as we consider the various patterns of group organization to which individuals may be exposed.

## Group Organizational Patterns

Man is continually engaged in a process of satisfying his basic survival needs. At the same time he feels compelled to explore the outer unknown fringes of his world because of his discomfort in the presence of the unknown. This feeling probably stems from the fact that the unknown contains both promise and threat. It holds the promise of greater need satisfaction while it holds the threat of possible reduction of need satisfaction. Man must know what the unknown holds in store for him, of good and evil, and thus he continues ceaselessly to explore.

Man satisfies some of his needs through others, that is, others are the means or control the means by which he satisfies many of his needs. Thus man is a *dependent* creature. He also strives to be an *independent* creature, free of the power which others wield over him as a result of their control of the means of his need satisfaction. But another fact is of equal importance. While he satisfies his needs through others, others are satisfying their needs through him. Consequently, men are also, by virtue of this fact, and whether they wish to be or not, *interdependent* creatures. This factor of interdependence will be the focus for the remainder of the discussion. We shall consider what function it serves for the individual, what kinds of group organizations are best suited for its accomplishment. Finally, we shall consider how a person must behave in his interpersonal and group relations in order to permit a high order of interdependence.

Not only is interdependence essential to survival, it also appears to be the only means of insuring optimum need satisfaction for the individual. It is not enough for the individual to strive to satisfy his needs through his inner resources and through those of others;

he must at the same time strive to be a source of need satisfaction for others. It also seems clear that the more he is able to satisfy the needs of others, the greater will be his own need satisfaction. This fact, we know, has led some individuals and groups to the belief that complete self-denial, complete devotion to the welfare of others, is man's highest achievement, the only source of complete satisfaction.

In the part of our discussion of the process of interpersonal interaction where we considered the three situations typical of the various balances of power that can exist between the two interacting parties, we noted that the behavior which led to the most satisfactory interpersonal relationship was that which attempted to augment the means of need satisfaction of the other party.

When A had the balance of power it was usual for A to use reduction in his relations with B, but it was more conducive to better interpersonal relations if he used augmentation as well. We noted that while both methods might elicit the desired behavior from B, offering to help B buy the bicycle tended to result in positive feelings between the parent and child whereas threatening to deprive him of his Saturday movie might create feelings of resentment and some kind of retaliatory behavior.

When B had the balance of power, we found that the only recourse available to the weaker party, A in this case, was to enhance his usefulness to B, to become more indispensable to B by making himself the means by which B satisfied more of his means.

In the situation where the balance of power was almost equal between the two, it was even more evident that the only interpersonal behavior which led to a satisfaction outcome was that in which each worked for the other's welfare, or in which both worked cooperatively for a common goal. The satisfaction thus attained was greater even after it was shared than either could have gained alone.

Now this factor of interdependence, this mutual concern of one person for the welfare of others, does not apply to the behavior between two persons only. It applies equally to group situations in which a large number of persons are related to one another in an interdependent network of relationships. Here again, the individual will receive from the group in proportion to his contribution to the need satisfaction of other individuals and the group-as-a-whole. Interdependence, therefore, can and must extend even beyond intra-group relations, for a group cannot succeed in satisfying the needs of its members from its inner resources any more than the individual can be self-sufficient. Groups, too, are interdependent upon one another as also are networks of groups. The idea of interdependence, which is expressed ultimately in the concept of One World is not an idle dream. It is a biological fact. Although we are far from achieving the goal of interdependence through cooperative endeavor even in the simplest interpersonal relation, it is, nevertheless, the goal toward which we must continue to struggle in all of our interpersonal, our group, our inter-group and international relations.

In the struggle for more complete self-realization and in response to the biological fact of interdependence man has affiliated with others in groups and in clusters of groups. Affiliation, of course, implies organization and interdependence implies special forms of organization. Unfortunately, the form of organization most appropriate to an interdependent relation has not been easy to conceive nor is its nature yet entirely clear. Man has experimented for centuries with a great many different forms of organization in the search for that which would be most satisfactory, for that which would permit the highest degree of interdependence and the fruits of interdependence, which are the greatest good for the greatest number. It is impossible in such a discussion as this to survey the infinite variety of organizational patterns that have emerged. They tend to group by types, however, and it is possible to select for analysis three or four types that are fairly representative. We shall consider two varieties of paternalistic organization, a third which we shall call anarchistic and a fourth which we shall call democratic-participatory.

## Paternalistic Organization

If someone or some part of the group assumes major responsibility for the welfare of the other group members we have the basis of the paternalistic pattern of organization. Whoever assumes the parental function in the group may do so because he is believed to possess some special endowments which qualify him to assume this

role. He may be older, more intelligent, better educated, more experienced, or more skillful than the other members in the organization. These superior endowments tend to give him power over
lesser-endowed members and this is the source of his authority.
It is a pattern of organization characterized by relationships similar
to those we observed in an earlier section where A had the balance
of power over B. As we noted then, it is subject to many hazards.

Let us consider a few of them more specifically. In the paternalistic organizational pattern communication tends to be one-way,
from the top down. The one in authority usually appraises the
situation, determines what is best for the group, formulates policies
and procedures and hands them down as arbitrary directives.
Families in our culture are perhaps the most typical example of this
pattern of organization, but other examples might include certain
religious groups, the military forces, the classroom, the factory.

There is usually a good deal of planning done in the paternalistic
form of organization, very often indeed more than is desirable.
Most of it is done by those in authority leaving little share of the
planning process to those in subordinate positions. Clear directions
are given as to what to do and how to do it.

The group members are kept in a subordinate relationship until
they are able to demonstrate their superiority in some respect over
others by virtue of which they, in turn, earn the right to assume
the authority role.

The dangers and limitations in such a superior-subordinate relation are obvious. The authority figure can very easily be, and very
often is, tempted to use the group for his own ends, to be concerned
about his own need satisfaction to the neglect of others. If he sub-
mits to this temptation he will very likely use reduction more frequently than augmentation with the result that the group will detract
from, rather than enhance, the general need satisfaction of the
members. There is a tendency, too, for the one in authority to grow
more and more out of touch with his subordinates. Each tends to
withdraw from the other to such an extent that the planning that is
done at the top may fit less and less the needs of the situation at the
bottom. A single routine, or procedure, tends to be applied generally
to many situations for some of which it is inappropriate. In infant

care, for instance, a feeding schedule which has been found to work with the first child may be used with subsequent children even though it does not meet their physiological needs.

There is danger, too, in the tendency for one in authority, in planning for others, to base his treatment of them on the treatment to which he has been subjected in the past. Some housemothers in a state correctional school for girls tried very hard to impose upon the girls standards of dress and behavior which the adults had been brought up to accept as proper. These demands were made, despite the fact that the girls came from very different cultures where such standards were either inappropriate or meaningless.

Perhaps the most serious danger in the paternalistic pattern, however, is that it may make the group members permanently dependent, incapable of making responsible decisions. Creativity in the individual may be stifled and his attainment of a satisfactory degree of maturity seriously limited. Feudalism, in whatever form it has emerged in the world, is stark evidence of the dangers inherent in the paternalistic pattern of organization.

## Modified Paternalistic Organization

We turn now to another form of organization which seems to be essentially paternalistic and yet it is at least in one respect somewhat different. Wilson and Ryland, when discussing the role of the social group worker, quote a portion of a jingle which they feel describes the relationship of the worker to the group. According to the jingle, the worker or the authority figure in performing his function will "Love them and limit them and help them to achieve." [13]

Now this jingle can be interpreted in at least two ways, one of which could characterize the "modified paternalistic" pattern of organization, while the other might define the fourth of our organizational forms, the democratic-participatory. In the case of the former, the jingle may be interpreted in the following manner. The adult person related to the group "accepts" the individuals as he finds them. He may not "like" their behavior, but he "accepts" their worth as persons. He "loves" them. Because he accepts their worth, he wants them "to amount to something" and because he is a person

[13] Wilson, Gertrude, and Ryland, Gladys. *Social Group Work Practice*. Boston: Houghton Mifflin Co., 1949, p. 85.

of conviction and principle, he has a conception of what "amounting to something" means in terms of this person's or this group's behavior. He has goals for them which he hopes he can help them to attain. As he works with them he finds some of their behavior leading toward the goal. This he encourages. He finds other behavior leading away from the goal. This he discourages by "limiting" them. As time goes on, he finds to his satisfaction that the group members are gradually accepting as their own, the direction he has indicated and, as they do, he relaxes the limits and exerts his efforts toward "helping them to achieve." In this way they move toward the goals he has set for them and which they have now accepted as their own.

Many groups of children and adolescents are organized on this modified paternalistic basis. The common factor in all of these groups is the presence in the group of an adult person, a parent figure, who has certain aspirations for the group, clear-cut behavior patterns he wants them to follow and certain decisions to which he wants them to come when issues arise.

In the case of a group of adolescents at an early stage in their development a series of questions may arise around some activity, let us say, a dance. There may be such questions as these: Who shall be invited to the party? What will be the theme? How shall we decorate? What type of music shall we have? How much will we charge? What shall we do if some guests bring liquor? At what time will we close the dance? Now the adult *"knows"* the proper answer to all of these questions. On the basis of his knowledge of the club, he judges that it is ready now to consider some but not all of these questions. He feels that it is ready to decide who shall be invited, which really means that he is confident that it will choose to invite other adolescents of whom he approves. Because he is not sure, however, about its ability to make sound judgment with respect to the other questions, he makes these decisions for it. Later, as the group is "ready," it will be allowed to make the other decisions. Indeed, once convinced that the group has reached a stage where it will not make an "inappropriate" decision, with respect to any of these questions, it will be encouraged to give free reign to imagination and creativity. It may be allowed complete freedom, for instance, to express ideas in decorating the hall for the dance. Finally, it may earn the right to decide all the other questions with respect to the dance and thus to an outside observer it will appear to be completely self-directing.

There is a fundamental difference, however, between a group which has internalized adult values and appears to be self-determining and one which is truly so. It is this difference which distinguishes the modified paternalistic and the democratic-participatory patterns of organization. To an uninformed observer the adolescents would appear to be self-determining. Actually, they had demonstrated their willingness to make responsible decisions, meaning they had internalized the goals and behavior patterns which an adult had decided were appropriate for them.

It seems clear, therefore, that these first two forms of organization are essentially the same, although somewhat different in outward appearance. Both are paternalistic. This is not bad, necessarily, for in the socializing process children and youth need adult guidance. However, there is in it the hazard of overdependence upon adults. There must be real opportunity for group self-determination, initiative and the assumption of responsibility, if growth is to occur.

## The Anarchistic Pattern of Organization

Before we turn to a consideration of the alternative interpretation of the jingle, "Love them, limit them and help them to achieve," let us pause to consider the very different pattern of organization which we are calling anarchistic in this discussion. Perhaps it is inappropriate to use the term organization in describing it, because anarchism is essentially the negation of organization. Where the paternalistic pattern tended to be formal and rigid, the anarchistic, in contrast, is almost completely fluid and informal. It is based upon the laissez faire principle of allowing the natural forces in the situation to interact freely to produce what they will. Where there was tendency toward overplanning in the paternalistic pattern, there is likely to be little, if any, planning in the anarchistic pattern.

Essentially, anarchism is the expression of self-centered behavior. In any anarchistic pattern each individual is trying to achieve his goals in his own way with little regard for others. Very young children playing in a sandbox are good examples. Each wants what he wants when he wants it with interaction occurring whenever his interest in a play object coincides or his plans conflict with others'.

It has been observed that adults who are attracted to the anarchist patterns tend to be persons who behave more in response to their emotions than to their intellect.[14] Although capable of feeling and reacting, they tend to avoid logical reasoning. The necessity to analyze a situation and then to plan a course of action is both difficult and unpleasant for them. They are much more adept in the action phase of the group's activity although incapable of sustained effort in one direction. Such people are potentially creative because of their impulsiveness and spontaneity but seldom realize their creative possibilities because of their inability to analyze and channel their creative talents.

It is difficult to cite examples of this organizational pattern because such are rare in any extreme form in our culture. The "bull session" and "gab fest" come close to it. In these there is no plan and no defined goal except to express one's ideas. Each person reacts in a chain-like fashion to each new stimulus and each new idea. Occasionally, there may be a logical thinker in one of the sessions who tries to hold the group discussion to a single course for a time. He will likely fail or if he is successful his efforts will not be appreciated.

The inadequacies in such a pattern are obvious, of course. In the first place, if imposed upon a group, it may be very threatening and very frustrating to group members who constitutionally need more definite structure. Many find it frustrating for the additional reason that such a pattern is often productive of little more than emotional release. Finally, even those who like the freedom and fluidity of the anarchistic pattern are probably generally dissatisfied because this kind of group experience has not greatly extended their means of need satisfaction.

It would be unfair to infer, however, that such a pattern has no value. There are times and situations which call for an optimum of spontaneity and creativity. There have been occasions in every science when progress has come to a standstill because no further

[14] Pressman, Frank, Jr., and Miller, S. M., editors. "Participation, Culture and Personality." *Journal of Social Issues.* 5:10-11; Winter 1949.

movement was possible based upon the premises developed up until that time. The usefulness of these premises has been exhausted. An entirely new idea, a new theory, a new way of looking at the facts is demanded. Here, and in similar situations, the anarchistic pattern which frees one for a "new look" is ideally suited even though it may produce only the *germ* of the new idea.

## The Democratic-Participatory Pattern of Organization

Having discussed two types of paternalism and the anarchistic pattern, we come finally to a consideration of the democratic-participatory pattern of organization. As we indicated earlier, to "Love them and limit them and help them to achieve" is adequate to describe the relationship between the adult person and the members in this pattern of organization only if it is interpreted in a special way.

This interpretation is based upon three related convictions. The first grows out of the belief that each individual has within him the seeds which determine, in large measure, his destiny. You cannot produce growth in any living thing; it is there and you can only cooperate with it. Therefore, one should not provide goals for people or groups; instead one ought to help them find their own goals. Related to this is a second conviction that one has no right to impose goals or beliefs on another. We may believe, for instance, that divorce and mercy killing are wicked, to which beliefs we have a perfect right, but we have no right to impose them upon another. Finally there is the conviction that we have no right to impose our services upon another unless he voluntarily seeks those services or unless the "greater good" indicates that we must impose our services upon a dangerous few.

Basic, then, to the democratic pattern of organization is the idea of group self-determination. In the democratic pattern the group itself assumes responsibility for its own welfare; it plans its own course of action; it assumes responsibility for its actions. Group self-determination, so defined, would seem to consist, then of two components: (a) *participation* by the members in all aspects of life about them which affect them and (b) the *assumption of responsibility* by each of the members for all of their corporate actions.

Principally, however, this pattern of organization is distinguished from others by the special role which the leader or the outside agent plays in the group. He does not occupy a position of authority and dominance. Rather, he has the position in the group of a *servant-enabler* by which we mean that he performs in the group the service of which he is capable and which is necessary for the group's present welfare. What is also important, he performs this service by group sanction.

The servant-enabler approach was recently tried in the college classroom. In two sections of the same course, running concurrently, the instructor in presenting himself at the beginning of the semester, offered to function, within the limits of his ability, in whatever manner the class felt would be most helpful. One of the classes was relatively small, consisting of ten fairly mature and experienced persons. They came to the course with fairly clear questions in mind, definite ideas of what they wanted to discuss and areas they wanted to explore within the general content area of the course. They expressed a wish to be allowed to develop their own curriculum and to use the instructor both at this stage and later as a resource person and a consultant. They decided that fifteen minutes at the end of every two-hour session were to be used by the class to measure progress, to reset their goals and possibly to redefine the use of the instructor from time to time. Between classes two of the members, serving in rotation, met with the instructor and planned how to open up the subjectmatter area in the next session. Very often in these steering committee sessions further direction was given to the instructor as to the role he should play.

The other was a somewhat larger class of twenty-five members, many of whom were a little younger with less experience. In this case, when the instructor presented himself to the group, they elected to use him very differently. "The whole area of this course is very new to us," they said. "We have very little idea of what it is all about. Would you, the instructor, propose an outline for the course which we will react to and possibly modify?" This was done and then they asked that he take an active part in the first few sessions in directing discussion until they had a chance to "find their way." They wanted to become self-directing they said, but not immediately. These instructions were followed out for several weeks until the instructor began to notice signs of apathy and heard some of the members remark that the class seemed to be different than it had been in the beginning. This was his cue to seek further guidance as to his role. At the end of one class session he distributed slips of paper on which each member was asked to indicate how he thought the direction of the class was determined. The form which was used is shown in the figure below:

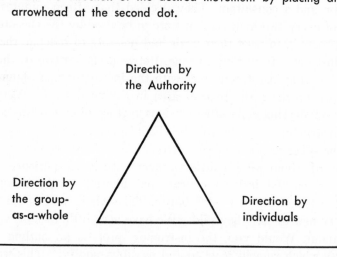

*How is the direction of this class determined?*

1. Indicate by placing a dot on the diagram, below, the kind of leadership pattern the class is experiencing at the present time.

2. Indicate with another dot joined to the first by a line, the kind of leadership pattern which you would like to see and think could be achieved in the next month.

3. Show the direction of the desired movement by placing an arrowhead at the second dot.

Direction by
the Authority

Direction by
the group-
as-a-whole

Direction by
individuals

The results were tabulated as shown in the next figure. It was found that the dots which indicated where the class thought they were at present were grouped in Area I on the triangle and the dots which indicated where it wanted to move in the next few weeks were grouped in Area II. The class members indicated, almost without exception that they wanted to move in the direction of more group self-determination.

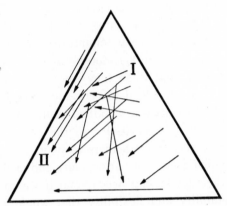

The results were shown to the members and they were asked to discuss what they meant in terms of future planning of class procedures. Out of the discussion came several concrete suggestions. They wanted to continue to follow the original course outline, but to have a steering committee meet each week to plan with the instructor and to make recommendations two weeks in advance about outside reading and preparatory projects. A few class members expressed the feeling that the steering committee should not do too much planning. They felt its job should be to find the best way of initiating discussion in a given content area then to allow the group complete freedom to explore the area in its own way. There appeared to be general acceptance of this idea and the steering committees followed the directive for the remainder of the semester.

Some will say that such group self-determination with the adult playing the servant-enabler role can be used only with very mature people. Another example may serve to show this opinion to be unfounded. At a summer camp for boys ranging in age from 9 to 12 years something similar often occurred. A series of evening programs around the campfire had been conducted by one or another of the cabin groups, or by groups of the counselors, or by the program director, each affording a different degree of group self-determination. At one campfire the boys were asked how they wanted the special Saturday night campfire to be planned and conducted. They said that they wanted the program director to be in charge and they suggested that he choose the songs which he thought they would want to sing and which he thought they sang best. This would seem to show that even a group of young boys knew what they wanted and even appreciated their own immaturity and their inability to assume too great a degree of self-determination. They realized that they were dependent, that when they were allowed too much freedom of decision it did not lead to very satisfactory results, and so they asked for the support that a skilled adult could give them.

If we could develop a sensitivity to the cues that groups give regarding the roles they want leaders to play; if we could develop techniques by which groups of various ages and degrees of maturity could indicate their leadership needs; and if we could develop the degree of adaptability and flexibility that would be required, we might very well be able to help groups of all ages realize advanced forms of this democratic-participatory pattern of organization.

In such a pattern the manifest activity of the group, that which an outside observer might see, could be almost identical with that which would result from the modified paternalistic pattern. There is an essential difference, however. In the modified paternalistic organization, the parent figure determines the limits that will be placed upon the group, whereas in the democratic-participatory the group and the leader together determine the limits which they will place upon themselves or which they will ask the leader to place upon the group. This is not a new procedure for it is just what we do when we elect legislators to pass legislation empowering police officers to prosecute us if we violate traffic laws. This is what we do in wartime when we give the President extraordinary powers to place limits upon us. It is true, of course, and this is of crucial importance, that as we give these powers to another we always reserve the right, in a democratic society, to take them away when they are no longer required.

The democratic-participatory pattern is both similar to and different from the other patterns described. Where there was planning without member participation under paternalism, and member participation without planning under anarchism, there is planning through member participation in democracy. The planning is done by the persons or the representatives of the persons who will be affected by the plan. As in the paternalistic pattern, there is form and structure but it is functional, that is, it fits the needs of each particular situation. Because each unit is autonomous and operates within a general structure, each unit is functionally different in some respects from all others. Where authority stemmed from the top down through the organization in the paternalistic patterns, under the democratic pattern authority rests with the autonomous units at the bottom, and power is delegated up through the organization through various bodies empowered to integrate, but not irrevocably to control, the constituent parts.

The possibility of creativity and spontaneity which we recognized as the sole value in the anarchistic pattern is guaranteed in the democratic method, for the group can elect to modify temporarily its organizational structure to permit spontaneity.

We have described the democratic-participatory pattern of organization as one in which the group assumes major responsibility for setting its own goals and procedures. The adult person or status leader relates to the group as a servant-enabler. He helps the group as the group wants and needs help, and he gives the kind of help requested if it is within the limits of his ability and function.

Such a pattern or organization invites a number of obvious criticisms for it seems to have serious limitations under certain circumstances. We must face these criticisms squarely, see what they are and what to do about them.

1. *The group may not know what it wants to do.*

Very often the group members, unlike the boys around the campfire, do not know what they want, or because they have never experienced a certain activity are unaware that they might be interested in it. Children who have never tried the water, who have never camped out may not know how much fun they can have. Because of this, they will probably never ask for help in learning swimming or campcraft. In such circumstances, particularly where parents look to camp to expand their children's interests, it seems appropriate for the adult person to expose each person or give each camper a taste of all the activities but to allow him to decide those in which he wishes to continue.

2. *The group may know what it wants to do but does not appreciate the consequences of its action.*

For example, a cabin group of fourteen-year-olds was reported to be smoking in the woods. Smoking by boys of this age was prohibited for health reasons and for reasons stemming from the philosophy of the sponsoring agency. Smoking in the woods was prohibited generally because of the fire hazard. The director spoke with one or two of the boys who had been smoking and found that they felt that there was no reason why they should not smoke, since they did so at home and their parents approved. The director took no action but suggested that a meeting of the entire senior section of the camp be held where there could be a full discussion of the question and a reconsideration of the present ban against smoking. They met in the senior clubhouse around the fireplace and fully discussed the whole question. The boys carried the burden of the discussion and brought out the fact that, although they were allowed to smoke at home, the sponsoring organization had standards against smoking for its own reasons and that many parents sent their boys to the camp because they approved these standards. The matter was not settled that night. The boys who had been smoking asked if they could remain for a while after the others had left for bed. They wanted to talk alone about the matter. The director and all the others left. What the boys who remained did is not known, but the next day they asked to see the director. When he met with them they gave their remaining cigarettes to him, asking him to keep them until they went home. They had decided it was best for everyone for them not to smoke while at camp. The director told them that he was perfectly willing for them to keep the cigarettes in their own cabin. The boys said they were not sure they could trust themselves, so he agreed to their request. Thus the matter was settled by the boys deciding to operate within the limits set for them by the camp. They had been helped to see the broader consequences of their action and had made their decision accordingly.

Suppose, however, that they had insisted upon their right to smoke while in camp? By their insistence they would be asking the servant-enabler to change the policy which would have left him with two alternatives. Either he could have taken steps to change the policy if he too believed it was inappropriate, or he could have told them that the service they asked of him lay outside the limits which he was able or willing to perform. The request might have exceeded his ability limits because of the trust placed in him by the agency or it might have exceeded his own limits because it violated a value he held strongly. If he had, for either reason decided to uphold the policy, the boys would have been obliged to conform or to leave camp if they felt that strongly about the issue. But again it would have been their decision.

There is a subtle but important difference between this approach and that which we described in the modified paternalistic pattern. The boys were helped to see the limits within which they operated but they were allowed to choose whether they wished to be bound by these limits. Their right to decide whether or not to remain in the situation was not violated. The director played the role of the servant-enabler within the limits of his position.

3. *The group does not ask for help.*

In the classroom situation described earlier there were times when the instructor felt that the group needed help and wanted it, but, for some reason or other, did not ask for it. In this situation the instructor indicated to the group the kind of help which he was willing and able to give at that moment if they wanted it. This does not seem to be a violation of the servant-enabler role, particularly if he created a permissive enough atmosphere to make it possible for them to reject his offer if they did not think it would be helpful. One effective technique is to present a group with several alternatives from which it may choose.

4. *The group does not give a true indication of what it wants.*

This is a much more difficult situation because, although the group has asked the servant-enabler to perform a certain service, this is not what it really wants. The larger of the two college classes previously considered is an excellent case in point. It will be recalled that the class had indicated that it wanted to be more self-determining and that the procedure had been planned accordingly. It had indicated that it wanted a minimum of structuring in class sessions to insure greater spontaneity and creativity. This, too, was done. The results, however, in this case were somewhat disastrous. The group from this point on seemed to deteriorate. Discussion in class was sporadic and forced. Some class members seemed to "freeze" and were unable to participate. Some members became apathetic, some very critical and over all the sessions hung an atmosphere of tenseness. Finally, in the last session, by class request, the situation was discussed and some surprising facts came out. Although the class members had indicated that they wanted greater group self-determination, they had said so because they felt that "this is what they *should* want" or this is what the instructor "wants us to want." Furthermore, it was found that only a few, the more vocal members, had wanted a minimum structured situation. The majority, although they had shaken their heads in agreement, had really not wanted it. Here, then, was a case in which the servant-enabler was functioning on invalid data from the group. It would seem very clear from this that we need better techniques for determining real feelings in the group. Until we develop them, however, we must do the best we can, allowing as many opportunities as possible for the members to communicate their real desires.

5. *The group is in imminent danger.*

There are times when immediate action is demanded. There is no time to present alternatives for group decision. A story is told which aptly fits this situation. A social worker stood on the bank of a river near a spot where a man was floundering. The man disappeared below the water and reappeared twice, while the social worker wrung his hands in despair. Before disappearing for the third time, the man managed a feeble "help" whereupon the social worker dived in and saved him. When he had the man safely on the bank, he said, "Thank God, you finally called for help." This is probably unfair to social workers for they, too, realize very well that there are times when one does not wait for the cry of help. When a child or a puppy ventures out on the street amid the traffic, the adult does not hesitate to act. The servant-enabler will also act in situations like these, but whenever he does he will take steps to see that the person who needed help develops sufficient self-discipline to make such unsolicited "rescues" unnecessary in the future.

It is obvious that the servant-enabler will rescue a drowning man or a threatened child, but what will he do in a situation where a club is launched upon a plan which he knows will certainly cause it to have an unsuccessful dance, for instance? This is a situation where a failure probably will do them no harm and may have a good effect on the group. The servant-enabler is thus faced with this additional decision of whether the imminent danger is serious or not. How will he decide what is serious and what is not? Is the servant-enabler not subject to the same hazard as we noted in the benevolent autocrat in the modified paternalistic pattern who tended to be over-protective? Clearly he is. Unavoidably he must make a subjective judg-ment as to whether or not to act in each situation. If the situation is one which will lead to permanent impairment of an individual's or group's means of need satisfaction, it is a situation which calls for direct and immediate action by the servant-enabler. By "permanent" impairment we mean that which would require therapy of some sort to repair the damage.

By way of summary the actions which the adult must take if he would play the servant-enabler role as we have described it are listed.

The servant-enabler:

1. Helps the group to help itself
2. Gives, within the limits of his ability, that help which the group indicates it wants
3. Acts in response to implied or non-verbally expressed requests as well as those verbally expressed
4. Describes service which he is prepared to give, and which he thinks the group needs, along with other alternatives and allows the group to accept or reject his offer
5. Exposes the group to untried courses of action
6. Helps the group see the consequences of present actions
7. Acts without group sanction only when he perceives the situa-tion to be one fraught with danger of permanent impairment of need satisfaction for the group. Wherever possible or necessary explains afterwards the reason for his action.

Of all the forms of organization we have considered, this latter form would seem to present the greatest possibility for the optimum satisfaction of human needs. It makes great demands upon the members, for all must participate and all must assume their measure of responsibility, but the resultant group self-determination guarantees that what is accomplished by the group will more completely meet the needs of all the members.

The democratic-participatory method will be as effective as the group members and the servant-enabler make it, for in the long run it depends upon the members' ability to behave according to the demands which such a pattern as this puts upon them. We return again, therefore, to the individual and his behavior, to a consideration of the kind of member behavior which is required for democratic participation.

Essentially, it requires the abandonment of an old and the acceptance of a new attitude toward what it means to be a member of a group. One of the greatest obstacles to democratic participation is the notion, so commonly held, that some of us are just followers while others are the leaders. In a democratic group there is no such dichotomy between leader and follower. Leadership is one of the accompanying responsibilities of membership in a democratic group. The leadership of the group is *every* member's responsibility.

Each group member has some skill, some knowledge; each group member has some functional role which he is able to perform. From time to time, the activity of the group or the state of the group demands that certain functions be performed. By definition, in a democratic group every member is obliged to perform any function for which he has particular aptitude. These functional roles, performed by group members as needed by the group, are in reality the instrumentation of group-self-determination. This is the means, the only means, by which democratically determined goals can be realized in the groups of which one is a part.

Benne and Sheats have listed the following functional roles which they believe cover the variety performed in a group-discussion situation:

## Group Task Roles

The initiator-contributor, the information seeker, the opinion seeker, information giver, opinion giver, elaborator, coordinator, orientator, evaluator-critic, energizer, procedural technician, and recorder.

## Group Building and Maintenance Roles

The encourager, the harmonizer, the compriser, the gatekeeper and expediter, the standard setter or ego ideal, the group-observer and commentator, and the follower.

## Individual Roles

The aggressor, blocker, recognition seeker, self-confessor, play-boy, dominator, help-seeker, and special interest pleader.[15]

Anyone who has observed a discussion group or a committee closely, particularly a productive one, will notice that at some time or another almost everyone in the group performs one or another of these roles. If, indeed, we defined leadership as "the performance of any functional role that moves the group," we would find that the leadership had been shared by most of the members. If one observed the group long enough, one would probably notice, too, that it tended to look to certain of its members when particular functions needed to be performed. Members would begin to be cast habitually in certain roles. The important point to be remembered, however, is that the dichotomy between leader and follower in a situation like this is meaningless and even misleading.

Many people believe that the productivity of a committee depends upon the ability of its chairman. This is probably true if one holds the leader-follower notion and places all responsibility on the leader. But in a democratic group such is not the case. The productivity of the group depends upon the extent to which all the members assume responsibility for leadership, upon the ability of the group to mobilize its resources, upon its ability to cast members in functional roles appropriate to the situation, and upon its ability to reorganize according to the demands of the changing situation.

## Democratic Behavior

Thus we come finally to a point where we can summarize our entire discussion in a brief statement on democratic behavior. First of all are five assumptions upon which the statement is based:

1. The motivating force behind all behavior arises from man's effort to satisfy his basic survival needs.

2. Men satisfy their needs through one another, hence are inevitably interdependent.

3. The more one can be the means of satisfying the needs of others, the greater will be one's own need satisfaction.

4. Men form groups as a way of facilitating the process of mutual need satisfaction.

[15] Benne, Kenneth D., and Sheats, Paul H. "Functional Roles of Group Members." *Journal of Social Issues*. 4: 41-49; Spring 1948.

5. The individual is the most reliable judge of his own needs and, therefore, the one who should largely determine his own destiny.

On the basis of these assumptions we have advanced an argument which holds that the group organization most conducive to the attainment of optimum need satisfaction is one in which the group is self-determining, in which each member assumes the measure of responsibility of which he is capable and participates actively in all aspects of the group's life, again according to his capacities and special abilities. This is the democratic-participatory pattern of organization. The behavior demanded of anyone who wishes to function in such a group will require in addition to the assumption of responsibility mentioned above, an active concern for the welfare of others as well as, and perhaps before, his own welfare. This kind of person is very rare, we know, which may explain why the implementation of democracy is so difficult and so slow. Our greatest hope for developing such persons is first to provide, in infancy and early childhood, conditions in which the individual will feel accepted and secure. This is the firm base upon which a mature adult can develop. Secondly, in order to permit democratic behavior to emerge, the servant-enabler rather than the superior-director role must be assumed in the relations of individuals and groups.

# Bibliography

BENNE, KENNETH D. "Leaders Are Made, Not Born." *Childhood Education* 24: 203; January 1949.

BENNE, KENNETH D., and SHEATS, PAUL H. "Functional Roles of Group Members." *Journal of Social Issues* 4: 41-49; Spring 1948.

CANNON, WALTER B. *Wisdom of the Body.* New York: W. W. Norton and Co., 1932.

CARMICHAEL, LEONARD, editor. *Manual of Child Psychology.* New York: John Wiley and Sons, 1946.

COYLE, GRACE. "Definition of the Function of the Group Worker." *The Group* 11: 11-12; May 1949.

COYLE, GRACE. *Group Work with American Youth.* New York: Harper and Brothers, 1948.

DEERING, IVAH. *Let's Try Thinking: A Handbook of Democratic Action.* Yellow Springs, Ohio: Antioch Press, 1942.

GORDON, THOMAS. "What Is Gained by Group Participation?" *Educational Leadership* 7: 220-26; January 1950.

GUY, GEORGE V. "Group Study Procedures: A Selected Bibliography." *Educational Leadership* 7: 266-69; January 1950.

HARSH, CHARLES M., and SCHRICKLE, HARRY G. *Personality Development and Assessment.* New York: Ronald Press, 1950.

HENDRY, CHARLES E. *Decade of Group Work.* New York: Association Press, 1948.

JENKINS, DAVID H. "Research in Group Dynamics." *Social Education* 12: 347-49; December 1948.

KELLEY, EARL. *Education for What Is Real.* New York: Harper and Bros., 1947.

LEE, IRVING J. "Why Discussions Go Astray." *A Review of General Semantics* 4: 81-88; Winter 1947.

LEWIN, KURT. "Dynamics of Group Action." *Educational Leadership* 1: 195-200; January 1944.

LEWIN, KURT. "Field Theory and Experiments in Social Psychology." *American Journal of Sociology* 44: 868-96; May 1939.

LEWIN, KURT. "Field Theory and Learning." *The Psychology of Learning.* Forty-First Yearbook, Part II. National Society for the Study of Education. Bloomington, Ill.: Public School Publishing Co., 1942, Chapter 6.

MCGREGOR, DOUGLAS, and OTHERS. "The Consultant Role and Organizational Leadership." *Journal of Social Issues* 4: 2-53; Summer 1948.

MURPHY, GARDNER. *Personality—A Biosocial Approach to Origins and Structure.* New York: Harper and Brothers, 1947.

MURRAY, HENRY A. *Explorations in Personality.* New York: Oxford University Press, 1938.

NEWCOMB, THEODORE M., and HARTLEY, EUGENE. *Readings in Social Psychology.* New York: Henry Holt and Co., 1947.

PLANT, JAMES S. *Personality and the Cultural Pattern.* New York: Commonwealth Fund, 1937.

PRESSMAN, FRANK, JR., and MILLER, S. M., editors. "Participation, Culture and Personality." *Journal of Social Issues* 5:10-11; Winter 1949.

SHERIF, MUZAFER. *An Outline of Social Psychology.* New York: Harper and Brothers, 1948.

SIMKHOVITCH, MARY K. *Group Life.* New York: Association Press, 1940.

SLAVSON, SAMUEL R. "Group Work and Mental Health." *The Group* 11: 4-11; May 1949.

STEINZOR, BERNARD. "The Intent Behind Behavior: A Study in Group Dynamics." *Educational Leadership* 5: 301-306; February 1948.

STOGDILL, RALPH M., and SHARTLE, C. L. "Methods for Determining Patterns of Leadership Behavior in Relation to Organization, Structure, and Objectives." *Journal of Applied Psychology* 32: 286-91; June 1948.

THELEN, HERBERT A. "Engineering Research in Curriculum Building." *Journal of Educational Research* 41: 577-96; April 1948.

THELEN, HERBERT A. "Group Leaders Look at Frustration." *Educational Leadership* 7: 260-66; January 1950.

TOLMAN, EDWARD C. "The Psychology of Social Learning." *Journal of Social Issues,* Supplement Series No. 3; December 1949.

WILSON, GERTRUDE, and RYLAND, GLADYS. *Social Group Work Practice.* Boston: Houghton Mifflin Co., 1949.

YOUNG, KIMBALL. *Sociology, A Study of Society and Culture.* New York: American Book Co., 1949.

ZANDER, ALVIN. "On the Symptoms and Survival of Senile Groups." *Educational Leadership* 5: 319-22; February 1948.

# CHAPTER THREE

# The Related Fields of Health Education, Physical Education and Recreation

THE three fields of education to which this yearbook is devoted have been shaped by the demands of the world in which we live in the twentieth century. They have been designed to meet some of the personal and group needs of children, youth and adults living in today's world. In the previous chapters there were opportunities to think about the kind of world in which we live, to explore the basic needs of human beings and to analyze how their needs are fulfilled in relations with others. In the light of these discussions it is timely to consider the three fields as they have evolved in our country and as they are now contributing to life in the United States.

Health education, physical education and recreation are not, of course, separate fields. They have some elements in common, others which are disparate. In this chapter both the common ground and the special areas of functioning are evident as each of the three fields is described in turn and the possible contributions of each to the education of the individual are discussed. In line with the subject of the yearbook, when considering the possible contributions, emphasis is placed upon the concern of each field for developing democratic human relations.

## HEALTH EDUCATION

### CHARLES C. WILSON

Man's life on earth seems to be a constant struggle against the forces of adversity. He is not a self-sustaining animal at birth. He is born in a state of dependence and remains so for the better part or all of his life. He must be cared for as an infant and only through a careful process of nurture and education does he achieve any semblance of control over the influences which would destroy him.

As Hearn has pointed out in the previous chapter, man emerges only with great effort from the infant state of complete dependence to a type of life where, with the help of others, he is able to be master of his fate to a considerable extent. In this endeavor the evidence shows him to be somewhat successful. As Paterson indicates "The world population as viewed from continent to continent, exhibits enormous variations in health and efficiency, wide variations in genetic or acquired characters, and dramatic variations in social circumstances from famine to plenty." [1] It is with some assurance and some hope that one may believe that in the more civilized states the contribution of health education to man's welfare has been to improve the health and efficiency to which Paterson refers. It is evident that in those world areas where school and public health education programs have been developed the health status of the people is vastly improved over that of less enlightened populations.

In the United States the improvement has been marked. It may be measured in terms of life expectancy (from 30 to 70 in 150 years), in reduction of death rates (from 12.2 to 10.0 in this century), in the reduction in the incidence or the control of certain diseases (smallpox, diphtheria, the venereal diseases, tuberculosis), in the discovery of significant therapeutic drugs, in the improvement of the standard of living, in the extension in the usage of labor-saving and timesaving devices, and in dozens of other ways. In many respects, life is lived better and more healthfully today than it was two hundred years ago and it is lived longer.

Not that there are no significant problems remaining. There are some killers and cripplers still to conquer such as heart disease, cancer and poliomyelitis. There are problems attendant upon the sedentary life which will require the concerted efforts of several generations to penetrate. There are problems attendant upon the increasing prevalence of mental disorders which indicate total or partial failure of large numbers of people to satisfy their basic needs

[1] Paterson, Robert G. *Foundations of Community Health Education.* New York: McGraw-Hill Book Co., 1950, p. 27.

in our complex, rapidly changing, industrialized, competitive, yet interdependent society. There is no reason to be overjoyed at the health status of the population but there are some reasons to be sanguine.

What forces have operated favorably upon the health of people? The tide of health, of epidemic and pestilence, of plague and famine ebbed and flowed for centuries. As populations changed from rural to urban, commerce from land to sea, as medicine and surgery evolved and, principally, as the conscience of people awakened to their responsibility for others, favorable forces began to exert strength over the forces unfavorable to health and survival. Paterson cites the eighteenth century as the era when the chief thinkers ". . . emphasized the importance that health, education, sanitation, hospitals, schools, libraries, and parks must no longer depend upon chance benefactions but must become the serious business of the state." [2]

This transition in thinking marked the birth of the modern era of improved health and better living for the great populations of Europe and the United States. The next two centuries brought tremendous gains. Semmelweiss, Harvey, Pasteur, Lister, van Leeuwenhoek, Nightingale, Jenner and scores of others contributed vastly to the expansion of our knowledge or the improvement of our services. Physiology, chemistry, psychology, medicine, hygiene and many specialized areas made advances with incredible speed, once the shackles of the Dark Ages were removed. In fact, so great were the advances, the twentieth century opened with a lag between discovery and application which still remains. Today, there is much more helpful scientific information available (in nutrition, disease control, child nurture, sanitation) than the people use. It is a breathless race between the forces which sponsor research for man's benefit and those which aid him to use what is available. Both are winning in their joint contest with the forces which would prematurely destroy man.

In every listing of the forces which operate to improve man's health, education is prominently mentioned. The school has continuously been in the center of this effort for as long as schools have

[2] *Ibid.*, p. 41.

been organized. The culture of every civilized people has been transmitted from one generation to the next by means of organized education and within that culture the story of man's health and his struggle to protect and improve it has, of course, been told. Education in health is an ancient enterprise. Its manifestations today are widespread in schools, in the activity known as school health education, and in public life as public health education.

The educator stands strategically placed to bring to the school and public groups the results of the scientist's investigation—the accumulated experience of the race in life improvement. To the extent that the educator goes about this business with zeal and energy to that extent the public benefits. If he undertakes his task with fear and timidity, in lethargy and neglect, to that extent people will remain in ignorance, and in danger of disease. Let educators shirk their duty in regard to the transmission of their segment of our culture, let public health workers fail to present the story they have to tell, and both must accept responsibility for a community in which the level of healthful living is lower than it should be or needs to be. Stupidity about disease, about diet, or life adjustment, or parenthood; ignorance about family, or cancer, or safety can be changed by the forces of education. The scientist is doing his part. The educator must do his.

What does the school do to meet this challenge? In general it seeks "to bring to bear upon the individual life the best in information and service from the scientific world so as to preserve, protect, and develop . . . life." [3] It seeks (a) to develop a program of instruction founded upon an appraisal of needs which, when organized into a curriculum and taught by skilled teachers, will meet these informational needs, and (b) to organize a program of services, likewise based on revealed needs, which will bring the talent of skilled medical, dental and educational personnel to bear on the problems presented so that individual needs for service will, in the end, be met. The purposes of the school health program are "distinctly educational in nature and remain within the purview of the school as an educational institution. The program seeks (a) to inform, (b) to assist in rendering children fit to receive an

[3] Oberteuffer, Delbert. *School Health Education.* New York: Harper and Brothers, 1949, p. 30.

education, (c) to give them experience with the best of scientific health services, and (d) to secure for them a school environment favorable in every respect to their growth and development." [4] If such objectives can be achieved the school may well take pride in the contribution it makes to the health of the population.

What are the means, the detail of the program by which the school achieves these ends? The school that contributes most to the health of its pupils, and to the community in which it is located, conducts numerous diverse activities that are coordinated with the efforts of parents to guard and promote the health of their children and with the programs of official and voluntary health agencies. For convenience, the various aspects of a total school health education program can be considered as (a) Healthful School Living, (b) Health Instruction, and (c) Health Services. Each of these parts is related to the others and each needs to be developed if a balanced and effective school health program is to be attained.

## Healthful School Living

If children and young people are to live healthfully while they are in school, consideration must be given to the development of an environment that facilitates their optimal growth and development. Protection and improvement of health require that all school programs show in the methods employed the application of knowledge concerning the mental and emotional health of children and youth. There must be adaptation to pupils' interests and capacities; there must be experience in achieving, in receiving recognition; there must be opportunities for self-expression and for belonging to groups; there must be concern for the developing personality of each boy and girl and the social adjustments each one is making.

Provision for a healthful environment involves the application of knowledge of environmental sanitation and of other factors that affect health, safety and well-being. School buildings must be constructed and equipped so that there will be no hazards to life or health. Consideration has to be given to safe water supplies and safe sewage disposal; to heating and ventilating; to toilet and

[4] *Ibid.*, p. 31. For other good statements of the objectives in health education see the bibliography on page 114 for writings of Brownell, Coops, Grout, Turner, Williams and Abernathy.

washing facilities; to illumination both natural and artificial; to play areas that are sufficiently large to prevent accidents due to overcrowding; to seating that prevents fatigue and encourages good posture; to appropriately located and adequately equipped lunch rooms and kitchens. In addition, attention must be given to the decoration of classrooms and the landscaping of school grounds so that they will be attractive as well as safe.

School lunch rooms deserve special attention because of their great importance to healthful living. Eating should be a pleasure and should be done under circumstances that are favorable to physical and emotional health. Pleasant as well as clean eating facilities, good lighting, attractive decorations, will help some pupils to develop standards which they may later strive to secure in their own homes.

Actually, healthful school living implies awareness of the impact of all aspects of school life on the health, growth and development of each pupil. The health and personality of the teacher are important and so are his methods of teaching. Ways of evaluating pupil progress need consideration, as do the methods for marking. None of these can be overlooked for their effects on healthful living. To name all the factors having positive and negative results on the health of pupils would mean to list every phase and happening of school life.

### Health Instruction

Any experience that influences understanding of health in any way is a part of health education. On the other hand, health instruction, or health teaching, refers to programs definitely organized to promote certain specific learnings in the area of health. Methods for organizing and conducting health instruction vary from school to school and with grade levels, depending upon the particular curriculum pattern of the school. In a single school examples may be found of incidental, integrated, correlated and direct health teaching.

Incidental health instruction involves the utilization of a particular occurrence or situation to help pupils secure information or understanding or to encourage the development of appropriate attitudes or desirable practices. A campaign by a health agency, the occurrence of a case of poliomyelitis, the visit to a school of a dentist, an accident to a pupil, or the opening of a new housing development are "incidents" which the alert teacher can utilize for this type of instruction. Such procedures are especially effective in the lower elementary grades but are appropriate at all levels. This type of teaching does not need to be "accidental" for the well-prepared experienced teacher can readily anticipate the incidents which will occur, and be prepared to expand and develop the interest which they create.

In some schools health instruction is integrated within a "core" or "central studies" curriculum. In this plan children consider broad problems which in turn involve investigation of what would otherwise be studied separately as social studies, science, reading, health, writing or arithmetic. Practically all large problems or "centers of interest" have health implications that can be developed by the teacher who is aware of them.

Correlated health instruction involves a planned relationship between two or more areas of the curriculum. Health may be correlated with biology, general science, home economics, social studies, physical education, and other areas. Conversely, instruction relating to health may be broadened so as to contribute to other areas. Correlated instruction is possible and desirable at all school levels.

Direct health teaching includes all units or courses that have a definite focus on health. A unit on selection of foods, a project on "Health in our Country," a course in "Health for Americans," "Modern Health Problems," "Home and Family Life," or "Health and Human Relations," are illustrations of direct health teaching. Specific units or courses are needed wherever the curriculum is organized on a subjectmatter basis, as is true in most secondary schools. Regardless of the instructional plan used, an effective school health program assigns health a place of major importance in the curriculum.

## Health Services

Formerly, many persons considered school health services as functions of physicians, dentists and nurses, but present day concepts hold that effective programs of school health services can be developed only as teachers accept responsibility for important parts of the program. Guidance personnel and psychologists are used in the program more frequently than in previous years and emphasis is placed on developing teamwork among all those who share in the program. Health services included in the school health program of most modern schools include provisions for (a) the care of emergency sickness or injury, (b) specific procedures for the prevention or control of communicable diseases, (c) health appraisal and (d) health counseling.

## Health Education in Relation to Educational Objectives

Growing interest in the development of school health programs stems from increased recognition of individual growth and development as objectives of education. Optimal growth requires that the individual be as healthy as possible in view of his inherited endowments. Increased interest also grows out of efforts to relate instructional programs to real life situations. Health education is centered on the quality of life of each person. It respects the individual and fosters a realization of all his potential abilities and achievements.

Health education is in the vanguard of efforts to center attention on the complete development of each child and on providing conditions, equipment and programs that facilitate normal growth, maximum health and greatest happiness. To the extent that health education efforts are successful, the next generation of men and women will be healthier, stronger and happier than any who have lived previously.

An authoritative commission has stated that the educated person "knows the basic facts concerning health and disease . . . protects his own health and that of his dependents . . . and works to improve the health of his community." [5] This statement indicates in general terms the ways through which the school health program contributes to the education of the individual. Part of the individual's education stems from learning facts and developing understandings related to health and to disease. He learns how food, activity, sleep and relaxation influence health and he learns how disease can be

---

[5] National Education Association, and American Association of School Administrators, Educational Policies Commission. *The Purposes of Education in American Democracy.* Washington, D. C.: the Commission, 1938, p. 61.

prevented. He learns, too, how the human organism functions and how it is affected by environmental conditions.

But learning facts and developing understandings are only part of the individual's education, for he must also learn to act. This is implied in the phrase "protects his own health and that of his dependents," since to protect he must act. The school health program helps the individual to learn desirable health practices and to use professional health services when necessary. Furthermore, health education helps individuals develop concern for community health. Students learn that their own health depends in part on the health of others and that, in turn, their health influences others with whom they come in contact.

## Concern with Developing Democratic Human Relations

The school health program must be concerned with democratic human relations and with the use of methods that exemplify desirable human relations. Interest in health implies concern for the condition of each individual and for his relations with others. Each individual is accepted as a unique person, with characteristics and traits different from all other persons. His personality is respected, and his growth and development guided along directions that enable him to capitalize on his particular endowments.

Contributions of the school health program to the development of democratic relations vary in degree according to teaching methods and program content. Greatest values come from the use of methods which involve teacher-pupil planning and which give students responsibility for making decisions. The good teacher of health does not impose a predetermined program on his pupils; he has them share in program planning. Furthermore, he encourages pupils to find their own answers rather than providing them with ones that are ready-made. He encourages group projects, through which children learn how to work with others by actually doing so. Concern for the welfare of others grows out of consideration of specific school and community health problems, as, for example, when a class undertakes study of the question, "What can we do to make our school, our homes and our community safer places in which to live, play and work?"

To the need of democracy for an informed population, school health education makes its own and singular contribution. It brings to young people the best of scientific developments as they affect human life. It provides them with knowledge and experiences and with motivations which enable them to remain strong, for strength in its broadest sense is fundamental to the securing and the preservation of freedom.

# PHYSICAL EDUCATION
## Jesse Feiring Williams

Physical education is an old and fundamental education. The first physical educator was the parent who taught his son to throw a spear, to climb a tree, to leap a brook, to do all those things that were important for youth to learn in the tribal life of uncivilized man. Over the centuries the civilized social scene has changed tremendously, ways of living have profoundly altered, and new stresses have pressed upon the old biological patterns of man. And yet the patterns remain; the organism still retains the structures, organizations, and functional demands that long ago appeared. The need to learn how to throw a spear has passed but the need to throw remains; the need to climb a tree is gone but the urge to climb appears in every child; the need to leap a brook rarely occurs but the necessity to leap arises again and again in the urgent jumpings and leapings of youth. The patterns developed by nature are old and fundamental forms that emerge out of a tribal past and insistently make their demands in a highly industrial and complex present.

It has been the unfortunate heritage of physical education to conceive of its programs in physical terms alone because its activities were so obviously physical. When mind and body were thought of as two separate and disparate entities, physical education was obviously an education *of* the physical; in similar fashion mental education made its own exclusive demands. But with new understanding of the nature of the human organism in which wholeness of the individual is the oustanding fact, physical education becomes education *through the physical*. With this view operative, physical education has concern for and with emotional responses, personal relationships, group behaviors, mental learnings, and other intellectual, social, emotional and esthetic outcomes. Although important and not to be neglected, it is quite insufficient to develop a strength of muscles, bones and ligaments, to acquire motor skills, and to secure physical endurance. The dichotomy of body *and* mind has been abandoned in scientific circles. Physiology, psychology, sociology and modern philosophy recognize the fact of organismic unity. Furthermore, not only is the individual a whole but he is also one with his environment so that the total situation includes the whole person in all his aspects and the environment with which he reacts and interacts in all his responses.

This recognition of man's organismic unity and environmental dependence has required that physical education be *in fact* an education through the physical and hence take into account not only the technical learnings of a physical experience but also the associated and concomitant learnings that inevitably accrue. It is therefore absurd to limit one's objectives to physical outcomes; other outcomes emerge also. Recognition of the whole does not require minor respect for the physical; by virtue of the activities themselves the physical will always have a major role. Nor should there be any apology for its prominence in the proper education of young people. Anyone disposed to regard the physical lightly should remember that the physical was present at Bataan and Okinawa, as well as courage and intelligence, and persists as a part of everything that is good and true and beautiful. Nothing could be meaner than to miscall it. It asks for no supremacy, knowing full well the ugly distortion in the human being when it has an exclusive role. The balance and harmony sought by the Greeks is, in modern terms, an education of the whole person in which the physical takes its proper place in the unfolding of the intellectual, social, emotional and esthetic powers of the individual.

This emphasis upon the education of the whole person runs the risk that the physical may be neglected because of the pressing demands of the intellectual and because of the high compensation that an industrial society pays for mental skills. Nevertheless, that risk should be run. Force and strength without humane direction are too terrible to contemplate. All persons should know that vigor and vitality of peoples are dependent mainly upon muscular exercise for their development and entirely for their maintenance, and that, aside from the conditioning influences of heredity and favorable nutrition, vigorous physical education is the indispensable means today for national strength. But it should never be forgotten that vitality that is ungenerous, beastly and knavish is no proper objective for any division of education. Let the sponsors of physical education have deep convictions about the tremendous importance of vigor and vitality in peoples; let them assert, time and again, and everywhere, the strategic and imperative role of muscular activity in development, but let them guard against an unworthy exclusiveness that leaves them devoted to strength with no cause to serve, skills with no function to perform, and endurance with nothing worth lasting for.

It is apparent on every hand that the accumulated social inheritance presents a staggering load to be acquired by each new generation. When youth had only a few skills to learn or one or two legends to memorize the task of education was simple indeed. Now selections must be made. Likewise in physical education the great wealth of material in physical activities, the wide range of objectives, the increasing mobility of local situations demand careful selection of material. All motor experiences are physically educative but some are worth more in effects produced and in kinds of effects than others. With these considerations in mind a well-known definition of physical education should be stated here: "Physical Education is the sum of man's physical activities selected as to kind, and conducted as to outcomes." [6]

This definition takes into account the fact that a selection of activities must be made and that outcomes are important. Selection as to kind requires appreciation that activities vary in value and hence that some are obviously better than others for securing the outcomes desired. When one chooses one thing from among many, then unless caprice controls, standards are necessary to which the activity is referred. Standards change from time to time in relation to the dominant ideas and urgent needs of people. Although

[6] Williams, Jesse Feiring, and Brownell, Clifford L. *The Administration of Health and Physical Education*. Philadelphia: W. B. Saunders and Co., 1947, p. 20.

muscular and mechanical needs persist, it is not practical to use only the standards that serve such purposes. The social and moral necessities of today place upon all forms of education the responsibility of keeping selections broad and inclusive enough to minister to these necessities also. Certainly these grim days do not require any "back to the body" movement, but rather a selection of physical activities that contribute to democratic human relations, that will offer opportunity for the individual to be tolerant, generous, kindly and friendly, that will encourage manifestations of self-reliance, independence and adventurous spirit, and that will make primary the goal of a strong and positive personality.

And the phrase, "conducted as to outcomes," means of course that the outcomes needed by America today will be sought. There will therefore be emphasized physiological results, growth and developmental outcomes, neuromuscular skills, interests and attitudes and habits. Habits and attitudes of healthful living and interest in wholesome recreation are the concern and responsibility not only of health education and recreation but of physical education as well. While health education and recreation will devote more time to the development of healthful habits and attitudes and recreational interests, their achievements will always be conditioned by the patterns of social life that other forces help to shape. To the proper purposes of health education and recreation, physical education has a unique opportunity to contribute in its training and conditioning routines, in its athletic ideals, and in its functional leisure-time skills.

## Contributions to the Education of the Individual

It is fortunate whenever education can state precisely and with assurance the contribution that any of its disciplines can make to the development of the individual. With respect to physical education this statement can be both precise and assured. Moreover, the conditions which control are known. It is therefore possible to state the contributions which physical education makes to the education of the individual and at the same time to indicate the conditions under which those contributions may be expected to achieve success.

The contribution may be stated in the following four categories:

(a) development of organic systems, (b) development of neuro-muscular skills, (c) development of interest in play and recreation, (d) development of standard ways of behavior.

The development of the organic systems of the individual to their highest functional levels is dependent upon physical activity that uses vigorously the large muscles of the trunk and hip joints. The demands made by these muscular masses call into play all the vital organs and stimulate them to increased activity as they attempt to meet the demands of the muscles. The source of vitality of a person is the functional power of these organs. Both the anatomical facts and human experience testify to this relationship. Moreover, there is not an alternate route that one can take. The development of the vital organs is dependent solely upon the use of the large muscles. And there is a strategic time for this development to take place; it must occur in childhood and reach its fulfilment in youth.

The small muscles of the arms make little contribution to this effect and mild exercises are of little value. To gain development of the great organic systems the child must run and jump, climb and hang, pull and push, wrestle and test himself with others of his kind. Strength and vitality come to those who have expended effort in physical activity.

The second development is the acquisition of neuromuscular skills. All sorts of skills may be learned but those that contribute to the education of the individual are functional ones. These are utilitarian and recreational. The utilitarian skills are the controls that bring a mastery over such acts as walking, sitting, standing, lifting weights, climbing stairs, carrying objects and other neuromuscual coordinations employed in daily life. The recreational skills cover a wide range of sport, dance and self-testing activities. And all these skills are functional. While it is possible for the individual to learn many other coordinations, they make no educational contribution unless he can use them either in vocational or avocational life, or unless they serve as essential precursors of subsequent functional development. This latter hypothesis has no standing in physical education since it is well established that skill is not a general quality but a specific one. Individuals do not learn to run in general, they learn particular ways of running.

The third development is the awakening and enrichment of interests in play and recreation. All young children express early their interest in play. To the casual observer the play may appear to be mere "fooling" but it is nature's way of development. As maturation prepares the individual for higher levels and as experience teaches new controls, the acquisition of skill arouses the individual to the possibilities of a motor experience. Now new interest arises and expands. Learning such a simple game as hopscotch may be enough to lead the individual to spend many hours in this activity, while rope jumping opens up many intriguing coordinations that beckon the jumper to practice for hours until satisfaction comes. It is from such simple experiences in childhood that the individual goes on to handball, swimming, golf, tennis, dancing, and numerous other recreational activities that comprise a means of wholesome expression for the leisure hours that come to adults.

And this development of interests in play and recreation relates directly to the two preceding contributions since the interests that arise involve activity of the large muscles and the skills that are learned are truly functional ones. Moreover, the relation of skill in an activity to interest and participation is direct. The dub in any motor experience develops no interest and soon drops the activity because it provides no adequate satisfaction. It should always be remembered that proficiency and participation go together.

The great effort in physical education should be made to get boys and girls out of the dub class and into the enjoyment level of activity. It is probably a mistake to spend time and money on the development of stars and champions; it is always a mistake to do so when this effort means a neglect of the group for the development of a few. Certainly, no public educational effort can justify in a democracy the development of a few fine athletes and neglect of the mass which results in a large number of physical illiterates unable to enjoy wholesome motor recreations because they lack the necessary skills. But of course in a democracy there should be no restraint placed upon the highest development of which an individual is capable. Individuals are not equal in ability and some can achieve much higher levels of performance than others. These should have their chance but only after there is an adequate opportunity for all boys and girls to get out of the dub class and into the enjoyment level.

The fourth contribution to the education of the individual is the development of standard ways of behavior. Behavior patterns are learned. All experience leaves a behavior deposit in the attitudes and habits of individuals. Physical education is not the sole means of teaching standard ways of behavior; all experiences of the individual make their many contributions. But physical education is a kind of experience about which young persons care and care greatly. Learning to be generous, fair, kindly, friendly and tolerant when participating in vital activities is learning that takes and lasts. The opposite is also true. At times this crucial area for the learning of standard ways of behavior fails to teach the standards that society expects children to learn and succeeds in teaching other patterns that society deplores.

The essential condition for the development of standard ways of behavior is good leadership. Teachers with a purpose to improve the behaviors of youth are always confronted with the realities of present habits and practices. The difference between the *ought* and the *is* reflects the continual struggle of man over the centuries to achieve higher levels of humane civilized life. But improvement of living in any phase of life depends upon persons who exemplify behaviors that are better for men and women than the present patterns of any cultural scene, and who can make these appear to youth as good and desirable. Indeed, the mores of any people are changed only by leaders and it is the clear responsibility of administration to select and support leaders who will be for youth examples that youth may imitate. Generous and fair sportsmanship defeated in this world is defeated forever and it is in this world that it is defeated. It is defeated by coaches and teachers who fail to be examples of excellence, by parents who neglect to support desirable behavior, by citizens generally and the press that exploits the commercial and professional aspects of sport with little regard for the development in youth of those responses which shape fine character.

## Concern with Developing Democratic Human Relations

The need for democratic human relations exists everywhere in the world, in the most abject tyrannies and even in the professedly democratic countries. In the United States a democratic philosophy has shaped its short course in the history of civilization; and respect for the individual, equality before the law, freedom of worship, press, and assembly have made real progress in America. But much remains to be done; restriction of opportunity for racial and religious reasons denies the equality and inalienable rights of man, and class animosities and prejudices destroy that harmony a nation needs.

Physical education should begin its campaign for development of democratic human relations by substituting democratic administration for arbitrary and authoritative administration wherever it exists, by making real effort to eliminate racial and religious bias on the playground, and by intelligent planning of programs to reduce opportunity for needless conflict. These three areas of action should be explored further.

Quite naturally, physical education carried over into administrative practices the patterns of formal gymnastics that shaped its programs for so many years. When the proper procedure in teaching physical education was to command someone to do an act, it was not easy to sit down with colleagues and arrive at policies after discussion of different points of view. This kind of authoritative action readily transferred to the athletic field so that coaches behaved as czars and players were puppets to do exactly as they were told. In some of the more highly developed sports such as football the fun has gone out of the play and all that remains is the foolish pride of being on a "winning team." The basis of democratic administration is full opportunity for differing views to be heard. At times, the members of a group will be unable to agree upon a policy, and yet a decision must be made. At those times, the administrative head must take the responsibility for a temporary decision with the avowed purpose to reopen the policy for discussion at another time after additional experience. One element in democratic administration is the absence of finality about policies where disagreement exists. Let the minority realize that its views are respected enough to be heard again and that there exists the spirit of full cooperation of the minority with majority decisions.

The effort to eliminate racial and religious bias should operate in all aspects of the activity program. Too often programs that might come to grips with the basic issues in the complex problems of human relations are conducted without purpose. The remedy lies in the correction of faulty attitudes of teachers and in their developing real convictions regarding the worth of personality.

The intelligent planning of programs to reduce opportunity for needless conflict should take into account the techniques of sociometry. Sociograms may help a great deal in organizing the class into a harmonious group. There is an increasing body of literature available describing good practices in intergroup education and analyzing methods of group work. Much of this material is drawn upon in subsequent chapters. Those in physical education who really want to assist in the important task of developing democratic human relations can turn to this literature for helpful suggestions about procedures. Before they use this material with profit, however, they must have developed two understandings: first, they must understand the basic facts about behavior, such facts as were stressed in the previous chapter; secondly, they must have accepted the view of the field of physical education as education *through* the physical, not *of* the physical. They must have insight into all aspects of the contributions physical education may make to the development of the individual.

## RECREATION

### George Hjelte

Recreation finds its definition in the vast collection of activities which are voluntarily engaged in by all the people, young and old, rich and poor, urban and rural, cultured and uneducated. It comprises activities in all the fields of individual and group expression from the simplest and most natural to the artificial and most complicated forms of human experience. Thus recreation runs the gamut from the natural playful physical movements of the child to the highly organized competitive athletic sports of youth; from imitative make-believe play to expertly produced drama of the stage; from shaping of crude forms in the sandpile to chiseling of a fine likeness in stone; from discordant singing in self-amusement to superb rendition of a classical composition; from hasty reading of a daily newspaper to complete absorption in a literary masterpiece. All of these activities define recreation broadly but not inclusively. None is recreation in the full sense unless it is practiced in the spirit of play. Joy must be a concomitant of effort in recreation. The innate satisfaction of self-realization must derive from the absorption of the individual in the recreational activity.

Recreation is both objective and subjective. There is that recreation which belongs to and proceeds from the individual and which is the expression of his own peculiar mental, emotional and physical impulses. It is the outward manifestation of his own thoughts, his feelings and his innate and learned capacities for action. It acts in relation to others or toward the shaping of the individual's environment—it is objective. On the other hand, there is that recreation which is subjective in that it consists of observation, contemplation, and reflection upon the recreation of others. It is an experience which takes place within the subject—it is subjective.

Both types of recreation are experienced by everyone. Some are devoted more to the one than to the other. Objective recreation is preferred when one possesses an exuberance of energy or when developed capacities, having been suppressed, drive one to express them. Subjective recreation is frequently preferred when refreshment from toil is desired or when relief from boredom is wanted. The one is developmental, creative and re-creative of powers; the other is passive.

The abundant life is, of course, the one which is expressive of all of the individual's capacities for action, some on a plane of high skill and all conforming to good taste according to the standards of a cultured society.

Those who believe in recreation as a dynamic force in the direction of the good and satisfying life, deplore the fact that there is a paucity of real objective recreation in the life of the people, and a seeming superfluity of subjective recreation. Most people have not acquired a sufficient repertory of recreational interests and skills and nearly all are habitually given to watching while others are active. There is insufficient opportunity generally for people to pursue their own interests in objective recreation together, and on the other hand there are always present blatant advertisements, raucous announcements, intriguing promotions, and promising enticements to amusements and light and frivolous entertainment.

This situation is a result of our industrial organization. Amusement and entertainment can be dealt with as a commodity to be produced and sold. When the techniques of mass production are applied, mass attendance must be developed, hence great efforts must be employed to entice the customers. Large budgets are made available for artificial stimulation of interest. Larger profits lie in the path of mass production of commodities or services. By multiplying the number who are on the receiving end of the chain—that is, the consumers—and minimizing the number of performers, the profits increase proportionately.

One of the results is the growth of a vast industry which caters to a credulous public seeking amusement and entertainment. Staggering figures are published weekly giving the attendance at motion pictures, television, athletic contests, horse racing and other audience-pleasing events. The sum total of hours thus spent leaves little time for participation in recreation that is truly developmental. The very expertness of the performers who entertain and amuse in itself tends to repress amateur expression. The average individual is so appalled by the obvious comparison of his own inexpertness to the skill of the exhibitionists that self-consciousness possesses him to the extent that he shrinks from displaying his own clumsiness. His refuge then is doing nothing himself and being content to take his recreation vicariously and subjectively. Fortunately, this insidious effect is not operative upon children. In this there is hope and challenge for those who through recreation see an opportunity for the development of a happy, competent and truly cultured society.

The traditional recreational heritage of the people is not the product of the machine age. The great works in music, art and literature were the creations of people who devoted themselves to the arts of leisure and who were not subject to the enticements of amusement and entertainment which abound today. The musical forms, dances, crafts, games, sports and contests which have survived through the ages and which become the basic play patterns of children are the products of folk life in the simple community of yesterday. Prior to the machine age, with limited facilities for communication and transportation as well as for mass entertainment, people were left to their own devices for entertainment. Through the processes of individual and group activity they created characteristic ways of singing, dancing and contending in physical playful combat from which emerged a national leisure-time culture representing often the finest sensibilities and reflecting the elevated thoughts, the deepest feelings and the highest ideals of a community or a nation.

In American early folk life similar processes were at work. Among us everywhere were people steeped in the cultural traditions of other nations. The carry-over of foreign habits into the new life in America was not easy. More often the old was discarded in a grasping for the new. But the scene in a new industrial society has not been conducive to the same grass-root process for the development of folk life and the propagation of recreational forms that have lasting value.

It is neither pleasant nor popular to "view with alarm," yet searching analysis is necessary if we are to progress. Changing times call for adaptations of old forms and old organization and for the promotion of new programs and new institutions if the higher goals are to be achieved. It is true that some compensations are evident. The development of a great national culture is in large part dependent upon two basic prerequisites—wealth and leisure. The well-rounded culture of ancient Greece flourished in an age of conquest and an age when socio-economic organization favored the creation of a leisure class who cultivated the arts of leisure. The same was true of England in the Elizabethan period from whence have come so many of our cultural traditions surviving to this day. The modern machine age has created wealth in America and a distribution of wealth hitherto unequaled. It has also brought about a division of time wherein limited hours need be devoted to the compulsions of daily living and increasing time for leisure remains. In a free society this leisure may be devoted to the service of mankind or to its destruction, to its elevation or to its profanement. Herein lies a grave challenge to education in our day.

That the germs of human wastage and social destruction flourish in the recreational life of the people cannot be questioned. The moral degradation and depravity of people is apparent in their devotion to profane and tawdry amusements and entertainments, some giving expression to the baser instincts and unbridled impulses. The popular taste in commercially conducted entertainment as revealed by the advertisements in the daily press leave little room for pride and self-respect. Meanwhile the news columns are replete with reports of crimes and misdemeanors stemming from debauchery in leisure time. Much of the latter is due to intemperance by a people who, lacking the ability to use leisure interestingly, seek satisfaction or temporary detachment from reality, as the case may be, by the use of artificial stimulants, mostly alcoholic beverages. The cumulative effect through habitual alcoholism is no doubt the greatest wastage of human potentialities and the biggest debit in the account of human happiness today. The need for the exercise of self-control in the pursuit of happiness through recreation and of the upgrading of the common taste through educational means is imperative if the leisure which has been wrought from the human toil and resourcefulness of the ages is not to result in the ultimate deterioration of the race. The oft-quoted statement "Civilization is a race between education and the forces of destruction" finds application here.

The full implication of these reflections and considerations is that recreational education must become a fundamental of general education for all. Universal education must seriously concern itself with "preparation for the worthy use of leisure time," and not be content with mere lip service to this goal. It must join hands with other forces to banish recreational "illiteracy."

## Contributions to the Education of the Individual

In order to give direction and guidance to any purposeful educational program in recreation it is helpful to state the goals or objectives of the program. These may be thought of as the ultimate or final goal and the immediate educational goals. The ultimate and the pervading and correlating objective of recreational education is the achievement of human happiness through individual self-realization. The immediate objectives are (a) physical health, (b) mental health, and (c) group (social) adjustment. These are not exclusively the role of recreational education but other programs directed toward these goals would do well to utilize recreation as a means. It is difficult to recall any broad educational objective which cannot be subserved by recreation. It is important that recreation shall not be conducted and pursued in such a manner as to impede the achievement of goals of other educational programs and that it shall contribute positively to the educational goals of other fields of education. Recreation may be good or bad according to the goals which it serves, the quality of its expression, and the standards to which it conforms. To be considered as a positive educational force, it must be organized and conducted with educational standards, objectives, and ideals constantly in mind.

The ultimate objective of education for leisure, namely human happiness, implies that all people shall have the opportunity to develop resources within themselves for a satisfying leisure and a joyful, happy and balanced life, and to achieve full group membership in a democratic society. Opportunity to develop means not merely the exposure of the individual to the world of activities which comprise our recreational heritage. It means the exploration of the individual's capacities and discovery of his individual needs and interests. It means the drawing out of his enthusiasm and interest. It means the teaching of elementary knowledge and basic skills. It means the social adjustment of the individual, for most recreational activities are enjoyed and essentially practiced in the group. It means the organization of a program of participation graded according to the age of the participants and to the individual capacities and needs. It means the provision of facilities capable of accommodating all as they participate in the efficiently organized program. The full implications of this primary concern of education for leisure are almost overwhelming and go far beyond what has yet been apprehended by educational authorities. In short, it calls for a mass program equal in its appeal and its expansiveness to the program of mass entertainment which can serve but a small part of the total recreational and leisure time need, however high its standards might be placed.

Recreation may contribute to dynamic physical health. The ability to function physically in a manner equal to one's potentialities is largely a product of activities which develop neuromuscular skills and the power of organic functioning. These outcomes may be achieved through other activities than those practiced in the recreational manner, but the easier and more pleasant manner, and thus the one that largely produces its own motivation, is to organize recreational activities with this objective directly in view.

Recreation should contribute positively to mental health. The mentally well person is one who finds a happy outlet for his impulses and emotions and whose thoughts and actions are free from abnormalities. Recreation of the right sort may provide such an outlet and may discipline one's thoughts and actions in the channels of normality. Persons who manifestly are recreationally educated are generally healthy personalities and, contrariwise, mentally maladjusted personalities are most frequently personalities who play abnormally or whose recreational capacities are undeveloped. The positive value of a well-ordered recreational regimen in the treatment of mental disorders has been eloquently proved in the results of treatment in the veterans hospitals. It has also helped to make cures of mental illness permanent. The mental health of people is commonly judged by their behavior in leisure time. The most frequent admonitions to achieve peace of mind and sane living are to play wisely and well.

The third immediate objective of recreation is group adjustment. Recreation is to a great extent practiced in association with others. No other activities of life are so completely cooperative. In a society in which mutual interdependence is inherent as a condition of existence, the cultivation of the ability to succeed cooperatively in group endeavor must be accorded high importance.

## Concern with Developing Democratic Human Relations

In a democratic society a high degree of group adjustment on the part of the general citizenry is essential. Nowhere among the democratic nations is this more important than in the United States of America because of the heterogeneous character of our population, composed as it is of many minorities representing different racial and cultural backgrounds. The burden of bringing about a condition of mutual acceptance and of developing cultural unity as well as mitigating intergroup conflicts falls primarily upon education. Education in the human relations desired is a process of learning to put democratic ideals into practice.

Among the various activities which comprise the total program of education none is as capable of demonstration and practice of democratic ideals as recreation. By tradition in America, choices in recreation are freely made, without compulsion. The place an individual earns among his fellows in a recreational group is determined by his conduct toward his associates and the level of his skill and performance. He must assume individual responsibility in and make his maximum contribution to the group enterprise. He must recognize and adapt himself to the contributions of others. He achieves personal security through the joint effort. In recreation, intergroup tensions due to accidental circumstances of birth, color, nationality, religion, are almost nonexistent among the "recreators," albeit not among spectators. There are frequently competitive tensions related to the rules of play, but rarely the other tensions which are so destructive of continuing good human relations.

The theoretical assumptions which underlie this line of reasoning are deserving of profound research to the end that there might be developed sound principles of guidance for enlightened recreational leaders. Although from the standpoint of the recreator, most recreation is intensely purposeful, leaders of recreation have not yet organized, conducted, and guided recreation effectively with a view to the accomplishment of definite objectives. More has been done in the adaptation of recreational activities to serve specific objectives in the field of mental therapy and hygiene. Even this work is conducted without the benefit of adequate research and experimentation. The field of recreational research is wide open to those who would contribute to education and human welfare.

The full use of recreation as an educational force has only begun to be realized. Its traditional quality of freedom acts as a resistant to its purposeful organization, but organization under the direction of wise leaders need not impair its virtues. The development of recreational interests, skills and appreciations among children and youth is still left pretty much to chance. This statement is not meant as an indictment of the schools and the several youth-serving agencies in whose programs recreational activities are the core. "Preparation for worthy use of leisure" has long been accepted as a fundamental objective of education, nevertheless, as yet the application is not universal. There is a searching inquiry to discover what vocational interests each pupil may have and what his probable degree of success may be in any of a variety of vocations, but the choice and pursuit of avocations is left to whim and caprice.

We still worship at the shrine of drudgery. One who shuns pleasures and subjects himself to the discipline of seemingly endless toil is often held up to emulation. The dignity of recreation practiced for its own inherent worth needs to be upheld. There is a need for counseling children from time to time in the wise selection of hobbies and for providing them aid in pursuing them. Impulses to follow a hobby often die for lack of facilities or for lack of knowledge of how to procure them.

The environment in which people live is generally ill adapted to leisure-time activities. Urban neighborhoods are completely artificial. There is little within them to inspire the soul, nearly all vestiges of unsullied nature having been wiped out. Space is decidedly at a premium and whole neighborhoods are permitted to be built without provision of a playground or park. The city planning and urban development movement grows at rapid pace, but it will require generations to rebuild our cities. Meanwhile, the schools constitute the largest single resource for the practice of recreational activities on a large scale. The keys must be thrown away and the gates swung open in order that each school may become a center of neighborhood recreation.

The privilege of "leading the people out of bondage to the commonplace" may not be accorded exclusively to the schools. Even assuming an extension of adult education and preschool education, the universal educational system cannot and should not occupy the entire field of education for leisure. The pattern of leisure time organization which has developed in American life seems well suited to our American ideals and to the essential democratic concept of recreation as an area of life where freedom of choice and expression must be preserved at all cost. In an age requiring increasing regimentation of many activities in the interests of mutual protection, mutual aid, vocation, and subsistence, it may well be that the field of recreation and leisure may become the last refuge of the democratic spirit. Hence, it is appropriate that recreational organization shall be heterogeneous with a free assumption of prerogatives by the home, the church and the community and by a multitudinous collection of voluntary national and local organizations.

That this is the American way in recreational organization is apparent to anyone who studies the pattern of organization for leisure in American life. Characteristic of this pattern is the existence in every community of numerous groups, large and small, temporary and comparatively permanent, each group built upon some identity of interest, enthusiasm and desire upon the part of its membership. The number of such groups defies any effort to catalog them. Taken together in their activities they represent a cross section of American leisure-time interests and participation. They represent "the building blocks of American culture," which it is hoped may be wisely shaped and laid one on the other to build a cultural edifice of great dignity in a nation which has recognized since its beginning the right of all to "the pursuit of happiness."

## Bibliography

AMERICAN ASSOCIATION OF SCHOOL ADMINISTRATORS. *Health in Schools.* Twentieth Yearbook. Washington, D. C.: the Association, a department of the National Education Association, 1942.

AMERICAN YOUTH COMMISSION. *Youth and the Future.* Washington, D. C.: American Council on Education, 1942.

BRECKENRIDGE, MARIAN E., and VINCENT, E. LEE. *Child Development.* Philadelphia: W. B. Saunders Co., 1943.

BROWNELL, CLIFFORD L. *Principles of Health Education Applied.* New York: McGraw-Hill Book Co., 1949.

BURNS, CECIL D. *Leisure in the Modern World.* New York: Century Co., 1943.

CANNON, WALTER B. *The Wisdom of the Body.* New York: W. W. Norton and Co., 1932.

CASSIDY, ROSALIND. *New Directions in Physical Education for the Adolescent Girl in High School and College.* New York: A. S. Barnes and Co., 1938.

CHAMBERS, MERRITT M. *The Community and Its People.* Washington, D. C.: American Council on Education, 1940.

COOPS, HELEN. *Health Education in Elementary Schools.* New York: A. S. Barnes and Co., 1950.

DEWEY, JOHN. *Human Nature and Conduct.* New York: Henry Holt and Co., 1922.

DIMOCK, HEDLEY S., and TRECKER, HARLEIGH B. *The Supervision of Group Work and Recreation.* New York: Association Press, 1949.

GROUT, RUTH. *Health Teaching in Schools.* Philadelphia: W. B. Saunders Co., 1948.

HALDANE, JOHN S. *Organism and Environment.* New Haven: Yale University Press, 1917.

LEWIN, KURT. *A Dynamic Theory of Personality.* New York: McGraw-Hill Book Co., 1935.

LINDEMAN, EDUARD C. *The Goal of American Education.* New York: Farrar and Rinehart, 1940.

LINDEMAN, EDUARD C. *Leisure—A National Issue.* New York: Association Press, 1939.

LUNDBERG, GEORGE A. *Leisure: A Suburban Study.* New York: Columbia University Press, 1934.

MEYER, HAROLD D., and BRIGHTBILL, CHARLES K. *Community Recreation.* Boston: D. C. Heath and Co., 1948.

MORGAN, CLIFFORD T. *Physiological Psychology.* New York: McGraw-Hill Book Co., 1943.

NATIONAL EDUCATION ASSOCIATION and AMERICAN ASSOCIATION OF SCHOOL ADMINISTRATORS, EDUCATIONAL POLICIES COMMISSION. *The Purposes of Education in American Democracy.* Washington, D. C.: the Commission, 1938.

NATIONAL EDUCATION ASSOCIATION and the AMERICAN MEDICAL ASSOCIATION, Joint Committee on Health Problems in Education. *Health Education.* Washington, D. C.: National Education Association, 1948.

NATIONAL EDUCATION ASSOCIATION, DEPARTMENT OF SUPERVISORS AND DIRECTORS OF INSTRUCTION. *Mental Health in the Classroom.* Thirteenth Yearbook. Washington, D. C.: the Department, 1940.

NEUMEYER, MARTIN H., and NEUMEYER, ESTHER S. *Leisure and Recreation.* Revised edition. New York: A. S. Barnes and Co., 1949.

OBERTEUFFER, DELBERT. *Physical Education.* New York: Harper and Brothers, 1951.

OBERTEUFFER, DELBERT. *School Health Education.* New York: Harper and Brothers, 1949.

PATERSON, ROBERT G. *Foundations of Community Health Education.* New York: McGraw-Hill Book Co., 1950.

ROMNEY, G. OTT. *Off the Job Living.* New York: A. S. Barnes and Co., 1948.

RUGG, HAROLD. *Foundations for American Education.* New York: World Book Co., 1947.

SLAVSON, SAMUEL R. *Recreation and the Total Personality.* New York: Association Press, 1948.

SOROKIN, PETER. *Society, Culture and Personality.* New York: Harper and Brothers, 1947.

STAFF OF THE PHYSICAL EDUCATION DEPARTMENT, University of California, Los Angeles. *Group Process in Physical Education.* New York: Harper and Brothers, 1951.

STRANG, RUTH, and SMILEY, DEAN F. *The Role of the Teacher in Health Education.* New York: Macmillan Co., 1946.

TURNER, CLAIR. *School Health and Health Education.* St. Louis: W. V. Mosby Co., 1947.

WILLIAMS, JESSE FEIRING. *Principles of Physical Education.* Fifth edition. Philadelphia: W. B. Saunders Co., 1948.

WILLIAMS, JESSE FEIRING, and ABERNATHY, RUTH. *Health Education in Schools.* New York: Ronald Press, 1949.

WILLIAMS, JESSE FEIRING, and BROWNELL, CLIFFORD L. *The Administration of Health and Physical Education.* Philadelphia: W. B. Saunders Co., 1947.

# CHAPTER FOUR

# Democratic Leadership

ROSALIND CASSIDY

THIS chapter closes Part I on Basic Point of View. Its purpose is to draw out of the preceding chapters the threads which will make clear the basic principles of the particular kind of leadership demanded if democratic human relations are to be developed by teachers and leaders in the areas of health education, physical education and recreation. These threads come from the very texture of what we know about our present-day society and the people who are living in it, making it and remaking it. Threads must come also from the nature of our educational field. We are teachers and leaders in health education, physical education and recreation. Thus the objectives and educative tools of these fields also define the leadership task for which we are responsible.

This chapter must be seen as serving a further purpose. It precedes the second part of this yearbook which is devoted to the application of principles of leadership in a democratic society. Therefore, it must state leadership principles both as summary and as direction for action.

## Changing Conceptions of Educational Leadership

In our time we have lived through a period when the generalization that "the pattern of education is made by the culture" has been made very clear. Mussolini's Italy and Hitler's Third Reich have shown us cultural patterns which demanded a rigid pattern of education and as rigidly defined the role of the teacher and youth leader required to serve that pattern.

Since the turn of the century we have seen in our country changing concepts about the individual-in-his-society, how he must be educated and by what kinds of teachers and youth leaders. Two powerful over-all forces have been changing our view about ourselves and our society. One of these has resulted from the rapidly developing technology, the other is the result of the research in biology, psychology, anthropology and psychiatry. The first has given us a changed concept of our world and our relations with others both at home and abroad. The second has given us a changed concept of the human individual and his close relation with his culture. Thus we have come to accept an on-going interactive concept of personality and society and think of personality as "the flowing continuum of organism-environment events." [1] We now see that "the nature of the self system an individual acquires in the course of socialization depends largely on the kind of personalities he is associated with and the culture after which his activities are patterned, what the significant people in the environment think of him and the ways in which the socialization program is carried out. It is now being increasingly recognized that almost all human actions are 'ego-involved' and that the picture or conception that one has of himself has a great deal to do with one's behavior in a given situation, no matter whether one is aware of the processes involved or not." [2]

## Today's Demands

If the individual is "made" by the culture and the pattern of education is one of the most potent means by which these concepts and beliefs in the culture become a part of the individual, then we must examine our society and ask what kinds of persons are needed for American citizenship? Educators today are increasingly aware that "We must equip young people to respect the worth of the individual, to work together for common purposes, and to apply the method of intelligence to the difficulties we face in living together, to the controlling of our material environment and to the

[1] Murphy, Gardner. *Personality—A Biosocial Approach to Origins and Structure.* New York: Harper and Brothers, 1947, p. 21.

[2] Kluckhohn, Clyde, and Murray, Henry A. *Personality in Nature, Society and Culture.* Cambridge: Harvard University Press, 1948, p. 439.

use of our mounting scientific and mechanical inventions and discoveries for the welfare of mankind. In short, our major function should be to help young people understand and practice the democratic way of life in a technological age." [3]

The demands of our society and our day make imperative the belief in, understandings in and skills in democratic human relations. There is a new urgency about this imperative demand in a world where man has learned to use atomic energy for war and destruction. It becomes increasingly clear that education's primary task now is to teach human beings how to get along with one another.

## The Democratic Way

If we are to clarify the contribution of health education, physical education and recreation to democratic citizenship, we will have to state as directly and clearly as we can what we believe to be the elements in this democratic way. Jefferson first stated them as "self-evident truths," Adams called them "The American Dream," Myrdal "The American Creed," Dewey "The Democratic Ideal." [4] They rest on a deep conviction of the uniqueness, dignity and worth of the individual person; responsibility for one's own actions; concern for the welfare of others; faith in the effectiveness of cooperative action; the belief that government is controlled by the citizens for the good of all and is not a value or end in itself.

When we try to state the demands upon citizens in the United States in the understanding and use of the democratic process, we find categories used in the recent study made by the National Association for Physical Education of College Women of value. These are:

I. *Belief in the Uniqueness and Worth of Each Individual*
   Acceptance of self.
   Acceptance of differences.
   Empathy as a plus value beyond tolerance or sympathy.

[3] National Education Association, Department of Supervision and Curriculum Development. *Leadership Through Supervision*. 1946 Yearbook. Washington, D. C.: the Department, 1946, p. 2.

[4] See: Adams, James Truslow. *The Epic of America*. Boston: Little, Brown & Co., 1931. Myrdal, Gunnar. *An American Dilemma*. New York: Harper and Brothers, 1944. Dewey, John. *Democracy and Education*. New York: Macmillan Co., 1922.

II. *Responsibility for One's Own Actions*

    Acceptance of mature action as a goal.

    Willingness to accept the results of one's action without alibi or evasion.

    Sensitivity to the results of one's actions upon others.

III. *Belief and Skill in Cooperative Action*

    Belief that planning and working together is an effective method, evidenced in habitual use of cooperative methods.

    Acceptance of majority rule.

    Protection of minority opinion.

    Belief in the emergent results of group thinking and action.

IV. *Awareness of Democratic Principles and Ways They Are Learned in Everyday Experience and Evidenced in One's Actions*

    Explicit emphasis on democratic principles in educational experiences.

    Emphasis on relationship of beliefs to action in planning, acting, evaluating.[5]

The Citizenship Education Study, sponsored by the Detroit Public Schools and Wayne University, has developed the five qualities of the good citizen in the following statement:

"The Good Citizen. . . .

"Cherishes democratic values and bases his actions on them.

"Recognizes the social problems of the times and has the will and the ability to work toward their solution.

"Is aware of and takes responsibility for meeting basic human needs.

"Practices democratic human relationships in the family, school, community, and in the larger scene.

"Possesses and uses knowledge, skills, and abilities necessary in a democratic society."[6]

"All of these statements define for us the need for educating for responsible, cooperative participation in all aspects of personal and social living." [7] Our ever-present problem is *how* this may be accomplished.

[5] National Association for Physical Education of College Women. *Practices of Promise in the Understanding and Use of the Democratic Process.* Supplement to Annual Proceedings. The Association, April 1949, p. 13.

[6] See: The Citizenship Education Study publications. *Understanding Democracy* and *Five Qualities of the Good Citizen.* Detroit: Detroit Public Schools and Wayne University, 1948.

[7] Cassidy, Rosalind. "Contributions of Physical Education to Democratic Citizenship." *Journal of Health, Physical Education and Recreation.* 21: 218-19+; April 1950.

## The Three Areas

In considering the problems of education in a democracy it is important to view the objectives, materials and methods of the educational areas with which we are concerned. We must examine health, physical education, and recreation programs to see what hazards and what opportunities are present in the preparation of boys and girls for democratic citizenship through the experiences of these three areas of education.

All three are centered in concern for the person and his fullest development as a healthy, effective, social person. There is emphasis on regard for each individual and for individual differences. The objectives of the area cannot be obtained without cooperative action. There is a high premium on responsible self-direction and initiative in game and dance activities, committee work, health practices.

The body, as a symbol of the self, is central in the experiences of these areas, therefore there is a unique opportunity for educating for the acceptance of one's self as a worthy person. Here is an essential for truly democratic action in accepting others and for valuing differences. The quality of the instrument determines the very quality of one's life, while the understanding and skills in the use of the instrument determine one's effectiveness in society.

These are areas of action and feeling. The activities are highly charged and dynamic for either good or bad for the participant. They are therefore areas in which the potentiality for desirable learning is great and the acceptance of responsibility for directing this learning toward democratic ends is imperative.

These fields have great possibilities for democratic, cooperative action, while at the same time they are constantly threatened by the authoritarian patterns of response-to-command systems of an earlier day, the all powerful "coach" patterns of highly competitive athletics, the very pattern within the game structure itself where the official must blow the whistle and give the penalty. If effective education for American citizenship is to be achieved, all of these aspects must be seen realistically in relation to present-day educational demands and aligned with democratic principles.

## Implications for Leadership in Health Education, Physical Education and Recreation

It is now clear, as we review our "foundation" statements concerning facts about people in our present-day United States of America within its close and threatening world relationships, that leaders must be well-adjusted, secure personalities with a possessive belief in democratic principles evidenced in behavior with other people. The leader must be a person who sees himself as advisor and guide in a process of group action directed toward best development of the individuals concerned. The direction is toward responsible self-direction of the learner whether it is in a health education class, on the tennis court or around the campfire.

In thinking and talking about leadership with teachers and play leaders as we are in this volume, we must realize that we are often shifting our attention from the "adult person" or the "authority figure" in the leadership role to the person, whoever it may be, who at any given time carries the leadership role for a group. There are different manifestations of leadership. However, the principles of democratic leadership are the same, with the difference centered primarily in degree rather than in kind.

The following statement contrasting what the leader is and is not states basic directions for both the "authority figure" and for the spontaneous leaders who emerge in the process of group action. It is weighted *in degree* rather than *in kind* to indicate a description of the "authority figure" or the "adult person" in the group situation.

### Summary of the Leader as Guide in Group Experiencing[8]

| THE LEADER | THE LEADER |
|---|---|
| *Is* | *Is Not* |
| A person who | A person who |
| believes in himself | lacks confidence in his own ability to do the tasks for which he has taken responsibility—lacks courage to reach out into new experience. |

[8] Baxter, Bernice, and Cassidy, Rosalind. *Group Experience—The Democratic Way.* New York: Harper and Brothers, 1943, p. 13-15. Permission to reprint granted by Harper and Brothers, 49 East 33 Street, New York, N. Y.

| THE LEADER | THE LEADER |
|---|---|
| *Is* | *Is Not* |
| A person who | A person who |
| believes in others | has little concern for others—is primarily interested in himself—does not enjoy being with others in social activities. |
| believes in the development of the individual through cooperative group experiences and demonstrates this belief in his relationship with others—realizes the importance of the kinds of experiences and therefore gives attention to the quality of all experiences selected. | feels insecure in opening up problems for group discussions and decisions—who likes to tell everybody what to do—brooks no questioning of his decisions—dislikes to explain the why and wherefore of decisions—does not let others take responsibility but directs and carries out most of the activities himself—is not one who believes that "discipline" is shown by thought-through, fully understood shouldering of responsibility and self direction in an enterprise, whether the goal is shared or individual; but rather, is one who thinks it is shown by immediate unthinking obedience to the leader's order. |
| is well prepared in his knowledge of the human organism and in its social setting—continually studies individuals in groups to gain insights into their behavior and best ways of releasing power and growth. | considers a study of case histories, backgrounds and other forces playing upon individuals in his group unnecessary (sees only the momentary action and fails to see it as symptomatic of a larger cause or need). |
| creates a climate conducive to a relaxed and trusting feeling on the part of individuals. | |

THE LEADER

*Is*

A person who

helps the members define a shared purpose in which each feels a responsible part and desire for accomplishment.

helps each to see his best contribution and best ways of making it.

brings about a rearrangement of working situations and re-direction of goals for the greater freeing of the "space" in which individuals interact and for greater freeing of individual tensions and insecurities.

emphasizes the satisfactions in shared planning and shared achievement.

develops responsible and self-directing individuals who carry leadership responsibility where goals undertaken call for their particular abilities.

All the facts about our social commitments and about how individuals learn most effectively to solve problems and to be more responsible self-directing persons point to a concept of leadership as guidance in experiencing. Guidance does not mean doing something to another person, telling him what to do; it means helping him to act for himself. "Specifically . . . it is guidance to define problems, to plan, to investigate, to organize, to express, to evaluate *for one's self*. All of these activities may be encouraged by the teacher guide through many means, adjusted to the nature of the particular situation and persons involved in it. To the extent that students forge their own definitions and plans, investigate for themselves, organize, express and evaluate under their own power—to that extent the student is experiencing and learning first hand (which means at the best)." [9]

In a recent study made by a staff group to improve its own concept of the role of the teacher, the statement on the next page was formulated by the recorder of one of the summary sessions. It illustrates the concept of leadership we hold for the person related to a group in a supervisory-consultant-enabler function.

## Principles of Democratic Leadership

Principles are fundamental beliefs which, to be valid, must be based upon fact. We call that base our educative foundations and in our professional areas find our foundation facts primarily in psychology, anatomy, physiology, sociology and anthropology.

Whenever we consider principles, we press back our foundation facts as we have in this book, declaring step by step our factual bases for the declaration of principles. The factual areas we are here concerned with are the present-day people within our United States society within its larger world. Our consideration of this factual base is necessary in order to arrive at and state principles. For example, the early chapters of this book have shown very clearly the commitment of the democratic culture in which we live. From that commitment we derive the first two of the principles listed later—the principle of *Personal Involvement* and the principle of *Individual Worth*.

Principles when consciously accepted serve as the basis for decision and action. Educational principles serve as guides in selecting experiences within the educational structure. It is true that decision and action in education as elsewhere are often based on "best opinion," "hunches" or "emotionalized beliefs" rather than on scientifically proved and documented fact. However, the important thing for educators is to evidence a willingness to examine the bases for their action and to move in the direction of establishing a factual base for educational action.

Therefore, in this chapter the basic foundation facts are reviewed.

[9] National Education Association, Department of Supervision and Curriculum Development. *Group Planning in Education.* 1945 Yearbook. Washington, D. C.: the Department, 1945. p. 150.

## Summary of the Meeting in Terms of Role of the Teacher[10]

The teacher in the Core Program must be able (or her role is):

| 1 | 2 | 3 | 4 | 5 |
|---|---|---|---|---|
| To have the long view. See the outer structure and the end goals in teacher education and in the UCLA structure and to relate experiences pre and post. | To have a growing knowledge of the needs of her group and to take them where they are. | To have a belief in and skills in the democratic process and use it as a method. | To put skills on its movement base and learn general principles as the basic most important skill. | To create a climate for best learning. One in which the individual achieves inner security. |
| Belief in and competence in group planning in area, between areas and with department group. | To be a resource<br>Stimulator<br>Frustrator<br>Presenter<br>Reassurer<br>Revealer<br>Relator<br>Generalizer<br>Clarifier | Skills in sharing with students. | To move each student along in skills in P. E. and skills in teaching P.E. and in readiness for directed teaching. | |
| To be able to put principles into practice. Use methods the girls are to learn to use by using them. | Individual and group guidance. | To give students full overview and to see basic principles to extend horizons. | | |
| To facilitate goal setting and problem solving paramount. | Evaluation. | Self-direction is learned by being given responsibility in self-direction. | | |
| To aid in knowing how to use resources—people, books, etc. Wide knowledge and own security. | | | | |
| Ability to work with others to execute and plan in preparation. | | | | |

*The teacher is responsible for guiding situations so that best learning takes place. She must facilitate learning; must guide so that student does the learning and gains her best development in relation to her needs, to others and to demands of the end goal—a teacher certificate.*

[10] Recorder's notes taken on December 5, 1949. Staff meeting, University of California, Los Angeles, Department of Physical Education, Division for Women. Mimeographed, Department File. Permission to reprint granted by Dr. Carl Haven Young, Chairman of the Department of Physical Education, University of California, Los Angeles.

Principles are derived and stated. From these declared principles the action implied is stated and examined. This process is somewhat belabored, yet its importance to educators is imperative. It is a method of work, a method each one can use in clarifying his own action. It is spelled out here in this pivotal chapter since all programs for developing democratic relations described in later chapters are concerned with action based on these stated principles.

Principles considered in the first part of this book about our society, the educational fields with which we are concerned, and leadership demands which must guide our action, may be stated in the following way:

### The Principle of Personal Involvement

1. Accepting this principle would mean that leaders must have a responsible personal commitment to democratic process. They must be continuously developing a workable philosophy of democratic action. It means that they are committed to acting upon more complete understanding about human beings within the social context. They are interested in the quality of interpersonal relationships.

### The Principle of Individual Worth

2. Accepting this principle would mean that leaders see group experience as the means to achieve individual competence in democratic human relations. They value each individual and see his development as the important goal of leadership responsibility.

### The Principle of Field Relations or "Climate"

3. Accepting this principle would mean that interacting field relations are seen as central, that the atmosphere or "climate" of a situation is seen as an over-all important aspect of the field.

### The Principle of Guided Group Interaction

4. Accepting this principle would mean that the concept of leader as group *guide* is central. It means that the leader starts where the group is and moves toward self-directed action by the group. It makes possible a wide range of methods to meet group needs.

### The Principle of Goal-Centered Activity

5. Accepting this principle means helping the group to define and accept its own problem or goal as the only possible way to achieve

a shared cooperative way of working. This is the leader's constant concern in starting and continuing with a group.

### The Principle of Shared Responsibility

6. Accepting this principle would mean that responsible participation by each member is basic. It means that decision-making and democratic group self-determination and direction are essential. It includes the concept of social responsibility. It means that the leader-member role is shifting and that each one carries responsibility for whatever supporting role he assumes at any given time.

### The Principle of Continuous Evaluation

7. Accepting this principle means that the efforts of the group to set up a goal and to evolve effective ways of together achieving that goal demand a commitment to ways of appraising progress and the methods used to obtain such progress. This is essential to moving along in problem solving.

## Guide Lines for Action

Seven "cardinal" principles for democratic group leadership have been stated. These can be elaborated into action statements for leaders and teachers in the areas of health education, physical education and recreation as shown in the following statements. However, the important meaning of these concepts comes only when leaders and teachers themselves begin to list significant action descriptions under these principles or, even better, to restate both the statement of principles and their action descriptions.

### The Principle of Personal Involvement

1. Leaders must have a democratic philosophy. They must be developing an ever more workable philosophy of democratic action based on strong belief and increasing understandings of human beings within their social settings. They must have a responsible commitment to democratic relations.

2. Leaders must believe in the worth of their task and see it in the larger view and social need.

3. Leaders must have a clear concept of how learning takes place, how behavior is changed, how personality develops.

4. Leaders must have a growing understanding of the larger social framework and of the national and local culture patterns. They

must understand that the person behaves as a responding organism within a social context.

5. Leaders must increasingly understand the meanings of context, seeing relationships and interaction within a field as central—the nature of response changing both individual and field.

### The Principle of Individual Worth

6. Leaders must hold the individual as of worth and must see group experience as a means, not an end, in the development of individuals for democratic citizenship.

### The Principle of Field Relations or "Climate"

7. Leaders must understand how children grow within their particular culture and what developmental tasks are required at the various growth levels and in the several class levels.

8. Leaders must be aware of the need for maintaining a democratic "climate" if responsible behavior is to be achieved. It must be an atmosphere encouraging all to participate and contribute.

### The Principle of Guided Group Interaction

9. Democratic leadership is guidance toward responsible behavior.

10. Leaders must understand the several levels of cooperative behavior and move from where the individuals are toward responsible, cooperative democratic behavior.

11. Leaders must value youths' goals and purposes and create a climate for best learning in terms of starting from these goals.

### The Principle of Goal-Centered Activity

12. Leaders must provide action in problem-solving situations as responsible participants. They must see this as an essential to democratic learning. The problem or goal must be seen as the integrating center.

13. Leaders must study youth needs and realize that all behavior is purposive. It is an effort to achieve one's goal and therefore is symptomatic of need.

### The Principle of Shared Responsibility

14. Leaders must see leadership as one of the group roles to be shared within the group, changing with the demands of the problem to use the competencies of all group members.

### The Principle of Continuous Evaluation

15. Leaders must help the group to share responsibility for making its own rules for best conduct, for planning and evaluating and for training its members for most effective participation.

Since these are largely stated for the "adult person" type of leader and we have pointed out that the difference is in degree rather than kind, it is suggested that teachers and leaders rework these with action statements for group members who are not in the "adult person" role. This will aid in seeing one's own role and in identifying the degrees of difference between the leader and one who is not the leader in the group situation.

# Bibliography

BAXTER, BERNICE, and CASSIDY, ROSALIND. *Group Experience—the Democratic Way*. New York: Harper and Brothers, 1943.

BRADFORD, LELAND P.; BENNE, KENNETH D.; and LIPPITT, RONALD. "The Promise of Group Dynamics for Education." *National Education Association Journal*. 37:350-52; September 1948.

BROUWER, PAUL J. *Student Personnel Services in General Education*. Washington, D. C.: American Council on Education, 1949.

BROWN, IDA S. *Training in Group Development with University Students—An Experiment*. Unpublished dissertation, University of California, Los Angeles, Calif., 1950.

BROWN, JAMES F. *Psychology and the Social Order*. New York: McGraw-Hill Book Co., 1936.

BURTON, WILLIAM H. *The Guidance of Learning Activities*. New York: Appleton-Century-Crofts Inc., 1944.

CASSIDY, ROSALIND. "Contributions of Physical Education to Democratic Citizenship." *Journal of the American Association for Health, Physical Education, and Recreation*. 21:218-19; April, 1950.

CASSIDY, ROSALIND, and KOZMAN, HILDA CLUTE. *Counseling Girls in a Changing Society*. New York: McGraw-Hill Book Co., 1947.

COYLE, GRACE. *Group Experience and Democratic Values*. New York: Woman's Press, 1947.

COYLE, GRACE. *Group Work with American Youth*. New York: Harper and Brothers, 1948.

DE HUSZAR, GEORGE G. *Practical Applications of Democracy*. New York: Harper and Brothers, 1945.

*Educational Leadership*. Journal of the Association for Supervision and Curriculum Development 7:79-144; November 1949.

ELLIOTT, HARRISON S. *The Process of Group Thinking*. New York: Association Press, 1928.

FOLLETT, MARY P. *Creative Experience*. New York: Longmans Green and Co., 1924.

GIRL SCOUTS, NATIONAL ORGANIZATION. *Leadership of Girl Scout Troops—Intermediate Program*. New York: Girl Scouts of the United States, 1943.

HOPKINS, L. THOMAS. *Interaction—The Democratic Process*. Boston: D. C. Heath and Co., 1941.

KLUCKHOHN, CLYDE, and MURRAY, HENRY A. *Personality in Nature, Society and Culture*. Harvard University Press, 1948.

LEWIN, KURT. "Field Theory and Experiments in Social Psychology." *American Journal of Sociology* 44:868-96; May 1939.

LEWIN, KURT. "Field Theory and Learning." *The Psychology of Learning.* Forty-First Yearbook, Part II, National Society for the Study of Education. Bloomington, Ill.: Public Schools Publishing Co., 1942, Chapter 4.

LEWIN, KURT, and LIPPITT, RONALD A. *A Research Center for Group Dynamics.* New York: Beacon House, 1947.

LEWIN, KURT; LIPPITT, RONALD A.; and WHITE, RALPH K. "Patterns of Aggressive Behavior in Experimentally Created Social 'Climates.'" *Journal of Social Psychology* 10:271-99, May 1939.

LIPPITT, RONALD A. *Training in Community Relations Toward New Group Skills.* New York: Harper and Brothers, 1949.

MURPHY, GARDNER. *Personality—A Biosocial Approach to Origins and Structures.* New York: Harper and Brothers, 1947.

MURPHY, GARDNER; MURPHY, LOIS BARCLAY; and NEWCOMB, THEODORE M. *Experimental Social Psychology.* New York: Harper and Brothers, 1937.

NATIONAL ASSOCIATION FOR PHYSICAL EDUCATION OF COLLEGE WOMEN. *Practices of Promise in the Understanding and Use of the Democratic Process.* Supplement to Annual Proceedings, the Association, April 1949.

NATIONAL EDUCATION ASSOCIATION, DEPARTMENT OF SUPERVISION AND CURRICULUM DEVELOPMENT. *Group Planning in Education.* 1945 Yearbook. Washington, D. C.: the Department, 1945.

NATIONAL EDUCATION ASSOCIATION, DEPARTMENT OF SUPERVISION AND CURRICULUM DEVELOPMENT. *Leadership Through Supervision.* 1946 Yearbook. Washington, D. C.: the Department, 1946.

NATIONAL EDUCATION ASSOCIATION, DEPARTMENT OF SUPERVISION AND CURRICULUM DEVELOPMENT. *Leadership at Work.* Fifteenth Yearbook. Washington, D. C.: the Department, 1943.

NATIONAL EDUCATION ASSOCIATION and AMERICAN ASSOCIATION OF SCHOOL ADMINISTRATORS, EDUCATIONAL POLICIES COMMISSION. *Learning the Ways of Democracy.* Washington, D. C.: the Commission, 1940.

NATIONAL SOCIETY FOR THE STUDY OF EDUCATION. *Learning and Instruction.* Forty-Ninth Yearbook, Part I. Chicago, Ill.: University of Chicago Press, 1950.

NYLEN, DONALD, and BRADFORD, LELAND P. "We Can Work Together." *National Education Association Journal.* 37: 436-58; October 1948.

OLSON, WILLARD C. "Human Relations in the Classroom." *National Education Association Journal* 36: 640-41; December 1947.

ROETHLISBERGER, FRITZ. *Management and Morale.* Cambridge: Harvard University Press, 1942.

SLAVSON, SAMUEL R. *Creative Group Education.* New York: Association Press, 1937.

STAFF OF THE PHYSICAL EDUCATION DEPARTMENT, University of California, Los Angeles. *Group Process in Physical Education.* New York: Harper and Brothers, 1951.

TABA, HILDA, and VAN TIL, WILLIAM, editors. *Democratic Human Relations.* Sixteenth Yearbook. Washington, D. C.: National Council for the Social Studies, a department of the National Education Association, 1945.

TRECKER, HARLEIGH B. *Social Group Work.* New York: Woman's Press, 1948.

# Programs for Children

PATTRIC RUTH O'KEEFE, *Coordinator*
*Director of Health and Physical Education*
*Kansas City Public Schools*
*Kansas City, Missouri*

## 5. THE CHILD'S WORLD

EDNA W. BAILEY
*Professor of Education*
*University of California*
*Berkeley, California*

## 6. CONCEPTS AND ATTITUDES TO BE DEVELOPED

HELEN FAHEY
*Supervisor Health and Physical Education*
*Kansas City Public Schools*
*Kansas City, Missouri*

JOHN H. SHAW
*Associate Professor of Physical Education*
*Syracuse University*

## 7. METHODS

EDWINA JONES
*Supervisor Physical Education*
*Cleveland Public Schools*
*Cleveland, Ohio*

HELEN M. STARR
*Coordinator of Health*
*Minneapolis Public Schools*
*Minneapolis, Minnesota*

FRANCES WAYMAN
*Assistant Director Physical Education Department*
*Fort Worth Public Schools*
*Fort Worth, Texas*

## 8. EVALUATION

DELIA P. HUSSEY
*Supervisor Health and Physical Education*
*Detroit Public Schools*
*Detroit, Michigan*

IRMA M. PELZ
*Associate Professor of Health and Physical Education*
*New Haven State Teachers College*
*New Haven, Connecticut*

# THUS A CHILD LEARNS

• *Thus a child learns; by wiggling skills through his fingers and toes into himself; by soaking up habits and attitudes of those around him; by pushing and pulling his own world.*

• *Thus a child learns; more through trial than error, more through pleasure than pain, more through experience than suggestion, more through suggestion than direction.*

• *Thus a child learns; through affection, through love, through patience, through understanding, through belonging, through doing, through being.*

• *Day by day the child comes to know a little bit of what you know; to think a little bit of what you think; to understand your understanding. That which you dream and believe and are, in truth, becomes the child.*

• *As you perceive dully or clearly; as you think fuzzily or sharply; as you believe foolishly or wisely; as you dream drably or goldenly; as you bear false witness or tell the truth—thus a child learns.*—FREDERICK J. MOFFITT, Chief, Bureau of Instructional Supervision New York State Department of Education.

# CHAPTER FIVE

# *The Child's World*

EDNA W. BAILEY

PROGRAMS in health education, physical education and recreation directed toward developing democratic human relations at the elementary level, if they are to be effective, must be based upon insight into how growing boys and girls view the world about them and upon understanding their development as they move from infancy toward adolescence. It is the purpose of this chapter to contribute to this insight and understanding as a preface to exploring, in the next chapter, the concepts regarding democratic relations the child may be expected to develop and the attitudes, expressed through his behavior, which reveal the concepts he is forming in his relations with others.

There is so much to be said, so much ground to cover, so many research findings, that in a single chapter only a general picture can be drawn of the child's world and how he responds to it.

In our society, for all but the very poor, the child's world is a bountiful one in which all his needs and many of his wishes are met. The 40 million or more copies of children's books published annually in recent years, the quarter-billion comic books and the elaborate and expensive variety of play materials produced are sold in such quantity that the children of the well-to-do could not possibly be their sole consumers. With the nationwide reduction of paid employment of children under 14 or 16, our youngsters are in general a privileged class. Special foods, special clothing, special furniture, children's dentists and children's doctors, special teachers, playground and club leaders give evidence that children are big business, commercially and professionally. As the level of national prosperity rises, this important business grows bigger.

It is easy and natural for children, surrounded by plenty and sheltered from harsh necessity, to see their world as a beneficent home and to develop an unconscious faith that what they have not yet explored will be as safe, as kind and more exciting than the familiar aspects are. So they are free in spirit, and go adventuring in fancy with the radio, in the comic books, the fairy tales. They journey in imagination to far lands and develop sympathetic, understanding friendships with the strange children there. The popularity of pen-pals in European countries who exchange letters with American school children is a good example of this extensive, curious and yet warm-hearted friendliness. The impressive thing is that they feel no threat from these strange children, and no impulse to mistreat them, but rather a generosity much greater than would be shown to flesh-and-blood companions. So far as these children's personal world of fancy and imaginative flights is concerned, it is a place of security, plenty and good will.

Unfortunately, the picture is not so sanguine for all American children. The incidence of divorce and juvenile delinquency points to that portion of them who have come to be called the "under-privileged" and "problem cases." Many of these children do not have adequate food, clothing, shelter or space for play. But under-privileged children are to be found in mansions on the hill as well as in the shacks on the wrong side of the tracks. The divorced bank president and his wife may make their child feel insecure, unwanted and inadequate just as the deserted wife of a factory worker can make her child pay for deprivations and emotional disturbances she has suffered.

Research in child development has made it plain that the most important development for leading a satisfactory life, getting along well with oneself and others, is possible only through living in an emotionally stable and satisfying human environment. The children who enrol in schools come from homes with all degrees of stability and provision for the affectionate care which is the birthright of every child. There are neurotic, undernourished, insecure, disturbed children. The underprivileged problem cases seem to point out sharply the needs of all boys and girls for supporting and sustaining relations during the period when they are growing out of the dependency of infancy and early childhood. However, this brief description of THE CHILD'S WORLD is centered on the experiences and attitudes that characterize the ordinary well-adjusted child from six to 12 years old. We find it easy to forget, under the flood of case studies, that there are really a great many such children going to school, coming to playgrounds and summer camps.

When a baby is born he enters a complex world of people who have developed customs and mores, furniture, tools and the arts, skills for working and playing, attitudes, standards and values. The behavior of this baby will be shaped by the particular human environment into which he is born. Growing up is not only physical maturing; it is also social maturing as the child and youth acquire a particular share of the cultural heritage and learn the society's accepted ways of behaving.

A newborn human being is extraordinarily helpless, almost completely dependent on others for the maintenance, not to say the enrichment, of his life. A considerable fraction of us would never have drawn a first breath without vigorous "guidance"; no human infant ever found his mother's breast and essential food without help. Approximately a third of a normal life span is spent in growth and development of the individual in body, mind and spirit. Only with maturity does he attain the possibility of self-maintenance. To realize this possibility he must have developed considerable self-control. On the basis of his powers of self-control over his body and over his own behavior, he becomes self-reliant and gains self-respect.

Under good conditions of health care, intelligent guidance and affectionate security, growth from infancy to maturity means that the individual moves from dependence to relative independence. Between birth and the end of adolescence, any individual is to be found somewhere along the road from helplessness to self-maintenance. Anything we do for him which helps him toward independence is, other things being equal, a contribution to his welfare and happiness. Anything which keeps him content in dependence is, for a person in health and normally competent, a great disservice. In most children there seems to be a strong feeling for the value to them as persons of increasing independence. "Let *me* do it" is not ordinarily a plea, but rather a demand.

As Hearn has pointed out in Chapter 2, in moving toward independence the child has to learn to harmonize his dependence-independence needs in interdependent relations with others. The relations of mature adults are those of equals, parent-child or adult-child relations are not thus characterized. If the interdependent relations of equals are to be attained in adulthood, parents and others must provide the child leeway to move toward independence.

What determines the degree of self-sufficiency a child or an adult can maintain? For one thing, the range and quality of his sensory responses to the world about him. How wide is his world, how colored, how peopled? We are all, grown up or immature, at a loss in a strange place, with strange people and unfamiliar objects. To a child, the familiar world is a very narrow one; the unfamiliar presses in on all sides.

Other elements in producing a greater degree of adequacy are the person's abilities in motor performance and in problem solving. A baby has a complete equipment of muscles, but very little capacity for varied and precise movements. He finds the simplest problem is beyond his ingenuity—as, for instance, how to pick up another object when both hands are full. Along with this ineptness at problem solving goes a limitation of attention; he can attend to a situation only very briefly. Most hampering of all his handicaps, he is bound to the present moment. He has little memory of what lies behind him, even less capacity to look ahead. Past experience is of slight use to him; future goals are meaningless and unrealized.

These are some of the important reasons why young children are relatively helpless and, therefore, almost wholly dependent. As their horizons of time and space are expanded and their ability to use body and mind in fruitful activity is increased, they approach competency in life situations and a relative independence.

However, there are adults in full possession of their abilities, with adequate bodily equipment and mental capacities, who do not attain independence as individuals. They are handicapped by failure to organize their attitudes and emotions and by inability to control their impulses, to postpone satisfactions, to accept defeat, to endure frustration and still remain in command of themselves. The experiences and guidance which encourage the development of self-controls lead the child along the road to inward independence and self-respect which goes with it.

## Defining Self and the World

A child's world is typically a world that is beyond his actual powers, but tantalizingly within his grasp, as of tomorrow. Everything is of interest to him until he has got the feel of it, until it is no longer strange; then he is off to new explorations. A young teacher once said, "The most astonishing thing about these children is their intent absorption and the amount they can learn about something new to them. The most baffling thing is how completely done they are with it in about fifteen minutes!"

The child's world is a challenge to his powers—to see, hear, smell, taste and touch, but above all to handle, to manipulate. There is also the urge to classify and to name, going back to the expression "What's that?" of the three-year-old. Especially in boys, a budding scientific curiosity appears, with much interest in collections, in model making and a great variety of construction projects. To gratify these tastes, a child is willing to work hard at learning to use tools, at acquiring good command of his body, at reading difficult material and learning new words and new skills in counting and measuring. The challenge of his world lifts him to new heights of achievement in his efforts to master it and make it familiar.

Because of the strength of these driving interests in exploration, when his world is a secure and friendly place the youngster in early school years is typically disdainful of danger, but gets into plenty of it. The leading cause of deaths during this period is accidents. This lead is so great that the number of deaths from accidents exceeds the numbers from the next four causes added together. As we have seen, this liability is implicit in the sense of security, so essential to his personal integrity, with which he explores his world. Therefore, his protection must come from adult carefulness and from specific training which makes certain items of safe behavior automatic. The signs do not say to children: "Danger! Autos coming!" They say to drivers: "Danger! Children at play!" and that is as it should be. There are many other situations where adults must take the responsibility, knowing that the need for carefulness, the stark danger of the adult's juggernaut-filled world, is not comprehended by citizens of the child's world.

When we remind ourselves that a child's business is to move from dependence to independence, his sense of values becomes more comprehensible to us. We understand more sympathetically the high priority for him of everything which widens his world in space and time, and of every effort which gives him better command of self and environment. Faegre has described these traits of elementary-school children more successfully than most writers:

> He is on the way to becoming a self-contained, self-directing, self-motivating person. Still close to his parents, still appreciating attention, love and sympathy, he is striking out for himself, making friends, showing individual tastes, exploring many fields—a lively, eager, able, light-hearted and often maddening creature. He is tremendously interested in the things and life about him. As he approaches the teens he will become interested in himself, but now his thoughts are mostly turned outwards toward the practical, material world. Experimentation leads children everywhere; it urges them into using every one of their senses. They discover the sweet taste of the growing ends of grass blades, and sample pungent, tangy pine needles. They make leaves squeak, tear apart paper-thin birch bark layers. . . . They burrow into the haystack, climb on top and come hurtling down with dust in their hair. They run, panting, after the fire engine, hoping the fire will be a big one. When the plumber comes to the house, they're right under foot, watching. And when a street is being paved, every operation is followed by fascinated eyes. . . . Soap is something to work up a lather with, rather than something to get clean with. . . . Sending away for samples, saving box tops or coupons, making collections of anything and everything . . . haunting the back premises of grocery stores in the hope of getting boxes to build with. . . . These are almost as characteristic of our 6 to 12-ers as eating is.[1]

## Learning Through Play

From the earliest days of child study, observers have been impressed by the spontaneous, self-initiated activities of children, carried on apparently for the fun of the activities themselves, not for any specific purpose or ulterior end. This kind of activity has

[1] Faegre, Marion L. *Your Child from Six to Twelve*. Children's Bureau Publication No. 324. Washington, D. C.: United States Government Printing Office, 1949. p. 1, 3.

been called play and distinguished, somewhat unsatisfactorily, from work. Work has been described as activity which is definitely channeled, often under the direction of others, and directed toward a specific accomplishment. All agree that the chief difference between work and play is found in the motives behind the activity. Sometimes work is obviously play and among older children there are occasions where play seems to be work. These are useful terms, though not precise ones. Perhaps it is difficult to state the distinction precisely because a child's activities grade smoothly from one to the other classification and human pleasure in exercise of human powers is so great that most work carries for healthy persons an overtone of play; it is to some extent a self-rewarding though an imposed activity. To make a man's work bitter to him is a shocking mismanagement of his life; and to interfere with the child's legitimate freedom in play is a sure way to stunt his development, impoverish his personality and make hazardous his future.

A child's wide-ranging interests are revealed in the amazing variety of play engaged in by children from eight to 10 or 12. They are not keen for style or finish in their performances. Once they have got the hang of the game or stunt or hobby, they are off on the track of another. So rich is the variety of their world, and so tempting, that a nine- or 10-year-old is likely to cheat on time for the essentials of living, those very essentials which absorbed practically all his time and energy as an infant. He now thinks of sleeping and resting as bores, inactivity suited to babies and the aged but a frightful waste of time for childhood. Eating he enjoys, but it must be done in a hurry. As to baths, as the 10-year-old sees them, they take time that could be better used.

In a sense, play is a child's major occupation, just as earning a living is his father's. This is true in consequence of his anatomical and physiological immaturity. From infancy to puberty, a child literally operates a machine, himself, in which the controls differ from those of an adult or even, in most cases, of a pubescent. He has, long before birth, the full neuromuscular equipment of the adult, functionally related to skeletal attachments which, while partly cartilaginous or membranous rather than bony, seem to offer adequate support for action. But the use he makes of this neuromuscular equipment and the service it renders him are limited by the relative immaturity of the cortices. At the same time, exercise of his motor abilities absorbs his interest and attention to an amazing degree, gives him satisfaction, even joy, in full measure. This absorption and delight in activity appears at its height from the time of learning to walk and talk, on through preschool and early school years. His powers relating to visual efficiency, to language, to manipulation and to locomotor activity come to be based on adequately developed equipment somewhere between eight and 12 years.

Human beings and other higher vertebrates are so constituted that we are most intrigued by activities which are just coming to be possible to us in the ordinary course of development, depending on the extent to which the nerves through which we organize and integrate our behavior are finished off anatomically. We work at such activities with abandon, with absorbing interest and with whole-souled enjoyment. Once the neuromuscular equipment is complete and our command of it assured, we lose some of our zest for activity as such and begin to regard our performances as means to ends rather than ends in themselves. We come to this stage during puberty, in the normal course of events.

Olson has expressed economically one aspect of this developmental characteristic: "Action and growth are inextricably intertwined. The level of maturation determines in part the nature and direction of activity and the exercise in turn stimulates and perfects growth and integration of behavior." He adds, with a straight face, "The affective coloring of play makes it important for mental hygiene." [2]

The type of play depends upon children's age, their sex and what their environment offers. There is no doubt that skilful supervision of play and intelligent provision of equipment and space will greatly enrich the play of children, and thereby their personalities, as well as foster social growth. The social development of children is, outside of home and school influences, almost wholly dependent on their play opportunities.

Play life and school life have been, in past times, in conflict. Modern emphasis on an activity program has gone a long way toward arbitration of this conflict. Such a program recognizes the aptitude

[2] Olson, Willard C. *Child Development*. Boston: D. C. Heath and Co., p. 87.

of middle childhood for wholehearted effort along lines for which readiness exists, and seems to take account of that inability to direct, analyze and polish the learning which is the companion to the child's joy in those activities which are just coming under control. From the standpoint of knowledge of child development, the activity program and emphasis on gearing the program to each child's readiness is sound educationally for early years. Beginning with the fifth and sixth grades there is basis for a policy which expects more power of self-criticism and self-direction. This is increasingly true through later childhood and youth, though these advances in self-control are, in many children, somewhat negated by the onset of puberty.

The variety of play interests is very great. Space is an essential if locomotor and manipulative play is to be encouraged. Running games like tag, kick the can, hide and seek, cops and robbers, pom-pom-pullaway—all these take space. They have increased interest from five or six years of age to 11 years, after which there is a marked decline of interest in both sexes. Baseball and tennis increase in interest up to puberty, in both sexes. Boys are increasingly interested in football, horseshoes and marbles, girls in such activities as jumping rope and long ball; London bridge, drop-the-handkerchief and farmer-in-the-dell lose their attraction, while checkers and other board games gain. Games with playing cards begin to be popular about 10. Dramatic or imaginative play, engaged in by both sexes at the preschool level, is less popular with boys than with girls and may disappear before 10. Little girls play house and play school interminably, little boys almost never after school days are begun. Interest in dramatic play is heightened by lack of equipment and space for games and construction play. It is as if the children are thrown back on fancy when access to the real world is barred. It has been shown that cramped space and lack of equipment also favor quarreling and rough-housing, with bullying an unhappy accompaniment.

It takes time for children to develop the idea of "sides" or teams and of playing games in any organized way. Along with this new interest, a child takes sharper notice of individual differences in excellence. Competitive impulses are strengthened while at the same time he is learning cooperation with his team. This represents extraordinarily valuable learning in the field of social behavior. Anderson describes the general process:

A game or contest has rigid rules which are well-defined and well-administered—probably more so than are rules of conduct in any other area of human affairs, even including government. As a result, the child acquires not only the skills needed for a game of sport but also knowledge of the activity and of its rules. Although the process is gradual and largely informal, its completeness causes some to wonder as to what would happen if similar methods could be used for regular school work.[3]

Some claim that similar willing subjection of impulses to law and order comes in participation in music and dancing, especially in group activities. Whether the discipline of team games and of the arts can be made to function in personal relations generally depends on many things. But it seems plain that the child's world widens to include his contemporaries in terms of partners and opponents in games and in terms of others who move with him in the lawful patterns of the game, the dance, the school chorus or the percussion band.

For children who live in cities, the opportunity for free activity is greatly limited by the cramped quarters in which their explorations must be carried out. This does not refer merely to apartment-house dwellers. Anything less than a room of his own, plus a basement or an attic and garage and an acre or so of land not too much cluttered up with landscaping, seems cramped to a 10-year-old. There is a long history of warfare in one city between the director of parks, who thought parks should be beautiful to see, and the director of recreation, who thought parks should be good for playing in. The rural youngster is more fortunate in having elbow-room for his activities and freedom for explorations.

The part played by time as well as space in a child's development toward independence has been mentioned previously. As he gains strength and endurance, he feels the pressure of too little time for play as definitely as spatial restrictions. Various tasks encroach on his day. Some of these relate to personal care, health maintenance, food and rest and sleep; others are involved in schooling. Since he lives in a family, there are chores which he recognizes as work.

[3] Anderson, John E. *The Psychology of Development and Personal Adjustment.* New York: Henry Holt and Co., 1949. p. 378.

## Work in the Child's World

At first, learning how to wipe dishes and set the table is as challenging as any other self-testing experience; but once learned there is no further challenge in it and it becomes work. If well-taught, children accept work as a natural part of their lives as the long, long days of the preschool child are swiftly shortened into the brief crowded days of school children. Whether a child likes work, tolerates it, shirks it or hates it, it becomes a part of his day, sharply distinct from the other part which is playtime. It almost seems as if those hours were colored differently, the few hours when the youngster is free to play. A reasonable balance between work and play makes both kinds of activity more enjoyable, and most children seem to be aware of this enrichment of playtime by work periods. A school child's day has work in it; during these years he is learning satisfaction in work, seeing variety in work, earning rewards for work. Teaching him to work is like breaking a colt; if it is done skilfully he will not fight the saddle and bridle.

Besides the services which children give as part of cooperative group living, there are opportunities to work for pay. Children get a lift out of earning money outside their homes. In our society, gainful employment of children, except in agriculture, is severely restricted as to kind of work, hours and age of worker. These regulations are not uniform for all the states, and even in any one state interpretation and enforcement vary from year to year and in different regions. At first glance, it seems the rules should be simple prohibitions against any gainful employment for children under 12, or 14, or 16, or 18; and a green light for all after the agreed age. However, we are fumbling toward a pattern of employment which will permit a long, carefully graded and individualized set of experiences in earning money for all normal, healthy youngsters. We are recognizing that personality is enriched and citizenship developed by giving youngsters something to show for their efforts, something earned on the open market. No ordinary amount of money given a child by parents and friends can build in him the self-confidence and self-respect he gets out of gainful employment. If an adolescent is to be employable, the child he used to be must have begun to learn the lessons of being employed, giving and getting satisfaction, earning money. It is a true golden opportunity that childhood offers. Especially for men, successful vocational adjustment conditions success as persons in a democratic society. From six to 12 years, work becomes steadily a more significant part of the child's world. He learns to meet responsibility, to turn in a good job, to understand and handle money, to take satisfaction in earning, all of which experiences and attitudes make him more tolerable to a future employer. Should he himself become the employer, the self-confidence and self-control he has developed are nonetheless useful. There is considerable change between the sixth and twelfth years. At six work claims little of the child's time and no one counts on him much for a contribution. At 12, work requires a considerable fraction of his time and what he accomplishes is important to him, to his class at school or his Scout Troop. These are the years when he is learning to pull his share of the load and like it.

One consequence of a normal child's free and easy feeling about his world is the difficulty he experiences in learning that his world consists in part of other people's property. While recognition of property rights is found among all peoples ever studied and even in many of the higher vertebrates, there is no evidence whatever that children are born with a sense of mine-and-thine. Learning this distinction is dependent upon the development of a recognition of the difference between self and not-self, setting the limits of the individual personality as against all the rest of the universe. There is no doubt this takes a good deal of doing and the boundaries of the personality never are quite sharp. The old slippers, the worn coat, the cap and hair-ribbon seem to be a part of the children, both to us and to them. When a child past seven or eight is apparently careless about property rights, or steals, it is not usually because he is ignorant. He may have been badly taught, so that the part of his world which is not his has been made to seem arbitrarily denied to him. His drive for independent action and self-maintenance then seems to him blocked by this business of "don't touch," "that's mine!" If well taught, he appreciates that respect for the property of others is the price of their respect for his; but his passion for investigation, manipulation and use of objects is still thwarted in regard to all the things which he knows belong to others.

Property rights in money are extraordinarily important in our society, and are not well taught. A piece of money is as abstract in significance as a numeral, or a flag. A child's respect for money has to be taught as we teach accuracy in arithmetic and reverence for the flag. Until a child has understood and learned to handle money affairs, until he has legitimate access to money of his own and freedom in its use, almost all paths to self-maintenance and self-respect are barred to him in our society. Before adolescence, in our culture, this is a play relationship; a child under 10 cannot, according to law, steal or commit any other crime. But that does not change the importance of practicing skills and developing attitudes relating to money. Money is in the child's world, just as there are occasionally sticks of dynamite within his reach. How to handle dynamite, what it is good for and its disconcerting potentialities would need to be learned well in a culture where dynamite was universally present. In teaching a child safety measures we put the responsibility on the adult. The same reasons hold for expecting parents and teachers and older children to safeguard a child's contacts with money during the years he is learning how to deal with it. Then, if a child's world contains other people's property and other people's money, it will also have in it his own property and his own money. No one has a right to rob a piggy-bank for ready cash.

Closely related to money and property rights is the place in the child's world of gambling. Without money and property conventions, gambling could not exist; perhaps the converse holds. Spicing a game with the pleasure of acquisition seems harmless enough to some and certainly is a very general practice. "Playing for keeps" develops in children's games and the little shops present slots in which to drop pennies with certainty of getting something and the delightful possibility of getting a great deal. How is a child to reconcile this with the general structure of property rights? Fortunately, he is not especially alert to inconsistencies. There is also a kind of fairness and lack of discrimination about Lady Luck. She is as likely to favor the ragged as the sleek. This goes well with a child's feeling that this is truly a great, wide, wonderful world in which anything may happen and often does.

It is a fact that unhappy, disturbed children frequently steal, not because they do not know better, not because they want what they take, but in an impulsive, wild effort to work out an inner conflict. In cases like this stealing is a symptom, and one of the most difficult with which adults deal. The child's motives are not conscious ones, but blind. To help him, the conditions causing him pain must be done away with before his stealing will stop. The stealing is a blundering attempt to set something right in his life. The something may have nothing to do with property at all. It is frequently deprivations or frustrations in the area of the child's relations with others.

Learning to understand and cope with the world, achieving understanding and acceptance of one's own self and developing satisfying relations with others are human goals continuous with life itself. During the years of childhood major steps are taken toward their accomplishment. The world is explored in efforts to learn what "it" means. The boundary between self and nonself becomes increasingly clearer and the child gradually learns to define "me." Through his relations with others he gradually comes to understand what "we" means. As these developments are taking place, physical growth goes on apace and he develops controls which are the tools he requires to move steadily toward adequacy in himself and adequacy in his relations with others.

## Aspects of Development

### Physical Growth

Rapid physical growth characterizes the years from birth to the age of six. However, the rate becomes progressively slower. In middle childhood boys and girls alike enter on a period of regular, uneventful growth in size, modified perhaps by the seasons, halted by illness but restored with a rush by convalescence. The child's basic energy consumption is less in the first six years and decreases steadily until the beginning of the rapid growth which precedes puberty. He has grown circulatory organs and an alimentary and respiratory tract considerably larger in proportion to body size and energy demands than he had at four or five. His slower rate of growth makes less demand on him for tissue building; he will add in a year less than his baby sister will put on in six months. This state continues for most boys into the early teens. For girls it may end as early as nine or 10 or 12. Then the preadolescent spurt in growth, set off by endocrine changes involving among others the pituitary, the thyroid and the gonads, makes heavy drafts on food, time and energy. At this growth stage skirts are too short, sweater sleeves do not reach the wrists and shoes are always too short as feet grow like a puppy's. One girl, aged 12, outgrew five complete outfits during one school year. But this experience comes for most children after or toward the end of childhood. There are many years when a few clothes are worn out—not just outgrown, when the youngster can see himself in the mirror without a shock, when hands and feet, legs and arms, turn out to be about where he last noticed them and reasonably manageable.

Such economical growth requires less rest and sleep. The fortunate youngster who takes his time about the prepubertal spurt will actually need less sleep than brother and sister in the early teens. He is less awkward, less self-conscious and in better command of himself.

At six the body proportions of boys and girls are still very different from those of the adult. At 12 the youth comes closer to adult size relationships and a more graceful form.

Middle and late childhood is the time when children get the teeth that will have to do them for life. They start losing their baby teeth about the time they go to school and cut the first permanent ones some time between five and seven. By the age of 12 or 13, the average six-year-old's 20 baby teeth have been lost and 28 permanent teeth have appeared in his jaws.

This whole process has some unpleasant aspects. It does not improve the appearance of the first-grade children whose toothless grins are a usual sight. There is a certain amount of recurring discomfort as each one of the 28 teeth makes its entrance. It could be four a year for seven years, but they rarely come with such regularity. The new teeth are attacked by decay at an average rate of almost two teeth a year through this period. It is also not uncommon to find a lack of harmony in the size of the teeth and the size of the jaw they must occupy. Toward the end of childhood comes the period of braces and retainers for those families which can afford to provide orthodontia. For the rest, there begins a lifelong unpleasantness impairing nutrition, damaging good looks and self-respect. One competent school dentist estimated that, in a city school population of 75,000 there was needed 4 to 6 million dollars worth of orthodontia. He did not attempt to estimate what it would cost to take care of all the cavities. Teeth are a lot of trouble to a school child, first and last. And all the dental care children do not receive is shown in the state of their dentition in adult life.

Things are also happening to a child's bones during these years. The epiphyses of the long bones are closing the cartilaginous gap which separates them from the shafts, and new units of ossification appear. At six years there are about 300 bone masses. At 12 there are approximately 220 separate bones. This steady bone building and consolidation makes heavy demands on the child's nutritional stores, especially of calcium and vitamin D. When the calcium balance of the organism is disturbed, there are disturbances affecting the whole personality.

Toward the end of childhood, youngsters have practically adult weight of the brain and anatomical completeness of the central nervous system. Vision, the latest of the senses to mature, is at its best at this time, barring structural defectiveness or abuse. The lymphoid tissues, related to resistance to infection, attain a weight double that of the adult. The muscular system is anatomically complete. The individual has, by 10 or 12, good command of as wide a variety of motor skills as he has opportunity to learn.

During the early years of this period, children suffer a very great deal from communicable diseases. Half of all the cases of communicable diseases reported to health departments occur in children aged five to nine, inclusive. These illnesses are made up chiefly of measles, mumps and chicken-pox, scarlet fever and whooping cough, plus upper respiratory ailments and digestive disturbances. The fifth and sixth grades, however, show remarkable gains in freedom from these illnesses.

Whooping cough and measles are yielding in some degree to immunization procedures, so that at least their severity is lessened; scarlet fever is less virulent than formerly. These are the years when rheumatic fever appears. But curves of mortality and mor bidity dip sharply from six to 12, so that the death rate for children from 10 to 12 is the lowest of the whole life span. Through puberty there will be a slow rise, both in deaths and in illness. This relative freedom from illness undoubtedly contributes to the zest and enthusiasm, the alertness and the readiness for adventure, which characterize the 10 to 12 age group. It is possible, too, that this general high level of bodily well-being weakens the appeal of conventional health teaching for these children. Now, and for some years to come, health is no motive in and for itself; it appeals only where improved condition permits gains in athletic prestige for boys or grace and good looks and social acceptability for girls. Curiosity is a stronger motive at the fifth or sixth grade than health-seeking; it may be capitalized upon in health instruction.

The development of the reproductive system follows a time-table of its own. The organs of reproduction are completely formed before birth; sex cells are not discharged until sexual maturity at the time of puberty. Sex organs grow in size somewhat during the first four years, reaching about 6 percent of adult weight. No further change occurs in size until the onset of puberty, when very rapid increase brings these structures to full size by the time the individual has attained maximum height. Generally, puberty begins earlier in girls than boys, although boys are more variable as to the timing of development. In the fifth and sixth grades some girls are beginning to show the rapid growth in height and the changes in body contours which mark preadolescence. There are also a few early maturing boys. At nine, there are not likely to be any pubescent children in a group. At 11 there will be approximately 20 percent of the girls and an occasional boy. At 13 years of age all but 20 percent of the girls will have entered puberty and perhaps half the boys. At 15, most of the girls are sexually mature and all but 10 percent of the boys are mature or pubescent. At 17 there will be 10 percent of the boys still pubescent and all the rest mature. For any one child, the whole process of pubescence, involving anatomical, physiological, psychological and social changes, will extend over a four or five year span.

Interest in genital organs and a varying amount of sex play are characteristic of children throughout this whole period. Sex play occurs from earliest childhood to adolescence, most frequently between ages eight and 13. About one-third of the boys who engage in such play keep it up for as long as five years and more than half carry on such activity for a year or two only. The higher the educational level, the shorter the duration of this type of play activity. The least frequent kind of play at all ages from five to 15 is coital (3% to 13%), next heterosexual (6.5% to 23%) and homosexual (6% to 29%). Sex play is usually taught a youngster by a slightly older boy or girl, and is carried on with a child near his own age. In a group of boys 10 to 12 years old, about 40 percent will be carrying on more or less sex play; about 20 percent will be engaged in homosexual, 23 percent heterosexual and 13 percent coital play. Before and after these ages, the percentages decrease markedly; but in any group of elementary school children there will probably be found a limited amount of sex play.

Preadolescent sex intercourse occurs in a small percentage of cases, but there is a marked difference here in the play of boys from higher educational levels and those from lower levels. According to Kinsey, "With the lower-level boy, pre-adolescent coitus may occur with some frequency and it may be had with a variety of partners. For the upper-level boy, the experience often occurs only once or twice, and with a single partner or two." [4] This statement is borne out by numerous studies. It is important to keep in mind in formulating sex education programs.

By 12 years of age, about a fifth of the boys will have begun to develop pubic hair, will have had ejaculations, will show voice change and will have begun rapid growth in height. More of the girls will have begun to be pubescent, and to show other secondary sexual characteristics. But while the girl becomes sexually mature, in the sense of discharging at regular intervals ripe ova which are capable of fertilization and development, most girls do not become mature in sexual behavior or interests for some time after menarche.

From infancy to maturity we can never justify ourselves in leaving out of our conception of children the influence exerted on their whole natures by their reproductive endowment. There is a very wide range of individual difference here, and the influence of home, church and community differ with the socio-economic level, educa-

[4] Kinsey, Alfred C.; Pomeroy, Wardell B.; and Martin, Clyde E. *Sexual Behavior in the Human Male.* Philadelphia: W. B. Saunders Co., 1948, p. 173. See Chapter 5 for summary of the literature.

tion, religion, housing and recreational pattern. Few generalizations apply to all children, but it may be said: they are male and female, most of them are sharply aware of sex differences before 10 years of age and are deeply influenced by this awareness in all the details of everyday life and the dreams of tomorrow. Neither we nor the children can ignore their sexual development, which began soon after their conception.

Many writers emphasize the difficulties parents and children find in moral evaluation of the sex conduct of children. Handling the genitals is probably universal in infancy and early childhood and also probably brings more pleasurable sensations than other explorations of the anatomy. This handling of the genitals may be an incidental or chance happening, a playful pastime or a compulsive nervous habit. The question before parents and teachers of primary school children is what attitude to take toward the child and toward this behavior. Social disapproval is strong, amounting to revulsion and disgust in many people. This disapproval produces a feeling of guilt in the child. Formerly there was a notion that masturbation caused insanity but there are no grounds for such a belief. Shall parents and school personnel therefore ignore this behavior, regard it as a normal part of development or attempt to limit it by building up disapproval of it in the child's own mind?

There is general agreement among child psychologists that lasting damage to a child's personality may be done by condemning the behavior and making him feel he is bad. He becomes skilful at hiding behavior that is frowned upon. Where children are stimulating themselves to excitement purposely and habitually, parents and teachers have the responsibility of improving the situation in which the individual child finds himself, minimizing minor pressures and enforced inactivity and increasing opportunities for social contacts and constructive play. If the child's response is not improved, expert help is needed. While it is true that masturbation is nothing to be shocked and horrified about, it is equally true that it is a mode of play which is not especially rewarding in enrichment of personality and which may make a child socially unacceptable.

Sex experimentation and mutual sex play of various kinds occur to some extent with most boys and with about a fifth of the girls.

There is no more usefulness in punishment of this play than there is in regard to masturbation. Teachers and parents should be prepared to encounter this behavior in early school years with equanimity. It is the same kind of challenge as masturbation: provide better supervision, better and more stimulating environmental situations for play, for social activities and for general developmental progress. Such behavior and the feelings it arouses are given undue importance by adult discussion. In these years it is play, a little different in the child's mind from other play, but still play. Sex impulses are not urgent or of critical significance in childhood; this is the time for orientation and wholesome comprehension of sex behavior as an element in human life. Where the child's play runs into excess or into socially undesirable behavior, he should be protected from his own immaturity without being burdened with guilty anxiety or embarrassed humiliation. As with safety precautions to avoid accidents, the responsibility in this sector of a child's responses is on the adults who are in charge of his days.

By 12, most girls and boys have become aware of moral codes and the obligations of each sex in sex relations. They have developed ability to postpone satisfactions and to seek long range goals. They are capable of high idealism. Decency and modesty seem natural to them. Where they behave otherwise it is ordinarily due to the influence of the behavior of adults and, especially, of older boys and girls.

## Motor Skills

By the sixth year the child has come a long way from the dependence and inadequacy of infancy, but he has still a long way to go to reach the goal of maturity. For the next five, six, seven years he appears to concentrate his whole being on developing motor performance and, to a lesser degree, to gaining a command of language, the magic tool human beings depend upon for solving problems and for a variety of creative activities.

For the infant and young child, the center of life and effort is vegetative, nutrition and growth far over-balancing other kinds of activity. In childhood, organismal attention centers on motor activities. A very large part of the child's time is spent in perfecting performance. During his preschool years he has acquired good control over his body; he is able to sit or stand well-poised, he can attend to all sorts of motor behavior which were beyond him in early childhood. This improvement is not made solely through the use of large muscles; some of the tiniest and most delicate muscles in the body are the very earliest to come under control. Watch the tiny baby learning to see one object with two eyes or, a bit later, picking up threads or pins off the rug with thumb and forefinger. But many motor performances require, not only small muscle activity but precise muscular coordination, large and small. This can only be accomplished against an anchorage of firm body-carriage. Little girls playing jacks or hopscotch are using both large and small muscle groups; most particularly, they are not using unnecessary groups, and by inhibition are attaining skill and a measure of grace. Children not only learn to ride a bicycle, but figuratively to ride it upside down and backward. A performance once learned is used as something to be embroidered and elaborated, for the sheer joy of achievement. From the end of the rapid growth of early childhood to the beginning of rapid growth in prepubescence, this is the all-absorbing, wholly satisfying activity. It has been said that a child's hands are "skill hungry."

During middle childhood certain basic elements which enter into many motor skills improve quite considerably with age. Three such elements are speed, strength, coordination. Speed increases very rapidly from three and one half years of age, when a child's response is three times as slow as that of the average adult, to six and one half years, when it is about 50 percent slower than adult response. Reaction time has not only become much quicker, but it is more consistently quick. Through the elementary school years the child gains steadily in speed. At 12 he has come within 10 percent of adult time. Some of the gain over early childhood is a gain in ability to understand and to attend to a stimulus. But after eight years of age the gain seems to be wholly a gain in speed. This speed of reaction is of great practical importance, especially in games and sports. It also has some bearing on the kind of game a child can learn at any given developmental level.

In *strength* there is a rapid increase with age, paralleling increase in muscle tissue, especially during middle childhood. From six to 14 years the increase in strength of grip, for instance, is consistently rapid in both sexes, and at about the same rate. Girls gain little after puberty, while boys continue for 10 years or so to make gains. At all ages most boys surpass most girls in strength. But during elementary school years the boys have only slight advantage over the girls.

In *coordination,* involving accuracy and rhythm of performance, both boys and girls show marked increases from early childhood to puberty, after which there is a slow increase to early maturity. Boys are superior to girls in practically all tests of accuracy and skill, but up to 11 or 12 years the difference is not great. From then on the boy's performance is on the average very much better. Anderson points out, however, that these differences are due rather to the boy's superiority in strength than to any lead in basic motor coordination, "since pure tests of coordination, which do not involve either speed or strength, show that girls perform as well as boys at all age levels. . . ." [5] All the long range studies made of various motor performances by the two sexes have suggested that the impressive differences between them are related also to differences in motivation. It is, as is easily observed, difficult to keep up interest in competitive tests of strength and skill in girls in their teens. These appeal strongly to adolescent boys and young men. Demonstrated superiority in this area gives a boy prestige among his associates of both sexes. This is not true for girls.

All studies of development agree on two things: that middle childhood is preeminently the time there is the greatest interest in both sexes in acquiring sensori-motor skills, the variety being endless, the choice determined mainly by local factors of popularity and supply of equipment; that through this development, and this only, can the child establish himself as an independent, self-respecting, self-confident personality. "Skills are assets with which the person moves on into the later domains of his life and on which he builds his future." [6]

[5] Anderson, John E., *op. cit.*, p. 137-38.
[6] *Ibid.*, p. 152.

## Language Skills

By the time a child enters school he has lived through the most rapid period of speech acquisition; he has learned to use speech as play material, as a facilitator of social contacts, as a way of getting things done by others and a means by which others signal him to action. He usually has a basic vocabulary estimated by strict standards at around 2500 words. By a more flexible means of assessment he has some degree of acquaintance with at least 10 times that many words. He lives, as one writer has said, "in a linguistic bath"; he is rarely silent for more than four minutes. When he is not talking, and often when he is, he is surrounded by the speech of others. He has an enormous amount of practice in talking and listening. His vocabulary seems to be limited chiefly by the vocabulary he hears; he learns the words geranium and photograph as he does cat and dog, if given the opportunity.

All this practice in using his vocabulary has been relatively unhampered by criticism. He has been encouraged to talk in early childhood and later he has been at worst tolerated or ignored. He enters school in an active language-acquiring stage, the mechanism involved reaching anatomical maturity between seven and nine. His interest and pleasure in speech are correspondingly keen. But he meets two obstacles. He enters a large group, many members are strange to him; the vocabulary and manner of speech which were adequate for home and playmates usually prove unequal to the new situation. His immediate task is to learn the speech of his peers, and the way it is used. But because he is one of a group, he must learn not to talk for what seems to him an interminably long time. An educational policy which takes children at the age of peak interest in development of motor skills and language and sets up an ideal conduct for them such as "Sit still and behave, and don't whisper" is regrettable.

From six to 12 children will, at the very least, double their vocabularies. They will lengthen and elaborate the structure of sentences. A child adds another dimension to his use of language: he finds it serves him as a means of thinking and of problem-solving. He learns the abstract language of numbers and, with luck and good teaching, he finds it useful. He learns to write and to compose.

When these learnings are in step with his readiness for them, his personal esteem and self-confidence are definitely enhanced. When too early he is frustrated, confused. This strikes at the heart of his feeling of being equal to life. This is not all that he suffers by these failures; these skills with language are indispensable tools for his formal education, and for his adult life in our society. If he makes heavy going of these acquisitions, he suffers anxiety and loss of status.

By intelligence test scores, girls have been found to be consistently superior to boys in language skills. There are fewer girls who are nonreaders, nonspellers, nongrammarians. Girls have also an unenviable superiority in the use of language as a weapon. By the time the twelfth year is reached both sexes are using vilification in place of blows, but the girls depend on this method of combat more than do boys.

A major problem of education is how to conduct formal schooling in such a way as to encourage the individual to solve problems independently, to feel confidence in his own abilities as good enough to take care of situations he finds himself in and, above all, to enjoy using his best wit and wisdom. There is evidence that men and women act on the basis of their feelings, not of their intelligence. Certainly this is not universally true; but if it applies to most adults, in full possession of their powers, it reveals a tragic lack in their development. This failure is in part the school's failure, as the eight- or nine-year-old's world is full of challenging situations which he feels he is capable of handling, but there is too often a competent and experienced adult ready to take over. Where more effective methods of instruction are used, children display ability in solving problems and there is opportunity for growth in this ability.

Anderson, recognizing present difficulties in the way of numbers, teachers and space, goes on to say:

When the time comes for such education, we will be amazed by the extent and amount of responsibility that young people can take, by their capacity to manipulate and run complex affairs, and by their ability to solve specific problems. One is often astounded at the increased ability of school-age children to express themselves freely and forcibly, and to tackle problems by group techniques. Children of nine or 12 now prepare and make speeches, run school papers, manage clubs, and handle many complex relations with an ease that is surprising to persons who have known children of other generations.[7]

In the process of moving from dependence to independence, keeping alive zest for using all his resources of body, mind and spirit to solve his problems is of very great significance. It is in childhood, and especially in later childhood, that all his powers, except those of reproduction, come into play. Typically, a child of this stage will "try anything once," even using his head. Whether he tries it again and again depends on the grown-up's reaction to his first efforts. Faegre has put a finger on certain elements in this situation when she points out that a child's

. . . growing ability to think and reason for himself are sometimes disconcerting. It upsets our notions of our superiority—when our children begin to question our opinions and to have very definite ideas of their own.

" 'I'm quite as big for me,' said he,
    'As you are big for you.' "

This is really what scares many an adult off. . . We feel secure in our bigness and power—important in contrast to smallness and helplessness . . . As children grow out of complete dependence, they begin to think and reason for themselves.[8]

All too often, these beginnings are unwelcome. The story of a child's achievements, in relation to his ability and desire to think and reason for himself, is often no credit to us who guide him. Then, in the teens, he is suddenly "almost grown," and we say he has no more ability to look after himself and do us credit than a mere child. Constructive thinking, problem-solving effort, is always hard work at any age. A child's world may not be too much shadowed by our discouragement of his tentative beginnings in intellectual independence, but his future is.

## Relationships with Others

A child's world has people in it from the moment of conception. From early childhood, interest in persons is keener than interest in things. Personality is an outcome of social experience, definable

[7] *Ibid.*, p. 191.
[8] Faegre, Marion L., *op. cit.*, p. 1.

chiefly in terms of reactions to and by other persons. Social approval is the greatest reward and social isolation the most severe punishment short of death.

A child's behavior in any situation is modified one way or another by the pressure of other children or adults. Social development is not only related to changing modes of response to other persons, but to the effect of the presence of others on behavior which is not interpersonal. The effect may be inhibitory, but more frequently it is stimulating, inciting and exacting. Children eat better when other children are present and also eating, unless the social facilitation gets quite out of bounds and the meal becomes a mob scene. This mutually stimulating effect on each other has great possibilities for good and evil. Children are increasingly under the sway of age group influences from seven or eight through puberty. At adolescence, the opinions and values of the peer group are all powerful. But before other children influence the child to marked extent the matrix of his personality has been set, in the first years of life, by his relations with his mother and father and other members of the family group.

## Family Relations

A great deal of research has been done on the first years of the child's life and in the last decade many of the findings have been incorporated in books drawing implications from them for educating the young child. A "new look" in child raising has resulted. No longer are prescribed, rigid routines for eating and sleeping followed by the up-to-date parent; rather are these regulated according to the individual child's rhythmic pattern of need for eating and sleeping. Rocking the baby is once more respectable, not simply because of the pleasure it gives the mother, but because it is a way of meeting the child's need to be fondled and cuddled and gain feelings of being wanted and loved.

It is now understood that it is through the parent-child relation that the individual should gain feelings of security, acceptance, belonging and adequacy which will stand him in good stead the rest of his life in developing satisfying relations with others. Rejection by one or both parents usually means a warping of personality, means that the rejected one endeavors to make up for deprivations and lack of acceptance and consequent feelings of inferiority by "taking it out" on others. He finds it necessary to be aggressive toward others, to exploit them, to move against them in various ways, or he moves away from them, withdraws into himself and makes up for unsatisfactory real relationships in a fancied world he can structure to suit himself.[9]

Even the relationships with others of the child who is loved and wanted are affected by parents' attitudes and values. For example, he learns, more through actions than their words, to have respect for others and their rights, or to limit that respect to only those who are in the same social group or of the same color or religious belief.

The child's ideas about the relations of the sexes will be sharply affected by the relationship of father and mother. He learns how men treat women from his father's behavior toward his mother. He learns how women respond to men from his mother's response to the father's treatment of her. The learnings will be of one kind, when the father-mother relation is a partnership in the full sense of the word, a sharing of the jobs of home building and rearing of a family, when father and mother obviously enjoy one another's company and extend this enjoyment to include the children and the partnership to include them as well. The learnings will be of a different kind when the home is dominated by an authoritarian father or by an over-protective but equally dominating mother, when reasoning does not prevail but emotions rule and there are bickerings, inconsistent demands upon the child so that he becomes confused and fearful, not knowing just what are the right roads toward attaining the much desired approval and acceptance of his parents.

In the family group, relationships with brothers and sisters influence this first shaping of the child's personality. One child may dominate another; there may be rivalry among the children for the parents' attention and approval; the attractiveness or achievements of one child may be used to shame another or as a standard of what is expected of him. There are both positive and negative results possible from such relationships with siblings. Whether the outcomes in personality development are positive depends upon the

[9] Healy, William, and Bronner, Augusta P. *New Light on Delinquency and Its Treatment.* New Haven: Yale University Press, 1936, p. 4-5.

trust and confidence the child has in the love, affection and protective care of his parents. Possessing these, he can weather the tyranny of an older child, vie with brothers and sisters for attention and admire the attractiveness and achievements of a sibling providing him a model to emulate.

When the child comes to school at the age of five or six, he brings with him attitudes towards others he has built up largely through his relationships in the family group. However, even before entering school his horizons have widened to include other children of his neighborhood in his play life. Entrance into school marks an increase in the number of peer relations and the definite increase in effect of these relations upon his behavior.

## Relationships with Other Children

Children in early preschool years show interest in other children but not in relating activities to those of others. The earliest stage of social play seems to be just watching others; later comes parallel play, which is playing with the same materials as others in their presence. For example, a group was given a box of shells; in less than two minutes each child had his own pile of shells and was playing with it. Much later, each began to notice what his neighbors were doing with their shells; there developed some competition for larger piles of shells. Riding tricycles together is another kind of parallel play that usually develops into racing each other, a simple kind of competition. By kindergarten age, children can operate for short periods in groups of two and three, carrying on common projects in a loose kind of cooperation with division of labor. Children learn through these patterns of group play a good deal about getting along with other children.

## Group Relations

Beginning in about the third grade, children begin to form clubs spontaneously. There are secrets and officers. These clubs disintegrate in a few days but new ones are formed. In later childhood and early puberty the groups last longer, have stricter and more elaborate rules, and often feel the need of a private abode such as a clubhouse of some type. These organized groups of children can be cruel to their own members, impose harsh treatment on their neophytes and generally imperil the welfare of their members if unsupervised. But there seems no doubt a real need for belonging to a social unit and submitting to its discipline, as is shown by children's interest and loyalty to these clubs and gangs with their secrecy and mumbo-jumbo.

Groups such as Scouts, Camp Fire and Y's often satisfy this interest, with the added advantage of a good program of activities and comradely adult supervision. But such groups lose their attraction after puberty for most boys and practically all girls. During adolescence youth is still interested in organizations, but shifts to hobby clubs and special interest groups. Interest in these often lasts throughout life. The influence of club membership is apparently wholesome, unless the club happens to be focused on undesirable activities, such as sex play or thievery. "The desire for esteem and social reinforcement from others with common interests is so strong that unless opportunities are provided under good auspices, the needs will be met by organizations under bad auspices." [10]

Reference has been made to the development of ability to cooperate with other children. This is rudimentary at three and develops steadily as competitive behavior through childhood and youth. Children enjoy cooperative competition, or competitive cooperation, through the whole range of play and school life. In any activity which involves some division of labor, timing one's actions in relation to those of others and obeying signals, there are throughout childhood conflicts and repeated disruption of group effort with resultant failure or varying degrees of success. At seven, several authors have noticed a tendency to quit the group or to sulk. By eight, the children are more likely to muddle through the situation; although there may be much bickering, the play goes on. From childhood to adult life with its diplomats and negotiators, the struggle for effective cooperation goes on.

Authorities in the field of child development state that there will be much friction, complaining, tale-bearing, name-calling and combat and that caution should be exercised in entering these conflicts. Indirect means for reducing friction through changes in the situa-

[10] Anderson, John E., *op. cit.*, p. 349.

tion in which the children are operating should be employed. When there is not room enough for moving about without physical collision or there are not enough tools and materials for the project, there is more trouble and less effective action in the group enterprise. It is also noticed that when a group exists too long at a time, the amicability-span appears startlingly short. A cooperative project in which there is division of labor, leadership and timing of action on the part of three or four children is comparable to a rope-walking stunt for an adult; it is barely within the limits of human capacities.

Investigators warn that the outcome of attempts at cooperation is not necessarily beneficial to the participants. Gesell says: "If adverse behavior (as tattling, cheating, sulking, ganging-up, etc.) is not kept in bounds and if it is not resolved in its immediate context by the children with the legitimate help of an adult, the overall trend (of social development) can be unfavorable. The years five to ten can breed delinquency and poor citizenship." [11]

Any children's group attempting cooperation has a better chance of succeeding if a leader who can win acceptance appears. Such leaders do appear from the beginnings of group activity at three and wherever two or three try to carry out an enterprise involving division of labor. There is at first a ready assuming of the role, as in most simple games where each player has an opportunity to take the lead in turn. Even in a nursery school group, some children do better as leaders than others. Some, because their fellows do not want them in the group, and some, because they do not want to be involved with others, seldom experience the responsibilities and joys of leadership.

Traits which characterize leaders of children's groups have been studied and found to change somewhat with the age level of the group. Young children like the child who is physically active and a voluble talker. This child may take the lead through aggressive methods or he may be resourceful in seeing new and interesting things to do and getting along with other children. Among older children, leaders are likely to be somewhat brighter than the rest, taller and heavier, better dressed and better looking. They often are good talkers and more daring than other children. They have

[11] Gesell, Arnold, and Ilg, Frances. *The Child from Five to Ten*. New York: Harper and Brothers, 1946. p. 386.

better control of themselves and are not so likely to lose their patience or temper. However, children choose their leaders at fifth- and sixth-grade level in terms of special abilities suited to the project under way. This fits in with the tendency noted earlier to shape clubs in terms of hobbies or special interests.

There are other elements besides general or special excellence involved in leadership success, as was shown in an early study by Terman (1904).[12] He found that leaders tended to be children who were conspicuous, though not necessarily conspicuously good. More recent studies, using a variety of sociometric techniques, find a few children who push steadily and gradually to a position of prestige by what looks like a planned campaign of choosing the right friends or associates and thus gaining social visibility and a chance at leadership. This seems to mean that one of the characteristics of a good leader is a persistent desire to be in a prominent position, to have prestige, to be acceptable and admired. In early childhood this alone will put him in office for the brief tenure children's groups offer. In later childhood he will need in addition some special excellence or skills in an area valued by his mates. A problem of education is to help every child to become acceptable as a leader in some respect because of particular competencies.

*Peer Friends.* Children form attachments for other children within the larger group of club, gang or clique. These friendships are, after school age, usually with children of their own chronological age, of about the same mental ability and the same physical vigor. Young children choose their friends from among near neighbors, since they do not have a wide range of acquaintance. In later childhood they have a wider field from which to choose, and are more likely to look for similar tastes and interests rather than just taking the youngster who lives nearby. A good deal can be told about a child by studying his chosen associates who reflect his qualities to a certain extent. That is why they are picked to be his chums.

Most investigators of children's close associations agree that good friends quarrel more frequently with each other than with other children in their group. In early school years quarrels lead to attempted bodily aggression toward each other; later the "fight-

[12] Terman, Lewis M. "A Preliminary Study in the Psychology and Pedagogy of Leadership." *Pedagogical Seminary* 11: 413-51; November 1904.

ing" is done through name-calling and taunting. Quarrels do not last long unless interfered with, when they tend to rankle and recur. The more social the child's nature, the more likely he is to be involved in many quarrels. Fortunately, these quarrels are quickly forgotten.

In prepubescence a strong attachment often develops for a pal or chum. A boy and his chum become inseparable companions, a girl and her girl friend dress alike, talk alike and where one is the other is apt to be found. "Can Mary come too?" "I will if Joe will," express this friendship. It is a sustaining relationship for the boy or girl who feels that adolescence and adulthood are not too far off and who is beginning to look at loving and protective parents with an eye to getting free of their apron strings. Having a companion who is in the same stage of peering into untried paths sometimes becomes the most important relationship in the child's life at this period.

*Boy-Girl Relations.* It is generally agreed that by school age a child has made an intellectual discrimination between the sexes, has recognized his own sex and has begun to see what being a boy or a girl involves in present behavior standards and what significance the fact of sex has for his future. Faegre states, however: "On the surface (the child) seems fairly indifferent to sex during these years. We may not see much evidence of sex interest, or activity that can be called sex activity, except as boys and girls tend to draw apart and mingle less with the opposite sex." [13] The most complete statement of observed sex behavior, knowledge and attitudes for each year from six to 12 is given in various publications from Dr. Arnold Gesell's Child Development Clinic, Yale School of Medicine. In regard to the development of a child's concept of himself, Gesell says that this depends upon the impact of other selves and "is intermeshed with the phenomenon of sex. This does not mean that the whole, far ramifying structure of the self is built about a single framework of sex. . . . Sexual functions do not necessarily play a despotic role in the patterning of child development. . . . (We must) see the facts of sex in perspective and recognize the subtle

[13] Faegre, Marion L., *op. cit.*, p. 100.

gradations by which they are incorporated into the total development of the individual self." [14]

A few youngsters at six want to be of the opposite sex. A child may know that only females have babies yet he, as a boy, may be upset because he can never have a child, or he may even be fearful that a baby is growing inside him. . . . A six-year-old girl dressed like a boy may demand to be called Johnny and play with a truck. From this beginning through puberty both boys and girls, who are never all-boy or all-girl, must work at discovering what are the assets and liabilities, opportunities and limitations of this life which the sex of each makes possible. He and she must also learn to find proper pride and satisfaction in these prospects.

The six-year-old has had several years of asking questions about his own and others' bodies, and about where babies come from. By the time he comes to school these have been answered well enough for his peace of mind or he has learned these things are not to be talked about. He has learned that you marry a member of the opposite sex, but he may announce that he is going to marry his mother or sister or the little girl next door. He knows babies follow marriage, but is more interested in "how the baby gets out" than in its conception. The facts of intercourse are beyond his grasp. He may want his mother to have another baby, but he does not pay much attention to the slow changes in her during pregnancy. He sometimes gets some ideas about birth through watching dogs and cats bearing their young.

All authors, and most families, have noticed the development of modesty and a new demand for privacy through the seventh and eighth years. A little boy may refuse to use the toilet at school if there is no door on it and he no longer wants to share a bath with a brother or sister. He appreciates a chance to dress and undress in privacy.

At six, boys and girls play together without any more difficulties than same-sex groups have. There are boy-girl friendships in preschool groups which may last some months or even years and which have a quality different from sex-like attachments, but show nothing of self-consciousness or silliness. At seven children may become

[14] Gesell, Arnold, and Ilg, Frances, *op. cit.*, p. 309.

involved in elementary love affairs, with recognized pairing-off, writing notes with tender assurances, even planning marriage in the very dim future. There is nothing very personal about this, it has the air of a game played tentatively. Gesell tells of a seven-year-old who had no boy friend, "wailing to her parents, 'What is the matter with me? I'm not in love.' " By eight, this girl-boy relation is becoming a dominant interest, and acquiring a more romantic color. "Boys recognize a pretty girl, and girls chase handsome boys, much to the boys' delight." [15] They resent being teased about these attractions and attachments, and become secretive on the subject. There are "engagements," and planning for future homes in some detail as to house and garden and furniture. In doll play, family life is mimicked. Overt group sex play may develop, usually led by older children. These groups are especially likely to form where play is unsupervised and somewhat poverty-stricken as to opportunities, but they may form under good environmental conditions as well.

The eight-year-old has a great many questions to be answered about babies and where and how they appear. An avalanche of questions may be launched when the child finds his parents will answer frankly. Both sexes are ready for knowledge of the father's share in reproduction before 11. Girls are thought to be more inquisitive than boys and somewhat more precociously knowing. Between eight and 10, both boys and girls arrive at ability to understand human reproduction.

During the years from seven to nine, there begins a definite preference in sex of playmates, and a resulting segregation of boys and girls in play. Girls draw away quietly though consciously. Later, around nine, boys become rough and boisterous about excluding girls. Among nine-year-olds, Gesell says the spontaneous groups are nearly always single-sexed, birthday parties are by choice limited to one sex, and "each sex cordially disdains the other." "Girls don't count!" "Boys are loathsome creatures." "I enjoy watching them." [16]

Individual differences in maturity become important after eight. Most girls are nearer maturity than most boys, but individual differences are also striking. Gesell says: "The psychology of a ten-year-

[15] Gesell, Arnold, and Ilg, Frances, *op. cit.*, p. 149.
[16] *Ibid.*, p. 193, 205.

old girl is significantly distinguishable from that of a ten-year-old boy of equivalent breeding and experience. The girl has more poise, more folk wisdom, and more interest in matters pertaining to marriage and the family." [17] There are marked sex differences in play interests and skills and in choice of radio programs, movies and reading. With the tenth year, these accumulated divergencies are heightened in significance by a full-blown sex antagonism, freely expressed and sincerely felt.

By the 12-year-old level, boys and girls show they have formulated ideals of admirable persons of both sexes. These differ as day from night. For the boy, appearance, "good-looking," is not important; it is crucial for the girl. The boy must be skilful and daring, good at games, the girl feminine and ladylike.

In reference to the child's progress from helplessness to independence, his acceptance of his sex role and his increasing mastery of himself in regard to sex behavior are essential elements in his achievement of success as a person. He needs clear concepts of changes from childhood to maturity, of human reproduction, sex intercourse, conception, pregnancy, birth, nursing, weaning and of menstruation and seminal emissions. He needs also to know the psychological aspects of sex behavior and to have a working familiarity with the game of teasing, flirting, courting, what is right and wrong and why, in relation to sex conduct. Ignorance gives no basis for freedom, but it is true that a child, just because he *is* a child, can only gain a very superficial kind of understanding of some aspects of sex development and relations. But what he can grasp, the experiences he is capable of, seem to be important for his welfare, seem to set him free emotionally to move into adolescence.

## Adult Leadership

Several good observers and thoughtful students of child development emphasize the need for skilful adult attention to this whole process of social development. Because it goes on primarily in situations outside the classroom and the home, it is all too likely to be unsupervised; or it may be stultified by over-organization under a dominant adult. The whole process is of critical importance

[17] *Ibid.*, p. 213.

to the success of the individual as a person and as a future member of a society that struggles to become more truly democratic.

The best thing we can do to further the welfare of children is to provide social situations where individuals regardless of origin, wealth, poverty or "background" are free to find their own level of associations. That will also be the level where individual potentialities have the best chance of being realized. It is a matter of pride to those who work in and for public schools that these can, and often do, provide free social situations and help children to take advantage of them. The social acceptance of Negroes in music, in sports and in entertainment has probably been advanced by free access to extracurricular activities and sports in the nonsegregated schools which are the rule in many of the 48 states.

This chance for a child to find himself by finding congenial associates does not just happen. While need and opportunity are greatest at the high-school level, later childhood can profit by being related to a reasonably large school, drawing pupils from varied backgrounds and giving them a chance to try out many interests, musical, dramatic, athletic, artistic. Many youngsters are interested in various kinds of construction and for others the satisfaction of growing things, to sell or to use or to enjoy. Children are ready for the social development these opportunities make possible when they are in the fifth and sixth grades; although children's parents can open up the various activities to them, they are not in the best position to help youngsters find companionship and prestige with their own age group through these achievements.

It is recognized as important to see that certain children in a group are not always at the end of the procession, to help them find a place in the sun if not at the head of the line. The methods which are effective aim at two developments: improvement of some special abilities which are valued by the group and overcoming reluctance to assert oneself and take responsibility. Jersild, who has observed social behavior in elementary school groups over a considerable period of time, is convinced of the usefulness of these methods in bringing a child to a fair degree of social adequacy.[18]

Between five and 12, a child has gained increasing mastery of himself and increasing success in living and working with his

[18] Jersild, Arthur T. *Child Psychology*. Revised edition. New York: Prentice-Hall, 1946. p. 224-28.

fellows. But as he progresses, the complexity of his tasks continually outstrips his gains; his reach is typically greater than his grasp. But he can see and feel his own achievements and increasing adequacy. Under reasonably intelligent guidance and with a measure of good luck as to companions and environment, he feels joy in living and confidence in meeting the future that waits for him beyond adolescence. There are none of the responsibilities and few of the joys of adult life with which he has not made tentative acquaintance. Under good conditions, his courage is high and his zest keen. The goal, of such independence as an interdependent creature like man may know, is not far distant.

## Bibliography

ANDERSON, JOHN E. *The Psychology of Development and Personal Adjustment.* New York: Henry Holt and Co., 1949.

BRECKENRIDGE, MARIAN E., and VINCENT, E. LEE. *Child Development.* Revised edition. Philadelphia: W. B. Saunders Co., 1943.

CARMICHAEL, LEONARD, editor. *Manual of Child Psychology.* New York: John Wiley and Sons, 1946.

FAEGRE, MARION L. *Child Care and Training.* Minneapolis: University of Minnesota Institute of Child Welfare, 1947.

FAEGRE, MARION L. *Your Child from Six to Twelve.* Children's Bureau Publication No. 324. Washington, D. C.: United States Government Printing Office, 1949.

GESELL, ARNOLD, and ILG, FRANCES. *Infant and Child in the Culture of Today.* New York: Harper and Brothers, 1943.

GESELL, ARNOLD, and ILG, FRANCES. *The Child from Five to Ten.* New York, Harper and Brothers, 1946.

HEALY, WILLIAM, and BRONNER, AUGUSTA P. *New Light on Delinquency and Its Treatment.* New Haven: Yale University Press, 1936.

HURLOCK, ELIZABETH. *Child Growth and Development.* New York: McGraw-Hill Book Co., 1949.

JENKINS, GLADYS G.; SHACTER, HELEN; and BAUER, W. W. *These Are Our Children.* Chicago: Scott, Foresman and Co., 1950.

JERSILD, ARTHUR T., and ASSOCIATES. *Child Development and the Curriculum.* New York: Bureau of Publications, Teachers College, Columbia University, 1946.

JERSILD, ARTHUR T. *Child Psychology.* Revised edition. New York: Prentice-Hall, 1946.

KINSEY, ALFRED C.; POMEROY, WARDELL B.; and MARTIN, CLYDE E. *Sexual Behavior in the Human Male.* Philadelphia: W. B. Saunders Co., 1948.

OLSON, WILLARD C. *Child Development.* Boston: D. C. Heath and Co., 1949.

TERMAN, LEWIS M. "A Preliminary Study in the Psychology and Pedagogy of Leadership." *Pedagogical Seminary* 11: 413-51; November 1904.

# CHAPTER SIX

# Concepts and Attitudes
# To Be Developed

HELEN FAHEY

JOHN H. SHAW

THE primary concern of every educator should be the quality of living that is experienced within the school. Learning is influenced by living. It is impossible to educate for democratic living by having children live in an autocratic atmosphere during the hours they are at school. "Good human relations are those ways of mutual human behavior which by common consent are recognized as essential to promoting and safeguarding the desired quality of human living." [1]

Democracy is a way of living more than it is a kind of government. Democracy involves the right of each individual to live his best and to give his best to those with whom he lives. As teachers there is the realization that no individual can live his best or give his best if he does not respect human personality or if he in turn is not respected.

The fields of health education, physical education and recreation are excellent channels through which this ideal of social living can function. The responsibility for developing good human relations is, therefore, an important task for every teacher or leader of health education, physical education and recreation. Where good social living prevails, good human relations are being developed. Children who play harmoniously together, planning and carrying out group

[1] Kilpatrick, William H. *Better Human Relations.* New York: Freedom Pamphlets, Anti-Defamation League of B'nai B'rith, 1949, p. 3.

[ 157 ]

action, abiding by group decisions, meeting each problem as it arises, are gaining an understanding of democratic human relations. Children who are alert to needs and changes on the playground may well grow into adults alert to the needs of people in an ever-changing world.

Special care in the organization of physical education classes must be exercised to insure a democratic atmosphere. Marching, calisthenics and formal gymnastics, especially when taught in over-crowded quarters, may be handled in an autocratic manner and this relationship between pupil and teacher carry over into the entire program of physical education unless one guards against it. Winslow has pointed out this tendency in his survey of New York State Schools, "A large number of teachers were observed who evidently conceived their role to be that of a disciplinarian and drillmaster, and maintained authority by the use of sarcasm, nagging, ridicule, and dogmatic domination." [2] The teacher who gives the most to the child's world is one who shares ideas, shares responsibility, is as willing to discard or accept ideas through evaluation as the children are. In a democratic set-up, this teacher is as often a player on a team as he is the director of the game. It is significant that children prefer play leaders who occasionally play with them to those who just direct or supervise activity. It is necessary for the teacher to be accepted as a member of the group rather than an outsider. Playing with the group particularly in an activity in which the teacher is proficient aids this acceptance.

"Every adequately organized and planned activity has a purpose, a goal, a directive and an inventory. When this goal has been established in response to interest and needs, plans are made toward accomplishment. When the goal or objective has been achieved the progress and results are evaluated." [3] To help children in developing democratic relations with others the adult guide needs to have specific objectives in mind. A list of such objectives for the teacher or leader of children is offered. Subsequently each of these objectives is related to the concepts children may be helped to form in the words children use to express them.

---

[2] Winslow, C. E. A. *The School Health Program.* New York: McGraw-Hill Book Co., 1938, p. 26.

[3] O'Keefe, Pattric Ruth, and Fahey, Helen. *Education Through Physical Activities.* St. Louis, Mo.: C. V. Mosby Co., 1949, p. 27.

## General Objectives

Each individual must be given a feeling of security by being accepted, loved and appreciated, and in return must respond by giving love and by accepting and appreciating others.

Each individual must have and show respect for the rights and privileges of others.

Each individual must have a place in the group, must assume the responsibility of contributing to the group's action and must share the responsibility for the group's decisions.

Each individual must experience success through achieving his optimum development in proper relation to the group's welfare.

Each individual must have the opportunity as a member of a group to face problems, to undertake their solutions and to evaluate the results.

Each individual should develop a feeling of appreciation of racial, religious and national differences.

Each individual should gain knowledge of and develop respect for the cultural contributions of other groups.

Each individual must understand his potentialities and limitations and be capable of adjusting to them.

Each individual must experience unfamiliar situations so that he can learn to adjust to changed conditions. There is no need to fear the unfamiliar.

The adult or teacher objectives in the area of human relations will be repeated with the listing and exemplifying of specific concepts that children may possess or may be encouraged to develop through the elementary-school years. Each objective will be presented as it has meaning and understanding for the age group being discussed. Concepts are presented as they may be developed in health education, physical education and recreation programs for children.

## Development of Concepts and Attitudes

Objective: *Each individual must be given a feeling of security by being accepted, loved and appreciated and in turn must respond by giving love and by accepting and appreciating others.*

### Concepts and Attitudes—Primary-Age Child

When I am friendly to a playmate he is friendly too.
The teacher is friendly even when I am not.
It is fun to play with other boys and girls.
When a playmate does something well, I should tell him so.
I like to hear my work is fine.
I am happy to be with these boys and girls.

### Concepts and Attitudes—Intermediate-Age Child

How can I be popular with my classmates?
When I do good work I want praise or recognition.
Other boys and girls like to receive credit and recognition for work well done.
School is sometimes a good place and then again it is not.
The teacher usually understands me, but not always.
I should be friendly even when others seem unfriendly.

The six-year-old says, "Mary, will you bounce the ball back to me if I bounce it to you?" "Shall we let Tommy play?" "I can't climb a rope, Mrs. Ellis." The good teacher provides an environment conducive to good play. Good play reduces tensions, helps everyone to have fun, feel happy and be himself. Good play means adequate materials, space and a place to play. There are many balls of different sizes, jumping ropes, a ladder, a castle tower to climb and boxes for building. There is instruction in how to throw the ball or how to climb a rope. Each one is encouraged to play with a classmate or in a group. Each child is secure in that he is asked to do that which he is capable of doing. His performance is accepted with, "You knew you were tagged, Mike." "Try keeping your hands on the rope just in front of your face when you climb, Jill." "I believe you reach too far up the rope with your hands." "Try again." Praise, companionship, recognition and love bring security to the young child.

What happens when a child experiences failure is very important. He must learn that sometimes many, many repetitions are necessary before success is achieved. The instructor and classmates must present an attitude of helpfulness rather than a critical or sarcastic one which leads to feelings of insecurity. Too many instructors fail either personally in this respect or in controlling the reaction of the class to individual performances. Children should learn to profit from their failures.

All children want to be liked and the older child is often willing to put his desire into words. "How can I be popular, Miss Smith?" "How do you make friends?" "Some days I do not even want to go to school." All are questions and statements that have confronted the teacher of the 11- and 12-year-old group. Such expressions indicate their desire to become more poised, to gain confidence in themselves, to like and to be liked.

One teacher helped her class by studying the social structure of the class. Each child was requested to list his five closest friends and to list five people with whom he wanted to be friends. From this sociogram the teacher knew the popular members, the isolated, friendless ones and the cliques. Through seating arrangement, work in groups and guidance in choosing teams for sports she was able to see that each child received favorable attention from some classmate and that each child felt wanted, liked and secure.

When the teacher, parent or leader is sensitive to situations, an awareness is developed that there is always some play situation in which a child can excel or at least feel needed by his group. A little time spent in adjusting the situation unobtrusively will often result in his being successful and gaining status. The large, slow-moving boy may make a good soccer goalie, a position others may not care for because of the limited physical activity associated with playing that position. This position suits the boy's capabilities and temperament perfectly. Making such adjustments is largely a matter of alertness on the part of the teacher and being aware of boys and girls as individuals rather than concentrating on the perfection of skills to the exclusion of other learnings.

Objective: *Each individual must have and show respect for the rights and privileges of others.*

### Concepts and Attitudes—Primary-Age Child

Some children do better work and play better than I do.

Everyone in the group can use our supplies.

I can show you how to make this.

When I am chosen leader I cannot do this.

Some children can do what I can do.

All of us should take turns.

Some things belong to others.

### Concepts and Attitudes—Intermediate-Age Child

Each classmate has a right to contribute his ideas.

Everyone in the group should have an equal opportunity.

Classmates are dependent on each other and upon the teacher.

Regardless of who it is, each member of the group has a right to express his ideas and members should grant each one this right.

Every privilege carries a responsibility.

Ideas as well as materials should be shared.

Classmates do not want to be bothered when they are busy.

Learning to share materials, to follow rules, to accept each child for his unique contribution is a developing process. A child moves slowly from interest in self toward interest in the rights and privileges of others. The five-year-old walks into the kindergarten, picks up all the dolls and takes them to one corner of the room. As other children reach for a doll a cry of "that is mine" can be heard. The teacher finds it a slow process to help him understand that other children like dolls and that each should have the privilege of playing with them.

The idea of taking turns and prior rights to certain articles must be given careful consideration. Some things cannot be satisfactorily shared but must be enjoyed individually. Fair play should be stressed. Appealing to an individual's sense of justice often works well as "How would you like it, John, if the situation were reversed?"

Developing a sense of shared responsibility for the care of equipment is important. "John brought the ball out—he should go get it," is often heard at the close of a play period. It must be pointed out that "someone else may have hit it over the fence but there will be no game tomorrow if the ball is lost—the equipment belongs to all of us and everyone enjoys playing. If we take care of the ball we have more fun and learn more. Be a good sport and do your share."

In some situations where the equipment is taken to the playground during the play periods the child taking it should be made directly responsible for returning it. This is his responsibility which must be assumed with the privilege of having charge of the equipment.

The nine-year-old may also be confronted with such a problem as this: if his foot were not on the base before the ball was placed there, he was "out." Arguments may arise until someone remembers that Tommy is the leader. He must make the decision as to the outs. Tommy is faced with the realization that carrying the ball and being the leader are privileges accompanied with responsibilities.

Objective: *Each individual must have a place in the group, must assume the responsibility of contributing to the group and must share the responsibility for the group's decision.*

*Concepts and Attitudes—Primary-Age Child*

I will work with boys and girls in my group.

This is our problem.

Let us find the best way to do this.

I can do this by myself or I cannot do this by myself.

The group decided what to do and we all did it.

I must help the leader.

I am the leader—what shall we do?

*Concepts and Attitudes—Intermediate-Age Child*

We can accomplish more by sharing responsibility and by co-operating with our classmates.

As a member of a group I should give my opinion in discussions, as silence means acceptance of the group's ideas.

It is better to try to get agreement of the whole group than let the majority rule. If the group accepts its responsibility then control of our actions will come from within the group.

My classmates think I am dependable and responsible.

"In the morning when we come to school we look clean and neat, but at noon we are messy." "Our work gets soiled and when we go to the auditorium to sing, Mrs. Black's pupils look at us." "We need to comb our hair and wash up." These are remarks heard in Miss Hall's room. The teacher agreed and thought the group should do something about it. Plans were immediately started. The girls wanted a dressing table but the boys thought it was sissy. Finally the boys agreed to the dressing table if they could have a bachelor corner in the room with a mirror. Four girls with help from a mother made the skirt for the dressing table. The boys got a mirror for the girls and a mirror for themselves. They refinished both mirrors. Jane brought hand lotion. One boy said, "We all can't use the same comb," and a girl said, "We look silly standing in line so long waiting to wash our hands." The group finally decided to:

have a small box in the locker for combs and pins.

look at the school clock and wash hands between 12:50 to 1:00.

take turns looking in the mirror and not look in it forever.

use a little hand lotion if needed.

accept the plan that unless everyone looks neat the whole group would not go to chorus.

The decision was made by the group and it was a difficult one to adhere to. Nancy said, "I was ready to go to sing at 12:45 and then because Tom never came in until too late I didn't get to go." Members reminded Nancy that she was the one who made the suggestion concerning missing chorus so she couldn't complain.

After this experience the class decided that it was not fair to penalize an entire group for the lack of neatness of a few and so voted that only those failing to clean up should miss the opportunity to sing.

The group described made the important discovery that even though a solution is reached cooperatively it may not always be a good decision; decisions have to be considered in terms of their results; a group may make mistakes and profit by its mistakes just as individuals do.

A difficult conception for children to develop is the understanding that when one is a member of a group he has a definite responsibility in formulating the group's plans and in making decisions. When he makes no contribution or does not dissent, he continues to be responsible for the group's decision. There are too many adults who attend vital civic meetings and leave stating, "I didn't agree with the committee members and although I didn't take part in the discussion like some, I want my friends to know I do not like what is being done." A different concept of responsibility in a democracy is needed and children should be helped to develop it through their group experiences.

Objective: *Each individual must experience success through achieving his optimum development in proper relation to the group's welfare.*

*Concepts and Attitudes—Primary-Age Child*

I made it myself.

I have to wait my turn.

I can bring things to school for everyone to see and use.

If you see work you would like to do go ahead and try it.

It will help my friends.

Our group was the best.

*Concepts and Attitudes—Intermediate-Age Child*

I should show I am a responsible person.

My responsibility shows in the work I do.

Attacking new problems helps me.

What is good for most people in the class should be considered when making plans.

Other children want to be leaders and they should be leaders sometimes even though I want to be.

Our class has good ideas.

The development from "I" to "we" is a difficult transition for young children to make, although among kindergarten children pride in accomplishment of the group and solicitude for the welfare of the group are noticeable by the second semester of the first year. "Mrs. Johnson, we all want to climb the ladder and there are too many on it" is an expression familiar to any primary teacher. What needs to be done may bring forth many suggestions. "We must wait our turn." "Let the one in front go half way across the ladder before you start." "Keep in line but don't let the line get under the ladder." "Someone might get hurt if he pushes."

Even a six-year-old realizes that he has a responsibility toward his group regarding health. Remarks such as these are heard:

"I stayed home because I had a cold and I didn't want to give it to someone else." "Mary should cover her mouth when she coughs."

Boys and girls of 11 and 12 years of age are capable of assuming the responsibility of assisting children in the primary grades, to conduct recreational activities before school in the morning and at noon. Leaders may be assigned to rooms and the leaders see that equipment is available. They help the children organize and play their games. The leaders often become interested in the welfare of the younger boys and girls and in winter months see' that they are dressed adequately for outdoor play. They enjoy working with the children in different school activities.

For a variety of reasons the tendency is strong to assign leadership responsibilities to the few who are superior. Many times it becomes apparent when the situation is studied that the superior children need the experience of leadership less than the average child. Every child should have experience in assigned leadership. Care must be exercised in the assignment of responsibilities that a child does not have duties in which he will fail or feel inadequate because of lack of knowledge, skills or experience. Careful supervision is necessary particularly for those who need this experience most. The children who tend to assume leaders' positions usually should be put in a position where the value of being a member of a group working under someone else becomes apparent. These boys and girls need to learn to be supporting members of a group as well as its leader. It is difficult for some of these children to relinquish leadership to others. In this respect they are no different from the adult who does not permit leaders to emerge in the children's group because he is unable to relinquish authority, is afraid of losing control or needs to dominate others. In the completely democratic group, leadership is a quality of group membership. It cannot become this pervasive quality if the status or assigned leader leaves little opportunity for others to assume leadership. This is a point fully developed by Hearn in Chapter 2. A review of his discussion is recommended in connection with leadership in programs for children.

Stress should certainly be placed on the need to select the one best qualified to lead in a particular situation. Tendencies to select on the basis of popularity, good looks or athletic ability rather than demonstrated worth in terms of the immediate needs of the group should be questioned. It is desirable to point out the consequences of such action. This must be done tactfully without "loss of face" for the chosen one. The group should be helped to profit by its mistakes. A basketball team may be selected on the basis of friendship rather than ability in the sport. The defeat received will quickly show the folly of such action.

Objective: *Each individual must have the opportunity as a member of a group to face problems, to undertake their solutions and to evaluate the results.*

*Concepts and Attitudes—Primary-Age Child*

This is a problem.
What can we do about it.
This is what I want to do about it.
What do you think should be done?
How do you know this?
Let us work together.
How did it come out?

*Concepts and Attitudes—Intermediate-Age Child*

When a problem arises the group should think critically about it.
Opinions of many classmates should be sought.
Solution to a problem is usually easier if the group works together.
The results should be considered.

Children need to develop habits of self-analysis, self-discipline, cooperation, concern for the rights of others, responsibility and critical thinking. Problems should be attacked from the angle of "what happened and why?" Questions like: "Who started it?" "Who was to blame?" foster narrowness and defeat.[4]

Joe was a good pitcher but he could never be depended upon. When a game was arranged with Miss Ables' room it was lost because Joe wasn't there to pitch. Everyone blamed Joe and Joe resented it. After the indignation subsided, Miss Brown questioned

[4] Association for Supervision and Curriculum Development. *Organizing the Elementary School for Living and Learning.* 1947 Yearbook. Washington, D. C.: The Association, a department of the National Education Association, 1947. p. 171.

Joe. She learned that Joe's mother had taken a job and that Joe had to get up and get breakfast for his two little sisters and himself. This made him late. Miss Brown asked if he thought the class might help him with his job.

After due consideration Joe decided to ask his classmates for help. "I could come by and get the girls dressed, but I couldn't do any cooking," said Nancy. "What do you cook, Joe?" The breakfast part seemed easy as Joe made toast and served milk. "I sure would hate to come to school on that," said one. This led to a lively discussion on what you should eat. The students were surprised to learn that few in the class could prepare a nourishing breakfast.

Good breakfasts were discussed and one boy brought a Fred Harvey breakfast menu for children. Soon a small electric stove was brought to school and various cereals. Different ways of preparing eggs were demonstrated. The importance of citrus fruit in providing vitamin "C" was discussed.

When interest in a good breakfast lagged, Bob asked the group, "How does this help Joe?" The children decided that:

Joe would have to be responsible for getting up sufficiently early to prepare the breakfast. This meant giving up reading late at night and getting to bed earlier.

Two of his school friends would go by and help him with the dishes and in getting the younger children off to nursery school.

Nancy evaluated the experience by saying, "We wanted a ball pitcher and ended up learning to cook and eat good breakfasts."

Objective: *Each individual should develop an appreciation of differences.*

### Concepts and Attitudes—Primary-Age Child

Some children in the group are colored.

Why doesn't Hulda talk as I do?

I like him just because I like him.

She is my best friend but she can't come home with me.

### Concepts and Attitudes—Intermediate-Age Child

Should only white children come to this school?

Do I dislike him because he is of a different race?

Am I prejudiced?

What makes us different?

How are we alike?

I should not have the same prejudices as my parents.

His opinion is as good as mine.

A person should be judged by what he does and not because of his race, nationality or color.

"Let's make this an all-American team, Jay, all white and all American," said Bob, as Jay began to line up a team for giant volleyball intramurals. Mr. Hay, the teacher, quietly asked Bob if he would do an errand. Later when Bob returned and started to enter the game Mr. Hay suggested that he watch for awhile. Bob got tired of watching and asked Mr. Hay why he couldn't enter the game. "No reason, Bob, except your hair is red and we are not having redheads on this team." By the end of the game Bob was provoked. Mr. Hay asked, "Was it fun to stay out of the game?" Bob answered, "No, and it wasn't fair." "Wasn't it as fair for you not to make the team because of your red hair as it was for Jack not to be selected because of his skin?" asked Mr. Hay. Bob still felt that he had the right because he was an American. Upon questioning about what made him on American, it was learned that Jack's ancestors were in America before Bob's.

Mr. Hay wanted Bob to understand how the other fellow feels when he suffers from discrimination. In schools where an atmosphere of cooperation and respect for all prevails, primary boys and girls accept each other as equals with little thought of sex, color or nationality. Prejudices and undemocratic attitudes are developed as the results of other influences or reflections of adult attitudes. As children grow older an awareness of adult prejudices begins to penetrate their thinking. This is a time to deal with prejudices as they arise. Stories derived from anthropology enthral 11- and 12-year-olds. If children through social studies, science and health education can study and evaluate present and past reasons for discriminations, their thinking may become less biased.

Too often in studying these problems the tendency is to emphasize differences. More emphasis needs to be placed on likenesses. Differences stem from different climatic, economic, social and educational experiences. The common origin of man can be stressed and the differences seen as enriching human life. It would be a dull world if all were alike.

Objective: *Each individual should gain knowledge of and develop respect for the cultural contributions of other groups.*

*Concepts and Attitudes—Primary-Age Child*
I like stories about Dutch, Irish and Mexican children.
Play that Russian record again, please.

*Concepts and Attitudes—Intermediate-Age Child*
We go to different churches although we worship one God.
In many ways people of other countries are like us.
America is made up of many races.
Each race has made a contribution to America.

Children can understand that regardless of where people live they live in families, build houses, raise food, make clothing, enjoy games and recreation, produce and exchange goods and services, transport and communicate, worship, create and appreciate the beautiful. People differ in the ways they do these things.[5]

The fields of health education, physical education and recreation are rich in opportunities for studying the culture of people from other countries and for appreciating the contributions made by races and nationalities to our civilization.

Tom, from the primary grade, found an arrowhead on a walk with his father. Eagerly he returned to school on Monday to tell the group, "Indians once lived here." Immediately his classmates became interested in learning about Indians and becoming Indians. Papier-mache masks, feather head-dresses, painted burlap costumes, tom-toms and tents were made. Indian dances were learned and everyone enjoyed being an Indian.

Sally went to Mexico for Christmas vacation and brought back a sombrero and some Mexican victrola records. No one could dance to them so finally Charles and Conchita from a Junior High School came over and taught the Jaraba Tapatio. Someone asked if the chili she ate gave her the beautiful complexion and much to everyone's surprise Conchita said that she didn't like chili.

Jack, who is the best runner in the room, found some statistics on Olympic performers which led to such a heated discussion that

5 Association for Supervision and Curriculum Development, *op. cit.*, p. 178.

everyone began consulting reference books, encyclopedias, and health education readers. By the time all the information was organized the group had a better understanding of early life in Greece, the supremacy of the Japanese swimmers in the American Olympic meet, what countries entered the last Olympics, and the influence of food on physical achievement.

To know people is to understand them and understanding is necessary for appreciation.

Objective: *Each individual must understand his limitations and potentialities and be capable of adjusting to them.*

### Concepts and Attitudes—Primary-Age Child

I can do this.

No matter how hard I try, I cannot do it.

Sometimes I have to try over and over again.

Maybe I can find someone who can help me do it.

I can't run fast but I am the best speller in class.

### Concepts and Attitudes—Intermediate-Age Child

Capabilities should be known.

Limitations must be faced.

Might should not be the ruler.

Some new things can be accomplished with practice and help.

"Well, little girl, you are walking with crutches, but some day you will be running up and down this hall," said a lady visitor to Mary, age eight, in a school for crippled children. "No I won't, lady, I'll always walk on crutches. I can't run in kickball, so Jimmy runs for me. I bet I can beat you playing Canasta." The visitor was shocked. Mary had a small limp and had been such an interesting guide that the lady wanted to say something nice to her. Mary knew that the small limp was to mean amputation later. She had faced the fact that she could not walk or run as other eight-year-olds could do. Maybe that is why she decided to learn to play Canasta. By learning it during the summer she was ahead of the others. She could beat some of the older boys and girls. She also taught many schoolmates to play. The attitude of Mary and many of her schoolmates was, "I have one arm or I will always sit in a wheel chair, so what? It is my responsibility to find out what I can do and then do that job as well as I am able."

Many people underestimate their capacities and very few realize their optimum development. Somewhere along the path of growth from childhood into adulthood the urge to learn, to explore the unknown, is deadened. With children care must be taken not to assume that limitations exist which do not actually exist. The real potentiality of each child for further development is an unknown quantity. Each one needs to be helped to explore his potentiality fully. Encouragement, some successes, recognition of achievement, freedom to try himself out without fear of ridicule, with the understanding support of adults and his peer group whether he succeeds or fails, are important elements in the help required.

Objective: *Each individual must experience unfamiliar situations so he can learn to adjust to changed conditions.*

### Concepts and Attitudes—Primary-Age Child

I do not want to stop what I am doing.
I do not want to try it.
This is new to us.
I am afraid.
I like it.

### Concepts and Attitudes—Intermediate-Age Child

I must be willing to try new experiences.
When I do not like an experience I should try to make the best of it.
It is sometimes necessary to do things I do not like.
Until I have given it a fair trial I won't know if I like it.
It is fun to have new experiences.

If children shy away from new experiences it is usually because they fear insecurity, failure, or loss of face. When they feel secure in the group and know that understanding and help are available in new ventures they will not usually hesitate to try something new. Insecurity, failure and fear of loss of face are due to unpleasant past experiences either fancied or real. The girl who does not want to play volleyball with her group because she jumps rope so well with the younger children does not want to attempt something new because she may not be successful. The young boy who has his mother come to school to learn why he was not chosen on the basketball team that played another class cannot face an unpleasant experence. Nothing constructive will be accomplished in these cases by thrusting the children into new experiences until the learning climate is so revised for them that they no longer feel insecure or fear failure. They may still fail but the stigma is no longer attached to such failures.

Children must learn that change is constant, inevitable and usually desirable. It should be welcomed rather than feared. Everyone prefers to do those things he does well, but learning to do other things or having new experiences broadens and enriches life. Living in school cannot remain static. It ought to be a continuously changing, challenging process. For "We learn what we live, we learn each response as we accept it for our living purposes, and we learn it in the degree that we live it. And what we thus learn we therein build at once into character." [6]

## Bibliography

ASSOCIATION FOR SUPERVISION AND CURRICULUM DEVELOPMENT. *Organizing the Elementary School for Living and Learning.* 1947 Yearbook. Washington, D. C.: The Association, a department of the National Education Association, 1947.

BROWN, SPENCER. *They See for Themselves.* New York: Harper and Brothers, 1945.

COWELL, CHARLES C. "Mental Hygiene Functions and Possibilities of Play and Physical Education." *Elementary School Journal.* 50: 196-203; December 1949.

COWELL, CHARLES C. "Play Behavior and Personality Analysis." *Educational Research Bulletin,* the Ohio State University. October 20, 1937.

DE HUSZAR, GEORGE B. *Practical Applications of Democracy.* New York: Harper and Brothers, 1945.

ENGLISH, O. SPURGEON, and PEARSON, GERALD H. *Emotional Problems of Living.* New York: W. W. Norton and Co., 1945.

GESELL, ARNOLD, and ILG, FRANCES. *The Child from Five to Ten.* New York: Harper and Brothers, 1947.

GESELL, ARNOLD, and ILG, FRANCES. *Infant and Child in the Culture of Today.* New York: Harper and Brothers, 1943.

HOPKINS, L. THOMAS. "Atmosphere for Learning." *Teachers College Record.* 46: 99-105; November 1944.

HOPKINS, L. THOMAS. *Interaction: The Democratic Process.* Boston: D. C. Heath and Co., 1941.

---

[6] Kilpatrick, William H., *op. cit.,* p. 25.

HOSKING, ELIZABETH. "Developing Good Human Relations." *School Executive.* 68: 51-52; December 1948.

HUSSEY, DELIA P. "The Play Route in Human Relations." *Childhood Education.* 25: 157-60; December 1948.

JERSILD, ARTHUR T., and ASSOCIATES. *Child Development and the Curriculum.* New York: Bureau of Publications, Teachers College, Columbia University, 1946.

KALLEN, HORACE M. *The Education of Free Men.* New York: Strauss and Co., 1949.

KILPATRICK, WILLIAM H. *Better Human Relations.* New York: Freedom Pamphlets, Anti-Defamation League of B'nai B'rith, 1949.

KNICKERBOCKER, IRVING. "Leadership—A Conception and Some Implications." *Journal of Social Issues.* 4: 23-40; Summer 1948.

LASKER, BRUNO. *Race Attitudes in Children.* New York: Henry Holt and Co., 1929.

MAYFARTH, FRANCES, editor. *Adventures in Human Relations.* Washington, D. C.: Association for Childhood Education, 1948.

MIEL, ALICE. "A Group Studies Itself." *Teachers College Record.* 49: 31-44; October 1947.

MURPHY, GARDNER. *Personality—A Biosocial Approach to Origins and Structures.* New York: Harper and Brothers, 1943.

O'KEEFE, PATTRIC RUTH, and FAHEY, HELEN. *Education Through Physical Activities.* St. Louis, Mo.: C. V. Mosby Co., 1949.

OLSON, WILLARD C. "Human Relations in the Classroom." *National Education Association Journal.* 36: 640-41; December 1947.

OLSON, WILLARD C. "The Improvement of Human Relations in the Classroom." *Childhood Education.* 22: 317-25; March 1946.

OVERSTREET, HARRY A. *The-Mature Mind.* New York: W. W. Norton and Co., 1949.

PRATT, CAROLINE. *I Learn from Children.* New York: Simon and Schuster, 1948.

STRATEMEYER, FLORENCE B.; FORKNER, HAMDEN L.; and MC KIM, MARGARET G. *Developing a Curriculum for Modern Living.* New York: Bureau of Publications, Teachers College, Columbia University, 1947.

SUERKIN, ERNST H. "Human Relations in the Classroom." *School Executive.* 68: 49; October 1948.

WINSLOW, C. E. A. *The School Health Program.* New York: McGraw-Hill Book Co., 1938.

# CHAPTER SEVEN

# *Methods*

EDWINA JONES
HELEN M. STARR
FRANCES WAYMAN

THIS chapter is addressed to all adults concerned with the growth and development of children at the elementary-school level who have any part in programs of health education, physical education and recreation.

In the health education program the classroom teacher is the key person, but there are in many schools professionally trained health personnel, such as the school medical advisor, nurse and health coordinator to help the teacher select, plan and carry out desirable learning experiences, to perform certain specific health activities and to guide the teacher in day-by-day health counseling and follow-up of health needs of pupils. The alert classroom teacher coordinates and integrates the work of each of these individuals in the total health curriculum, in order to secure the best possible program for boys and girls.

In the physical education program the classroom teacher may or may not be the key person. This program may be in the hands of a special teacher of physical education or a responsibility of the classroom teacher. There are arguments for and against specialization at the elementary level but the arguments over who should do what fade into insignificance when emphasis is placed on what is done, regardless of who may be engaged in the doing. It may be more difficult for the special teacher to see the "whole child"; on the other hand he or she may have an understanding of children's needs and purposes that surpasses the classroom teacher's. It may be more difficult for the classroom teacher to acquire techniques for perfecting physical skills of children, so essential for them to acquire; on the other hand, the classroom teacher may have a collection of trophies for outstanding performance in some physical activity and better than average ability to help children acquire physical skill as well as discernment into and skills for democratic relations.

In the field of recreation the key person may be the playground supervisor or director, the sponsor or leader of a club or youth organization or, again, the classroom teacher who may take responsibility for after-school recreational activities.

There are other adults at the elementary level who should have equal concern with the child's developing relations with others. The job of total child development cannot be delegated to a part of the curriculum or to an isolated class period at some particular time during the school day. The varied numerous learning opportunities needed for pupils to achieve the necessary skills and understandings demand the concern of all. This need is well stated by Alice Miel:

> It is abundantly clear that no school subject such as history, geography, or civics can be expected to do the job of democratic socialization. Neither can the best integrated course in social studies carry the full burden of the social education of children. The task is too big to accomplish in one year of life or in any one period of the day or in one of life's many settings. From the morning greeting to the farewell at the end of the school day, every school experience must be utilized for social learnings. In addition, these experiences must be reinforced by positive socializing experiences in the home and the community.[1]

To help in this socializing process those in the field of health education, physical education and recreation may make use of experiences having great potentiality for developing democratic relations because the experiences are geared to children's interests and concerns in everyday life. The health education program can and should be planned around real life experiences of the child in the community and home as well as in the school. These experiences are readily at hand—eating, sleeping, medical care, playing safely and getting along with others. There are many opportunities in physical education to help pupils to live and conduct themselves

---

[1] Miel, Alice. "Toward Democratic Socialization." *Childhood Education.* 26: 50-51; October 1949.

toward others in a more democratic manner. The games, self-testing activities and rhythms of the physical education program have potency for learning situations because they are allied with the child's play interests and his positive attitude toward physical activities. Recreational activities are even more potent in this respect because of the voluntary aspect of participation and maximum freedom.

It is apparent that democratic human relations should not be taught as a subject but should be developed as part of the working and playing situations indigenous to particular fields. It is apparent that democratic human relations must be considered as a way of life in every hour of the day. The problem is to make the experiences with which we are concerned a part of this way of life.

The question to be considered is: What ways are there at the elementary level to promote this desirable way of life? Methods are considered ways of doing things. They imply the use of many specific procedures which in this chapter will be called techniques. The first problem in relation to over-all method and particular techniques is how to select them or what bases to use in selecting them.

## Selecting Methods and Techniques

There are certain principles governing the selection of methods. They have long been employed in the teaching of subjectmatter and are equally applicable to teaching for developing democratic human relations. The principles are derived from what is known about growth and learning.

1. It is impossible to separate what is taught from the ways of teaching. The "what" for the child is not only the matter the teacher is presenting, it is at the same time the tone of his voice, his direct or implied expectations of him, the responses of other children around him and many other elements.

2. There is a direct relationship between techniques employed and the outcomes attained. When planning, the teacher must know the outcomes he seeks, the procedures demanded to achieve these outcomes and the means through which he and the children may evaluate achievement. This is an important principle for developing

democratic relations. To get certain desirable outcomes teaching must be directed in specific ways to achieve them. This assures better results than if they are left to chance or considered the "halo" results of good teaching directed toward attaining other outcomes.

3. To secure best learning the teaching techniques must be used which lead to a maximum of enjoyment and success and a minimum of drudgery and failure. To experience enjoyment is to experience the desire to act. Success stimulates further effort. Drudgery often means lack of purpose and failure often brings avoidance of effort in situations where further failure is anticipated.

4. Learning must be viewed as an activity of the learner as opposed to passivity. This means the learner participates actively in what is to be learned rather than sitting passively and listening as he is told how to brush his teeth or practice good sportsmanship or be kind to animals. Through wise choice of method and techniques teachers should give children opportunities to apply and practice the skills of democratic living instead of continually trying to tell them how to live democratically.

Attention has been called to these principles and they have been explained briefly because they have been followed, or at least been given lip service, for some time by teachers and leaders at the elementary level. The principles should be kept in mind as underlying bases for selecting methods and techniques.

### The Goals To Be Attained

Method must be thought of as a definite process to accomplish a desired goal. Having a clear picture of the understandings, attitudes and skills we want pupils to acquire to live effectively directs selection. The concepts and attitudes to be developed were explored in detail in the previous chapter. These should be considered now in terms of selecting methods and techniques. For example, if the teacher wants each child to learn to respect the rights and privileges of others, he selects ways of doing things that show recognition on his part of individual rights and privileges. He uses guidance techniques to help the child do unto others as he would be done by.

There is more to the selecting of means suitable to attaining certain ends than thinking in terms of what the teacher wants for the child. To be an effective learning situation the child must want or purpose to learn. Therefore, a part of method must always be selecting ways of interpreting the desirable outcome in concepts and attitudes the child can understand and make his own objectives, because they are within the context of his own experience. Many suggestions for the kind of concepts and attitudes that might be utilized as goals in the area of democratic relations were made in the previous chapter. There are undoubtedly many more that are not listed. The alert teacher finds the appropriate ones within his particular teaching situation.

## Understanding Children

Determining the goals to be attained precedes choice of method, but the study of the needs, interests, experiences and purposes of children antedates both. This study has both a general and a particular aspect. The teacher comes to a certain class with knowledge of children gained through his preparation to teach and through observation of children already taught. He is enabled through this knowledge to set up in advance certain desirable goals and to plan in considerable measure how to attain them. But the process is never ending. As he works with the children he goes on learning more about them. He modifies his goals and helps the children to set theirs in the light of his understanding of this particular group.

The age of the children, their different stages of development, their past experiences, the abilities they have developed and not developed, their personalities and needs are all factors influencing the selection of method. The efficient teacher never ceases studying the children themselves. He keeps informed of new research on growth and learning. Only in this way can he base his selection of method on understanding the boys and girls he teaches.

There are other bases for selecting method such as the limitations of facilities and space and the teacher's own skills, but in democratic relations these are of minor importance compared with making selection directed by understanding of the children concerned and the goals they may be helped to set and to attain.

## Patterns of Method

Method must be related to changes in children. These changes are called outcomes. Any changes that have taken place will be reflected in pupils' behavior, in the responses they make in a particular situation. Pupil responses are as much a result of the way in which the teacher conducts the class, or the climate in which learning takes place, as they are a result of the goals to be achieved. The way the teacher operates in the classroom is the strongest factor influencing the climate of learning and pupil reaction. The relationship between teacher and pupils, between pupil and pupil, is expressed in the way they treat each other, conduct themselves in the classroom or on the playing field, respond to directions or criticisms, and participate in the activities. As the activities and the responses are repeated in the same pattern day after day, a definite interaction pattern is evidenced within a group. The teacher may by his choice of methods set the stage for a particular pattern of group responses.

In recent years there have been several groups of educators in the country making intensive studies of group responses and group action. One such group has analyzed the patterns which the teacher encourages by the way he conducts his classes.[2] Patterns are described which range from one definitely teacher-centered and controlled to one in which the acme of group participation is reached, being entirely pupil-centered with the teacher in the role of guide as well as an active group participant.

A teacher concerned with developing democratic relations must analyze and evaluate the interaction patterns existing in her own classroom. To aid in such an undertaking, descriptions of the method patterns as analyzed in the article, "Group Discipline," will be given and discussed.

### Adult Rule, Child Obedience

In this pattern "the teacher assumes that he holds absolute authority and that the pupils should respond unquestionably with the demand behavior, and he acts accordingly."[3] The authors of

---

[2] Cunningham, Ruth, and Associates. "Group Discipline." *NEA Journal*, 38: 12-13; January 1949.
[3] *Ibid.*, p. 12.

"Group Discipline" go on to say that "if we want to make sheeplike conformists who will be good followers of Hitlers, it is easy to see how it can be done." [4] The continued use by the teacher of methods which foster this kind of response on the part of pupils shows that "on the whole the group accustomed to obedience patterns seems to comply with unquestioning obedience." [5] Individual pupils who do not conform readily to this pattern of teaching are viewed by the teacher as disciplinary problems and "if the group has known a pattern, either at home or at school, which involved self-direction, the reaction is violent aggression against each other, the curriculum, teacher, the school, or against all of these factors." [6] As a result, the pupils are products of a learning environment in which the teacher makes all the rules and insists on the pupils obeying them regardless of individual differences or varying needs. Sometimes pupils are punished or ridiculed if teacher-set rules are not obeyed.

In recreation situations the autocrat has a poor time of it if children are accustomed to a different pattern of group participation. They are free to come or not to come to the club meeting or the team practice. They will drop out or if they do attend they can give the autocrat a bad time. When children have already been conditioned to unthinking obedience to adults, the autocrat directing a recreational activity serves to perpetuate and reinforce responses undesirable for democratic living.

When health education becomes a command-response experience the pupils hear, "Wear your rubbers or stay after school," "Eat this particular food whether you like it or not, because it is good for your health." "Report to the doctor for vaccination!" "Check with the nurse to see if you are well enough to be in school." "Do as I say; don't ask questions." As a result of this type of teaching many individuals never learn to take responsibility for caring for their own health, nor do they gain self-direction in securing needed medical care or a feeling of responsibility for the health of others. They are being taught that someone else will tell them what to do about their health when the time comes. After they leave school no one is there to command or order them to carry out certain health

[4] *Ibid.*
[5] *Ibid.*
[6] *Ibid.*

practices. They may go for years without seeking much needed medical advice, because of the negative and resistant attitudes toward health developed through their early school or home experiences. Are these the people who accept without question the directions and advice of quack medics? Are they the ones who practice self-medication, as a result of directions of patent medicine ads on the radio or in newspapers without seeking reliable medical advice, or obey without question the health advice of uninformed friends? They are the ones if they have been taught blind obedience to someone else's commands in health education.

What about physical education situations? Here as in health education the full and undesirable harvest is not reaped until later years. The child may tolerate the autocrat and conform to commands to get on with the business which is his central concern, playing a game or practicing a stunt. Later as the need and urge toward physical activity lessens and, as too often happens, he is continually subject to response-command situations in the secondary schools, there is rejection and rebellion. Many individuals never learn under this method pattern to understand the importance of physical activity in their lives. They never feel responsible for making their bodies skilled instruments for working and playing. After leaving school, when self-direction is required, they do not possess it. They do not know how to plan and carry out a program for healthful living.

There are times in a democracy when people must conform to rules and regulations for their own good and the good of others. It is essential that children learn to adhere to certain regulations protecting health and insuring safety. It is equally essential, however, that children understand the reasons for the rules. Often pupils can help to set up the rules which must be obeyed. It can be clear to them that those who violate the rules must experience the results of the code of penalties which they helped formulate.

If methods are continually employed which focus attention on the teacher, such as drills, lectures, group testing, teacher demonstrations, reading by the teacher, reading or practice assignments, this teacher is fostering response-to-command behavior. There is little relation between these responses and the need for pupils to gain skills in democratic human relations.

## Planless Catch-As-Can Procedures

"There is no attempt by the teacher to control or organize the group." [7] As a result, "the reaction of the group is evidenced as disintegration of group cohesion with intense rivalry for power by aggressive group members and withdrawal from the group by nonaggressive members." [8]

A teacher who permits a pattern of group response such as described above to develop violates all the principles of sound education. In addition, he jeopardizes any opportunities for helping pupils achieve goals in democratic human relations by allowing a pattern of interaction to exist which is alien to everything which makes for group unity and cohesion. Competition between members of the group for recognition and power prevents any effort in cooperative work toward common goals. Particularly in the area of individual and group adjustment, the teacher who allows the learning environment to be controlled and directed by a few aggressive group members, who have only their own needs and interests at heart, is violating the basic principles of democratic living and is fostering rule by might instead of right. The nonaggressive pupils take no interest in class activities and as a result do not participate actively. These pupils may be very valuable members of the group, but they learn to avoid participating and become fearful and distrustful of any type of group efforts. Other members of the group may learn to be deceitful, to lie so as to get the attention of the power group or they may become the object of bullying techniques by the aggressive members. This type of teaching tends to produce individuals who gain selfish ends by being aggressive and inconsiderate of the rights of others. It is a grave mistake for any teacher to think that in a learning environment where pupils have entire freedom to do as they please that this is providing education for living in a democracy. This method pattern results in selfish behavior on the part of individuals and little or no sense of responsibility for the welfare of others.

[7] *Ibid.*
[8] *Ibid.*

## Teacher Planning with Individuals

"There are teachers who interpret planning as a process of individual pupil-teacher interaction. Each individual, in turn, has an opportunity to plan a course of action with the teacher. This is usually coupled with a teacher-rule pattern for all but the one individual engaged in planning with the teacher." [9] As a result of this type of teaching, "The group as a whole reacts as in Pattern I, except that if the reaction is hostility, it is further aggravated by interpersonal competition." [10] A pupil who is a product of the type of experience where the entire emphasis in the teacher-learning process is placed on the teacher and one individual student cannot in the true sense become educated democratically. Acquiring and practicing democratic skills involve a group. For example, making the school a safe place in which to live cannot be achieved by a teacher and an individual pupil in a tutorial type of planning conference. The use of this method not only violates the basic principles of cooperative planning in solving problems common to the group, but it is repetitious and time consuming. The group response to this type of interaction pattern is one in which the pupils are conditioned to seek someone in authority for an answer to their questions, instead of an experience in which the group concerned attempts to solve problems through unified group effort. By utilizing these individual methods, the teacher tends to develop undesirable competition among members of the group, which results in pupils striving to please the teacher rather than working for the welfare of the group. Pupil responses to this type of teaching are bound to be highly individualized, self-centered and self-concerned. There is little or no feeling of responsibility to the group; nor is there concern with helping other members.

Pointing up the inadequacies of this pattern of method for developing democratic relations does not mean denying a place in the learning process for individual conferences, individual projects, individual help and the like. The use of the conference technique with emphasis on privacy often gives a child an opportunity to discuss problems of a personal nature with someone who understands and is willing to listen. It is a way to help the child gain

[9] *Ibid.*
[10] *Ibid.*

confidence and security, to overcome fears or perhaps to go to the proper source for medical advice.

By the nature of the activities this pattern of method is more apt to be overstressed in health education or in classroom situations than in physical education and recreation where much of the activity required is group action. This type of teaching may be characterized by individual pupil demonstrations, oral reading by students, individual activities and projects, interviews, teacher going from pupil to pupil around the room, and individual pupils going to the teacher for help and private interviews.

## Adult-Directed Group Planning

In the adult-directed group planning "the teacher designates the area and scope of group planning. The teacher who provides opportunities for self-direction too far beyond the capabilities of the group will find he is creating insecurities such as those of the "catch-as-can" pattern, while the one who is providing less scope than the class can handle is tending toward adult rule." [11] A sense of insecurity on the part of each member of the group and within the group itself is a very important factor for a successful program of cooperative learning. This means that the learning activities participated in by the pupils must be within their capabilities and understanding and that the group be given only as much self-direction as it can handle intelligently.

Expecting adult behavior from elementary school-age pupils in planning and conducting their own activities is the sign of a poorly informed and inadequate teacher. The continuous selection of problems beyond the capacities of the group or below the level of group activity results in responses of disinterest or resistance to the group process. The teacher has failed to see that pupils need help in learning the techniques through which groups solve problems that face them day by day in the school, home and community. Planning a picnic—including selection and preparation of food, selection of the site, discussion of safety precautions, provision for individual needs and securing the necessary funds offers a real life problem for teaching democratic human relations and the

[11] *Ibid.*

processes involved in their attainment. Through these experiences, the teacher must continually guide the pupils to meet and solve the problems on a cooperative basis. Without this guidance and help, he is developing a pattern of group interaction similar to the second one discussed which leads to a state of chaos and lack of respect for members of the group.

## Group Self-Management Through Group Planning

"The group which is able to develop goals, plan attainment of goals, cooperate in achieving them and evaluate progress is the group which learns, grows and disciplines itself." [12] These are skills for group work required for democratic relations. To achieve the unified group effort of individuals the interaction pattern used by the teacher must call for a group response which evidences cooperation, group self-discipline and harmony on the part of members. According to the yearbook, *Toward Better Teaching*, cooperative learning is efficient because "members of a democratic society need to know how to carry on cooperative group activity, to give and take, to make choices and to come out with solutions that represent the best thinking of the group." [13] Self-management through group planning is characterized by committees at work, group and panel discussions, dramatization, planning sessions, group projects, division of larger groups into working groups.

Observers report that teachers who appear to be successful in guiding pupils to operate effectively as a group tend to use all of the five method patterns described. The choice of pattern depends upon the immediate need, purpose of the group, experience, and skill of the teacher. However, the last two patterns described which are concerned with cooperative planning, action and evaluation seemed to be the best ones for teaching democratic relations.

It is apparent that the preparation of the teacher for utilizing methods for cooperative learning must be included along with gaining special competencies for teaching in a particular subject field. A good way to envision what this preparation must encompass and what understandings and skills the teacher on the job should have

[12] *Ibid.*
[13] Association for Supervision and Curriculum Development. *Toward Better Teaching.* 1949 Yearbook. Washington, D. C.; the Association, a department of the National Education Association, 1949, p. 6.

is to consider the basic concepts of cooperative learning as stated in *Toward Better Teaching:*

Cooperative learning begins with establishing rapport.

Cooperative learning gives pupils experience in setting goals together.

Cooperative learning encourages all concerned to make group decisions and assume responsibility for these decisions.

Cooperative learning provides for a division of responsibility among individuals or small groups.

Cooperative learning gives pupils an opportunity to gather and distribute materials.

Cooperative learning extends beyond the classroom.

Cooperative learning provides for group evaluation of progress toward goals.[14]

## Particular Techniques

It is always helpful when discussing a list of particulars to have some way of classifying them. This is true of techniques useful in promoting cooperative learning for it is impossible to discuss all of them. Teachers have a way of devising or improvising techniques to fit a particular situation as well as drawing upon known and reliable procedures. This means that new techniques are developed and become known so that a list given today will not be complete tomorrow. The classification selected for use here is taken from Raths' "What Is Teaching?" He discusses the operations carried on by a teacher as (a) Clarifying, (b) Show-How, (c) Security Giving, (d) Culturally Unifying and (e) Enriching Community Living.[15]

### Clarifying Operations

The teacher helps pupils "see more clearly what they prize and cherish, what they abhor; what they believe and what they reject as false; what they worry about, how they are thinking and planning, what they are doing." [16] Here the group develops a meaning of health as more than freedom from disease. Here the group sees perfecting skills in terms of ability to play the game. Here the group sees respect for the rights and privileges of others as a way of receiving as well as granting individual rights and

---

[14] *Ibid.*, p. 51.

[15] Raths, Louis E. "What Is Teaching?" *School Bulletin* No. 3. Minneapolis Public Schools, September 30, 1948.

[16] *Ibid.*

privileges. Values as to each one's responsibility for his own health, his own improvement in skills, his own behavior toward others, are stressed. The role of the individual in planning for and securing help in making progress is discussed and defined by the group.

In discussions differences of opinions occur. These are clearly analyzed so that each one sees the need for tolerance, understanding and the recognition of individual differences in meeting problems common to the group. Thought-provoking questions which challenge the children to draw upon their own knowledge and experience are aids in stimulating discussion. In the clarifying process the teacher sees that the pupils are aware of the means used to arrive at the solution of a problem. This is, of course, intimately related to evaluating what was done.

Besides general discussion directed toward clarifying the meaning of something, whether the "something" be the total problem to be solved or a very particular matter such as standing behind the safety lines on the baseball diamond or the best way of responding to an umpire's decision that seems unfair, the teacher uses other techniques of value. Whenever desirable he searches for pictures, charts and films to make visual the point to be clarified. He works with small groups as one of each group, not as an adult director, and utilizes opportunities to help the pupils clarify the meaning of what they are doing for themselves. He provides the same type of help to individuals also, focusing on helping the child to find the answer rather than telling it to him.

## Show-How Operations

The teacher helps pupils "to learn how to do certain things, to practice how under competent supervision, and to learn how with appropriate skill." [17] Physical education teachers are usually prepared with show-how techniques in relation to motor skill. They know that children must have sufficient time and opportunity for meaningful practice; they know that success and enjoyment stimulate effort; they know that well-timed demonstration and redemonstration are required with perhaps individual correction to prevent wrong learning; they know the satisfaction a child feels in being

[17] *Ibid.*

able to bat well or execute a perfect handstand. They know that skills bring social recognition and are therefore desired, especially by boys. Show-how techniques pertaining to motor skills are extremely important in the lives of the children and for democratic living. Studies show how much the status of a boy or girl in a group depends upon skill in playing games. Other studies show that the recreational sports of adults are in great measure those for which they learned the skills in childhood.

But there are other kinds of skills children should be acquiring for which the teacher needs show-how techniques. These are skills for working with others, skills for leadership, skills that a health educated person needs to acquire. Many of the requirements for perfecting physical skills apply to these other areas. There must be time and opportunity for practice, success and enjoyment in achieving, guidance in the practice with explanation, demonstration, correction as needed.

For example, it is very important for children to understand the health examination and to acquire certain skills in relation to it. Learning how to be an intelligent examinee at a health examination can start in the early grades by inviting the doctor and nurse to demonstrate the examination in the classroom. Later, as part of the unit, pupils can be given the opportunity to learn the skills required in taking a health examination, such as learning to write a health history. Respect for the doctor, etiquette at the examination, ways to make an appointment, responsibility for meeting the appointment, honesty in answering questions and following recommendations of doctors are skills which the alert teacher can help the children acquire.

Similarly, show-how techniques are applied to developing leadership and developing the qualities of active participation as a member of a group. The group activities themselves, including committee and small groups, can serve as illustrations of skilful and unskilful action. The starting point must be helping the children to understand the requirements for leadership and for good group membership, in a particular situation. Then there must be practice accompanied by evaluation, by the leader himself, by the teacher and group participating, of the leader and of themselves. In present-day group work research there is a tendency to abandon the leadership-followership concept in favor of considering every member of a group co-responsible for the group's progress and a leader in situations where he is called upon to lead. In the course of completing a group project or solving a group problem there will be many leaders. The teacher's job is to help the children spread the leadership as broadly as possible and this can be done by aiding individuals to acquire very specific knowledges and skills enabling them to fulfil a leader's role to the satisfaction of themselves and the group in particular situations.

The only sound way to provide leadership experience for all children is to help them attain competencies making them acceptable as leaders by the other children. There is nothing to be gained and harm may be done by allowing a child unqualified for a particular position of leadership to assume it. This goes for the popular boy or girl who is selected by the children regardless of suitability for the job to be done as well as for the boy and girl whose "turn" it is to be the leader whom the children would never otherwise consider as leader because he is a "dub" or "too bossy" or a "fraidy cat." This point brings us directly to the next type of teacher operations.

## Security Giving Operations

Because of the fact that "identical or conceptual learning, sometimes even motor types of learning, involve so much challenge to the personalities of pupils that, to facilitate learning, teachers must carry on operations which contribute to a feeling of security in the challenging situation. Students must feel free to learn, to change; they must have some emotional assurance in a situation which carries a challenge." [18]

Feelings of security arise out of being wanted, belonging, of being adequate to meet life situations. A child moving to a strange city or town, coming to a new school, longs most of all to be one of a group, to be called by his name, to share in the successes and failures of a group. Fundamental to his happiness is the speed with which he comes to feel accepted by the other children and a part

[18] *Ibid.*

of the group. Getting-acquainted games the first week of school are helpful starts. The newcomer's name will be learned and he has a chance to learn the names of the other children. Then the teacher watches carefully to see how the new boy or girl fares. He is particularly careful to avoid situations in which he might be ridiculed for his performance or not chosen by the other children. In a friendly climate, in which the teacher-pupil relations are those described in the last method pattern, the children will aid and abet the teacher in making the newcomer feel at home and at ease.

A child's security can be endangered by the expectation that he attain standards beyond his ability to achieve. A goal which is within range of eventual achievement is a stimulus to interest and a challenge to work. A standard which is outside that range dulls interest and inhibits effort. It is the leader's role to see the child as an individual with his own level of achievement and potential achievement which are different, maybe higher, perhaps lower, than most other children's.

The matter of belonging must be seen as a group affair. A teacher who finds rejection in the group will need to examine its group living. The experiences offered, the control devises and interaction patterns employed—all will be factors determining whether or not belonging can be developed for every member. Children seek scapegoats against whom they can display resentments they cannot express to adults who exercise power over them. The example of power leads them in turn to seek power over others. There is far less of these types of behavior patterns in an environment in which there is cooperative learning and their judgments are considered and encouraged. Even in such situations there may well be children who are less accepted than others, whose sense of belonging is tenuous. The trouble may lie outside the school, in home and family relations; it may simply be lack of skill; it may be differences from the majority in race or religion; it may be a handicap or unattractive appearance. The teacher can only try to discern the cause for lack of full acceptance, then do what lies within his power to remove the cause.

In health education, the teacher can meet the need for belonging by being interested in pupils as individuals as well as group mem-

bers; being aware of their health problems and helping them overcome them. He can help a child understand his health status and
know his health lacks and strengths. He can do this through the
use of a Health Worksheet on which the pupil can record and study
his own progress. This type of teaching eliminates competition to
reach an absolute standard set by the teacher. Pupils learn that
individuals vary in their health status and need to carry out different
programs of correction. In health teaching there is thus opportunity
to help children have an understanding of individual differences
and to check the feelings of insecurity which may arise in a child
who realizes he is different from others.

Another kind of security operation lies in becoming acquainted
with the background of each pupil. In case the child needs assistance in securing lunch tickets, this can be done quietly. The pupil
and his family can be guided to sources of free and low cost medical
and dental care. Pupils are taught that it is not a disgrace to accept
health services without cost if they or their parents cannot get
work or are not able to work. An alert teacher will teach children
their responsibility as members of a democracy to help others
receive basic service in the area of health. He will also see that
each one learns to carry some responsibility regardless of his
economic status.

An excellent report of how to carry on teaching in this area is
contained in *Human Relations in the Classroom,* by Bullis and
O'Malley.[19] This is a series of lessons in human relations for classroom use, which can be carried on by the average teacher without
a great deal of outside preparation and study. Such topics as
"Assuming Responsibility," "Cooperating with Others," and "How
Personality Traits Develop," are treated as lesson topics. This is
an excellent source for teacher help, recommended for use on the
elementary level.

## Culturally Unifying Operations

The teacher helps pupils understand individual differences and
"that experience tends to make us uniquely personal individu-

[19] Bullis, H. Edmund, and O'Malley, Emily E. *Human Relations in the Classroom.* Wilmington, Del.:
State Society for Mental Hygiene. 1947. p. 1.

alities." [20] He is concerned with the classroom experiences that help "provide more opportunities for greater unity to emerge from group interaction." [21] The unity comes out of working for a common goal in which individual differences are not only tolerated but welcome. John can do some things. Mary can do others. The Mexican child shows the other children how to weave baskets for the class party. The Negro child has great skill in producing a poster when needed. Appreciations for the contributions different members make have their origin in the children's interest in attaining the group goal. To be genuinely felt the goal must be the children's own and not teacher imposed. The teacher helps the children to see the various contributions and to express their appreciations.

## Enriching Community Living

Through these operations the teacher carries forward projects "which help to solve community problems." [22] The teacher utilizes the problem-solving approach which is basic to cooperative learning. Pupils are encouraged to select problems which are real to them and have meaning for them. With the guidance of the teacher they set up the goals to be achieved, define and carry out a plan of action, and evaluate the results. These problems on the elementary level might be such projects as a study of backyard playgrounds and the making of plans adaptable to yards of different size; making our home a safe place in which to live; learning about our health helpers in the community; surveying neighborhood recreational opportunities prior to summer vacations and learning about community and privately operated camps.

It can readily be seen that the teacher concerned with developing democratic relations uses many and varied techniques. It is never possible to describe these techniques step by step as the techniques for teaching spelling or a motor skill may be described. This is because they deal with variable, human behavior and are different as behavior changes and situations vary. General concern for the area of human relations and experimentations will result in more explicit aids to the teacher. Already, some progress has been made in this respect. In the meanwhile, the teacher concerned with this area

[20] Raths, Louis E., *op. cit.* p. 1.
[21] *Ibid.*
[22] *Ibid.*

may take as his starting point the principles of learning listed at the beginning of this chapter. He may see and understand the patterns of interaction possible in working with children and the merits in developing responses through cooperative planning and action in a permissive climate. Above all, he can base his procedures on the known fact that children have to live democracy in order to gain an understanding of it and to develop the concepts basic to democratic relations with others.

## Bibliography

AMERICAN COUNCIL ON EDUCATION, COMMISSION ON TEACHER EDUCATION. *Helping Teachers Understand Children.* Washington, D. C.: American Council on Education, 1945.

ASSOCIATION FOR SUPERVISION AND CURRICULUM DEVELOPMENT. *Organizing the Elementary School for Living and Learning.* 1947 Yearbook. Washington, D. C.: the Association, a department of the National Education Association, 1947.

ASSOCIATION FOR SUPERVISION AND CURRICULUM DEVELOPMENT. *Toward Better Teaching.* 1949 Yearbook. Washington, D. C.: National Education Association, 1949.

BAXTER, BERNICE. *Teacher-Pupil Relationships.* New York: Macmillan Co., 1941.

BAXTER, BERNICE, and BRADEN, ANNE. *An Overview of Elementary Education* Boston: D. C. Heath and Co., 1945.

BIESTER, LILLIAN L.; GRIFFITHS, WILLIAM; and PEARCE, N. D. *Units in Personal Health and Human Relations.* Minneapolis: University of Minnesota Press, 1947.

BROWN, MERLE S. "The Role of the Teacher Today." *Childhood Education.* 26: 70-73; October 1949.

BULLIS, H. EDMUND, and O'MALLEY, EMILY E. *Human Relations in the Classroom.* Wilmington, Del.: State Society for Mental Hygiene, 1947.

BURTON, WILLIAM H. *The Guidance of Learning Activities.* New York: Appleton-Century-Crofts, Inc., 1944.

CITIZENSHIP EDUCATION STUDY. *Democratic Citizenship and Development of Children.* Detroit: Detroit Public Schools and Wayne University, 1949.

CUNNINGHAM, RUTH. *We, the Children.* Washington, D. C.: National Education Association, 1945.

CUNNINGHAM, RUTH, and ASSOCIATES. "Group Discipline." *National Education Association Journal.* 38: 12-13; January 1949.

CUNNINGHAM, RUTH, and ASSOCIATES. "Johnny Doesn't Belong." *National Education Association Journal.* 37: 578-79; December 1948.

CUNNINGHAM, RUTH, and ASSOCIATES. "Leadership and the Group." *National Education Association Journal.* 37: 502-503; November 1948.

DE HUSZAR, GEORGE B. *Practical Applications of Democracy.* New York: Harper and Brothers, 1945.

DRISCOLL, GERTRUDE. *How to Study the Behavior of Children.* New York: Bureau of Publications, Teachers College, Columbia University, 1941.

ELLIOTT, MERLE. "Patterns of Friendship in the Classroom." *Progressive Education.* 18: 383-90; November 1941.

FENTON, NORMAN. *Mental Hygiene in School Practice.* Palo Alto, Calif.: Stanford University Press, 1943.

FOSTER, JOSEPHINE C., and HEADLEY, NEITH E. *Education in the Kindergarten.* Second edition. New York: American Book Co., 1948.

HOPKINS, L. THOMAS. *Interaction: The Democratic Process.* Boston: D. C. Heath and Co., 1941.

JONES, EDWINA; MORGAN, EDNA; and LANDIS, PAUL E. *Easy Steps to Health.* Chicago: Laidlow Brothers, 1950.

JONES, EDWINA; MORGAN, EDNA; and LANDIS, PAUL E. *Your Health and You.* Chicago: Laidlow Brothers, 1950.

JONES, EDWINA; MORGAN, EDNA; and STEVENS, GLADYS. *Methods and Materials in Elementary Physical Education.* New York: World Book Co., 1951.

LA SALLE, DOROTHY. *The Guidance of Children Through Physical Education.* New York: A. S. Barnes and Co., 1946.

LIGON, ERNEST M. *A Greater Generation.* New York: Macmillan Co., 1949.

MIEL, ALICE. "Toward Democratic Socialization." *Childhood Education* 26: 50-51; October 1949.

MINNEAPOLIS PUBLIC SCHOOLS. *Living and Learning in the Elementary School.* Minneapolis: Minneapolis Public Schools, 1949.

NATIONAL EDUCATION ASSOCIATION and AMERICAN ASSOCIATION OF SCHOOL ADMINISTRATORS, EDUCATIONAL POLICIES COMMISSION. *Learning the Ways of Democracy,* Washington, D. C.: the Commission, 1940.

RATHS, LOUIS E. "What Is Teaching?" *School Bulletin* No. 3. Minneapolis Public Schools. September 30, 1948.

SHEVIAKOV, GEORGE and REDL, FRITZ. *Discipline for Today's Children and Youth.* Washington, D. C.: Department of Supervision and Curriculum Development, National Education Association, 1944.

TAYLOR, HAROLD A. "Education and Human Relations." *School and Society.* 69: 345-47; May 1949.

TRAGER, HELEN, and RADKE, MARIAN. "Guidance for Human Relations Education." *Childhood Education.* 25: 210-15; January 1949.

*What Schools Can Do—101 Patterns of Educational Practice.* New York: Columbia University Press, 1946.

WICKMAN, E. KOSTER. *Children's Behavior and Teacher's Attitudes.* New York: Commonwealth Fund, 1928.

# CHAPTER EIGHT

# *Evaluation*

Delia P. Hussey
Irma M. Pelz

**M**ANY concepts and attitudes basic to democratic relations with others were analyzed in Chapter 6. In Chapter 7 methods were described for helping children to become increasingly democratic persons through the development of these concepts and attitudes. What remains to be explored in this chapter are answers to the questions: How may we know that the methods employed are effective? What ways are there to find out the degree to which children are developing the concepts and attitudes which they must develop if they are to become democratic persons?

Children are in the process of becoming socialized; they are learning how to behave in our particular society in order to lead effective, adequate, satisfying lives within this social context. It is very important for the adult leader of children, and for the children themselves, to know whether the learnings taking place actually help the children to understand and practice democratic behavior. Evaluation thus becomes an indispensable part of educating for democratic living.

## The Process of Evaluating

A common definition of evaluation is this: evaluation is the process of appraising experience in terms of the objectives set at the outset. An examination of this definition, an analysis of the meanings incorporated in it, is one way to describe evaluation. We shall see what meanings such an analysis brings to light.

First of all, the definition states that evaluation is a process. Webster tells us that process is a series of actions or operations definitely leading to some end. Thus we shall expect evaluation as a process to be made up of operational steps, each step's function prescribed by the end for which the process operates. A beginning point, then, in describing evaluation, is to list and explain the steps involved.

The next thing the definition reveals is the end. The process of evaluation operates to appraise experience. It is important to note that there are no limitations placed upon the kinds of appraisals to be made. The implication is that any kinds of appraisals may be undertaken that seem suitable. Thus, in evaluating we may test and measure, where we have tools to do this; we may observe and interpret what we have seen; we may question, rate, confer, record, report, discuss, in fact use any means that seem to be ways of finding out what we would know.

The definition does place one limitation upon what may be done when evaluating; experience has to be appraised in terms of objectives. In other words the standards or criteria used as a basis for appraisals must be derived from the objectives which directed the planning and carrying out of the experience. The criteria must be the behaviors which will demonstrate or show that the objectives are being achieved. Such criteria are seen as desirable outcomes.

When evaluating, progress made toward reaching all the objectives set up will be appraised. The children will be helped to find out what they have accomplished, the skills learned, the problems solved, the facts acquired, the tournament games lost and won, the picnic given, the health survey made.  They will also be helped to clarify how they worked together to accomplish the ends in view, how assignments were fulfilled, the contributions of group members, errors in planning, successful planning and a host of other factors specific to the situation.

The experience being appraised is a totality in which the "what" and the "how" are interrelated. However, in the discussions to follow, of the steps in evaluating and the techniques that may be used, the total evaluation program carried out by adult leader and group is not being completely considered. In the main, the focus has to be upon aspects of evaluating which pertain to finding out about the relations being developed among children that, in turn, will show whether the concepts and attitudes basic to democratic relations are being developed.

## Steps in Evaluating

1. Objectives are stated.
2. Desirable outcomes are listed.
3. Ways are selected or devised to appraise outcomes.
4. The appraisals are made.
5. The findings are interpreted.
6. Objectives are revised on the basis of findings.
7. Desirable outcomes are re-listed.
8. Etc.

In any discussion of evaluation, the statement is sure to be made that it is a continuous process. The listing of the steps involved makes clear that this is the case. Over and over again the steps are repeated as any group works together to set objectives, make plans, try with insight, evaluate, recast objectives, make plans for future action.

*Stating Objectives.* In the process of evaluating, it is the children's objectives which must be clarified and stated. This is made mandatory by the principle of learning that tells us that children learn as they purpose to learn and that, in any situation, they select and learn those things they believe will serve their purposes and meet their needs.

Of course the adult leader has goals *for* the children in the area of human relations, based upon all that he can find out about the needs, problems and interests of a particular group. These goals direct the guidance he provides in helping the children to understand their own needs, purposes and interests and to set their own objectives. Teachers and other adults sometimes make the mistake of assuming that the goals they have for children are actually those of the children. This is usually far from the fact. So the wise adult is willing to begin where the children are and trust to the socializing process, in a friendly permissive climate with his understanding guidance, to bring about changes in their purposes in the direction of more democratic relations with others.

The adult may use any words he wishes to list and describe his own objectives for children. He may borrow from the writings of the founding fathers, from famous historical documents, from John Dewey and others, to clarify his thinking about democratic values, democratic relations, democratic methods. But he will not make the mistake of thinking that the children will be able to understand, and accept as their own, these objectives expressed in general abstract terms.

A child's vocabulary largely describes specifics. Abstract words and phrases, such as respect for the rights of others, responsibility, integrity, are understood only when translated into action. The right of each child to have his turn on the swing is the beginning of an understanding of "respect for the rights of others." Willingness to clean up after a school party or following through the plans of a committee to successful completion are specifics which carry the meaning of the word responsibility. In setting up objectives with children, the use of a vocabulary which the children can understand cannot be overstressed.

Objectives are always set in relation to a particular situation. They may be long-term goals, covering the time the group will be together; they may relate to short-term projects carried out within the total program; they may be immediate aims to be accomplished during the day's work.

LaSalle in *The Guidance of Children Through Physical Education* gives many examples of children setting their own goals after realization of needs. For example, in one case, the children realized that they were missing the first part of their physical education period by allowing noise and confusion to exist. Through discussion, the teacher and children stated the problem, arrived at their objective, made suggestions for improvement, tried these out, evaluated the results, made further plans and finally achieved their goal, namely, less noise and confusion and more time for play.[1]

The scope of the objectives set will determine the scope of evaluation. This is readily understood in terms of physical activities. If the objective is "learning to play newcomb or netball," evaluation will be much more inclusive than if concern is specifically

---

[1] LaSalle, Dorothy. *The Guidance of Children Through Physical Education*. New York: A. S. Barnes and Company, 1946, p. 129-34.

centered on "learning to serve the ball" and ways to estimate progress in learning to serve. Objectives in the area of human relations have this same difference in scope. Many specific objectives are set in the course of a program, each specific related to and contributing to the larger goal which children may gradually come to understand and accept. They understand and accept as they build many particular experiences in democratic living into a generalized concept of what being democratic means.

*Listing Desirable Outcomes.* The adult leader lists desirable outcomes, that is, he lists behaviors that will show that the objectives are being attained. In the process of evaluating he helps the children to see the ways of behaving that are desirable for them in the light of the objectives they have set themselves.

The adult's thinking might follow this pattern as to objectives for these children:

1. A sense of achievement through optimum development in relation to the group
2. Increased ability to face and solve problems with the group and to evaluate results
3. Increased ability to accept those who are different; better understanding of themselves
4. Willingness to face unfamiliar situations which call for adjustments to change
5. Respect and recognition for the contributions of others
6. A sense of belonging to the group with a sharing of responsibility for what the group does
7. Consideration for the rights of others.

In this situation, these are some outcomes which will show that these objectives are being reached. The outcomes are stated in question form.

1. *A sense of achievement through optimum development in relation to the group:*

Does the physical examination show him free from defects?
Is there effective follow-up where defects are present?
Does he have adequate opportunities to experience success?
Does he seek fun and what forms of fun does he seek?
Is he growing in appreciation of related areas through reading, dancing or listening to music?
Is he interested in improving his skill in activities?

Is his activity geared in terms of subsequent reward and recognition or some of it self-motivated and spontaneous?

Is he given opportunities in activities to do what is natural and highly valued for his maturity level, that is, rolling on the floor, bumping others, running, dodging, jumping or climbing?

Does he have adequate opportunity to experience many types of activities?

How many types of activities can he do well?

Has he enough skill to maintain status with his group?

Is he growing in independence of adult control? Is he able to proceed on his own?

Does he feel important in his group in at least one function?

2. *Increased ability to face and solve problems with the group and to evaluate results:*

Does he recognize a problem and then participate in its solution?

Does he react to discipline with understanding?

Deos he feel that he has been fairly treated?

Does he like to finish what he starts out to do?

Is he able to compromise in serving group interests to solve a problem?

In similar fashion the adult leader may go on to list desirable outcomes in relation to other objectives. In any particular situation, with any particular group of children in mind, the listings can be much more specific than is possible here.

Having clarified for himself the outcomes desired, the adult leader is on the alert for opportunities in day-by-day operations to help the individual child and the group to see the ways in which they need to behave in order to do what they want to do. Ways of being responsible then become, not just ways the teacher says you should or must behave, but ways that will help to accomplish something you want very much to do.

In evaluation children are helped to consider their behavior toward others in the context of the specific objectives they have. They learn through their successes and mistakes. They learn more and best with the kind of guidance that makes for more trial with success than trial and error.

*Selecting or Devising Techniques.* Elaborate instruments and procedures are not ordinarily called for in programs for children.

Simple ways of finding out what they need to know are indicated. As often as not the children themselves may devise the technique. Examples are: listing a series of questions to be answered by each member of the group, deciding upon the items to be included in a rating scale, describing the ways a leader should act in a given situation, working out headings to be used for self-appraisal. The development of the instrument for evaluating may be in itself a learning experience directed toward consideration of ways of behaving democratically.

Whether the techniques are selected or devised, there are two important bases for using them. Obviously, they must be suited to the level of understanding of the children with whom they are used. Just as obviously, they must be selected because they will provide the information sought.

*Making the Appraisals.* Evaluation is immediate and spontaneous —"We forgot to ask John to play, so it is our fault that he went home." "Mary and Dora just finished this poster. Isn't it a beauty?" Evaluation is a planned procedure in a day's work: "After we have tried out this plan of practicing the game, shall we meet back here and see how the plan worked?" Evaluation is stock-taking from time to time on the road toward a long-term goal. "At the end of the term we want to entertain our parents at a square dance party. What have we learned so far that will help us to give a good party?" Evaluation is final appraisal after a project is completed or a problem is solved. Estimates are made of successes and failures, what was done that could have been done better, how assignments were fulfilled and the like.

Evaluation is most meaningful to children when it follows hard upon the heels of action. The following description illustrates this point and also shows that evaluation need not be a formalized procedure.

It was traditional for the fourth grade to conduct a field day. Through discussion, the class agreed upon an outline for the event to which other school groups were to be invited. A central committee was set up to plan details with the teacher.

The central committee organized a number of other committees according to interests and the abilities of class members to carry out particular tasks.

Goals were set up and these were outlined in the following way:
1. Everyone is to participate, visitors as well as hosts.
2. All are to have a good time.
3. Members of the fourth grade shall be individual hosts to one or more visitors.
4. All events are to start and stop on time.
5. Recognition is to be given to individuals and groups wherever possible.
6. All details are to be taken care of so that no last-minute preparation will be necessary.
7. Committee chairmen are to be alert and take care of any unforeseen situation that may develop.
8. Each committee is to evaluate its own part in the program and make suggestions for improvement.
9. The general committee is to evaluate the whole day and make suggestions for improvement.

The main goal was: "All are to have a good time." If this was to be achieved, it was necessary that each child be included in the division of responsibility. Proof of this came with evaluation. Jane, chairman of the planning committee, said, "I found that I had nothing to do except to take part in netball because everyone did what he was supposed to do." Barbara, a quiet child, said, "This was the best day this year. John made a good leader. He saw to it that everyone had his turn, even if the time was short." Mary, in a surprised voice, reported, "All the girls told me what a good time they had. They want us to visit them in turn. Maybe we have started something." Harold, the snack chairman, contributed, "Everyone helped to clean up. I hope Mary's mother makes cookies for us again." Al said, "The umpire was late and we didn't get started on time at our court. Maybe we should have written him a note instead of just telephoning him." To which Bill replied, "That was my job. Next time maybe I'd better write." "Write what we call a 'confirming note,' " the teacher contributed.

Thank-you notes from the visitors gave the class an additional sense of satisfaction in achieving the main goal. The central committee placed brief written recommendations in the teacher's log book for the consideration of next year's fourth grade.

There are no hard and fast rules governing how to make appraisals. A free discussion may bring out all the necessary points. On the other hand, the preparation of a form for discussion or for self and group appraisal may well serve to sharpen thinking regarding the matters to be covered.

*Interpreting Findings.* When a test for a motor skill is given, the good teacher is careful to see that the children understand how it is scored and discusses with them what the scores received mean for progress made and future practice. Similarly, the findings from a rating scale to self-appraise behavior in the dressing room, or from a discussion of how a project was carried to completion, are considered with the children. As much as possible the interpretation should come from the children. The adult leader's role is to see the place where the children's insight leaves off and through asking leading questions or providing specific information help them to understand more fully what the findings mean. Relating the results of one kind of evaluation to those of another is often helpful to increase this understanding. For instance, findings from observation and a self-appraisal form may be related or a sociodrama may be designed to clarify the points made in a discussion of group organization to conduct a tournament. The purpose, of course, of interpreting findings is always to clarify the base for further planning and action.

*Revising Objectives.* When this step has been reached in evaluating, the group is back at the beginning of the process and the process starts anew. It is sometimes difficult for children to understand this, to understand that their purposes change. It is even difficult for some adult leaders to comprehend this fact, particularly when they are accustomed to preplan for children down to the last detail. The adult leader who takes the children into the planning is better able to see how their needs change and their purposes are modified and changed in a situation designed to be responsive to these changes. Someone has called the flexibility in program planning required to make the program fit the changing needs and purposes of children "playing by ear." It means alertness on the part of the adult leader to see what is really happening in a given group and willingness to abandon the security of knowing in detail for a long time ahead what activities will be undertaken. This adult, within the framework of the situation which places some restrictions on what activities may be undertaken, encourages the children to plan their own program with his guidance and to carry out and evaluate their own plans.

## Techniques for Evaluating

Any instrument or procedure that helps the adult leader to understand children is an evaluation technique. Any instrument or procedure that helps children to understand themselves better is likewise an evaluation technique. The list discussed here has been delimited to those techniques which seem to be useful in programs for children to evaluate the jobs being done in developing democratic human relations. The techniques to be considered are:

Observation
School records
Conferences and interviews
Diaries and autobiographies
Interest finders
Self-appraisals
The wishing well
The sociometric test
The sociodrama

### *Observation*

Observation is probably more frequently employed by the adult leader than any other evaluating technique. Judgments are continually being made regarding children's behavior. Learning to observe accurately is a first requirement of those who use this technique. A second one is to bring to the observation of any child's behavior all that may be learned about him and the situation in which he is responding. A third requirement is scrupulous care to separate what is observed from opinions about what the behavior means. Whether the behavior is described only in the adult's mind or is described as an anecdotal record, the distinction between what occurred and interpretation of what occurred should be kept clear.

A great deal of observation is incidental, especially when beginning to work with a group of children. The technique is used to provide clues to children's difficulties, abilities, attitudes toward themselves and toward others. As the adult comes to know more about the children, continuously collects information about them from many sources, observation is directed toward finding out some particular thing about a child or the group. For example, a teacher suspects from previous observation and from other sources that a child grows angry when he cannot have his own way because he has learned this behavior brings results; he puts on an act. Observation then becomes focused on finding out how the child behaves when the anger is disregarded by the other children.

Of course, judgments made through observation must be checked against findings from other evaluating procedures and verified through repeated observation. What is learned about a child through observation should be put to use along with other findings. The following story illustrates how one teacher put the findings to use.

Pete lost his arm in an accident when about the age of four. He was in the fourth grade when he came to a certain elementary school. During the physical education period he would retire to a corner and no amount of encouragement could get him into activity. His class was just about to start soccer. The teacher took Pete aside one day and told him that this was a game in which the feet were used and in which the hands were of comparatively little value. Pete looked interested. She got out a ball and showed him how the feet were used in dribbling. She encouraged him to try it and he shyly and awkwardly made the attempt. Every day she spent some time with him during free play.

When the group started to play soccer, Pete was already skilled in the use of his feet. There was no other player who could knee the ball as well as Pete. He was elected captain of the team. When the soccer season was over and the class was going into lead-up games for basketball, Pete had much more courage. He found that he could catch a ball using a knee and his one arm. He was a happy boy, no longer to be found alone in a corner.

## School Records

Immediate sources to turn to for background information about a child who is being observed are the school records. Health examination findings, past successes and failures in school work, home background are types of information provided. The child's pattern of growth and development since he entered the school may be studied from these records with consequent increase of insight into why he behaves as he does. The use of cumulative records is a technique familiar to all teachers, although it cannot be said that all teachers make full use of these sources of information.

## Conferences and Interviews

Conferences and interviews are occasions, usually prearranged, for talking over the needs and problems of an individual child in order to see possible solutions. The following kinds may be identified:

Child-adult leader
Parent-adult leader
Child-parent-adult leader
Child-psychiatrist, psychologist, doctor, dentist or school nurse
Child-parent-professional person
Child-parent-professional person-adult leader.

In interviews with children it is well to use an indirect approach to the problem of concern, putting the child at ease and establishing rapport by talking about some activity in which he is interested. Children, like adults, are often reticent in revealing their inner thoughts and motives. To secure reliable information and help the child requires tact based on sympathetic understanding. Criticism and censure should be avoided. Whatever the child says should be treated seriously and should be accepted. What is said may not be what the adult desires the child to say. If the interview is in a friendly climate it will be the child's own views of the problem and as such tells the adult the starting point for moving toward solving the problem.

When conferences with other adults are held, with teachers or professional persons, personal reactions to individual children should be kept to a minimum. A student teacher was asked by her supervisor, "How are the bad boys getting along?" In surprise the student replied, "Which ones do you mean? I did not know that there were any." Conferences among adults should be more than "gab fests." They should be terminated by decisions regarding next steps to be taken to help the child and assignment of responsibility for taking the steps to the person most acceptable to the child as a guide.

Teachers in the elementary school are urged to visit the homes of their pupils and many of them follow the recommendation. Sometimes these visits are not satisfactory to the teachers or to the parents. The success of the visit is mainly the responsibility of the teacher. A visit to any home requires careful planning. The booklet, *Sociometry in Group Relations,* gives an excellent procedure and form for home interviews.[2] Teachers who have not studied this technique will find useful suggestions in this booklet.

## Diaries and Autobiographies

In helping a child to solve some types of problems it is often a good procedure to ask him to keep a diary over a period of time in which he writes down what he does about the problem each day. This procedure is suited to such problems as eating a nourishing breakfast, cleaning up after play or refraining from teasing younger children.

Sometimes a child may be asked to write a description of an incident in which his behavior got him into trouble with other children or school authorities, or in which he gave evidence of being disturbed. Such descriptions often reveal the child's view of the situation and his evaluation of his behavior. The adult is thus enabled to help him to see what he needs to do about it.

## Interest Finders

The use of various types of instruments to find out about the interests of children is, like using school records, a familiar technique. A check list may be devised, giving the children opportunity to express their preferences by numbering the activities listed in the order of their choices. "Like or most want to do," "Dislike," "Indifferent," "Don't know" may be used to determine interest when the children write in under the headings their selections from a list of activities provided them. The information obtained, when tabulated, may be used with a group of children to assist them in planning their activities. It has direct usage in helping each child decide what he wants to do.

## Self-Appraisals

Children evaluate their own behavior and that of others, sometimes consciously, sometimes without being aware of it. Adult

[2] Jennings, Helen H. *Sociometry in Group Relations.* Washington, D. C.: American Council on Education, 1948, p. 37-42.

leaders may help them to do this in very strategic ways as the following example illustrates.

John was twelve years old and was in the sixth grade. He was well liked by the boys in his peer group and was highly skilled in games and sports. Shortly after the fall term started the teacher of physical education noticed that John asked to be excused on the days that dancing was being scheduled. This aroused her interest and she began to observe John more closely in other coeducational activities of the program.

After his team lost a volleyball game he was heard making the remark, "The girls spoil our team." In the progress of a game it was quite usual to hear him say, "She just stands there." In choosing committees or in electing leaders the teacher noticed that he never chose, nominated, or voted for a girl. When girls made overtures or friendly gestures to him (he was a nice-looking boy) they were completely ignored or left standing there with their remark or question unheeded. Other teachers in the school said that they had not seen him participating in any activities with girls but it had not occurred to them that it was unusual.

The physical education teacher found out from the mother that John had a younger sister (nine years old) who took dancing lessons at a private studio. When company visited the home Jane was always called upon to perform. John continually taunted and mocked Jane in what he called her "sissy dancing." John's problem was becoming very clear to the teacher and her next step was to help John understand it also.

One day the opportunity to talk to John presented itself. The following conversation took place:

Teacher: You played a very good game today, John. Is basketball one of your favorite activities?

John: Yes, I like it but I'm also crazy about baseball and touch football.

Teacher: What activity do you like least?

John: I don't like dancing, particularly with girls.

Teacher: That surprises me because usually good sports people are good dancers.

John: Well, it's sissy stuff and besides, I don't like girls.

Teacher: Did anyone ever tease you about a girl, John?

John: Sure they did and just because I showed a new girl where the library was.

Teacher: Well, we've all been teased at some time or other but usually it's just in fun. Most boys forget it as soon as they see that it doesn't bother you.

John:     Well, anyway, girls can't play games.

Teacher:  That is one reason I wanted to talk to you, John. I need
          your help. I want to get three or four of the boys
          to help coach some of the girls in throwing and catch-
          ing a baseball. Will you help us out?

John:     Girls have butter fingers. How can you expect them to
          catch?

Teacher:  Some girls are very good players and I'll bet that you
          can help more of them play a better game.

John:     Well, what will I have to do?

The teacher provided time for three boys, including John, to
work on lead-up games with some of the girls. She observed John
closely and soon found registered disgust change into something
like pride at the progress the girls were making. "Gee! Mary can
sure sling that ball," he was heard exclaiming to other boys.

The teacher's next step was to invite a man instructor who taught
folk and square dancing in a nearby high school to come to an
after-school party for the sixth grade. A demonstrating group of
high-school students came with him and one of the boys was the
captain of the football team. John wasn't going to attend the party
at first but other boys teased him and his curiosity got the better
of him. The high-school students showed some good vigorous
dances that were simple enough for sixth-graders to perform. The
fact that a man instructor was teaching dancing was a surprise to
many of the elementary-school students. The demonstration was
thoroughly enjoyed and at the end all of the students were invited
to participate.

John edged to the door but not before he was pulled by Mary
(the girl he coached) into a set. He was so bewildered that he made
no move to leave the set for fear of being teased by the other boys.
Although embarrassed and awkward at first he soon found that
others were completely engrossed in the fun and the activity. He
found himself laughing and not minding any more when he turned
in the wrong direction.

The physical education teacher talked again to John and was
encouraged with his casual remark, "Girls aren't so bad and neither
is dancing." He was seen asking help in dancing from some of the
girls just as he had given help in coaching baseball. Instead of
being pulled out to dance by a girl he now asked different girls
to be his partner. He began to talk about dancing at home. He told
his father that someday he was going to do it just as well as the
high-school football captain.

Group self-appraisals are most frequently made through discussions centered in how the group carried out a plan. Another technique, involving more time but sometimes very useful, is to construct an appraisal form for each child to evaluate his part in the undertaking, then to compile the responses to get a picture of the group's evaluation of itself as a whole. If the children share in constructing the form and have responsibility for making the tabulation the procedures have increased value. Rating scales, questionnaires or descriptive statements may be used in this connection.

## The Wishing Well

A Wishing Well Test may be secured from The Ohio State University or an adult leader may construct one for use with a particular group. This instrument is designed to discover what children need and want. Eight basic needs are represented in the twenty wishes making up the Ohio State University wishing well. The needs are:

The need for belonging
The need for achievement
The need for economic security
The need to be free from fears and aggression
The need for love and affection
The need to be free from guilt
The need for sharing and participation
The need for a world outlook

The boys and girls are asked to place an "X" before every statement which expresses something for which they wish. They are told not to write names on the papers. If there is some valid reason for wishing to know how individuals respond the teacher may code the papers.

The items on the test are arranged in groupings of eight, each corresponding to one of the needs listed above. Such wishes as the following are included:

I wish my class in school really wanted me there.
I wish a few children would want me as their very best friend.
I wish others thought my work was improving.
I wish my parents paid more attention to me.

## The Sociometric Test

This test provides a technique for understanding natural groupings in a class and for seeing an individual's associations in the group pattern. The students are asked to express first, second, and third choices of other individuals with whom they would like to be associated in a particular situation. Groupings may be different in a classroom, on a committee or in a play group. When the choices for an actual situation are diagrammed the result is a sociogram. Groupings may change even in the same situation depending on the time when the choices are made. It is not a test in the usual sense of the word. In some cases rejections of those not desired in a particular situation are asked for, but this technique involves great understanding and tact on the part of the teacher.

The adult leader may find the sociogram useful in obtaining improved play group situations, for team work, committee work, squad work, or dance composition. It will also be of assistance in knowing and helping the children who are rejected at certain times by the members of the group. Putting this knowledge to work, he regroups on the basis of choices made, then observes to see whether the new groupings give more children a sense of belonging.[3]

## The Sociodrama

The sociodrama is a technique in which children are provided opportunities, through role playing, to live or relive experiences of common interest to the group. A related technique is the psychodrama, used mostly by psychologists. In the psychodrama the emphasis is on the personal or private life of the individual; in the sociodrama the emphasis is on the problem of concern to the group. Teachers and recreation leaders are rarely encouraged to use the psychodrama, since its unskilful use may do great harm to disturbed children. The sociodrama, however, is being used with increasing value as teachers gain skill in the technique.

The situation or problem chosen for exploration in a sociodrama must truly represent group concern and desire to explore. Spontaneity is the keynote of success in role playing, success estimated by the insight gained into the causes of difficulty or into possible solutions. Children may volunteer or be assigned the roles to be played, but in either case, for best results they should want to play

[3] See Chapter 16 for a detailed discussion of sociometric techniques. See also Staff of the Physical Education Department, University of California, Los Angeles. *Group Process in Physical Education.* New York: Harper and Brothers, 1951, Chapter 7.

the roles and they should be concerned about the problem under consideration.

Many situations arise in health education, physical education and recreation which can be effectively explored through the sociodrama. Some examples are situations in which the children cease to have fun; situations in which certain types of behavior on the part of one or two irritate the others; situations in which the group becomes confused and does not see clearly what it needs to do to make progress. Through the sociodrama the adult leader may find out a great deal about the interactions among children in a group and gain insight into the behavior problems of individual children. He often obtains help, also, in improving the social climate. This is possible with a better understanding of the relations developing and changing within the group.[4]

In ending this survey of some of the many techniques for evaluating, it may be fruitful to re-emphasize that children's problems in human relations are not discovered by the use of any one technique alone. Observation needs verification; what the child says in self-appraisal or writes on an interest questionnaire needs to be checked against his observed behavior. The situations in which the child is responding need to be studied. Attitudes, such as those in regard to accepting differences, may be expressed in positive or negative behavior, according to the emotional drives aroused in different situations. A home visit combined with the results of a health examination and a sociogram may entirely alter a judgment arrived at through observation. Teachers and leaders must bring to the guidance of children in the area of human relations all that they can discover about each child. Then comes the process of using the information to help each child and the group continuously to evaluate progress being made in working with others, in getting along with others, in belonging to the group, in all the other aspects of behavior revealing a growing understanding of democratic human relations.

[4] See Chapter 16 for a detailed discussion of the sociodrama.

# Bibliography

ADAMS, THOMAS R. *Education for International Understanding*. New York: Institute of Adult Education, Teachers College, Columbia University, 1949.

AMERICAN COUNCIL ON EDUCATION, COMMISSION ON TEACHER EDUCATION. *Helping Teachers Understand Children*. Washington, D. C.: American Council on Education, 1945.

BONNEY, MERLE E. "Popular and Unpopular Children: A Sociometric Study." *Sociometry Monograph*, No. 9. New York: Beacon House, n.d.

BRIGGS, THOMAS H., and OTHERS. *The Emotionalized Attitudes*. New York: Bureau of Publications, Teachers College, Columbia University, 1940.

BROWNELL, CLIFFORD L. *Principles of Health Education Applied*. New York: McGraw-Hill Book Co., 1949.

BURTON, WILLIAM H. *The Guidance of Learning Activities*. New York: Appleton-Century-Crofts, Inc., 1944.

CALIVER, AMBROSE. *Education of Teachers for Improving Majority-Minority Relationships*. U. S. Office of Education, Federal Security Agency, Bulletin 1944, No. 2. Washington, D. C.: United States Government Printing Office, 1944.

CITIZENSHIP EDUCATION STUDY. *Democratic Citizenship and Education of Children*. Detroit: Detroit Public Schools and Wayne University, 1949.

DE HUSZAR, GEORGE B. *Practical Applications of Democracy*. New York: Harper and Brothers, 1945.

DIMOCK, HEDLEY, and OTHERS. *Camping in a Democracy*. New York: Association Press, 1941.

FENTON, NORMAN. *Mental Hygiene in School Practice*. Palo Alto, Calif.: Stanford University Press, 1943.

FOSHAY, A. WELLESLEY. "Evaluating Social Learnings." *Childhood Education* 26: 65-69; October, 1949.

GILCHRIST, ROBERT S. *Building Friendly Relations*. Columbus: The Ohio State University, 1947.

HILDRETH, GERTRUDE. *Child Growth Through Education*. New York: Ronald Press, 1948.

HOLLINGSHEAD, ARTHUR T. *Guidance in Democratic Living*. New York: Appleton-Century-Crofts, Inc., 1941.

HUGGETT, ALBERT. *Growth and Learning in the Elementary Schools*. Boston: D. C. Heath and Co., 1946.

JERSILD, ARTHUR T.; TASCH, RUTH J.; and OTHERS. *Children's Interests*. New York: Bureau of Publications, Teachers College, Columbia University, 1949.

LA SALLE, DOROTHY. *The Guidance of Children Through Physical Education*. New York: A. S. Barnes and Co., 1946.

NATIONAL EDUCATION ASSOCIATION AND AMERICAN ASSOCIATION OF SCHOOL ADMINISTRATORS, EDUCATIONAL POLICIES COMMISSION. *Learning the Ways of Democracy*. Washington, D. C.: the Commission, 1940.

POTASHIN, REVA. "A Sociometric Study of Children's Friendships." *Sociometry* 9: 48-70; February 1946.

PRESCOTT, DANIEL, editor. *Emotion and the Educative Process*. Washington, D. C.: American Council on Education. 1938.

SEIDENFELD, MORTON A. "The Role of Mental Hygiene in Health." *Journal of Health and Physical Education* 18:295-96; May 1947.

SHEVIAKOV, GEORGE, and REDL, FRITZ. *Discipline for Today's Children and Youth.* Washington, D. C.: Department of Supervision and Curriculum Development, National Education Association, 1944.

STAFF OF THE PHYSICAL EDUCATION DEPARTMENT, University of California, Los Angeles. *Group Process in Physical Education.* New York: Harper and Brothers, 1951.

STRATEMEYER, FLORENCE R.; FORKNER, HAMDEN L.; and MC KIM, MARGARET G. *Developing a Curriculum for Modern Living.* New York: Bureau of Publications, Teachers College, Columbia University, 1947.

TRAGER, HELEN, and RADKE, MARIAN. *Guidance for Human Relations Education.* New York: Bureau for International Education, 1942.

WATSON, GOODWIN. "What Are the Effects of a Democratic Atmosphere on Children?" *Progressive Education* 17: 336-42; May 1940.

*What Schools Can Do—101 Patterns of Educational Practice.* New York: Columbia University Press, 1946.

# Programs for Adolescents

RUTH ABERNATHY, *Coordinator*
*Associate Professor of Physical Education*
*University of California*
*Los Angeles, California*

9. THE ADOLESCENT'S WORLD

CHARLES C. COWELL
*Professor of Physical Education*
*Purdue University*

10. CONCEPTS AND ATTITUDES TO BE DEVELOPED

BERNICE MILBURN MOORE
*Consultant, Homemaking Division,*
*Texas Board for Vocational Education*
*and the Hogg Foundation for Mental Hygiene*
*of the University of Texas*

11. METHODS

DOROTHEA DEITZ
*Teacher of Physical Education and Health*
*Oneida School*
*Schenectady, New York*

ROSE STRASSER
*Instructor, State University of New York,*
*The State Teachers College at Brockport, New York*

HARRY C. THOMPSON
*Assistant Director of Recreation*
*Great Neck Public Schools*
*Great Neck, New York*

12. EVALUATION

RUTH ABERNATHY
*Associate Professor of Physical Education*
*University of California*
*Los Angeles, California*

DOROTHY ZIRBES
*Teacher of Physical Education*
*Central High School Needle Trades*
*New York, New York*

You see youth as a joyous thing
About which love and laughter cling;
You see youth as a joyous elf
Who sings sweet songs to please himself.
You see his laughing, sparkling eyes
To take earth's wonders with surprise.
You think him free from cares and woes,
And naught of fears you think he knows,
You see him tall, naively bold.
You glimpse these things, for you are old.

But I, I see him otherwise—
An unknown fear within his eyes.
He works and plays and never knows
Where he is called or why he goes.
Each youth sustains within his breast
A vague and infinite unrest.
He goes about in still alarm,
With shrouded future at his arm,
With longing that can find no tongue.
I see him thus, for I am young.

—BY AN OKLAHOMA HIGH SCHOOL BOY.
Nellie B. Sergent's *Younger Poets:*
*An Anthology of American*
*Secondary School Verse.*

CHAPTER NINE

# The Adolescent's World

CHARLES C. COWELL

ADOLESCENCE is a focal point in education because it is a focal point in human development. It is a period of physical and emotional maturing through which youth must pass successfully before they can be considered adult in every sense of the word. During this developmental period, youth break away from their infantile moorings and face a world of reality in which they must learn to make a place for themselves. They seek less dependence on home and parents, search for greater personal freedom of expression, put aside their childish emotional attachments and set out to conquer a world of their own. Naturally, the growing dignity that comes with self-recognition of individuality makes adolescents less amenable to external authority or direct suggestion.

In speaking of the adolescent's journey toward normal emancipation, the late G. Stanley Hall pointed out that children are not small adults and that one cannot hasten the development of the tadpole into a frog by cutting off its tail. Each developmental period in childhood and youth, although not too clearly defined, has a purpose in which certain developmental tasks must be performed. During adolescence the centers of interest and affection should transfer gradually and imperceptibly from the self and parents to peer friends and the common interests of the great world outside the home. As the process of maturing continues, attitudes toward life and human relations cease to be childish; adolescents now want to think for themselves, to make their own decisions and to shoulder responsibility.

The adolescent seeks diligently for opportunities of self-discovery and to gain some insight into his respective capacities to do some one thing well—something that is really worthwhile, something of *his own* choosing. Furthermore, the adolescent desires social success. He wants to do something really significant in the social groups of which he is a member. Although he rejects adult standards and controls, he fears ridicule and loss of popularity and is very dependent upon conformity with his peer groups. In such groups, the adolescent learns to understand and to accept others and how to manage his friendships and other human relations.

Oversensitive and self-conscious as a result of increasing size, skin eruptions, body odors and normal psychosexual development, the adolescent searches for new meanings and new values by which he may define his place in relation to other human beings.

In our complex culture, adolescents face many inevitable conflicts. There is the old and the new; the ancient good of the old testament and the newer and higher good stressed by later authorities. There are the traditions and beliefs of fathers and grandfathers and the newer truths of modern science. There is the effort to inculcate a wise choice of health practices and there are the questionable "ads" extolling the practices of athletes and of "people of distinction."

## Principles of Adolescent Growth

In the days of G. Stanley Hall we were taught that adolescence is a period of "storm and stress." As the difficulties of youth multiplied in our complex industrial society and these were recorded in the cumulative records of our schools and in juvenile courts, theorists were more than ever convinced that "storm and stress" inevitably accompanied adolescence and that it was chiefly biological in origin.

Study and comparison of adolescents in many societies indicate that there are relatively few universal adolescent characteristics. Concepts and principles developed by research in psychology and social anthropology suggest that the problems and conflicts of adolescents in our society, though they have a biological base, are unnecessarily stressful because of the social factors blocking the road to adulthood.

## A Biosocial Process

The term biosocial implies that something is biological and at the same time social. The adolescent as a biological organism operates in a cultural setting. He responds to other personalities as fully as he responds to food. The hunger cycle belongs to sociology as well as to biology. Murphy reminds us that "turning red is a biological event which may be due to a circulatory disturbance; turning red at an embarrassing remark is a biosocial event." [1] Constant interaction of organic and environmental forces makes our social world. The social order, in turn, molds personality. Neither culture nor the responses of human beings to it can change greatly without one modifying the other.

The developmental growth of the adolescent is a biosocial phenomenon; it, like personality, is an aspect of the social process. The difficulties and problems of American adolescents are, to a great extent, due not to their being adolescents but to their being adolescents in America. Situations act upon the individual, and his personality is an expression of the situation in which he is functioning. For example, Hartshorne and May found in their studies of deceit that no factor was more important in relation to honesty or deceit than the behavior of the group of which the student was a member. [2] The morals and ideals of his peer group are always strong determinants of the adolescent's behavior.

What the adolescent strives for and how his efforts are expressed are determined by the culture patterns which surround him. He wants to "grow up," to be adult, but we make it very difficult. In our culture, the adolescent in an adult world pays a fairly high emotional price for being socialized. The hampering restrictions of an adult culture, which limit opportunity for the adolescent to use his budding capacities and to be accorded a status more in harmony with his development, are highly frustrating factors. The strong tendency of adolescents to set up their own clubs, sororities and fraternities gives evidence of their efforts to fill the roles we often deny them in our culture.

[1] Murphy, Gardner. *Personality—A Biosocial Approach to Origins and Structure*. New York: Harper and Brothers, 1947, p. 139.

[2] Hartshorne, Hugh and May, Mark A. *Studies in Deceit*. New York: Macmillan Co., 1928.

Nonfunctional high-school curriculums, the lack of opportunity for work experience and for finding a job after graduation, the conflicts between standards and philosophy prevalent in one decade contrasted with another, and therefore between parent and adolescent, the rapid changes in our physical environment and the resulting "cultural lag," are all cases in point and sources of adolescent conflict.

Research studies based on adolescent interviews, problem check lists and similar devices suggest the sources of conflict. Among the problems listed are the following:

1. Lack of practical work experience.
2. Uncertainty of a job after graduation.
3. Ill at ease when trying to speak to a group.
4. Parents too strict about permitting attendance at evening affairs and in use of the family car.
5. The absence of "dates"; the behavior on "dates" and the degree that they should physically express their feelings.
6. The failure of parents to discuss sex questions.
7. The concern about making the world a "better place in which to live."
8. Inadequate facilities for wholesome recreation and play.

The cultural inconsistencies youth face are the causes of many conflicts. We as adults help to create the conflicts by encouraging in youth high levels of aspiration, then failing to make available the resources through which the aspirations might be attained. This is aptly described by Murphy and Newcomb when they picture our culture as one which, in turn, asks the young person "to be the center of attention, to get out of the way, to accept absolute authority, to show his independence of authority, to sacrifice himself for the larger group, to be self-sustaining and independent, to love passionately and to achieve financial success." [3]

The adolescent, as an organism trying to make adjustments, uses what is biologically relevant or of value in the environment to relieve tension and maintain internal equilibrium. If the environment provides goal resources in the form of activities, space, facilities, equipment and trained sympathetic leadership, basic drives and tensions will be resolved by integration into wholesome situations.

[3] Murphy, Gardner; Murphy, Lois Barclay; and Newcomb, Theodore. *Experimental Social Psychology.* Revised edition. New York: Harper and Brothers, 1937, p. 327.

Acceptable social behavior should result. Conversely, if the environment is "delinquent" and devoid of socially approved goal resources, the organism seizes upon whatever resources are available. In the search for excitement and adventure, being chased by the "cops" for tampering with the gum-vending machine might take the place of "Run, my good sheep, run!" It is a fact that delinquents appear for the most part in the "delinquency areas" where there is a "delinquent" culture. Mental health "spot maps" tend to indicate a similar relationship to the cultural setting.

## A Unified Organism Does the Growing

Personality evolves as a whole around a central plan or goal and is not a summation of traits. The synthesis of values, purposes and desires with respect to a goal or life plan is an important factor and determinant of personality. On the playing fields we speak of physical growth, emotional development, absence or presence of dynamic drive, sociability and other components of personality, but the really important factor is the dynamic organization within the individual, the interrelationships among these components. Considering any one item, out of its relationship to others, at its face value is a questionable practice, for these relationships are always evolving and changing. Any one aspect of development in isolation from other aspects brings little understanding of either the part or the whole. All aspects are interrelated in the total developing personality. This principle of growth is the source of the conviction that no matter what the field of education, there must be education of the "whole child." This makes mandatory shifting the center of attention from subjectmatter to the needs, interests and goals of the child or youth being educated.

Even though growth is a unified process, different aspects of growth show variations in rate. Emotional growth may lag behind physical. Physical maturing may be slower than intellectual growth. Different parts of the body grow at different rates and change at different periods. During childhood, collars and shoes are constantly becoming too small but caps wear out; in adolescence shoes wear out but trousers and skirts become too short. Personality is a "whole" and evolves as such. Yet it must be seen as being made up at any given time of parts that have not developed at the same rate. We must expect different aspects of development to show differences in stages of maturity. Just because an adolescent boy is six feet tall does not mean he is sexually mature or emotionally adult.

## Each Boy's and Girl's Growth is Different

In any group of adolescents of the same chronological age we find a variety of physiques. Within each individual member of the group we likewise find an *individual* growth pattern. The processes of emotional-physical-mental-social growth are unique in each adolescent. The term "average" never refers to any one individual.

Social values of the group and the importance and meaning that the group in any given culture attaches to marked deviation from the average or central tendency in height, weight, adipose tissue, or ways of thinking and behaving, often give the adolescent a warped image of himself. One of our educational functions, therefore, is to aid him in developing scientific understandings about individual differences. He must be helped to see that to be different is not to be abnormal or either superior or inferior. Because of their insecurities adolescents are afraid to be different. It is often difficult or impossible for them to accept others who differ from them. With a secure place in their age group and the emerging of an adult self, it becomes possible for them to "be themselves" and at the same time to grant to others diversity of expression. Understanding and acceptance of individual differences are essential to the democratic way of life.

## Maturity Is the Goal

Growth is thought of as progress toward maturity. Maturity may be seen as the type of behavior appropriate to the chronological age of the individual. The two-year-old who still crawls rather than walks is immature in this particular respect. The adolescent who feels that he can never make a move without first asking "mama" is still dependent and emotionally and socially immature. Aspects of maturity, like those of personality, are relatively easy to detect, but it is difficult to define maturity as a total concept. The chief criterion of maturity as it applies to human relations lies in the ability of the individual to exhibit sociocentricity, interest in others, rather than egocentricity, the focus of attention upon the self. Absorption in causes and goals unrelated to self-seeking and vanity is a favorable sign. The ability to be smilingly objective about himself, to weigh his personality assets and liabilities in comparison with what his classmates say of him, is a test of the adolescent's growth toward maturity. Maturity also implies some integrative factor best represented by a unifying philosophy of life, made up of intellectually formulated principles controlling thinking and actions, which represents the individual's conception of his place in the scheme of things. An adolescent with long-range purposes and a plan to achieve them, plus the actual use of the goal resources available to start him "goalwise," is showing progress toward maturity.

Qualities of maturity are implied in certain behavior patterns which become aims of education in a democratic society, such as:

1. Considering the rights of others.
2. Cooperating with others.
3. Discovering and accepting one's own inadequacies and improving upon them if possible.
4. Assuming responsibilities inherent in democratic freedom.
5. Solving problems by thinking them through rather than resorting to emotional solutions or escapes.
6. Accepting individual differences without assignment of superiority or inferiority.

Arrested development may occur at any stage in the life of the individual. Many adolescents live the emotional lives of children, and many adults live the emotional lives of adolescents. Those genetic phases of development in emotional and social maturity more closely involved in human relations may be suggested in terms of behavior as shown in the chart on the following page.

## Defining a New Self

The self or ego usually refers to the individual as he is known and understood by himself. To the young child, the self is localized as the physical body and the social controls are something external to him. Gradually and in time the self is referred inward and he learns

| Child | Adolescent | Mature Person |
|---|---|---|
| Beginning to like play in small groups and some interest in team activities. | Decided preference for group games by boys. Girls have had this experience and now prefer more individual sports activity. | Enjoys activity of complex organization. |
| Gradually widening social contacts, but still rather egocentric. Group consciousness weak. | Allegiance swings to his group, but is not very stable. | Permanent interest and social values well developed. |
| Relatively little interest in the opposite sex as "pals." | Permanent friendships begin. Friends of the opposite sex; dating. | Makes wise choices and abides by them. |
| Interests change from asocial to social; from interests in immediate environment to the wider community. | Increasing consciousness of growth toward a new and independent personality. | Able to initiate a task and carry it to completion. |
| Codes of moral conduct as exemplified in the Scouts, and similar groups are accepted. | Group and group status are major concerns. Desire for recognition is strong. | Able to organize his behavior in relation to more remote ends. |
| Social groups, based on interests, rather unstable and change as interests change. | Interest in opposite sex based on sex consciousness. Most girls dating and most boys willing but still somewhat afraid of showing their real interests. | Able to inhibit emotional response and defer gratification of an immediate desire. |
| Goals and purposes rather immediate. Values sought are not deferred values. | Organizations are not always democratic despite the drive toward group activity. | Has developed a philosophy which gives him a satisfactory "world picture" and an understanding of himself in relation to this picture. |
| Personal sacrifice for the good of the group rather difficult. Rights of others frequently ignored. | Social groups become more stable. Social values still superficial. | Action dependent on reflective thinking and suspended judgment. |
|  | Curious and interested in understanding the intricacies of human relations and "doing the right thing" to foster them. Searches for models and ideals. | Shows concern for the rights and personality development of others. |

that he is a "person" able to exert some controls over people and events. He learns what people are in contrast to things.

Since the self becomes a source of satisfaction and dissatisfaction, self-criticism becomes possible. The self-image becomes a value, judged by and formulated largely by values expressed in the world about the child. His successes and disappointments, his conflicts, desires, hopes and ideals begin to shape his personality.

In zero weather the child puts on additional clothing to protect his body. Similarly, he employs many protective devices such as excuses, "sour grapes" attitudes and many rationalizations in order to guard his inner picture of the self. Educationally, our task is to provide goal resources conducive to the achievement of wholesome personal values and self-realization in harmony with the broader social goals of democracy as a whole. Self-realization for the adolescent means the formulation of a plan which will produce the wished-for self.

## Leaving Childhood Behind

In the various poorly-defined stages or periods of emotional growth, the individual's center of affection and interest shifts gradually and imperceptibly. The picture of the self is strongly influenced by the early and vague conceptions of those with whom the child is closely identified.

In the immediate family, the growing child assimilates the feelings of those about him. Later, in other primary or face-to-face play groups, the picture and value of the self grow. Finally, the secondary group, including the world of television, radio, movies, political organizations, clubs, fraternities and causes which make deep impressions on the adolescent, storm and attack his value systems as he becomes aware of the vast number of distinct personalities in the world about him.

The adolescent's experience of his own developing self, emerging from the interaction of a growing, changing organism with its environment, is often perplexing. The fact that the individual is identified with his group and accepts its structured pattern of values gives him a picture of himself which is largely defined by the values prescribed by his group. The acceptance of himself as a person depends, to a large extent, upon how others accept his personal variations, his physique, his ideas, his behavior traits and various ways in which he may differ from the expectations of the group.

## Physical Development

Rapid and uneven growth is characteristic of adolescence. The girl by 16 years and the boy by 18 years are attaining very nearly mature height and weight and maximum muscular coordination. For girls, the maximum increase in the rate of growth occurs about six months before the menarche and increments of growth practically cease at two and one-half years after the menarche. Data for boys show similar results when the onset of pubescence is the criterion.

The boy's physiological lag of one year behind the girl shows itself in factors related to physiological maturity. Physical growth, social interests and value systems in both sexes appear related to and dependent, to a certain extent, upon the instigation of hormones accompanying sexual maturation.

Since in any given high-school grade there are apt to be some individuals in the beginning and some in the end of the puberal growth cycle, and since much doubt, worry and concern evolve around the individual's pattern of growth in relation to classmates, friendly guidance and understanding with respect to youth and physical development are required of parents and teachers.

Growth anxieties often appear in adolescence as a result of physical maturation coupled with social pressures and the cultural importance unduly attached to temporary physical variations. In girls, menstruation, the development of the breasts, the broadening hips, a growth spurt which often makes them tower over the boys in their classes, their interest in boys and dancing and the disinterest of the boys in them all lead to the conclusion that the boys do not like them. The campaign for acceptance is then stepped up by a new "hair do," lipstick and other subtle techniques.

Since in any given age group there are many different stages of physiological change represented, there is much worry about being "normal" when comparisons are made. The girl whose breasts have not begun to develop and the boy who has not yet experienced his growth spurt become much concerned when others of her or his age group have given evidence of already achieving these stages of physical maturity. The patterns in body type, skill, skin, dress and the like which his peers accept as appropriate determine the degree of individual frustration of the adolescent's self-ideals and his emotional reactions to new situations.

Temporary body disproportions may cause temporary anxiety, and may even be the source of persisting deep-seated emotional disturbance. Ignorance and lack of understanding may lead to serious misconceptions of growth changes and their resultant effects upon the pattern of the self-concept. Perceptions of the physical self as a male or female and the meanings attached to these perceptions before and during adolescence form the matrix of personality. Whether the adolescent is self-depreciating, unduly humble, feels inferior or is confident and self-assertive will depend upon his actual or imaginary experiences in the past. Like other concepts, the self-concept is capable of change and it is the function of education to change it in the directions compatible with wholesome personality development.

Since, in adolescence, youth observe the differentiation of personalities as female and male, the attitudes of one sex toward the other, as well as the acceptance of one's own sex, are strongly influenced. The implications for coeducation for satisfactory heterosexual development and the development of understanding in human relations are here evident.

## Changing Relations with Adults

As the adolescent recognizes himself as a unique personality with distinctive characteristics, he drops the "nest habits" of the young child and the ready acceptance of the judgment of father or mother. Struggle toward autonomy and self-determination, with tendencies toward achieving, dominating and mastering the environment are characteristic of the normal development of the human being. Life and the process of growing up involve increased autonomy and eventual independence from parents and the acquisition of new means and methods of achieving autonomy.

The over-aggressive and the rebellious adolescent at school is sometimes the child of the overly strict and authoritarian parents.

Finding no place to assert his independence at home he uses the school as a place for asserting the independence denied him in the family.

When conformity and unquestioning obedience are asked, the adolescent is blocked in his struggle to grow up and rebellion and defiance, delinquency and anti-social behavior are apt to appear in his relations with others. At the other extreme, his responses may take the form of fear of all assertiveness, surrender of personal autonomy, defeatism, feelings of guilt, insecurity and neurotic illness.

Rebellion and argument are unpleasant symptoms of the blocking of adolescent strivings to escape from childhood dependence, but both are normal and hopeful signs. By protesting parental decrees, by arguing and by questioning authority, the adolescent announces that he is growing up, does not want to remain dependent, but desires to think for himself and stand on his own feet. As long as the adolescent is willing to let others live his life for him, his mental, emotional and social development will be arrested; he is prevented from moving in the direction of normal independence and then on to interdependence in his relations with others.

There are ways for adults to meet the adolescent's need for autonomy and minimize expressions of rebellion and frustration. An allowance, a chance to earn, to budget and select one's clothes, being included in family and school planning are modified and socially acceptable expressions of autonomy. Specialists in psycho-drama speak of "restructuring" the situation, giving the adolescent a chance to act out a part, to liberate himself in arranged situations which permit him to be himself and to grow. The physical educator and recreational leader consciously using such techniques on the playground and in the gymnasium may also provide situations in which the adolescent may fulfil his desire to grow up.

Much of the reluctance of adults to meet the adolescent's demand for independence is created by the ambivalent behavior of the boy or girl. Adolescents are confused and inconsistent—brash and asser-tive at one time, shy and retiring at another. One day the adolescent demands the rights and privileges of an adult; the next day he asks mother what tie he should wear, what time he should get up, whether or not he should go out for track. The next evening the same adolescent may claim the right to decide for himself where he shall spend the evening, with whom he will go out and at what time he expects to return.

Another source of the reluctance is the inability of some adults, parents particularly, to give up the power and control they have exercised hitherto over the child's comings and goings. Their need to dominate causes them to fail to meet the adolescent's need to get free, to learn to decide for himself, to take control of his own life. The adjustments of parents to their adolescent sons' and daughters' changing relations to them are not nearly so difficult if the adults have always encouraged their children to make decisions with understanding of consequences and to share in family decisions and planning; in other words, treated them as persons who must learn to take responsibility for themselves and for others as well. Even so, there are adjustments to be made. More than this, there are steps to be taken in helping adolescents to overcome social blocks to adulthood, steps that will aid them to become economically independent and able to assume responsibilities of establishing homes of their own.

*Creating a Self-Image.* The kind of person the adolescent idealizes and accepts as a model or ideal gives some indication of what he as a self is trying to become, how the world looks to him and what he is trying to achieve in his struggle to fill the role of an adult. Adolescence finds the girl in close identification with her mother, the boy with the father. Then comes the necessity to reject the parent in the struggle to establish an independent self. Other persons are selected as models for the personality the adolescent seeks for himself. He prefers persons he knows such as the athletic coach, a teacher, an older boy, but he also accepts movie stars, athletes, scientists or characters in novels. The selection may cause important changes in his personality as he strives to be like the ideal. Emulation may be so inclusive as to affect dress, speech, choice of profession, personal habits, attitudes toward others. The need of adolescents for a model, a hero or heroine to emulate, makes clear how important it is to them for developing democratic human relations that the adults they associate with, who might be these models, be democratic and mature persons.

*Entering a Peer Culture*

The adolescent's experiences in his own age groups as he is socialized by the different value systems operating in his peer group at various stages of development are powerful preparatory factors in readying him for an adult world.

Research by Tryon[4] indicates how the adolescent group's behavior, its objectives, its standards of values, its rules of behavior and methods of securing conformity, its relation to the adult society, all undergo change as development progresses from late childhood to maturity. These changes in values, changes in things desirable or sought after, represent way stations on the march toward that intangible goal of adult maturity.

Values, in Tryon's study, were represented by those characteristics which pubescents and adolescents considered desirable in each other. For example, seventh-grade boys admired skill in games, daring, ingenuity in leading and directing games, boisterousness and rough and ready appearance. As ninth graders, they still admired skill, courage, strength and aggressiveness almost as much, but personal untidiness had become unpopular. Boisterousness and seeking the center of the stage were looked upon as "childish." Social ease and personableness began to share honors with strength and skill and aggressiveness.

At the twelfth grade, the outstanding athlete needs little else to retain his position. Brains minus social skills are not admired, but a socially poised or mature boy with a good academic record is popular. Being honest and capable in what one undertakes is a mark of acceptability.

The seventh-grade girls who are demure, prim, ladylike, pretty, friendly, tidy and submissive are well accepted if they are happy and buoyant. "Tom-boys," daring and jocular, are accepted but not especially admired. The ninth-grade girls who are good sports and attractive to boys are very acceptable and the girls who were most admired as seventh graders for being ladylike may not now be the group's ideal of social attractiveness. The socially active girl with many friends, popular in large groups, is now admired.

As twelfth graders, the girl who is well groomed and has achieved

4 National Society for the Study of Education. *Adolescence.* Forty-Third Yearbook, Part I. Chicago: University of Chicago Press, 1944. p. 217-39.

fully her feminine role is the model. Sophistication and glamour, plus attractiveness to boys, plus poise, polish, and consideration for others, place the girl high in social acceptance. Belonging to a special clique having prestige and being popular with a desirable boy bring her reflected prestige and admiration.

*The Herd Period.* Despite the fact that standards of qualities which make for acceptance vary from culture to culture and from period to period within a given culture, group approval is the most powerful influence in adolescent behavior. Strong pressure to conform to the value system of the upper group is evident, side by side with the desire to be independent of adult standards and controls. This trend, in contrast with autonomy, has been called "homonomy" by Angyal[5] and is based on the experience of being a part of meaningful groups such as family, social group and a meaningful world order. The tendency to conform, to unite with and participate in and fit into such groups is a powerful motivating force in human relations.

The school and neighborhood, as social laboratories for youth, find them learning the ways of adult behavior, organizing their own athletics and social activities, selecting their own leaders, dancing, enjoying "bull sessions," playing social games. By such means do adolescents set up a peer world of their own which they may control and in which they assume the roles and independence denied them in the world of adults.

Childish loyalty is based somewhat on the trend toward autonomy or independence. The young child and the immature youth are loyal to those individuals and groups which satisfy their immediate needs and gradually give them a feeling of individuality and security. Individuals and groups, in this sense, are used as instruments in establishing independence. At this stage the attitude is still quite egocentric. The social status and the confidence in one's own power and importance which one seeks, can be given only by others. The resultant good is a social good because it represents valuation by members of a group. In this sense people in groups are used as tools and invoke loyalty only as they may be used as such.

[5] Angyal, Andras. *Foundations for a Science of Personality.* New York: The Commonwealth Fund, 1941, p. 172.

The growing active loyalty of maturity begins to make its appearance in adolescence. At this stage, other people are recognized as values in themselves. The other person or group, or an ideal for which the group stands, may have greater motivating power than individual desires. To share and participate in something which the adolescent regards as greater than his individual self is a big step in human relations. Loyalty to the family, the little play group, the team, the school, the state, the nation and finally to humanity, are crude examples of gradation in social attitudes. The concrete ideal of the hero or model gives way to abstract ideals or principles. The adolescent no longer sees himself in the part of another. He has found himself. He has learned to live with others and still retain his personal integrity. To get along with others, be able to adjust to them, and at the same time be unafraid to be a unique personality, indicate moving out of the "herd period" and of having successfully achieved one of the developmental tasks of adolescence.

*Relations with Own Sex.* Early adolescence is the period of intense friendships. In earlier years, through experience in the primary or face-to-face groups, boys and girls have played different roles in different groups. They have been leaders, "isolates" and sometimes dominators of groups. By group reaction and their respective status roles, they have come to create a self-image which leads to feelings of various degrees of inferiority and degrees of self-acceptance or self-rejection.

Strong friendships among adolescents reflect some desire to choose as friends those who are like themselves and of the same sex. Most psychologists would consider this "buddy" and "pal" stage a normal period through which adolescents pass in our culture, and consider it a transient phase in the development of the child's love growth. The degree of harmfulness lies in the intensity of the feeling of possession which one person has toward the other. It has been suggested that "The meaning of intense love-friendships and crushes for adolescents is not yet entirely clear; they may reflect both the projection of the child's needs for affection and the sublimation of growing emotions that in another culture might have more immediate sex expression."[6]

---

[6] Murphy, Gardner; Murphy, Lois Barclay; and Newcomb, Theodore, *op. cit.*, p. 644.

The next normal stage in psycho-sexual development is for the opposite sex to absorb more and more of the adolescent's interest, affection and attention.

*Boy-Girl Relations.* The results of anonymous opinion polls and problem checklists, when the respondents are adolescents, show how strong is the desire to "get along with others"; over half of all adolescents "wish they were more popular," "want to make new friends," "want people to like them more." Each sex is concerned about "not having dates." Girls are concerned about "not having boy friends"; boys are concerned about "not having girl friends." Boys are bashful about asking girls for dates. Both sexes are concerned about how far they should go in love relations, about "going steady," whether they must "pet" to be popular. Girls want to improve their figures; boys want to improve their body builds.

From childish egocentricity to strong "crushes" and intense friendships with "buddies" and "pards" of like sex to the heterosexual period where one is experimenting and learning the ways of mate selection marks the path from childhood to adolescence.

In our culture, in practically all instances, young people select their own marriage partners. The large numbers of marriages which fail suggest that education for family life has not been adequate. Delayed marriage, due to the heavy economic responsibilities of marriage, the ideal of "rugged individualism," long periods of courtship, the automobile, the "drive-in" theater, the romantic love idealized in our movies and soap operas, and general lack of friendly and understanding supervision place unduly heavy responsibilities of control on the sexually mature adolescent.

The degree of failure in marriage among Americans seems to indicate that a rather immature system of values frequently surrounds the marriage relationship. We do not seem to understand what is involved in building social awareness and mutual respect for a relationship which should enhance the personalities of each partner. Adolescents fail to see that boys and girls will have different tasks in adult life and that they are equally valuable and mutually related to successful family life and parenthood.

Success in marriage seems related to emotional and social maturation during adolescence and to the choice of a mate who is likewise emotionally and socially mature. Often special help is needed which the school should attempt to supply genetically, not only in units related to education for family life, but in the way youth live in the school as reflected by its over-all educational purposes for meeting the needs of life in America.

## Paths to Adulthood

The protracted period of infancy in the human gives a longer period of role playing. Out of this role playing there gradually develops the integrated self of self-consciousness. The different roles a youth takes in an organized game have a relationship to one another and each player must know something about the role of the others in the scheme of things. Were this not so, it would never be possible for a team or other cooperative group to become an integrated social group—one whose members are bound together by the integration of numerous individual abilities searching for achievement of common goals and purposes. Mead mentions the importance for youth to develop the attitude in which each one is everyone else on his team—a "generalized other"—and in terms of which he sees and defines *his own place* in the group.[7] In a highly-organized team game such as the activities of life the same process of development of the self is involved. Team work is a term we apply to many life situations in which a self is developed and expressed in cooperative enterprise.

Social sensitivity and social awareness are learned gradually in a social structure in which these qualities of human relations are considered social virtues. As the social setting provides conditions and stimuli for cooperative undertakings, youth have opportunity to assume the attitudes of groups and communities and see their own responsible attitudes in their social relations.

As developmental social tasks of greater complexity are gradually faced by boys and girls, a broader base of social awareness and social feeling is built. Gradually they develop concepts of their relations to the whole of human striving and a clearer picture of their respective parts in the melody of common social purposes.

Preparation for marriage is required and the school should do its

[7] Mead, George H. *Mind, Self and Society.* Chicago: University of Chicago Press, 1934, p. 135-226.

part to provide it, not only in units related to education for family life but also in all the ways of living and learning included in the curriculum.

*Self-Understanding.* As indicated earlier in this chapter, there are changing patterns, not only of physical growth, but also in the conceptions of the self. The self-concept created in early childhood is worked over and changed in numerous ways; self-regarding attitudes and social attitudes toward others are in a state of flux and become strong factors in the motivation of behavior. This behavior as exhibited in school and society is understandable to the student, parent or teacher only as the *source* becomes known. Plant suggests that we see the personality as a river . . . "and at any point its currents, its debris, its power are known only as one understands the sources from which these spring."[8]

As the growing organism perceives, thinks about, and responds in action initiated by the self, considerable change in the self-concept results. It is no wonder that the adolescent feels queer, new and different. As the adolescent notes changes in anatomical patterns and stature in himself and others—as he notes the disproportion, the awkwardness, the new signs of power, his new perceptions change greatly the meaning pattern of the self-concept and what he himself means to himself.

An important educational function for parents and teachers is to clarify for adolescent boys and girls the wellsprings of their actions, and to indicate that sometimes faulty interpretation of their perceptions of themselves accounts for peculiarities in social behavior and for their unhappiness. Parents and teachers must understand the structure of selfhood and build wholesome self-concepts. This is important at a period when changing meanings in the self-concepts, self-feelings or self-regarding attitudes are particularly subject to distortion as a result of the seemingly erratic course of physical development.

It is important in a culture which is both demanding and inconsistent in what it values and what it rewards with social recognition.

*Economic Independence.* Growing up in America involves the ability to make a living and opportunities to put the ability to work.

[8] Plant, James. *Personality and the Cultural Pattern.* New York: Commonwealth Fund, 1937, p. 8.

Havighurst speaks of this developmental task as achieving assurance of economic independence in which the goal is "to feel able to make a living, if necessary. This is presumably a task of boys in our society, but it is of increasing importance to girls."[9]

*Heterosexual Adjustment.* The developmental task of accepting boys as boys and girls as girls is not always as simple for the growing boy and girl as it sounds. As sex attraction becomes a dominant force in the maturing adolescent, a natural and normal development is away from predominant interests in groups of his own sex and toward the opposite sex.

New feelings, interests and internal pressures have to be built into a new design for living. Into this design for boys, come girls; for girls, come boys. Exalted desires, ideals of loyalty and devotion well up to prepare the adolescent for the next developmental task, that of active expression of the protective and nurturing feelings of parenthood.

The social experimentation in choice of friends, in making tentative conclusions about what qualities one most wants in a friend or future mate of the opposite sex, is important for normal heterosexual adjustment. Possessiveness and jealousy are common outcomes of these adolescent heterosexual experiences. "Going steady" is a big issue at the high-school level, for young people do not realize that they are still finding out about people—boys about girls and girls about boys. The design for each is still incomplete because it is based on incomplete knowledge of the people with whom each best gets along. Mutual regard, tenderness and devotion between sexes are built, tested and learned to a large extent in these adolescent years.

*Participation in Community Life.* It is an old aphorism that "one learns to swim by swimming, to talk by talking," yet we sometimes expect to teach citizenship by having students memorize social-science lessons. Being "mayor for a day" as the Hi-Y "takes over" the city is related to preparation for and participation in community life, but is a rather weak prescription for citizenship.

Many research studies of observed adolescent behavior in America interpret responses as direct aggression against the hampering re-

[9] Havighurst, Robert J. *Developmental Tasks and Education.* Chicago: University of Chicago Press, 1948, p. 37.

strictions imposed by our culture. Biologically adults, but treated sociologically as children, our young people are often robbed of their self-confidence and hindered in developing social responsibility—retarded in their social development. Much of the adolescent behavior observable in American adults might be eliminated at the adolescent period if our high-school boys and girls could find expression in *real* community functions for leadership, initiative and independent planning of action.

In contrast to many primitive cultures in which community education plays a major role in the education of youth, our culture is slow to recognize the ability of our youth to carry on adult duties. The result is frequent evidence of frustration, with either its accompanying aggression and cynicism or withdrawal, submission and discouragement. The little worlds which adolescents set up and in which they may "play" at being adults are important and necessary, but they must be seen as stepping stones to the real thing.

During the war, many adolescents were wanted, given worthwhile tasks, recognized as valuable contributors to society and achieved responsibilities commensurate with their abilities. Educators could ease the paths to adulthood for boys and girls and advance our national social outlook and maturity level immeasurably if we ceased reminding our youth that they are "too young to know what they are talking about" and "too young for real responsibility."

*A Value System.* The pathway to a mature value system is determined by a number of factors. We value objects, conditions or experiences only as long as these yield satisfaction to us and no longer. Havighurst suggests six ways in which we form values.

1. *Through the satisfaction of physiological drives.*

We value food in relation to the satisfaction of the hunger drive. Children value climbing in relation to the satisfaction of the activity drive.

2. *Through satisfactory emotional experience.*

Certain forms, patterns of color, melodic patterns and rhythms are pleasant for some people, unpleasant for others. Our aesthetic appreciations are the result of values we have learned.

3. *Through concrete punishment and reward.*

One values the act which brings money or a treat and if consistently so rewarded. However, "this method is apt to be ineffective in turning an initially unpleasant act into a pleasant one."

4. *Through association of something with the love or approval of persons whose love and approval are desired.*

Game skills bring the approval of one's age mates and therefore come to be valued. Dressing neatly and having well groomed hair is appreciated by the girls, therefore the boy of 15 comes to value these things. At nine, grooming holds little or no value for him.

5. *Through inculcation by someone in authority.*

"The Ten Commandments are handed down from the supernatural or fearsome authority, or the catechism may be impressed upon the child by the stern pastor who is a surrogate for God."

6. *Through reasoning or reflective thinking.*

Analyses of social conditions and human behavior result in the seeing of relationships or possible social and individual consequences. In evaluating a work of art, certain aesthetic principles are applied. Judgment is arrived at concerning its value.[10]

Havighurst suggests that the fourth and sixth modes of value formation are most relevant to education at high-school and college levels. Close attachment or identification with those with whom students have close relations and who have prestige in their sight are powerful "value formers" for youth. A rough genetic sequence of these "value formers" is suggested by Havighurst as follows:

1. Parents
2. Teachers and parent-surrogates, such as club leaders and adult neighbors
3. Successful age mates and persons just older than the individual
4. Glamorous adults such as movie stars, soldiers, airplane pilots, athletes, outlaws
5. Heroes read about, such as Abraham Lincoln, Florence Nightingale, Louis Pasteur
6. Attractive and successful young adults within the adolescent's range of observation.[11]

The goal for adolescent and adult alike is a set of values, a philosophy in harmony with the best modern scientific knowledge of the nature of a Christian democratic society, the nature of man and the nature of the learning process.

[10] Havighurst, Robert J., *op. cit.*, p. 56-57
[11] *Ibid.* p. 58.

Philosophy—a value system—is a "rudder," a determinant of human behavior and human relations. Self-confidence and sociability are alike the foundation stones of sound mental health and good human relations as well as a mark of a mature philosophy of life. The adolescent's belief in regard to himself and his relations to his peers are the fundamental determinants of what he does, and both are strongly subject to educational influences.

## The Needs of Adolescence

The adolescent is a biological animal in a cultural setting. As such, he is subject to two directional forces. As a biological animal he inclines unconsciously toward goals prescribed by his own internal constitution, such as activity, food and rest. As a purposeful member of a society, he inclines consciously toward goals representing social values which satisfy such motives as success, mastery, achievement, adventure, approval, recognition and love. Motivation toward these latter goals is biosocial and strongly influenced by the value and prestige attached to them by the adolescent's age mates.

The adolescent's success in his social relations, his success in solving problems of life, making adjustments and maintaining internal equilibrium will depend upon the success with which he meets his "needs" by finding socially acceptable channels for expression of the biological and social drives mentioned above. Schools meet the needs of adolescents when they provide the objects, conditions and experiences necessary for their satisfaction. Needs are always personal and inseparable, one influencing another. The trends of growing organisms toward autonomy or self-assertion on the one hand and toward sharing and merging into a social group on the other develop readiness to tension. The organism in its various functions is dependent for need satisfaction upon the resources of the environment. Needs, like purposes, are personal and integral with their goals or objects. In the development of human personality, it is exceedingly important that we, as teachers and leaders of youth, be concerned with the questions of how students attempt to achieve certain goals and meet their needs, how they defend their egos, how they try to achieve superiority, excel, and gain security.

## The Concept of Need

Needs are not abstractions, they are personalized. The goal, the purpose of the individual is integral with the need. The simplest definition of need is "the absence of something which if present would tend to give satisfaction." A need is the immediate outcome of certain internal and external occurrences and is therefore basically related to culture. Needs vary from culture to culture and with individuals in terms of their respective levels of development. A need is evidence in behavior of certain basic drives and tensions operating within the organism. Needs are directional tensions of individuals. A need, then, in its implemental sense becomes any requisite to the normal wholesome functioning of an individual in a given culture.

A need exists when the environmental factor, which is necessary to carry out a given function, is absent or insufficient. A need is a distress situation. Needs tend to put the organism into a state of restless activity, of striving toward a goal; they provide motive power. With the attainment of the goal, the series of activities is completed or closed, tension is released through motor channels and the normal equilibrium of the organism is restored until the individual finds himself in a situation that will give rise to another need. Needs have been variously classified, but it is simplest to classify them in terms of their origins.

Prescott classifies the needs of developing children into three categories representing three major aspects of life. These categories of need are:

1. Physiological—"When describing needs that spring primarily out of structure and dynamic biochemical equilibrium."

2. Social or status—"When describing the relationships that it is essential to establish with other persons in our culture."

3. Ego or integrative—"When describing needs for experience and for the organization and symbolization of experience through which the individual will discover his role in life and learn to play it in such an effective manner as to develop a sense of worthy selfhood." [12]

Between the point at which the individual feels a need and his purpose to meet it lies a certain void. This void between where the

[12] Prescott, Daniel, editor. *Emotions and the Educative Process.* Washington, D. C.: American Council on Education, 1938, p. 113.

person is and where his goal lies represents the instrumental usage of the need concept. Here, playing basketball, having a "girl friend" or belonging to a club might be examples representing the *means* or *instruments* for making drive satisfaction possible, the implemental usage of the term "need." We might say that "John needs to play basketball," "he needs a girl friend" or "he needs to belong to a club." When a teacher helps a student define his goals, helps provide opportunities and conditions as resources and suggests a path leading to a goal, he is helping the student to implement his needs.

*Needs in Our Culture.* Cultural or normative needs are those expressing social standards or norms. They represent the demands made upon the individual by society and not the demands of the individual upon the culture. The first type is illustrated in such statements as, "Johnny needs Latin!" or "Johnny needs to learn table manners!" Wright feels that this type of need exemplifies projected adult requirements and values and the absence of motive power on the part of Johnny.[13] We think here of teacher objectives. These become student purposes when we have somehow turned cultural requirements into organismic needs.

Organismic needs, on the other hand, are receiving greater emphasis as we learn about human personality from research in child growth and development and the newer findings in psychiatry and mental hygiene. The fundamental forces within the personality which are behind satisfaction-seeking behavior are being studied. Education in many places is being redesigned to meet individual needs.

Theoretically, some of the tensions resulting from what Prescott classifies as physiological, social or status, and ego or integrative needs might be illustrated in the manner of the chart on the following page.

Like organismic needs, purposes are *within* the individual, but he is *not always* conscious of the goals or conditions which would satisfy his needs and relieve him of feelings of disturbance, discomfort, desire or unrest. The function of the teacher then becomes that of helping the students to define their goals clearly and to map out the path which will lead them to goal satisfaction. We must provide experiences, materials and conditions that lead to goal

[13] Wright, Herbert F. "How the Psychology of Motivation Is Related to Curriculum Development." *Journal of Educational Psychology:* 39: 149-56; November 1948.

| *Disturbing Situations* (Causes of tensions) | *Goal Resources* (Implemental usage) | *Goal Satisfactions* (Resolution of tensions) |
|---|---|---|
| Threat to bodily comfort (pain, hunger, sex demands, need for sleep). | Our function as teachers is to help to provide the goal resources in the form of conditions, materials, experiences and opportunities which shall make desirable goal satisfactions possible for the adolescent. How goal resources may be provided and how learning experiences may be organized is the burden of the two chapters to follow. | Improved health, physical well-being, rest, marriage. |
| Being bored, finding life dull and monotonous; inactivity; wanting physical "play"; unsatisfied curiosity. | | New adventure, exploration, experience, zestful activity, creativeness and self-expression. |
| Feeling of weakness and failure, feeling of inferiority. Feeling of being thwarted and disappointed. | | Success, mastery and achievement. A sense of leadership and power. |
| Being unwanted, being unloved; rejection by one's peers; loneliness; being "left out." | | Being loved and given intimacy and tenderness by those whose love and approval we seek. Having a sense of belonging to a larger social unit; sharing and participating in group ventures. |
| Being ignored or looked down upon; regarded with scorn, contempt, disapproval; being emotionally insecure. | | Being looked up to, recognized and approved, admired and appreciated; having status in one's group. |
| Lack of orientation in life; uncertainty of ideals and goals worth following; uncertainty about one's purposes and abilities in life, and an unclear picture of the conscious "self"; a muddled attitude toward the "major" issues of life. | | A clearer concept and picture of himself; clear ideals of life accomplishment and of self; clarification of masculine and feminine roles; acceptance of one's bodily characteristics; a philosophy of life which gives consistent direction to behavior and life; religious belief; unity of purpose. |
| Being worried, anxious, fearful that he will be deprived of goal satisfaction, that his needs will not be met; threats to one's security. | | Peace of mind, security, release from tension; some well-defined purposes and a stable philosophy of life or religious belief. |

realization. We must help the student create new purposes and extend or modify old ones. To reach goals, students need goal resources. Abilities, chances, opportunities, favorable conditions are necessary in order that needs be satisfied.

## Needs in the Area of Human Relations

Adolescent needs in the area of human relations have been implied, if not named, in previous discussions. As a matter of fact, it would be impossible to name all of them. Here, instead of trying to do the impossible, it seems better to reiterate the major developmental tasks to be accomplished during adolescence and to emphasize that the needs of adolescence arise out of their efforts to accomplish the tasks. The developmental tasks having direct bearing on their needs in the area of human relations are:

To accept themselves

To accept others and be accepted by others

To win independence

To create an adult value system

To accept the reality of interdependence and its implications for working with others.

In accomplishing these tasks the adolescent needs to develop a separate self that is worthy of respect and acceptance; he needs to belong; he needs to be free to learn to take responsibility for himself and others, to be self-directing and self-managing; he needs to learn to work productively and cooperatively with others and to play with them joyously and creatively; he needs to be helped to solve the problems resulting from individual differences centered in sex and in struggles to achieve and receive recognition so that he increasingly understands that satisfying relations with others in a democracy are built on the foundation stone of respect for personality, all personality. As he is done by, the adolescent is apt to learn to do. Parents and teachers do well to ponder this fact.

## Leadership of Adolescents

Adolescence represents a focal point of development and the last period where considerable direct educational influence is still possible and where there is enough plasticity of personality to make major changes in the direction of behavior. The adolescent rebels at domination but is constantly looking for goal resources in himself, in others (age mates, parents and teachers), in materials, in conditions and experiences which will help him find answers to his problems and meet his needs. He wants help in establishing clearcut goals, but before this he needs and wants help in understanding himself and becoming aware of what his needs really are.

Once a friendly guide makes him conscious of his needs, helps him find the resources with which to establish goal satisfactions, helps him see the paths toward his goals, the most important function of educational leadership has been performed.

## Qualities of the Leader

**A Mature Person.** Considerable has already been said in previous sections concerning maturity and the criteria for maturity. The ability to delay one's overt responses, to exhibit self-control, to stand on one's own feet, to be economically competent and independent, to take responsibility, to cooperate with others, to make one's own decisions, to have a wholesome heterosexual attitude and a point of view on life—a philosophy characterized by unity and consistency—are the marks of a mature and adequate adult.

Suggestions and models are eagerly sought by adolescents as they grope for some sort of self-image of the kind of person they idealize or want to become. The conscious selection of the traits to imitate and the devotion to the ideals embodied in a given personality are very potent forces in the developing self and in behavior. The adolescent is fortunate who has good models in parents, teachers and leaders. The courage, skill, honesty, democracy, friendliness and other traits and principles represented by these virtues and in these people might well be generalized and accepted by the adolescent as guide lines as they become objects of desire and purpose and come to represent what the adolescent thinks of himself.

Ideals are potent factors in a stable personality. One lives hygienically, not by specific habits, but when hygienic living has become an ideal, a generalized habit. Democracy as a way of life will function only as it becomes an ideal. A few very old proverbs exemplify this: "Character is caught, not taught," "What the parent is speaks far more loudly than the techniques which he employs," "Most values are 'caught' from other people."

*An Understanding Person.* Understanding refers to the fund of meanings one has built up. The leader in health, physical education or recreation can be effective in changing the behavior of people in the direction of desirable goals to the extent which he:

1. *Understands the culture in which he lives.* Culture is the system of ways in which people behave, defines what is "proper" or "improper," including knowledge, beliefs, values, art, morals, law and custom or any other capabilities of men acquired by social inheritance.

The social group transmits to the adolescent its powerful taboos, values, interests and standards for satisfying his needs and attaining prestige and acceptance. Since adolescent behavior is in large part the result of the society in which youth grow up, we must become interested in the social structure as well as the individual if we are concerned with human relations. We are part and parcel of the culture in which we live. How various biological impulses become socialized by the provision of satisfactory channels for this process is one of the chief concerns of physical educators and recreation leaders functioning as applied social scientists.

2. *Understands the nature of the individual—in this case, the adolescent.* The validity of what educators do depends upon the validity of the principles by which they determine their procedures. Science, the search for functional relationship between facts, has established principles and has enabled us to base our beliefs and practices on facts rather than on superstition, tradition and hearsay.

From research in growth and development; from psychiatry, mental hygiene and human biology; from social psychology, sociometrics and functional analyses in sociology; from cultural anthropology; from the study of the learning process come principles which if applied in education would help immeasurably in improving mental health and human relations. The function of schools is to close the gap between what science has found out and the application of the principles. *This is our job* as teachers.

3. *Understands his own field.* Professional understanding of one's job implies the ability to understand and apply principles. The sources of many of these have been mentioned in the preceding statements. These are applied to understanding the nature of the individual and the nature of society. In addition, we must understand and be able to apply principles of organization and administra-

tion and principles of method—how learning experiences are organized. Whatever we do will be free from error only to the extent to which we employ tested and verified principles. Without them we cannot really understand our jobs.

Those working in the fields of health education, physical education and recreation should understand the potentiality of these areas for leadership of youth. This potentiality rests upon:

1. The large numbers of contacts and the consecutive periods of contact with the same students. Leadership cannot operate in isolation; people must be in association with each other.

2. The nature of the activities in which students, teachers and leaders engage. In physical education and recreation these are biologically and socially "prepotent," representing strong individual and social values to the adolescent. They seek to satisfy their needs in human relations by means of them. They use them as goal resources.

3. The informality of the student-teacher relationships in these activities.

4. The physique, the athletic and craft skills, the vitality and the values stressed tend to cause adolescents to identify themselves with the teacher having prestige in their sight. The idealized hero or heroine with educational insight may be very effective in guiding youth toward maturity.

5. At one time, all that was asked of the educator was that he know his subject. Sometime later he was asked to know his subject and also to know Johnny, the pupil. Today he is asked to know not only his subject and to know Johnny but to know himself as well.

Most problems of adjustment in school are bipolar—one pole the teacher, the other the pupil. We as teachers tend to interpret what we know in terms of what we *are* and what we *feel*. If the teacher feels insecure and must compensate for this insecurity by demanding obedience, showing authority and other signs of immaturity, the circular reaction of human relations begins and in this case it will not be a happy one.

Strong, independent, stable and well-socialized men and women are invariably those who as children were accepted and secure and who had parents and teachers who were well integrated personalities and were neither too dominant nor too submissive. Teachers who do not understand themselves can hardly understand their pupils. Schools are therefore rightfully concerned with the kind of teachers who are, in considerable measure, responsible for the development of democratic human relations among children and youth.

The skilled leader in human relations is one who is sensitive to the needs of individuals and is able to integrate the superior abilities of individuals toward a common goal. The good coach does exactly this—develops an integrated social group. Individuals have various abilities but each member contributes his ability toward the common goal. Each individual has the opportunity to grow to his full stature through participation and each develops a sense of mutual interrelationship and appreciation of the values of differences among men and women.

Democratic educational administration does not imply lack of leadership. It integrates the various abilities in faculties about the common educational purposes of the school. It calls forth, uses and encourages initiative, resourcefulness and enthusiasm of every member of the school. The democratic teacher, coach or recreation leader as an administrator must be not only an originator of ideas but a coordinator of the ideas of others.

The intelligent cooperation upon which the success of democracy depends must be learned in the schools. Democracy has many roots in a million playgrounds, athletic fields, gymnasia and summer camps. How firmly these roots take hold depends largely upon the quality of leadership which members of our respective professions supply. Democratic "climate" produces democratic children. Authoritarian "climate" produces authoritarian children. We now have the principles by which we may produce any climate we wish—we can be our own climatologists.

## The Guidance Required

*The Leader as Friend.* Pestalozzi once said, "Secure the love of the child and his education is an easy matter." The analysis of 14,000 letters written by children in grades two to 12 in response to a nation-wide radio contest on "The Teacher Who Helped Me Most," listed in rank order the following qualities in teachers which children found desirable:

1. Cooperative, democratic attitude
2. Kindliness and consideration for the individual
3. Patience
4. Wide interests

  5. Personal appearance and pleasing manner
  6. Fairness and impartiality
  7. Sense of humor
  8. Good disposition and consistent behavior
  9. Interest in pupils' problems
 10. Flexibility
 11. Use of recognition and praise
 12. Unusual proficiency in teaching.[14]

The children have here described the qualities of a mature adult —a well-integrated individual who feels secure and adequate and who is emotionally and socially mature. They also value this type of teacher because he or she represents the kind of person who satisfies their needs in human relations, helps them meet their needs and solve their problems.

Psychiatrists and clinicians have found that unless they can somehow get rapport with a patient and get his active cooperation, successful treatment is doubtful. Education comes from within. No one can educate another. The mental health, personality and example of the teacher are of basic importance in maximum motivation. The patterns of behavior, the attitudes developed, the value concepts and ideals crystallized in adolescents are in large part the result of the quality of human relations existing with their age mates and with their teachers.

*Self-Direction the Key.* Guidance functions of the school, since they deal with human personalities, cannot be compartmentalized. These functions are related to the curriculum, methods of instruction, the school health program, physical education and recreation, home and community relations and a myriad of others. All are concerned with the same thing, helping the adolescents understand themselves, their abilities and interests, helping them extend, create and change their long range purposes, helping them see the paths to these goals and helping them find within themselves and in their environment the goal resources to get where they want to go.

The final goals of guidance are self-responsibility, self-discovery, self-realization and self-direction in a democratic social order.

[14] Witty, Paul. "An Analysis of the Personality Traits of the Effective Teacher." *Journal of Educational Research* 40: 662-71; May 1947.

## *Leadership in Our Fields*

The educational aims of health education, physical education and recreation for the adolescent should not fail to include self-discovery, self-revelation and opportunity for self-assertion under friendly guidance. Distorted meanings in the concept of self, self-depreciation or self-negation due to peculiarities of physical development should be of real concern to workers in the three related fields. In adolescence, changes in size and form, together with new stimulations from developing organs, bring observable changes making the adolescent feel queer and new and different. The adolescent's beliefs in regard to himself and his relationships toward his peers are the fundamental determinants of what he does. The educational leader not earnestly searching for the principles of human development which help him to understand the dynamics of human personality and the structure of human relations is like the blacksmith not knowing the principles of metallurgy; he will never get us very far.

Situations act upon persons. We as leaders and applied social scientists on the athletic field, in the gymnasium or in the craft shop must study the situations that act upon adolescents as fully and as systematically as we would study internal physiological changes. Whether we observe neurotic behavior, exemplified by frustration and aggression or similar evidence of "storm and stress," or whether we observe evidences of good mental health and personal-social adjustment indicative of satisfactory human relations, depends upon the capacity of the situations we set up to provide free expression and opportunity for the satisfaction of basic personality needs in a socially acceptable and educationally desirable manner. Powerful natural impulses cannot be destroyed. Our task is to alter their modes of seeking expression—i.e., aggression may find its outlet in football. Status may be achieved by contributing to a common goal through group membership. Camping may provide adventure, excitement and new experience.

If we believe in the principles of mental hygiene, situations in physical education, athletics and recreation must be so structured socially that adolescent goal realization in the area of human relations is encouraged and not frustrated. This means that we must help the student find goal resources within himself, within others and within the situation. Goal satisfaction must become a possibility. We must create social situations so that chances, conditions, materials and experiences are available for use by adolescents seeking to meet their needs as they try to achieve real maturity.

What we *are* as teachers speaks so loudly that the student cannot hear what we *say*. The teacher as a leader must be a goal resource and a model for the student. The student must identify himself with what the teacher represents and the teacher must represent what he teaches. The technique of identification is effective in our fields and stresses the importance of coaches, teachers and recreation leaders as models and ideals, as guides to conduct and achievement, to social sensitivity and democratic human relations.

## Bibliography

ANGYAL, ANDRAS. *Foundations for a Science of Personality*. New York: Commonwealth Fund, 1941.

BENEDICT, RUTH. *Patterns of Culture*. Boston: Houghton Mifflin Co., 1934.

CASSIDY, ROSALIND, and KOZMAN, HILDA CLUTE. *Counseling Girls in a Changing Society*. New York: McGraw-Hill Book Co., 1947.

CLAYTON, ALFRED S. *Emergent Mind and Education*. Teachers College Contributions to Education No. 867. New York: Columbia University Press, 1943.

COWELL, CHARLES C. "Physical Education as Applied Social Science." *Educational Research Bulletin*, The Ohio State University. 16: 147-55; September 1937.

COWELL, CHARLES C. "The Guidance Functions and Possibilities of Physical Education." *Journal of the American Association for Health, Physical Education and Recreation*. 20: 238-39; April 1949.

COWELL, CHARLES C. "Mental Hygiene Functions and Possibilities of Play and Physical Education." *Elementary School Journal*. 50: 196-203; December 1949.

FLEMING, CHARLOTTE M. *Adolescence*. New York: International Universities Press, 1949.

FURFEY, PAUL H. "The Group Life of the Adolescent." *Journal of Educational Sociology*. 14: 195-204; December 1940.

HARTSHORNE, HUGH, and MAY, MARK A. *Studies in Deceit*. New York: Macmillan Co., 1928.

HAVIGHURST, ROBERT J. *Developmental Tasks and Education*. Chicago: University of Chicago Press, 1948.

HAVIGHURST, ROBERT J., and TABA, HILDA. *Adolescent Character and Personality*. New York: John Wiley and Sons, 1949.

KOZMAN, HILDA CLUTE; CASSIDY, ROSALIND; and JACKSON, CHESTER O. *Methods in Physical Education*. Philadelphia: W. B. Saunders Co., 1947.

LYND, ROBERT S., and LYND, HELEN M. *Middletown*. New York: Harcourt, Brace and Co., 1929.

LYND, ROBERT S., and LYND, HELEN M. *Middletown in Transition*. New York: Harcourt, Brace and Co., 1937.

MEAD, GEORGE H. *Mind, Self and Society*. Chicago: University of Chicago Press, 1934.

MEEK, LOIS H., and OTHERS. *The Personal-Social Development of Boys and Girls*. New York: Progressive Education Association, 1940.

MORENO, JACOB L. *Who Shall Survive?* Washington, D. C.: Nervous and Mental Diseases Publishing Co., 1947.

MURPHY, GARDNER. *Personality—A Biosocial Approach to Origins and Structure*. New York: Harper and Brothers, 1947.

MURPHY, GARDNER; MURPHY, LOIS BARCLAY; and NEWCOMB, THEODORE M. *Experimental Social Psychology*. Revised edition. New York: Harper and Brothers, 1937.

MURRAY, HENRY A. *Explorations in Personality*. New York: Oxford University Press, 1938.

NATIONAL SOCIETY FOR THE STUDY OF EDUCATION. *Adolescence*. Forty-Third Yearbook, Part I. Chicago: University of Chicago Press, 1944.

PLANT, JAMES S. *Personality and the Cultural Pattern*. New York: Commonwealth Fund, 1937.

PRESCOTT, DANIEL, editor. *Emotion and the Educative Process*. Washington, D. C.: American Council on Education, 1938.

REDL, FRITZ. *The Need Concept and Its Place in Educational Planning*. Division of Child Development and Teacher Personnel, Commission on Teacher Education. Washington, D. C.: American Council on Education, 1940. Mimeo.

WITTY, PAUL. "An Analysis of the Personality Traits of the Effective Teacher." *Journal of Educational Research*. 40: 662-71; May 1947.

WRIGHT, HERBERT F. "How the Psychology of Motivation Is Related to Curriculum Development." *Journal of Educational Psychology*. 39: 149-56; November 1948.

# CHAPTER TEN

# Concepts and Attitudes
# To Be Developed

BERNICE MILBURN MOORE

ADOLESCENTS and their world have been described and analyzed
from the point of view of physical, emotional and social
growth. From this has come insight into an important stage in
the growth process, through which all pass physically but at which
some become blocked emotionally, socially and intellectually.

Of particular importance to the transition from adolescence to
maturity is the development in concept-attitude structure which
has to do with the premises on which behavior is based. Increasing
maturity in the sense of the ability to function as self-disciplined
and responsible persons in a democratic society is the growth-goal
for adolescence.

Development of democratic relations is dependent upon democratic attitudes and values so closely integrated into personality
that they are always discernible in behavior with and toward others.
Such attitudes and values arise out of experiences with mature
persons who live them skilfully. Teachers, parents, youth leaders
and ministers are of major importance in this developmental aspect
of adolescence; nor are the teachers the least of these. How teachers
teach, their objectives, their own relationship patterns are of the
utmost importance to the maturing youth. Nowhere are these influences felt with greater impact in the educational process than in
the fields dealing with persons and their basic relations with themselves and with others—health education, physical education, recreation and home and family life.

Though maturity as a dynamic concept has been described in the previous chapter, perhaps it will not be amiss to redescribe it in concepts man has developed for its description over the ages he has used language. This vocabulary is shaped by the culture out of which it is formed, and in the concepts of that particular culture.

The mature person in a democratic country is the man who knows and understands the meaning of freedom. He lives with independence and with integrity. He has honor and he is loyal. He believes and practices justice in his human relations to the best of his ability and understanding. He has a philosophy of life, a value structure which directs his attitudes and his acts. He has full knowledge of the meaning and implications of words which have become concepts in his own society. His conceptual thinking is worthy of the dignity and character of mature man. His value-attitude pattern is oriented around respect for self and respect for others as well.

## Conceptual Thinking of Adolescents

The ideal mature man, as heretofore described, never exists as a real person. He is a value toward which persons strive throughout life. Individual man, the living functioning being, measures up in some aspects of maturity and down in others. But he does have one very important aspect in common with the never-realized ideal. His thinking is more highly conceptual than personalized. He is socially oriented rather than personally oriented.

Value judgments, in the mature, are based on broad experience and basic human understanding. Attitudes are positive and creative rather than negative and destructive. Actions have a high degree of consistency with concepts, values and attitudes. Judgments, therefore, tend to be fair and tolerance broad. Relationships, with such socially related persons, are understanding and sympathetic. Permissiveness arises from faith in fellow men and from conviction in the validity of the philosophy of live and let live.

Emotion is not absent in the thinking and acting of the mature person, but he demands facts as the basis for decision. Decisions may be in error, since every human makes errors in judgment and interpretation, but reasons and emotions have balanced out in decisions reached. Fanaticism is not used as an escape from problems which must be faced. Convictions are held, but they can be and are often changed.

Keys to such personality integration are numerous, but one of the more important is the development of conceptual thinking out of rich, varied and broad experience. Concepts are nothing more nor less than the idea of what a thing in general should be. Concepts are "mental images" of things formed by "generalizations from particulars," to quote Webster. The broader the experiences in "particular" from which the "generalizations" are derived, the sounder the value pattern on which the particulars are generalized, the more mature is the emotional-social-intellectual life of the individual.

Conceptual thinking is, of course, thinking in terms of the abstract. It is thinking of a situation or an act *plus*. The *plus* side of the picture is its implications, its ramifications and its generalizations. However, to come to understand the implications, the ramifications, and to draw generalizations from a situation or from an act, demand breadth of understanding based on wide and various experience. As Harry Overstreet puts it, the knowledge links to the environment must be strong.

## Adolescents and Personalized Generalizations

Adolescence is a period of personalized particulars. Generalizations, values and attitudes up to this period of development have been taken in large part from parents, teachers and other adults. However, childhood age-mates and those slightly older should not be overlooked in the understanding of the formation of attitudes and values even in childhood. But rarely are these questioned regardless of source.

During the teen trek toward independence—independence in action, in thinking, in making decisions, in behavior—the individual begins to question and throw aside the imposed and often authoritarian conceptions of good and bad, right and wrong, man and woman, grownup and child. He also begins to feel his way, more than think his way, toward new concepts out of the breadth or meagerness of his own youth experiences.

*Self-Centered Adolescence.* Adolescence is a period of growth where attention and concern are centered on self. Physical growth and change create a new awareness of body. Not since the person was a small child, literally in process of discovering himself, did he feel as conscious of himself as a physical being. Arms and legs seem to get in the way. New body contours, the budding promise of maturation, are very evident to the youth. He feels they are equally evident to others. Concern is felt if change is not as rapid as he assumes it to be in his fellow youth, and concern is felt if development appears to be more rapid. On either hand, consciousness of physical self is a part of his years of rapid maturation.

For the majority of children in the culture, childhood is a period of family-centered living. Always what the family does, what the family thinks, what the family gives is of greater importance than what any other group does, thinks or gives. Children find their play around home base and families see that play is home based. The first concern of children is primarily with acceptance by the family and security in the family. And the next is, of course, acceptance by the neighborhood play group. Protection by parents, or surrogate parents, is a part of everyday living, and it is an essential protection on physical, emotional, intellectual and social fronts. Children, no matter what their social class, must be taken care of for physical survival and for emotional and social security.

Adolescence is a period of peer group-centered living. Youth in the teen years is tremendously interested in and greatly impressed by the life of its own age group and the security which comes from belonging. The individual begins to take a position in his own age group similar to that which he will attain among adults when he reaches adulthood.

Wise parents during this period of transition from childhood to adulthood continue their protective role, but with a difference. Adolescents still need to be guarded against the full impact of adult responsibility and the irresponsibility of immature and unhealthy adults. But protection by parents or teachers cannot and should not be obvious. The more subtle the guidance toward acceptable living and away from the dangers of living, the more accepted it is by the adolescent.

Adolescence has as one of its characteristics a high degree of impatience. It is impatient with itself, its world and with the elders in its world. To be grown up is considered a highly desirable state. To be neither grown up nor a child is both confusing and irritating. Nor does our society offer much assistance in going through this period of "neither-nor." Adolescents do not have a place of their own in our culture. No "real jobs" exist save continuing with "the preliminaries," as one wise young person expressed it. This leads to an increasing attention to self because of the mounting desire to "get somewhere" and "in a hurry."

Children tend to think in action words and terms. Their values and their attitudes are from their elders. They accept and they do. When childhood is past and adolescence becomes reality, concepts begin to develop in terms of expanded horizons and age-mate influences. Value judgments begin to be analyzed and new values formed. But interpretation of concepts, of generalizations, of attitudes and of values, tends to remain centered about self. These are highly personalized. Interpretations of implications are in relation to the immediate youth future and to their immediate value to youth rather than in long range goals as viewed against their social worth.

## Attitudes, Values and Personal Conflict

All living is governed by the attitude-value duo. Attitudes are the tendencies of individuals to act toward a given situation or given persons in a given way. Values, on the other hand, are the directing forces toward or away from which we act. Values away from which we act are those which we deem detrimental to society. Youth learns the negatives as truly as the positives in our value situations. Values always color attitudes; and attitudes always color values. Equilibrium between the two is essential for mature living and peace of mind.

Many of the conflicts of individuals and most of the conflicts of groups arise out of disequilibrium between attitudes and values. Values may be held which are inconsistent with attitudes and actions. Attitudes may not support instilled values. As Gunnar Myrdal [1] has pointed out in *An American Dilemma,* it is just such a

[1] Myrdal, Gunnar. *An American Dilemma.* New York: Harper and Brothers, 1944.

conflict of attitudes and values which dominates intergroup relations in the United States today. In a democracy with its basis in
Christian doctrine, the brotherhood of man and the integrity of
personality are accepted as essential values for "the good life."
But our attitudes toward different national and color groups and
our actions resulting from our attitudes are diametrically opposed
to our value structure, to our philosophy, to our faith. Until attitudes and values are harmonized, conflicts within the individual
and among groups will be embittered by an attempt to justify an
uneasy conscience.

Adolescents find themselves in a not too different situation in
relation to their attitudes and values toward their families and
toward other dominant adults in their sphere of influence. Children
in our society are supposed to respect parents, older relatives,
teachers, ministers, group leaders and, in general, other adults.
Obedience and respect have often been confused in their meaning.

"Mother knows best" has been drilled into the child as a social
fact. Father is respected because he is "father," not because of
his own worth. Teachers are well-informed and better trained.
Youth leaders must be given help in order to "keep the group"
functioning. Ministers are men of reverence. Grandparents must
be treated with proper dignity because of their age.

Teen age youth begin to question . . . and rightly so . . .
whether "mother always knows best"; whether father is really all
his position in the family implies; whether "what teacher says is
always so," whether all youth leaders must be supported even if
they are bunglers in their human relations. But because acceptance
of values given by adults has been a part of childhood, a guilty
conscience over this questioning becomes a very real part of
adolescence.

The more common form of youth action which indicates the
questioning attitude is that whatever the family does is wrong.
Parents become deeply concerned over this particular phase of
intellectual and emotional growth. They tend to take personally
the criticism the adolescent centers upon them, not because they are
all wrong, but because they happen to be immediately available
as the target for youth's developing critical attitude. Teachers come

upon the same cynicism, the same attitude of "prove it or I don't believe it," but in a less emotionalized, less personalized and less articulate form. Difficulties in relationships arise if the adolescents themselves are troubled or made to feel guilty because of their questioning of heretofore accepted absolutes. They are troubled by their sudden ability to see the family with penetrating clarity. They are somewhat frightened at their desire to get away, to do and to live differently. Nonetheless, what they are experiencing is one manifestation of the desire for independence. Granted they express it adequately and emotionally, if not understood by parents and teachers the resulting conflict between their newly-formed attitudes and their family values, arrived at through their years of childhood, may lead to severe emotional difficulty. The adults should offer help in resolving the conflict by accepting its manifestation for what it is—a part of the intellectual-emotional growth process.

## Adolescent and Mature Concepts and Attitudes

An examination of positive values accepted more or less universally in our culture will illustrate the transitional state of adolescent thinking and the emotional content of this thinking.

### The Adolescent Wants "To Be Free"

*Freedom.* Freedom is a fundamental value in a democratic society and a fundamental concept for mature functioning in such a society. Freedom to the adolescent is a highly desirable and personalized goal. Interpretation of freedom for him is "to be free," "to be free from restraint," "to be free from authority," "to live without being disciplined." Since the adolescent feels himself an independent being "bounded only by his own skin," as a wise philosopher put it, his concept of freedom is equally person-centered.

Adults who have grown out of emotional, social and intellectual adolescence recognize freedom as a relative, a social fact. Freedom is never freedom from authority, but freedom under the rules of the particular society. Freedom is never without discipline but with self-responsibility and self-discipline. Maturity accepts the fact that all living is social, that all personal desires are adjusted to desires and wishes of others. Recognition is gained that complete freedom would mean anarchy. Freedom in a democracy is freedom controlled and limited to equal opportunity to be as free as living well with others will permit. In other words, the mature person in our society accepts the reality of interdependence and as Hearn pointed out in Chapter 2, has achieved a satisfactory balance between his dependence and independence needs.

Transition from the interpretation of freedom as the adolescent sees it, "freedom from" to freedom as the mature adult sees it, "freedom within," is one of the major essentials of growing up. Many adults never make this necessary step in their conceptual thinking. Their attitudes, therefore, remain on the level of "fighting authority," of "demanding freedom," of "resentment of interference." On many fronts in our social life we find the reality-fact of living with and doing with others in definite conflict with a value structure which holds "every man for himself" as its central thesis.

*Independence.* Independence is one of the most desired attributes as far as the adolescent is concerned. He sincerely, and sometimes desperately, wants to be the master of his own fate. But many things in our society are against an early assumption of independence. The primary block is economic. Jobs for teen agers who, of necessity, must work, are limited. Jobs for teen agers who would like to work are even more scarce. Apprenticeship is almost a thing of the past, and when it remains a part of job training, apprentices are usually young men or women out of school.

Educational demands have also played a part. In-school years have been lengthened by families themselves for all youth, but compulsory school age has been steadily rising farther and farther into adolescence. College training is not only considered essential for the lower middle-class and upper middle-class youth, an assured fact for the upper-class boys and girls, but is more and more becoming recognized by the upper-lower status group as a necessary stepping stone to rising in the class structure.

Again, as the science of human relations becomes more and more developed, understanding is being gained that emotional and social, as well as economic security must be furnished adolescents through their transitional years into adulthood.

Independence for the adult means some measure of economic sufficiency, self-determination, self-control, and a degree of social responsibility. Independence, as dreamed of by the adolescent, is the freedom to "do as I please," "to determine my own next steps," "to make up my own mind." To accomplish each of these entails economic independence, an educational level sufficient to brook stiff competition in earning a living, and emotional maturity sufficient to withstand the shock of adult social life.

Adolescent independence is sensed as a highly desirable state for the individual. Little thought is given to responsibilities which go with such a state. Independence to the adolescent is somewhat feared, since it is more sensed than understood. Even though youth live with independent adults in the home, in the community and school situation, rarely do they seem to gain from such experience the full implications of freedom from economic, emotional and social protection as afforded by the family and by society. Rarely do youth, and too rarely do many adults, realize that independence in itself arises out of interdependence with others. No individual is ever successful or a failure in and of himself. His own temperamental set combined with the impact of his experiences with the people with whom he lives determines how independently he may live and how successful or how unsuccessful his independent living may be.

Charles Horton Cooley, one of the great pioneers in social psychology, calls personality "our social selves," or "our looking glass selves," which even makes our personality a product of dependence on and with others. He says we behave or act as we think others would wish us to act.[2] Social roles, therefore, are played by each in relation to the others in his life. What we are is what we judge others expect and want us to be. To gain this concept of self is a sophisticated process. To come to full realization of it is definitely a sign of maturity. Judgment of what others expect of us, to be valid, must be based on experience in satisfactory human relations on many fronts. Only in this way is consistency in behavior obtained. Only in this way is independence within interdependence really achieved.

[2] Cooley, Charles Horton. *Social Organization: A Study of the Larger Mind.* New York: Charles Scribner's Sons, 1909.

## The Adolescent Wants "Fair Play"

*Justice.* Justice is something the adolescent usually understands in relation to his own age group, to his peers. How the rules are applied to his fellows at school, at home and in sports is important as the applications relate to himself and to those of his associates whom he respects and admires. Justice, interpreted in the light of mature democratic experience, is concerned with justice before God, justice before the law and justice in the economic and social order. If justice as an ultimate value is accepted by the culture in which persons live, then its interpretation is always in terms of justice for each person and justice for all as well. The adolescent sees it as justice for himself and for his own age group as meted out by his elders.

*Equality.* Perhaps no concept in democratic philosophy is more difficult to understand than that of equality. Adults, in chronological age and mature in many phases of their emotional development, no less than youth, find themselves confused over what equality in a democratic society really means.

Equality, to the adolescent, tends to be interpreted as "Exactly the same as," or "not different from." Companions are "equal" if they dress alike, act very much alike, use much the same vocabulary, date in an almost ritualistic pattern, and belong to similar groups of peers. Physical differences, discrepancies in intellectual interests and attainments, and especially social variations identify one in the adolescent world as "inferior" or "beyond the pale." Many adults find it equally difficult to accept variations in appearance, intellectual performance and social attitudes and values without judging the different as superior or inferior.

Equality, as a concept of democratic living, of necessity must be based on something other than sameness. By the very nature of man, men are not and cannot be identical. Individuals differ in capacities, certain temperamental characteristics, as well as in physical appearance. Opportunities for growth and development vary as widely as do those of the child of the multi-millionaire and the street sweeper. In addition to social and economic status, the community and its schools, churches, recreational facilities and general emotional climate are determining factors in individual differences. Denial of differences as social and emotional facts does not establish equality in the meaning of identical as a fact in democratic society.

As Herbert Agar has so well pointed out in *Time for Greatness,* mature individuals have clarified their conception of what equality means in a society based on democratic principles. Equality, Agar says, is equality in something: in opportunity to grow and develop, to learn and earn, to share in what the culture has to offer; equality in justice and before God.[3]

Again, equality in a democratic society may be interpreted by the mature person as "comparable in performance," "adequate for" and "sufficient unto" the demands of living. This interpretation of equality accepts individual differences as a fact, but accepts as well the potentiality of the individual to become an emotionally and socially mature adult.

Equality, thus interpreted, demands fundamental understanding of individual differences and acceptance of them. Morever, it has within it an appreciation for the minute division of labor in a democratic and technological society and the contribution of each segment of the society, no matter how small, to the welfare of the whole. Fundamental security within self is essential also to see that equality does not mean "one cannot afford to be different" or cannot afford to accept the contributions of those who are different as of equal importance.

When the adolescent has come to the point of inner security and personal growth where he can afford to differ from his peers, he has taken a long step toward understanding equality in its social meaning. When he can afford to be seen with and have friendship for those who differ from him, still another step toward mature conceptual interpretation of equality has been taken. When he can accept with tolerance ideas, attitudes and behaviors which do not fit into his own little world, he has completed his transition from a personalized definition of equality as "the same" to the socialized interpretation of "comparable in performance," "adequate in handling situations," and "sufficient unto" the demands of living.

[3] Agar, Herbert. *A Time for Greatness.* New York: Little, Brown and Co., 1942.

## The Adolescent Wants To Belong

*Loyalty.* Loyalty is a value in the teen years. The paramount loyalty of the adolescent is usually to his own age group. Many of the conflicts in this period of development arise out of conflicting loyalties to parents and to age-mates, out of loyalties to values of mother and father as contrasted to newer values being tried out by youth of similar age and development. Some teen-agers never get to the developmental task of solving such conflicts. Loyalty, as fidelity to a set of principles and to groups of persons who live by these principles, is of later development.

*Integrity.* Outstanding characteristics of adolescents are inconsistency in behavior, fluctuating values and changing attitudes. No doubt some of the inconsistency arises out of conflicting claims of peer affiliation and adult authority. Behavior from day to day varies with mood, with current demands and with new experiences. Behavior at home with the family may be exemplary, but outside the control of family and with the peer group it may leave much to be desired. Behavior in school may be erratic and unpredictable, but behavior on the football field or in social activities may be consistent and always recognizable as stemming from the same motivating force.

Adolescents have difficulty in understanding integrity as a quality of being complete, of being consistent, of being undivided in one's attitudes, values and behavior. Integrity might be described as the "core of consistency" which identifies the personality as the same personality in each situation or which identifies the individual of many social roles as a total and consistent unit.

The adolescent is in process of choosing his values, of setting up his goals, whereby his behavior may become predictable in the light of these. He cannot be expected to act with the consistency of an adult. He is only coming into an understanding of what integrity means. He is in process of trying out responses to situations until he finds those which fit him more comfortably into participation with his fellow men.

Integrity or consistency in behavior is desirable from the point of view of the adolescent because it offers more individual comfort in living. It is an essential from the viewpoint of the adult because one cannot be trusted to carry out one's share of responsibility in living when behavior varies from day to day or situation to situation. The adolescent wants the security of integrity in behavior and sees it as a hazy goal. The adult demands integrity in his fellow men so that dependence can be placed in them for their share in the solutions of the problems of living.

To obtain predictability, to obtain wholeness of personality, to acquire consistency in role playing regardless of the social situation, to gain personal integrity and completeness, is a never ending process throughout living. But when attitudes become social, when values become selfless rather than self-centered, such integrity is more nearly achieved. Here again can be seen an illustration of the personalization of experience into self-centered thinking which is characteristic of adolescence in contrast to the mature value pattern of the adult.

## Building a Philosophy of Life

A philosophy of life is nothing more nor less than a set of principles or values by which the individual attempts to live. These principles or values by which the individual attempts to live as interpreted by the adolescent have one end in view. They must be principles which assure belonging, which assure acceptance, which make for popularity with fellow teen-agers. Because the adolescent needs reassurance and assurance of himself, because he has his fears and his very real insecurities, because he feels himself neither "fish nor fowl" in the adult world toward which he is growing, he must feel acceptance by his own group. Principles of living, therefore, which make for unpopularity, which make for behavior different from that of the major part of his age group, cannot be allowed to enter into his philosophy of life. Hence "drips" are those adolescents whose behavior is more nearly in line with adult attitudes and values and in conflict with peer group demands.

Adults have learned that principles or values lived by with consistency and integrity in all behavior very often do not lead either to belonging in their age group or to acceptance by their peers. Need for reassurance in maturity is less, of course. Or rather it arises from other than personalized sources. Small children are dependent upon their parents for their security. Adolescents turn from parents to their own age-mates, but nonetheless gain their feeling of security from others rather than from being sure of competence in self. Men and women find their security in their belief in themselves, in their ability to handle their problems, in their achievement, in their relationships with other adults.

## Adolescent and Mature Relations

Human relations, in all their variations, have their basis in an all important concept, the concept of self. Self, as psychiatric, psychological and sociological study has revealed, in the life of the child, is self-centeredness. The concept is that of "I" and "mine." Association with others, the adults serving childhood needs, is association for self-gratification and self-comfort. "We-ness," the social self, is not achieved, if ever, until the relatedness of the individual to his fellow individuals and to the society created by him and them is realized and understood.

Maturity and immaturity might well be described in the pronouns of "I" and "we." Self-centered, narrow, in-turned living identifies the individual whose concept of self has never expanded out of the "I" centered concept of childhood. Social-centered, outward turned, broadly tolerant living is accomplished by those who see themselves as related to others, as interdependent with others, as literally the products of life with others.

Stages of growth, of course, are discernible in the concept of self as in any other. The infant is the complete egoist. The child discovers "I" because there are other "I's." The adolescent is still chiefly "I" centered, but is rapidly learning the importance of "we." The mature adult sees himself always in relationship with others—children, youth or adults.

### Family Relations

Family relations, for the adolescent, are often fraught with danger as far as making adequate transition from the "I" to the "we" way of thinking and acting is concerned. Many parents tend to treat as immature and foolish the ideas expressed by their adolescent sons or daughters. Concepts of adolescents may be fully mature for the growth stage in which they are. This should be recognized. Maturity needs to be seen as a dynamic for growth rather than as a static condition to be gained and eternally held.

Criticism of family and home should be understood as development of the ability to see the family and home objectively. A little humor instead of hurt feelings can balance negative criticism. Families are not perfect. Family members are not perfect. Insight is always considered a measure of individual maturity. Insight as to strengths and weaknesses in the family is an equally valid measure of maturity though not so often used. When youth are learning to look at the family from an outsider's point of view, it is definitely a sign of growth and maturation. Young people may need help to see the family's strengths as well as its insufficiencies. They should not be made to feel guilty because they are critical.

Actually it is this critical attitude toward family which makes possible the improvement of family living. If each generation accepted as perfect the behavior and practices of the last, no change would take place. Each younger generation should be helped by the older to understand family and community as they really are. Thus opportunity is offered for betterment of human relations in both these areas.

Democratic families are the first assurance that adolescents will become mature adults in their conceptual thinking and reasoning. Such families live with consistency between their democratic values and their attitudes and behaviors.

## Boy-Girl and Man-Woman Relations

Conceptual development and growth can be seen, as well, in the differences between the value structure surrounding boy-girl relations as contrasted with man-woman relations in adult living.

Adolescent girls measure their personal success in terms of attractiveness to boys, in numbers of dates, in so-called popularity. When dates are not numerous or do not come with any degree of regularity during adolescent days, acute feelings of inferiority develop and serious problems of behavior may arise to overcome this very real feeling of insufficiency in a much desired human relation. Boys, and girls as well, find it necessary to be popular with the other sex if they are to "rate" in their own youth community. Timidity, awkwardness, inexperience, lack of opportunity for association with the opposite sex on an every day basis, may lead to all manner of unsocial behavior in other situations.

Standards of what it takes to be popular and how popularity is defined are set by the middle class. However, as Margaret Mead has stated in *Male and Female,* the tendency in each class group in the culture is toward publicized, glorified, fictionalized middle class patterns.[4]

With greater freedom than any group of adolescents in history, teen-agers find themselves face to face with problems of petting— to pet or not to pet; how far to go and when to stop; "does one have to pet to be popular" or "to be a good scout"; who sets the limits, boy or girl. Marriage, to the adolescent, very often appears as the way out of this dilemma. Marriage, to many adolescents, means freedom from controls in sex relations and freedom from restraints of home and parents. Nor is this concept of marriage surprising when one remembers preoccupation with physical development, with sexual maturation, with freedom and independence, which are very real developmental tasks of youth.

Younger adolescents often have no real concept of the relationship of boy-girl dating and petting other than its immediate value in personal rating. Few have an understanding of boy-girl adolescent experiences as a prelude to successful marriage. Few have a positive set of values in regard to sex relations which holds them steady as they build toward satisfactory sex relations in marriage. Marriage as the relationship of man and woman for the mutual development of personalities, as the basic relation for the creation of new life, as the mutual sharing of responsibility, as the basic social-affectional relation in all human living, has not become apparent to them. Why it has not since they have lived in families where parents are married is one of the puzzling questions of the day.

## Community Problems

It must be recognized that a youth world does exist. In our culture, this adolescent society is too much isolated from the adult world

---

[4] Mead, Margaret. *Male and Female.* New York: William Morrow and Co., 1949, p. 281-95.

into which it leads. Full acceptance of the adolescent is assured only by his peers, and not always by them if he follows too closely the demands of adults. Adults tend to accept him on a childhood level one day and expect him to act on an adult level the next. Too rarely do parents, teachers, ministers, youth leaders and others accept the adolescent as an *adolescent*.

Time to youth is the immediate. Goals are goals for today. To-morrow seems a long way off. To bring tomorrow closer, chances to share in adult living should be a part of youth life. At the same time, no attempt should be made to force adolescents into adult-hood with no real transition 'from childhood. Values desirable for adult living in a democracy are implanted in individuals from childhood. Acceptance without evaluation is the child's reaction to them. Evaluation on the base of limited experience is the adoles-cent's reaction to these values. Evaluation on the base of broad social experience should be the adult's reaction to them.

Experiences which adults may offer youth toward social per-spective in living are of two different types. Associational experi-ences, formal and informal, real and vicarious, are extremely im-portant. Actional or active experiences, where the immediate is interpreted in the light of ultimates, are equally important.

Associations with adults which are most important to the adoles-cent are those with parents, teachers, recreational and religious lead-ers, and with "the boss" if the boy or girl is working. At no period in living do adults need to display their own emotional balance and their own value structure more clearly than when they are working with adolescents. Children may not realize inconsistencies be-tween attitudes and values in adults. Youth never miss the implica-tions of the act as counter to the value expressed or implied.

## Objectives in the Area of Human Relations

The content of concepts, the value orientation of concepts, like the adolescent himself, is in process of growth and development during the teen years. The developmental aspects of thinking-feeling-understanding pass from the direct action words and thoughts of childhood to the personalized conceptual thinking of adolescents, to the socialized concepts and values of mature adults.

As no stage in physical growth can be skipped or eliminated, so no stage in the developmental process of use of knowledge and experience in thinking should be skipped. The important question is not what to do to make the concepts and values of adolescents less personalized, but how to be sure that conceptual thinking passes successfully through this stage in development to the broadly oriented, other-centered reasoning and thinking so necessary for successful democratic living. Determination must be made as to what kinds of objectives leaders and teachers of adolescent youth will foster which will assure this desirable development. Life adjustment education, so much in the forefront today, is stressing practical values in the school experience for youth. No longer do educators talk of "what we teach youth," but they talk of "youth and their needs." Youth and their developmental tasks and what teachers have to offer for more effective living are becoming the keynotes of curriculum planning. The school is a supplement to family teaching in most instances. But educators are more and more realizing that in many cases the school must be a substitute for family inadequacy if youth are to have opportunities to grow into adequate maturity.

Personal and social adjustment, progression toward vocational competence, citizenship, and marriage and the family are recognized as the four main areas in living for which youth need to be educated. No small part of this education has to do with the richness of experience which makes concepts "intelligent generalizations from a wealth of particulars." It makes values and attitudes easily translatable into behavior. Personalities coming under such influences tend to become integrated wholes.

A first requirement in developing concepts and attitudes in the adolescent toward the accepted democratic values is maturity in concept structure of the adults with whom he must associate. An understanding of the adolescent himself by the emotionally mature adults in his life is a second essential. Still another aspect of the situation is the need for adults to realize there are progressive steps in development of the ability to think and act, as there are progressive steps in physical growth.

Guidance for the child is direct. Guidance for the adolescent must of necessity be indirect and subtle. If youth are to take their places as adults of integrity and equality, controls of their thinking should be loosened. Opportunities need to be given for the expression of ideas and feelings. Chance must be given for concepts to be shared and socialized.

## A Democratic Climate

Adults, whose influence upon adolescents is direct or indirect, have tremendous responsibility to create by their own acts, by their own way of living, a democratic climate in which youth experiences take place. Teachers are no less sensitive to critical evaluation by youth than parents. Evidence of this is the effect of independent thinking on test grades. Too many times when youth fail to give back what the teacher has put out as fact, grades suffer. If youth have the temerity to question teacher-stated fact, teacher reaction is as direct from grades as it is indirect from smouldering resentment of parents.

If adolescents are ever to pass through their period of personalized conceptual thinking into socialized concepts as a basis for thinking, broad experience with reasoning, criticism and evaluation is necessary both at home and at school.

Too often it is at this point where "the perpetual adolescent" is developed. If he attempts to evaluate his family or school or his relationship to it, he is stifled by adult irritation and resentment and may well give up. If he is cut short by their unwillingness to listen to and discuss his ideas, he may quit trying to develop ideas. Even more important, he may react with an intense sense of guilt. Trying to see groups, institutions and individuals as they are may become to him something undesirable or "bad." To avoid guilt feelings, he may quit thinking. Here may develop unreasoning or passive acceptance. Here may develop acceptance with underlying aggression. Here may arise a Pollyanna attitude toward life, living and the pursuit of happiness. Any one makes for adult immaturity.

Teachers, by their very position in society, represent authority. If they are insecure in themselves they cannot cover it. If they are arrested adolescents in their own thinking and action, it will show through. Their authority with adolescents will be expressed in domination, in superiority, in arrogance, in impatience. If, however, they are secure in themselves, their thinking and actions become their authority. Their integrity, their wholeness, shows through to youth in every relation. Their controls of youth are the controls of equalitarian understanding, of social justice, of personal integrity. Parents and teachers can "get by" with immature behavior with youth. Recreational and religious leaders are forced to display maturity or they are apt to be left to their own devices.

Mature adults have interests broader than self. Insights into themselves and into the world in which they live are objective. They have the ability to accept emotions as a normal and healthy part of living. Skill at meeting frustrations is their skill in problem-solving. Attitude-value patterns are in harmony. A philosophy of life guides actual behavior rather than verbal behavior. Youth need help to learn these facts of emotional maturity from the emotionally mature in their transitional years.

Adult associates who display selfishness are of no help to youth. Those who have neither insight nor humor concerning themselves or their world are a liability. Fear of emotional experiences and attempts to repress them by grown persons who are youth leaders offer little toward sound emotional maturation of adolescents. Cynicism, fanaticism or boredom as ways of meeting frustration furnish unhealthy examples to be followed by youth. Facing problems and working them out is a positive contribution. When so-called mature individuals think one way, talk another and act still another, their inconsistency is evident to adolescents with whom they work.

A philosophy of life, which is nothing more than verbal mouthings of well-worn platitudes, offers little as an example to be followed. Experiences where youth are given the responsibility for their own performances in action and for their own mistakes should be wide and varied during this period. Interpretation of these experiences by understanding adults in terms of value and meaning should be a part of them.

### Self-Direction and Self-Responsibility

Implicit in the creation of a democratic climate by democratic action of all concerned is that all procedures, methods and techniques employed with youth lead to self-direction and self-responsibility.

Instead of resentment of the desire for freedom by youth, adults should understand freedom as something every individual wants and needs. Parents should help in the attainment of freedom and independence. Action and thought of adolescents should be as free as they are capable of handling at their particular growth stage. Even more, opportunities should be planned and given for assumption of responsibility. Self-discipline is learned. The privilege of making one's own mistakes and taking the consequences is necessary for growth.

At the same time, if authority of adults over youth is handled as social control rather than as personal control, a real step forward is taken. Direct control belongs to childhood. Social control is a part of adulthood. Adolescents need to learn from adults that freedom does not mean without controls. Freedom is always relative to the authority imposed by society on those who compose it. Critical attitude on the part of the adolescent should be fostered by older persons. Positive criticism as well as negative should become understood. An objective critical attitude is expected of mature men and women. One does not and cannot learn to be objective and critical unless one has the opportunity to learn how to analyze and weigh situations. Attitudes should come to be seen as directly related to values. Realization that there are negative values away from which we live as well as positive values toward which we live is a sign of maturation.

Again, work habits at school and in the home should be developed out of many opportunities to do worthwhile tasks. Value in work done should lie not only in what it does for the boy or girl but also in what it does for the group. Work habits at school should be understood as preludes to work habits on the job. They are a part and parcel of the same thing.

## Cooperation and Sharing

Many opportunities should be offered adolescents to work and play together, boys and girls, boys with boys and girls with girls. Group projects which have as their main emphasis cooperative sharing should be many and varied. Experience is the basis of all thinking and reasoning. Persons do not think in a vacuum.

To offer youth opportunity to pass from a person-centered world
to a social-centered one, they need experience which helps them
to see themselves as a part of a total social pattern. Too often
adolescents see themselves as isolates in a social picture. Moreover, they need to be assisted to gain long range perspective. "Preliminaries" should be sold to youth. Adults may offer opportunities
for them to see their ultimate value. Adults may well help youth
gain an understanding that "what is best for me right now" must
always be seen in relation to "what is best for all of us right now
and tomorrow."

*Boy-Girl Relations.* Opportunities for happy, normal, gay work
and play experiences, boys and girls together, should be many.
Dating is only one aspect of training toward mature man-woman
relationships. Men and women in our society work shoulder to
shoulder on jobs, in communities, at home, in parenthood. To gain
respect for each other as persons, as well as members of different
sexes, demands many and varied mutual experiences. Similarities
in capabilities, in emotional maturities, in social adaptiveness, can
be discovered through association.

Such experiences help youth see sex differences in proper perspective. Sex relations are only one part of man-woman relations.
Teaching of relationships between sexes has been weighted entirely
too heavily from the point of view of the physical and from the
point of view of negative values. When emphasis is placed on growth
toward emotional adequacy, sex tends to take its normal place in
the scheme of things. When social effectiveness and intellectual
breadth become ends for good living, positive attitudes toward
men and women result. Attitudes and values in relation to sex
become positive goals to be achieved in adulthood. To far too many
youth, sex relations are interpreted as negative acts to be avoided
in adolescence and youth.

Positive values and attitudes toward sex do not arise out of
knowledge of physiology and hygiene. A basic knowledge of the
psychology of sex is necessary. Even more necessary to mature
happiness in marriage is a set of attitudes toward men and women
which have as their basis mutual respect. An understanding of the
comparable contributions of each sex to the on-going and well-being

of society is a necessity. Emotional stability on the part of each is essential in meeting problems of everyday living as well as the more intimate problems of marriage and parenthood.

Discussions of a wide variety of problems of living between boys and girls cannot be overemphasized. Such discussions are effective in development of attitudes and values, which make for happier relations between men and women on the job, in the community and in marriage. Sharing of ideas, points of view, agreements and disagreements do much to develop objectivity. The guidance of understanding, intelligent adults gives a broad base for concept content.

*Democracy in Living.* To achieve for youth an interpretation of democracy as a way of living demands that it be lived every day. Family, school, church and recreational groups should offer demonstrations of equality, justice, cooperation, integrity and tolerance. Social situations in which youth are participants need to constantly illustrate skill in human relations.

Democracy demands two things: respect for the individual regardless of his age or ability, and respect for the needs of individuals in groups. Teen-agers feel themselves as highly individualistic. They need desperately to have their personalities respected by adults. They need, as well, participation in groups in order that group needs may be seen in relation to the satisfaction of individual needs.

*Education for Family Life.* Home and family life education for youth and for adults in the United States is widening the horizons of understanding of millions of parents and future parents. They are coming to see the necessity of democratic values lived every day in the family if democracy is to survive as a way of government. Moreover, this same education helps parents and future parents to understand that democracy is a way of life which offers the individual opportunity to develop to the height of his potentials for his own personal fulfilment and for his most effective social service to his community, his nation and his world.

*School Relationships and Social Growth.* Again, responsibility for self in group participation can be practiced in every school situation if the teacher is alert to possibilities. Independence of action in the interdependent group is always a possibility. Freedom to plan, to make decisions, to succeed and to fail are all potentials in every health education, physical education and recreation group, in every homemaking class, in every social science situation. Co-operation as a method of meeting individual and group needs is always there when the group leader has maturity to act and be cooperative in relation to youth. An understanding of self in relation to other selves can always be gained in informal, active, effective participation. Learning of physical needs, of emotional and social growth, of home and family, of the community and society offers self and social understanding.

Health education, physical education and recreation in high school and in college, as well as homemaking education and the social sciences, carry a large share of the responsibility for furnishing a wealth of rich experiences to youth toward selflessness in living rather than toward self-centeredness. By the very nature of these educational areas, they treat of the stuff of everyday living. By the informal method of teaching, by the consistent use of democratic practices in relationships, through the laboratory technique in gymnasium, on the playing field, in the homemaking cottage, in the project oriented social science division, a wide variety of stimulating social and personal experiences in human understanding are possible. Moreover, because of the close contact and intimate association of youth with teachers—more on the counselor-youth base than most classroom teachers—associational experiences between the adult and youth world are more real and more possible. When health is understood as total health—physical, emotional, intellectual and social—when health is seen as the opposite of "dis-ease," when human behavior is understood as symptomatic of underlying needs, when developmental tasks of each age group are understood, then experiences offered to youth will always be geared toward development into intellectual, social and emotional maturity symbolized by a body efficiently managed and thoroughly understood.[5]

[5] Sincere appreciation is herewith expressed to Dr. Carson McGuire of the Department of Educational Psychology and Dr. Harry Estill Moore of the Department of Sociology, The University of Texas. These two offered many helpful suggestions and ideas which have been incorporated in this chapter.

# Bibliography

AGAR, HERBERT A. *A Time for Greatness.* New York: Little, Brown and Co., 1942.

BLOS, PETER. *The Adolescent Personality.* New York: Appleton-Century-Crofts, Inc., 1941.

BOSSARD, JAMES H. S. *The Sociology of Child Development.* New York: Harper and Brothers, 1948.

CASSIDY, ROSALIND, and KOZMAN, HILDA CLUTE. *Counseling Girls in a Changing Society.* New York: McGraw-Hill Book Co., 1947.

CLOTHIER, FLORENCE. "The Challenge of a Protracted Adolescence." *Vassar Alumnae Magazine* as reprinted in *Child-Family Digest* 1: 3-5; October 1949.

COLE, LUELLA. *Attaining Maturity.* New York: Farrar and Rinehart, 1944.

DAVIS, W. ALLISON, and HAVIGHURST, ROBERT J. *Father of the Man.* Boston: Houghton Mifflin Co., 1947.

DOLLARD, JOHN D. *Caste and Class in a Southern Town.* New Haven: Yale University Press, 1937.

DOLLARD, JOHN D., and ASSOCIATES. *Frustration and Aggression.* New Haven: Yale University Press, 1939.

FRANK, LAWRENCE K. "This Is the Adolescent." As reprinted in *Child-Family Digest* 1: 52-59; September 1949.

HAVIGHURST, ROBERT J., and TABA, HILDA. *Adolescent Character and Personality.* New York: John Wiley and Sons, 1949.

HOLLINGSHEAD, AUGUST B. *Elmtown's Youth.* New York: John Wiley and Sons, 1949.

HORNEY, KAREN. *The Neurotic Personality of Our Time.* New York: W. W. Norton and Co., 1937.

HORNEY, KAREN. *Our Inner Conflicts.* New York: W. W. Norton and Co., 1945.

LANDIS, PAUL. *Adolescence and Youth.* New York: McGraw-Hill Book Co., 1945.

LLOYD-JONES, ESTHER, and FEDDER, RUTH. *Coming of Age.* New York: Whittlesey House, 1941.

MEAD, MARGARET. *Male and Female.* New York: William Morrow and Co., 1949.

MYRDAL, GUNNAR. *An American Dilemma.* New York: Harper and Brothers, 1944. 2 vols.

OVERSTREET, HARRY A. *The Mature Mind.* New York: W. W. Norton and Co., 1949.

PLANT, JAMES S. *Personality and the Cultural Pattern.* New York: Commonwealth Fund, 1937.

SCHUMACHER, HENRY C. "Mental and Emotional Disturbances in Adolescence." *Journal of Child Psychology* as reprinted in *Child-Family Digest* 1: 10-20; July 1949.

STRANG, RUTH. "Manifestations of Maturity in Adolescence." *Mental Hygiene* 33: 563-69; October 1949.

SYMONDS, PERCIVAL M. "Changes in Sex Differences in Problems and Interests of Adolescents with Increasing Age." *Journal of Genetic Psychology* 50: 83-89; March 1937.

YOUNG, KIMBALL. *Personality and Problems of Adjustment.* New York: F. S. Crofts and Co., 1941.

ZACHRY, CAROLINE B. *Emotion and Conduct in Adolescence.* New York: Appleton-Century-Crofts, Inc., 1940.

# CHAPTER ELEVEN

# *Methods*

DOROTHEA DEITZ
ROSE STRASSER
HARRY C. THOMPSON

I N THE previous chapters, attention has been given to the meaning of adolescence with its characteristic rapid physical changes, problems in emotional and social growth and ambivalent and inconsistent behaviors. Growth has been discussed in terms of maturation goals as a biosocial process by a unified organism proceeding at an individual pace. The developing concept of self, the nature of the "wants" of adolescents in terms of freedom, discipline, independence, fair play, loyalty and integrity, and a philosophy to live by have been presented. Implications have been drawn for the development of objectives in the area of human relations; a democratic climate, self-direction and self-responsibility, cooperation and sharing with others were seen as essential.

It is the purpose of this chapter to clarify the problem of methods to use to create a democratic climate, to help adolescents to become increasingly self-directing and responsible and to give them opportunities to share with others in cooperatively planning for and carrying on their activities in health education, physical education and recreation situations. The chapter will consider in turn the climate, the process of method in general terms, the participation of individuals in the process and possible outcomes. These discussions will be followed by applications of the methods in planning for adolescents and working with them.

## The Climate

Everyone has had the experience of walking into a room in which there were a number of people and becoming immediately aware of a "feeling tone." In one instance it may have been friendly and hospitable while in another there may have been overtones of hostility or lack of concern. The atmosphere felt was not necessarily directed toward the one who entered but rather seemed characteristic of the particular situation.

Climate is very real, it exists and it can be identified. Climate affects each individual and in turn is modified continuously by everything that happens in and around it. Leaders have all experienced what happens to a study group when the fire engine goes by or when someone enters and interrupts a hot discussion. The climate certainly changes.

The variety of climates that can exist in a given situation have also been a matter of common experience. The important thing is to be able to identify climates and to recognize some of the forces which are operative. One of the major jobs of those who work with adolescents is the insuring of the kind of climate in which young people may move most effectively toward maturity.

### Characteristics of a Democratic Climate

A group that has achieved a dynamic, friendly and relaxed atmosphere is moving in the right direction. If the group is purposeful, if it recognizes and attacks problems and if it becomes increasingly self-motivated toward the achievement of common goals, further progress toward creating a democratic climate is being made. In addition, there should be evidence of enthusiasm, zest and pleasure. In a very real sense, learning and sharing and doing are fun. In a democratic climate the feeling tone is a happy one. Participants give evidence of growth through accepting differences, maintaining individuality, sharing responsibility, cooperating in group action and of "we-ness" and high morale.

This type of climate does not arise out of a vacuum and on occasion is created by accident rather than deliberation. The problem is to create it and to maintain it at a level conducive to the most effective learning.

## Important Factors Influencing Climate

Certain factors seem to be very influential in creating climate. Among them are the kind of leader, the kind of framework in which the group operates and the purposes of the group.

*The Leader.* As Hearn has pointed out in Chapter 2, the group is important to the adolescent for in it he can work out his fears and confusions and gain support during his period of conflict with adults. Expert adult leadership is required. But the adult working with adolescents has two strikes on him before he gets started; first, because he is an adult and for this reason generally rejected, and second, because by the very nature of his assignment he has a status role. The resolution of these two difficulties is somewhat interrelated. The kind of person the leader is and the kinds of understandings and skills he has and uses will have an impact on the way he handles the status aspects of his role.

It has been shown that at least three types of social atmosphere can be deliberately created through the use of autocratic, democratic or laissez-faire leadership patterns.[1] The resultant behaviors on the part of the participants in terms of aggression, submission, frustration, irritability and idleness on the one hand and friendliness, "we" feeling, individuality and self-direction and self-responsibility on the other indicate clearly that working with young people in our society requires both the understanding of and the working toward the creation of a democratic climate.

As a person the leader must be mature, friendly, understanding, fair in decisions and judgments with limitless patience and faith in people sparked by a sense of humor. He must be able to let young people struggle with a problem and make decisions, yet know when to assist if direction is not sure, when required decisions are beyond the experience of the group and when probable consequences will be unrewarding. On the occasions when it becomes necessary to say, "No, that can't be done," the important thing is not that an authoritarian decision has been made but rather what happens next. Is the situation handled so that the decision is accepted because of understanding or is it a matter of "I said it and that's it."

[1] Lippitt, Ronald A., and White, Ralph K. "The 'Social Climate' of Children's Groups," in Roger Barker; Jacob Kounin; and Herbert Wright, *Child Behavior and Development*. New York: McGraw-Hill Book Co., 1943, p. 485-508.

The latter obviously is out of place in a democratic climate. The question then becomes: Which is more important—the *time* required for clarification or the *learning* of the group?

*The Framework.* The expertness or inexpertness of the leader may be modified by the type of situation within which the group must operate. For example, the master teacher who operates democratically may have slow going with a group which has known only authoritative action. It might take some time to develop an easy, friendly, working climate in a formal and rigid school which places emphasis on grades and on achievement scores in terms of national norms. The skilled recreation worker might find the group slow to attack problems in a framework based on laissez faire. In other words the climate in which the group operates will be affected by the larger situation. Not only will experiences of the group be different as it comes together, but also the expectancies of the individuals in the group must be taken into account. An adolescent who has not had experience may think the teacher who acts in a democratic way "easy," "soft" and either lazy or stupid. The leader in such a case needs skill, understanding and forbearance. His job will be much more difficult than in a situation which itself has a democratic climate. There are secondary schools and youth centers in which all activities are cooperatively planned by the administrators, the staff and the boys and girls. There are many others in which the job is done from the top down and doing what one is told to is the most commendable behavior. Because of the influence of the framework upon the climate of a group, those who are adherents of the democratic method do well to seek out others of like mind to do what may be done to change the climate of the total situation.

*The Purposefulness of the Group.* As has been indicated, the democratic climate consists of more than sweetness and light. It is, rather, an atmosphere conducive to good work and progress toward goals. A common goal or purpose which all share in developing and accept as their own is essential. The effect of the common goal on the morale of a group is easily seen in the difference in enthusiasm, zest and effort. For example, a group decided that it would like to go on a hike and "cook out." Committees developed as if by magic, directions and locations were investigated, recipes and menus checked, recommendations cleared with families and the leader, the actual hike undertaken with purpose and hilarity, the food cooked and eaten with humor, appetite and satisfaction. High spirits held through the cleanup and the long haul home. Contrast this with a required class in physical education or in health education in which the group comes together not by choice, with a variety of purposes and with attitudes toward the class that range from eagerness to frustration. In the one instance the climate developed with ease while in the other there will undoubtedly be some problems encountered before the group finds a common interest. It should not be inferred that all voluntary groups automatically evolve a democratic climate, but rather that in required situations the leader must assume much more responsibility, plan much more carefully and use a much greater variety of techniques in assisting the group to find a common base for action. It is not the "requirement" that creates resistance but the multiplicity of interests or "hidden agendas." This brings out the need for considering the process through which group purposes are developed and plans made to attain them.

## The Process

The use of group process in education is consistent with the concept of democracy as it is being interpreted today. Democracy is seen as a way of life which seeks to give every person his share in the making of the society to which he belongs. The classroom, the athletic field and the swimming pool may be the laboratories where practice of democratic principles has a priority rating. Through the medium of group process democracy may become an active reality in the lives of growing youth.

Group process is exactly what its name implies, progressive activities carried out for, by and in a group. Each member is entitled to share and has responsibility for sharing in the planning and carrying out of the progressive activities. One teacher states this really means just "putting the adolescent on the steering committee for his own program." The group process seeks to develop the many persons within its numbers toward a given goal without sacrificing the suggestions, ideas or abilities of any individual through neglect or intolerance. The process seeks to utilize the combined thinking of the group toward achieving purposes common to the interests of all within the group. These purposes change as the group learns and a change in plans is dictated by evaluation of the course of action being pursued.

## Preplanning

Any teacher who wants boys and girls to learn in his classes plans in advance for this learning. There are differences, however, in the kind and scope of preplanning when group process is to be the method of work. The differences may be illustrated by the questions two teachers or leaders might phrase as a basis for advance planning. One might ask: What are the goals these boys or girls should achieve? What activities are good for them? What do they have to learn in this class? How shall I set up the program for these ends? The other might ask: What do the students want and need from this program at this time? What do they understand about their own capacities and limitations? In what areas can there be freedom of choice? What can they expect from the program and how can they get it? What do they understand about the program and their relations to it? Where are they in ability to plan, to share and to work together?

By the very nature of preplanning both of the leaders would obtain information about the adolescents who would comprise the group. In a school situation, they would probably review school and departmental records relating to medical examinations, illnesses, family background, mental and aptitude tests, cumulative and anecdotal records of course experiences and behaviors. It is after the data are reviewed that the paths in planning would begin to diverge. This divergence would be related to the basic beliefs of the leader concerning such statements as: democratic behavior arises out of opportunities to behave in democratic ways; young people find security and assurance in group action; young people can make sound decisions within the boundaries of their experience and maturity; young people should have opportunities to become increasingly self-directing and to assume responsibility for the results of their actions; young people should become increasingly aware of the nature and rate of their progress toward goals.

Probably the key to the amount and kind of decisions made in advance by the teacher or leader rests upon his understanding of the actual maturity and experience of the group. He does as much prestructuring of the program, and only that much, as is necessary to get the group off to a good start. Some preplanning is a must. Effective leadership does not operate "off the cuff." Adolescents have a right to information as to what the program is about and what their share in it is to be. This preplanning is obviously related to the climate and the factors which strongly influence it. Criteria for sound preplanning would include:

1. Knowledge of the experience and expectancies of the boys and girls in the group.

2. Awareness of the wants and developmental tasks of adolescents.

3. Acceptance of the adolescent as a biosocial unifying and unique organism.

4. Awareness of the relation of means to ends.

5. Expertness in analysis and use of professional "tools."

6. Recognition that group progress is dependent upon the understanding and acceptance of goals.

## Setting Goals

The degree of success which may be associated with the functioning of most youth groups appears to be determined by the range of planning and organizing they themselves do under proper guidance and counsel. The first step is a statement of goals. These goals are not dead-end purposes but show the direction in which the group is moving. They may be signposts toward a more remote but desirable aim. They must be real in the sense that there is possibility of successful attainment. Successful achievement leads to further effort toward larger aims. Goals should be flexible and should not impose limitations on group action if evaluation indicates they need to be changed. They must be constantly redetermined in the light of the progress made by the group in group thinking, participation and action. The goals set by any group should represent the thinking of the many and be evaluated continuously in terms of their benefit to the group and to the individuals in the group.

In determining the goals for a group, especially in a group which is newly organized, the teacher plays an important role. Students without experience in the group process often need much help in thinking through group purposes, but as the group grows in ability to determine purposeful goals by itself, the teacher becomes less prominent. As the group grows in its ability to formulate its own worthwhile goals, it is a sign that its members have become more integrated and cooperative. The members of the group have grown in consideration of the welfare of the whole group membership and, as individuals have grown in self-discipline and control of impulses and desires, changes have taken place in those to whom participation in a group formerly meant aggressive leadership, frustration or submission.

In the final analysis individuals cannot become a group until they have been able to develop common purposes that each can accept as his own. At this point the group begins to find a "we-ness" and basis for high morale that is increased as it moves toward the achievement of the goals set. This is true whether the goal is to run a table tennis tournament, to learn about mental health or to develop skill in football fundamentals.

## Making Plans

Once the goal has been determined, then it becomes necessary to make plans to attain it. The question becomes: "What shall we do to reach the goal?" Subsequent group action rather closely approximates the steps taken in problem-solving, in that there is a goal and there is an obvious need for a plan. The steps would include:

1. Identifying and clarifying the problem or problems involved in the achievement of the goal. This would entail a sharpening of focus and analysis of the goal in order that members of the group have a clear understanding of what the goal actually is.

2. Finding the facts that relate to the achievement of the goal. For example, it might be necessary to find out what facilities would be available, and what would appear to be the outlay required in terms of human energy, time and money.

3. Applying the facts to the problem. It might be that the goal would need redefinition and further clarification as the group reviews the various factors involved.

4. Drawing conclusions. The group would consider the various aspects of the problem and the facts obtained, and would then begin to evolve procedures for a direct attack on the problem.

5. Acting on conclusions. Committees are appointed. All individuals share in the action, and resources of the group are continually explored in light of the needs of the group. This is the trial period of the plan.

6. Evaluating and replanning. Action is checked to see whether or not the group is moving toward the goal that prompted the plan in the first place.

The listing of the steps may be somewhat confusing as in reality the lines are not sharply drawn. For example, judgments are being made and redirections proposed throughout the making of the plan and in taking action. Evaluation is not the sixth step but rather a part of the larger whole of plan making. Steps 2, 3 and 4 may be so closely related that it is difficult to distinguish where one begins and the other ends. While there undoubtedly is a starting point as well as an ending point for the action of the group toward a given goal, it should be noted that learning just does not happen that way. One of the problems imposed upon the leader or teacher is that of considering the on-going quality of learning and the fact that objectives of adolescents change as learning takes place.

A physical education teacher reported the following as an example of the introduction to group process:

A boys' physical education class was having difficulty. John, James and three or four others wanted to play basketball every class period because they excelled in it. Tom and Joe and several others wanted to spend some time practicing the skills necessary for them to become good basketball players. The remainder of the class was more interested in learning and practicing tumbling skills. How, then, could this class be organized to fulfil the needs and desires of the students? With only one gymnasium to work in, each must compromise. Yet each should have the opportunity to participate in the activity which was most meaningful to him.

To meet this problem the teacher introduced group process. Progress in becoming a group with a unified purpose was slow and at times discouraging, but with faith in the ultimate realization of the group goals, he continued to encourage the boys to set up their own goals for class activities. In doing this, the students learned that some of their individual goals had to be redirected to fit in with the goals of the group. Slowly the class developed some concepts of democratic living, cooperation, sharing and consideration of the rights and privileges of others.

The planning process includes the participation of all the members of the group. It involves a consideration of the wants and the abilities of group members. It requires that recognition be given to the various roles or jobs involved in achieving group ends and further that the meaning of consensus be clear.

This type of process makes it necessary for the members of the group to assume responsibility for communicating their ideas to the group and for moving the group ahead. In the beginning an inexperienced group will require time to learn to work together. This involves group discussion. All members should gain sufficient confidence in the group to be able to participate effectively. This means that each person should be aware of the characteristics of good group discussion if it is to bring about the group interaction and integration needed to achieve the group goals. These characteristics are requisite to satisfactory growth of the group members:

1. Participants should attempt to keep the discussion centered around the problem being discussed.

2. Participants should make their contributions brief.

3. Members of a group should be willing to listen, to consider seriously the contributions of others.

4. Individuals should attempt to be sensitive to the group process or operation in order that they may help to solve problems by performing various roles as needed.

5. All members should feel a responsibility for leadership in the group.

6. Participants should maintain an objective attitude toward other personalities in the group.

7. Members should be willing to subordinate personal motives to that which is best for the group as a whole.

8. Individual members should be willing to compromise if they can do so without sacrificing values.

9. The members of the group should be willing to apply self-analysis to determine their own growth in ability to be a worthy member in and of the group.

## Carrying Out Plans

The way in which plans are carried out may well be the most rewarding as well as the most revealing aspect of group process.

At this stage the effectiveness of the plan is demonstrated and the ability of the group members to assign and accept responsibilities is shown. The kinds of jobs individuals volunteer to undertake or are asked to undertake also reveal the degree to which the group and its members have moved toward accepting the reality of differences and the qualities needed for a particular assignment.

If the individuals have become a group in the sense of common goals there will be no rebellion or aggression toward the plans. There will be critical evaluation of them, however. Members of the group recognize that the success or failure is in a large measure dependent upon the way in which every member performs his part in the whole. Each member of the group is responsible for contributing to the success of the entire project.

## Evaluating and Replanning

In a real learning situation evaluation is concerned with more than a consideration of the end product. As a matter of fact, evaluation gets underway the first time the group meets. Conclusions are formed and judgments made throughout the whole process. The goals are discussed and challenged in the light of the views of the group members, each step in the planning is subject to variation and change as the group grows. This continuous checking can assist the group in its movement toward the larger goals which may not be clear in the beginning. Here the development of all within the group may become of more importance than achievement by the few, as the group explores through discussion and activity the concept of "giving every person a share in the making of the society to which he belongs." That this same society or group, as it were, should not seek to stifle the opportunities for expression of those who possess unusual abilities and skill is a challenge which can be met by continuous evaluation and replanning.

The group must become cognizant in its discussions that not only is the achievement of its goals important, but also the media and activities utilized in achieving the goals need evaluation. A group should not be satisfied with the attainment of specific goals, but should be continuously in the process of growth toward achieving more worthwhile ones. This leads to replanning and further action.

## The Participation

The group process may be said to be functioning well when each member assumes responsibility for the success of the group activity. This acceptance of responsibility by the individual may necessitate assuming consciously or unconsciously the roles which he can best perform. These roles will vary for each individual from time to time and, as group members become skilled in the techniques of group process, they can assume roles conducive to promoting and facilitating better discussion and more creative thinking by the other members of the group.

### The Status Leader

The most versatile participant in the group process should be the teacher or leader; the leader, who by the very nature of his job responsibility, has a status role. This is particularly important in getting the group under way. He should be resourceful, calm, tactful, gracious, forceful and level-headed. He must have quickness of apprehension, depth of comprehension, breadth of sympathy and a sense of humor. He must be able to assume, as the situation demands, the roles of coordinator, opinion seeker, encourager, evaluator or critic. His participation in the group process is the result of reflective study of the group's problems and needs, consideration of possible ways of meeting these needs and solving these problems, and establishing inner vision to light the pathway toward purposeful goals.

The status leader's role will change as the group develops understanding of the group process and as it grows in ability to assume some of the roles assumed by the teacher or chairman to initiate and perpetuate the group process in the class. Some of the duties which will need to be performed by the leader in the early stages of development of group discussion will be:

1. To open the discussion with a brief statement of the problem and to stimulate contributions by directing questions to the group.

2. To summarize or reformulate contributions to give the group time to rethink the point made.

3. To supply illustrations when a member of the group states a principle

and to generalize when a member of the group gives specific illustrations to provide time and opportunity for understanding.

4. To give recognition for each contribution made.

5. To emphasize aspects of the various contributions significant to the thought.

6. To interpret and integrate diverse contributions.

7. To meet the pauses that sometimes occur by asking pertinent questions to stimulate discussion.

8. To interpret and integrate from time to time and at the end of the discussion.

9. To control individuals who disregard the conditions of the discussion and tend to monopolize.

10. To insist that members of the group speak in voices which can be heard by all.

11. To prevent emotional clashes and harmonize incipient conflicts.

12. To state clearly the decision reached in the solution of the specific problem under discussion.[2]

## Other Leaders

As the group develops skill in solving its problems by the group process, the members can assume many of the functions performed by the teacher in the initiation of the method. The group may elect its own chairman and delegate the status leader to the role of participating member. However, the teacher may still need to assume the leader role from time to time.

## The Resource Person

In solving a problem or planning a class activity through the group process, the occasion may arise when the members of the group are not experienced enough to solve the problem by themselves. Then it is that the teacher assumes the role of the resource person; another person who is an expert in a particular field might be called into the group to fill the role; group members often serve in this capacity. The resource person is one who is able to contribute information or other assistance as the need for it arises in the group.

[2] Heffernan, Helen. *Technique To Be Used in Solving an Educational Problem by the Discussion Method*. Sacramento, Calif.: State Department of Education, 1944.

## Other Roles

In the operation of group process, it is usually helpful to have a group recorder whose duties are to keep a written record of the progress of the group and to assist during discussion by restatement of the problem and by summarizing contributions pertinent to the problem. The records may be kept as elaborately or as simply as the group wishes.

When a group becomes conscious of its ways of working together and a desire develops to improve, the use of an observer often helps it to define the specific ways in which it needs to improve. The person filling the role of observer is freed from involvement in what is happening to give full attention to *how* it is happening. Observers' reports on how decisions are reached, how leaders filled their roles, how group members filled various other roles, frequently serve to clarify for individuals and for the group better ways to accomplish what they want to do.

The members of the group have various roles or responsibilities to perform in the utilization of the discussion method as a learning technique. Individuals will be needed to suggest new ideas or different ways of approaching a problem, to ask for clarification of facts which are authoritative about the problem or to evaluate the group accomplishment or proposals in terms of certain criteria. Members can learn to assume these various roles as they develop in ability to participate in group thinking and planning.

The group process, if used correctly, should not provide an outlet for the individual who endeavors to satisfy some personal need which is not pertinent to the group functioning or the group purpose. Such individual roles as those performed by the aggressive individual who expresses general disapproval of all plans, the opposition booster who adopts a negative, opposing attitude without reason, the attention seeker who calls attention to self through boasting and pointing out personal achievements, the dominating individual and the special interest advocate have no place in the group process. These boys and girls should be encouraged to take a less selfish and more democratic attitude toward the group thinking and discussions. They should not be ignored if good human relations are to be maintained, but should be utilized for whatever special contributions they can make to the group purposes and encouraged to identify themselves more with the group.

As group members gain in competence and confidence they will assume a variety of group roles. They will also gain in recognition of the roles taken by various members and become increasingly sensitive to such contributions.

## The Outcomes

Advocates of group process consider that it fosters specific values conducive to worthy membership in a democratic society. Recognizing as it does the dignity, worth and talents of each individual in the group, it is a process containing values basic to democratic living. Some of the values accruing from the group process are as follows:

1. It awakens a sense of responsibility toward others and the group's responsibility to the individual.

2. Each individual can contribute to the solution of problems according to his ability and experience.

3. People can recognize and solve problems together more effectively than can one individual.

4. The individual is enabled to develop the fullest realization of his potentialities through the encouragement of self-direction.

5. The exchange of ideas between group members results in progress both quantitatively and qualitatively.

6. It presents avenues for greatest satisfaction of personal and group needs such as sense of belongingness, recognition and achievement.

7. Decisions are more rapidly accepted and result in more effective action when they evolve through group interaction.

8. Human relations in all areas from family to world organization can function on a higher level through group interaction.

9. It is one of the most successful methods in creating situations through which learning takes place.[3]

## Planning for Adolescents

Many teachers and leaders throughout the country have developed ways in which they work for and with young people. In planning

[3] Group Values Committee. *Values of Group Process.* Summer Workshop, University of California, Los Angeles, 1949, mimeographed. Permission to reprint granted by Dr. Carl Haven Young, Chairman of the Department of Physical Education, University of California, Los Angeles.

programs for adolescents there is background work which must be
done with administrators, parents and the community as a whole,
if understanding and support are to be gained and extended. The
planning for boys and girls being considered here is not so much
the advance planning done by teacher or leader in preparation for
meeting a group; it is the planning which may be done to insure
a more democratic framework in which particular groups operate.
The cooperative planning of administrators, staff, parents, expert
consultants and lay citizens is required to develop this democratic
framework. Those who actually teach and lead adolescents are
immeasurably helped to lead their groups toward democratic outcomes when they themselves are participants in democratic planning
of all concerned with meeting the needs of adolescents.

## A School-Community Recreation Program

There are many opportunities for the development of more democratic human relations through a school-community recreation
program and there is evidence that general relationships within the
community can be improved as more and more individuals participate in the project. This is another indication that common goals
and group centered action can serve as powerful incentives to democratic action in the larger sense.

*The Advisory Committee.* Where the school and community are
jointly responsible for a recreation program for all age groups, the
utilization of an advisory committee has been found most helpful.
These committees are composed of adults representing a cross-
section of the community. Such a committee serves in an advisory
capacity to the staff people directly responsible for the recreation
program. Community recreation advisory committees can assist
greatly with the problem of meeting the needs and interests of
the community. These groups, by and large, are much closer to a
situation than are boards of education or other civic authorities who
have broader and wider responsibilities demanding their attention.
These committees will not only observe more clearly the needs of
the community in terms of specific phases of the program but will
also relieve other municipal boards of much time-consuming activity
required in the development and promotion of the program.

The procedures and techniques involved in the working mechanism of advisory committees are rather simple. The committee may advise directly a superintendent of schools or other executive bodies on matters concerning the program; or it may submit recommendations indirectly through the director or assistant director of recreation, who in turn would pass such recommendations on to the official civic authorities.

The advantages of pursuing the advisory committee plans are obvious. Those responsible for the recreation program are benefiting as a result of recommendations made, and at the same time the community can realize its part in the development of a suitable recreation program. Community and school relations are developed on a higher plane and there is better understanding among all groups.

*Utilizing Lay Resources.* School-community relations can be measurably improved and developed through lay participation in planning and conducting programs. There is usually a great deal of talent lying dormant within a community which comes to life only upon request. Surveys and investigations will usually result in the discovery of resources which had never been tapped. These resources, when wisely used, will develop and enrich and increase the scope of a program. In most cases those who possess such talents and skills are most willing to be of service to the community through serving as leaders or resource people.

Volunteer lay leaders can and will be of invaluable assistance in furthering the program providing that they are familiar with the purposes, policies and procedures and understand their part in the whole. This orientation should be carefully planned and carried out through group action. As individuals contribute to the project through the investment of their own time and energy they seem to develop a belongingness that results in strong and well rounded support for the school-community program.

Not only should the assistance of individuals be utilized, but the support and active aid of various community groups and organizations should be sought. Such groups already have a rallying point or purpose common to the members of the group. Here again it is possible to add a larger goal that makes for "we-ness" in the community as a whole. Service clubs, parent-teacher associations, church organizations and other groups are in most cases willing to assist professional personnel in developing a broader and more meaningful school-community recreation program. These various organizations through group action have established themselves in the community and are able to aid in ways not possible of accomplishment by the individual. They can assist with large scale projects because of the representativeness of their membership. Not only the recreation program but the entire community will gain through the action of a variety of groups toward the accomplishment of a common goal.

*Staff Operations.* The importance attached to the part the professional staff plays in developing and maintaining better human relations is beyond exaggeration. Experience alone supplies the answer as to the value of a capable staff personnel. One poorly trained, uninterested staff member can break down more favorable relations in one day than a dozen well-trained staff members can build up in a month.

Human relations in the field of recreation can best be built up by those responsible for the program through a sincere interest in the participants and the kind and quality of service rendered. The personality and attitude of the leader toward other individuals under his or her supervision are most important. It must ever be remembered that in the field of recreation participation is largely voluntary and, as such, carries with it objectives which are peculiar to this field. The enjoyment which results from recreational activities, along with the opportunity for a more fruitful use of leisure time, provide a base from which professional personnel can lead toward better human relations. However, another base also is required. All staff members sharing in over-all planning of the program which they are expected to carry out leads to personal commitment, enthusiasm and effort for the success of plans. It is part of developing the democratic framework in which they serve as leaders of youth.

*The Youth Groups.* People of all ages enjoy the experiences and satisfaction of self and group accomplishment. The need for assisting in some way to solve problems, complete projects, build and conduct programs and assume important responsibilities is inherent in most individuals. Particularly in the area concerned with young adults and teen-agers is it important that this feeling of "self doing" take root. Youth organizations and youth center groups in particular are very much concerned with their part in being responsible for the conduct and organization of their own programs. Better relationships between the professional personnel and the participants will exist in situations where there is cooperation and where the program is definitely identified with the participants and not with an overzealous professional staff. Guidance is necessary with all age groups. However, a supporting behind-the-scenes type of assistance that comes forward as needed will be more acceptable and consequently more helpful to youth.

The planning of particular programs, election of officers, setting up of rules and regulations and other activities concerned with the administration and conduct of the program should be shared responsibilities of leader and group. This democratic procedure is of value to all concerned. In order for youth programs to be successful, it is necessary to have such programs based on sound educational principles and objectives. The youth center, for example, must be more than a hand-out. There must be a challenging program, diversified in its activities so that the needs and interests of a maximum number of participants will be met. Groups which function on a democratic basis will move toward developing and maintaining better human relations among themselves and in the community as a whole.

## A Secondary School Situation

Many secondary schools have set up curriculum councils, composed of administrators and staff members, which guide and coordinate the work of many other groups in planning for the various areas included in the curriculum. Some schools include students in all planning groups at all levels. The trend is away from the general telling the colonel what to do, the colonel telling the lieutenant, the lieutenant telling the sergeant and the sergeant telling the private who does the job. The development is toward fulfilling the ideal that "all who have a share in carrying out plans should have a share in making them." The teacher who believes in using democratic methods in the classroom is immeasurably sustained and supported by the use of democratic methods throughout the school.

*The Administrator Needs to Know.* Even in situations that involve all staff members in goal setting, in making and carrying out plans, there is need for reporting and interpreting the results of stock-taking in particular programs. Sharing works both ways. As a way of securing the administrator's understanding of the program, one teacher made a practice of submitting regular reports to him. In one of these reports after outlining in brief the activities and organization of the physical education program she made these comments:

1. 203 (77%) of a total of 263 girls in school have taken part in the after school program in which 229 intramural games have been played. 91 girls (38%) have had opportunity to meet and play with girls from other schools. 20 girls made letters this year.

2. Team play, team work, cooperation and loyalty have been developed. Relaxation, fun, friends, have contributed to personality integration. We believe that our program builds new interests and skills as a barrier against delinquency. Our girls who are interested in athletics are not our "problems." Rather our problem is how to reach *all* girls with an "interest."

3. As you suggested, the real proof of growth in poise and an understanding of the body as an expression of the real self may best be gained by comparing the entering students with those about to leave.

4. Leaders have done a magnificent job for the benefit of all girls in Oneida and show individually the value and power of their preparation and experience. They have been an inspiration.

5. You might be interested to know that 220 outside-of-school hours for clerical work have gone behind this year's job in physical education.

6. The cadet teachers tend to give breadth to our program possibilities and I believe we give them very valuable experience.

7. Our big softball sportsday at Oneida in which 7 schools participated is a joy to all of us. You would have been proud of the job the Oneida girls did in organizing and carrying through their plans.

8. Spring festival "peaks" the inside work.

Thank you for your cooperation. Please feel free to make suggestions for improvement.[4]

*Parents Need To Share, Too.* Probably the largest potential community contribution parents make lies in their understanding and

[4] Excerpt from report of Dorothea Deitz to Principal, Oneida School, Schenectady, New York.

guidance of their children. A part of this understanding and guidance rests upon what they know and support in the school program. In reviewing the report which follows it might be said that it is only an example of good public relations technique. So it is, if by that is meant the utilizing of a variety of ways to let people know about the program and then working toward a sharing of ideas and plans. This report to parents was mimeographed in a two-column folder with an attractive frontispiece. The results were good in that parents raised questions and made suggestions. The students seemed pleased not only at the idea of the report but also at the response of their families.

### Oneida "Can Do" in Sports

We are all agreed on one thing—Americans want "the best" in education for their youngsters. But what will they need most, 10 or 25 years hence?

If every branch of the armed services for both men and women used sports as both morale builders and body conditioners, you can be pretty sure that sports will play an ever-increasing part in these two respects in our school program too. Can you think of any better way to buy insurance against juvenile delinquency? Can you name many good athletes who turned into delinquents? Did you ever hear of 75 to 90 youngsters staying, voluntarily, an hour after school day after day for anything other than athletics? (If we had two gyms we could keep twice this number both interested and busy—off the streets, loath to go home.) Why? Because youngsters like "to do"—but they have to know how.

Our plan in sports is to build a broad intramural program which offers both a choice of activity, and also a challenge for all levels of performance, so that every youngster can play, with some chance of success, in competition graded to his level of ability. Then, to challenge those "top performers" we like to run invitation games with "Honor teams" from some neighboring school.

This kind of after school program, presupposes a sound *daily* instructional period. Learning is fun! The better anyone can perform, the more pleasure he gets from the game. (Judge yourself by your proficiency in either bridge or golf and the resultant pleasure from either.) Consequently our policy is to teach skills, scoring, rules, etc., during the class periods and then organize for each grade in this after-school program. For example, this fall Oneida boys and girls played 72 games in volleyball; 3 leagues for boys, 3 leagues for girls, and a championship team for each. Then we picked the "honor team" players for the games with our neighbors. This same system goes on for each of the seasonal periods (2 months each) during the entire school year; every season has its own sports. Boys and girls who participate accumulate points toward their school letter which is awarded at the end of their third year of competitive participation.

You as parents have a right to *insist* that your programs in physical education really produce for your children. What products? A strong efficient body, stamina and endurance, moral courage, physical skills and coordination (Americans kill 40,000 people annually by "mistakes" in driving), specific techniques for wholesome recreation, opportunities for social contacts, and training in leadership. These we try to give you at Oneida.

Your child "can do"—how *well*, will depend on how soon you give us that basic daily period, and the space we need to do the job right. "Can you?"

It is a pleasure to add that as we go to press, plans are under way to enlarge the scope and range of activity at Oneida.

## Working with Adolescents

An example of group planning in which an attempt was made to provide for the variety of interests in a class group is illustrated by the following situation.

### A Boys' Activity Class

A group of ninth-grade boys was selected by their classmates to serve on the preplanning committee for the indoor season of the physical education program. They meet with Mr. Johnson, the physical education teacher. The beginning discussion might run something like this:

Jim: "Let's start with basketball."

Mr. Johnson: "Since we've just finished ten weeks of soccer should we limit ourselves to another team game?"

Joe: "But we need a chance to practice basketball. After soccer a basketball will feel so different."

Fred: "Yeah . . . I couldn't even make a basket right now."

Art: "I'd like to do something besides basketball all the time— how about some conditioning exercises?"

Mr. Johnson: "We didn't spend much time on conditioning prior to soccer and basketball is another game involving running. What about all-round body development—are there other activities that should be considered?"

Fred: "We could do some tumbling or some apparatus but we'd sure need some warm-ups and conditioning."

Joe: "Maybe we could do some basketball drills along with the warm-ups."

Mr. Johnson: "Those are good ideas. What about badminton or some other activity you can do out of school . . . how should we divide up the class time so we can do the different activities?"

Jim: "I think we ought to spend some time learning to dance better . . . the freshman dance is coming up—it's no fun being a dope."

Art: "And maybe we could get the girls' class so we could have partners."

Joe: "It's sissy stuff—but if you guys want to—O.K. . . . we'd still have four days for other stuff like basketball."

Fred: "How about tumbling and badminton?"

Jim: "Maybe we could start with warm-ups and conditioning every day."

Mr. Johnson: "How would it be to spend 15 or 20 minutes at the beginning of class on conditioning and skills practice. Then if we divide into squads, by using the short courts we could rotate squads. Two would play basketball, two would play badminton, and the rest could work on tumbling. Intramural basketball and badminton would provide for additional practice and playing time for anyone who signs up. Squad leaders would be responsible, and I'd circulate from squad to squad. We could do this for four weeks and by then we'd know what to plan for the rest of the season."

Art: "Sounds O.K. to me. We'd all get a chance to do something that we want to do and we could change it if it didn't work."

Mr. Johnson was aware that basketball and other team sports had been emphasized in the school, and further that the community was interested in the team activities. He wanted to satisfy the wishes of the students to play basketball but in addition wanted them to experience a broader program of physical education. He had found out that authoritative planning didn't work so he had turned to group process in order to get more cooperation and sharing of ideas in the group. Since some class members had experience in other activities and liked them some variety was suggested.

Further discussions centered about the size of the class, the best way to organize groups within the class so that each person could have an equal opportunity to participate in all activities, how to motivate those students who might not be interested in learning to dance or to play badminton or to tumble, how leaders might be selected, etc. This was done so that a constructive plan could be presented to the entire group for consideration and changes or additions made according to the group needs or wishes.

When the plan was presented to the large group, the class agreed to try it for the four weeks suggested. Warm-up and skill activities were to be combined wherever possible. Squad leaders were to be chosen by the class and all class members were to sign up for the squad of their own choice. The maximum number on a squad was to be 8 so that all members would have an opportunity to play each time the squad played basketball. In badminton, a rotation system was worked out so that players rotated on the court with a new person replacing a player after each four points made. In this way, the group felt that more equal opportunities to participate would be given to all class members. Dancing did not present much of a problem because everyone could participate at the same time. However, the squad idea proved helpful in designating partners for dancing, particularly at the beginning of class since the girls' classes also were organized on a squad basis. The boys in squad number 1 were to dance with the girls in the girls' squad number 1, squad number 2 with 2. The next week, boys' squad number 1 would dance with girls' squad number 2, the next week with number 3, etc. Squad leaders were to learn how to direct tumbling activities, including safety precautions necessary such as spotting, and to assist in refereeing games.

At the end of the three weeks the class as a whole met to evaluate the program. The group expressed the opinion that too many activities were being offered in one week and that it would be wiser to concentrate working on these activities in units. However, the majority wanted to continue with the social dancing for one period a week. It was agreed that the warm-up and skills practice time in each class period was important and should be continued. The combination of basketball and tumbling was to continue. Badminton was to be omitted and a three-week period was to be set aside before the end of the 10-week season for a unit on badminton skills and techniques. Additional time would be utilized in the intramural program for practice in playing the game. The group recognized the fact that badminton skills were important and requested additional time for a movie and expert demonstration over and above class time.

Other areas than the one described in the above example offer opportunities for the utilization of the group process in the physical education field. A dance class is often requested to participate in assembly or other school or community programs. For example, a folk dance class is requested to participate in a program. The group, in order to make an effective appearance, must meet together to plan the dances most suitable for presentation, the personnel of the group taking part, the costumes to be worn, the most effective arrangements necessary, and the like. The presentation of such a program promotes many understandings and appreciations in the field of human relations and international understanding. Few people can actually participate in dances without becoming more tolerant and appreciative of other cultures.

Activities such as folk, square and ballroom dancing are essentially social. The group process could therefore tend to break down many of the tensions of the adolescent level by helping, through these activities, to make adjustments to members of the opposite sex a casual and expected experience. This will tend to help students to have a happier and more healthful outlook on life.

The planning of other extraclass activities such as the intramural program, field trips, joint youth and adult recreation programs are further areas in which the group process in physical education can be used. Some teachers in schools, rejecting group process methods give as a reason the heavy teaching loads they carry. These teachers are wont to say, "It is all right at the college level; students are more mature and the numbers a teacher has to deal with are not so large." "It's fine on paper—but impracticable. There isn't time." Some other teachers have surmounted these very real difficulties, first by believing that *saving time* by telling students what to do instead of helping them decide what to do does not make authoritarian methods good enough; second, by perfecting the organization of the program so that students especially prepared for the jobs share leadership responsibilities. An outline is presented which was made by a teacher for preparing students for assigned leadership jobs:

The leaders come from the rank and file of class members who have demonstrated self-responsibility, cooperation, teamwork, self-direction, desirable individual choices and work patterns, and who come closest to the behavior for best human relations, who have competency in one or more of the physical activities in the program.

Leaders may be selected in a number of ways:
   by group vote,
   by arbitrary choice determined by a special ability,
   by rotation—different one for each activity or sports season,

by expressed desire for such experience and with qualifications, by a rating scale for those qualities considered most important by students in the school.

The leader preparation should include:

1. Experience in effective planning for reaching goals.

2. Methods of organization and presentation of the activities through which goals are attained.

3. Techniques for getting groups under way, for getting attention and maintaining interest of members within a small group.

4. Ways to work with a slow learner.

5. Space-plans for practicing skills and playing of games (usually by duplicator, ditto machine or mimeograph).

6. Psychological "tips" on widening opportunities for self-direction, service and satisfaction for both classmates and self.

7. Short cuts to efficient organization for intramural programs (developed through the democratic process):

    a. Schedule for field and courts with the games schedule.

    b. Previous knowledge of pinny or shirt teams and direction of goal or basket.

    c. Assignment of referees and umpires by system of rotation to avoid delay.

    d. Rotation order for timers—and foreknowledge of length of playing period.

    e. Direction of moving on and off field and courts to save confusion and time.

    f. Knowledge of equipment assignment and responsibility.

8. Duties of team captains and assistant captains.

9. Methods of scoring, officiating and checking of equipment.

10. Make-up of schedules and tournaments.

11. Methods of representing the group; sensitivity to needs.

12. Practice in becoming articulate.

13. Methods and plans for conducting discussions.

14. Essentials of accurate correspondence and minutes.

15. Self-evaluation as leaders—ratings.

16. Extras for enrichment of their own program; leaders' trips and conferences with other schools.

Actual experience in leadership will of necessity begin slowly for new members of the leaders' corps and should always be provided carefully so that success is assured. For example, a new leader may work as an assistant to a more experienced leader or in a simple skill situation when the primary purpose is "warm-up" and a "feel of the fingers on the ball." With increasing experience comes additional range of service. Can the teen-ager be entrusted with responsibility? Is he willing to help others? Give him this opportunity, with training, to be of service to the group and watch him grow in poise and stature, and begin to feel the possibilities of his contribution to the future. Adeptness in democratic human relations can be vitally interesting! The teacher is now a leader and has time to move freely among the group, guiding in actual face-to-face situations, keeping a balance on individual choice and group pressures and increasing awareness on the part of each student of his own relationships with his fellows.

The health education, physical education and recreation activities which are organized democratically are more difficult to carry out than is the traditional type of class. The group process is slow until students acquire skill in it. Students will be hesitant at first to give creative expression to their activities. However, the democratic teacher or leader is rewarded by seeing adolescents grow and develop as their needs and wants are met and satisfied. Watching boys and girls move toward developing democratic relations with others is ample reward to the teacher or leader who believes in group process as a method of work.

# Bibliography

AUER, J. JEFFRY, and EWBANK, HENRY. *Handbook for Discussion Leaders*. New York: Harper and Brothers, 1947.

BARKER, ROGER; KOUNIN, JACOB; and WRIGHT, HERBERT. *Child Behavior and Development*. New York: McGraw-Hill Book Co., 1943.

BAXTER, BERNICE, and CASSIDY, ROSALIND. *Group Experience—The Democratic Way*. New York: Harper and Brothers, 1943.

BENNE, KENNETH D., and SHEATS, PAUL H. "Functional Roles of Group Members." *Journal of Social Issues*. 4: 41-49; Spring, 1948.

BENNETT, BRUCE L. "Physical Education and Social Learning in the Secondary School." *Journal of the American Association of Health, Physical Education and Recreation*. 20: 452-53; September 1949.

BIESTER, LILLIAN L.; GRIFFITHS, WILLIAM; and PEARCE, N. D. *Units in Personal Health and Human Relations*. Minneapolis: University of Minnesota Press, 1949.

BURTON, WILLIAM H. *The Guidance of Learning Activities*. New York: Appleton-Century-Crofts, Inc., 1944.

CASSIDY, ROSALIND. *New Directions in Physical Education for the Adolescent Girl in High School and College*. New York: A. S. Barnes and Co., 1938.

CHATTO, CLARENCE I. "Health and Physical Education for Democratic Living." *Journal of Health and Physical Education.* 17: 466-67; October 1946.

CHISHOLM, LESLIE. *Guiding Youth in the Secondary School.* New York: American Book Co., 1945.

CITIZENSHIP EDUCATION STUDY. *Problem Solving.* Detroit: Detroit Public Schools and Wayne University, 1948.

COLLINS, LAURENTINE B.; CASSIDY, ROSALIND; and OTHERS. *Physical Education in the Secondary School.* New York: A. S. Barnes and Co., 1940.

COYLE, GRACE. *Group Experience and Democratic Values.* New York: Woman's Press, 1947.

DE HUSZAR, GEORGE B. *Practical Applications of Democracy.* New York: Harper and Brothers, 1945.

HEFFERNAN, HELEN. *Techniques To Be Used in Solving an Educational Problem by the Discussion Method.* Sacramento, Cal.: State Department of Education, 1944.

HERRON, JOHN S. "Human Relations, Democracy and Physical Education." *Journal of Health and Physical Education.* 17: 510-11; November 1946.

JENNINGS, HELEN. *Sociometry in Group Relations.* Washington, D. C.: American Council on Education, 1948.

KOZMAN, HILDA CLUTE; CASSIDY, ROSALIND; and JACKSON, CHESTER O. *Methods in Physical Education.* Philadelphia: W. B. Saunders Co., 1947.

LYSTER, ALVA M. *Social Problems of the High School Boy.* Austin, Texas: Steck Co., 1935.

NATIONAL ASSOCIATION FOR PHYSICAL EDUCATION OF COLLEGE WOMEN. *Practices of Promise in the Understanding and Use of the Democratic Process.* Supplement to the Annual Proceedings: the Association, 1949.

NATIONAL EDUCATION ASSOCIATION, DEPARTMENT OF SUPERVISION AND CURRICULUM DEVELOPMENT. *Group Planning in Education.* 1945 Yearbook. Washington, D. C.: the Department, 1945.

NATIONAL EDUCATION ASSOCIATION and AMERICAN ASSOCIATION OF SCHOOL ADMINISTRATORS, EDUCATIONAL POLICIES COMMISSION. *Education for All American Youth.* Washington, D. C.: the Commission, 1944.

NATIONAL EDUCATION ASSOCIATION and AMERICAN ASSOCIATION OF SCHOOL ADMINISTRATORS, EDUCATIONAL POLICIES COMMISSION. *Learning the Ways of Democracy.* Washington, D. C.: the Commission, 1940.

NATIONAL TRAINING LABORATORY IN GROUP DEVELOPMENT. *Report of the Second Summer Laboratory Sessions.* National Education Association and Research Center for Group Dynamics. University of Michigan Bulletin No. 3. Washington, D. C.: Division of Adult Education, 1948.

RADIR, RUTH. *Modern Dance for the Youth of America.* New York: A. S. Barnes and Co., 1944.

SKUBIC, ELVERA. "A Study in Acquaintanceship and Social Status in Physical Education Classes." *Research Quarterly.* 20: 80-87; March 1949.

STRANG, RUTH. *Behavior and Background of Students in College and Secondary School.* New York: Harper and Brothers, 1937.

STRANG, RUTH. *The Role of the Teacher in Personnel Work.* New York: Bureau of Publications, Teachers College, Columbia University, 1935.

TRAXLER, ARTHUR. *Techniques of Guidance.* New York: Harper and Brothers, 1945.

# CHAPTER TWELVE

# *Evaluation*

Ruth Abernathy

Dorothy Zirbes

Wᴵᴛʜᴵɴ the framework of their needs, it is the job of the teacher or leader to use the tools available to assist adolescents to clarify where they are in the learning situation, where they want to go and how they may reach their objectives. This means stock-taking at the beginning, numerous appraisals along the way and final estimates of progress made. Evaluation is three dimensional in a time sense; it takes place concurrently with setting goals, planning and carrying out plans; it takes place whenever the group feels a need to pause and see how far it has come in achieving stated ends; it takes place when a project is completed or a problem solved.

It is difficult for some persons to understand how all the steps in group process operate continuously, yet in actuality this occurs. A good comparison is that of the earth rotating on its axis at the same time that it moves in a definite orbit around the sun. The general goals of a group will prescribe the direction the group wishes to go, but within that prescribed path there is a daily recasting of specific objectives, replanning and acting. Evaluation accompanies each phase of the daily operations as well as the over-all process.

It is the purpose of this chapter to focus on the ways in which some of the outcomes of health education, physical education and recreation may be investigated and interpreted. The more quantitative aspects of evaluation dealing with program outcomes such as increased health knowledge, accuracy in archery or participation in a greater variety of recreational pursuits will be considered only as they relate to outcomes in the area of human relations.

Some teachers and leaders may recall when evaluation was really simple. In physical education, for example, there was a time when students stood in straight rows and responded to commands and each lesson was evaluated by two criteria, precision and perspiration. Now it is not so simple for we are concerned with what happens to the individual in relation to "living" goals. Evaluation in this larger sense is conceived to be that part of the learning process in which the adolescent shares with the leader the responsibility for looking at, checking on and drawing conclusions from his direction, his progress and his behavior in relation to the goals which were agreed upon.

If the group plans, then individuals in the group form judgments sooner or later and such judgments may be sound or unsound depending upon the basis upon which they are formulated. The job is to select or devise instruments or techniques which may serve as a basis for reasonable judgments. These judgments are the interpretations of where the group is, how far it has gone and how it operated. They may range from judgments formed through a study of mean scores to those based on the candid reports that the student makes at his own dinner table.

While the judgments formed on the basis of a student's comments at home might ultimately affect the program he was discussing, the problem of more immediate concern is what happened to the student himself. What did he know, how did he behave, how did he interpret the changes in himself? Were the changes in keeping with his wants and with social needs? Was he able to see the consequences of his own acts? Was he able to appraise the progress of the group and his own progress with a reasonable degree of accuracy? These questions relate to the on-going quality of learning as well as to the process through which learning takes place. They indicate recognition that the student does his own learning and, further, that evaluation is not something that is done to him. Evaluation is shared.

## Setting up Criteria for Evaluating

Literally, evaluating means deciding the worth of some action, thing or process. It is the assigning of value or lack of value in some degree. Obviously, the assignment of value or worth has to be done in the light of some criteria on which to base a judgment. The way in which criteria for evaluating are derived from goals in group process is not always clearly understood. It is also not always apparent why criteria set up by one group will not be the same as those derived by another, even when both groups have the same general aims. It is essential to see how criteria for evaluating are derived from goals.

Let us say that the general goals of a bowling club in a teen center have been identified as:

To improve ability to bowl
To run a bowling tournament for the center

In order to move toward achieving these aims the members of the bowling club will need to know where they are in their ability to bowl and where they are in their ability to organize and run a tournament. In the initial appraisal each goal is analyzed to deduce and list the knowledge, skills and understandings entering into the abilities involved. These might be listed as:

To improve ability to bowl
   knowledge of rules
   skill in bowling
To run a bowling tournament
   knowledge of suitable tournament forms
   knowledge of tournament scoring
   understanding how to assign responsibility
   skill in organizing committees
   skill as a participating member of a committee
   skill in umpiring

From among the items listed in this first analysis of what elements make up the goals they wish to attain, a given group sets up its specific objectives according to the needs of that group. Needs change as planning and carrying out plans to attain the objectives go on; objectives are changed when needs change. Carrying the bowling club example a bit further may help make this clear. A year ago, when this club was formed, its members did not know how to bowl nor did they know the rules. But that was a year ago, and they have progressed in skill and in knowledge of the rules. The objectives now set call for more definitive knowledge and skills of a higher level. The needs have changed and the objectives have changed. In other words, the analysis of goals into specifics does not take place once for all at the beginning, but is repeated as learning occurs and new needs are understood.

In several instances the need for clarification of goals and specifically in the statement of objectives has been mentioned. It has been pointed out that this careful statement of purposes and steps involved in attainment is an essential prerequisite to effective learning, in that there is less waste motion in getting under way and in knowing what to do next. Attention has also been given to the fact that the goals change as progress is made just as the bowler changes his objective from trying to hit the head pin to the more productive "putting it in the pocket." These objectives also indicate what is to be evaluated. For example, criteria of the bowlers might be stated as skill in hitting the pocket, picking off the 1-3-7 spare or sharpening a hook rather than knocking down more pins. The *how* should be involved or implicit in the objective or criterion.

Criteria for evaluating how the group is operating are set up through the same type of analysis as that described for bowling. When and if the group sets a goal for itself such as "good discussions," "being effective as leaders," "being a productive committee member," each of these will be analyzed to see what the group needs to do to improve and the ways defined become the criteria for evaluating progress.

## Techniques for Evaluating

Many techniques are now available for use in evaluating. They range from the simple to the complex, from the objective to the subjective and from written tests to observations of game skills and social behaviors. Techniques range from those designed for use in the research laboratory to those involving such simple questions as "Is this objective really pertinent to the goal?" The former probably would be applicable to work with adolescents only to the extent that they accepted participation in an experimental study as a goal or to the extent that such study was in keeping with the goals previously determined.

The problem is to choose or devise instruments that will meet the needs of the group at a given time, in a given situation and in terms of the purposes that group has accepted. This means the selection of those techniques which will provide best the information required. For example: a rules test in basketball is not indicative of game ability. Nor will it give information as to skills in human relations or social behaviors. On the other hand, an instrument designed to appraise strategy in a game situation may also point to certain personality traits and to attitudes toward others. Likewise, techniques designed to estimate behavior toward others, positions in the group, fulfilment of the leader role and the like may be of aid to the leader in revealing clues to possible problems in the development of game strategy.

Another aspect of selection has to do with the applicability of the techniques in terms of time and resources. Sometimes the best instrument in terms of a given criterion may not be usable in a given situation because the group is too large or it is beyond the understanding of the group. The actual clock time required for explaining, discussing, understanding and using the instrument may be more than the group can afford to devote to it in terms of other objectives to be evaluated. This factor in selecting techniques might be more simply stated as, "Don't bite off more than can be chewed," but rather stick to the essential and assist the youngsters in deciding upon those essentials. This involves the role of the leader as a resource person.

Techniques should also be selected in the light of group interests. A part of the group might be vitally interested in evidence of their individual growth toward a given goal while the others might give evidence of complete boredom at the very idea. The reasons for such diversity might include lack of clarity in the goal, lack of acceptance of the goal by a part of the group, the instrument itself might not be understood or might not be related to the goal which had been accepted. A further factor might be that the goal accepted might not be suitable for the group, in the sense that it might be beyond the ability of the group to achieve. Obviously an instrument devised to check progress toward such a goal would also be unsuitable. This is another aspect of the need to be sure that the goals set are realistic and possible of attainment.

Finally, in some areas if the leader waits to select only those techniques that are known to have what is called reliability, few if any selections will be made. The reasons are two-fold, first, a reliable instrument does not yet exist, or second, if one is available it is too complicated to use in the ordinary group or class situation. The requirements for special equipment, the numbers to be tested at a given time, the complexity of scoring and the difficulties in interpreting all might serve to make the instrument an unwise or impossible selection. The leader cannot afford to wait. The group is there and in action. The goals have been determined and the objectives set. It is the job of the leader or the teacher to work with the group in selecting or devising as sound an instrument as can be obtained. While he will work as always within the framework of his own best understanding of need and direction, it should be clear that his recommendations must be based on fact rather than "feel." Sensitivity in or to a group is not enough. The leader must assume responsibility for a continuing review of research in his own and related fields in order that the evaluation procedures will be as sound as current knowledge can make them. In any event, findings derived from an "unproved" instrument should be interpreted with caution. The members of the group should understand the limitations and should consider the findings in the nature of clues which will entail further study, analysis and verification by other means.

The following discussion of useful techniques is presented on the assumption that teachers and leaders will make use of the variety of tests that are usable in their fields as well as collect general background information that is available about the adolescents concerned. Among these would be skill tests, knowledge tests, data from health examinations, family histories and other cumulative data from the counselor's office, school or department records. Such data may on occasion provide the verification needed in order to interpret the findings of the techniques to be described.

## Observers' Reports

The effective leader or teacher is continuously involved in observation and in drawing conclusions concerning the behavior observed.

The anecdotal report is an example of the effort to objectify such observations. It is concerned primarily with the behavior of an individual and used serially as a basis for interpretation can be most helpful, particularly as the process and findings are shared with the individual concerned. This technique to be sound should be carefully planned. Decisions as to what is to be observed, how much and how it is to be recorded and summarized should precede its use. Implicit in this is the fact that judgments will be made in the light of some value system, and for this reason it is advisable to clarify thinking as to the purpose of each observation and the criteria involved. The health teacher in relation to studies in nutrition may encounter problems that make it advisable to observe and record behaviors incident to the school lunch program. The coach concerned with the need for more hits and runs will observe and analyze movement; for example, in batting and base running.

Some teachers have found that students can also develop individual records with profit in terms of increased acuity in observation, and heightened incentive. The role of the leader is to aid in interpretation and to assist the student in *doing* something about the behavior observed.

This observer technique is now applied for the purpose of assisting the group to recognize the influence of behavior on process, on the effectiveness of discussion and carrying out plans. The observer's report in this instance would include a description of climate or "feeling tone," individual responses, the action of the leader and other roles. The report should emphasize process rather than content and serve as a review of how the group operated.

Even the simple observer's report requires that the observer have some preparation and competence. The following are important facets of this role:

He must be able to "see" what goes on in the group and to record it. This means that he must recognize the possible impact of his own needs on what he is able to observe and record.

He must recognize that the "feed back" must be adapted to the level of the group to which he is reporting. He must be able to start with group operation and as security is gained the experienced observer may move toward reporting member roles.

He must indicate progress or lack of it as indicated by getting off the subject, staying problem-centered, lacking clarification, making decisions.

He must be able to tell the difference between friendliness in a group and real progress toward the goal.

He must be able to stimulate the group to evaluate and to make decisions concerning the points observed that affect group action.

It will be noted that these guide lines for observers are centered in *how* the group operated, *how* things happened. With adolescents it is not necessarily advisable to go beyond this to interpreting *why*. This requires experience in group process, maturity and objectivity on the part of both the group and the observer. If not done on a mature and objective level, it results in destructive criticism of individuals. On the other hand, the how may be reported as a matter of fact with emphasis on "we"—*we* did not, or *we* did, and *we* should do.

Making a guide sheet for use in observing is sometimes helpful. A series of questions or statements are listed covering the factors or points to be observed, under which comments may be made. For example, questions dealing with how well the group planned might include: Were the objectives clear? Were they set by the group? Was there evidence of consensus? Were plans clear? How many were proposed? Was consideration given minority opinion? Was provision made for evaluation? Was replanning based on evaluation? What resources were used? Relative to evaluation, questions might be: Were the criteria clear? Were comments based on fact rather than opinion? Were comments objective? Were comments to the point? Were proposals made for future action? Was accomplishment clear in terms of goals? What resources were used? Getting under way in discussion might well involve questions which are indicative of preplanning, such as: Was the problem clearly stated? Was there time and opportunity to discuss and clarify various aspects of the problem? Was there evidence that the group knew what was expected of it? Was there evidence that the group knew what to do? Was allocation or limitation of time made clear?

## Recorders' Reports

A recorder's report provides a record of the activities of the group. It may be as inclusive as the group desires and in keeping with the ways it is to be used. Such a report differs from that of the observer in that it includes a recording of the decisions that were made, who was to undertake what assignment, what issues, ideas and opinions were expressed and what action was taken or not taken. It is used to assist the group in keeping its direction clear and staying with the main issues involved as well as to give direction and obtain action relative to the correction or approval of the report itself. If the report has been planned to serve as a summary of group action and to provide clues for replanning it can be so used to advantage.

The purposes which the report is to serve should be developed by the group in the light of its own needs. If it is to be used for the purpose of interpreting the effectiveness of group functioning then the recorder should assume responsibility for seeing that the report includes such points as the effectiveness of communication, the assumption of responsibility by group members for improving group functioning through participation in decisions, accepting varying roles and thorough understanding of group purposes. The "we-ness" of the group is evidenced by the exchange of ideas, the development of long range plans toward goals and the ability to handle conflicts that arise. Another indication is the use of resources from both outside and within the group.[1]

## Questionnaires and Checklists

Various types of questionnaires and checklists have long been used in health education, physical education and recreation. Examples are the interest inventory and the activity-experience inventory. These instruments are particularly useful when it is desired to get information from many individuals. If properly constructed they are easy to summarize. The method of responding can be checks in *yes* and *no* columns, choice on a descending scale as 1-2-3 or other variations. These techniques are helpful in group process in that they may be short cuts for obtaining group opinion or pooling information about a given procedure or problem.

[1] For additional information regarding observers' and recorders' reports see National Training Laboratory in Group Development. *Report of the Second Laboratory Session.* Ann Arbor, Mich.: National Education Association and Research Center for Group Dynamics, University of Michigan, Bulletin No. 3. Washington, D. C.: Division of Adult Education, 1948.

## Rating Scales

Under the heading of nonquantitative and nonobjective instruments of evaluation, may be classified the kind of rating scales which are constructed by leader and group together to define and specify desirable behavior traits. Adolescents are often anxious to know what is expected from them in the way of social behavior by their peers and by adults. They are reassured by knowing what broad ideas like sportsmanship, getting along with others and citizenship mean in terms of action. The process of constructing and using a rating scale is an excellent device for stimulating a purposeful and enlightening discussion of socially acceptable behavior patterns. When the group members become really involved in the making of a scale they are more apt to do their self-ratings and ratings of others thoughtfully. Also they are ready to gain the most from such follow-up procedures as personal interviews where the rating may be the subject of the conference. An example of how such a rating scale was made in a senior high-school volleyball class may serve to illustrate these points.

At the beginning of the volleyball unit during a planning discussion, one boy mentioned "cooperation" as a desirable objective ("I like to play on a team where all the guys cooperate"). Heads nodded and some mention was made of the idea from time to time. When evaluation procedures were being set up for midterms, it was suggested that cooperation should be included as a part of self and team ratings. During the ensuing discussion, many ideas of cooperation were presented, some definitions attempted and innumerable examples brought up. The boys began to have a common understanding of the concept in *action* terms. The elements selected for the rating constituted a summary of the discussion and were (a) playing one's own position and not hogging the ball, (b) being prompt and ready to play at the start of each playing period, (c) trying to improve each day, (d) backing up teammates during play, and (e) making constructive suggestions to: (1) individuals, (2) the team, (3) the whole class.

A similar process was used in constructing a scale for skills analysis. The wholesome effect of making, doing and interpreting the ratings continued during the life of the group in whatever activities they engaged, because a background in vocabulary and meanings about cooperation had been established in the group.

Another example is presented below showing how a rating scale was developed as a result of a problem that arose in a group. The example points to the difference in potential for learning between the admonition, "I won't have this," and group decision regarding a needed change in behavior.

The dressing room was a mess, something really had to be done. When the class came together the problem was presented and it was discussed in some detail. A survey committee was selected by the group to make a preliminary study. The committee worked in the dressing room and compiled a list of the words used and the actions observed which it felt provided evidence of the attitudes of class members toward the dressing room situation. This was reviewed with the class. From the list of its own words and actions the group developed a rating scale or appraisal form which it then used to serve as a basis for needed replanning. The resultant change in the dressing room was quite probably more the result of an increased awareness of the problem and group responsibility for it, gained through construction of the rating scale, than the result of using the scale for self-appraisal.

The value of rating scales is proportionate to the depth of meaning to the group using them. Prepared scales may appeal to a teacher as a short cut and as a means of covering many points comprehensively. However, the effect on a group is apt to be superficial and temporary. The values of making the scale are sacrificed and meaning may be obscured. The "home made" scale may not be scientifically constructed but has the advantage of coming directly out of group life and therefore being understood in a fresh, immediate sense.

Very similar to rating scales are instruments which provide for making one among several choices. These are similar to the multiple choice knowledge tests on which correct scores are made as the right answer is selected from among several. Situations in which these instruments might be used to evaluate behavior are: being a committee chairman, organization of a team, planning with group, practicing skills, keeping score, the shower and dressing room, the toilet room, watching a game, losing a game, forming a dance set, awaiting turns, close or wrong decision in a game. With the situation given, the problem becomes one of clarifying behavior choices. The situation and choices given as example indicate the way in which items are clarified. The number of situations on a given instrument will depend upon what the group wishes to find out about its own behavior.

| *Situation* | *Behavior Choices* |
|---|---|
| | Fringe—no activities |
| | Fringe—lone activity |
| Free play period | Sabotages activity of others |
| | Joins with others |
| | Takes leader and member roles |

## *Sociometric Test*

Among the newer techniques is the sociometric test which reveals a great deal about the relationships among group members. A working group may then be organized on the basis of the information obtained. A retest at a later date often shows progress made in becoming a real group with greater acceptance of individuals made possible through congenial smaller groupings. This technique is not described here, since it is explained briefly in Chapter 8 and in detail in Chapter 16.

## *Final Appraisal*

The group will need to devise procedures which may be used to summarize the findings of all the techniques used. The purpose is to provide an over-view of progress made toward all of the goals. Such a summary prepared by the group or by a committee with the leader serving as a resource person throughout, when it has been revised and approved by the group, would be descriptive of group operations and accomplishments.

## Using the Techniques and Findings

Care should be taken to insure that a given technique is used, scored and interpeted in keeping with the rules governing that particular type. There are differences, for example, among a true-false test, a skills test, an observer's report, a rating scale and a questionnaire. With a skills test there are specific leads that must be done before the test is given. There must be explanation of what the test is, how it is to be scored, either demonstration or practice in doing the test and a warm up before the test begins. The rating scale requires some competence in judging the trait or characteristic observed; this then would imply that preparation of a differing type would be required. There is a great deal of difference in forming judgments on the basis of a series of bull's-eyes and on behaviors supposedly indicative of cooperation and sharing. Anecdotal records require a degree of skill and studied serially may be interpreted by the teacher or leader with more confidence than could the same person interpret a student diary or autobiography. The observer's report at even the more simple descriptive level must be based upon objective criteria and must record what actually happens.

The time or when to evaluate arises out of process. When the leader plans with participants a part of that plan is finding out from time to time how they are getting along. The group that operates effectively and without "going it blind" or getting "fog bound" will see places where it will need to make use of evaluation techniques in order to take stock. This points to the need for flexibility as well as an awareness of when such rethinking or double checking is necessary.

In spite of the importance of appropriate selecting and proper use of techniques, the really significant phase of evaluation lies in what is done with the findings and what happens as a result. Since increasing maturity is the ultimate goal, the moving ahead of the group and the individual members toward evaluating behaviors objectively and realistically is a prime requisite of the learning process. The way in which findings are anticipated, understood and accepted also bears a relation to what will be done about them. If the findings are used in such a way that they become frustrating and defeating to the group or individuals, then it is improbable that the next steps will be toward larger and more rich experience in the area of the objective evaluated. This response of the participants to evaluation is probably closely associated with the climate or "feeling tone." If it has been permissive, democratic and supporting, the chances are good that morale will be high. High morale in turn will serve as a stimulus to use the findings for further learning.

Findings, to be effective, must be interpreted in the light of their meaning in relation to the goals. The individual and the group have changed. The questions are, how much and in what direction? For in terms of this change, needs also have changed. This means that replanning is necessary. Once again the on-going relations of goal setting, planning, carrying out plans, evaluating and replanning become evident. With adequate guidance in using the findings from evaluation the relationships become clear to the group.

In school situations the findings from evaluation should comprise the basis for marking. Marks, as symbols of progress or lack of progress, seem to be inevitable in the present school situation. At best marks are but symbols of value judgments derived from some evidence about a partial aspect of growth toward the goal. At worst, marks become the goal, with consequent distortion of values on the part of the learner. Probably the best that can be done is to provide as sound a base for marking as possible and to attempt to make it meaningful to both students and parents. This rests in part on process and in part on the techniques used in evaluation.

Students are involved and consequently should share in planning relative to marking. The group can assist in the development of criteria upon which the marks will be based; the individual can share in estimating his own progress. By comparing his own estimate with that of the teacher, if both understand and reconcile differences, it is possible that the mark will have more meaning. Through class and individual sessions on marking the student may gain insight into his progress and the factors that entered into the mark given.

As the student understands the significance of his marks he is better able to interpret them to his parents. The teacher can also aid in this understanding through the use of anecdotal notes to parents or conferences with them.

## Self-Appraisal of the Leader

While the evaluation of the group and of individuals within it will provide many helpful clues for the leader both as to his own and the program's efficacy, there is a need for periodic stock-taking by the leader himself. This would be based on essentially the same questions that have been discussed in relation to selecting techniques, namely: What are the goals? What should be evidence of attainment or criteria? What progress has been made?

It has been demonstrated in every discussion of group process that the leader's attitudes and actions are the most crucial factors for success or failure of the method. It is not easy to appraise the attitudes and actions of oneself. Willingness to do so is a first step. Efforts to appraise honestly and objectively must be made. Questions the leader might ask himself are:

Am I mature, friendly and understanding in dealing with adolescents?

Am I fair in decisions and judgments?

Do I have patience and faith in people?

Have I a sense of humor?

Can I let the youngsters struggle with a problem and not "butt in" unless they get stuck, or the job requires a skill they do not have? (Am I sure they don't have the skill?)

Do I use my professional preparation in helping adolescents move toward goals they have accepted?

Do I take advantage of the best methods in the light of what is now known about learning?

Do I really assist young people in finding out for themselves the need for self-direction and self-responsibility—do I give them a chance to find out?

What do I really believe about people?

What do I really know about adolescents? Physical, social and emotional problems of growth? Understanding the characteristic ambivalent and inconsistent behaviors?

What do I really know about the developing concept of self in the adolescent, do I really appreciate his needs as a biosocial organism?

Do I have a full appreciation of the *wants* of the adolescent in terms of freedom, discipline, independence, fair play, loyalty, and integrity?

Do I understand the problem of the adolescent in attempting to develop a mature value scale and his effort to gain a philosophy to live by?

Do I really conceive of my professional tools being for the purpose of assisting the youngster toward a variety of goals including improved human relations?

Am I mature, is my value scale mature, do I know the philosophy I live by, am I a democratic human being?

The following list was developed by a physical education teacher for the purpose of checking the program:

1. Efficient use of teaching time without pressure
2. "Life" and dynamic climate (a test of climate)
   a. do youngsters want to get into it; are they unhappy if they are absent; do they come willingly on Saturday?
   b. how many doctors' excuses does the program support?
   c. what do restricted people do?
3. High lights and interesting "extras" like:
   sports nights and demonstrations
   (perhaps using proceeds for college scholarships)
   pamphlets to parents on programs and procedures
   letters to parents pointing up long-spots for youngsters
   visiting days for parents
   teas for mothers
   father-son ball games
   mother-daughter banquets
   out of town trips with teams—leaders
   news reports—use of radio
4. The variety of activities, knowing that desirable student outcomes are better where variety exists
5. Opportunities to evaluate behavior patterns and build concepts, traditions, spirit, direction
6. Strengths and weaknesses of program possibilities due to time, space, facilities
   a. reports to principals, superintendents and boards of education
   b. recommendations for improvements
   c. temporary stop-gaps—maybe renting outside space, etc.
   d. long-range planning in terms of desired pupil outcomes for members of a democratic society
7. The kind of public relations job that each teen-ager will do at the family dinner table
8. Development of the whole child; is everything he does in school favorable educational experience?
9. Measurement and self-evaluation and the method and meaning of grades
10. The necessary revisions of curriculum
11. Community understanding, interest, support.

This chapter has sought to give some answers to the question: What ways are there to find out the degree to which adolescents are developing the concepts and attitudes basic to democratic relations with others? A number of ways have been described but no one of them is held to be a "must" for evaluation in group process. The only "must" involved is the fact that adolescents learn better through doing than being done to. They learn as they have opportunity and become able to share, responsibly and cooperatively, in whatever evaluative procedures are selected or devised by leader and group.

## Bibliography

BURTON, WILLIAM H. *The Guidance of Learning Activities*. New York: Appleton-Century-Crofts, Inc., 1944.

CHISHOLM, LESLIE. *Guiding Youth in the Secondary School*. New York: American Book Co., 1945.

COWELL, CHARLES C. "Diary Analysis: A Suggested Technique for the Study of Children's Activities and Interests." *Research Quarterly*. 8: 158-72; May 1937.

CRAWFORD, JOHN E., and WOODWARD, LUTHER E. *Better Ways of Growing Up*. Philadelphia: Muhlenberg Press, 1948.

CROW, LESTER, and CROW, ALICE. *Our Teen Age Boys and Girls*. New York: McGraw-Hill Book Co., 1945.

DIEDERICH, PAUL B. "Evaluation Records." *Educational Method*. 15: 432-40; May 1936.

ERICKSON, CLIFFORD E., and HAPP, MARION C. *Guidance Practices at Work*. New York: McGraw-Hill Book Co., 1946.

KOZMAN, HILDA CLUTE; CASSIDY, ROSALIND; and JACKSON, CHESTER O. *Methods in Physical Education*. Philadelphia: W. B. Saunders Co., 1947.

KUHLEN, RAYMOND, and BRETSCH, HOWARD. "Sociometric Status and Personal Problems of Adolescents." *Sociometry* 10: 122-32; May 1947.

MC CLELLAND, F. M., and RATIFF, JOHN A. "The Use of Sociometry in Promoting Social Adjustment in a Ninth Grade Home Room." *Sociometry* 10: 147-53; May 1947.

MIEL, ALICE. "A Group Studies Itself." *Teachers College Record*. 49: 31-43; October 1947.

RATHS, LOUIS B. "Criteria for a Program for Evaluation." *Educational Research Bulletin*, The Ohio State University. 17: 846; March 16, 1938.

RAUTMAN, ARTHUR L. "The Physical Education Teacher as a Personal Model." *Journal of the American Association of Health, Physical Education and Recreation*. 21: 10-14; January 1950.

STRANG, RUTH. *Behavior and Background of Students in College and Secondary School*. New York: Harper and Brothers, 1937.

STRANG, RUTH. *Counseling Technics in College and Secondary School*. New York: Harper and Brothers, 1941.

STRANG, RUTH. *Reporting to Parents*. Practical Suggestions for Teaching Series No. 10. New York: Columbia University Press, 1947.

WRINKLE, WILLIAM L. *Improving Marking and Reporting Practices in Elementary and Secondary Schools*. New York: Rinehart and Co., 1947.

# Programs for Older Youth

BEN W. MILLER, *Coordinator*
*Executive Director, American Youth Hostels*

13. THE PERIOD OF LATER ADOLESCENCE
ROBERT T. KRETCHMAR
*Assistant Professor of Physical Education*
*The Ohio State University*
MARIE NOGUES
*Associate Professor of Health, Physical*
*Education and Recreation*
*Mills College, California*

14. CONCEPTS AND ATTITUDES TO BE DEVELOPED
MARY ELLA CRITZ
*Instructor of Physical Education*
*State University of Iowa*
MARGARET E. EVERETT
*Instructor of Physical Education*
*State University of Iowa*
MARGARET G. FOX
*Associate Professor of Physical Education*
*State University of Iowa*
ELIZABETH HALSEY
*Professor of Physical Education*
*State University of Iowa*
M. GLADYS SCOTT
*Professor of Physical Education*
*State University of Iowa*

15. METHODS
ALMA M. HAWKINS
*Associate Professor of Physical Education*
*George Williams College*

16. EVALUATION
MARGARET DUNCAN GREENE
*Assistant Professor of Physical Education*
*University of California*
*Los Angeles, California*

*. . . it is reasonable to assume an over-all purpose toward which all men can devote their lives. . . . What is such a purpose? For our day, it is the endeavor to improve society for all men. But lest the Hitlers lay claim to this same goal, there is needed some test by which to resolve conflicting values. This test can be whether a given course of action tends continuously to produce a social order in which the values are good will, understanding, mutual recognition of interests, reciprocity, and cooperation among men. The course of action that does so is good, and should have the right of way. Whether or not this is the ultimate purpose of life for all time, it is the one which stands the best chance of capturing the imaginations of the young people of today. They seem potentially to be socially minded. They are less concerned than former generations with personal glorification and ultimate salvation, with the goals of glory, power, and wealth. When they sense the maladjustments in society today, and the opportunities for creating a better life on earth, they respond with eager desire to participate.* ALGO D. HENDERSON, Vitalizing Liberal Education

# CHAPTER THIRTEEN

# The Period of Later Adolescence

ROBERT T. KRETCHMAR

MARIE NOGUES

T HE period of later adolescence has been defined by some authorities as encompassing the ages 19 to 21.[1] We shall consider this
period, however, in a broader sense by giving attention to those
individuals whose ages range from 18 through 22—the college age
group. This is a period in which young people are approaching
maturity. Age, of course, is no certain indication of the degree of
maturity which a person has attained. A better indication is the
manner in which he meets his own problems and the obligations
which society imposes upon him.[2]

The behavior of these young men and women, like the behavior
of their younger brothers and sisters, is determined by their efforts
to fulfil their needs. Their characteristics and ways differ from
those who are younger because they have somewhat different needs
and face different problems. Practically all have more independence than they have previously known. Along with this greater
independence they often develop feelings of uncertainty and insecurity. In a sense, "the chips are now down." Many feel they are
now in "the game" and all that has gone before has been merely
preparatory. Let us look more closely into the characteristics and
problems of these young people.

[1] Schnell, Dorothy M. *Characteristics of Adolescence.* Minneapolis: Burgess Publishing Company,
1946. p. 46.
[2] Goodenough, Florence L. *Development Psychology.* New York: Appleton-Century-Crofts, Inc.,
1945. p. 534.

# Where Are They?

## *Physical Growth*

During this period (18-22 years) physical growth is for the most part completed.[3] Some of the young men will continue to grow in height until the age of 20. Most of the young women have attained their full stature by the age of 18. Both men and women have completed sexual maturity with the exception of a few very retarded individuals. Glandular changes no longer cause the acne and pimples so upsetting previously.

These youth differ considerably from their younger teen-age brothers and sisters in that they have a "pulled together" look about them. No longer do they appear as the awkward gangling adolescent who is all arms and legs. They have become physically coordinated and integrated. Older adolescents have far less need than younger for assurances that they are normal physically. In most instances they can see that this is so.

## *Understanding Themselves*

These young people are now becoming increasingly aware of themselves as individuals with strengths and weaknesses. Many at this time are forced to take a realistic inventory of their personal assets and liabilities. The high-school graduate who seeks a job is immediately brought face to face with his abilities in comparison with the abilities of others. The youth who enters college likewise becomes immediately aware of his abilities—primarily academic— in comparison with others. For example, freshmen in one university receive various tests during their first quarter in residence, including a college aptitude examination, a general culture test, a current affairs test, an English proficiency examination, a mathematics placement test, and a reading proficiency examination. The results of these examinations are given to the students in the form of percentile ratings. In other words, the entering student is soon made aware of his ability in these various areas in relation to the ability of others. Regardless of the significance, validity, or reliability of these tests, it must be recognized that they affect the

[3] *Ibid.* p. 499.

student's understanding and appraisal of himself. All of this is not to condemn these tests. Certainly the warning of the Greek philosophers to "know thyself" is meaningful. Young people today are inevitably forced to face situations in which many of their shortcomings as well as their strengths will appear obvious.

Also the attainment of physical maturity during this period may affect the individual's appraisal of himself. Here again young people are brought face to face with reality. The young man of small stature who as a boy dreamed of becoming a college football star now realizes that perhaps he cannot even make the squad.

However obvious the strengths and weaknesses of these young people appear, many of them have considerable difficulty in appraising their own capabilities. Sometimes they underrate their abilities. A college freshman consulted her adviser twice within the first three weeks of the quarter to talk with him concerning withdrawing from school. She was obviously in a state of great anxiety. Scholastically, she was discouraged. Actually, she had no sound basis for her concern. According to prognostic instruments employed by the college, the evidence suggested that she was not only capable of completing college work, but also of achieving scholastic success and recognition. Her score on the psychological examination, a college aptitude test, was 71 percentile; her score on an English proficiency test was 91 percentile. Yet this individual was discouraged and actually felt incapable of passing her course work. A check with her instructors revealed that she was doing very satisfactory work.

Sometimes members of this group overrate their abilities. One young man, unattractive in appearance, particularly self-conscious, shy, nonsocial and devoid of any apparent qualities of leadership, decided he would prepare to become a dean of men in a college. Ignoring suggestions from teachers and friends he went on to graduate school to take work in educational administration. Upon completing the M.A. degree, he searched in vain for an administrative position in a college. Undismayed, he returned to graduate school to continue study for a doctorate in educational administration. This individual of superior scholastic ability obviously lacked insight concerning his vocational potentialities. There are others like him in this age group. Despite the numerous situations which tend to make evident to these young people their abilities and limitations, it is clear that many of their number need help in understanding themselves.

## Winning Independence from Parents

For various reasons, some geographical, some social, some economic, some biological, most of these young people gain increasing independence during this period. The young man who now has a full-time job and is able to pay his parents for room and board gains new feelings of independence and pride. The college student away from home for the first time is often overwhelmed with his newly-won freedom. To many young people increased freedom and independence are neither easily given nor received. The over-protective, often immature, parent does not graciously foster his child's independence. To the children of these parents even geographical distance does not bring freedom. Many college students, although many miles from home, are still dominated and directed by their parents.

There are a surprising number of students following particular college curriculums because of their parents' desires rather than their own. The desires of these students will frequently eventually prevail, but in many instances it is not until after failure has occurred in the curriculum selected by the parents. When asked, "Why did you not begin this program in the first place?" they answer that their parents wanted them to prepare for a vocation in another area. For boys this often means the vocational area of the father or an uncle.

Some young people are hesitant to seek independence from their parents. They are fearful of the insecurity which may come with this independence. Some have become so accustomed to the protection, guidance, and direction of their elders, they encounter difficulty developing any other type of relationship with their parents. Much anxiety displayed by college freshmen is due largely to the absence for the first time of their "problem solver," mother and/or father. We all know the extreme "Mom's boy" or "Dad's girl" type of young person. Often these young people enter the period of later adolescence as anxious, shy, timid individuals, unused to associating with others and without having had to take responsibility for themselves or others.

In some instances athletic teams, clubs, sororities, fraternities, or dormitory life will assist these young people in developing independence from parents and to become more out-going in their relations with others.

Youth who seek employment after graduation from high school, like their college friends, encounter some difficulty in their new freedom. The people with whom they work may not seem so kind as family or school associates. They sense hostility in their new environment. They realize that they are on their own and feel that they must prove themselves.

Luckily a great many of these young people are caught hold of by life and helped to grow outward and expand almost in spite of themselves. A few, however, even though placed in the best of circumstances, cannot use the opportunities that are available. They are too shy, self-conscious, or fearful to risk the competition that is inherent in the situation. Some are too aggressive, masking feelings of inferiority by challenging and provoking others, getting themselves disliked for this behavior. Often the period of later adolescence offers a youth his last chance of catching the attention of persons or groups that may help him. After adolescence people tend to consider him a grown-up person, an adult, and capable of taking care of himself.

## Heterosexual Adjustment

To some young people courtship, marriage and parenthood come within this period. For others this is a time of preparation for these responsibilities, a time in which interest in members of the opposite sex is narrowed in anticipation of selecting a partner for life. In some respects modern society has made it difficult for young men and women to make the adjustment to one another. In early America small community gatherings, church parties, sleigh rides, barn raisings, husking parties, and barn dances offered considerable opportunity for young men and women to meet, and learn to know one another within a stable, understood social situation. The loss of neighborly contacts among people, caused by urbanization and the tendency of large numbers to move from place to place, has changed the picture. In many instances today, young people are forced to rely on chance meetings at school, at work, upon the street or in taverns. The changed situation has not gone unheeded. The scope of co-recreational activities on the weekly social calendar of many colleges and universities—mixed swimming parties, folk dance frolics, roller skating parties, sports nights, all-university dances, to name a few—is evidence of efforts to provide opportunities to college students for meeting and getting to know members of the opposite sex. Nor are these opportunities available only to the young people in college. Noncollege young men and women help plan and participate in social functions of churches, "Y," recreation departments, and various club groups.

Many in this age group have made satisfactory heterosexual adjustment, that is, they have accepted themselves as man or woman, in great measure because they have been accepted by the opposite sex and are sought as friends, companions and lovers. Some have yet to complete this developmental task as is very evident to those who work with college students or groups of young working men and women.

Those who are ready for marriage and have, in addition, selected their marriage partner face a particular sex-social dilemma.[4] In our society biological maturity and economic independence do not coincide. Marriage is delayed several years for many young couples because of financial factors. Sometimes, parents are willing to help financially in order to make earlier marriage possible. Sometimes, young people solve the problem by both working, taking turns at going to school to complete their education in a variety of partnership patterns that are becoming more and more prevalent in our society.

However, there are an unknown number in this age group who are deterred from seeking marriage for financial reasons. This places restrictions upon their relations with the opposite sex and, sometimes result in various undesirable expressions of sex drives. This pushing upward of the age when marriage is possible, too far above

[4] Pressey, Luella C. Some College Students and Their Problems. Columbus: The Ohio State University Press, 1929. p. 1.

the age of biological readiness for marriage, especially among the professional and semiprofessional groups, demands the creation of new social patterns in which young people can operate. What these patterns might be is only dimly seen. What they will be cannot be predicted.

## Selecting, Preparing For and Carrying Out Life Work

Most young people give thought and consideration to their vocational future while in high school and, in some instances, while still in junior high school. It is not, however, until the period of late adolescence that selection and decision in this matter are forced. A large number of them are not ready at this time to make a decision and few of them in the working world are confident of the wisdom of a particular vocational choice. The great amount of shifting about from job to job would indicate that many of them are still groping in their search for a vocation. Their college friends apparently fare no better. They, too, for the most part, are vocationally uncertain. Witness the great amount of transferring from one college curriculum to another. Perhaps this problem is aggravated in many schools by requiring the incoming student to declare immediately his field of specialization. Thus a decision is forced before many are prepared to decide wisely.

This uncertainty about a vocation or career is not surprising. These young people are in a period of becoming increasingly aware of their strengths and shortcomings. They may find that goals established in an earlier period are unrealistic. They may find that they have aimed either too high or too low. One whose boyhood ambition was to become a train engineer may now decide to enter a college of engineering. Another who dreamed of becoming a big league ball player decides now to become a teacher of physical education. Another realizes that he does not have sufficient ability in chemistry to become a doctor. And so it goes with college or non-college youth.

The tremendous amount of change in vocational goals during this period is evident to anyone who guides college youths. In every large university there is a continual flux of students from one college to another. A student who started in the college of engineering decides he would rather be a teacher than an engineer and transfers to the college of education. Another student who is in the college of education decides he would like to get into the area of sales and merchandising and transfers to the college of commerce. Transfers are continuous and in all directions.

The young woman faces a particular difficulty in this area because of the uncertainty of marriage. Is she to prepare for a career? Is the expense and time involved in preparing for a career justified if she is contemplating marriage? Many young women resolve this difficulty by recognizing that preparation for a career is good security for even the married woman. Once this point of view is reached, the big question still remains unanswered: what career?

Fortunate indeed are the young people in this period who see eye to eye with their parents concerning vocational choice. For the majority of this group the choice is difficult enough even with parental understanding and cooperation. The young men in this group who are married may face further difficulty because of critical and unsympathetic in-laws. One young man's father-in-law, a successful lawyer, persistently disparaged the profession of teaching, suggesting that the young man give it up for something more lucrative. In addition to respecting the father-in-law's judgment, the young man feels some obligation to consider his wishes because of the financial assistance he is giving. Yet this young man feels in his own heart that he would be happier in teaching than in any other profession. His dilemma is repeated many times among young people in later adolescence.

In spite of the numerous difficulties which youth encounter in making a vocational selection, the majority of them do come to a reasonably satisfactory decision before the close of this period. Some have reached a clear decision early in the period and are preparing for or working at the vocation of their choice with confidence and enthusiasm.

## Their Use of Leisure

The bulk of the leisure time of these young people is spent in dating, reading, listening to radio, sports, movies, and dancing.[5]

[5] Mooney, Ross J. *A Study of Student Needs in Non-Academic Areas.* Columbus: Bureau of Educational Research, The Ohio State University, 1924. p. 49.

As evidenced from this list, much of their leisure time is spent in association with members of the opposite sex.

"Y" groups, fraternities, sororities and other social clubs often play a significant role in their leisure time. Dances, parties, and picnics which these groups sponsor are high lights in the lives of these young men and women. Unfortunately for the noncollege youth, a dearth of suitable social clubs exists in many communities.[6] This condition is particularly true for rural youth.

The interest of young people in sports has a definite pertinency to the subject of this yearbook. Numerous studies have been made relative to the interests of college men and women in sports. Beise, Toogood, Wiedemann, and Mason, among others, have made such studies.[7] Their findings would suggest that the activities most popular with college women are swimming, tennis, golf, riding, archery, and skating. The preferences of men are basketball, golf, swimming, tennis, football, baseball, and bowling. Perhaps it is significant that all of the activities preferred by the women and four of the activities preferred by the men are suitable for coeducational participation.

Mason asked 1040 men attending a state university whether they would be interested in coeducational physical education in such activities as tennis, golf, badminton, dancing, and swimming.[8] A total of 85 percent answered in the affirmative. Burkle points out that the force motivating young women toward a home and children is basic in their lives and for this reason women often prefer recreational activities such as bowling and badminton, since learning these activities will increase their opportunities for male companionship.[9]

This does not suggest that all young people are vitally interested in sports and that all physical recreation should be coeducational.

[6] Rainey, Homer P. *How Fare American Youth?* New York: Appleton-Century-Crofts, Inc., 1938. p. 89.

[7] Beise, Dorothy, "A Comparative Analysis of the Physical Education Background, Interests, and Desires of College Students as an Evaluation Procedure," *Research Quarterly*, 11: 120-34; December 1940.

Toogood, Ruth, "A Survey of Recreational Interests and Pursuits of College Women," *Research Quarterly*, 10: 90-100; October 1939.

Wiedemann, Inge L. and Howe, Eugene C. "Undergraduate Attitudes with Regard to Physical Education Activities at Wellesley College." *Research Quarterly*, 8: 15-32; March 1937.

Mason, James G. "A Study of the Interests of Men Students in the Physical Education Program and a Comparison with Similar Pre-War Studies," Unpublished Master's Thesis, The Ohio State University, 1947.

[8] Mason, James G. *op. cit.*, p. 83.

[9] Burkle, Louise E. "Planning Recreation Activities for Women," *Industrial Bulletin Service*, Washington, D. C.: National Recreation Association. (Reprint of speech delivered at Industrial Recreation Conference, January 27 and 28, 1946.)

Terman's study showed that some young men and women have little or no interest in sports. These youths, however, do not characterize this age group. The high mutual interest of young men and women in each other and in sports explains in part the popularity of co-recreational activities in communities and on college campuses.[10] The question to raise is whether opportunities are adequately provided them on every campus and in every community.

## Developing a Philosophy of Life

At this age many youth give their first serious thought to social values, moral interpretations, codes of conduct, and standards of behavior.[11]

By later adolescence many of these young people have begun to evolve a value system of their own. Just as they once rejected, or at least questioned, parental values and eagerly accepted the values of their age-group, so now with emergence into adulthood imminent, they question peer standards and values. They are exposed more and more, some in first jobs, others in college activities to associations with adults who hold diverse beliefs. In these associations with adults they are accepted more and more as grown-up persons. Much behavior of their "herd period" of a year or two ago seems silly now. In other words with maturity and the ability to form generalized concepts they are thinking for themselves. What are they to believe? Who should they believe? What is the truth? What is truth?

For some, a clash between their evolving philosophy of life and the beliefs, attitudes, and conventions of their parents is again inevitable, as it was in earlier adolescence.[12] A number of the group will at this time forsake the religion of their parents. One who has seen young people in the throes of making these breaks realizes the great emotional conflicts involved. Some of these young people will break with the political philosophy of their parents. The son of a successful republican may fervently embrace the idea of the "welfare state."

[10] Terman, Lewis M. and Miles, Catherine C. *Sex and Personality.* New York: McGraw-Hill Book Co., 1936, Chapter IX.
[11] Wrenn, Gilbert C. and Bell, Reginald. *Student Personal Problems.* New York: Farrar and Rinehart, 1942, p. 20.
[12] Pressey, Luella C. *op. cit.,* p. 1.

Although there are cynics in their number, the bulk of these young people are idealistic in their outlook. Often their idealism clashes with reality. Those who fail to recognize that such a conflict is inevitable and lifelong become considerably disturbed.[13] Some may for a while become quite skeptical. A few will assume a pseudo-cynicism because they believe it a mark of sophistication and intelligence. But this usually passes as they grow older.

## Where Are They Going?

Young people of later adolescence are headed at varying rates toward adult responsibilities and a place among men and women. Often the attainment of this goal is confused with their achievement of physical and legal maturity. Age and physical status, however, are not truly indicative of social and psychological maturity.

What are the characteristics of the social and psychological maturity for which these young people are striving? The two—social and psychological maturity—are interdependent and interrelated. If they are referred to here as if they were entities in themselves, it is only for the purposes of analysis. It is difficult to conceive of a person who is socially mature and psychologically immature.

Perhaps the essence of social maturity is the ability to recognize the needs of others and realize the importance of their fulfilment. The socially mature person recognizes that his happiness is interrelated with the happiness of others. The psychologically mature person is not overly preoccupied with his "self" and its satisfactions or too greatly absorbed with his ego. He acts with consideration for the long-time satisfaction of the entire group of persons involved. In his association with members of the opposite sex he is not ashamed or fearful. He is not unduly preoccupied with the thoughts of sex. He attempts to solve his own problems without immediately appealing to others for help; he does not flit from one problem to another without ever focusing his efforts and attention on one; he does not live continually in a world of fantasy and wishful thinking.

[13] Wrenn, Gilbert C. and Bell, Reginald. *op. cit.*, p. 20.

The conflicts between the standards and values of home, peer group and adults with whom youth associate, the discrepancy between their ideals and reality, the pressure of increased competition on the job and in college, and the striving for complete independence have fostered within them a measure of uncertainty and insecurity. However, they have come a long way from the self-centeredness and emotional instability of their early adolescent years. Now they have greater stability in emotional reactions, increased poise in social relations with both their own and the opposite sex, more direction in the expending of effort, and greater curiosity about the purpose of life.[14] They are on the brink of accepting adult responsibilities and taking their place in the world of men and women.

## Their Needs and Problems

### Basic Needs Common to All

All people, regardless of age, have certain basic needs such as need for food, shelter, clothing, acceptance by others, and distinction before others. They express themselves in varied and infinite ways in seeking the fulfilment of these common needs. Age, past experience, environment, and personal attributes all affect the manner in which they satisfy their needs. A child of two needs clothing almost solely for purposes of bodily warmth; a college student seeking the favor of a particular girl needs clothing for additional reasons. This suggests also an interrelatedness among people's needs. The need for clothing is often closely related with the need for acceptance by others. The proud new home owners are satisfying not only their need for shelter but also their need for status with others. Because of this interrelatedness among needs it is difficult to find an adequate way of classifying them.

All the needs of the late adolescent group, as of any other age group, are not unique and different. The uniqueness and difference comes largely in the ways these young people attempt to handle their needs. Young men and women reveal their true characteristics and individuality in attempting to accomplish the following tasks.

---

[14] Hartmann, George W. *Educational Psychology*. New York: American Book Company, 1941, p. 93.

*Accepting One's Self.* This particular need takes on new meaning at this age inasmuch as the young person is now fairly well aware of his physical, mental, and emotional potentialities, limitations, abilities and failings. It is not easy to understand why some of these young people, whose abilities are marked and unquestionable, apparently encounter difficulty in fulfilling this need; whereas others with obvious shortcomings move rather confidently and surely ahead. One young student, a physical education major with a 5'2" stature, was not only handicapped in athletics but also the object of many facetious remarks. He was a particularly popular student, confident, happy, apparently at peace with himself. Another young man who was good looking, well built, athletic and intelligent, felt so inferior and insecure that he was referred to a psychologist.

Often success and achievement in one area, despite failings in others, will foster a person's acceptance of himself. The mechanical ability of one young man, the dancing ability of another, the mathematical ability of a third might be the keys to their self-acceptance. For this reason it would appear wise for those who are associating with young people to recognize and commend their successes and achievements. The comments, opinions, actions of others toward them have crucial bearing upon their appraisal and acceptance of themselves. It is now recognized that a person's feelings toward himself are basic to his relationships with others. Self-respect is necessary to respect others. It is therefore very essential in helping students develop democratic relations with others to help them to understand, respect and accept themselves.

*Being Accepted by Others.* It is largely from the desire to be accepted by others that young people seek membership in sororities, fraternities, church groups, and various community organizations. It is also for this reason that many of them dress alike by wearing such articles as saddle shoes, bow ties, corduroy jackets, sweaters, and denim trousers. There is a feeling of security in belonging—in being a member of a group. There is also a sense of recognition in being accepted by a group. Belonging and recognition contribute to the need for self-acceptance.

Many individuals can recall clearly the great anxiety they felt the first day they reported for a new job, or the day they arrived at college. In circumstances such as these we are wont "to grapple to our souls with hoops of steel" the first person to accept or befriend us.

The young person on the job is particularly concerned with acceptance by the boss, just as is the young college student with acceptance by his instructors. It is unfortunate that in both these situations this acceptance and recognition are often rather tardily and indifferently given. It is regrettable that in large college classes today instructors find it difficult, if not impossible, to recognize and identify students as individuals. In these situations the student often is nothing more than a name on the class roll book. A study by Mooney revealed that 25 percent of the students questioned indicated that they knew no one faculty member well enough to ask him to write a letter of recommendation. A total of 34 percent felt they knew no teacher personally. Many suggested the desirability of more "human" faculty-student relations.[15] The responsibility here rests not alone with the faculty. In a large university it is necessary for the student also to assume some obligation in fostering student-faculty relationships. Faculty members should attempt to know the students as individuals and encourage the students to make themselves known. Informal conversations before and after class are helpful. An occasional tea, luncheon, party, or picnic can foster improved understanding between faculty and students. Often faculty members tend to minimize the significance of these obligations. However, the instructor who identifies these young men and women as individuals and accepts them on a fairly adult level is helping to satisfy some of their basic needs.[16] Respect for personality, friendliness, and concern for others take on new meaning when considered in respect to the insecure young man or woman striving for acceptance and recognition.

*Accepting Others.* Just as it is important for these young people to accept themselves and to be accepted by others, so also it is important that they accept others. To accept others of various opinions, religions, and races, to be tolerant of their foibles, and to refrain from being too critical of them is a mark of maturity. In observing

---

[15] Mooney, Ross T. *op. cit.*, p. 42.
[16] Mohr, George J. "Psychiatric Problems of Adolescence," *Journal of American Medical Association*, 137: 1589-92; August 28, 1948.

young people closely, it is found that those who continually belittle and berate others are often not accepted by others and are actually having difficulty accepting themselves.[17]

Young men and women at this time are moving into new situations which bring them face to face with others of different nationality and religion. Their ability to accept others may be severely tested. The young man who for years has heard his parents debase Negroes may now find himself working next to a person of this race. The college freshman of Catholic faith may have a Methodist for a roommate. These new experiences, coupled with an increase in competition—economic, social, and for some, athletic and scholastic—may make it difficult for these young people to accept others. Not all their activities, however, are competitive. Cooperative efforts come into play in their games and sports as well as in their club and social group activities. These cooperative activities in the community and on campus are potentially fine media for them to learn to accept others who differ from themselves.

It is essential for these young people to accept others not only for the sake of their own happiness, but also for the welfare and promotion of democracy as well. The democratic process requires cooperative social action. Cooperation and acceptance of others have their roots in experience. A young person cannot effectively be verbalized into accepting another. Situations must be provided in which he can see and feel the interdependence which exists among people and the need for recognizing and respecting others.[18] Unfortunately, the experiences now provided for these young men and women often promote cooperation and the acceptance of others on a very limited scale at best. Some young people can cooperate fairly well with members of their own family or church group, or club, or fraternity, or athletic team, but distrust completely anyone outside their own limited fold. Many people never mature beyond this point.

It would appear that world citizenship and understanding is the logical ultimate goal of cooperation and the acceptance of others.

[17] Stock, Dorothy, "An Investigation into the Interrelations Between the Self Concept and Feelings Directed Toward Other Persons and Groups." *Journal of Consulting Psychology,* 13: 180; June 1949.
[18] Hullfish, Gordon H. "The Basic American Dilemma." *Journal of Health and Physical Education.* 17: 582-84, December 1946.

Much can be done in the period of late adolescence to foster the achievement of this objective.

## Feeling Adequate To Meet Life Situations

Although these young people often appear confident and carefree, upon closer examination they may be found to be seriously concerned about their ability to meet impending responsibilities. Thoughts of establishing a home, of developing economic independence and of attaining success in their chosen occupation make these youth pause and wonder about the future. In this respect they differ considerably from their younger brothers and sisters who live more from day to day.

Most of this older group now realize that they have enjoyed considerable protection and shelter from the responsibilities of independence. Parents and teachers have in some measure served them as "problem solvers." For the most part these young people have worked out satisfactory solutions and adjustments to their current problems of living. But will these solutions prove adequate for the new problems they will face?

Their concern for the future can be aggravated by such matters as poor health, over-solicitous parents, complete economic dependence, and failure to meet satisfactorily their current problems and needs. Also the value which our society places upon material success adds further to the concern of these young people. The young man is aware that the efforts of his father or father-in-law to direct him into a particular vocation are prompted largely by concern with material success. All of this complicates the anxiety of the young man as he approaches his first job and economic independence.

Those young people who enjoy a measure of success and adequacy in their current living activities have some fortification and assurance as they look to the future. For this reason it is important for every young person to experience success and recognition in at least one activity. For some it might be found in their ability to repair a radio; others might find it in their ability to play a piano or to ski, to play golf or to dance. The possible activities are limitless. None of them is insignificant in respect to developing confidence.

## Problem Areas

The needs of young people define the areas in which their problems lie. College students have been found to be concerned with such problems as being too self-conscious, the inability to make friends, getting low grades, too few dates, too little social life, inability to make the varsity team, taking things too seriously, poor appearance, wanting a more pleasing personality.[19] These problems stem directly from their needs to accept themselves, to be accepted and accept others, to feel adequate in meeting life's situations.

Those older adolescents already in the world of work reveal the same basic needs and concern with much the same problems, though the problems take shape in a different social context, hence are expressed differently, have different factors in them and call for different solutions. Many of these young men and women leave farm and rural communities to work in the cities. They make their way largely on their own. Others take jobs when leaving high school. Working youth's problems are centered in employment per se; the slightest economic depression is immediately reflected in loss of jobs by young workers. Their problems are centered in vocational choice and adequacy on the job, in making social contacts and making their leisure hours re-creative and enjoyable, in finding a mate and establishing home and family.[20] As yet adequate planning for assistance to this age group in the areas of work and play has been done neither at the community level nor by state and federal governments. The recreational needs of these young people are poorly served in many situations. The fact that their work contributions may be less and less needed in an increasingly technological society, except in times of war, has not as yet been comprehended to the extent that long-term plans have been developed to meet this situation.

The emergence of the individual out of later adolescence into adulthood with some degree of real maturity means that the young

[19] McKinney, Fred. "Case History Norms of Unselected Students and Students with Emotional Problems." *Journal of Consulting Psychology.* 11: 258-69; September, October 1947, p. 263.

Hunter, Ruth A., and Morgan, David A. "Problems of College Students." *Journal of Educational Psychology.* 40: 90; February 1949.

Mooney, Ross T. *Manual To Accompany the Problem Check List, College Form.* Columbus: Bureau of Educational Research, The Ohio State University, 1942, p. 41.

[20] Bell, Howard M. *Matching Youth and Jobs.* Washington, D. C.; American Council on Education, 1940.

man or woman has completed the developmental tasks of adolescence. Those who evidence attaining maturity have won emancipation from their parents and view themselves as independent persons; they have accepted their sex and established satisfying relations with the opposite sex; they have set goals for themselves in the area of work and are moving toward attaining the goals; they have considerable security—in themselves and in their relations with others; they are accepted in groups of which they are members for social, political or economic reasons; they have developed a value system of their own which gives them principles and direction for living. This list of accomplishments sounds academic and abstract, yet within it is contained the explanations for the characteristics, problems and behavior of young people in later adolescence.

## Implications for Leadership

Health education, physical education and recreation can provide experiences through which older youth may in part meet their needs and solve their problems. How adequately these needs are met and how functional the guidance process is depend upon the vision, competence and maturity of leaders in the three fields. This age group is seeking to attain maturity and to whom else should they look for guidance than to mature adults? Unless professional workers are well along the road to maturity, they should not presume to guide. The tools of guidance in the hands of an insecure, prejudiced, unskilled person would develop frustrations and have disastrous results. All professional workers should ask themselves a few pertinent questions:

Do I enjoy a sense of happy security in my work and social life, or do I have feelings of inferiority that drive me to compete in a hostile manner rather than to attempt to cooperate with my fellow workers?

Am I aware of my powers and my limitations or do I ignore them and repeatedly meet defeat which I blame on others?

Am I an independent, self-reliant adult, able to make wise choices, to function effectively in normal and in difficult situations, or am I dependent upon others and easily upset by difficulties?

Do I make an effort to enlarge my store of knowledge in order to keep abreast of the times or am I content with what I learned in school?

Do I recognize my responsibilities and execute them effectively or do I shun responsibility and effect slip-shod results?

Do I enjoy a well-balanced life or is mine a one-sided life?

Do I get real satisfaction from living or am I merely existing?

Do I have a sympathetic concern about my fellow man or am I still concerned largely with the self?

Have I developed a philosophy of life which is based on firm beliefs and principles or am I in doubt about what I consider real values in living?

Do I have a wholesome understanding of my sex nature and its relation to my own and the opposite sex or is my sexual development still in the adolescent stage?

Do I have a realistic understanding of my place in the scheme of things or am I just teaching health education, physical education or recreation?

In other words, how nearly have I myself attained maturity? To what degree have I accepted and acted upon principles of democratic leadership, the principles of personal involvement, of individual worth, of field relations or climate, of guided group interaction, of goal-centered activity, of shared responsibility, and of continuous evaluation?

Students are asked to evaluate their progress. Should professional workers not honestly evaluate theirs from time to time? Many could not truthfully answer all of the above questions in a strong affirmative. They should, however, be able to recognize their weaknesses and be willing to work for improvement.

This older youth group looks to its leaders for guidance and it expects well-rounded, well-informed leaders. Competence within the chosen field is taken for granted. A leader who is incompetent in his field soon loses the respect of this age group. However, competence in a chosen field is not enough. The whole area of human relations is one with which workers must be familiar if they are to carry out their work successfully. If they are to meet the social objectives of the program they must understand people as individuals and understand how they function in groups. Then they must be able to effect guidance in such a way that the individual grows and the group benefits.

The professional workers' education has been a broad one. Besides the specific subjects in their own field they have had work in allied fields such as psychology, anatomy, physiology, sociology, psychology, guidance and the arts. This preparation alone should make them aware of what goes on about them. As leaders they must be aware of community needs and problems—the community may be a college campus, a large industrial plant, or a city or town. Unless they are aware of these community needs and problems, they have not gained insight into the needs of the individual who is a member of that community. Active participation in community affairs is essential if one is to gain the necessary knowledge. Too often a leader loses sight of the surroundings and is concerned only with the activities that go on in his own plant.

This step from plant to the community is a minimum responsibility. A well-informed person today cannot rest content with concern for community life. Everyone is influenced by events in other parts of our state, our nation, and other countries of the world. Matters of national and international importance have deep concern for all those who are to guide youth effectively. Professional workers cannot play ostrich and bury their heads in modern health units, physical education plants and recreation centers.

The public associates athletic skill with the fields of physical education and recreation. If one is engaged in an activity program, skill in those activities taught is a valuable aid in teaching. Occasional participation on the part of the teacher or leader motivates the class—often the better the performance, the more effective the motivation. The mere possession of motor skills however, is not sufficient. Leaders must be able to help students to acquire these skills and also wholesome attitudes toward activity so they will participate willingly in leisure hours. The purpose is not accomplished if one has merely taught skills. To help students to meet their needs, one must go beyond this point. One must be able to guide others to acquire the knowledge, understandings and skills necessary for satisfying relations with others in groups and in person-to-person relations. The very acquisition of a sports skill may be the tool that will help a student find security in his group. A student should be helped to acquire skills in working with members of his group and gaining recognition there. This means that all workers should understand the group process in relation to their fields, examine their methods and evaluate the outcomes in terms of what is happening to the individual in relation to the group. Through programs of health education, physical education and recreation older youth should be helped to understand and respect themselves, to assess their own abilities, to successfully reach goals set within the limits of these abilities, and to learn how to work with others for the realization of planned and shared objectives.

This whole area of leadership is beset with problems. How much direction should be given? How much freedom should be allowed? No one formula can provide the answers. Successful guidance toward democratic freedom comes through many experiences in working with many types of groups. Two things are certain: few groups or individuals will attain functional maturity in human relations if the policies are dictated by the leader; nor will they, if the leader's guidance is nonexistent or of poor quality. Those who have chosen to work with groups of people have the responsibility to learn to do it in a way that will benefit and not harm them.

The older youth group in schools has the advantage of personnel trained in guidance. A physical education department should establish positive relations with the guidance department, the health center and any resident department that exists on the campus. Every effort should be made to establish student-staff relations on an adult level. Our general campus students must see staff members as mature and understanding adults who are more concerned with them as individuals than the possessors or nonpossessors of motor skills. Staff discussions on problem cases can often suggest areas of guidance which will be helpful to the students concerned. Staff members should take the initiative in calling case conferences on students, when they feel the cooperation of other instructors on the campus would be helpful. Planned guidance is necessary if staff members hope to see results. A cheery smile or a casual greeting has its place, but it does not solve a real problem. Effective guidance is time-consuming and time must be allotted for it if students, all students, are to be effectively helped.

Democratic human relations cannot be honestly advocated when departments are administered in a dictatorial manner and staff members, supposedly mature adults, cannot themselves adjust satisfactorily to the small group known as "the department." If a department believes that it has a responsibility in the development of mature citizens and if it believes that democratic human relations are desirable, it must communicate that feeling and that attitude to those whom it contacts. Example supports belief. This places a responsibility upon the administration in the matter of staff selection, in-service training, staff relations, and student-staff relations. If relationships with the older youth group are to be effective they must be friendly, unassuming, understanding and yet command their respect. Professional workers must be able to work together effectively as staff members and must be able to work with their program participants. Participants should have an opportunity to share in the planning of the program which is designed to meet their needs—it might be a sports club, a seminar, a dance class, an industrial league, or a special interest club. A staff which offers stimulation to the participants in its program is well-rewarded for the effort involved. The participants see mature, democratic human relations in a successful situation and have a basis for future application. They are part of this functioning group.

The concern of professional workers in health education and physical education with the older youth in industry is not as direct, nor are opportunities to help them develop democratic relations with others as numerous as those recreational leaders have or can create. These leaders are challenged by the voluntary aspects of their programs to attract youth to their activities and hold them through increased interest, skill and satisfying human relations. Hjelte has pointed out in a previous chapter that in our society many commercial agents dispensing passive, vicarious, sometimes sensational even degrading entertainment and amusement compete for youth's leisure hours with other educational and recreational agencies promoting active, social, creative, rewarding activities. It is becoming increasingly clear that more success will be achieved by the second group of agencies as they better meet a first demand of youth, to plan and carry out their own activities.

In many areas much has been done *for* youth. It is a grave question whether enough has been done with them as active participants in the democratic process of planning and carrying out recreational programs for themselves. Those professional workers who are charged with the education of future leaders in the three fields have an additional responsibility.

Those who presume to develop future leaders are faced with even greater problems. They have the responsibility of guiding students who will later put into practice the principles and the methods formulated while working with them. How crucially important then, for learning through experience, become matters of staff selection, staff relations, major selection, student-staff relations, in-service training, placement, and follow-up. The democratic-participatory pattern of group functioning is called for in all aspects of the major program.

In the main, these college-educated men and women are the group upon whom future leadership in education, in the community and nation will fall. What eventually happens to these young men and young women, what eventually happens to our communities, our state and our nation is in considerable degree a test of the leadership ability of those who are now helping to prepare these young people for teaching and leading children and youth to live effectively as members of a democratic society.

## Bibliography

BEISE, DOROTHY. "A Comparative Analysis of the Physical Education Background, Interests and Desires of College Students as an Evaluation Procedure," *Research Quarterly* 11: 120-34; December 1940.

BELL, HOWARD N. *Matching Youth and Jobs*. Washington, D. C.: American Council on Education, 1940.

BENNETT, MARGARET E. *College and Life*. New York: McGraw-Hill Book Co., 1940.

COLE, LUELLA. *Attaining Maturity*. New York: Farrar and Rinehart, 1944.

ENGLISH, O. SPURGEON, and PEARSON, GERALD H. *Emotional Problems of Living*. New York: W. W. Norton and Co., 1945.

GOODENOUGH, FLORENCE L. *Developmental Psychology*. New York: Appleton-Century-Crofts, Inc., 1945.

HARTMAN, GEORGE W. *Educational Psychology*. New York: American Book Co., 1941.

HULLFISH, GORDON H. "The Basic American Dilemma." *Journal of Health and Physical Education*. 17: 582-84; December 1946.

HUNTER, RUTH A., and MORGAN, DAVID A. "Problems of College Students." *Journal of Educational Psychology* 40: 79-92; February 1949.

JOHNSON, WENDELL. *People in Quandaries.* New York: Harper and Brothers, 1946.

KELLEY, JANET AGNES. *College Life and the Mores.* New York: Bureau of Publications, Teachers College, Columbia University, 1949.

LANDIS, PAUL. *Adolescence and Youth.* New York: McGraw-Hill Book Co., 1945.

MC KINNEY, FRED. "Case History Norms of Unselected Students with Emotional Problems." *Journal of Consulting Psychology* 11: 258-69; September-October 1947.

MITCHELL, ELMER D., and MASON, BERNARD S. *The Theory of Play.* New York: A. S. Barnes and Co., 1939.

MOHR, GEORGE J. "Psychiatric Problems of Adolescence." *Journal of American Medical Association* 137: 1589-92; August 28, 1948.

MOONEY, ROSS J. *A Study of Student Needs in Non-Academic Area.* Columbus: Bureau of Educational Research, The Ohio State University, 1939.

MOONEY, ROSS J. *Manual To Accompany the Problem Check List College Form.* Columbus: Bureau of Educational Research, The Ohio State University, 1942.

OVERSTREET, HARRY A. *The Mature Mind.* New York: W. W. Norton and Co., 1949.

PIERCE, WELLINGTON S. *Youth Comes of Age.* New York: McGraw-Hill Book Co., 1948.

PLANT, JAMES S. *Personality and the Cultural Pattern.* New York: Commonwealth Fund, 1937.

PRESSEY, LUELLA C. *Some College Students and Their Problems.* Columbus: The Ohio State University Press, 1929.

RAINEY, HOMER P. *How Fare American Youth?* New York: Appleton-Century-Crofts, Inc., 1938.

REMMERS, H. H., and SHUMBERG, BENJAMIN. *Examiner Manual for S.R.A. Youth Inventory.* Chicago: Science Research Associates, August 1949.

SAUL, LEON J. *Emotional Maturity.* Philadelphia: J. P. Lippincott Co., 1947.

SCHNELL, DOROTHY. *Characteristics of Adolescence.* Minneapolis: Burgess Publishing Co., 1946.

STOCK, DOROTHY. "An Investigation into the Interrelations Between the Self Concept and Feelings Directed Toward Other Persons and Groups." *Journal of Consulting Psychology* 13: 176-80; June 1949.

TERMAN, LEWIS M., and MILES, CATHERINE C. *Sex and Personality.* New York: McGraw-Hill Book Co., 1936.

TOOGOOD, RUTH. "A Survey of Recreational Interests and Pursuits of College Women." *Research Quarterly* 10: 90-100; October 1939.

WRENN, GILBERT C., and BELL, REGINALD. *Student Personal Problems.* New York: Farrar and Rinehart, 1942.

# CHAPTER FOURTEEN

# Concepts and Attitudes
# To Be Developed

Mary Ella Critz      Margaret G. Fox
Margaret E. Everett     Elizabeth Halsey
M. Gladys Scott

WATCH young men and women on their way to the office, store, or factory. See them going about a college campus. Whether they are walking alone, in two's, or in groups, their actions, their talk or silence bring them closer together or set them farther apart. Consciously or unconsciously, they express interest, curiosity, acceptance, friendship; or indifference, coldness, hostility, aggression.

Follow them, in your mind, as they go into their jobs, and later as they leave for their homes, boarding houses, dormitories, fraternities. Follow them out into the evening's recreation, the night class or the library, the committee meeting or town forum. Try to sense the atmosphere of human warmth or coldness, the "social climate," which each one enters in each situation. Try to feel the changes and developments in the social climate and the actions which bring about such changes. It is only when one thinks concretely about these things which are the essence of human relations that one can begin to understand and control them. To know why a social climate changes for better or for worse is one of the most important things a teacher can know. To improve the social climate of a school is one of the most important things a teacher can do.

The social climate of a school or any group is the whole pattern of person-to-person relations of the human beings in the group. It develops through feelings, words and acts. In this chapter an attempt is made to describe the behavior, the words and the acts of older youth who are successful in learning how to establish democratic human relations. Also the ideas, ideals and feelings expressed by their visible behavior are discussed. Young men and women are followed into the situations of everyday living. This approach is a way to see the goals which teachers and leaders may set for helping to develop democratic persons through experiences in health education, physical education and recreation. However, there is a preliminary step to take before considering specific concepts and attitudes to be developed. Human relations in any society are accounted good or bad, desirable or undesirable, according to the values of that society. The values in our society, derived from science, religion and the democratic philosophy itself, are explored as a base for the discussions which follow.

## Principles of Democratic Living

"We believe in the human spirit. We believe in reason and the inquiring mind. We believe in the moral law and the supremacy of God." [1] From these beliefs, from these three main sources of values, have come certain principles basic to what we hope is the American way of life. All of the principles are familiar, and to each we have been trained to give service. Lip service, however, is not enough. It must be service of all our powers. Therefore, as we read, let us think critically, apply, and as soon as may be let us act.

*1. Human integrity comes first.* Humanity in oneself or others is always considered an end, never a means to an end.[2]

Dave has great social assets, but is avoided. He is fond of tennis and bridge and excels at both games. Whenever possible he plays against slightly inferior opponents and runs up the score with obvious satisfaction and satirical, gloating comments. He is critical of his partners' mistakes and coaches them continuously in a very direct, not to say pointed, manner. Both opponents and partners are used as means to one goal: demonstrating Dave's unquestioned superiority.

The coach of our football team refuses to take chances with his players; to him they are something more than a means to winning games. They have careful medical supervision and the doctor's word

---

[1] Lilienthal, David E. *This I Do Believe.* New York: Harper and Brothers, 1949, p. 12.
[2] A simplified statement of the Ethical Imperative of Kant.

is law. No boy plays without unqualified medical approval. Coach Brown considers the boy's future health more important than any game at any stage of the season.

Sue is a likable, charming student. She knows how to use her charm to raise her grade point average. She is relying more and more on personality, less and less on work, so her own very fine mind will probably never be developed. She does not respect humanity in herself.

**2. The welfare of all is the goal of each.** It may be secured through organized justice; equality before the law, equality of opportunity for full development, and mutual respect and help.

A physical education major was having some difficulty with his fourth grade class practicing a relay race. Number two in the file would not stay behind until touched off by the runner. The teacher then asked each team to discuss the reason for this rule. A suggestion that number two start as soon as the runner had turned to come back was voted down because it would be dangerous. The ten-year-olds came up with the answer, "A fair chance for everyone." If this teacher had not been conscious of game rules as "organized justice," he might have let his group develop law-evading techniques and a general attitude of carelessness toward rules of the game.

In the wiring room of an electrical equipment factory, the quicker workers often helped out others who were behind in the day's output. Although this practice was thought to be more distracting than helpful, it was appreciated by the workers. "I think it's a good idea to help a fellow out once in a while. I know I appreciate it. It makes all the difference in the world. It's a funny thing. I'll be working along and be behind, and I'll feel all fagged out. Then somebody comes over and starts in wiring on my equipment with me, and you know I perk up to beat the band. I don't know; it just seems to put new life in you, no matter if he only helps you for a couple of levels. I can pick up and work like the deuce then, up 'til quitting time." However, help was not often given to loafers or workers who did not reciprocate.[3]

Youth of college age do not have equality of opportunity for education. Discrimination is prevalent in our colleges: (a) the high cost of college attendance discriminates against sons and daughters of parents in low income levels; (b) Negroes, Jews, Mexicans, and Orientals are barred by the "quota" system and indirect methods of discrimination; and (c) restrictions on out-of-state students prevent youth who grow up in rural states from an equal opportunity for education in the health sciences such as medicine,

[3] Roethlisberger, Fritz J., and Dickson, William J. *Management and the Worker.* Cambridge: Harvard University Press, 1939, p. 505-506.

pharmacy, dentistry and psychiatry.[4] A few states are legislating against these practices.

3. *Freedom is the individual's right and privilege.* Freedom should be balanced by responsibility up to the limits of his capacity. The freedoms of the adult in thought, speech, action, and religion require the mature individual's ability to make his own decisions and control his own conduct in the interest of the general welfare.

The long process of development toward emotional maturity is marked by lags and spurts. Normally older youth are in a "spurt" period. Pushed on by the definite requirements of a job, by the independence of living alone, or by the stimulating experiences of a college environment, they seem to grow up over night. But it is not an easy change. Suddenly the family shelter is gone. There are no interested neighbors. The young man in the city can come and go as he pleases, to his rooming house, to work, to play—no one marks his movements. He is not identified. In fact, he is practically anonymous. This is liberty at last. Of course, it may also be license and it may be unbearable loneliness. The freshman girl who comes from strict parental control to the comparative freedom of a large dormitory is often confused. Other girls have other standards, other values. She has to review previously unquestioned standards of conduct and make her own decisions.

Youth who come through such experiences with most substantial development and least damage are those who have practice in initiating ideas and carrying out plans, in discussing social values and in self-discipline.

4. *While the will of the majority prevails, the rights of the minority must be respected.* Sunday morning service in the girls' camp was nondenominational, but a few Catholics were taken into town so they might attend their own church.

One boy in the club was always arguing on the other side. Usually the other boys let him talk because they understood his need for attention. However, when they had much to consider, they adopted a rule limiting each boy to one speech of one minute.

5. *Individuals differ.* If we are to make the most of our rich diversity in human resources, we must accept persons of various races, colors, creeds, opinions, nationalities and levels of ability, wealth and social status; we must respect the contribution each person is able to make. To accept a person who is different means that the differences do not affect us emotionally. We do not have to reject the person but can associate with him as naturally as with those who are more like ourselves.

[4] President's Commission on Higher Education. *Higher Education for American Democracy.* Vol. II, *Equalizing and Expanding Educational Opportunity.* Washington, D. C.: Superintendent of Documents, 1949.

When Emily found that she had to work with an armless veteran in the chemistry laboratory, she asked to be transferred—"just couldn't take it." Mary changed places with her readily enough and she had no trouble. She simply accepted the way Bob did things, admired his dexterity and never pitied him.

The senior high-school girls in a wealthy suburban town were having a tea for their mothers. They also invited Mrs. James, a very popular colored woman who was the local Y-teen worker. Everything went well. As they were leaving, one mother was heard to say to her daughter, "Marilyn, why didn't you tell me Mrs. James was colored?" "Why, Mother, I didn't think it mattered."

6. *The mature mind is free from prejudice, rigidity, stereotyping, and delusions of infallibility.* Have you traveled in Europe? Didn't everyone think you were wealthy? You were unmistakably an American, and all Americans are rich. Ask a good Irishman and you'll learn quickly that all Englishmen are so-and-so's. All football players are dumb. All girls majoring in physical education are mannish; all college professors are stuffed shirts. These are stereotypes and, of course, untrue.

7. *Mature minds have the capacity for creative thinking.* Mature persons, coming together for a common purpose and working with mutual respect for diverse experiences and opinions, will readily harmonize their differences. In addition, they may go far beyond mere compromise into the realm of new developments and experimental planning.

The above principles must now be applied to world problems. Solutions demand better ways of working together. This brings a sobering responsibility to educators. They should ask themselves, what are we doing about it? Specifically, what are we doing to equip young people to meet situations such as these?

a. Local bowling alleys discriminate against colored players.

b. Recreation authorities do not permit colored and white individuals to swim in public pools.

c. There is a social war between the "independents" and "Greeks" on many campuses.

d. Certain teachers in a department "know all the answers," have the one right method to solve any or all problems, discourage discussion, demand and get identical answers to essay-type questions.

e. Some colleagues get along well with students or young instructors but are antagonistic toward any person of higher rank or greater authority.

f. The chairman of a student government committee is expected to do all the work unless he specifically assigns parts of the job to others.

g. A student-staff committee meeting taking up an urgent problem loses a promising start in free discussion because of a number of "this-may-be-what-he-wants" contributions.

h. At meetings of professional workers in our three fields there are very few colored people in attendance.

i. "We do not hire Jews."

j. He is a fine man but a Catholic and will never be elected.

k. Do the work as you are told—ideas are out.

l. This teen-center is going to be run efficiently and a youth council can't do it.

*8. Changes in the world of people and of things are continuous.* Persons and societies must recognize and adapt to change if they are to succeed—or even to survive. Successful adaptation to change is based on the scientific method. This means: (a) critical inquiry into answerable questions; (b) objective, accurate, and organized observations; and (c) deferred judgment based on reasoned analysis of observations.

*9. The scientific pursuit of truth must be sustained and incorruptible.* The principles of science have direct bearing on human relations. In recent discussions of world problems, however, science has often been described as the arch-enemy of humane procedure. It has been said that mankind's existence is endangered by the success of science in developing weapons of destruction.

It is clear that we need to give more attention to the ends for and the arts of living. Then, science becomes our tool and the scientific method our procedure for best achieving the goals. Experts in the field of human relations emphasize the importance of scientific attitudes in daily living.

Predictability then is not only the polestar of the scientist, around which revolve all his purposes, theories, and procedures; it is also the bedrock foundation of sanity, of adequate everyday social and personal adjustment. It is not to be implied that science, in its highly refined and technical aspects, is to be mastered in its entirety before one is to be considered sane. What is implied is that science, as general method and as basic orientation, does tend to make for foresight and general adequacy in the behavior of individuals and of groups.[5]

Teachers of health education and physical education are responsible for helping their students to generalize and apply learnings in the biological sciences. Are they sure that students gain from these experiences scientific attitudes as well as useful knowledge of facts?

[5] Johnson, Wendell. *People in Quandaries.* New York: Harper and Brothers, 1946, p. 83.

a. Are students alert to differences and changes in persons a... situations?

b. Are they ready to challenge authority, to experiment, to test tradition by their own experience?

c. Do they ask specific, significant questions, and obtain all relevant facts?

d. Do they keep open minds, considering impartially all available facts, and then reason out the best answers available to them at that time?

e. Do they consider these answers as qualified and limited by their own points of view, rather than as universal truths?

f. Are they ready to act on the basis of these answers although they recognize them as tentative and subject to continuous review?

*10. Sportsmanship is applied religion.* Church and home alike tell the child that he is his brother's keeper, that he should treat others as he wants to be treated. This basic concept becomes the living spirit of a game whenever opponents treat each other with respect, recognize that each side has the same right to the satisfactions of a well-played, spirited game, promoting the best performance of each team and of each player.

The analogy is obvious. Cooperative, responsible behavior is just that, wherever it is practiced, on the playing field or in the Security Council of the United Nations. The world sadly needs large numbers of people possessing the skills to harness competition within the framework of cooperation for the good of all peoples.

## Specific Concepts and Attitudes

There are many concepts and attitudes which older youth may acquire through health education, physical education and recreation, enabling them to live and work with others in the democratic way. Again, let us try to visualize this group—on the job, off the job, in the living situation and in the community.

### On the Job

Industrial studies have recently discovered that the man on the job is a human being. Earlier emphasis in research, on fatigue, illumination, ventilation, rest periods, time motion, and other physical conditions of work, is being supplemented by the study of employee attitudes and relationships. In the well-known research at the Westinghouse Hawthorne plant covering a variety of experiments over a period of years, it was found that in one situation, where a small group of workers developed good attitudes toward each other, felt their work to be important, had some share in planning new procedures, and were under informal supervision, production rates continued to increase although physical conditions of work were experimentally varied. Another group, which was suspicious of management's innovations in the interests of efficiency, organized informally to protect their human associations by restricting their output, although this action also restricted their pay. Mayo concludes that the individual worker does not always follow logically his own economic interests, but is actuated "chiefly by a passionate desire for an intimate and routine relation with his fellows at work." [6] Hoslett lists in order of frequency a series of 28 factors affecting employee morale.[7] Pay appears twelfth on the list. The top 10 can be summarized by saying that these employees wished to be treated like human beings: to be given help when necessary, to be encouraged to offer suggestions, to know whether their work was improving and to be given a fair hearing and a square deal in the case of grievance.

Employers are considering social factors. Two studies of employees' failures, by Southard and by Brewer, respectively, trace the majority of these failures to social rather than technical incompetence.[8]

Some of the ways of doing things which characterize the socially competent young worker are:

1. He works responsibly; takes his own share of the job, gets it done with dispatch and adequate initiative.

2. He thinks objectively; does not overestimate nor underestimate his own capabilities; does not overestimate the capabilities of his friends nor underestimate the capabilities of others.

3. He keeps an open mind; is not prejudiced against change: even if innovations are made by management, he evaluates them on the basis of facts rather than hostility or fear.

4. He accepts other persons on the job, even if they differ from him in religion, color, nationality, social and economic status, and

---

[6] Mayo, Elton. "Research in Human Relations," *Personnel* 19: 264-65: May 1941.
[7] Hoslett, Schuyler D. *Human Factors in Management.* Parkville, Mo.: Park College Press, 1946, p. 136.
[8] Reported by Menninger, Karl A. *The Human Mind.* New York: Alfred A. Knopf, 1930, p. 434.

ability; is able to look up the line without rancor, on his own level without fear, and down the line without contempt; recognizes the importance of differences.

5. He learns from his job; takes suggestions from supervisors or co-workers; respects expertness; turns his failures to his own profit by analysis and correction; avoids an alibi, does not rationalize.

6. He faces reality, lives in the shop instead of a castle-in-the-air.

7. He wants new experiences; takes on any new assignments: thinks "is this more interesting?" rather than "is this more work?"

8. He has a clear-cut goal for himself; knows what standards he must reach on the way; revises both goal and standards as he becomes more mature and realistic in his outlook.

9. He cooperates; is a good team member in his work-room, on his union committee, or in his industrial basketball league; is loyal to his group.

10. He respects himself; asks to be treated like a responsible human being; wants a chance to exchange ideas up and down the line as well as in his own division; wants to participate in making decisions.

## In School

Each of the above points applies directly to youth at school as well as youth at work. In addition, the following responses to campus situations characterize the socially competent college student:

11. Since attending college is his job, he works responsibly at his courses; knows he is being paid, in part, from both public and private sources; realizes that he owes society, his family, and himself a good return on a sizable investment.

12. He organizes his time; plans days so he is not too hurried in contacts with people.

13. He learns as he goes; applies what he reads and hears; discusses and digests new ideas; does not live in his books, but lets his books live in him; can even listen to dull lectures and learn from them.

14. He works honestly; steals no man's words nor ideas; is no apple polisher and is not afraid to treat his instructors like human beings, ask for help and take advantage of their suggestions.

15. He works objectively with others; is free from envy or condescension; discovers, "It is easy to work with those you like and respect, possible to work with those you do not like but do respect, as for those you neither like nor respect, well, if you really want to, you can work with them, also."

16. He works scientifically; challenges, experiments, compares, guards against his own personal bias, reasons out the answer on the basis of evidence; checks it by further experiment.

## Off the Job

Quitting time is coming, and none too soon. Most employees have been anticipating the factory whistle, the store's closing gong, for at least half an hour. The young ones go about as if two persons: one winding up the day's work, the other racing ahead to "meet the date." Finally the doors open, the signal comes, work compulsions are lifted for sixteen hours, and workers feel free to enjoy that part of the day when they "really live"—or so they tell themselves.

What do they do when they "really live"? They do any one of a multitude of minor variations on a recreation theme which is fairly general for our country. The chances are about 10 to one that, if they stay at home, it's the newspaper or the radio, and, if they go out from home, it's the movie or the automobile.[9] Except for motoring, this is vicarious rather than real experience, but it is relatively cheap, available and effortless. It does not fill the bill, however. It is not what people say they want nor what the scientists say they need.[10] What people want and need are more active, creative, varied and sociable forms of recreation. They need recreation which will give them these things:

1. Enjoyment and satisfaction.
2. Physical activity.
3. An outlet for aggressive feelings.
4. Exploration of new experiences, new learnings, growth, and development.
5. Full expression of personality.
6. Attaining some kind of success.
7. Social contacts with individuals and groups.
8. Escape from reality.
9. Creative achievement.
10. Service to community.
11. Strengthening of moral and ethical codes.

[9] Numerous studies on recreational pursuits of American youth and adults report similar findings.
[10] Menninger, Karl A. *Love Against Hate.* New York: Harcourt, Brace and Company, 1942, Chapter 7 on play.

This last need is acute with older youth. Nearing independence from family guidance they are apt to lose the guidance of their religion and their partially established moral codes. Particularly in off-the-job living this tendency appears.

Jane Cole has "met the public" with a smile all day at the glove counter. She has fitted hands—clean, dirty, jewelled, strong, flaccid. She has fitted her own services to the varying moods of the customers who are "always right." At five o'clock she meets Bill at the bowling alley. The first satisfying crash of falling pins helps her to forget how her feet hurt. But she can't forget her dream of last night in which she was bowling at the strangest pins. Each one was topped by the head of an exasperating customer! Suddenly she sees Mrs. Van Blank's head on the corner pin, the only one left. Her second ball hits it squarely: she was never so sure of a spare before.

Young Thompson was a quiet, self-effacing newcomer who seemed to belong in the cashier's cage and would probably remain there. He was persuaded to become treasurer of the Community Chest drive, and before he realized it was making sound suggestions about procedure which were heard with respect. The novel sensation of speaking with authority led him to use all his planning and organizing ability for the drive. He even overcame old habits of reticence and learned to speak to groups. His community contacts in this and later drives were a source of pride to Thompson and greatly astonished the bank officials.

What are some of the specific ways of thinking and acting characteristic of a youth who maintains good human relations while satisfying his own needs in recreation?

1. He likes people; enjoys being with them; lets them know it and so gets along well with both boys and girls; makes new acquaintances readily but keeps his old friends; is selective but not exclusive, does not like discrimination on grounds of superficial differences; never tries to use people to his own advantage.

2. He likes the feeling of activity; enjoys sports and dance; knows a lot about outdoor and indoor games and how to get people to participate; likes to watch big games and highly skilled play; plays and watches in a sportsmanlike manner.

3. He likes the feeling of skilled movement; the lift over the hurdles, the whack of a squarely hit golf ball as it rises in a long high straight drive, the plunk of an arrow in the gold, the freedom of his body slipping through water; enjoys the sensation after exercise of general relaxation and mild fatigue.

4. He likes new experiences; is alert to new ideas; knows how to follow them up and learn more about them; develops interesting projects; is receptive to, but not controlled by new sensations.

5. He likes to discuss ideas—to hold bull sessions; can argue good naturedly, listen and concede.

6. He likes to make things: a piece of furniture, a wallet, jewelry, a boat, a garden, a picture, a poem or a play; whatever it is, all his imagination and ability go into it.

7. He likes to do things with a group, can lead but doesn't have to; can follow, but doesn't have to; likes a warm feeling in the group and helps to make one.

8. He likes to let off steam; when worked up or mad, kicks a ball, knocks down tenpins, splits wood; does not take it out on people.

9. He likes to excel; works up some hobby and becomes an authority or an expert performer; keeps his head about it; is a keen but fair competitor.

10. He likes to "get away from it all" occasionally; picks harmless ways to do this: movies, theater, travel, reading fiction; avoids destructive ways such as drink and dope; knows he can't live much of his life "away from it all," or even in daydreams.

11. He likes to laugh and have fun; refuses to take himself or anyone else too seriously; is good company; knows how to listen, whether or not he can talk entertainingly.

12. He wants to find the right girl; dates with many; treats each one as a person worthy of respect, not just as part of his experience.

13. He wants to respect himself; avoids being at odds with his conscience; develops his code of ethics, harmonizing it with social custom, and lives up to it.

## In the Living Situation

Older youth usually change their living situations in such a way that adjustment is needed. Whether the small intimate family group is exchanged for a large college dormitory, or for an anonymous rooming house, the youth no longer is the center of attention. He is just one among many. The warmth of family ties has been replaced by the coldness or indifference of a large group. He must now take a long step toward that attitude characteristic of intellectual maturity but difficult to acquire: he must begin to accept the fact that the world will largely be indifferent to his fate.[11]

[11] Cole, Luella. *Attaining Maturity.* New York: Farrar and Rinehart, 1944, p. 21.

Even if he starts to work in his own town and lives at home there will be adjustment problems. As a wage-earner, who has to take responsibility on the job, he will assert independence of parental control. But, in many cases, parents will still think of him as a child who needs protection. If protection is excessive it may be as devastating in its effects on the maturing personality as is out-and-out domination by parents. Youth need help instead of hindrance in the transition from dependence to independence. If hindered, the young person will rebel, or at best live in constant friction at home. If his rebellion against parents is suppressed, it will come out in his relations with others of authority. A skillful leader will detect in the rude, antagonistic young person someone who may need help in understanding his parents' problems.

The youth leader may help also when youth start to assert the ego by casting aside normal behavior restraints. At this time conventions seem "stuffy" and something to be ignored. An older person may be able to interpret conventions as necessary to permanent satisfactions in living. Cole states that without conventions society promptly degenerates into the social anarchy of a frontier town. Conventions admittedly inhibit one's personal liberty, but they compensate by giving order, dignity, and safety. The chief trouble with the nonconformist is that he isn't very bright. He fails to see in his revolt against society the mechanism of the escapist who is running away from something he will not face. And the fundamental trouble with his bright new world is that it will not jell, because it has no traditions or conventions to hold it together.[12]

After all, conventions describe socially considerate behavior. Older youth should be growing toward consideration for others and away from the adolescent's self-centered thoughtlessness, his hasty decisions, his emotional ups and downs, and his headlong pursuit of new thrills. On the basis of socially considerate behavior (the ethical imperative again) older youth may form close and permanent friendships, make satisfactory sexual adjustment and develop successful family relationships in which they themselves fill the adult role of parenthood. Direct education for this role should be available, since so many families of yesterday and today have produced mentally

[12] *Ibid.*, p. 67.

immature adults. From his observations as a psychiatrist in World War II, Menninger considers that "America's future greatness is threatened unless life in many of her families is helped to become more healthy." [13]

Some specific attitudes and concepts which characterize the socially considerate older youth, in his living situation, may be described as follows:

*In his parents' home:*

1. He takes responsibility; pays at least nominal sum for board and room; keeps his own room neat or has other regular household jobs.
2. He develops respectful independence; asks for his own key; makes his own decisions; entertains his own guests, but at his parents' convenience and his mother's invitation; volunteers information about his own doings but politely discourages cross-examination.
3. He is courteous; accords his family the same good manners he would show to outsiders; considers their reactions to his actions.
4. He knows how to harmonize differences; doesn't "blow his top"; suggests family councils for talking things over; tries to understand the reasons for others' words and actions; is open to other points of view; concedes when honestly convinced.
5. He respects his family as persons; knows something about their interests; listens to their problems; is proud of their successes.
6. He adjusts his habits and routine to the needs of the family; if a late riser, gets his own breakfast and cleans up; when coming in late is quiet; doesn't play his radio or use his typewriter after the family has gone to sleep.
7. When home on visits or vacations he makes definite "dates" with the family; doesn't fill his calendar so they never see him.

*In the dormitory or fraternity:*

8. He lives within bounds; tries to keep rules, but asks to have impossible ones changed; yields to majority decision; is willing to listen to minorities—within reason.
9. He respects his roommates as persons; never tries to use them to his advantage nor lets himself be imposed upon; respects the personal property of others.
10. He takes responsibility; contributes to group discussions and

[13] Menninger, William C. *Psychiatry in a Troubled World.* New York: The Macmillan Company, 1948, p. 409.

group projects; if he votes for a project involving hard work, does his share to carry it out.

11. He has a balanced pattern of friendships; is selective but not exclusive, and avoids discrimination on the basis of superficial differences; makes friends outside as well as within his living group.

12. He is objective; tries to meet hostility on an intellectual basis —to understand why others act as they do; controls emotional responses.

*In the boarding house or rooming house:*

13. He is a good customer; is realistic enough to know his land-lady is in a business situation; expects her to make a fair profit, but refuses to be exploited.

14. He respects house rules and the property they protect.

15. He is highly selective in his friendships; develops casual ac-quaintanceships easily, but takes plenty of time in developing more intimate friendships.

16. Learns to rely on himself for good company, when necessary.

## *In the Community*

This country believes in the democratic way of life. We have fought at least three wars to maintain it. Some observers including Menninger, point out, however, that, although thousands of our youth have died for democracy, few are ready to live for it:

Men who fought at the risk of their lives to maintain certain prin-ciples have returned to a state of apathy or indifference toward the further maintenance of those principles. Many feel pessimistic about wielding any influence in changing things against the odds of rumored 'strong lobbies,' 'business groups,' and 'labor pressure.' Few will trouble to express to their Congressmen their thinking about how to improve our country's status. Fewer still will stimulate others to do so. They are too busy with their own problems, their own interests, to discover their own potency in changing the situation. Social ills which do not directly touch them are like the starving people in India—left outside the field of their concern.[14]

Menninger goes on to say that the principle of improvement is basic to mental health: self-improvement, family improvement, and community improvement.

Today the war of ideas is putting democracy to a new test. Can we convince the nations of this world that freedom works? Can we demonstrate the compatibility of security and liberty? Perhaps so,

[14] Menninger, William C. *op. cit.*, p. 358.

if we can put our own house in order, and if we have the wisdom to chart a course in foreign affairs consistent with our democratic beliefs.

To the first of these jobs every American must contribute. For the second each of us must hold his leaders responsible, but let them know that we are in favor of trying new ways. No person can afford indifference. Alert adolescents in high school social science courses are far from indifferent. But when they go to work, their immediate problems close in, no group stimulates discussion, the apathy and cynicism of older workers smother youth's interest.

Even if they go to college and graduate to positions of responsible leadership, most youth are not stimulated to be interested in public affairs. Why? Because too often college administrators and college teachers are not so interested; because work in college is highly specialized and play in college is athletic or social in the frivolous sense. The specialized study of American society, to which almost every college student is exposed in at least one course, does not have the generalized, permanent effect of making him an active citizen. To develop this effect would mean organizing indirect teachings in other courses as well as in the informal educational opportunities which are so rich and varied on the college campus. These indirect and informal learning situations occur often in physical education and recreation. We need to be aware of our "teachable moments" and be ready to use them.

First, let us list specific ways in which older youth may think and act in order to promote democratic human relations in the community. We mean, of course, not only the small neighborhood community, but the city, state, nation, and the "community of nations."

1. He uses his knowledge of society; accepts and acts on the principle that democracy is based on mutual *interdependence* between the individual and the community.

2. He takes responsibility; willingly does his share as an individual to promote community welfare.

3. He feels a debt to society; believes that taxes used for his education and lives sacrificed for his freedom may partially be repaid through his contribution to social change and improvement.

4. He has a broad view; has interests that go beyond self, family,

and neighborhood to city, state, national, and international problems; resists isolationism as dangerous to mental health of individual or community.

5. He is sensitive to social justice; works toward equal opportunity for all regardless of differences in race, religion, nationality, economic level and status.

6. He seeks status in service; gives talents to group projects as substitute for personal supremacy and power.

7. He understands democratic leadership; is effective in selecting good leaders, accepting the leadership of others or giving leadership himself according to the situation.

8. He is a good mediator; handles opposing points of view objectively without regard to own emotions; knows difference between compromise and appeasement, how to use compromise and how to prevent appeasement.

9. He uses democratic techniques to secure group action; clarifies issues, secures factual material, communicates it through various channels, provides free discussion, summarizes and distributes outcomes of discussion, organizes and carries out action; is critical of propaganda, prejudice, stereotyping, infallibility, etc.

*In his own town:*

10. He is an active member of community groups; prizes free association as the privilege and responsibility of free men; gains experience in college groups, small club or neighborhood organization for larger groups and wider social action.

11. He works with all groups; in any project makes sure that different interests and areas are brought together in spite of differences in background.

12. He works for sane athletics and takes part in a sensible athletic program as part of community recreation and physical education; i.e., general participation, equal use of facilities by all levels of talent and avoidance of overemphasis and commercialization of top-flight players.

13. He understands competition and knows the values and dangers of competition; controls hostile and overaggressive tendencies in any form of competition; is particularly alert to substitute cooperation for hostile competition between community agencies.

## Generalized Concepts

The foregoing descriptions of behavior in specific situations may be considered as specific outcomes desired by teachers and recreation leaders who deal with youth in their late teens and early twenties. They might be added to and still not include all possible goals toward which good programs in our three fields are aimed. It is clearly impossible even to list over-all pertinent behavior patterns. At this point, it is more profitable to ask ourselves: What common threads underlie the complex behavior patterns of well-socialized youth? What general concepts should we, as guides, strive to develop in young men and women which they may take from one specific situation to another?

Some of these concepts, along with examples of leaders' objectives in regard to helping young people develop them and examples of youth's expressions of attitudes revealing understanding of them, are listed below.

| Leaders' Objectives | Generalized Concepts | Youth's Attitudes |
|---|---|---|
| To set an example of im-partial treatment of all and to help youth to study reasons for hostile or anti-social behavior by themselves or others. | OBJECTIVITY | When I work in a group I'm forgetting my own likes and dislikes and figuring out *why* the other guys react the way they do. |
| To make class and game schedules and assign-ments clear; to help youth leaders do the same in project organiza-tion; to insist each does his job on time. | RESPONSIBILITY | I'm keeping a calendar so as to remember what I have to do and when. I'm not joining anything I don't care to work for, but I can't resign from the U. S. A. or my own town —and I don't want to. |
| To be approachable, a good listener, and let young people talk their way to a solution of their own problems. | INDEPENDENCE | I'm not bothering my folks with all my private problems, but I'm not trying everything the other kids try either. A man has to figure out right and wrong for him-self, but he's got to live with his conscience, too. |
| To know resources for vocational and recrea-tional guidance; to help youth clarify their ex-pressed goals and under-stand their unconscious drives. | GOAL-DIRECTION | I want a job that's inter-esting with good pay that I can do. I can take tests for that. I want a girl— the kind I'll marry some day. I probably won't find her for a while. |

| Leaders' Objectives | Generalized Concepts | Youth's Attitudes |
|---|---|---|
| To encourage self-directed study and exploration of community resources; to define propaganda and stereotyping and help youth detect and discount them. | FLEXIBILITY | I like to get new ideas from people, but I won't believe everything I hear or read. I check it the way I learned to do at school. What are the facts? What do they mean? |
| To use the ethical imperative as a guide in dealing with youth, i.e., never exploit them or let them exploit their own lesser gifts. | RESPECT FOR HUMANITY | No use trying to climb up on the backs of the other fellows because then they'll do the same thing to me and it's just a dog fight. Everyone ought to have his chance, and it's more interesting to know what a fellow wants to be than just to push him off the road or pat him on the back. |
| To study groups so as to spot the lonely, the less-sought individuals; to give them guidance or send them where they can get more expert help; to insure that they get club and team experience. | CAPACITY FOR COMPANIONSHIP | I like a crowd and I like to be taken in by them. Can't always be the big shot and can't be everyone's best buddy. I don't like the campus politician. He's your best friend today but he won't remember you next week. I want a few best friends who are real. |
| To discuss historical and factual material in class; to encourage informal study and reports in recreational groups so as to build appreciation of the values of a democratic society. | DEMOCRATIC VALUES | I wouldn't want to be a cog in a machine, a number in an army, or just a yes-vote in an election. I want to be a man, myself, and to do my part toward supporting myself, my family, and my government. If what we have learned at church and school is right, then we can treat everyone like that in this country and have a good chance for progress—if there's peace in the world. |

| *Leaders' Objectives* | *Generalized Concepts* | *Youth's Attitudes* |
|---|---|---|
| To practice democratic procedures in organizing and leading programs; to study ways of guiding youth leaders to skill in these same techniques; to hold leaders' institutes to practice democratic discussion, planning sessions, committee work, presiding over large groups, using parliamentary procedure, etc. | DEMOCRATIC PROCEDURES | I like a committee that gets to work without just talking or fooling. Everyone has to put in, though, not just leave it to the chairman. If the majority votes to do a job, everyone has to do part of it. |

On the basis of the principles of democratic living, the behavior of young people of college age has been described to show how they think and feel and act when they are truly democratic persons. Of course, there are no young people who entirely fit these descriptions. There are none now; there were none in the past generation. Will there be any in the next? None that fit the picture in every way. But there will be change. "You can't change human nature" is often said in despair of or in excuse of human actions. The statement is unscientific. Research in evolutionary biology reveals that human nature does change. Moreover, human beings change in the course of their lifetime. As of the present, human beings will change or probably be exterminated.

While our technicians are concerned with instruments of death, teachers and other leaders of men must concern themselves with instruments of human change. Youth must be educated to understand the direction change must take; they must be educated to move in this direction through the practice of democratic human relations.

No leaders deal more directly with youth than those in the fields of health education, physical education and recreation. No leaders deal with more intense emotions or more delicate problems of balancing competition and cooperation. None, then, has greater responsibility for what youth learn in this area of democratic relations.

# Bibliography

BAXTER, BERNICE, and CASSIDY, ROSALIND. *Group Experience—The Democratic Way.* New York: Harper and Brothers, 1943.

CASSIDY, ROSALIND, and KOZMAN, HILDA CLUTE. *Counseling Girls in a Changing Society.* New York: McGraw-Hill Book Co., 1947.

COLE, LUELLA. *Attaining Maturity.* New York: Farrar and Rinehart, 1944.

HOLLINGSHEAD, AUGUST B. *Elmtown's Youth.* New York: John Wiley and Sons, 1949.

HOSLETT, SCHUYLER D. *Human Factors in Management.* Parkville, Mo.: Park College Press, 1946.

JOHNSON, WENDELL. *People in Quandaries.* New York: Harper and Brothers, 1946.

KANT, IMMANUEL. *The Fundamental Principles of the Metaphysics of Ethics.* New York: Appleton-Century-Crofts, Inc., 1938.

LILIENTHAL, DAVID E. *This I Do Believe.* New York: Harper and Brothers, 1949.

LIPPITT, RONALD A. *Training in Community Relations Toward New Group Skills.* New York: Harper and Brothers, 1949.

LOVE, LESTON L., and OTHERS. *Student Planning in College.* Columbus: The Ohio State University Press. 1941.

LYND, ROBERT S., and LYND, HELEN M. *Middletown in Transition.* New York: Harcourt, Brace and Co., 1937.

MC WILLIAMS, CAREY. *Prejudice.* Boston: Little, Brown and Co., 1944.

MENNINGER, KARL A. *The Human Mind.* New York: Alfred A. Knopf, 1930.

MENNINGER, KARL A. *Love Against Hate.* New York: Harcourt, Brace and Co., 1942.

MENNINGER, WILLIAM C. *Psychiatry in a Troubled World.* New York: Macmillan Co., 1948.

NATIONAL EDUCATION ASSOCIATION and AMERICAN ASSOCIATION OF SCHOOL ADMINISTRATORS, EDUCATIONAL POLICIES COMMISSION. *Learning the Ways of Democracy.* Washington, D. C.: the Commission, 1940.

OVERSTREET, HARRY A. *The Mature Mind.* New York: W. W. Norton and Co., 1949.

PLANT, JAMES S. *Personality and the Cultural Pattern.* New York: Commonwealth Fund, 1937.

PRESCOTT, DANIEL, editor. *Emotion and the Educative Process.* Washington, D. C.: American Council on Education, 1938.

PRESIDENT'S COMMISSION ON HIGHER EDUCATION. *Higher Education for American Democracy.* Washington, D. C.: Superintendent of Documents, 1949.

ROETHLISBERGER, FRITZ J., *Management and Morale.* Cambridge: Harvard University Press, 1942.

ROETHLISBERGER, FRITZ J., and DICKSON, WILLIAM J. *Management and the Worker.* Cambridge: Harvard University Press, 1939.

WARNER, W. LLOYD. *Democracy in Jonesville.* New York: Harper and Brothers, 1949.

# CHAPTER FIFTEEN

# *Methods*

ALMA M. HAWKINS

T HE over-all method being discussed in this chapter is the group process. This is a method of work in which the group itself, guided by teacher or leader, sets its own goals, plans and acts to attain them, estimates results and replans on the basis of findings. The basis for selecting this method of work is that it has proven to be the most effective for developing democratic concepts and attitudes and for learning the skills in working democratically with others; it is also proven to be, when it really operates, the most effective method for learning subjectmatter, for problem-solving and for carrying out specific projects.

With the use of group process many specific techniques and tools must be selected or devised to accomplish the various steps in group planning and action. These specific procedures will be selected for older youth, as for all age groups, according to their usefulness for moving toward objectives as determined in a particular situation and their suitability in relation to the needs, interests, capacities, previous experience and goals of a particular group. In group process the techniques and tools are not selected and used in a preconceived routine pattern, but are employed as the situations demand in an ever fresh and unique manner. Group members share in determining which ones will be used.

Group process as a method of work may be used with older youth in any and all situations with which teachers and leaders in health education, physical education and recreation have concern. The discussions in Chapters 7 and 11 dealing with methods of developing democratic human relations in health, physical education and recreation programs respectively for children and adolescents are helpful in presenting examples of these situations and the approaches used with younger individuals. As the individual grows older some principles and methods are even more applicable. For example, it is even more applicable for older youth to learn to take responsibility for their own health through the use of group process in health education. Physical education and recreation programs also offer unique opportunities for older youth to learn to work in groups. Activities such as sports, swimming, dramatics and dance have a natural appeal to most of them. Keen interest leads to a real concern for what goes on in the group or class. Many of these activities call for a high degree of interaction among participants who work not as individuals but in relation to others in the group. The high degree of interaction necessitates some kind of planning and direction. This interaction brings older youth face to face with real problems in group relations. They may encounter trouble as they play on a team, participate in a tournament, select partners in social dance or work on a group study in dramatics or in modern dance. In such situations, offering opportunity for significant learning, group process is an effective method to help a group plan and carry out activities as well as solve problems.

Out-of-class activities sponsored by a physical education, athletic or recreation organization also offer many situations which call for close working relations and concern for others. The executive committee of an organization usually has the responsibility for planning activities that will best meet the interests of all students. The wise executive group will try to utilize every opportunity to have many youth participate in planning and carrying out the program. Committees may be appointed for special activities such as outings, play days and banquets. Captains of intramural teams may be asked to assume responsibilities outside of the game period and thus become an important channel between the executive group and the participants. Inactive teams may act as officials, scorers and timekeepers, thus assuming some responsibility for their tournament. Skill teams may be selected by students who participated in tournament play rather than by the sports manager and advisors.

Problems in human relations may arise at any level of activity.

The executive committee as well as sub-committees and activity groups must be sensitive to them. The problem may involve tensions and divisions that have developed around town and resident students or fraternity and independent groups. It may relate to the allocation of budget or clearing calendar dates with other campus organizations. It may center around decisions on questions such as whether or not to accept an invitation to send players to a state badminton tournament which limits participants "to members of the Caucasian race." As a group struggles with problems such as these it can learn to make decisions in the light of values and in terms of what is best for the group.

In community centers, on playgrounds and in youth centers there are similar opportunities to permit and to help young people do what they emphatically assert in every survey that they want to do—"Organize and carry out our own activities." It is a well-known fact to youth-serving organizations, highly successful in many cases in meeting the interests of younger boys and girls, that they lose their memberships during the teen years. This happens, even though groups are encouraged and helped to plan their own programs within the structural framework, goals and purposes of a particular organization. Older youth, generally, do not seem to want even this much prestructuring in their voluntary activities.

Public and private recreation agencies will meet the needs of older youth to greater extent as they concentrate less on planning programs *for* youth and devote their resources and skills more to planning programs *with* youth. Because of the voluntary aspect of recreational programs, many more leaders in this field than in health education and physical education are using group process methods. Teachers in colleges and universities are apt to say of this, "It's all right for recreation leaders. They do not have to cover a certain amount of subjectmatter or give grades in terms of mastery." The evidence is beginning to pile up that there is more and better learning of content through group process as teacher and group gain skill in its use. Sharing responsibility for planning and conducting their own activities, in addition, provides opportunities for practicing democratic skills for working with others, so essential for our citizens to have. In general, how can this best be done? The following discussion is designed and organized to show the steps in group process and to explain and illustrate some of the techniques and tools useful in guiding a group.

## Getting Started

Forty men and women have signed up for social dancing. The activity may be offered as one of the classes in the physical education service program; it may be offered as a feature of the campus recreation program; it may be offered by some community agency for out-of-school young people. In any case, the teacher or leader has three questions to answer before the group meets:

1. What do I know about these young people that will help me to plan?
2. What preliminary planning is necessary before I meet the group?
3. What orientation does the group require? In regard to the activity? In regard to themselves as a group?

### Finding Out About Group Needs

A class may be designated as a beginning activity but seldom does it happen that all people in the class have the same background. In the case of social dance some students will come with no background in any form of dance and may find extreme difficulty with rhythm while others will have had experience with a brother, friend or a club group. Some may have had experience in another form of dance such as square dance. The experience background of a group in an activity including individual abilities and disabilities is an important factor to be considered in planning and teaching.

The teacher of a college social dance class will be in a better position to understand the students' early response to the activity and to the group if he knows why students are in the class. Some may have elected the course because they want to learn to dance. Some may want to improve their meager skill. Some may have registered because they are required to have one course in dance, and others may be there because social dance is a part of their professional education program. Some may be in the class for a combination of reasons.

For those who are in the class on an elective basis, the need for the activity and the desire to learn are obvious. For others the desire to learn may or may not exist at the beginning of the term. The teacher's first problem may well be how to create a desirable setting for learning.

Unless the teacher is a complete stranger to all members of the group, he is likely to know many particulars about the group before he meets it. These data, whether based on casual acquaintance or on more direct contact with members of the group in or out of a class, will add to the preliminary background information which is valuable for the teacher to know.

*Resources of the Teacher.* The previous experience of the teacher and his general information about older youth, including their needs, their problems and the experiences required by this age group, represent the framework of his efforts. The discussion in Chapter 13 presents a basic orientation in the needs, problems and desirable experiences in the period of later adolescence. The implications for leadership are also presented there.

In addition to the general information above, one of the most fruitful resources for the teacher is the cumulative records of the student. These include the guidance record, the health or medical record, the physical education record and general observations. The guidance office usually will be the most complete source of information concerning the student. These records will help the teacher learn something of the individual's home and school background, his potential ability and present level of experience, his problems, successes and failures and his personal and vocational desires. Such records often reveal important information such as specific interests or hobbies, desire to become proficient in certain recreational activities or volunteer leadership with some community group. For example, a student may have assisted with singing in a settlement club group, a Red Cross swimming class for crippled children or a playground softball team. This type of information can assist the teacher in understanding behavior and needs as they arise in a specific class.

The health or medical record including the observations and objective measures of the physicians and nurses should furnish information concerning any special assets, liabilities or special needs of an individual. These records should answer such questions as: Are there any activities in which an individual should not take part? How much should be expected of him? Should the activity be expanded in any way? This resource should be available throughout the year so that information concerning illness, accident, worry or general student load will reach the teacher at the opportune time.

The physical education record may indicate the student's desires and previous experience in activities, as well as his response to them including successes, failures and problems. It may also give some insight concerning his attitudes and behavior revealed through these activities.

An information sheet, or checklist, concerning specific physical education interests and experiences may be filled out by each student at the first class meeting. This device has frequently been used in swimming classes and should be valuable with activity groups.

Another source of information is the teacher's observation. During the first class period the teacher should make careful note of individual ability. This not only discloses something of experience background but also ability. Some will move with coordinated bodies and a good feeling of rhythm while others will have great difficulty perhaps due to special handicaps.

*Resources of the Recreation Leader.* Sources of information about participants will vary in different community agencies but are usually more limited than those available to teachers. Leaders in some community situations may find almost nothing available to them while in others a little seeking may reveal important sources.

The registration form used by many agencies frequently supplies significant information concerning experience and family background. Some agencies require a health examination before participation in activity. The YWCA, for example, uses this not only as a protective device but as an educational tool. Settlement houses and other groups that stress work with clubs will have narrative records which reveal interests, attitudes and working relations with peer groups. Parks, playgrounds and Boy Scouts will usually have activity records. Some agencies have a close working relation with local schools and share information. These various sources would indicate that often information concerning participants in a program is not pooled in any central spot. Frequently pertinent information will rest in files unless the leader exerts a little effort to find it.

*Studying Needs a Continuous Process.* Finding out about group needs begins in advance but goes on thereafter as the teacher guides the group. Both students and the leader share and contribute in this on-going process as is illustrated below and also in the discussion of the later steps in group process.

An early class period may be used for group exploration of individual interests and needs. Students and the teacher or leader may discuss their own concerns and what they hope to achieve. Together they attempt to get an overview of the interests of the group. During this process the teacher or leader not only secures information but also has an opportunity to observe the participants. The manner in which they express themselves and react often gives insight into the depth of interest, the degree of tension and the relationships with others in the group.

As the class gets under way, the teacher will find it a real advantage to have scheduled conferences or informal chats with each student. Students will talk more freely during these contacts than in class. Frequently they may wish to discuss personal problems which may have a direct effect upon learning, group relations and general effectiveness. Help in solving these problems may have a definite effect upon class work.

The group or class situation changes constantly. As a result of day-to-day experiences, entirely new needs may arise and take precedence over earlier planning. In other words, the teacher and the group cannot do a good job of planning during the first week and then relax, feeling that their course has been charted. Often students do not really become aware of their needs until they have had some experience with the activity and with the group, or until some outside force affects their thinking. In a basketball class members may become aware of their need for greater skill in foul shooting and working together as a group after they have played with a visiting school and discovered their inadequacies. Students in social dance class may grow concerned about the skill in leading and about proper etiquette as their all-school dance draws near. Students in an archery class may become interested in the repair of equipment after some of them have learned that as camp counselors they will be expected to take care of equipment.

As students have experience in an activity, they will develop larger concepts and see the aspects of work that were not discernible at first. This means that the leader and members of the group must constantly be alert to new and changing needs. The emerging of new needs should be recognized as a sign of growth.

## Preliminary Planning

Those who are unfamiliar with democratic methods often have the impression that these methods require no advance planning on the part of the teacher or leader. Those who adhere to traditional practices are apt to label democratic ones time-wasting and chaotic because of this supposed lack of planning. It is important for anyone desiring sincerely to use democratic methods to understand the teacher's role in planning. The teacher or leader does plan, not only in advance but along the way as well. The difference between this planning and the traditional type is that the first is flexible, plans change in response to group needs and group action; in the second, plans are made once and for all for a program, complete in advance, and are carried out as an orderly sequence of lessons, assignments, practice periods, etc., according to the nature of the subjectmatter. The second is neat, tidy and comfortable for the teacher or leader for he always knows what the next step will be. The plan once made may be used over and over again. He is not put to the trouble of making a new plan for a new group. Using democratic methods in planning is not simple and easy, for the teacher or leader knows that any plans made will be modified or completely changed by the group. Nevertheless, in advance the teacher does not leave getting started to chance. He prestructures what *may* happen and often does, but stands ready to abandon any procedure with evidence that the group is able and willing to take over the situation for itself.

In advance of the first meeting with the class the teacher or leader will make an agenda of things to be done to be ready for the group. The listing will include a statement of his goals for the group, plans for orientation of the group, needed supplies, physical arrangements. These are all familiar procedures to the experienced teacher.

*Goals for Students.* As long as there have been teachers and those to be taught, the former have set goals for the latter; they have had in mind things they feel the students should learn and planned a program accordingly. Using democratic methods does not change this setting of objectives for students. On the basis of whatever advance information he has gained about a group, the teacher or leader clarifies for himself what he hopes the learning outcomes will be. For example: in the social dance class the teacher might list his goals for the group as:

1. Effective use of the body—coordinated poise and movement with quality;
   a. Skill in fundamental movements or steps,
   b. Understanding of rhythm and ability to work to different rhythms—waltz, fox trot, rhumba, tango, and
   c. Skill in leading and following;
2. Understanding of and skill in creative use of dance skills;
3. Development of confidence and ease in working with other individuals, especially members of the opposite sex; and
4. Concern for others and skill in working with a group.

In setting these goals, when using group process, the teacher does not lose sight of the fact that they are his goals, not those of the individuals in the group. He knows that each young man and woman will come to the class with purposes of his or her own and that he must help the group to clarify what these are. Using democratic methods he does not superimpose his own goals upon them. He knows that best learning is attained when the learner sees the relation between the experience offered him and the fulfilling of his own purposes, and that superimposing his goals for students upon them, as in traditional practice, does not produce best learning.

*Arrangements To Be Made.* Outside of the usual concern for needed materials and care for the physical environment, there is an additional point to be considered when group process is the method. The teacher or leader wants group participation from the beginning. He will need to arrange the situation for the first meeting so that it permits a maximum of group interaction.

Students arranged in rows facing the teacher may be an effective arrangement for some phases of teaching in social dance or other activities but it does not establish a good situation for discussion. Neither is it wise to hold discussion with students scattered informally about the floor, as they often are in social dance or team sports. It is difficult to hear, concentration is poor, and usually they just wait until they can proceed with the activity.

For good group response the group must be brought together in a place with adequate ventilation and good lighting, but not facing windows. Most groups will automatically assemble facing the leader. This may establish easy relationship between the leader and group. Group process, however, does not mean interaction between leader and members of the group, but rather interaction between members of the group. A circular arrangement with people facing each other will work more effectively. The leader can become a part of the circle. This makes it possible for discussion to move from one member to another and does not make it necessary for the leader to come in except at points where he can make a contribution. The arrangements for group discussion should not be left to chance any more than any other phase of the class period. The leader should be familiar with the space to be used and have a plan for setting the stage for the discussion period.

## Orientation

Orientation of the group means finding direction. It involves an understanding of the group's needs and preliminary planning previously discussed. It also involves early efforts in seizing opportunities for positive group interaction, in helping group members feel secure and in minimizing any period of floundering while group patterns are being observed and developed.

*Climate Is Important.* Democratic human relations reach their fullest development in a free or permissive atmosphere. In such a climate each individual is respected and considered to have potential capacity for growth. Each is encouraged to think, work and contribute in terms of that which he believes is best for him and the group. A democratic climate tends to free persons so that they explore various avenues of thinking and acting which lead to new understandings and growth.

A desirable climate does not just happen. The type and quality of feeling tone in any group are dependent to a large degree upon the philosophy of the leader. The leadership may be guided by autocratic, laissez faire or democratic principles. In the autocratic pattern, the leader determines all policies and procedures. He expects the group to accept these without questioning. Various steps in the activity at hand are presented one at a time with little reference to relationships and future use. The leader makes all assignments and remains aloof from the group. In this type of environment, the individual may quickly discover that his contribution to the group is not considered as valuable as that of other members. Those eager to make a place for themselves in the group learn to shape their responses and work around the opinions of the leader and avoid expressing ideas that deviate from the accepted pattern. Obviously this type of climate does not encourage a person to express and clarify his own feelings or to try out his own ideas. Young people in such an environment usually lack initiative and depend upon the leader.

The leader may choose to play a passive role which results in a laissez faire pattern. This is in direct contrast with the autocratic pattern. Under this type of leadership, the group has complete freedom to make decisions concerning activity and procedures. The leader assumes no responsibility for guiding discussion or assisting with evaluation of individual or group results. With this type of freedom, students tend to shift frequently from one activity to another and often feel at a loss as to what to do.

The democratic pattern, though centered in a permissive atmosphere as described in the opening paragraph, uses freedom in a very different sense than that experienced in the laissez faire pattern. Democratic leadership makes it possible for members of a group to share in determining policies and making decisions concerning activity at all possible points. They work with persons of their own choice and together the group determines division of responsibilities. A unique difference lies in the role of the leader. He participates actively in the group and assumes the responsibility of a guide.

During discussion periods he assists the group in broadening the scope of thinking and discovering a wide range of possibilities. He contributes to the discussions in attempts to make wise choices. He guides group discussion so that steps for action emerge and the group sees these in relationship to the individual and group objectives. Thus the group proceeds as a cooperative enterprise.

Climate affects learning. A democratic climate created through skilled leadership and a wise use of freedom provides a setting for experiences of the highest quality. Best learning takes place when the task at hand is meaningful. The individual needs to have clearly formulated goals and to see the relationship of his work to these.

The leader sets the stage for the pervading climate. Each group or class brings together individuals with different interests, purposes, attitudes, patterns of behavior and levels of experience. All of these act as powerful forces affecting the group relation. The teacher as leader of the group must not only recognize these individual differences but attempt to understand them and help others to understand and accept them. With a belief in the potential development of all persons, he should proceed to work toward blending differences and creating a desirable climate.

The leader's relation to the group often exerts more influence in developing good relations in the group than do fine sounding words. His ability to respond to all students with warmth and interest as well as to demonstrate consistently through action a real respect for all individuals serves as a potent force in the development of an environment that helps students grow in understanding and respect for all.

Likewise, the manner in which a leader deals with a trying situation arising from behavior problems will have a significant influence upon attitudes in the group. The leader seeking to establish a permissive atmosphere would not resort to a technique that would "put the student in his place" as might be expected under autocratic leadership. Instead he would try not to reject the individual as he attempted to work through the situation toward more desirable patterns of behavior.

The group shares in the responsibility for developing a desirable climate. The democratic process moves toward higher levels of operation as the members of the group grow in their understanding of the responsibility of an individual to a group. Through wisely guided experiences individuals learn that the privilege of freedom carries responsibility and that personal gains obtained from a group are dependent upon contribution. The skill and level of maturity displayed in the functioning of a group are dependent upon the previous type and quality of experiences. Therefore it is important that the leader adapt his methods to the functioning level and current needs of a group.

There are a variety of ways in which the leader can help to establish a friendly, permissive atmosphere. Anything he can do to develop the feeling of identification of individuals with the group, a recognition of shared purposes, a feeling of moving forward toward common goals, will add to the atmosphere in which work *can* go forward. During the first day, for example, the teacher of the social dance class might help insure a right atmosphere in these ways: arrive ahead of the students and talk informally with them as they assemble; spend some time getting acquainted; clear details so that all are sure of what is expected of them; discuss the general nature of the class and the method of planning and proceeding; have the group participate at this point; listen and respond with interest to each student's comment; begin teaching in an informal manner; start with a phase of the activity that all can do with a fair degree of satisfaction; make suggestions to the group, not individuals; avoid making difficulties of any individual noticeable to the group; proceed as though their problems are not unusual; quickly establish the feeling that he is not going to ask them to do things beyond their ability, that he is interested in helping them learn, and not there to condemn. This is done not so much through words, but by what he does and the manner in which he does it.

*Ways To Get Acquainted.* There are innumerable ways to help group members become acquainted. A particular method may be called into use by the nature of the group, the beginning atmosphere as it gathers and the time available for social intercourse. The group members may find that they know one another, with few exceptions, or the group may spontaneously take responsibility for each member getting acquainted. In any case the feeling of identification with the group should become tangible. The teacher predicts, senses and seizes the best opportunity to assist. On the basis of his skill and experience he is flexible and can adapt his techniques. The teacher of the social dance class is particularly fortunate in being able to use innumerable "social mixers" combining physical skill with the social situation.

*Exploration of the Activity or Problem.* Exploration is the beginning period in which planning and experiencing are interrelated. Initial plans are discussed. Group participation and response are encouraged. Resources are made known. Group members are helped to sharpen special problems. The present achievement level of the group is investigated and general progress to a new level is approached. The teacher of the social dance class faces a relatively simple task in this exploratory phase of group process. He needs to discover what skills the group knows, the possibilities of new learnings, and relate these data to a group approach. In other activities this exploratory phase might be a much more involved and more lengthy step. Especially would this be true if the group members had no familiarity with the activity.

## The Group Sets Its Own Goals

Setting goals demands rigorous self-examination as to purposes and intentions. It is based on democratic participation of all. It is not leader dominated. The leader advises, stimulates, contributes and suggests in the setting of goals which are generally related to the participants' needs and interests.

A group may have sharply defined individual or group problems. These in turn may require individual activities as well as group projects for their solution. However, a collection of individuals is not a group until common purposes have been accepted by all as goals which they wish to strive to attain with others. Group goal-setting involves drawing out of the group as a whole a series of goals and activities or ways of achieving them which are closest to the real needs and interests of the individuals involved.

## Ways To Determine Common Goals

The process of goal-setting may be illustrated by again thinking of the social dance class. This time an actual situation is described:

Following an opening discussion students were asked to think further about their own needs and to prepare a written statement outlining what they wanted to achieve during the term. The summary of these statements made by the teacher disclosed a wide range of interests and needs. Students wanted to develop skill in the waltz and fox trot; to improve style in dancing; to learn variations and "fancy" steps; to develop skill in rhumba and tango; to learn jitterbug; to develop confidence and poise; to learn about the origin of steps; to make new friends; to develop an easier relationship with members of the opposite sex; and to acquire information on methods of teaching that would help in part-time work. For example, some of the individual statements were:

Student 1. I want to acquire a feeling of security on the dance floor and have my partner have confidence in me, and to learn the waltz and the rhumba.   Student 2. To acquire credit in dance (I have never liked to dance, not even with my wife). Student 3. To learn a few basic steps, and to be able to feel more at ease in social situations and less out of place. Student 4. To acquire grace in dancing, to learn the tango and rhumba, and to make new acquaintances. Student 5. To learn different ways of dancing, to learn what steps to use with different tunes and how to recognize them, and to learn to dance so that I can gain more friends and be more sociable. Student 6. To learn jitterbug, rhumba and polka. Student 7. To learn the fundamental steps, to feel at ease dancing with a partner, to understand how to lead, and to learn about proper etiquette to use "on the floor" and when "sitting out." Student 8. To learn to dance so that I can lose the tortured feeling I now have when I dance, to improve enough so my partner and I can mix with other couples, and to help boys in the Hi-Y Club learn to dance.

As the students think about their goals for a class they tend to focus upon one or two things that are especially important to them. For example, it may be a concern to become more at ease while dancing or to learn jitterbug or rhumba. The teacher tends to see goals in a broader manner. He too will be concerned with helping students become more at ease but because of his experience he knows that the achievement of other goals is related to the achievement of this one. Therefore, he would add basic skills in the area of rhythm, steps and leading.

The group members then need the guidance of the leader, a more experienced person, as they discuss and set their goals. The wise leader will help them broaden their goals not by telling them what their goals should be, but by opening new avenues of thinking related to their problems and helping them discover fuller meaning of their goals.

The leader can help the group move from a long list of what seems to be an endless variety of individual interests to some sort of grouping or classification which will embody most of them. In the social dance class the group discussed this long list of individual interests and finally agreed that they would classify these under three large headings with a number of specifics under each. The following is the grouping that they used and called common goals.

1. Growth in basic skill and knowledges
(a) Rhythm, waltz, fox trot and variations; (b) rhumba, tango and samba; (c) leading and following; (d) dance in various situations; (e) creative use of materials; (f) quality and style in movement; and (g) etiquette.

2. Growth in the area of group relations
(a) Cooperate with activity of the group; (b) thoughtfulness and concern for all members of the group; (c) willingness to dance with all members; and (d) more at ease with members of the opposite sex.

3. Recreation—fun

The leader may have awareness of democratic procedures or group relations as one of his goals. Students, however, may not suggest this in their first statement. The alert leader will watch for the right lead in the early discussion period to open this area of need. For example, in the social dance class no one stated such a goal. During the discussion period someone suggested that they were concerned with developing easier relationships with members of the opposite sex. The leader raised the question as to how they felt this could be done. From this they moved into discussion of intergroup relations. Again the leader asked how they might run into trouble in this area. They suggested that some may want to dance with the same partner or not dance with less skilled people. From this discussion they decided that good group relations should be one of their goals.

This was a fortunate break in the discussion which the leader was successful in directing toward a new area of concern. Often, though, it may be necessary to wait until later experiences before the group has any realization of such a need. In a modern dance class, for example, this did not occur until the semester was well under way and the class was working on studies in groups of five to seven persons. At the end of the class period several students said, "We didn't get much done today." "We had lots of trouble working together." "Everyone had a different idea, went his own way, and we wasted a lot of time." This situation led to a discussion of group relations and the responsibility of an individual in a group.

## Group Planning and Action

After goals are tentatively agreed upon plans are made to achieve them and initial steps are taken to carry out the plans. This process is likely to be repeated a variable number of times depending upon the amount of time allocated to the whole project and the complexity of problems to be solved. Replanning is based on findings from evaluation. Revised plans thus represent a periodic cooperative effort to clarify and modify goals and see ways to attain them.

Whenever group planning and action are described in general terms, the process sounds very removed from actuality; to some it even sounds "fancy" and impossible of achievement. To take the description into the realm of experience, the following example is offered. It illustrates how one group worked out a difficult problem.

The bowling group which was open to all students had Negro and white students as active members. After several years of satisfactory experience in bowling at an alley, the manager informed the group that they could no longer use the alleys if there were Negroes in the group. All efforts to convince him that the alleys should be open to all students failed. The group went to all alleys in that section of the city, trying to make reservations for their mixed group. Always the managers came forth with the same reply —their regulations would not allow Negroes to use the alleys.

The executive committee studied the problem. They could see only three possible solutions: either to sponsor bowling at two separate alleys, thus providing for both Negro and white students; to continue using an alley open only to white students, explaining that it was impossible to secure an alley for all students; or to discontinue the activity. One member of the committee suggested that it might be wise to meet with some of the Negro girls and discuss the situation. The group agreed.

Such a meeting was arranged and the problem presented. Fifteen Negro girls and members of the executive committee carried their discussion of this problem and many others related to it over into a second meeting. It was the concensus of the Negro girls that sponsoring bowling at two alleys, separating the two groups, did not solve the problem. Finally one girl suggested the possibility of making arrangements for the entire group to bowl in an alley used by Negroes. This was a new idea and they felt that it should be explored. They agreed that they must either find a place for all or discontinue the activity.

Following this meeting, leaders presented the problem to the manager of an alley used by Negroes. He quickly understood the situation and was willing to cooperate. Even though his alleys were used heavily on Saturday afternoons he always managed to reserve adequate space for this group.

This solution came after many approaches had been examined and found lacking. Probably the most important factor contributing to a successful solution was the meeting of the Negro girls and the executive committee. It was here that they faced the problem squarely, the white girls seeking an answer, the Negro girls with ideas about what would lead to a satisfactory solution. Through these meetings the girls became more aware of certain values that must guide them in making a decision.

The preliminary plan of action for the social dance class involved general steps to be taken to meet common goals, specific teaching procedures and a planned schedule. It failed, however, to represent all interests that had been expressed by individuals. The group felt some responsibility to suggest ways that these more individualized interests might be met. For example, a few persons had expressed a need for help with methods of teaching. Since the curriculum offered a methods course and most members of the class were not interested in methods, it was agreed that class time should be used for other purposes. It was proposed: that those interested in methods make a special effort to observe the methods used by the teacher and to keep a notebook; secondly, that the teacher make helpful but brief comments on methods at appropriate points; and thirdly, that students feel free to raise questions at any time.

Similar attempts were made to help others develop a plan for meeting their individual needs.

With this planning as a background, the teacher and students proceeded with the task they had set for themselves. As they progressed they found it valuable to take time rather frequently to consider their progress in relation to their goals. These discussions helped to clarify their response to the activity and point up needs and set direction for the following class periods. A few of the problems and individual statements presented during these periods will best illustrate this phase of the work.

During a planning period, the group decided that the class work had been moving too fast and that they needed a day or two "to continue work on what we have learned so we can be sure of it and be able to use it outside of class."

As they were considering the use of the piano and recordings, they decided that recordings should be used more frequently because "it is more difficult to hear the beat in the recording. We need that practice so we can dance to an orchestra."

A consideration of methods used in changing partners brought the decision that they should not change so frequently when learning new material because "you had to get adjusted to each new partner and if changes were too frequent, you spent most of the time adjusting."

Problems in the area of group relations came to the attention of the group through statements such as these:

John: "Well, we could do better. I notice that when we have mixers, some cheat and do not change partners."

Don: "Some girls are very helpful but other girls make you feel that they do not want to dance with you. They seem to be just waiting to dance with a more skilled fellow."

Jane: "I was just trying to express my point of view. I didn't like it when he laughed at me."

As the group succeeded in getting problems such as these out in the open for discussion, they made some progress in altering their patterns of behavior.

The cooperative planning and evaluating used in the social dance class not only made for a better learning situation in dance but also provided real experiences in considering the interests of others, in making choices and in developing plans that were satisfactory to all. Growth through experiences like these thus contributes to better understanding of democratic living.

Many techniques are now available leading to greater effectiveness in group planning and action in carrying out plans. Much research is being conducted. Increasing help may be expected from this research in the analysis of member roles, good discussion techniques and the use of committees and resources.

## Group Roles

As group interest and concern develop through cooperative effort to achieve goals, and through work and play relations among group members, the teacher or leader has the opportunity to help the group take further steps in understanding democratic participation and relations. It is important for him to wait for this moment, however. Premature analyses of member roles may seem like "monkey business" to young people inexperienced in group process. A case is recalled of a teacher who, having had a stimulating and rewarding experience himself in group process methods, met his volleyball class for the first time and, after a brief explanation of various roles, said, "You will need a leader and a recorder. You should work out ways to use group members as observers and resource persons." The inexperienced group rejected the teacher's suggestions completely. It is noteworthy that it felt free to do this. The teacher, though not skilled, had by his own enthusiasm convinced the young people of his sincere conviction that they should share responsibility for planning their own program. The group took him at his word. Another group, not so convinced, used to taking cues from teachers "to get along," "make a good grade," might have docilely followed the suggestions, but with little understanding of what they had been asked to do.

When groups feel a need to examine and analyze how they operate, then is the time for the teacher or leader to supply them with information about group roles and help them to practice these roles to the end that they operate more productively and more democratically. If sharing in every step of the group process is genuine, the need is sure to arise.

Of course, groups have been known to reject the whole method and say, "Tell us what to do and we'll do it." This has been offered in defense of traditional practice, in spite of the fact that authoritarians would be the last to say that students should do what they want to do. For clarification of this difficulty, it is well to reread Hearn's description in Chapter 2 of the leader's role in various types of groups.

Research in Group Dynamics is providing us with many descriptions, examples and findings from experimentation regarding various member roles. This material is beginning to permeate educational fields and should result in increased understanding and improved use of group process methods.[1] This material is drawn upon in the following paragraphs.

*The Leader.* Principles for action in filling the leader's role democratically were evolved by Cassidy in Chapter 4. Belief in the need for personal involvement or convictions about democracy on the part of the leader, belief in individual worth, the importance of climate in guided group interaction, in shared responsibility and in continuous evaluation provide the leader with guides for the role he plays in the democratic process.

A paramount skill for those guiding group process is the ability to permit and encourage leadership to emerge from the group. There are thus in group process two types of leaders, status leaders and emergent leaders. The difference, however, is not one of kind but of opportunities for all to function in the leader's role. The status leader may jealously guard his prerogatives and restrict the leadership of others. The status leader is not necessarily the teacher or person officially placed in position as leader. The status leader may be a member of the class or group to whom others turn for direction, a person accepted by his peers as a leader.

"Every member a leader" has been interpreted for a long time as the right of each individual to have his turn being assigned leader. Many physical education teachers rotate leadership in a squad so that each member is captain or squad leader. This is often done in spite of the fact that some individuals are assigned respon-

[1] National Laboratory in Group Development. *Report of the Second Summer Laboratory Session.* National Education Association and Research Center for Group Dynamics, University of Michigan, Bulletin No. 3, 1948.

Lippitt, Ronald A. *Training in Community Relations Toward New Group Skills.* New York: Harper and Brothers, 1949.

sibilities they are unable to fulfil and are not accepted by others in the position of leader. When rapport and friendliness exist, the group will often sustain and support the inept person. More often his inadequacies and ineptness are glaringly revealed to the disgust of the other members and with disintegrative effects upon him.

This automatic rotation of leadership, in total or in part, is based on the leadership-followership principle. "Every boy and girl should have opportunities to develop leadership and be a good follower." This principle is being discarded in favor of "leadership as a quality of group membership." The reasoning behind the change is as follows: In democracy, responsibility for what happens through group action rests with the group. This is so for in democracy authority rests with the group, rests at the bottom, not at the top with the leader assigned to carry out the group's wishes. Where authority resides, there also responsibility rests. A follower's obligation is to carry out directions by the leader. If things go wrong, the leader is to blame. There is no such easy abnegation of responsibility in democracy, nor is there in a democratic group. Each member is responsible and serves the group as leader in both assigned and unassigned ways according to his ability. The assigned ways are familiar—being captain, chairman, manager and the like. Unassigned leadership is taken when a leader's plan is questioned, when volunteering to carry out a needed task, when mediating conflicting opinions, when taking responsibility for group progress in many specific ways. Leadership as a quality of group membership can only emerge as status leaders see their role as the "servant-enabler" described by Hearn in Chapter 2.

The understandings and insights an assigned leader should have which every group member should be developing have been listed by Barr, Burton and Brueckner as follows:

1. A leader is selected for a given special ability or fitness to lead a specified cooperative project. A leader has ordinarily demonstrated some ability or power better than the ability or power of other members of the group. This is the opposite of selection of a leader on the basis of seniority, political power, religious or social affiliations, and so forth. Any member of the group may become a leader at a given time.

2. A leader has the willingness and ability to create a truly cooperative spirit and procedure.

a. Ability to suppress natural primitive urges to mastery, dominance, and authority.

b. Ability to substitute the more civilized and mature urges to aid, encourage, inspire; to guide followers in defining, understanding, and attacking a problem (gets personal satisfactions thus instead of bolstering ego through dominance—which is childish).

c. Willingness and ability to secure sympathetic insight into the mental processes, attitudes, prejudices, ideals, motives, and aims of other individuals in group.

d. Ability to create an atmosphere of serious, critical analysis of problems and procedures.

e. Willingness to listen to, to understand, to try out if practicable, any well-thought-out proposal of a group member.

f. Willingness to recognize leadership in others—to accept it as a contribution to his group project and to allow others to take over the leadership temporarily or for the duration of the project.

g. Willingness to wait patiently for the more sure results which come from understanding the nature of learning; understanding the specific levels of the group members rather than to seek the quicker and so-called more efficient results of authority.

h. Willingness to recognize and to accept from colleagues intelligence and contribution superior to his own; willingness to accept with consideration and attention the contributions of slower and duller individuals.

3. A leader has better than average intelligence and emotional balance.

4. A leader has confidence in self, ability, aims, but also at times a profound feeling of humility, sometimes even distrust of self. Both attitudes contribute directly to leadership.

5. A leader has confidence in human nature, its improvability, the creativity of all individuals. A leader at times is profoundly critical of human nature, recognizing its dangerous shortcomings at given moments. Each attitude spurs to leadership.

6. A leader recognizes critical points in the democratic development of policy, recognizes when issues must be brought out into the open, thoroughly discussed and decisions secured. A leader recognizes even in the midst of democratic discussion, crises when agreement, vote, or even poll of opinion cannot be secured; recognizes emergencies in which it would be fatal to him to dodge responsibility for making decisions even authoritatively. A leader in these instances, however, recognizes that he

has taken responsibility and must take the consequences; particularly must he make frank statements as to what he has done and why.[2]

*The Resource Person.* The role of resource person is taken by any group member who meets the group's need for information, advice or critical analysis. The teacher of physical education who analyzes difficulties in perfecting a motor skill is a resource person. The group member who makes a study of regulations governing the use of municipal tennis courts and brings the findings to the group plays the role of resource person. The one who says, "In a similar situation this plan worked," and describes the plan, is serving as a resource to the group.

The status leader shifts to the role of resource person as leadership emerges in the group. The change in role is not static; leadership is assumed when needed. However, the more a group becomes unified in the pursuit of common goals, the more personal involvement and responsibility increase. Similarly the status leader more often plays the role of resource person, supplying the group with ideas, information and counsel as the need arises.

So far, it is the in-group resource person who has been considered. There are also out-group resource persons, those who are asked in from outside the group, because of the possession of some expert skill or particular knowledge, to help the group in a specific way.

*The Recorder.* It is usually easy for a group to accept the idea of having a recorder. Secretaries taking minutes at meetings are within their experience. The recorder, however, is not a secretary. His job is to take enough notes to remind him of what happened so that he can "feed back" to the group an account of the ideas expressed, points covered or left undecided. The recorder's report should give the content of discussion as related to the point at issue or the problem to be solved.

As a group makes plans, carries them out and evaluates results, the recorder may play an increasingly important role. His summary report of a planning session can serve to clarify for the group what it has decided to do. It may lead to an immediate evaluation of the plan with possible changes and modifications resulting. A discussion

[2] Barr, Arvil S.; Burton, William H.; and Brueckner, Leo J. *Supervision.* New York: Appleton-Century-Crofts, Inc. Second edition. 1947. p. 91-92. Permission to reprint granted by Appleton-Century-Crofts. Inc., 35 West 32nd Street, New York 1, N. Y.

leader may call for a recorder's report in the middle of the session as a way of revealing to the group a tendency to wander from the subject or for some members to block progress by quibbling, by expressing personal antagonisms and the like. Recorders should attempt not to interpret, but rather to state group action clearly.

*The Observer.* The function of the observer is to help the group to see *how* it is operating. The observer's role is

to watch the group during their discussion and then feed back to the group his ideas about what happened during their discussion. In order to give his full attention to the behavior of the group the observer does not participate in the general discussion. The assumption is, of course, that even though the group is deprived of the contributions of one of its members during the problem-centered discussion, the total productivity of the group can be profitably increased through utilizing this member as an observer. Sometimes groups bring in a specially trained person to serve as their observer, especially to get the observer role started and adequately identified. . . .

Non-participation of the observer is necessary to keep him from thinking about the subject matter rather than about the behavior of the group. To become involved in *what* is being said prevents focusing on the questions of *how* it is being said, its relation to the direction of the discussion, etc. The observer needs to maintain his vantage point of objectivity at almost any cost, yet without losing his feeling of membership in the group.

"The attention of the observer may be directed at a variety of behavior in the group. He notes the general level of motivation, the general work atmosphere of the group, the orientation of the group, leadership techniques, and other factors which affect productivity.[3] . . .

An observation sheet is often of aid to the person asked to observe a group. On the sheet are headings under which the observer makes his comments. The sheet may be prepared by the observer, by the group or by both together. The headings will represent the things to be observed such as the leader's techniques, amount of interaction among members, amount of digression from the subject. The headings may be in the form of questions such as:

What was the climate of the group—(a) formal or informal, (b) permissive or inhibited, (c) cooperative or competitive? [4]

[3] Jenkins, David H. "Feedback and Group Self-Evaluation." *Journal of Social Issues* 4: 50-60; Spring 1948, p. 53-54.
[4] *Ibid.,* p. 54-55.

With very little training and experience group members can serve to further group progress in the role of observers. The group, however, must be willing to analyze itself. Objectivity is required on the part of both the group and the observer. Objectivity grows, it has been found, in a permissive, security-giving climate, as the group becomes increasingly problem-centered, increasingly concerned with the project or problem in hand.

*Other Roles.* Group members play many other roles besides those described. These roles have been identified in considerable measure and described in Group Dynamics research as group task roles, group building and maintenance roles and individual roles. The purpose of the first is to "facilitate and coordinate group effort in the selection and definition of a common problem and in the solution of that problem." The roles in the second category "alter or maintain the group way of working, to strengthen, regulate and perpetuate the group as a group." Individual roles are not relevant either to the group or the functioning of the group, but are "directed toward the satisfaction" of the individual's needs.[5]

In the course of group operations each member will play a variety of roles. Skill may be developed so that members identify and play the roles required for the group to move ahead. In developing this skill the use of an observer, a person not involved in the matter at hand, will prove of great assistance. Bringing in an out-observer, especially to initiate the observer technique, often helps group members to see what roles they are playing and how to improve their participation.

## Group Discussion

There are many sources to turn to for detailed suggestions regarding leader and member roles in group discussion.[6] Many patterns for discussion are described which will help those who initiate group process methods to evaluate and guide discussions in their own situ-

[5] Benne, Kenneth D., and Sheats, Paul. "Functional Roles of Group Members." *Journal of Social Issues* 4: 41-49; Spring 1948.

[6] Auer, J. Jeffry, and Ewbank, Henry. *Handbook for Discussion Leaders.* New York: Harper and Brothers, 1947.

United States Department of Agriculture, Bureau of Agricultural Economics. *Group Discussion and Its Techniques.* Washington, D. C.: United States Government Printing Office, n.d.

ations. In the main these sources emphasize that the essentials for a good discussion are:

A problem the group is actively concerned to solve;
A leader who serves as a medium and guide for exchange of opinion, rather than as a speech maker and "director" of the group;
A recorder to note what is said and report back to the group.

In a discussion which gets somewhere group members are problem-centered; there is exchange of ideas among members as well as between leader and member; there is opportunity for each to contribute and the contribution of each is considered.

Breaking up into small groups of five or six members for brief discussion has been found to be a good technique for increasing individual participation and speeding up thinking about a problem. Such groupings have become known as "buzz" groups. Buzz groups should be carefully briefed on the matter to be discussed and how to report the thinking of the small group to the total group. Buzz groups may be organized on a variety of bases such as age levels, sex, interests, experience, point of view about the problem, sociometric findings. Random groups are formed by those seated near together forming small groups or by counting off the number of groups desired and the one's, two's and so on forming groups.

## Committees

The committee structure of organization is very familiar and needs little explanation here. A couple of points are worthy of attention, however. In group process, committee organization is a function of the group, though the responsibility may be delegated to a leader or chairman at times. Committees then operate in the same pattern in which the total group operates—to set goals, plan and act, report back to the group. Evaluation follows by the committee and by the group.

A second point is that by using the familiar committee structure, through the organization of a class planning or steering committee, a good starting place is found for introducing group process methods. It is a way of starting with procedures with which most older youth have experience, then guiding them toward more and more sharing in planning and carrying out of their own programs.

# Bibliography

ANDERSON, RUTH H. "Skills for Social Living." *Educational Leadership* 1: 144-47; December 1943.

AUER, J. JEFFRY, and EWBANK, HENRY. *Handbook for Discussion Leaders.* New York: Harper and Brothers, 1947.

BARR, ARVIL S.; BURTON, WILLIAM H.; and BRUECKNER, LEO J. *Supervision.* New York: Appleton-Century-Crofts, Inc., 1947.

BENNE, KENNETH D. "Leaders Are Made, Not Born." *Childhood Education* 24: 302-308; January 1948.

BENNE, KENNETH D., and SHEATS, PAUL. "Functional Roles of Group Members." *Journal of Social Issues* 4: 41-49; Spring 1948.

BERNSTEIN, SAUL. *Charting Group Process.* New York: Association Press, 1949.

BREEN, MARY J. *Partners in Play.* New York: A. S. Barnes and Co., 1936.

DE HUSZAR, GEORGE B. *Practical Applications of Democracy.* New York: Harper and Brothers, 1945.

FENTON, NORMAN. *The Counselor's Interview with the Student.* Palo Alto, Calif.: Stanford University Press, 1943.

GILES, HARRY H. *Teacher-Pupil Planning.* New York: Harper and Brothers, 1941.

HOPKINS, L. THOMAS. *Interaction—The Democratic Process.* Boston: D. C. Heath and Co., 1941.

JENKINS, DAVID H. "Feedback and Group Self Evaluation." *Journal of Social Issues* 4: 50-60; Spring 1948.

LIPPITT, RONALD A. *Training in Community Relations Toward New Group Skills.* New York: Harper and Brothers, 1949.

LLOYD-JONES, ESTHER, and SMITH, MARGARET R. *A Student Personnel Program for Higher Education.* New York: McGraw-Hill Book Co., 1938.

NATIONAL INSTITUTE OF SOCIAL RELATIONS. *It Pays To Talk It Over.* Washington, D. C.: National Institute of Social Relations, n.d.

PRICE, RUTH. *Creative Group Work on the Campus.* Bureau of Publications, Teachers College, Columbia University, 1941.

STRANG, RUTH. *Group Technics in College and Secondary School.* New York: Harper and Brothers, 1938.

TRAXLER, ARTHUR E. *Techniques of Guidance.* New York: Harper and Brothers, 1945.

"Two Lessons of Group Dynamics." *Educator's Washington Dispatch.* Washington, D. C.: 1948.

UNITED STATES DEPARTMENT OF AGRICULTURE, BUREAU OF AGRICULTURAL ECONOMICS. *Group Discussion and Its Techniques.* Washington, D. C.: United States Government Printing Office. n.d.

UTTERBACK, WILLIAM E. *Decision Through Discussion.* Columbus: The Ohio State University Press, 1948.

# CHAPTER SIXTEEN

# *Evaluation*

MARGARET DUNCAN GREENE

T HE purpose of this chapter is to define principles and illustrate
techniques of evaluation. Emphasis is placed upon methods of
evaluation which in and of themselves are dynamic learning experiences and which offer the most development of democratic human
relations at the older youth level. Illustrations are drawn from the
specific fields, but, it is to be hoped, in such a way that applications
to many situations can be envisaged. This chapter is written from
the point of view of teacher and class. However, there are no aspects
of the process and techniques which are not equally applicable in
nonschool situations or out-of-class activities.

## Evaluation Readiness of the Older Adolescent

The normal six- or seven-year-old has what is called "reading
readiness" by the primary school teachers. He has the experience
background to attach meaning to symbols and the physical eye and
muscle-nerve development necessary to start learning the skill of
reading. In an analogous way, the older adolescent has what might
be termed "evaluation readiness" in the area of developing democratic human relations. He has enough social and intellectual maturity to begin to understand evaluation of relationships and to
share in the appraisal process.

The late adolescent shows his readiness for evaluation especially
as he acquires social maturity. He has passed the ego-centered
childhood stage and has emerged recently from the early adolescent
phase of wanting to be exclusively with a small gang of his own
sex. He wants to be with those of the opposite sex and to mix with

[ 403 ]

different kinds of groups. He has a new and tremendous need to understand himself, but the expression of this need is no longer just ego-centered. So many of his cues for understanding himself come from his observation and learning about others that he begins to have a genuine concern and consideration for his fellow man.

The move that the older youth makes toward living constructively and democratically is furthered by his participation in the world of adult ideas and concepts. He reads many of the same books, newspapers and periodicals, he listens to the same radio programs and he takes part in the same recreational activities. He understands and uses the vocabulary of the adults close around him, and with help he can absorb technical and abstract ideas. He is ready to try to understand for himself what democratic human relations mean. He begins to see many things from an adult point of view because he lives more and more in an adult world. As he reaches toward the adult world, he also begins to be evaluated in terms of adult standards of conduct and performance.

One of the reasons that the older youth is able to build more and more bridges into adulthood is that he is growing in his ability to benefit from the evaluation phase of the learning process. As a youngster he was often too completely involved in the experiencing or the living through of a situation to see the meaning of his experience. The older adolescent loses the precious, wide-eyed enthusiasm of the junior high B-7, but acquires in its place a reflective power of weighing, analyzing and considering what happens to himself and others. He is more willing to discipline himself to the careful learning and perfecting of such complex motor skills as shooting a basket, executing a football play, or performing a sequence of dance steps. Likewise, older youth with strong motivation will work patiently and unselfishly for the good of a community dedicated to a worthy purpose. He accepts and imposes long term goals upon himself, because when he comes to evaluating or accounting to himself, he wants results which he can recognize and respect. He is ready not only to share in the evaluation of things which concern him, but also to use considerable initiative in carrying out the process.

## Overview of the Evaluation Process

The teacher or leader who has studied his group of late adolescents carefully through the orientation and planning phases of the learning process knows something of their individual differences in social and intellectual maturity. He has ascertained something of their "evaluation readiness" in the area of human relations and can pitch the evaluation process at the proper level. Evaluation must start with this understanding of his group by the teacher. When he has gained a sense of where his group is, the teacher is ready to embark with his class upon the three steps in evaluation: (a) the clarification of educational purposes or goals, (b) the devising of methods that are appropriate to each of these objectives and (c) the interpretations of the findings.[1]

### Clarification of Goals

The clarification of educational purposes is the first job of the evaluators. It is the hardest and most important part of evaluation because it is the high point at which ideas must become specific and word symbols must be translated into action possibilities. Unless this first step is deliberately taken, evaluation becomes hit or miss and unrelated to what the group is trying to achieve. The task of seeing goals clearly is particularly difficult in the area of human relations because of their intangibility. It is easy to become lost in vague generalizations about democracy and humanity, and hard to discipline oneself and a group to setting clear specific goals capable of some degree of accomplishment and evaluation. The teacher or leader must make real the concepts of democratic relations and at the same time expand the vision of his students so that they see how the specific little daily happenings in their group projects have a deep significance and effect upon them.

The difficulty of specifying and clarifying purposes in the area of human relations becomes more apparent when compared with the relative simplicity of defining goals in skills areas. The goal of becoming a better volleyball player is easily broken down into improving service, setting up, court coverage, spiking and placing.

[1] Taba, Hilda. "What Is Evaluation Up To and Against in Intergroup Education?" *Journal of Educational Sociology*. 19-24; September 1947.

These techniques, though variable for individuals, are not hard to measure and judge when compared with becoming more friendly or growing in individual responsibility. The result of the situation is that the teacher or leader tends to find himself unable to do specific planning, acting and evaluating in the area of human relations. He approves objectives in that area but does not go beyond writing, thinking or speaking them. He concentrates his efforts on the more definite objectives of perfecting skills, learning rules and game strategy.

There is evidence that many teachers compromise when it comes to developing democratic human relations by being kind, friendly and considerate toward youth individually, but quite autocratic in the actual conduct of their classes. In a questionnaire given to 500 college freshmen and sophomores from public schools of California, over 80 percent affirmed that their teachers were (a) likable, (b) effective as teachers, (c) enthusiastic and (d) interested in them as individuals. However, according to answers made by these students on teaching methods, less than half of the teachers ever interpreted the purposes of the program, and a little over a third asked the students for their opinions about the program. Only 38 percent of the teachers emphasized the social aspects of the program as far as the students could judge. Three-fourths of the students said that their classes were well planned, but that in less than half of their classes were democratic procedures used or opportunity provided for creative or original projects (make up a basketball play, compose a dance, invent a game).[2]

The clarification of purposes describes the point at which the teacher or leader and his group must ask such questions as "What does being more friendly mean in this group?" "In what ways do people show that they are friendly?" "How are we going to know if we become more or less friendly?" "Aren't people friendly in many different ways?" "What shall be our criteria of evaluation for friendliness of our group and of individuals?" Such questions as these indicate that the group, while still in the planning stage, is passing judgment upon its goals or evaluating them.

The clarification of goals is a process that begins immediately

[2] Greene, Margaret Duncan. "Questionnaire on High School Experiences in Physical Education of Lower Division College Students," University of California, Los Angeles, Spring 1947. Unpublished.

with the beginning of any project or unit and is carried on throughout the project. This continual defining is especially important in the area of developing democratic human relations, because goals in this area change as experience takes place. As the group gains new insight and knowledge, the original goals are sharpened and expanded. The changing and growing may be confusing to both teacher and group unless the teacher is ready to move onto a new level of operation. It is the teacher's role as the more experienced member of the group to point up the need for adjustment of goals and then to consolidate the group's functioning on a new level.

## Methods of Evaluation

After the purposes are defined, the evaluators are ready to take the next step of selecting and using the instruments of evaluation. This second step was a challenging but comprehensible problem for the physical educator, recreation director or health coordinator of a decade ago who focused his attention on quantitative measurement. Health examinations were administered, defects discovered, totaled and compared from year to year by health coordinators. Recreational facilities were surveyed, participants were polled on their choices for recreational activities and actual varieties and incidence of participation were recorded and published by recreation directors, ambitious to measure the progress of the recreation movement. Physical educators gave innumerable motor ability, achievement and skills tests to evaluate skills. Quantitative measurement, begun in the field of physical education in the latter part of the nineteenth century by Hitchcock, Sargent and Seaver, and brought to a high peak in the last decade, added much valuable knowledge to the profession. The contribution of this type of research should not be underestimated. However, quantitative research gives very few cues to the teacher in search of instruments for evaluating human relations. Human relations cannot be measured quantitatively or even symbolically by the use of most pencil and paper tests. Human relations must be evaluated directly as they develop and grow.

Hilda Taba's advice in her discussion of evaluation in intercultural education applies to our evaluation problems. She says:

It will not be easy to develop instruments that are dependable, sound and appropriate at the same time. We need more descriptive evidence on the genesis of various attitudes, the influences that shape them, and the relation between verbal expression and overt conduct before we can afford to take short cuts. We also need to know more about how social attitudes affect personality structure before we can rely on instruments for diagnosis or educational stimulation. So let us do a lot more analysis of spontaneous reactions and let us spend more time watching our students before we try our hand at producing "objective" instruments.[3]

Two resources may be looked to confidently by professional leaders in this open field of trying to improve the instruments of evaluation. The first is a professional tradition as ancient as Greece of considering human beings as whole persons. While other educational fields have gone through periods of separating the mind from the body, we have endeavored to keep the human being in one piece. We should be able to use this tradition of seeing the total person to great advantage. Evaluation in the area of human relations depends to a great extent upon the power of the evaluator simply to see what is happening to and between people. Certainly it is the first step for anyone who wishes to improve his relationships with others. Careful observation and appraisal of other human beings are things the older adolescent must learn because this is a part of becoming adult.

The second resource that professional leaders can look to for help in methods of evaluation is the work that is being done in general education and psychology. For example, an issue of the *Review of Educational Research* (December, 1948) is devoted to evaluation. Digests of experimental work in other fields help interested teachers to get ideas for use in their own classes. A second resource is the research in group dynamics which has a great deal to offer in methods of evaluating group growth.[4] A third area of particular promise is found in the techniques of sociometry and role playing which will be discussed later in this chapter.

---

[3] Taba, Hilda, *loc. cit.*
[4] See bibliography at end of yearbook for works by Lewin, Lippitt, Benne and Sheats.

## Interpreting the Findings

After the teacher and his group of late adolescents have clarified their goals and selected and used their instruments of evaluation, they take the third and final step in the evaluative process—interpreting their findings. Again as in the second step, it is much easier to put one's finger on quantitative findings—number of defects corrected, number of baskets shot, number of new recreational participants. To see the significance of what has happened to oneself and others is difficult but not at all impossible. The teacher will find that the late adolescent is not inhibited in making sense out of things by the need to be scientific, restrained and not overly projective. He interprets forthrightly in a permissive atmosphere and often cuts sharply through to the truth.

The teacher often has a special job to do at this stage of evaluation. He may need to help to pull out the final significance of what has happened. Perhaps he does it by posing a few well-phrased questions which stimulate the group to probe deeply. If the point must be made immediately, he may speak directly of what he sees as the more experienced person in the group. This is particularly true when the teacher observes positive growth of which students are unaware. Students tend to be hard on themselves and one another and to see their shortcomings before their accomplishments. The teacher may wish to use an action technique like role playing to bring the findings more sharply into focus for the students. The whole interpretive stage of evaluation especially needs the skilful hand of the teacher because it is the point at which the group should consolidate its learnings and move ahead on a higher level of operation.

In class situations, part of interpreting findings is the process of marking. New learnings about people, emerging understandings of social concepts and growing relationships with others and similar intangibles must somehow be translated into letters or numbers. This difficult task is a reality in American education which must be faced constantly by teachers. The problem is not solved by having the teacher decide to grade on only those things which can be measured objectively and either to disregard such elements as learnings in the area of human relations or to weigh them in as a boosting or lowering value of the objective part of the grade as the spirit moves him on marking day. The problem must be faced squarely with students and they must participate in formulating marks for intangibles. Otherwise, they will come rightfully to the conclusion that intangibles can be separated from subjectmatter learning and are not very important when it comes down to brass tacks—the report card.

An excellent line of attack on the problem of marking is outlined and illustrated by Burton,[5] in which the class formulates a brief description of the kind of job a student should do to attain each letter grade. The description includes accomplishment in all objectives of the class. Students can then help to rate themselves and each other by trying to see how they fit into the pictures that have been set up and agreed upon as bases for marking.

The act of interpreting the findings carries the group into replanning on the basis of their evaluation. Replanning fulfils the purpose of evaluation, which is to find in an experience the basis of a more enlightened approach to further effort.

## Evaluation Techniques

In Chapters 8 and 12 evaluation techniques have been explored. Many ways to appraise progress with children and youth were discussed. The techniques explained—observation, rating scales, questionnaires, interviews, observers' and recorders' reports—are useful at the college level as well. It seems, however, more fitting to employ the space assigned to this chapter to a full discussion of newer techniques of promise rather than to duplicate, even in different words, what has already been done and what is familiar to most college and university teachers. For the reasons given, this section is delimited to consideration of sociometry and role playing.

### Sociometry

One of the most interesting and fruitful techniques to be developed during the past two decades for the study of group interrelations is sociometry. It is so admirably adapted for use in recreation and physical education that it is to be wondered why more use of this tool has not been made by our leaders and teachers.

[5] Burton, William H. *The Guidance of Learning Activities.* New York: Appleton-Century-Crofts, Inc., 1944, p. 484-86.

Sociometry may well be compared with chess. The steps in using the sociometric technique are fairly simple to learn, as are the moves of the different chessmen, and may be mastered in a sitting or two. The technique, like the game, can be done on a beginning level with safety, increasing enjoyment and insight. Each time the sociometric technique is used the results are different, just as each chess game turns out differently. The teacher soon realizes that there is an infinite amount to be learned about each group and, like the chess player, must learn to see pattern and meaning in the limitless variety of possible developments. The teacher has the edge on the chess player, though, because his "men" are real. He is studying people, not a game.

Sociometry is both an evaluative and a group guidance instrument in the hands of the teacher. The purpose of sociometry is to release the greatest amount of social energy within a group for cooperative action. With the aid of sociometry, the teacher can identify the social forces within a given group more accurately than by observation. Equipped with objective information on the status of group members and of the group interrelations, the teacher can arrange the most productive and harmonious working combinations within a group. Democratic human relations are fostered in a sociometrically structured group.

A brief description of sociometric techniques will be given in this chapter but the interested reader is urged to study *Sociometry in Group Relations* by Jennings.[6] This readable manual explains sociometry clearly, suggests applications and reports the most recent research. The periodical, *Sociometry,* begun in 1936, records current research.

The sociometric approach begins with an individual making spontaneous choices of those persons with whom he would most like to participate in a given situation. The teacher or leader prepares the group briefly and casually, but carefully, for the making of the choices by explaining that for the next class or group project he would like to arrange teams, committees or working units so that the members will be working or playing with those whom they most like to be with. He asks them to write down on a slip of paper

[6] Jennings, Helen H. *Sociometry in Group Relations.* Washington, D. C.: American Council on Education, 1948.

their own names followed by a list of their choices. The teacher assures the group that their choices will be kept completely confidential, and also that groupings will be made very soon according to the results. If it seems appropriate, he asks them to place at the bottom of the paper the names of anyone with whom they would prefer not to work. To make the situation a valid one, the teacher must have rapport with the group, he must word the question carefully ahead of time and he must be sure that the project for which the choice is to be made is actually going to take place in the near future. The length of time for which the groupings are to be maintained should be mentioned.

It is not hard to set the atmosphere and ask the right type of questions for good results in our fields. Such questions as these with appropriate introduction have been used:

During the six week volleyball season in our physical education class, which three persons would you most like to have for teammates?

List four boys (girls) with whom you would like to be in a square dance set for the parents' night performance next week.

Name three persons with whom you would like to room on the ski trip next weekend.

During the next two weeks in rhythms, we are going to be working on small group problems. Choose three persons with whom you would like to work. At the bottom of the paper put down anyone with whom you find it difficult to work.

Our class is going to visit various health agencies in small groups. With which persons would you like to make your visit and prepare your report for the group?

So many small, informal but deeply involved groups are used in health education, physical education and recreation situations that the sociometric test is easy to administer. Jennings, however, warns against using the words "sociometric" or "test" even with high-school students.[7] Also the teacher is to give no advice on how choices are to be made, as there are no right and wrong answers in sociometry.

The second step after administering the test is to arrange the choices in some kind of usable form. Jennings suggests two ways: first, the information on the slips of paper is tabulated on one

[7] Jennings, Helen H., *op. cit.*, p. 14.

graph sheet by listing the names vertically, then listing in the same order horizontally. The numbers 1, 2 or 3 are put in the proper squares to indicate the choices. Second, a graphic sociometric chart is made showing first, second and third choices as well as mutual choices. An example is presented here.

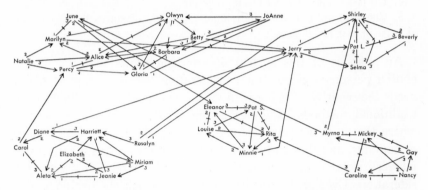

While making the tabulation form and constructing the chart, the teacher will be interested in checking his previous impressions of the group. He will see at once whether his group is knit together by a myriad of inter-connecting lines and mutual relationships which characterize a unified group, or whether the group is broken up into small, isolated units which have few or no communication arrows between them. Jennings devotes nearly a chapter to following up the cues of the sociograms. She has worked out a "sociometric analysis schedule," in which the teacher is asked to answer such questions as: What seems to account for certain pupils being the most chosen and receiving few if any rejections? What seems to account for mutual choices? Rejections? What do the majority of most chosen children have in common? [8]

The teacher searches for the answer to these and other questions which come to his mind as he works with the results, and his search goes on over a long period of time with observation and study. He must, however, start on the application step immediately, because students will have no faith in the sociometric process unless their expectancy for regrouping on the basis of their choices is fulfilled. In making the groupings, five steps are used which are based upon

[8] Jennings, Helen H., *op. cit.*, p. 28-29.

maximum choice satisfaction to as many individuals as possible.

1. Give the unchosen or seldom chosen person his first choice.

2. Give any pupil in a pair relation the highest reciprocated choice.

3. If a person is chosen by others but chooses none of those who choose him, give him his first choice.

4. Do not group any rejections together.

5. Check to see that each individual regardless of status is placed with at least one of his choices.[9]

An analysis of this system of grouping shows that the under-chosen person is given first consideration because he most of all needs the security of being with whom he chooses. This differs from traditional methods of group arrangement in physical education where the most popular persons are selected or elected as leaders or captains, and they in turn select their choices of teammates, with fringers, isolates, newcomers and motor morons receiving least con-sideration. Even where teams are arranged politely behind scenes by the teacher, with or without help of the leaders, those with the lowest status in skill or popularity are discussed and placed last. Sociometry reverses this procedure. The premise is that individuals are stimulated to do their best when they work with those whom they like. We gain strength and power in a congenial atmosphere and find ourselves at our best with our friends who understand us. The least chosen are favored because they most need the support of an encouraging atmosphere. The highly chosen, secure already in their position of acceptance and leadership, can afford better to be denied their first choice or second choice. They will have one of their choices, perhaps a reciprocated one, plus the support of those who choose them. This reasoning makes sense to the teacher who is primarily interested in the development of sound human relations. It will also convince the teacher who has observed that oftentimes the team with the most highly skilled players does not win the tournament; the team wins that gets along together and has "team spirit," a synonym for good interpersonal relations.

It should be pointed out that if this grouping system is used, captains or group leaders, instead of being chosen first will not be selected until after groups are formed. This is also a reversal of

[9] *Ibid.*, p. 45-46.

the usual procedure and has been objected to by teachers who want to get their roll books and cards made out early and who want to have captains elected as soon as possible in order to have a chain of command for class organization and regulation. In answer to this objection, it may be said that the inconvenience caused by the delay in electing captains is more than compensated for by the harmonious functioning of a sociometrically grouped class.

An additional help in analyzing the group, particularly after a retest, is the making of a *rank listing chart*.[10] The chart is easily made and shows the teacher at a glance the status order of the members of the group. While specific interrelations are not shown, the general picture of the group is. This type of chart, used in developing the Inglewood Project by Haas, is shown below as adapted for use in a physical education discussion group.

### Rank Listing Chart and Analysis

| Number of Person | 1st Test | 2nd Test | G-L | |
|---|---|---|---|---|
| 2 | 10 | 5 | L5 | |
| 6 | 8 | 8 | S | R1 |
| 11 | 7 | 9 | G2 | R1 |
| 8 | 6 | 6 | S | |
| 13 | 4 | 2 | L2 | |
| 14 | 4 | 2 | L2 | |
| 17 | 2 | 4 | G2 | |
| 9 | 2 | 7 | G5 | |
| 10 | 2 | 1 | L1 | |
| 16 | 2 | 3 | G1 | R1 |
| 4 | 2 | 2 | S | |
| 5 | 1 | 2 | G1 | |
| 1 | 0 | 0 | S | |
| 3 | 0 | 1 | G1 | R2 |
| 15 | 0 | 1 | G1 | |
| 7 | 0 | 0 | S | |
| 12 | 0 | 2 | G2 | |

Three choices were used of those with whom the group members would like to work. The G-L column shows "gains" and "losses" between the first and second test. "S" means same; "R" means rejected.

The comparison of first and second test figures shows a healthy growth in interaction as measured sociometrically. Over and middle chosen persons gave up some of their status so that choices were spread more widely throughout the group. Most significant is the fact that four of the six underchosen made gains although one of those persons also had two rejections. Only two persons in the group were unchosen compared to five on the first test. Three made gains in the middle group, one stayed the same, and two of the top of the middle group lost status. Only one of the overchosen gained and two maintained their same position.

[10] Haas, Robert Bartlett. "Group Work in Education—The Sociometric Approach," mimeographed notes used for lecture-discussion at Physical Education Workshop, Summer 1949, University of California, Los Angeles.

Old leadership apparently remained stable but permitted new leadership to emerge from the middle chosen group. The change in leadership shows growth and spreading rather than a rejection of old leadership. In three weeks time definite and reassuring signs of group interaction are observable.

Haas also suggests that the teacher have close by him a list of the underchosen and their choices so that every time an opportunity for little informal groupings comes up, they can be made advantageously.[11] Practice groups, couples to run an errand or take care of a piece of equipment, temporary committees, transportation groupings—such little episodes can be casually but valuably used by the alert teacher.

One of the most interesting results from using sociometry occurred with a group of thirty-six sophomore physical education major students:

The sociometric test had been administered to the group when they were low freshmen and again as high freshmen when three members had dropped out and three had been added. As freshmen, the group showed a healthy shift on the retest from popularity centered on a few, with nearly a quarter of the group unchosen, toward a spreading of choices more evenly throughout the group. Both tests showed a high degree of group inter-communication which was reflected in their strong unity and high morale.

In the sophomore year nine members of the original group dropped out and, coincidentally, exactly nine new ones were added. The sophomores had a difficult time getting started, particularly in arriving at a workable plan to achieve their goals. The first unit, a concentrated study of basketball, was not very successful and the group decided to do a field sports unit two days a week and a dance unit the other days. The staff suggested and the class approved the idea of determining the three field sports teams by the sociometric test. The test was given that day and the results charted.

The staff discovered that two relatively isolated cliques were in operation. The first clique of four made choices only within their group, though one choice was made into the group from outside. The second clique of three was likewise self-contained except that one of the three chose outside the group for her third choice which was not reciprocated. Five of the nine new class members were shown by the chart to be accepted, but the other four were

[11] Haas, Robert Bartlett. *Learning To Read Ourselves and Others: An Approach Through Sociometry and the Psychodrama.* Claremont, Calif.: Claremont Reading Conference, 1948.

unchosen in spite of the efforts of both the class and staff to absorb them. The sketchy group structure was a definite reflection of the difficulties the group had had in coming to decisions and in carrying out their plans to satisfaction. The cliques were no news at all to the staff, though their almost complete isolation from the rest of the group was a surprise. A check back to the charts for the freshman year showed faint outlines of the two cliques, but did not give a hint of how they would solidify under the stress of the second year's adjustments. The groupings were made according to the five suggested steps and the two cliques were teamed together plus the two weak links to the rest of the main group and three others attached to them. The cliques were placed on the same team, since they often mingled together. Their relationships did not show on the sociogram because only three choices were made, and none was left outside their cliques.

The class was ready for action the next day. The team lists were read and the staff watched carefully for reactions as the teams collected for the first time. The members of two of the teams, after a quick look around at one another, relaxed with happy, satisfied expressions without exception as far as the staff could determine. However, the faces of the third team with the cliques were studied. Their reactions might best be described as boredom. There were no surprises for them—as usual they were with one another and the project was pretty dull. Nevertheless, the whole group went to work promptly and got a good start on their unit of work.

Two days later the dance unit was begun, and when it was decided to work in small groups, the staff suggested a retest for the dance groupings. Retests are not usually done for a period of several weeks, but the staff reasoned that some kind of new groupings had to be made anyway for the dance groups and it would be a good chance to evaluate the effect of the first groupings.

The sociometric chart based on the dance choices was quite a different picture from the field sports chart. Throughout the group some changes in choices were made showing a wider acceptance of group members, though no dramatic changes in individual status took place except in the case of the two cliques. Revolt within these isolated units was apparent. Three from the first clique and two from the second clique chose out one or more times. The ones from each clique who did not choose out also lost status from within the clique. Both of them were from broken homes. Of the four underchosen new class members, only one remained unchosen.

Throughout the next four weeks the staff tried to observe the effect of the two groupings. Both study units were productive and efficient and a great deal of group satisfaction was gained from the successful trying out of the plans in both areas, but the morale of the whole group was higher in the dance activities. Although dance as an activity was less popular with them than field sports, the spirit during dance was much more similar to the kind of feeling that characterized the class during the freshman year. A sense of keen interest in one another's teaching techniques and skill improvement, a sense of expectancy and excitement over each day's lesson, pervaded the group. In the field sports unit, the clique group did not compare unfavorably with the other two teams on the days when they played. However, when their week came to plan for the practice and play of the other two teams, they had considerable difficulty in getting along together. They had many disagreements among themselves, some of which were healthy and others which were destructive. When things went wrong, they blamed one another or the staff.

The net result of the groupings was a widening of the clique structures. They sought new friends during their 10 hours a week together and stopped sitting together during discussion periods. Three out of seven became top class leaders during the next six months and sustained their position well. They had ability before, which the staff recognized, but it had been chained by their isolated positions as human beings.

Sociometry, in this clique situation, was a successful tool. The sociometric groupings gave the students enough insight into their own problems that it was not necessary for the teachers to deal with the problem in a personal way. The staff, with the information obtained by the sociometric test, was able to evaluate the class structure accurately and to watch it change with more patience and more objectivity than could have been done without sociometry.

## Role Playing

One of the techniques which is being used increasingly in an educational context is role playing. The term "role playing" will be used throughout instead of "sociodrama" or "psychodrama." These terms can be used interchangeably in many contexts. Role playing seems to be the best term to denote the kinds of situations presented in this material.

Like sociometry, role playing is a method which can be used safely and with much advantage by a sincerely interested teacher, but it is also a tool with complex implications which leads its users to a great deal of further study. Two basic references are given at the bottom of this page [12] for the reader, who is also referred to the quarterly *Sociatry* for current research in the field. The material in this chapter is confined to elementary techniques with which the teacher can experiment immediately.

The purpose of role playing is "to clarify and test the adequacy of social habits, skills, attitudes and values *in action*." [13] It is done by having members of a group act out real life situations under the direction of the teacher or leader who sets up the roles to be played, keeps the action moving and conducts the discussion, during and after the scene, on the interpretation of the roles. The following example illustrates how a role playing situation might be introduced and carried out with a group of older youths in our field. Suppose that in the basketball class round robin tournaments, in which the winning teams are to participate in the school-wide tournament, dissatisfaction arises because of a student referee's decisions and the feeling that some players are not playing a clean, fair game and are getting away with it. Instead of approaching the group with the usual remarks and discussion about learning to accept the official's decisions and about why they should play a clean game, the teacher sets up a role playing situation. Here he can evaluate the attitudes of the group *in action* and help the group move toward a satisfactory solution.

The teacher might start by describing a situation where the referee calls a personal foul on a boy, Jack, for personal contact. However, it is really George on the other team who was causing the foul. Jack accepts the penalty, but is not happy about it. In a few minutes, it happens again exactly as before and Jack is very upset because if it happens again he will be put out of the game. What does he do? The teacher might start the roles being played by asking the group if they have ever had that happen to them or seen it happen. From those who raise their hands, he selects two boys to play Jack and George, then a well-meaning but slow referee and other characters necessary to the action which the group might suggest,

[12] Haas, Robert Bartlett, editor. *Psychodrama and Sociodrama in American Education.* New York: Beacon House, 1949.

Zander, Alvin; Lippitt, Ronald A.; and Hendry, Charles. "Reality Practice in Education." *Psychodrama Monograph, #9.* New York: Beacon House, 1948.

[13] Harshfield, H. W., and Schmidt, J. P. "Playing Out Our Problems in Sociodrama." *Sociatry* 2: 365-67; December-March 1948.

such as a captain for each team, an umpire or a coach. The teacher asks Jack to start the action by trying to do something about the situation. The whole group might need warming up to the role playing, in which case the teacher would discuss informally with the cast some ways that Jack might try to solve his problem. When the group seemed clear on the action and their respective roles, they could start playing them out. The teacher allows the action to continue for a few moments until a solution seems to be suggested but not completed. The teacher may wish to interrupt the action if it gets off the point or bogs down. A suggestion from him or the audience group may clarify the roles.

After the action has been carried through in a fairly complete manner, the teacher conducts a discussion on how the roles were interpreted. He asks such questions as: Do you agree with how Jack played his role? Would you have done what he did? If not, how would you suggest it be played? If you had been in George's shoes, how would you have interpreted the role? How could the other players perform their roles in such a way as to change George's behavior? What does Jack say to George? What do the captains do? Does the coach come into it? Further developments of the plot might be suggested at this point, such as having the half-time whistle blow, which would give a chance for the situation to be talked over.

If the teacher has selected a really meaningful situation for the role playing sequence, and has kept it moving at first with suggestions, the class should be reacting strongly at this point and be bursting with reactions to the roles and suggestions as to how they should be played. The teacher can then replace certain or all of the original cast with new players of the roles. An excellent device is to switch roles within the cast. For instance, George should have the feeling of playing Jack's role, and the referee should play either of the boys' roles and Jack should play the referee's role. In that way, each person can gain some understanding of the other person's viewpoint and thus see his own role more clearly. The playing of such a role sequence as this one may take just a couple of minutes, so that during a class period many different persons would have a chance to play the roles. The teacher in his preplanning tries to anticipate several possible lines of action and to keep the role playing channeled along those lines. In this way the issues and implications become clear to the audience.

Role playing has many advantages to offer to both the teacher and the students. The teacher has a chance to observe students' *action* behavior, which is considerably more indicative than verbal opinions or answers given to please the teacher. Students become wholeheartedly involved in portraying their roles and identify themselves so closely with their roles that they reveal their real attitudes and values. The teacher has a chance to evaluate his students in the area of human relations in a dynamic setting.

For students, the greatest benefit comes from the chance to practice a variety of solutions to a given problem or conflict. In real life one does not often have a second chance, but in role playing one can try again. The student can observe or experience the consequences of various lines of action without actually having to face those consequences permanently. He may make mistakes and have a chance to find solutions which will really work when he needs them. An example of a typical boy-girl situation will illustrate this.

An after school co-recreational dancing group is concerned about the number who sit around the sidelines and watch instead of taking part. The group agrees that everyone wants to dance, but boys are shy about asking girls to dance whom they do not know well and the girls cannot ask the boys. The organizing committee has been asked by the group to try to solve this problem. The committee, after a discussion, decides that it will act as a host and hostess committee for the next week's dance. The advisor thinks this is a good idea, but wants to be sure that they actually have the social skills needed by good hosts and hostesses. Can they really handle the situations that they are going to meet? The advisor outlines the three following situations and suggests that they practice playing them through and then discuss them.

1. Roy, a host, asks Shirley, a complete stranger to him, to dance. How does he do this so that she really wants to dance with him? After the number is over, what is his next line of action?

2. Jack complains to the host that Harry is always cutting in on his girl and that she doesn't really like it, but does not know how to refuse. How does the host handle this?

3. Sally, an attractive hostess, asks John, a rude, conceited boy, for a dance. He replies to her invitation, "I'll pick my own, thank you." What does she do?

A number of other sequences could be arranged covering a whole variety of the social skills needed in this co-recreational dance setting. Students themselves can suggest the best situations taken from their own experience. After such roles are practiced by the group, some of them might well be presented to the larger group.

The outcome for the students of role playing to interpret boy-girl relations should be an increased understanding of joint responsibility in boy-girl activities. This type of understanding is particularly important for older adolescents to have as they approach the problems of courtship and marriage. To experience give and take between the sexes and to know first hand a few paths toward mutual consideration is reassuring and valuable for older youth. The teacher uses the seemingly trivial but very real life situations with which older youth are familiar to explore attitudes, discover values and develop social skills which have implications far beyond the role playing situation. The teacher has a chance to observe and evaluate behavior as it is revealed in the role playing and to use the findings in future work with individual students.

The two illustrations of role playing which have been presented are of student interrelationships. A third and final situation will be described to show student and teacher interaction. It is an example of how the teacher learns more about his own role from his students. The plot is as follows:

A student has received a "C" grade for the midterm. He feels that he should have received a "B" grade because he was present every day, was neat, clean and punctual, and cooperated in all the activities. He goes in to see the teacher, whose role is taken by a student. The student has been instructed to act the way he thinks a good teacher should deal with the student.

The resultant action should reveal to the teacher attitudes toward himself and teachers in general, and should help the students understand the teacher's role. It should also show the extent of the students' real understanding of the objectives of the program. Finally, the role playing situation could very well be the springboard for an excellent discussion of the evaluation program.

In every group's activities there is plenty of material for role playing. Whenever there are conflicts to be solved and skills in human relations to be learned, role playing can be used by the sincere teacher or leader with confidence. Lloyd Allen Cook, Director of the Inter-Group College Study for the American Council on Education, speaks encouragingly on the value of role playing:

Anyone can conduct it, do it better a second time, adapt it to any sort of human relations problem. . . . One learning outcome, evident in much of our data, is that neither students nor their teachers know very much of *use* in unifying conflicting views, in resolving personality clashes. Their lack of social skill is little short of astonishing; the rapidity of their learning, their obvious delight in it once the ice is broken, is equally startling.[14]

## Evaluation in a Subjectmatter Area

During the discussion of evaluation programs, one of the questions that is frequently asked in one form or another is, "How do our principles of evaluation apply in subjectmatter and skill areas?" Another is, "How can democratic human relations be fostered when objective material is being appraised?" Two projects will be reported which are experiments in the direction of trying to answer these questions—which, however, can only be answered satisfactorily through many, many experiments with varied groups in the different areas of our fields. The reports are again taken from physical education at the college level, lower division, but the material should be applicable to other situations.

The first project has to do with a class of low freshmen, prospective women teachers starting their individual teaching libraries and resource files. This project constituted their fifth objective, the other four in brief form being increasing understanding of self, of group action, of movement and of what teacher means. Not much was said in class about the fifth objective except that, at the beginning of the semester, the group agreed that even as freshmen they should begin to purchase books of their own choice in the field, collect pamphlets, subscribe to the *Journal*, buy records, own rule books, gather and arrange pertinent visual materials for display, save notes on methods of teaching, and, in general, build their resources for teaching. A date was set at the end of the semester for all materials to be brought in to be checked and graded as part of the semester's grade.

[14] Cook, Lloyd Allen. "The Frame of Reference in the College Study." *Journal of Educational Sociology* 21: 31-42; September 1947.

The day of the exhibit of materials arrived, and the staff and students alike were astounded with the quantity and variety of excellent resources that were spread out all over the gymnasium floor. The students had a most stimulating time inspecting each other's collections while the staff sweated it out checking and grading them, because staff had not yet learned to include the students in the grading process.

Early in the next semester, students began talking more about their files. Someone would obtain a good new book or pamphlet and show it around class informally. Soon students were asking each other to bring new material to class and tell how and where to obtain it and the cost. The bulletin board committee, which was changed every week, worked hard to outdo one another in original displays, which in turn gave ideas to the whole group on visual materials. Students who had found something valuable would volunteer to collect money and send for copies for those who wished them. Two very shy students made a recognized contribution to the group in this way. They found it easier to socialize with others when they had a definite small job to perform like collecting and distributing something tangible.

The staff invited the group to share in the grading and evaluation of the files at the end of the second semester. This meant that agreement had to be reached on what specific things should be in the files. Through student-led discussions the general areas set up for the first semester were broken into nine different categories, in which minimum coverage was expected of each person. Additional materials were to be concentrated in the area of the student's special interests. Originality and organization (usability and neatness) were also to be graded. Each student was expected to grade nine files, using a prepared form and a 3, 2, 1, 0 grade for each category. The scores were to be averaged by each team of nine graders and a grade obtained for each individual.

The staff invited major classes, faculty and administrators to drop into the files exhibit. The visitors were amazed with the wealth of pertinent material and were generous in their remarks to the freshmen. They asked many intelligent questions of the freshmen about how the material was collected and how it related to other class activities. The experience of talking with older prospective teachers, experienced teachers and administrators was their first taste of a kind of professional kinship. They had met many of the same persons socially, but never in such a purely professional relationship where they were on the giving, not the receiving, end. This was an additional kind of evaluation with plenty of democratic human relations.

Individual grades were determined by the staff as previously planned, but, in nearly all cases, were in agreement with those of the students. Some borderline grades were raised because the level of the group's achievement was high and, in some cases, represented outstanding improvement which the students who graded were not aware of. The students had graded on too rigid a curve. The staff grading was done with the full knowledge of the class.

In spite of all the positive outcomes of the exhibit and improved methods of grading, a great deal of dissatisfaction was evident, especially from those who were not producers of "A" files. In a discussion led by the evaluation committee chairman, some complained that those with a lot of good visual materials were graded higher than those with equally good notes. Those who had purchased several books carefully said they did not need to do extensive notes on the fields their books covered. Others said that they could not afford to buy books and therefore had a lot more work to do than those who could. Many objected to the files being graded at all because they were such a personal thing. Each prospective teacher needed different resources, and how could such an individual choice of materials be graded. Grading made it all competitive and destroyed the creative element.

When all these complaints and defensive reactions had been thoroughly aired, one girl asked what the purposes of the file were. Both staff and students began to clarify these purposes and to try to see how the files could best function for each individual. Raising the quality of the files received a great deal of attention with a de-emphasis on quantity. The question of grading was tabled until the next semester, but it was decided that the exhibition was valuable as a sharing experience. The sharing period was to be stressed more and a way devised for making suggestions for the improvement of each other's collections.

At the third exhibition during the sophomore year, the plan was to have four things happen: (a) each student was to check the completeness of six different collections and give each an over-all letter grade, (b) the grader was to write signed comments for each person, whose materials she evaluated, which meant that each student not only had the experience of judging others' work, but received six considered comments from others, (c) plenty of time was to be allowed for students to see the rest of the collections which they did not grade, and to take notes on things they wanted to know more about, and (d) a sharing session was to be held to evaluate the collections as a group and to exchange information freely.

The plan was carried out successfully and with satisfaction to the group. The high point of the project turned out to be the sharing session. The group was reaching a common understanding of the characteristics of good material. Their search was for functional material of high quality and they had been collecting long enough that they knew it when they saw it. They told interesting ways in which they had used their materials at summer camps and on their community projects when they had worked for eight weeks with a group of children under supervision. The project was still the building of a teaching library and resource materials, but it was being approached on a maturer level and with greater insight.

The stages in evaluation that the group went through more than anything else accounted for the growth in value of the project. Not too much happened as a result of the first exhibition because the staff did the evaluation and grading, thereby depriving the students of an integral part of the experience. The sharing that went on about resources during the next semester was evidence of a democratic skill in the making—combining a variety of resources for the common good. Instead of students hoarding their findings to gain credit for themselves individually, they learned to gain satisfaction by sharing their discoveries with their fellow classmates. Some evaluation of the quality of materials occurred at this stage but it was spotty.

When the staff had progressed sufficiently in their own concepts of evaluation, they took the students in on the process. The methods used at the second exhibition were too mechanical and rigid in their organization. The grading plan looked fine on paper but caused a lot of dissatisfaction. The discontent of the group caused them to return to the first step in evaluation which had never been completely taken—clarifying of the purposes for the files. When that hurdle was passed, the new methods of evaluation which evolved were not so mathematical and neat but were more meaningful and practical. The project at the end of the third exhibition ended on a high level with the concept of real sharing for a common purpose coming into its own.

## Evaluation in an Activity Class

The suggestion is implicit in the foregoing account of evaluation of subjectmatter materials that specific methods of evaluation must be found by teacher and students right within the structure of a specific project. Common sense methods were applied, refined by experience and growing insight. Techniques were developed and improved throughout the duration of the project as students and staff learned together. The account which follows may serve to illustrate a similar approach, but in the area of skills.

Thirty college freshmen students in a tennis class decided at the first of the semester that their common objectives were:

1. To learn to play tennis adequately to enjoy the game with other young men and women.

2. To know enough about techniques to be able to go on improving afterwards.

3. To know the rules and etiquette of tennis.

Fourteen of the students had played a little before, four indicated that they had played quite a bit, and twelve had never played before, although every person had watched a game being played and nearly everyone had played some badminton.

The teacher spent the first day in assisting them to become acquainted, and in helping the students to set up their objectives by asking them to discuss in small groups of six what they wanted to learn in the tennis class. A summary at the end of class resulted in a statement of their three objectives. The period closed with a suggestion by the teacher that the students purchase NSWA Tennis Guides by the next class meeting, and that they bring to class any pictures, articles, books or pamphlets on tennis for use in the class browsing corner in her office and for the bulletin board.

On the second day, after more getting acquainted was done and some materials shared, a short demonstration game was played by the experienced players to refresh the memory of the group on the procedure of the whole game. All those who wished then tried playing the game, using the four experienced players to answer questions on each court. Those who were absolute beginners were taken by the teacher for beginning work in how to hit the ball with the racket. The next three lessons were focused on directing the ball on the principle that the angle of the striking surface determined the direction of the ball. The grip, the backswing, the stance and the serve, the forehand and the backhand were analyzed and practiced with this principle kept foremost in mind. The sixth lesson was spent on a movie which reviewed techniques discussed during the week.

After this introductory period, the class was divided into five working groups of six each on the basis of sociometric choices. The teacher observed that the experienced players were all either average or highly chosen. Each group was asked to spend the next two periods making a working plan to last until the midterm period, based upon the individual needs of the group. Each group was to take stock of the abilities of the individuals in the working unit, collect a record of an analysis done by each individual of his own needs and formulate common group needs. The way each project was carried out was left up to each individual unit. A chairman and a recorder-reporter were elected by each unit and the process began.

The step that the teacher had structured the group to take was the clarification of goals. Each person was making specific for herself the purposes of the tennis class. She was doing a beginning estimate of what she herself could accomplish. In taking these steps with a small working unit, she was not only helping others to appraise their abilities, but acquiring a sense of her own needs in relation to others.

There was some objection on the part of the group that they did not know enough about the game to rate one another. The teacher reassured the group that they knew enough to make a beginning judgment, and that their understanding of the techniques would be greatly aided by analyzing others as they learned the techniques. She suggested that the groups start and see how much they could say about each other's strokes and that she would comment on their evaluations and help them. The next two class periods were not easy for the group. Some units seemed to be able to go right ahead and others took longer to discuss how they were going to carry out their ratings of one another. However, each group finished its job on the second day and the recorders took home the findings, including the individual self-analyses. They organized the material and went over their reports with their own unit during the first 10 minutes of the next class meeting. Common unit needs suggested by the recorders were revised and approved by the group. The rest of the period was spent in having each unit report to the whole group on their method of work, their findings and recommendations.

The working methods of each group differed considerably and a report of two of the units will indicate their trend. In the first group, two girls at a time played for a five minute stretch while the four others rated them on a 3, 2, 1 basis on grip, stance, forehand, backhand and serve. The ratings were recorded on a card which had the units' names on it, space for the ratings and space for comments. Each observer was to make a short comment on each item such as "starts swing too late," "always connects but ball goes in net," "does not throw ball same height for each serve" or "never ready for ball." This group had decided that each individual analysis should cover the same classifications and should reflect what the student had learned thus far about the techniques. The individual analyses of this unit were very complete, seemingly because each student had a sort of outline to work from and was encouraged to be specific. Individual analyses from two other groups were very sketchy because the groups had left the job up to the individual entirely.

The second group had two girls at a time playing with two observers and the other two playing with each other but analyzing themselves only. The observers did not use a mathematical rating, but simply recorded comments about the three strokes on three separate cards. The comments amounted to a short paragraph on each stroke and were very interesting to compare with the girl's own analysis also done on separate cards.

After the reports were presented, the teacher asked the group to make comments on what the reports implied for the way the class should be conducted until midterm. She asked that the comments be taken down by a recorder and given to a volunteer committee to organize and present to the group as an action plan. She asked them also to elect a class chairman, whose first job would be to organize the work of the volunteer committee with her help and lead the discussion of the plan the next period. This was a big step to take and involved not only the interpretation of the findings and replanning on the basis of them, but a transference of planning responsibility which she had carried for three weeks onto the group. The group had some preparation in its work with the small units, but still needed help from the teacher. She gave a great deal of support to the group, but more as resource person than as organizer.

During the rest of the semester the group carried out its plans and evaluated its progress at midterm and final periods. For midterm it adopted the general outline of the first group's methods of appraisal with some improvements. Self-analysis and grading were included. For the evaluation at the end of the semester, they made a few more changes and also requested the teacher to have final individual conferences. The evaluation procedures used by the group motivated their interest, were the basis for replanning and set the stage for their working as small units and then as a larger, democratic productive group. The actual plans were carried out in a similarly democratic way, with friendly relationships emphasized between the girls. The same group atmosphere and group process continued to operate during the evaluation phases of the tennis class.

Many other kinds of excellent evaluation projects not included in the scope of this chapter are doubtless being experimented with and worked out in our fields of health education, physical education and recreation. The intent here has been to review briefly the principles and process of evaluation and to present and illustrate some of the more promising techniques that are being developed by educational and psychological research workers. The particular techniques of sociometry and role playing were stressed because they are directed toward facilitating the development of human relations in whatever field they are applied. These techniques have helped teachers to work more specifically and definitely toward objectives in human relations which, though recognized as important, are nevertheless hard to clarify and approach.

## Bibliography

BURTON, WILLIAM H. *The Guidance of Learning Activities.* New York: Appleton-Century-Crofts, Inc., 1944.

COOK, LLOYD ALLEN. "The Frame of Reference in the College Study." *Journal of Educational Sociology.* 21: 31-42; September 1947.

HAAS, ROBERT BARTLETT. *Learning to Read Ourselves and Others: An Approach Through Sociometry and the Psychodrama.* Claremont, Calif.: Claremont Reading Conference, 1948.

HAAS, ROBERT BARTLETT, editor. *Psychodrama and Sociodrama in American Education.* New York: Beacon House, 1949.

HARSHFIELD, H. W., and SCHMIDT, J. P. "Playing Out Our Problems in Sociodrama." *Sociatry* 2: 365-67; December-March, 1948.

JENNINGS, HELEN H. *Sociometry in Group Relations.* Washington, D. C.: American Council on Education, 1948.

LEWIN, KURT. "Dynamics of Group Action." *Educational Leadership* 1: 195-200; January, 1944.

LEVY, RONALD, and OSTEN, RHEA. *Handbook for Group Development.* Chicago: Sociometric Research Associates, 338 Michigan Avenue, Chicago, 1950.

MOONEY, ROSS J. *A Study of Student Needs in Non-Academic Areas.* Columbus: Bureau of Educational Research, The Ohio State University, 1939.

MORENO, JACOB L. *Who Shall Survive?* New York: Beacon House, 1934.

PRICE, RUTH. *Creative Group Work on the Campus.* New York: Bureau of Publications, Columbia University, 1946.

SMITH, EUGENE R., and TYLER, RALPH W. *Appraising and Recording Student Progress.* New York: Harper and Brothers, 1942.

TABA, HILDA. "What Is Evaluation Up To and Up Against in Inter-Group Education?" *Journal of Educational Psychology* 21: 19-24; September 1947.

TROYER, MAURICE E., and PACE, CHARLES R. *Evaluation in Teacher Education.* Washington, D. C.: American Council on Education, 1944.

TYLER, RALPH. "Techniques for Evaluating Behavior." *Educational Research Bulletin,* The Ohio State University 12: 1-12; January 17, 1934.

ZANDER, ALVIN; LIPPITT, RONALD A.; and HENDRY, CHARLES E. "Reality Practice in Education." *Psychodrama Monograph* no. 9. New York: Beacon House, 1948.

# Programs for Adults

STERLING S. WINANS, *Coordinator*
*Director of Recreation, State of California*

## 17. THE ADULT'S WORLD TODAY

JAY B. NASH
*Professor of Education*
*New York University*

## 18. CONCEPTS AND ATTITUDES TO BE DEVELOPED

MILTON A. GABRIELSEN
*Associate Professor of Education*
*New York University*

WILLIAM F. MEREDITH
*Professor of Physical Education*
*University of Pennsylvania*

DOROTHY B. NYSWANDER
*Professor of Public Health Education*
*University of California*
*Berkeley, California*

## 19. METHODS

LAURIE E. CAMPBELL
*Associate Professor of Physical Education*
*University of Michigan*

WESLEY P. CUSHMAN
*Associate Professor of Physical Education*
*The Ohio State University*

WALTER ROY
*Director of Recreation*
*Chicago Park District*
*Chicago, Illinois*

## 20. EVALUATION

CHARLES F. WECKWERTH
*Director of Recreation and Camping*
*Springfield College*
*Springfield, Massachusetts*

LUCILE H. VERHULST
*Professor of Physical Education*
*Syracuse University*

*. . . The ordinary American is here—still rela-
tively free, still the final authority in public affairs,
still better fed, better clothed, and better housed
than the common man in any other country. If he
has been here since 1900, the mere fact that he has
survived means a great deal; for twice within that
period a coalition of empires has risen against him
to beat his political system down, once his economic system crashed about his ears, practically
every year some part of his social system has
given way and has had to be remodeled and rebuilt,
and for the past five years his form of government,
his economy, and his faith have been sternly and
relentlessly challenged by the most redoubtable
foreign power in existence. Yet he survives.*

*. . . This American may not be remarkable at all
for his beauty, or his wisdom, or his puissance;
but he is unquestionably remarkable for his dura-
bility. He is a standing encouragement to believe
that the worst has already happened, yet here we
are; and in the next half-century, that can certainly
not be fiercer, and may be far milder, it is impossible to fix a limit on what we may become.—*
GERALD W. JOHNSON, Incredible Tale

# CHAPTER SEVENTEEN

# The Adult's World

JAY B. NASH

FULNESS of life has been sought by mankind in all cultures and civilizations. Today it presents a problem and an opportunity. The extent to which it can be achieved for the average man will be the basis upon which this civilization will be judged by history. Some critics predict that our Western Civilization has reached its peak and is following Thebes, Athens and the Roman Empire down the western slope toward the end of another era. Other students of our time hold a more hopeful view that our Western Civilization is in a crisis and whether or not it perpetuates itself depends upon what individuals and nations do, the choices they make.

Life is a going-on process. It is active, achieving, accomplishing. Life activities never stop and the activities bring changes. The lesson to be learned in this for meeting the crisis in Western Civilization is that we cannot be content with fixed values or social forms already evolved. Certain it is that no group and no individual can permanently solve the problems of living. It is not possible to solve problems today and rest on the achievement. The problems of tomorrow will be different, requiring different solutions.

The unfinished business of life is life itself and constitutes its essence. When unfinished business ends, life ends. This is true both for societies and for individuals. In the Middle Ages people wanted values to be fixed. The totalitarian governments of the twentieth century demand fixed values and fixed social forms. Democracy has been opposed to this static conception of life. In theory it assumes a constantly shifting scene where adjustment, not conformity, is essential. In this shifting scene, in the past, democracy

[ 433 ]

has moved from taking all individuals into the social plan to taking them into the planning itself. Today, there is a threat that the democracies will not continue to move or will not move quickly enough in the adjustive process. Particularly in the United States there is a strong tendency to hold fast to that which has proven good in the past, to ways in which problems were resolved in the past. The solutions of yesterday will not be adequate to solve the problems of today. They can only be thought of as starting points for seeking new solutions.

For individual fulness in living there must be the same flexibility, the same reaching out, moving onward from the old to the new. There must be learning of new ways, expansions of horizons, as long as life endures. Psychologists assure us that learning is continuous with life itself, if the individual goes on exercising and developing his own powers. He can learn, he can change, he can solve new and different problems.

The French historian of art, Elie Faure, always referred to life as "A Dance over Fire and Water." The "fire and water" concept implies that there always will be risks in life. The individual attaining fulness, or the nation, for that matter, must have daring. There is drama in the uncertainty of the outcome. This drama is lived daily in our athletic games, our scientific research and in life itself. The child loves to flirt with danger. He piles one block on top of another and then another. An "it" is in all of his games from peek-a-boo to football. When the adult ceases to enjoy the contest—the dance over fire and water—he is hopelessly old. When civilizations cease to dare, to try new social forms, to seek new solutions to social problems, they too are hopelessly in decline.

It is apparent that education, whether it be called practical or cultural, whether it goes on in the home, in school or on the play-field, whether it be given from the standpoint of vocation or avocation, must be one intended for use in a going-on process. Education for a life that no longer exists will not help the civilization to perpetuate itself, because it will not help individuals to understand the times in which they live nor give them the tools for adjustment to new demands and new needs and the ability to solve new problems with daring and innovation.

It is late in the lifetime of the individual to educate him as an adult in problem-solving techniques and in understanding his world and the needs of himself and his fellow men. It is late for him to be acquiring the skills for working with others. It is not too late, however, and there is a chance through adult education programs to do a great deal in furthering the development of more democratic human beings.

## Some Characteristics of the Adult's World

It is essential for all those who are engaged with adult education programs to have insight into the conditions affecting adult life. A second essential is an understanding of the needs and requirements of adults in relation to these conditions and the process of changing them in the direction of fuller living for all.

### Life Expectancy Has Increased

Year by year the life span of people is increasing. The following table shows a larger and larger proportion of the population 45 and 65 years of age and over:

|  | 45 years and over | 65 years and over |
|---|---|---|
| 1860 | 13.1% | 2.7% |
| 1880 | 16.0% | 3.4% |
| 1900 | 17.8% | 4.1% |
| 1920 | 20.8% | 4.7% |
| 1940 | 26.5% | 6.8% |
| 1960* | 33.3% | 10.0% |
| 1980* | 40.3% | 14.4% [1] |

The important facts to be derived from these data are that the population is shifting toward the older group and by 1980 two-fifths of our people will be over 45, and one-seventh over 65. At the same time, the total number of people is also increasing. It has been conservatively estimated that the United States will have not less than 150 million people by 1980. By that time there will be

[1] United States Bureau of the Census. *Sixteenth Census of the United States*. Series P-S no. 3. Washington, D. C.: United States Government Printing Office, 1940.
* Based on probable increase in life expectancy. The preliminary report of the 1950 census indicates that these estimates and those which follow in the next paragraph are too low. The trend is more accelerated than had been anticipated.

not less than 60 million people 45 years of age and over and 21 million who will be 65 and over.

Fulness of life for these older people means more than comfortable animal existence. The lazy, purposeless life is a peril at any age. Life has a way of discarding or disposing of those who have no significant tasks to do. Financial security is no guarantee of fulness of life at any age. Retirement should be the time for men and women to pursue the elusive goals of unfinished tasks and un-explored but long beckoning paths. Our educational system must stand ready to help adults, not only as young men and women but all along the road to retirement and afterward. American society has been traditionally geared to the demands of youth, but already there has been some progress made in the field of adult education. Educators show considerable awareness of what the shift in age groups means and have made a start toward programs adequate to meet the needs of grown men and women.

## The Adult's World Has Enlarged

We often hear the phrase, "Television and the airplane have made the world smaller." In a certain geographical sense, yes, we can go from place to place more quickly but in a human relations sense, no, the world is larger. Not so very long ago, a trip to the county seat to market produce took 18 hours. On that trip one passed many farmhouses and met many people. They spoke the same language, they had common ideals and objectives expressed in common phrases. There was a certain unity. They helped each other at threshing time. They knew who were sick and joined with others to help in emergencies. They voted for people they knew. They worshiped in the same little church.

Today in 18 hours men can travel half way around the world. They may mingle with people who speak many languages and pro-claim loyalty to many gods. Thousands of years of background have set customs in the nations one can reach in 18 hours. Ninety per-cent of the people are hungry. Millions are insecure, and feel con-strained by forces they scarcely understand. Many are in slavery.

In this enlarged adult world "brotherhood of man" must become an ever greater reality or there will not be peace. "Love thy neighbor as thyself" is a concept deep in the gregarious concepts of men and has been stressed by most of the great religions. But in practice such brotherly love has been applied in a very restricted sense. It has not been applied to members of other racial, religious, nationalistic or political groups. One of the concepts of maturity in this larger world—one of the concepts of world citizenship—is the feeling for and the ability to practice brotherhood with people who speak other languages, have other social symbols and live under other conditions than our own. A test of maturity may well be, how big is your circle of brotherhood? Edwin Markham has dramatized this in his short poem:

> He drew a circle that shut me out—
> Heretic, rebel, a thing to flout.
> But Love and I had the wit to win:
> We drew a circle that took him in.[2]

Today's world is an interdependent one. To go on to the achievement of greater fulness of life we must work together for that end. Man is dependent upon the group and the group is all men.

## An Economy of Abundance

With the discovery of America and its early settlement it was assured that natural resources were unlimited to feed, house, clothe and contribute to the citizen's well being. One heard the phrase, "The great plains of America can feed the world." With confidence in this abundance Americans became careless. Other nations have shown lack of foresight. The story of unintelligent exploitation of natural resources is worldwide.

Now the adult world is brought face to face with the problem of meeting many of the basic, rock-bottom requirements of existence. The problem is gigantic and made more so as nations pour billions of dollars and use up more of their capital and resources in preparations for war. While the population of the earth has doubled, we have persistently destroyed the good earth's capacity to nourish us. Thus, we find great masses of people live one step from starvation.

[2] *Outwitted*, by Edwin Markham. Reprinted by permission of Virgil Markham.

The adult's world today contains many problems not faced by past generations. There is increasing need for the conservation of resources. There is need for new processes of production. Above all, there is need to solve the problems of distribution. We in the United States are among the most fortunate. We have learned how to produce enough for all our people with fewer and fewer man-hours of labor. We are learning that we can no longer waste and mine out our resources of timber, soil and metals. But we are still able to produce enough for ourselves and have some left over for others. And we must find ways through which the "one-third of the nation, ill-housed, ill-clothed and ill-fed," can be brought into sharing this abundance. We must find better ways of sharing with the rest of the world, both our know-how and our surpluses.

## Work in the Modern World

The adult's world of today is characterized by the minute compartments into which work has been divided. This has had two effects. Some individuals become specialists in a narrow field with limited opportunity to transfer. This gives rise to a definite pattern of insecurity. Primitive man, even the pioneer, could always turn to a simple vocation such as farming or hunting which would guarantee his family an adequate amount of food and protection. Today this is not possible. The adult world of work is rather terrifying. The great mass of people are employees dependent upon others, upon economic conditions for their jobs. It is no wonder young people often hesitate to assume the responsibility for the care and protection of children. One may be able to face hardships, even hunger, but no man can face the hunger of his own little children who depend upon him.

There is, also, as a result of this compartmentalizing of work, what may be called de-specialization, the breaking down of skilled jobs into many simple operations requiring little training to master. Much of this work is unsatisfactory to the worker. It is routinized, mechanical drudgery and leaves the worker uninspired, dulled, fatigued beyond the normal for the physiological energy expended. The fatigue is psychological. In this condition he is not receptive to active and creative forms of recreation.

The problem of unemployment in modern industrial societies—of millions, save in wartime—points up sharply how interdependent adults in today's world are. The unemployed live with fear and often with hate against those they look upon as competitors for jobs. It is a well-established fact that as unemployment increases minority groups in the population are pushed down the economic scale to the lowest paid jobs with the Negro at the bottom of the heap. Some, not all, of our practices of discrimination and prejudice against minority groups have their origins in economic conditions breeding fear and rivalry for jobs.

No democratic society can move toward fulness of life and tolerate large numbers of people whose work brings them no satisfaction of accomplishment and success and large numbers of unemployed over long periods of time. Idleness is corrosive in effect, demoralizing. In the French play, *The Harvest,* a lonely discouraged man, with no work, holds the sympathy of the audience. Like a crazed animal he beats himself to death against a cage of his own making. The moment he has work and companionship to appreciate it, he begins to grow in stature. He has a message. His body is erect. His eyes are bright. He belongs. He has significant work. The society must find more and better ways to provide significant work. Education's job in relation to this problem is to help children, youth and adults to understand the importance of work in their lives beyond earning a living and to help them prepare for vocations and professions according to their individual talents.

## Increased Leisure

It is only in this century that leisure time has become something more than the Sabbath day and a couple of hours on week days between work and sleep. There has come about a basic change in living patterns brought about by the shrinkage of the work day with the technological increase of production per man-hour and the shift from a rural to an urban society. Labor saving devices have had an influence also. The chores of children and young people have disappeared with the farmer's five a.m. to 10 p.m. schedule and the 12 to 14 hour factory, mine and mill day. Evidence of this change is seen in the emergence of the field of public recreation dedicated to helping people of all ages find fruitful and rewarding ways to use their increased leisure. Other evidence is provided by the many commercial amusement agencies and professional sports, both patronized by vast throngs of people—daily, weekly, yearly.

For fulness in living man must grow through doing, achieving, creating. He must be challenged, he must struggle, to gain the satisfactions of mastery. He must pursue success on higher and higher levels of accomplishment. These elements for growth are absent from much of his recreation today.

The tendency to "buy it," "to listen to it," "to watch it," is a sign of softness. To accept a challenge involves always the risk of failure. It is easier to drop back, to seek an escape—"do not try and you will not fail." Thousands of people in their search for status, for happiness, for a pattern of life which makes sense, for compensation through recreation, for too much tension and struggle in other areas of living, slip into the path of least resistance. The spectator takes no chances—he is always right. He needs no fortitude and develops no courage. The lures of the soft cushion or the concrete benches of the stadium become more and more attractive. Thousands of hours are spent each day sitting in motion picture houses. Trivial reading in the form of thrillers and true confessions become more and more available. Spectator sports, both amateur and professional, attract larger and larger crowds. It is apparent that both youth and adults in our society require a better education for leisure than they have thus far been provided if these vicarious, spectator forms of recreation are to shrink to a wholesome proportion in the total of recreational activities which must be, for fulness of living, predominantly doing, making, achieving.

## Devitalizing Tensions

The adult's world today is characterized by devitalizing types of tensions. Fear, insecurity and worry are man's greatest enemies from the standpoint of health. One of our medical men has indicated that all diseases in a sense are tension disorders. This is particularly so of heart disease, stomach and intestinal ulcers which are taking their toll and head the list of man's killers.

It may be argued that man has always had tensions—fear of

forest fire, enemy tribes, failure of crops and attack of wild animals. This is true but these fears were out in the open. The antagonist and the fear were recognized and man was adrenalized to meet the conditions. Modern fears are different. They are indefinite; they are goblins in the dark. The causes of these vague but pervasive feelings of fear are such that the individual can do little or nothing to change the situations and eliminate the tensions.

Man has been catapulted from an era in which life was simple into an era where life is overpoweringly complex. Economically, the individual is dependent upon others. In the main he no longer "makes" a living; he is employed and earns it. His livelihood and security are no longer largely under his control. Even children worry about this economic situation—"What will happen if dad loses his job?"

Another condition contributing to presentday fears and insecurities is the fact that we live and work to a great degree among strangers. Neighborliness, help in time of need, are not prevalent. People would help but they do not know the need. Among children and adults there is a widespread feeling of not being wanted, not being needed, not being a significant part of the life around them. Large numbers of families have no sustaining roots in community life. They move from job to job, always in temporary quarters, sharing little either in the rights or the responsibilities of citizens.

Still another contribution to these devitalizing tensions is our emphasis on achievement and success and competition. Mead points out that American children are early inoculated with the virus of competition. To win approval, to be loved, they must from the start learn to hold their own with other children. All too rarely is simple unconditional love granted them.[3] Psychoanalysts assert that the emphasis on competition over cooperation has made us a nation of neurotics. The number of the mentally ill grows larger yearly. One reason for this is the conflict and guilt in individuals, whose inclination is to treat their fellow men with kindness and consideration but who are forced into ruthless treatment of them by the culture's emphasis on competitive struggle for success.

The adult's world today is characterized by an attempt on the part of many to attain fulness of life through material things.

[3] Margaret Mead. *And Keep Your Powder Dry.* New York: William Morrow and Co., 1942.

Keeping up with the Joneses in the possession of more and better
bathtubs, automobiles, radios, gadgets of many kinds, provided
by technocracy, is a part of the success pattern. The trend toward
solving our problems through technocracy is an old one. Man has
dreamed of comfort and has assumed that by acquiring worldly
goods he could be forever happy.

Technocracy, when called upon as the maker of life, is the
insurer of death. Our mechanical system with its deadly and
deadening assembly belt is fast reducing work from a creative
integrating activity to a frustrating routine with neither beginning
nor end, wholeness nor adventure. We are witnessing a deadly effort
to escape its net by subscribing to shorter hours, higher pay, movies,
radio, television, printed thrillers and spectator sports. We are in
danger of being cut off from the forces of nature and of becoming
victims of a false philosophy of sheer individualism. This attempt
to escape is another factor in the immense increase of psychosis in
the modern world. This psychosis is rooted in a century of denial
of the forms which nourish the human soul. Those forces can be
identified as satisfying human relations through meaningful activities that build and nourish such relations.

Even with such a brief exposition as this of the problems of
living in today's world it is easy to understand the view of those
who declare our civilization is disintegrating. But we do not have
to accept this view. There is a saving factor. We know today far
more than any other civilization about the nature of man and his
needs and his relationships with the social and natural world.
If we wish to perpetuate our civilization we must put this knowledge
to work. We must place human life and living and human values
above all other considerations. Meeting the needs of human beings
in far greater measure is the only road toward fulness of life and the
preservation of our civilization.

## Adult Needs

Man is a biological organism and as such has needs in common
with all animals, for food, shelter, air. Like other animals he has
certain elemental drives for the preservation and reproduction of
life. But man is a special kind of organism with needs particularly

human. He has a highly developed brain and nervous system endowing him with the power to think, to create, and to evaluate what he thinks and creates. He forms judgments about his experiences, he constructs concepts to explain their meaning and he develops conscious purposes to meet his needs through these experiences as he understands them. He also develops something else—conscience or a moral sense, which tells him, if he will heed, when he is moving in the right or the wrong direction for his own well being and the good of his fellows. He moves toward maturity as he develops his strictly human powers to the full.

Maturity is a dynamic, never ending process. To go on maturing an individual has to maintain a forward look. It was stressed on the opening page of this chapter that no individual can permanently solve the problems of life nor can he attain or maintain normality by merely resting on past achievement. The human being is so constituted that satisfactions and development come through goal attaining rather than from the attainment itself. This point was fully presented by Hearn in Chapter 2 of this book. The growing individual always presses onward to other goals. A person says, "If I can achieve that goal, win that athletic letter, make that debating team, get that job, I will never want anything more in my life." Experience proves this to be specious. Once having achieved, the developing individual looks ahead to fresh worlds to conquer. Life's activities never stop for the maturing person. Life is a continuum of purposing, problem-solving, and replanning to meet the needs of self and others. This understanding is basic to a discussion of adult needs.

## The Adult Needs Health

The Constitution of the World Health Organization defines health as "a state of complete physical, mental and social well-being, not merely the absence of disease or infirmity." It continues that "the healthy development of the child is of basic importance and the ability to live harmoniously in a changing total environment is essential to such development."[4]

Body energy, neuromuscular skill and organic soundness are a

[4] Preamble to the Charter for the World Health Organization, 1946.

part of this conception of health. Emotional stability and good social adjustment are also contained within it. In fact, health has grown to be considered a total concept. Meeting the adult's needs to be a healthy person is tantamount to meeting all needs. This view of health had to come as more and more evidence has piled up confirming the psychosomatic unity of the organism. The relation between heart disease and worry and hurry have been made plain. Many other interactive psychophysical states have been determined. Emotional disturbances are just as certainly illnesses as are diabetes and pneumonia. So that when the statement is made that the adult needs health it is being said that the adult has needs that range from wholesome living and sane habits of eating and sleeping to satisfying relations with others and more success than failure in meeting the problems of living. The remainder of this discussion of adult needs may be looked at as analyzing the total need for health into some of its specific components.

## The Adult Needs Satisfying Relations With Others

Husband or wife, children, peer friends, neighbors, fellow workers are person-to-person relations through which an adult finds the satisfactions of being accepted and loved, of being valued for himself or herself. The fortunate individual moves in a warm intimate circle of such relations. With other adults the relations are those of equals. There is no psychological dependence of one upon another; there is no need to dominate or exploit others and use them for his own ends. There is helping and receiving help. There is mutual interest in common activities, mutual concern with common problems. There is loyalty, love and affection given and received. The mature adult not only welcomes the satisfactions and responsibilities of those intimate "linkages" with life; he understands, through experiencing them, the needs of other human beings for sustaining and supporting relations. Moreover, he is able to project the warmth and love received into an acceptance of all men as brothers having the same needs he has for satisfying relations. He is able to establish a balance in the "I-we" relation between himself and the social whole and groups within the whole.

Adjustment in the "I-we" relation is one of the most significant signs of maturity and the chaotic condition of the world indicates that few people have made the adjustment. If it were a simple choice between "I" and "we" or between absolute freedom and no freedom there would be no problem. But this represents the horns of a dilemma. Both choices are wrong. The right choice is somewhere between these two; but even the most mature man says, "Where is this point?" Bertrand Russell, writing on *Authority and the Individual* highlights the conflict in the modern world. Pushing too far on the authority side we have the centralized state, parentalism and possible loss of initiative and daring in the individual. Too much government or group control with guarantee of security may be crutches under the shoulders of men. And yet, the other extreme of letting the "I" go berserk is as bad. It means chaos whether it is called unlimited free competition, free enterprise or the jungle. The adjustment lies between these two extremes and America is trying to find it. As Russell indicates, equality is not enough. He says:

A society in which each is the slave of all is only a little better than one in which each is the slave of a despot. There is equality where all are slaves, as well as where all are free. This shows that equality, by itself, is not enough to make a good society.[5]

Russell hints, but does not go far enough, in calling attention to the fact that this middle course is well represented in the disciplines of science and in sports. In sports, for example, authority is vested not in a particular person or cross-section of society, but in the rules of games where everyone has a chance to have his voice heard. Deliberate violation of the rule is unsportsmanlike and lack of sportsmanship is an unpardonable offense. It should greatly hearten the people in health education, physical education and recreation to know that their teaching field represents one of the best opportunities to give people experience in choosing a middle course between two intolerable choices which have to do with world solidarity and permanent peace.

The individual must learn to adjust his interests and purposes to those of the group and today the group must be thought of as worldwide. He must do this to be accepted, to satisfy his own great need to belong, as well as out of regard for his fellows.

[5] Russell, Bertrand. *Authority and the Individual.* New York: Simon and Schuster, 1949, p. 49.

It is in the home that the child first feels this sense of belonging. It is in the home that the father and mother center their feelings of belonging. It is in the wider circle of friendships that the individual feels significance and security through belonging. It is in the still wider circles of community, national and world life that the mature adult feels a sense of belonging.

Primitive tribes went to great lengths to induct youth into the group. They recognized that this must be an emotionalized process, utilizing ceremony, song, magic spells, purification of "body and soul," and many other ways to tap the imagination. The stage settings were dramatic, with the dancing flames of immense camp-fires and all the mysticism and magic of darkness and shadows heightened by the rhythmic chants of hundreds of singers. Great flood tides of emotions were released. It was a time of decision, purging the individual of all selfish motives and, at the same time, a consecration of self to group ideals. These were *teachable moments* when life decisions were made, moments when halting, half-hearted good decisions became set in dramatic behavior patterns. Through contributions to tribal life, through work experiences, through dance and other religious ceremonies the adults of a tribe were tied together with strong bonds. Today to a large extent belonging is based upon achievement. The individual who does something significant, who is an outstanding craftsman or serves his group, belongs.

No man can grow to cultural stature without belonging; that is, without doing something significant for and in the group. Aristotle thought of the good man as the good workman, workmanship thought of in the craft sense as well as in the social sense. Man's feet are in the slough of despond, his head is bent low before the mirror of his companions until he has achieved—until men look up to him and say, "He has mastered." The area of achievement is so broad that every man, woman and child can acquire spiritual life from accomplishment.

This belonging concept has tremendous significance as it relates to many of the major problems of our day. It ought to be possible for an individual to accomplish regardless of race, religion or creed and gain a sense of belonging. If the boy in the home, school and community has a sense of belonging it is our greatest safeguard against delinquency and later against major crime. If a child handicapped by poliomyelitis or cerebral palsy or accident can achieve even in minor ways, a sense of normality is established. Belonging is a basic need of the child and the adolescent; it is no less a need of the adult. Man cannot live satisfactorily alone. He must draw spiritual strength from the group in which he lives and today the group-linkage must be worldwide.

## The Adult Needs Meaningful Activity

There is a drive in the organism toward activity. In the process of maturing this "set" toward activity becomes more and more related to the conscious purposes of the individual, to the extent that most adults will not for long engage in aimless activity. This is in contrast to the young child whose drive toward physical activity is largely organic in source. But it is not very long before what the child wants to do enters the picture and his activity becomes directed increasingly by awareness of purpose.

The purpose may be simply to have fun, but for meaningful activity purpose there must be. Emotions arising out of the way purposes are fulfilled give spark and power to human behavior for further endeavor, when needs are met in a degree satisfying to the individual. Emotions also block the efforts of individuals with feelings of persecution and frustration when there is too much failure in achieving their purposes, too little sense of belonging. In the past the tendency has been to play down, control and subjugate the emotions. Today it is recognized that the individual comes alive and alert under the emotional drives of desires and wants. The problem is seen as channeling these drives into ways that are socially acceptable and individually satisfying.

## The Adult Needs Exercise of All His Powers

The word exercise is here used in a very broad sense and refers not only to muscular movement but also to problem-solving, thinking, hating and loving. In this exercise, one of the basic biological laws of life comes into play—that which is used develops, that which is not used atrophies. This is the law of use and nonuse. The medical profession refers to the second as *the abuse of rest*. Rest beyond the amount needed for recovery is dangerous. The lazy life is a definite peril. George D. Stoddard points to three conditions which inhibit a continuous ability to think on more and more complex levels. He lists these as follows:

1. Bad health conditions (e.g., nutritional, endocrinal or infectious) which may retard children and bring adults to a full stop.

2. The mechanisms of escape, retrospection and rigidity which result in partial or complete regression to more primitive intellectual patterns.

3. A lack of mental exercise—a failure to undertake new abstract learning as appropriate to adults as schools and colleges are to the young.[6]

Prominent on this list of Stoddard's is the mechanism of escape. The individual escapes into areas in which he is already competent, avoiding new experiences because of fear of failure, fear of ridicule, fear of raised eyebrows and nudging elbows. The individual who keeps his hat in the ring, sets up new problems to be solved, continuously sharpens his skill and widens his circle of acquaintanceships and friends is setting the stage for moving always toward greater maturity. There is in this the implication for teachers and leaders of adults to provide friendly and challenging situations in which there is no need of the individual to accept fear of failure or ridicule, because he will see ways in which he can succeed and receive encouragement and help in the efforts he makes.

## The Adult Needs Meaningful Work

In the first section of this chapter work in our industrial culture for a great many people was seen as unintegrative, repetitious, routinized, monotonous, without understanding or visualization of the end product in many cases. This devolution from the sense of creating through the products produced by work and a pride in craftsmanship cannot be reversed, but it can be acknowledged and compensated for in several ways. The adult's needs for meaningful work can be met through social recognition of the contribution made by the work, through efforts to help him understand what he does as a part of a whole and through bringing him into the planning of his work. A number of recent studies made by indus-

[6] Stoddard, George A. "Patterns of Growth in Human Intelligence." *Proceedings of the National Academy of Sciences*, 27: 12; October 13, 1941.

trial firms on what makes the worker like to work have concluded that these are the ways to make otherwise dull jobs meaningful and purposeful to the worker.

## The Adult Needs Recreation

Frequently it is not possible for adults to do much about the jobs they do. Economic necessity constrains them to go on with dulling and uninteresting tasks. But they can do much to compensate for this through meaningful activity in their leisure time. Here again is an obvious implication for teachers and leaders of adults in our fields. Many of them do not have the resources for active, social and creative forms of recreation. Up until the last decade or two, opportunities for adult recreation were neglected. Today they are meager in many areas. It is difficult, late in an individual's lifetime, to develop understandings of recreation in the highest sense as in doing and achieving individually, as in making a chair or painting a picture. Similarly, the difficulty arises in social activities, such as putting on a play or learning to square dance. Results to date seem to indicate that the efforts to reeducate adults are worthwhile.

## The Adult Needs Skill

Recreationally, the adult tends to enjoy what he does well and to shy away from what he does not know how to do. In a study of some 2000 graduate students it was found that over 90 percent of their adult recreational habits were begun in childhood. In childhood they learned the skills needed for their recreational activities. A skill laid down in the nervous system is never lost. The individual who learns to walk on stilts, roller skate or work with tools will be able to pick up where he left off at any age, unless physical infirmity interferes. But adults can acquire new skills. Recreational programs for adults should provide them opportunities for these new learnings as well as the exercise of skills already perfected. Of course, what has been said about the adult's need for recreational skills and acquiring of new ones goes for vocational skills as well. However, this is an area with which workers in our fields have only limited direct concern.

## The Adult Needs Factual Knowledge

Another tool for meaningful activity on the part of adults is factual knowledge. The individual needs to recognize the use and limitations of this tool. Our understanding of facts changes with the advance of scientific research in every area of human life. Nowhere is this so apparent as in health and human relations. Day by day new advances in nutrition research and ways to combat disease make it mandatory to act in the light of these discoveries. Anthropology is giving us a broad basis of factual knowledge about the structure, capacities and capabilities of a wide range of people from various national and racial groups.

Facts become necessary if man is to live rationally and sensibly. Lester Ward, a pioneer sociologist, indicated the value of facts and at the same time their limitations from the standpoint of influencing behavior patterns. He likened facts to the rudder of a great ocean-going vessel, but added that unless the dynamic engines in the hold of the vessel were operating the rudder was useless. In life situations facts may be likened to the rudder and the emotions to the dynamic engines. We need both. One without the other leads to certain disaster. Edna St. Vincent Millay pointed this up so well in these lines from her poem, "Huntsman, What Quarry?"

> . . . Upon this gifted age, in its dark hour,
> Rains from the sky a meteoric shower
> Of facts . . . they lie unquestioned, uncombined.
> Wisdom enough to leech us of our ill
> Is daily spun, but there exists no loom
> To weave it into fabric. . . .

## The Adult Needs To See Part-Whole Relations

In the lines just quoted the poet infers that facts cannot organize themselves into a pattern of meaning. But there *is* a loom that can weave the fabric of life into a whole. This is the mind of man. In our time we have seen the mind of man well nigh overwhelmed by science and technology. New knowledge and new inventions have come so fast they have greatly outstripped our ability to understand their significance in terms of the ends for living. There is a need, as never before, for mature adults who can see part-whole relations and help the human race catch up with its own spinning of facts.

We have seen in this book how the child thinks in particulars, the adolescent in generalized particulars with himself as the focus and the mature person in generalized concepts or what we call abstract thinking. It is abstract because it is thinking about experience not reacting directly to it and it is not focused on self but on self-in-the-world. In this way the mature individual finds his own place in the scheme of things, assigns meanings to life; in other words, develops a philosophy providing him with ends for living and principles for action. He uses this philosophy as a framework to interpret further experience, changing his point of view as he continues to grow in insight and understanding.

One of the deterrents to real maturity is that individuals see only parts of life and not the relationship of parts within wholes. We expect a child to comprehend only the small circle of immediate contacts in which he lives. We expect his concerns to be with the immediate and the personal. The adult who retains the child's outlook and sees only his own small circle of life is not mature. These are the adults who will emphasize patriotism within national boundaries, when the relationship of the nation to the United Nations is the important thing. It is the part-whole relation the mature adult comprehends.

Overstreet in *The Mature Mind* discusses the relationship of parts to wholes under what he calls the concept of linkage.[7] The individual who sees wholes sees himself closely linked with his fellow men in his own community, with all peoples of the world who speak other languages and worship at other altars. He may see this linkage in terms of the spread of epidemics, world economy or the atom bomb, but the important thing is that he does see it and uses his insight to guide his own actions.

The implications, for adult education in this need to see part-whole relations, are two. One has to do with experiences that will serve to broaden mental horizons and increase the ability to general-

---

[7] Overstreet, Harry A. *The Mature Mind*. New York: W. W. Norton and Co., 1949.

ize in mature fashion. The other has to do with the experiences which will serve to develop skill in working with others. The individual alone, no matter how sincere, can do little. Many individuals, able to work effectively together, can do much. Man is gregarious and social. Fulness in living for the individual is inseparably tied up with fulness in living for his fellows.

The problems to be solved in today's interdependent world are problems in human relations. We Americans believe that by developing democratic human relations the solutions will be found. But this takes more than good intent; it takes skill in working with others, whether those others are members of a neighborhood council or tennis club or delegates to the United Nations Assembly. Democratic human relations are only understood as they are experienced in interaction with others. Skills in democratic action are learned, as are all skills, through practice. Learning situations for adults, no less than for youth, in the fields of health education, physical education and recreation, can and must be designed so that skills are acquired or improved with deepened understanding of democratic values, attitudes and behavior.

# Bibliography

ALEXANDER, FRANZ. *Our Age of Unreason*. Philadelphia, J. P. Lippincott Co., 1942.

ALLEN, FREDERICK LEWIS. *Since Yesterday*. New York: Harper and Brothers, 1940.

BEARD, CHARLES A., and BEARD, MARY. *America in Mid-Passage*. New York: Macmillan Co., 1939.

CARR-SAUNDERS, ALEXANDER M. *World Population; Past Growth and Present Trends*. Toronto: Oxford Press, 1936.

CHASE, JOHN W., editor. *Years of the Modern*. New York: Longmans, Green and Co., 1949.

CHERNE, LEO M. *The Rest of Your Life*. New York: Doubleday and Co., 1944.

CRAMPTON, C. WARD. "Live Long and Like It." *Public Affairs Pamphlets* No. 139. New York: Public Affairs Committee, 1948.

DEWEY, JOHN. *Freedom and Culture*. New York: G. P. Putnam's Sons, 1939.

GUMPERT, MARTIN. "Our Unknown Aged." *Nation* 171: 182-83; August 26, 1950.

HEARD, GERALD. *Man the Master*. New York: Harper and Brothers, 1941.

HORNEY, KAREN. *The Neurotic Personality of Our Time*. New York: W. W. Norton and Co., 1937.

HORNEY, KAREN. *Our Inner Conflicts*. W. W. Norton, 1945.

LILIENTHAL, DAVID E. "Youth in the Atomic Age." *National Education Association Journal.* 37: 370-71; September 1948.

LYND, ROBERT S. *Knowledge for What?* Princeton, N. J.: Princeton University Press, 1939.

MEAD, MARGARET. *And Keep Your Powder Dry.* New York: William Morrow and Co., 1942.

MUMFORD, LEWIS. *The Culture of Cities.* New York: Harcourt, Brace and Co., 1938.

NASH, JAY B. *Spectatoritis.* New York: A. S. Barnes and Co., 1934.

OVERSTREET, HARRY A. *The Mature Mind.* New York: W. W. Norton and Co., 1949.

PRESCOTT, DANIEL, editor. *Emotion and the Educative Process.* Washington, D. C.: American Council on Education, 1938.

RUSSELL, BERTRAND. *Authority and the Individual.* New York: Simon and Schuster, 1949.

SIZER, JAMES P. *The Commercialization of Leisure.* Boston: R. G. Badger, 1917.

STODDARD, GEORGE A. "Patterns of Growth in Human Intelligence." *Proceedings of the National Academy of Sciences.* 27: 12; October 13, 1941.

WRENN, G. GILBERT, and HARLEY, DUDLEY L. *Time on Their Hands.* Washington, D. C.: American Council on Education, 1941.

CHAPTER EIGHTEEN

# Concepts and Attitudes
# To Be Developed

MILTON A. GABRIELSEN
WILLIAM F. MEREDITH
DOROTHY B. NYSWANDER

IN THE previous chapter it was stated that the education of adults should be directed toward experiences that will serve to broaden mental horizons, give increased adequacy in work and play, increase the ability to generalize in mature fashion and develop skill in working with others. The next chapter is concerned with describing opportunities for adult education in the fields of health education, physical education and recreation and ways of working with men and women in programs designed to help them develop better understanding and greater skill in democratic relations. It is the function of this chapter to consider what concepts and attitudes are basic to developing democratic human relations at the adult level. As they are essential and basic, the concepts and attitudes become the desirable outcomes to be attained.

It is the intent to attempt to define and describe some of the more important concepts and attitudes. The purpose of this procedure is to clarify goals so that it may more easily be seen what the objectives in the area of human relations might be in programs for adults. It has been observed that teachers and leaders often do not utilize opportunities to help adults in this area, because they do not know how to go about setting particular objectives as they do specific objectives for the acquiring of motor skills or health information.

The concepts and attitudes basic to democratic relations at the adult level have already been discussed in previous chapters. They have been considered in programs for children, for adolescents and for older youth. This had to be done, for in considering growth in conceptual thinking and the behavior evidencing growth in democratic concepts and attitudes at each level, it was necessary to state what mature concepts and attitudes would be in order to point out the directions growth should take. It remains, however, the task of this chapter to consider these concepts and attitudes from the point of view of programs for adults.

Most adults are capable of some degree of abstract thinking. A statement such as belief in the worth and dignity of each individual is comprehensible to many. It would be understood by many more, if their educational experiences were directed toward developing the understanding. In health education, physical education and recreation we can do much more than we have done to help adults develop meanings regarding the democratic way of life, meanings that are not divorced from the situations we provide but arise out of them, and need only to be stated and considered with the larger implications for American citizenship and American life.

For this to happen the professional leader must himself understand the meanings and be able to draw them out of the particular experiences he designs with adults. Perhaps this chapter may add to the stock-in-trade of those leaders and teachers who have concern for doing a better job in the area of human relations at the adult level.

## Work and Play

The activities of adults in our society revolve around their work and play and the relationships with others involved in earning their living and spending their leisure hours in home and community life. To regulate these activities there is extension of relationships with others in functioning as citizens. A basic requirement for attaining satisfactions through work and play is skill. Skill is also a basic requirement in the area of human relations and for effective citizenship.

## The Meaning of Skill

The word skill as used here means the habit of doing a particular thing competently. The particular thing may be one of innumerable ways of using the body effectively; it may be related to the use of oral or written language; it may be pertinent to the pursuit of any art or craft; it may be a particular way of working with others, or fall into any one of many other categories. There are two understandings mature adults have regarding skill: skill is "know-how" and skill brings adequacy.

*Skill Is "Know-How."* Americans are world famous for their know-how in technical matters. It is characteristic of them, when a job is to be done, to study it, analyze it and devise ways to do it in the speediest, most efficient way possible. In other areas requiring skill or know-how, their attainment is at best mediocre. Many of them ineptly destroy good relations with others in groups without being aware that there are skills they might acquire which would greatly improve group operations. Many of them are recreational "morons" because of lack of skill. Some are far less healthy human beings than they need to be because of lack of skill in maintaining their fitness for living.

Educators must present a better case to adults regarding the possibilities and the necessity of acquiring needed know-how. While it cannot be denied that many skills are best acquired at earlier age levels, it must be recognized that these may be acquired at a later time, perhaps with greater difficulty, perhaps not. We have an obligation to set up situations which will provide instruction, facilities and time in every community, to the end that failures at an earlier level may be rectified at another. As a profession we face a grave responsibility for providing leadership and direction not only for children and youth now enrolled in schools, but also for adults who may be encouraged to return to the school and other educational agencies for further education. The leadership and direction should be motivated to help adults increase skill in the area of human relations as well as in the areas of health and recreation. This may be done as the instrumentality of programs to do the second is seen and utilized for developing democratic relations.

*Skill Means Adequacy.* The most essential know-how for adequacy in living a human being may have consists of problem-solving skills. John Dewey's explanations of the nature of thought and reason and many expositions on the scientific method have taught us that there are sequential, logical steps in problem-solving.[1] Through learning to use these steps skill may be acquired which the individual may employ to find solutions to his problems more satisfactory than he finds ordinarily by muddling his way through or letting things run their course, powerless to cope with his difficulties. The skilled person asks himself a series of questions:

What is the problem?
What do I know about it?
What else do I need to know about it?
Where can I get the information needed?
In the light of all information available, what are the alternative solutions?
Which solution seems best suited to my ends?
What plan do I need to make to reach this solution?
Did the plan work?

If the answer to the last question is yes, the problem is solved to the satisfaction of the individual. If the answer is no, the question becomes, which one of the other alternatives should I try?

Psychologists make it clear that because of the conflicts existing among the many needs human beings have, life is a continuum of problem situations. If we buy the suit we cannot use the money to buy those books we so greatly desire; we may even be unable to take that week-end trip we contemplated. Problems range from deciding whether to take a trip by plane, train, auto or boat to settling on a lifetime career or deciding upon ethical conduct in a crucial situation. The person equipped to think for himself, to think his way through logically, who knows how to go about getting facts or information when needed, demonstrates that skill means adequacy.

Social skills represent another type of know-how important to adequacy in living. Some of this type are allied to problem-solving skills. Social skills are thought of as including more than knowledge of suitable etiquette in different social situations. They include all the productive ways in which one individual may work

[1] Dewey, John. *How We Think.* Boston: D. C. Heath and Co., 1933.

and play with others. Skills such as those involved in leading group discussion, keeping discussion on the track, seeing the point of view of other persons and arriving at conclusions based upon the facts may be mentioned as examples. Ability to submerge oneself in the group, skill in recognizing the needs of the group and in making suggestions for contributions to group progress are other examples.

Knowing how another person feels, having some insight into what he is thinking and some idea of why he responds as he does, is a social skill bringing great adequacy in human relations. When this skill is fully developed it is known as empathy. Overstreet states empathy signifies:

. . . the imaginative projection of one's own consciousness into an object or person outside oneself. We sympathize with another being when we suffer *with* him; when we feel *with* him. But an empathic relationship is closer; we then enter imaginatively *into* his life and feel it as if it were our own. Though our bodily separateness remains, we effect a psychic identification. We stop being an outsider and become an insider.[2]

Overstreet continues as follows:

. . . Our everyday experience, in brief, testifies to the fact that empathy is one of our human potentials and that it can go far toward saving man from psychic isolation. Also, however, our everyday experience, and the desperate plight of our world, testify to the fact that the empathic potential remains chiefly a potential. Those whom it has genuinely released from immature egocentricity into mature socio-centricity are rare among us. The arrested development of the imagination is, perhaps, the most common tragedy of human existence.[3]

Other skills which are vital to adequacy are motor skills. These have been defined as "the harmonious adjustment of muscles to their action; it is teamwork among muscle groups."[4] Accepting this definition we see the contribution which skill in the use of the body may make to fulness of living on the part of any individual. "Butcher, baker or candlestick maker," the person with skill is equipped to enjoy life to a greater degree than the unskilled. Muscular strength, coordination and skill applied to the vocational field enable the individual to carry out his daily tasks without unnecessary

[2] Overstreet, Harry A. *The Mature Mind*. New York: W. W. Norton and Co., 1949, p. 65.
[3] *Ibid.*
[4] Mitchell, Elmer D., and Mason, Bernard S. *The Theory of Play*. Revised edition. New York: A. S. Barnes and Co., 1948, p. 237.

strains or drains, to function more efficiently and to leave the place of employment with a feeling of something accomplished, something done, without undue fatigue. He has energy left to be used in the enjoyment of wholesome leisure with his family and his friends.

In connection with the latter, skill plays an important role. The individual who has been properly educated has acquired skills through physical education and other activities which enable him to use his leisure to greater advantage. Re-creation comes only to the person who is able to enter into participation in an activity in such a way as to forget the problems of everyday life. A high degree of skill is invariably a factor in this process. Interest is based on satisfaction and satisfaction comes from the ability to perform well, whatever the field of endeavor.

Industry is recognizing increasingly the value of skill both from the standpoint of efficiency in production and the wise use of leisure time. The growth of industrial recreation has been an outcome of the realization on the part of management that skills and the opportunity for their use under wholesome conditions play a large part in the efficiency of the assembly line. Men and women who spend their leisure time in desirable recreational pursuits, who find no need or time for the roadside tavern or the neighborhood bar come to work in better condition for doing their work whatever it may be. There is less absenteeism, fewer accidents and production is maintained at a high level constantly.

It becomes increasingly apparent that there is a need for including desirable attitudes toward skill among the objectives of our educational programs for adults. They are important from the standpoint of continued participation as well as preparation for watching others perform. There is a place for watching others perform which often provides emotional release. We must be prepared for this phase to the end that we recognize and appreciate skilled performance in others, amateur or professional as the case may be, without losing sight of our own personal needs for activity, and the thrill of accomplishment.

The school must be regarded more and more as a place where adults may gain skills in better living. Health education, physical education and recreation, properly organized and conducted, have a great contribution to make not only as regards motor skills but also in relation to social skills and skills for problem-solving. Among desirable attitudes adults may be helped to acquire are: appreciation of skill as practical know-how for personal living; appreciation of skill as a means of contributing to group action; appreciation of skill as increasing group productivity; willingness to acquire skill when needed; appreciation of skill demonstrated by others.

## The Area of Work

In his discussion of the needs of man, Nash stressed the need to work not merely to make a living but also for creative expression and pride of accomplishment through craftsmanship. The primary need of man is to make a life worth living. This has been expressed down the years by the phrase "man does not live by bread alone." Mature adults understand work as a means of making a living, as a way of self-expression and as a contribution to society. Nash also made it plain that in many lines of work in our industrial society large numbers of people see little or no social significance in the jobs they do. Opportunities for self-expression in routinized tasks or for pride in craftsmanship, are minimized.

The fields of health education, physical education and recreation may contribute to developing mature concepts regarding work most directly in the education offered prospective teachers and leaders in these areas. These young adults are helped to get ready to earn a living. Ideals of professional service and understandings of the ways their work will contribute to their own growth and provide avenues for self-expression should be stressed and, happily, seem to be stressed in practically all programs for major students.

It is possible and there is a need for present and future professional leaders to expand these concepts and grant to the work other adults do, regardless of its nature so long as it has social value, recognition of it as a social contribution. Wherever it is possible help may be given adults to find fuller self-expression in the work they do. Too frequently the last is not possible, for the work is mechanical, repetitive action. The task then becomes helping them find channels for self-expression and additional social service in their leisure hours.

## The Area of Play

The adult's concept of recreation is conditioned to a large extent by his childhood and adolescent experiences in play and recreation. Man progresses in life through a definite growth cycle. The changes that occur during this cycle are not only physical but involve personality and behavior as well. Hence, maturity must be looked upon as a continuous process of building onto an ever-changing personality. Changes in personality are the result of experience. Attitudes toward recreation are developed largely through direct experiences. If the recreational experiences have been weak, misdirected, empty or second-hand, the attitude regarding the value of recreation will undoubtedly be distorted.

There is considerable evidence to indicate that man's attitude toward the potentialities inherent in recreation leave much to be desired. Choosing intelligently requires a conditioned intellect. A quick look at man's choices of leisure time activities reveals some astonishing facts which indicate that man is not choosing very wisely. Six billion dollars annually are bet on the horses. Ten billion dollars are gambled in other ways. Nine billion dollars are spent each year on alcoholic beverages. Eighty to ninety million people attend movies weekly. Countless numbers listen and view radio and television programs nightly. Millions avail themselves of the menu provided by spectator sports. All this indicates that the kinds of choices people make fall largely in the entertainment category.

It is apparent that all adults develop some concept of recreation, although it is questionable if many of them have been interpreting accurately its real potential for better living. It is essential for realizing this potential that the concepts regarding recreation include entertainment but contain much more. The concepts mature adults have developed would include such ideas as these: recreation at its best contains the element of play for play's sake, demands inner resources and requires outer resources in many instances.

**Recreation and Play.** The adult American still shows a residue of the Puritan's outlook on play as waste of time. He seems to find other reasons for his leisure activities than fun and pleasure that he gets out of engaging in them. Europeans with insight into this matter have often commented upon how hard Americans work at their recreation and how often the spirit of play is absent.

Adults engage in recreational activities to compensate for deprivations in other areas of living, to escape from the hum-drum routines of work, to enrich and broaden experience, to relax. These are wise motives and lead to meeting their needs. Recreation provides a fuller contribution to living, however, when these reasons for selecting activities are secondary to the pleasure and fun to be derived from the participation.

Adults need first of all to experience this enjoyment in their recreational activities; they also need compensatory activities, some that are creative and stimulating, some that are relaxing and release tensions, passive in nature. Any one adult will probably need all types in the course of his lifetime. Recreation literacy means ability to define needs in the area, select activities according to need and participate therewith.

*Recreation Demands Inner Resources.* Leisure should be looked upon as an opportunity for discovering one's self and developing latent talent, an opportunity for self-expression, an opportunity for release from tension and for satisfying many of the urges and drives inadequately met during the daily routine. Leisure can actually be the time in which "new people" can be made as personalities change.

Leisure is the sociological problem to which recreation is a partial answer. It was Parks Cadman who not so long ago said, "Tell me what you do in your leisure and I will tell you what you are." All people sooner or later will be confronted with the question of how constructive their leisure is. Nations in the past have fallen because of their inability to control or cope with the free time they have acquired. Idleness breeds discontent, crime and many other antisocial manifestations. Idleness is not leisure; it is a choice that man makes when confronted with leisure.

For too many years recreation has been interpreted to youth as something opposed to or different from education, with the first pertaining to physical activities of a joyful nature and the other concerned with intellectual and, to youth, comparatively dull activities. This is a false separation since both recreation and education have the aim of "fullness of life." It is a false impression for recreation is not limited to physical activities but includes the countless ways an individual may, with enjoyment, spend his leisure time. Educators have not sufficiently related their subjectmatter fields to the breadth of scope in recreation nor seen the inner resources for recreation they might help youth to develop. Science, literature, the arts and handicrafts have not been taught so that their potentialities for recreation were realized by youth. This failure has contributed to the lack of developed resources on the part of many adults for constructive use of their leisure. This lack presents a challenge for the recreational programs we design for adults. It is in the realm of social living and human relations that recreation finds its greatest potential. Everyone participates in recreation either as an individual or as a member of a small group or as a part of a large group. However, it is in small groups that adults most frequently seek to satisfy their recreational needs. With democratic leadership these groups have great potentiality for developing democratic relations with others. As the recreation leader looks at this potential of his field he might visualize recreation's contribution in this area in the following ways:

1. *Recreation can break down existing barriers:* At the square dance, the softball game, the swimming pool, on the golf course, and in other activities, it makes little difference whether the person is rich or poor, of different nationality or skin color. The ability to perform, achieve or produce determines the person's status in the group. The expression is often heard, "You know, he's really not such a bad fellow when you get to know him." Very often the getting to know him comes through joint participation in some recreational activity.

2. *Recreation affords an opportunity for recognition and appreciation:* As indicated above, the ability to perform at a high level of proficiency does more to tear down the barriers between people than almost any other single factor. The Negroes in America have gained more recognition and acceptance through sports, as exemplified by champions such as Joe Louis, Jesse Owens, Jackie Robinson, Buddy Young and many others. Bill Robinson, the famous tap dancer, was completely accepted, first, as a result of his achievement in dancing and, subsequently, as a man possessing fine personal qualities.

3. *Recreation participation involves adherence to certain rules and regulations:* The sport or activity that a person selects very often contains certain established rules that must be followed. If they are violated, penalties are incurred; thus, the basic elements of democratic living are practiced. When a group playing a game finds that the rules need modification they proceed to modify them in accordance with the consensus of the group. This emphasizes the group concept and places it above the individual's desire. It is significant to note in this connection that no team game which has received international recognition ever originated in a country possessing a complete totalitarian form of government.

In social or group recreational activities, the group prevails. The individual conforms to the desires of the group because he wants to be a part of it. In this way the individual learns cooperation which is the essence of democracy. Recreation teaches the person to be a good group member. As a matter of fact, being a good member is a prerequisite to being a good leader.

4. *Recreation provides a wide range of individual and group experience:* There are emotional outlets, physical benefits, social benefits and mental stimulation possible through recreation. It affords an opportunity for self-appraisal as well as a chance to observe and appraise the behavior of others. Whether it be in the shop, playground, gymnasium or camp, there are opportunities which, when wisely utilized, establish the basis for strengthening resources for democratic living.

5. *Recreation can establish direction:* People find themselves doing certain things as part of a group that they would seldom think of initiating themselves. Booing the umpire at a baseball game, standing up to cheer a performance, taking part in a group sing, playing softball at a picnic at the suggestion of the group are a few examples of how suggestion influences people to act. As Nash has suggested, we often need to be "kicked into action by a hostile environment." Once getting into the activity the experience can be so pleasing that the individual seeks to repeat the activity in the future; thus, direction is given to his recreation by the original suggestion of others.

The challenge faces the leaders of recreation programs. Too many are prone to follow a set procedure of operation which has been handed down to them. The individual should never be lost sight of in dealing with the group. One of the leader's main tasks is that of combating hostile and destructive attitudes in people and making a sincere effort to replace them with more desirable ones. These are "teachable moments" in recreation and they must be utilized by leaders to develop inner resources for democratic living.

*Recreation Requires Outer Resources.* It is the responsibility of adults in our society to authorize their governments at the various levels to organize and administer programs which will provide facilities and leadership as recreation resources for people of all ages. It is the privilege of adults in our society to make these provisions as private persons concerned with the recreational resources of some particular group in the population. Thus there are both public and private agencies furnishing the necessary leadership and facilities.

The concept that needs to be developed among adults in our population is that recreation resources are not provided for them by some abstraction called the city or state or the "Y." They are provided by adults themselves functioning as citizens, as church members, members of various organizations. This realization has come to many adults in neighborhood groups out of the neighborhood organization for civic defense during World War II. Such groups have gone on to work for better recreational resources in their immediate area. Often their efforts have resulted in community-wide concern for the resources being provided children, youth and adults.

A much better job can be done by professional leaders and teachers in our fields in programs for adults to help them conceive of providing recreational facilities and leadership as a responsibility of every citizen. They may be helped to understand better how community and neighborhood programs are organized and be assisted to evaluate the opportunities provided in their own situations. They may be helped to know what to do to take action when leadership and facilities are inadequately provided.

Having considered the concepts and attitudes health education, physical education and recreation may help adults to develop toward their work and play, concepts and attitudes that will lead to a fuller life for each individual, we turn now to considering relationships with others. There are concepts and attitudes to be considered in this area that direct behavior in work and play in home, school and community life.

## Relationships with Others

In this yearbook the point has been made on several occasions that satisfying relations with others in a democracy are based on respect for personality, all personality. The primary value in democracy is belief in the worth and dignity of the individual. It has previously been demonstrated also that man must respect himself before he can respect his fellows. He must understand and accept himself as a unique personality. Through this understanding and acceptance he learns to understand and accept other unique personalities who are like him in some ways and who differ from him in others.

It has also been shown that satisfying human relations are not built out of the exploitation of others, out of one individual using another to further his own ends. To come to his full stature of development and meet his needs for full living, each individual must have freedom to fulfil his own purposes within the context of social goals. Mature adults in our society understand: self-respect is basic to respecting others; individual differences enrich human life; mature relations are the relations of equals. These concepts underlie the democratic relations developed between men and women, between parents and children and among friends and neighbors. They are basic to democratic group process and the functioning of the mature adult as a group member.

## Men and Women—A Partnership

With respect for personality, with acceptance of differences without labels of inferiority or superiority and with understanding that the mature relations of adults are those of equals, the relationships of men and women are conceived of as a partnership in which together they build the common life of home and community.

In many countries of the world women are still held to be an inferior class. In the United States in spite of privileges they have still to attain full partnership with men. When that time comes the members of each sex will be permitted to do what each individual is best fitted to do, free of stereotyping of contributions as not manly, if a man cooks the dinner or sews a fine seam, or not womanly, if a woman prefers driving a truck to typewriting. Respect for personality demands accepting the person for what he or she can do best to contribute, without social expectations limiting what they may contribute.

The different biological contributions of men and women are another matter. They are facts, not to be denied—facts that a society moves counter to at its peril. But these facts are not to be confused with social assignments of masculine and feminine roles. The assignments differ in every culture, designing differently what a man may do and what a woman may do and keep social prestige. In a full and true partnership such expectations are minimized to the end that each may simply be himself or herself. The concept to be developed in this relationship is no different from that to be acquired for democratic relations with other groups who differ in color, class or nationality. Respect for personality applies to all these instances as does the concept of the relationships of mature people being those of equals. Assigning social superiority or inferiority on the basis of biological differences in sex, color of skin, kind of hair or any other physiological or anatomical manifestation has been found by science to be without justification. Within the limits of each one's biological inheritance, every person—man, woman, Negro, Hottentot, Chinese, Jew, Catholic, Lutheran and Holy Roller—is what he is by virtue of his interaction with his society. The design for democratic personalities must include the acceptance of this fact and democratic relations with others structured on the foundations so that the social environment, in turn, fosters democratic persons of both sexes, of any color, religion or nationality.

## Parent and Child—Growth Toward Partnership

In several previous chapters the concepts mature adults develop regarding the parent-child relationship have been implied. In Chapter 5 the importance for personality development of parental attitudes toward the child was discussed. In several other chapters the growth of the human being from a helpless, dependent infant to a mature self-maintaining adult was described. The concepts for adult education to be derived from these discussions seem to be: preparation is necessary for parenthood; the child is a separate entity, not an extension of the parent, and must be free to move through independence to the interdependant equal relations of maturity; attitudes are caught through the behavior of parents more than taught through their verbal admonitions.

The concepts and attitudes that need to be developed by parents are hard to acquire by those adults whose hostilities are such that their own lives are warped and the emotional disturbances are transmitted to their children. The vicious circle of the insecure parent producing the insecure child is difficult to break. It calls for many attacks. Education has narrowly conceived its task in this difficult and complex problem.

In health education, physical education and recreation there are opportunities that may be utilized to help parents become better prepared for their roles, to help them develop better relations with others, to help them to be free of tensions and anxieties in constructive recreation and to help them to understand that what they are speaks louder than what they say, even than what they do, in forming children's personalities.

## Friends and Neighbors

Human experience is shared experience. That life is rich which is sustained by the creation of a few deep friendships and many informal neighborly contacts. Belonging, feeling important to others, is thus satisfied. In programs for adults there are many opportunities to help adults to make friends and to increase neighborly contacts in informal groups—purposing to clean up the streets, make better gardens or improve play areas for children or themselves. Too much leadership in our fields has been directed toward administering programs for adults and too little directed toward helping adults do for themselves as friends and neighbors cooperatively working on common problems.

## Group Relations

It would be carrying coals to Newcastle to repeat here the many facts and concepts regarding democratic group relations already expounded in this yearbook. We may, however, look upon these relations from the viewpoint of adults who are full-fledged citizens and upon whom the responsibility lies for what our nation becomes. The concepts mature adults have developed regarding group relations, whether the group is a special interest neighborhood one or the peoples of the entire world, may be expressed as follows:

Interdependence is a social fact
Interdependence is a law of the organism
Democracy is consistent with the fact and law of interdependence and requires of the individual responsible, cooperative action with others to solve the problems common to all.

Barriers to developing these concepts are: ignorance, destructive emotional patterns, the autocratic pattern of our institutional lives in many homes, schools and communities. The breakdown of these barriers must come in all areas of living. The school must lead the way to the end that attitudes are developed showing willingness to cooperate with others, to contribute to group life, to share responsibility for group action, to consider the rights of the minority to be heard, to abide by the decisions of the majority, to challenge majority opinion while conceding it the right to direct action until such time as the opinion may be changed.

## Maturity

An attempt to say what concept mature adults have of maturity itself is in the nature of a summarization of the other concepts discussed in this chapter. To again quote Overstreet:

. . . A mature person is not one who has come to a certain level of achievement and stopped there. He is rather a *maturing* person—one whose *linkages* with *life* are constantly becoming stronger and richer because his attitudes are such as to encourage their growth rather than their stoppage. A mature person, for example, is not one who knows a large number of facts. Rather, he is one whose mental habits are such that he grows in knowledge and in the wise use of it. . . .[5]

Maturing, then, in the cultural sense at least, is a never ending process by which people adjust increasingly well to life's demands and life's situations. The helpless infant born into the world without choice must be taught the responsibilities of adult life. This implies a willing participation in the everyday "chores of life and a creative participation in the bettering of life."[6] The mature person accepts his human role. He is not dependent upon others but accepts the fact that the human experience is a shared experience; the human

[5] Overstreet, *op. cit.*, p. 43.
[6] *Ibid.*, p. 51.

predicament is a shared predicament. The world owes no man a living.

By the same token the mature person has no need to make others dependent upon him. He has no need to exploit others or to exercise power over them. He arrogates no specific and special rights to himself alone. The American way of life and the idea of world brotherhood, indicate the necessity for the realization of this ideal. Much of world conflict today is an outgrowth of failure to practice these principles. Nash suggests the answer here and points out the large contribution which may be made through the areas of physical education, health education and recreation in developing persons who have no need to exploit others.

Mature relations are the relations of equals; they are in a real sense democratic relations. So many groups react to one another as though observable physical differences were of import in the entirety of the socio-economic pattern. The mature individual recognizes his equals on the basis of what they can do and is not motivated by color or credo.

The aim of formal (organized) education in the United States today continues to be the development of social efficiency notwithstanding the differences in terms used by various writers. Social efficiency may be thought of as ability to "paddle one's own canoe" and at the same time to render aid to the less successful oarsman. This social efficiency may be fully realized in the willingness of each individual to be self-directing and self-responsible. The nation did not develop on a philosophy of "let George do it" but rather upon an acceptance by the majority of individual responsibilities as strong links in a strong chain. This responsibility continues to grow in importance as our national and international relations grow more complex. The mature mind recognizes the importance of granting to others the same powers of self-direction and responsibility. Growth of function comes with use. The greater the participation of thinking people, the greater the results in terms of social, political and economic development.

Furthermore, maturity will bring about a greater open-mindedness based upon a willingness to learn and to make changes consistent with this learning. This does not imply the "draughty" mind as visualized by the late Henry Suzzallo but a mind which adds constantly to its store of knowledge and makes responses to new situations which indicate progressive understanding of the world and its problems.

Finally, the mature adult sees himself as a part of the whole. He understands interdependence as a social and biological fact. He has acquired or is willing to acquire skill to the end that he may better solve his own problems and contribute to the solutions of problems he shares with others. He has skill in the areas of work and play which bring adequacy and enrichment to living. In short, he is a wonderful person, this mature adult. We have never met him, but we have met some few persons who have many of his qualities. There are many others with the potentiality for developing these qualities more fully, given opportunity to do so. It is with these opportunities we have concern in health education, physical education and recreation.

## Bibliography

BENEDICT, RUTH. *Patterns of Culture.* Boston: Houghton Mifflin Co., 1934.

BENNETT, MARGARET E., and HAND, HAROLD. *Designs for Personality.* New York: McGraw-Hill Book Co., 1938.

BETTELHEIM, BRUNO. *Love Is Not Enough—The Treatment of Emotionally Disturbed Children.* Glencoe, Ill.: Free Press, 1950.

BOWMAN, HENRY A. *Marriage for Moderns.* New York: McGraw-Hill Book Co., 1941.

BUCK, PEARL. *Of Men and Women.* New York: John Day Publishing Co., 1941.

CALIVER, AMBROSE. "Education of Teachers for Improving Majority-Minority Relationships." *United States Office of Education Bulletin 2.* Washington, D. C.: United States Government Printing Office, 1944.

CITIZENSHIP EDUCATION STUDY. *Five Qualities of the Good Citizen.* Detroit: Detroit Public Schools and Wayne University, 1948.

CITIZENSHIP EDUCATION STUDY. *Problem Solving.* Detroit: Detroit Public Schools and Wayne University, 1948.

COOK, LLOYD A. "Educating for Community Action and Unity." *Social Education.* 6: 304-308; November 1942.

DEWEY, JOHN. *How We Think.* Boston: D. C. Heath and Co., 1933.

ELLIOTT, HARRISON S. *The Process of Group Thinking.* New York: Association Press, 1926.

FOLSOM, JOSEPH K. *The Family and the Democratic Society.* New York: John Wiley and Sons, 1943.

GESELL, ARNOLD. *The First Five Years of Life.* New York: Harper and Brothers, 1940.

HARTFORD, ELLIS FORD. "Civic Leadership Through Clubs." *Social Education* 2: 91-93; February 1938.

HARTLEY, EUGENE S. *Problems in Prejudice.* New York: King's Crown Press, 1946.

KLUCKHOHN, CLYDE, and MURRAY, HENRY A. *Personality in Nature, Society and Culture.* Cambridge: Harvard University Press, 1948.

LIPPITT, RONALD A. "Better Human Relations." *School Executive* 67: 47-49; January 1948.

MC CLUNG, LEE ALFRED. "Race Riots Aren't Necessary." *Public Affairs Pamphlets* No. 107. New York: Public Affairs Committee, 1945.

MITCHELL, ELMER D., and MASON, BERNARD S. *The Theory of Play.* Revised edition. New York: A. S. Barnes and Co., 1948.

NASH, JAY B. *Physical Education: Interpretation and Objectives.* New York: A. S. Barnes and Co., 1948.

NASH, JAY B. *Teachable Moments.* New York: A. S. Barnes and Co., 1938.

OVERSTREET, HARRY A. *The Mature Mind.* New York: W. W. Norton and Co., 1949.

PRATT, GEORGE K. *Soldier to Civilian.* New York: McGraw-Hill Book Co., 1944.

PRESSEY, SIDNEY L., and ROBINSON, FRANCIS. *Psychology and the New Education.* New York: Harper and Brothers, 1944.

SLAVSON, SAMUEL R. *Creative Group Education.* New York: Association Press, 1937.

SLAVSON, SAMUEL R. *Recreation and the Total Personality.* New York: Association Press, 1948.

STRODE, JOSEPHINE, and STRODE, PAULINE R. *Social Skills in Case Work.* New York: Harper and Brothers, 1942.

TAYLOR, CATHERINE W. *Do Adolescents Need Parents?* New York: Appleton-Century-Crofts, Inc., 1937.

TEAD, ORDWAY. *The Case for Democracy and Its Meaning for Modern Life.* New York: Association Press, 1938.

WATSON, GOODWIN B. *Action for Unity.* New York: Harper and Brothers, 1947.

WILLIAMS, JESSE FEIRING. *Principles of Physical Education.* Fifth edition. Philadelphia: W. B. Saunders Co., 1948.

YAEGER, WILLIAM A. *Home, School, Community Relations.* Pittsburgh: University of Pittsburgh Press, 1939.

# CHAPTER NINETEEN

# *Methods*

LAURIE E. CAMPBELL
WESLEY P. CUSHMAN
WALTER ROY

IT IS late, but not too late, so the psychologists tell us, for most adults to develop understanding of democratic relations and to learn the skills for democratic action. Certainly the pressure for manpower during World War II, and the subsequent steps taken, proved that adults can learn new occupations and skills. The learning process for adults is no different than for children and youth. Adults learn what they purpose to learn. The difficulty is that by the time adulthood is reached the personality has been structured along definite lines. Adults tend to be less flexible than children and youth in changing their behavior patterns. They tend to respond to new influences in more firmly established patterns.

This is fine for developing democratic relations with others when the behavior patterns they have acquired in growing up are democratic ones. Their purposes to learn further will mean efforts to develop fuller and deeper understanding of themselves and others in a democratic setting. It bodes ill, however, for developing democratic relations with others when the behavior learned is made up of patterns of irresponsibility, dependence upon dogmatism for direction, authoritarianism, dependence upon others for decisions. It is not impossible, but not usual, for such persons to purpose sincerely to learn the ways of democracy. If they do, their interpretations of democracy are skewed to serve their outlook on life. Fortunately, large numbers of people in our society do not have extreme authoritarian personalities. Unfortunately, too, large numbers of people are not completely democratic. The bulk of adults in our society probably may be placed somewhere along a scale in between the two extremes. There is thus scope for education in this vital area.

It is doubly important that any educational program for adults be directed toward helping them grow in democratic understandings and skills. Not only is it important for the effects of their more democratic behavior in their relations with other adults; it is important because adults are the models and the mentors of children. This second point has been ably stated by Gesell:

Adolescents who will presently become voters and parents are of most immediate importance in education for democracy. But any long range view must take into account infants and children under 6 years of age. Throughout the preschool years there is an intimate interaction between the psychologies of the child and of the parent. Democracy is a way of life which demands tolerance and fair play. If we wish to lay the basis of such attitudes in young children we must begin with the education of the adults. The adults in their own behavior must furnish the models and the intimations of the democratic way. And the adults most responsible are, of course, parents and householders. For the 16,000,000 preschool children in America there is a corresponding number of fathers, mothers, grandparents, uncles and aunts. What all these adults and their communities do with and for this great army of children will have no small influence on the evaluation of our democracy.[1]

The crucial effects on the developing personalities of children of parent-child relations have been described in Chapter 5 of this book. That discussion, if applied here, illuminates the twofold significance of aiding adults in becoming more mature, more democratic persons.

## Opportunities for Adults

Many schools are now offering adult education programs. Public and private recreation agencies have expanded their child and youth-centered programs to include adults. Churches and industrial organizations are offering activities keyed to adult interest. More attention is now being given to the aged.

Cultural changes in the areas of work and play have brought about the increased concern for adults. Industrialization has meant

[1] Gesell, Arnold. *The First Five Years of Life.* New York: Harper and Brothers, 1940, p. 310.

additional education for the up-grading on the job or for new and different jobs. It has also meant increased leisure, more time to develop and follow hobbies, more time for education in the arts, for participation in dramatics, sports, handicrafts and a variety of other activities.

It is interesting to compare the patterns of fifty years ago with the trends of today. For example, the housewife in those early years spent her evenings performing household tasks such as sewing and ironing. Today her granddaughter leaves her dinner table to go over to the adult education center to study psychology or to the local recreation center to learn lapidary, or to the local high school for a swim in the pool.

Or consider the opportunities afforded the men of the family today in being able to take free instruction in golf from competent professionals. Consider his satisfaction gained from the camera club, garden club or the model building shop. Not only are there many opportunities for learning; social and psychological needs of the individual may be met. To this learning health education, physical education and recreation are making their contributions.

## Health Education

A major aim in health education for adults has been and is to bridge the gap between research and general understanding and use of the findings. The aim has been accomplished largely through the use of the standard media for public instruction, namely, newspapers, magazines, radio, motion pictures, posters and pamphlets. Information has thus been disseminated which health agencies believe the man on the street ought to have for his own welfare. There seems little doubt that the use of mass communication media has contributed to the improvement of individual, community and national health. Yet the gap between what is known by scientists and physicians and the information possessed by the people has not been closed. Perhaps it never can be as long as research continues. However, a marked expansion in the program to make research findings common knowledge is required. This way toward improving the health of the American people is a real contribution to democratic living even though, being a one-way communication, it does not aid directly in learning the ways of democracy.

Organized classes using group process methods are not common in health education for adults. Most classes at the adult level are informational in character, seldom are concerned with controversial issues, formation of policies or plans for action; but are devoted to providing specific knowledge of such things as first aid, infant care, nutrition, mental health, food handling. Concerned with this information, health educators have, by and large, continued in the paths of method trod by their academic friends who traditionally center their attention in subjectmatter rather than in the learner-in-the-learning situation. There is great scope for the adoption of group process methods in these health education classes. There is also great scope for the inclusion of controversial issues regarding health services, health care, community health problems.

There are indications that changes in methods are on the way. Professional workers in the field of health education are themselves learning the effectiveness of cooperative planning and acting to solve problems. Health committees and councils at local, state and national levels, conferences such as those held at Highland Park[2] and Jackson's Mill[3] and hundreds of workshops promoted by official and nonofficial agencies at the local level are bringing together medical, dental, school, public health and lay personnel to work on plans and policies for developing better community health programs. These experiences, as they are genuinely directed toward democratic planning and action, should help those sharing in them to see that the methods are most productive not only for the leadership in the field but for all adult groups concerned with any of the many aspects of health education.

## Physical Education

At the adult level, in general, the area of functioning which physical education and recreation have in common is stressed. Physical education teachers as well as recreation leaders organize adult

[2] Conference on the Cooperation of the Physician in the School Health and Physical Education Program, October 1947 and October 1949. Reports available through American Medical Association, 535 N. Dearborn St., Chicago, Ill.
[3] The National Conference on Undergraduate Professional Preparation in Health Education, Physical Education and Recreation. Conference Report available from the Athletic Institute, 209 S. State St., Chicago 4, Ill.

recreation groups. Physical education classes for adults most often have recreational aims, fulfilled either through participation in known activities or through learning new ones. Since this is so, the descriptions of these opportunities for adults are to be found under recreation.

Some advances have been made in offering other opportunities to adults through programs that have therapy and conditioning as aims. Schools and private agencies both have inaugurated such programs. Comparatively speaking, the number of adults who take advantage of these opportunities is not large. The question may be raised as to whether secondary school boys and girls, who eventually make up the bulk of the adult population, leave high school with clear understandings about their bodies as the instrument for living and the program they may make for themselves to maintain or improve their fitness for living.

## Recreation

Across the nation, in large cities, small villages and in rural communities, the number of agencies and institutions offering leisure time services for adults is greater today than it ever has been, and is constantly increasing. In large cities recreation departments are expanding their programs from the status of a children's playground program to include activities for persons of all ages. Municipal recreation departments now offer places for the men over sixty to play cards or checkers, and for women they offer sewing clubs, cooking classes and sports. Square dancing, folk dancing, social dancing, drama, music activities, handicrafts and hobbies are offered for people of all ages.

In the smaller cities such recreational activities are offered through the schools or through joint-operated agencies. In the rural areas the programs are keyed more to rural interest. For the most part the programs are promoted by the extension departments of the State Agricultural College and the Farm Bureau.

Private social welfare agencies also offer very extensive programs keyed to adult interest. The programs of these agencies vary more from agency to agency than do the public recreation programs. They offer citizenship classes, community education programs, health courses, public speaking, sports activities and many subjects of an academic nature.

Since the war there has been a great growth in the development of industrial recreation. In many instances a company's program will be closely integrated with the program of the community, in some places it IS the community recreation program. Many industries feel a great responsibility to provide their employees with livable communities and include recreation programs for the families as well as the workers. The movement in industry has its own association and journal. Many firms spend huge sums of money on these programs, have professional leadership and elaborate facilities. From the point of view of participation and volunteer leadership many industrial programs are ahead of other recreation institutions.

It is only in recent years that attention has been focused on the responsibility of government to provide recreation for adults. The early playground movement was in answer to child needs in the urban areas. Activities of a physical nature were stressed. The need for recreation in the lives of adults has gained rapid recognition in the past few decades due to urbanization and increased leisure time. Today it is accepted universally that it is a governmental function to meet the recreational needs of all citizens at local, state and federal levels. In the local community this recognition in terms of physical plant is evidenced in such facilities as municipal golf courses, swimming pools, tennis courts, skating areas, community houses, youth centers, picnic sites and many other developments.

Any description of recreational opportunities for adults today cannot omit the camping movement. Organized camps for children and youth—for girls, for boys, for mixed groups, for adults, for families are conducted by public and private agencies. There are municipal camps, school camps, state camps, those operated by youth serving organizations, those run by private persons for profit. Camp life may provide an ideal situation for education in democratic living. It has all the features to make it an excellent laboratory experience in how people may plan and work together cooperatively to develop the kind of community life they want. There are many camps operating on the thesis that this is the most important learning to be derived from camp life.

Whether the opportunities for recreation provided adults are offered by a church, a public agency, a private or industrial organization there are certain common features worth noting:

The programs must stand on their merit. The activity must offer a challenge; it must be educational; leadership must be good enough to attract participants voluntarily.

If the activity is to be successful, the facilities provided must be standard, and well maintained. Throughout all of these agencies, facilities, equipment and leadership are provided at a minimum cost.

The social aspect of the program must not be lost. People come together for social intercourse and to develop friendships. The program must include a "good time" and be of a socializing influence.

With these requirements, how are recreational programs organized? What must the worker do to plan, motivate and conduct recreational programs for adults? Naturally, any activity centers about the needs and the desires of the group or individuals to be served. In one community a garden club may be the immediate felt need upon which the whole broad program of adult activity may develop, while in another community a square dance, a singing club or choir, or even a critical social emergency may be the cause of the development of a leisure program.

For example, during the war, problems like emergency defenses, housing and bond drives brought people together who, though neighbors, did not know one another. Where such wartime activities were centered in a permanent community social center, many valuable by-products developed from wartime emergency activities. There should therefore be a cause, a need, a reason for people to be brought together. Such a center of interest can be developed through publicity, through door-to-door canvass or through one friend telling another of the program possibilities. In this manner, a nucleus can be established upon which to develop the program.

At this point the personality of the leader and the character of the institution starting the program are of the highest importance. Only by developing rather immediate satisfactions can the embryo group endure. Such satisfactions usually involve basic learning of the fundamental skills; a small degree of social satisfaction through the feeling of belonging to a compatible group, or a group that is "going places"; and a feeling of confidence in the leader and the institution or agency. Lacking these three elements, a new group surely faces a long uphill climb to a feeling of group security and satisfaction in the program.

*The Planned Program Approach.* These programs are planned, scheduled and conducted on a predetermined basis by the staff. The process operates in the following manner:

The staff inventories its facilities, examines its instructional abilities, reviews the needs and interests of the community and arranges a program to cover as many activities as their time periods will permit. Through community news organs, the radio, educational, religious and civic and social groups, they make known the activities to be presented. Starting dates are set and the activity begins. The activity may be a public speaking forum, an archery group, a group in woodworking, a camera club, a social recreation club, dramatic, outdoor sports club or other activities appealing to adults. Each activity group meets, and it is at this stage that the awareness of the professional worker to the possibilities of the group taking over planning its own program is important. His efforts may be in the following channels:

1. Through a planned approach, to make the group's first gathering an informative, interesting and satisfying experience.

2. To help the group to form a functional organization of its own.

3. Through committees and sub-committees to explore the different areas of interest in this particular activity.

4. To keep an open mind and be alert for changes in program or skills taught, with the group deciding the issues.

5. To give direction of the activity to the group as soon as possible.

6. To integrate the activities of the group with other activities in the agency, thus helping the group to become a part of the total agency program.

*The Less Formal, Unplanned Approach.* The handling of this group differs in the early stages in that the recreation worker uses the following methods to determine what the activity should be:

1. The recruitment of the group is slower. No previously announced program is used.

2. The worker discusses interests and needs by direct interview with individuals or in group discussion.

3. The group convenes and discusses common interests, making their decisions as to what they wish to do.

It is seen from this discussion of opportunities for adults to participate in health education, physical education and recreation programs that the needs and aims of adults in this participation are many and varied. They enrol in physical education and health education classes because they wish to acquire specific information or develop a special resource for leisure time; they join in many activities simply because they enjoy them or are interested in them; they participate in other activities because they provide opportunities for serving others or to make friends or for self-expression. It is doubtful whether it would occur to many adults to join a group or class for the purpose of understanding democratic relations better and gaining greater skills for democratic action. This last, however, must be an aim of the leader or teacher of the experiences which serve to fulfil the many desires of adults. With good guidance and appropriate methods the development of democratic relations can become, also, the conscious aim of the adults involved. It can become such an aim as a means for doing better the immediate project and it can take on larger meanings and "carry-over" values if attention is directed to the wider applications possible.

## Working with Adults

Adults, no less than children, have need for self-expression, recognition and acceptance as members of a group. Most physical recreation demands association with one or more persons which partially meets these basic requirements. If the experience is pleasurable, there is a tendency to be kindly disposed toward the members of the group. Interests shared among adults in a family group or adults in a neighborhood may lead from pleasurable experiences into more basic understanding, acceptance and goodwill. Such socialization is the basis of democratic living. The emergency of the war focused attention on the need for family and neighborhood organization for personal safety. Is the dynamic function of developing better human relations and good citizens for peace less vital?

We know that it is urgent for adults to learn and practice the skills of working together. The problems of the world today are basically problems in human relations. In this interdependent world we must learn to live and work together cooperatively or else—and the "or else" is not pleasant to contemplate. The quality of human relations rests squarely on the shoulders of adults as parents, as teachers and as leaders in all walks of life. Since life is a continuum, only concerted effort in the family, in the school and in the community will create an environment favorable for the development of individual characteristics and attitudes essential for democratic participation.

## Group Process

The science of group functioning is in its beginning. Most of the research in the fields of leadership and group dynamics is being carried on by psychologists and sociologists and the scientific literature is confined to the journals of these two fields. At present, the research is being directed largely toward the development of instruments to increase the efficiency of group work and techniques for evaluating the effects of various group methods. Health education, physical education and recreation leaders must keep in touch with the group work literature that will be increasingly forthcoming if they are to learn what techniques are most successful. Sources for much of this literature are centers such as the Personnel Research Board of the Ohio State University, now carrying on a 10-year study of leadership, and the Research Center for Group Dynamics, University of Michigan.

For group operations to be democratic there must be opportunities for the individuals who come together in order to share common learning experiences, to exchange points of view, define common goals and plan ways to attain them. Proper leadership, careful planning and effective techniques are necessary if the group is to mature.

It does not seem necessary in this late chapter to redescribe the steps in group process and techniques to use in carrying them out. The reader is referred to Chapter 2 in which Hearn describes the authoritarian, anarchistic and democratic-participatory patterns of group operation, also to Chapter 4 in which principles for leadership and guide lines for action are listed and discussed by Cassidy. Other chapters on methods in programs for children, for adolescents and older youth are sources to turn to for detailed discussion of the steps and techniques involved in group process. The discussions have full application to group process methods used on the adult level. There are, however, some techniques which may profitably be considered here from the point of view of adults with the presentation of some aspects of use not described elsewhere in this yearbook.

*Discussion Methods.* There are many kinds of adult discussion groups: informal, panel, speaker-discussion, forums and symposiums. Certain conditions seem to be necessary if a discussion group is to make a contribution to democracy in action. First, to have a discussion there must be a problem with which the group is concerned. It should not be a problem that can be answered merely by ascertaining a few facts. Topics dealing with policies, certain procedures and controversial issues are better. For example: "What are the common visual defects to be found in school children?" is a question that can be answered by science. "Shall our elementary teachers assume the responsibility of screening for vision?" not only demands knowledge of certain facts, but these facts must be considered in the light of certain conditions; different points of view must be aired and group agreement reached.

Second, for good discussion the topic must fit the group. It not only must be meaningful for the adults, it must be one about which the group as a whole has facts and opinions. If these conditions are not met, discussion turns to "chatter" and accomplishes little.

The third important condition is leadership. With groups possessing little or no skill, the effectiveness and value of good discussion depend upon the skill of the leader. He must understand that to promote discussion a well-lighted and ventilated room is essential and that participants should face one another. He must have the ability to keep the discussion progressing toward the goal, to explore all needs, to balance various views, to curb the too enthusiastic, to encourage the shy, and to act as a guide and not as a dictator.

Fourth, conclusions or plans for action should result. These may be no more than deciding that further discussion and study are necessary and appointing a "continuing" committee to make plans for further exploration. The participants, not the leader, must decide such things. A group that arrives at no expected outcomes leaves the participants with less not greater conviction regarding the value of discussion to solve common problems.

A formal group discussion is characterized by a set pattern of organization and usually by leadership that remains constant. Discussion is frequently limited to an interchange between the leader or leaders and members of the group. An informal group does not lack organization but its form is flexible, leadership is spread among the group members and face-to-face interchange of ideas among the members is possible and desirable rather than member-to-leader and vice versa.

In many adult activities, in both leisure and vocational pursuits, the commonest form of social and intellectual interchange of ideas is the small group discussion. The after-dinner family discussion, the classroom discussion, any situation where a small number of persons intensely explores a problem of common interest, can be considered a group discussion. Where such discussions are planned in advance, the problem in general is defined, a person is selected to lead the discussion and a summarizer or recorder is assigned to summarize the general attitude of the group on the question. These are valuable techniques for developing human understanding and greater insights, due to the intimate contacts of the members of the group. Face-to-face questions can be asked and opposing points of view can be approached directly. Of prime importance is a chairman or leader who can keep such discussion from developing into personal or subjective issues.

Methods have been developed to break up discussion groups into smaller units permitting more participation of each member in less time. The "buzz" group technique was explained in Chapter 15. For example, after a problem has been defined, small groups are formed for the purpose of suggesting ways or means which might lead to its solution. The leader often briefs these groups by giving them certain directives orally, or by distributing outlines to each group which directs the thinking on the essential factors relating to the problem. If, for instance, the problem under consideration was how a grant of money should be spent on community improvements, the leader might suggest what other communities had done under similar circumstances. If the money could not be used for certain purposes, such information would be given them. It might well be that several worthy projects already had been called to the leader's attention and he wished consideration of these with other suggestions members of the group might have. The function of briefing is not to curtail individual initiative and independent thought but to guide the thinking into productive channels.

Whenever a large group is broken into smaller groups to deliberate on a problem, it is customary to "feed back" to the total group. Directives as to their method of reporting back to the larger group are desirable. A spokesman is chosen from each group, as its representative, to give a summary of the discussion. In reaching a final solution to a problem or completing a problem, this process of utilizing small and large groups may be repeated many times.

While informal group discussions undoubtedly have greater value than the traditional formal discussion groups with which we are all familiar, there is no guarantee that the difficulties and obstacles present in the larger organization will be resolved or removed when numbers are reduced. The productivity of a group depends upon the ability of its members to work together cooperatively, and this is no small accomplishment. It is, in fact, so great an accomplishment that it has become one of the major areas of study for the social scientists.

Several formal patterns for carrying on discussions, particularly useful with large numbers of people, have been developed. The particular pattern selected for a specific occasion will depend on many factors. Of chief importance is the nature of the meeting, the audience which will attend, the advance planning possible, the nature of the subject(s) to be considered, the budget, the availability of participants and speakers. Some of these types of formal groupings are discussed in the following paragraphs.

1. *The Speaker-Discussion.* A very familiar pattern is the speaker-discussion which can be varied in the degree of formality to suit the number involved. It may be considered among the formal types of discussions, however, because it follows a set form. The speaker presents information on the problem in lecture form, after which the listeners engage in a question period. This type of discussion is common to the class room, church groups and conventions. It is frequently used on the radio. The disadvantage of this form of

group activity is that the speaker, in presenting his information, is limited by his personal experience and attitudes. Thus the impressions and attitudes formed may not be completely objective. Likewise, there is usually a gap between the speaker and the listeners, due to the feeling that the speaker *is* informed and the listeners are not.

This same type of discussion may ensue following a film presented in place of a speaker. The film-discussion avoids the personality problems presented in the audience's discretion toward the speaker. It nullifies the personal quotient involved in the speaker situation. However, in case of the elaboration of a minute point, the film may leave a gap, while the speaker may give some answer to almost any question.

2. *The Symposium.* The symposium answers some of the objections to the above speaker-discussion, inasmuch as three or more persons can speak on different interpretations of the problem. Thus a greater coverage of all aspects of the problem is possible. The audience may participate in a question period after the speakers have made their presentation. The symposium is used to a great extent on the radio, or at meetings where the subject is controversial and more than one point of view must be presented.

3. *The Panel.* If the problem before the group is complex with several points of view possible, the panel discussion is the pattern usually presented. In the panel discussion three or more persons with highly specialized information or knowledge on the problem are given an extended opportunity to speak from their own point of view or experience. The presentation of the members of the panel is usually conversational rather than a series of speeches. The leader attempts to give each member of the panel a fair opportunity to present his point of view, as well as to encourage questions between members after they present their statements. This type of discussion can be most constructive in creating attitudes and concepts necessary in our democracy through the behavior and conduct of those espousing various causes. If in the conduct of the panel they exemplify tolerance, understanding and objectivity, their adherents to the various points of view will also be inclined to view the problem in a more openminded way.

4. *The Forum.* The forum is similar to the speaker-discussion in that a speaker is presented, after which the audience may ask questions. The questions may be written or oral. Unless the audience is small, the audience participants are not usually encouraged to express their views. In this sense it is more formal than the speaker-discussion.

The forum may be supplemented with a film or a panel of experts or authorities. The town-meeting is a type of forum where two or more speakers present opposite views on a topic. The forum is used on the radio, and publicly, to present two or more sides of a controversy of interest to a large audience. The disadvantage of the forum or the town meeting is that it is frequently used to dramatize or propagandize issues before a large audience. Under such circumstances feelings rise to such a pitch that near rioting breaks out, and rather than developing understanding and insights it frequently fans hidden fires of dissension into real flames of hate and antagonism. The forum is too often used to arouse mass hysteria. Another disadvantage of the forum is that it lacks the intimate personal appeal of the panel.

## Use of Committees

Speaking generally, three types of committees may be identified with group process—the planning committee, the steering committee and the working committees. When an adult group forms to play volleyball, to study child development, to put on a play or for a variety of other purposes, the organization of committees is a function of the group. However, in the larger life of the community it often happens that action by the total group is not possible or not felt to be needed by the community. Individual adults or community agencies then take the initiative in organizing committees to consider problems about which community concern should be aroused. The descriptions of committee functions which follow have the second type of organization in mind, since committee structure within a functioning group has been discussed in a previous chapter.

*The Planning Committee.* The members of a planning committee may be representatives of an institution, educators, politicians or individuals in a community striving for civic betterment. Regardless of the motivation, the functions of the planning committee are usually similar in that they involve:

1. The definition of the problem or the need.
2. The definition of the source of participation or the groups to be served by the movement, whether it happens merely to serve a leisure time hobby or an important civic improvement.
3. The planning committee will usually develop a process or method for approaching the problem or filling the need.

4. The planning committee will usually develop a plan and strategy for action.

5. If the planning group is a part of a larger entity, such as a professional society, a social institution, an educational or business enterprise or the whole community, it may require approval of the larger entity before executing the action.

6. The planning body may be required to assemble resources, to develop a statement of the nature and importance of the plan in order to insure its success.

Through this process the leaders gain a greater understanding of each other and a clearer interpretation of their problems.

*The Steering Committee.* A planning committee may become a steering committee after the plan is approved. It is also possible for the planning committee to cease to exist after a plan is approved, and the steering committee comes into existence with authority to put the plan into motion. A steering committee is a group organized to pay close attention to the development of a plan after it is put into motion, and to make the project progress according to plan. The effective functioning of a steering committee depends upon the committee's understanding and insight into a plan. The steering committee must constantly observe all of the elements of the organization and be able to take remedial steps when any of the elements of the project are not proceeding according to plan.

*Working Committees.* The third stage in or development of the project involves performing the actual functions. Carrying out the plan is the responsibility of working committees under the direction of the steering, executive or planning committees. It is at this point that a statement should be made regarding the development of good lines of communications. The function of the steering committee should be to provide a channel of communication between the planners and the workers. Such a channel should provide for communication in both directions, in order that all elements of the plan can be carried out in terms of the general concept, and in order that the plan will be realistic, practical and economical in the light of the experience of the workers. Such supervision or relationship between planners, supervisors and workers should be a shared, constructive educational process, involving the creation of wholesome and enlightened concepts on all levels of functioning. In this manner the project can proceed to the greatest social or economic good. Within the hierarchy of committees, and within the committees themselves, when all are working toward the same objective and using democratic methods, the outcomes are greater understanding of individual differences, greater power through collective wisdom, and certainly greater progress through accomplishment.

## The Workshop

The workshop or work conference is a pattern of adult education that has become popular with educators as well as other professional groups. It is difficult to describe because no two workshops are ever alike nor should they be. Laura Zirbes in writing on the workshop idea says, "It gives people courage to invent and develop ways of getting teachers and others into purposeful, social learning experiences which they help to plan, improve and adapt. It gives them a sense of democratic self-help and of democratic group action while providing the content for professional advancement." [4]

The important elements of the workshop, elements which determine the very pattern of the workshop, are the participants and their problems. The workshop has the advantage over many educational methods in that the learners are in attendance because they recognize that they face certain problems in a particular area. They are purposeful, responsible people. Perhaps they do not see clearly all of the problems, but they recognize their general nature and realize that by getting together they are better able to define and solve them.

What might a workshop sponsored by a State University be like when it is run according to the principles previously discussed? First, it is the problems of the participants that determine for the most part the methods and staff of the workshop. The participants in a school health education workshop might be teachers, nurses, administrators, family physician and public health workers. If such is the case, representatives on the planning committee or workshop team should include representatives of these areas and if problems have not been solicited from actual participants, the workshop team can sketch out the most probable ones.

[4] Zirbes. Laura. "The Workshop Idea." *Childhood Education* 24: 402-403, May 1948.

Resource materials and resource people can be selected on the basis of the anticipated problems. Planning and arranging the physical setup ahead of time are important. Arrangements must be made for the use of the library, health service, training school and public health facilities. Housing the group to avoid isolation is desirable. Small meeting rooms, seating arrangements and blackboard space must be available. Facilities for leisurely eating and eating together are desirable.

Program over-planning must be avoided. A predetermined agenda allows for little democratic action and may interfere with effective learning. At least one session of the first day could be devoted to educating the participants in how group roles are played. A small group meeting could be staged to demonstrate the pattern of leadership-participation desired throughout the workshop. It could be planned so that the delegates could learn the part of the recorder, resource person, observer and other member roles. The remainder of the schedule for the first day or two should be flexible but should be aimed at having the group define and redefine its problems and the objectives of the working conferences.

After the purposes of the workshop are clearly defined the participants may be grouped. How they are grouped depends upon the needs and interests of the members. In a school health education workshop there might be one group of elementary teachers working together on a teaching program for their particular grades, another group might be made up of nurses and doctors working on problems in the health service area. There might be a group of special health teachers working on an industrial program in health and family living. In a short workshop of two or three weeks, probably more will be accomplished if the group with the same staff advisor stays together throughout the period, drawing on resource people as they are needed.

All the methods of adult education may be used successfully in the workshop if selected wisely. Individual study and library research are usually essential. Panel discussions on policies and procedures may be a must. Let us say the elementary teachers and secondary teachers in the workshop have come to the conclusion through reading and discussion in their informal groups that they have certain responsibilities in finding the child who needs medical care, but the question arises as to the extent of that responsibility in situations where the nursing service is limited. The workshop team in their daily meetings throughout the work conference note this common problem and may arrange a panel discussion on this controversial issue common to all participants. Again, the delegates may be brought together for general meetings so progress reports of each group may be given and suggestions and criticisms from delegates in other groups may be received. Films, lectures, demonstrations, laboratory experiments, all may appropriately be used within the workshop setup. The workshop process, according to Herrick, "accepts the point of view that, in a democracy, good learning is closely related to skills involved in problem identification and solution, in working and living with people, and with gaining an increased understanding of oneself and his world." [5] Space does not permit enumerating all of the many guides in how to run a work conference, but excellent suggestions are available in such pamphlets as "Two Lessons of Group Dynamics" and such studies as *Training in Community Relations*.[6]

## Leadership Required

It has been said that "Leadership is known by the personalities it enriches, not by those it dominates or captivates. . . . It is a process of helping others to discover themselves in achieving aims which have become intrinsic to them. The proof of leading is in the qualitative growth of the led as individuals and as group members." [7] Only in a democratic state would such a definition of leadership be accepted. It places high premium upon individual growth yet gives full recognition to the individual's responsibility for the general welfare. It implies also that there are two aspects to the leadership problem, namely, to help the individual toward worthy goals which he has discovered and wishes to achieve and to enable him to work cooperatively with others in reaching a mutually accepted goal.

All teachers expect that, because of their influence, changes in

[5] Herrick, Virgil E. "Workshop Patterns and Processes." *Childhood Education* 24: 426-29, May 1948.
[6] See Bibliography, p. 504.
[7] Tead, Ordway. *The Art of Leadership*. New York: Whittlesey House, 1935, p. 81.

students will be realized. Undoubtedly these changes do occur, though they may or may not be the ones anticipated. The definition of leadership given above, however, emphasizes a philosophy of growth which is based on self-discovery, self-determination and self-realization. It necessitates active participation on the part of the learner, be he adult or child. To achieve these ends, the leader's function is to so guide the individual that he will gain insight into his needs and problems and will be stimulated to formulate ways and means of meeting them.

Guidance of this type may be given to one individual or to a group of individuals. The approach may be direct as in an interview or conference with one person. Conversely, indirect guidance may be given to a classroom of children, to a staff of office workers or to adults in a recreation class. The assistance given by the leader should lead to self-appraisal, self-direction and self-management on the part of the individual or individuals concerned. This is true for all types of learning whether it be that of acquiring a physical skill or solving some vitally personal problem.

The second aspect of leadership is concerned with group achievement in reaching mutually accepted purposes and goals, with the resultant interaction of individuals in the group. The leader's role is to assist the group to so function that each individual has had a cooperative share in defining a problem, in analyzing its nature, in developing a plan of action, in executing the plan and in evaluating the outcomes. Techniques must be employed which will break down the formality of the initial gathering to bring about individual and small group contacts so that the people know each other. Tolerance toward others and an acceptance of each member of the group must be encouraged. All members of the group must be given a sense of "belonging" through shared planning. As the group becomes more cohesive the necessity for leadership from the officially appointed leader should become increasingly less essential. If these procedures have been democratically realized, individual as well as group growth may be expected.

Leaders must be well informed, intellectually honest, objective in their thinking, and have an abiding faith in people and a conviction that the collective wisdom and good judgment of the members of a group are almost always better than that of one person alone. All adults should come to feel responsibility as leaders. They must become sensitive to the group process and be willing to subordinate their individual desires and interests to the purpose of the group. As these understandings and skills are required, the officially designated leader withdraws from the active role of organizer, often assuming the role of resource person. However, no matter what role the trained leader is taking, he is always as much a member of the group as any other participant. When group process is really operating, all concerned, whatever happens to the individual roles, are completely within the group, sharing fully in all stages of group action and in the successes and failures which result.

It is a very well-known fact that adults in the main do not feel leadership responsibility, nor are they skilled in democratic group action. On the base of research, one commentator states:

"Against this background of desperate need for understanding and skill in group productivity is the really tragic picture of the almost universal inability of people to operate effectively in group situations. Anyone familiar with the average committee, with its difficulties in reaching decisions, its incomplete discussions and immature ideas, its personality clashes and emotional stress, and its inability to move from decision into action, should have no difficulty accepting this statement. This group inability has served to reinforce further the acceptance of the group leader as a group policeman ready to coax or bludgeon the irresponsible group member into productivity. The more the leader assumed police responsibility for group behavior, the more group members gained in irresponsibility for their behavior. Leadership thus emphasized the techniques of manipulation and control, and productivity was typically defined as the extent to which the leader could induce the group to accept his knowledge or decisions. The responsibility of the leader to help a group define its own problems, organize itself intelligently for production, and to train its own members to carry out group responsibilities has not frequently been considered. . . ." [8]

Those in a position to provide leadership to adult groups in health education, physical education and recreation should evaluate existing practices in their fields and their own practices in

[8] Bradford, Leland. "The Dynamics of Group Discussion." *Journal of Social Issues* 4: 2-7; Spring 1948.

particular, recasting their methods when necessary so that the experiences they offer adults will be in greater degree the much needed experiences for developing democratic human relations.

## Areas of Application

Methods in programs for adults may be said to have several applications. First of all they pertain to programs in which adults participate for recreation and self-improvement. Secondly, they pertain to parent education. Thirdly, they pertain to the efforts to improve community life. Consideration has been given to the first of these areas in describing the opportunities offered adults in health education, physical education and recreation. This section is concerned with parent education and community projects.

### Parent Education

Many authorities in adult education have voiced the opinion that democracy begins at home. Lyle has set up criteria for judging the extent to which democracy prevails in the home.[9] Adult health education, physical education and recreational programs have excellent opportunities to help parents understand how they may foster democratic behavior through learning experiences in family life. In organized classes, P.T.A. meetings, during teacher-parent conferences in the home and community, health education, physical education and recreational leaders should be continually impressing upon parents their responsibilities in home situations to teach democratic living.

The democratic home provides for a physical environment which promotes healthful living. If we are to develop unique personalities who function to their fullest capacities, we must provide a sanitary, pleasant and roomy home. In health education, we have often stressed the necessity of providing the sanitary and roomy environment in order to minimize the probability of disease and injury, but many of us have failed to impress upon parents the relationship of proper space, lighting, color and cleanliness to personality develop-

[9] Lyle, Mary S. *Adult Education for Democracy and Family Life.* Ames, Iowa: The Collegiate Press, 1944.

ment. Home visits provide the best opportunity for such teaching. At the time the health teacher, physical educator or recreational leader is in the home, practical counseling may be given as to how lighting might be improved or backyard play space better utilized.

The democratic home provides a pattern of family living that "furnishes stimulation to meeting new situations and problems with foresight and intelligence." [10] Certainly health education, physical education and recreational learning experiences offer problems for individual members that must be solved with consideration for future consequences to themselves and others. Immunizations at infancy and upon entering school, the young adolescent girl who faces the problem of wearing glasses, helping brother to adjust to a residual paralysis, financing the appendectomy and purchasing hospital insurance are situations the family must face that necessitate planning and foresight. The same can be said for such experiences as budgeting for a television set, bicycle or softball; planning the weekend picnic or joining an ice skate exchange pool.

Cooperative action is impossible unless we learn to respect the opinions and personalities of others. It is often easier for adults to settle disagreements by saying, "You can't do this because it isn't good for you," than by entering into discussions that allow different points of view or require lengthy explanations. Sam wants to go to school because today they have gym and music, his favorite activities. Sam has a cold. It takes time to explain to a seven-year-old that even though he feels well it is best to stay home, because if he goes he may pass his cold on to his friends and they will miss gym and music too. It is less time consuming to say, "Sam, you must stay home because it's good for you." Play provides marvelous opportunities for thinking for oneself. Mary, aged five, is making May baskets. Her mother has cut out the more difficult patterns and Mary is pasting them on the sides of the basket. "Mary," mother says, "the flowers are to be pasted standing up." "But I want to paste them this way," says Mary. "That isn't the way they will look best. Here, paste it this way," says mother as she pastes the flowers on. This mother is failing to let her daughter use ideas

[10] *Ibid.*

of her own. We must learn to respect the opinions and personalities of others. The home provides some of the best opportunities
for such experiences.

The democratic family shows concern for the welfare of others
in the community. Father, mother, brother and sister contribute to
the Community Chest drive; brother and sister help in the sale
of Christmas and Easter seals at school and mother is a Gray Lady.
Father is a member of the recreational committee now planning
for better facilities and an expanded physical activity program
for the summer. Brother was elected to the School Safety Patrol.
It can hardly be expected that a youth who has not been given an
opportunity to develop his individual capacities, to share his
experiences with others or to express his opinions and points of
view within the family group will become an active citizen in a
democratic society later in life.

From the developmental standpoint, it is vital that parents and
all adults who have contact with children and youth understand
the significance of play and physical activity in the formative years.
The natural demand to utilize energy through functioning is a
dominant characteristic of growing boys and girls. All those who
would guide youth in their various developmental stages may
utilize this drive and interest in promoting socially desirable characteristics and patterns of behavior. Most adults, however, need to
understand more completely the responsibility and opportunity
which is theirs. They need to assume a more active role in the
play life in the home and the community. They need to acquire
the techniques of leadership which will encourage growth rather
than dependence. They need to understand that their cooperation
and initiative are imperative if the goals of education are to be
achieved.

Through the medium of active physical games and sports, better
human relations can be achieved in the home. There are many
activities in which the whole family may participate. Here is
a common meeting ground and one which can promote family
solidarity and understanding. The parent who can be a partner
or opponent in a game, a companion in such informal activities
as hiking, exploring, fishing, sailing, coasting, skating and skiing,

is in a position to know the needs of the child and to guide his development more intelligently. Inasmuch as all learning is inter-related there is opportunity here to provide interest in the world of nature or outdoor life that may lead to a lifetime of enriched living. By establishing such contacts through areas which are of paramount interest to the child, there is the possibility of maintaining satisfactory relations in other areas of living.

The physical education and recreation leader can help to bring about such participation by promoting the kinds of activities in which families can participate. Attention should be focused on the opportunities for continuing these activities in the home and neighborhood. Demonstrations of backyard or neighborhood play areas might be set up. With the enlistment of the manual training department, help might be given parents on the construction of play equipment for these areas. Provision should be made for instruction in activities such as skating, skiing or swimming if facilities are available. All organizations promoting youth and adult programs should plan cooperatively to the end that the needs and interests of both are served.

The responsibility for interpreting the program and initiating action in this area of adult recreation rests squarely on the shoulders of the leaders in both physical education and recreation. If the conviction is strong that the enlistment of the services of parents and adults is essential, we may be entering a new era which will be characterized by better home and community life.

## Community Activities

Through sharing in community activities, tolerance and better understanding of individuals from different social, economic and racial groups may be realized.

In one large urban industrial center, square dancing has been offered in the summer parks and playgrounds over a period of years. The demand for continuing this activity in the winter months came from the participants on the many playgrounds. Neighborhood schools are used in many parts of the city where these groups, often totaling more than a hundred couples of all ages, dance weekly. Twice during each year an all-city square dance is held in a large industrial building. As many as eleven hundred people, including children in their teens, parents, grandparents, laborers, department foremen, managers of plants, people of all nationalities, races and creeds, dance the evening through. Many of the participants call the dances or contribute their musical talents to make the evening a success. The gallery holds many citizens from all walks of life. Frequent intermissions permit socialization, often in the groups demanded in the previous dance. When the musicians put away their instruments, the number of dancers leaving for their respective homes brings the peak traffic load for the evening.

Undoubtedly, the smaller weekly group meetings offer more to the participants in terms of personal relations than the all-city event. However, the interest, enthusiasm, skill and enjoyment in the execution of the dances of this large group of people recommends it as a community enterprise.

Certainly there are many American communities in which the citizens share in recreational activities. Frequently, all the resources in leadership and facilities of public and private agencies are called upon as a program expands. Coordination and cooperation in planning are required. Just as frequently, community projects requiring cooperative planning are concerned with more than participation in some particular activity. The following description is an example of such a project:

Some years ago, in a relatively small city (population approximately 40,000) it was recognized that keen rivalry existed between many of the social agencies because of competitive program offerings to the youth in the city. These programs were not all successful nor were they meeting the needs and interests of the city's youth. A Recreation Division was created by the Council of Social Agencies in an attempt to bring representatives of all the youth-serving agencies together to study the recreational needs of the boys and girls in the community, and to cooperatively plan activities which would meet these needs.

The early meetings of the Recreation Division reflected vested interests in types of programs, and a disinclination on the part of some committee members to see the problem as a whole. To secure the data essential to convince the group of its responsibility to the community at large a recreation survey was made by a committee appointed by the Mayor. The survey results, presented by persons outside the Division, showed startling inadequacies in cooperative effort and served to unite the group in working toward a common goal—that of serving all youth in the community.

Today this Recreation Division calendars all youth programs, so that conflicts are at a minimum. The program offerings have been broadened to include many activities. When vital issues are discussed, such as the creation of a Youth Center, representatives of the group concerned are invited to the meetings. Recently the Chief of Police was brought in to discuss his recommendation for a police officer to handle juvenile cases.

Though this Division still has problems, it has been instrumental in focusing on community needs, in securing cooperative action in the solution of many problems and in demonstrating that group discussion and action is the intelligent approach in community planning. Reflected also by the members of this Division is a concern for group welfare which was not demonstrated in the early years.

Recreation is not the only area in which community projects demand cooperative planning. In the main, the effectiveness of the health education program of a community depends on the interests and efforts of the community at large and not on the program of any one group. In this country the political-social-economic conditions have fostered the growth of many agencies interested in some aspect of health. These agencies have grown up more or less independently of one another, so there is overlapping of purposes and functions, duplication of efforts, and certain jealousies and misunderstandings. As the agencies have grown bigger and bigger, they have bumped into one another more frequently. Sometimes they have clashed, but more often they have chosen to work together cooperatively. One means of promoting a better working relation has been the community health council.

It is difficult to describe accurately what a health council is or how it functions. The Council on Medical Service and the Committee on Rural Health define it as a "community-wide committee which brings into one agency all local elements able and willing to contribute to better health planning." [11] The Council is an advisory and coordinating body and not an administrative one. Its aim is "to mobilize all the health resources of a community in a manner which will meet best the health needs of that community." [12]

Studies would seem to indicate that the general procedures of a

[11] American Medical Association. *The Community Health Council.* Chicago: American Medical Association, 1949, p. 5.
[12] *Ibid.,* p. 6.

community health council are to study the health needs, to learn of the immediately available resources, to suggest the best possible plan for the mobilization of these resources and to educate the public to the plan and inform it of any inadequacies as to resources and how additional ones may be obtained.

Studies would also indicate that it is not important who takes the initiative in forming the council. It is important that the council have community-wide representation, that the representatives subordinate individual and organizational desires and interests to the purpose of joint planning, that the health council grow out of a felt need within the community. If these principles are met, the health council can do much to help the community health education programs overcome duplication of effort, over-emphasis on special interests, inertia and indifference, misunderstanding, planless growth.

Of the coordination of agencies interested in health education programs, the American Association of School Administrators states:

Coordination means cooperation, working together with clear lines of delineation and articulation; it does not mean merging, subordination of the rightful interests of individuals and groups, or authoritarian dictatorship from any one agency. It means agreement upon the objectives desired and the acceptance of appropriate activities and responsibilities by each agency, based upon a clear understanding of what is to be done and upon a sane and sympathetic appreciation of the capacities of each group.[13]

The health council or committee, whether organized on the school, local community or state level, can help to promote such cooperation.

The health teacher or administrator in schools is not in a position where he can create overnight a community health council even though he may realize its need. The place for school personnel to begin is within the school itself. The school health program, including as it does health services and healthful environment as well as health teaching, must rely on the cooperation of health specialists and agencies in the community not under the jurisdiction of a board of education. Family physicians, dentists, public health nurses, health officers, welfare and voluntary health workers and their organizations have a rightful interest in the health of the school age child. Cooperation of these people and their organizations with

[13] American Association of School Administrators. *Health in Schools.* Twentieth Yearbook. Washington, D. C.: the Association, a department of the National Education Association, 1942, p. 297.

the school is essential for an effective school health program. Representatives of these organizations should be brought in on the planning of a school program at its beginning.

Every school should establish its own School Health Council or Health Committee. Organized on democratic and representative principles, under the authority of the principal school administrator, the School Health Council provides a simple, orderly and convenient administrative mechanism for determining and implementing wise school health policies in the light of local and immediate needs. Experience in many schools where such councils are now quietly and successfully functioning has already demonstrated their usefulness to the school administrator as well as their value to the children and the community. In the School Health Council should be vested the responsibility for planning the total health program of the school.[14]

The various community projects described have great social significance. As more and more laymen become involved, there are definite movements toward more articulate participation on the part of adults in community affairs. These programs and others of like nature are the concern of professional workers in health education, physical education and recreation both as professional people and as citizens. Leaders in the three fields must stand ready to serve in these movements anywhere along the line, to initiate projects when they see the need, to aid when projects are initiated by citizens who will benefit by the help of skilled, informed leaders. This chapter may be ended on a significant point for adult education in democratic living by describing the development of one such project in which democratic group planning and action were featured:

In the beginning two or three neighbors joined together to solve their garden problems. Other neighbors became interested. The community center offered a place to meet and a leader who called upon the resources of the community. The recreation agency publicized the new activity. A neighborhood Garden Club was created. From gardening interests the Club broadened its interests to cover a wider range of civic problems. The neighborhood club became a community club. It became active in promoting better streets, better subdivisions, better city planning, and ultimately, from such a small beginning, became a force to aid in insuring better living in that community.

[14] National Committee on School Health Policies. *Suggested School Health Policies.* 1946, p. 8.

## Bibliography

AMERICAN ASSOCIATION OF SCHOOL ADMINISTRATORS. *Health in Schools.* Twentieth Yearbook. Washington, D. C.: the Association, a department of the National Education Association, 1942.

ARMSTRONG, HUBERT C. "Teacher-Parent Conference." *California Journal of Elementary Education.* 11: 31-45; August 1942.

AUER, J. JEFFREY, and EWBANK, HENRY. *Handbook for Discussion Leaders.* New York: Harper and Brothers, 1947.

BURKLE, LOUISE E. "Planning Recreation Activities for Women." *Industrial Bulletin Service.* New York: National Recreation Association. (Reprint of speech at Industrial Recreation Conference, January 27-28, 1946.)

COMMITTEE REPORT OF THE AMERICAN PUBLIC HEALTH ASSOCIATION. *Community Organization for Health Education.* New York: American Public Health Association, 1941.

THE COUNCIL ON MEDICAL SERVICE AND THE COMMITTEE ON RURAL HEALTH. *The Community Health Council.* Chicago: American Medical Association, 1949.

ELLIOTT, EUGENE B. *Understanding Through Discussion.* Lansing, Mich.: Superintendent of Public Instruction, Bulletin No. 339, 1945.

FANSLER, THOMAS. *Discussion Methods for Adult Groups.* New York: American Education Association for Adults. n.d.

FANSLER, THOMAS. *Teaching Adults by Discussion.* New York: Service Bureau for Adult Education, New York University, 1938.

GESELL, ARNOLD. *The First Five Years of Life.* New York: Harper and Brothers, 1940.

GROOM, WILLIAM S. "The Health Council." *Journal of Health and Physical Education.* 17: 332; June, 1946.

HEMPHILL, JOHN K. *Situational Factors in Leadership.* Columbus: Bureau of Educational Research, The Ohio State University, Monograph 32, 1949.

HERRICK, VIRGIL E. "Workshop Patterns and Processes." *Childhood Education.* 24: 426-29; May 1948.

HOWARD, PALMER, and LIPPITT, RONALD A. "Training Community Leadership Toward More Effective Group Living." *Adult Education Bulletin.* 10: 168-74; August 1946.

INSTITUTE FOR ADULT EDUCATION. *Handbook of Adult Education in the United States.* Part 4, Section 2, "Media and Methods for Instruction," 1941, p. 253-80.

JONES, EDWINA, and STEVENS, GLADYS "Workshop Practices in Elementary Physical Education." *Journal of the American Association of Health, Physical Education and Recreation.* 20: 366-76; June 1949.

KELIHER, ALICE. "The Commission on Human Relations." *Progressive Education* 17: 497-504; November 1940.

KLEIN, PAUL E., and MOFFITT, RUTH E. *Counseling Techniques in Adult Education.* New York: McGraw-Hill Book Co., 1949.

LINDSTROM, DAVID E. *Democracy in Action.* Springfield: Illinois State Library, 1943.

LIPPITT, RONALD A. *Training in Community Relations Toward New Group Skills.* New York: Harper and Brothers, 1949.

LYLE, MARY S. *Adult Education for Democracy and Family Life.* Ames, Iowa:
The Collegiate Press, 1944.

PITCAIRN-CRABBE FOUNDATION LECTURE SERIES. *Modern Education and Human
Values.* Pittsburgh: University of Pittsburgh Press, 1947.

SLAVSON, SAMUEL R. *Recreation and the Total Personality.* New York: Association Press, 1946.

SMITH, BRADFORD. "In the Town Meeting Tradition." *Adult Education Journal*
8: 18-20; January 1949.

STOGDILL, RALPH M. "Personal Factors Associated with Leadership." *Journal
of Psychology.* 25: 35-71; June 1948.

TEAD, ORDWAY. *The Art of Leadership.* New York: Whittlesey House, 1935.

THE RESEARCH CENTER FOR GROUP DYNAMICS and THE TAVISTOCK INSTITUTE OF
HUMAN RELATIONS. *Human Relations,* Vol. I. London, England, W.1 (2 Beau-
mont Street): Tavistock Publications, Ltd., 1947. (Available in the United
States from The Research Center for Group Dynamics, University of
Michigan, Ann Arbor, Michigan.)

TRAGER, HELEN, and BROWN, SPENCER. *Making Democracy Work in Your Community.* New York: Bureau of International Education for Anti-Defamation
League of B'nai B'rith. n.d.

"Two Lessons of Group Dynamics." *Educators Washington Dispatch.* Washington, D. C., 1948.

TUCKER, EDYTHE. "A Functioning School Health Council." *Journal of Health
and Physical Education* 19: 321; May 1948.

ZIRBES, LAURA. "The Workshop Idea." *Childhood Education* 24: 402-403; May
1948.

# CHAPTER TWENTY

# *Evaluation*

LUCILLE H. VERHULST
CHARLES F. WECKWERTH

O NE wintry day about ten years ago while enroute between Providence, Rhode Island, and Springfield, Massachusetts, the bus stopped at a passenger pick-up station—an old inn. After leaving the bus to stretch our legs and experience a refreshing breath of biting cold New England air, we went inside the inn and there upon the wall over the fireplace was inscribed one of life's lessons hard to learn, "As we go through life, let us live by the way." Here at an unsuspected time and place was an old truth. Each of us attempts to illustrate by our choices of behavior how we individually "live by the way."

To live by the way undoubtedly symbolizes many things to many people. The word live implies more than mere existence. It suggests creative experience, ecstatic satisfactions, enjoyment through participation in some selected activity of human value. Such living may be experienced alone or with others. It is always enhanced when shared with others.

To evaluate means to estimate the worth of something or to appraise the results of something. Evaluation is thus a form of living by the way. When we evaluate, we pause in our doing and thinking to take stock. To evaluate in the area of human relations means even more to live by the way. It means taking time to become sensitive to the needs and problems of others as these are being expressed in our contacts with them. It means self-examination of our own responses to people as these occur and afterward. It is the purpose of this chapter to consider how these judgments may be improved either for the individual adult in self-appraisal, for a group as it participates in a given program or for the teacher and leader as he undertakes to find out the outcomes from a planned experience.

Previous chapters in this section of the yearbook have been concerned with understanding the adult's world of today, the beliefs and attitudes to be developed and the methods by which our programs might achieve these results. Evaluation is necessary to determine whether or not progress is being made or the desired outcomes are being attained. As such it is part and parcel of experience as well as a kind of end-product type of activity by which appraisal is made. It may be useful for several purposes. It is the means by which hypotheses upon which the program is developed may be validated. It provides information for understanding the individual participant in the program and for the individual to understand himself better. It is thus basic to effective guidance. It might be used to give a sense of security and satisfaction to all those responsible for the program and it provides a sound basis for public relations. Whether evaluation is undertaken by the individual or the group, or whether evaluation is made by an outsider to the group, the process suggests certain definite procedures.

## The Process of Evaluation

### Stating Objectives

The setting up of objectives to be attained in the program is the first step in the process of evaluation. Each individual participant and the leader with the responsibility for the group experiences will have purposes in relation to the experiences. These purposes must be clarified and merged in the setting up of common goals. The goals will be modified as the program gets under way and the needs of the group are better understood by the leader and the participants themselves.

Goals are frequently broad or general statements in order that they be inclusive enough to incorporate the different purposes of those concerned. This means that before evaluation can be undertaken the goals must be analyzed into specific objectives or the kinds of outcomes to be expected from the experiences. These outcomes are always in terms of changes in human behavior. Of course, behavior is thought of as including everything the person thinks, does or feels. In this sense passing or not passing a test is behavior just as much as giving a helping hand to a fellow participant.

Listing outcomes is not the simple task it may appear to be. The outcomes of any experience shared with others are so varied and interrelated that it is difficult to select any particular ones for evaluation. But the selections must be made and will be made in the light of the stated goals. Outcomes may be classified into such areas as facts or meanings, skills or abilities, needs or interests, feelings or emotions, thinking or problem-solving, attitudes or values, personal-social adjustments, and the integrative relations or a philosophy of life. Understanding the kinds of outcomes encompassed in a goal, it is possible to see objectives in terms of human behavior. An example will help to clarify this point.

In a graduate seminar the goals offered by the instructor and accepted by the group are:

1. To learn research techniques required for making a graduate study.
2. To receive help from the instructor and group in stating, defining, outlining and writing individual studies.

In the beginning the group is probably unable to break these goals down into many specific objectives which may serve as outcomes to be evaluated. A start is made, however, when the kinds of research techniques needed by each group member are explored and the ways in which each needs help are considered. The specifics listed will be directly related to the group's needs. There might be a need to explore the different types of research as a beginning step and knowledge of these types would become a first specific outcome to be desired under the first goal. Each individual would have opportunity to include under the second goal the specific outcomes which he hoped to attain.

In the course of making these analyses of outcomes desired, planning and carrying out plans to achieve them, questions about how the group is operating are bound to arise. If group process is the method used throughout, specific ways the group needs to improve operations will be included in the desirable outcomes to be evaluated.

Again these will be specific to the needs of the group. They may pertain to group discussions, the way assignments are carried out, the use of the instructor as a resource person, the objectivity of criticism of group members' work on individual studies.

## Selecting Experiences

The next step in the process of evaluation is the identification of situations in which individuals might be expected to display the types of behavior indicative that the objectives are being obtained. This step will not be difficult if the previous step has been thoroughly done. Suppose a recreation group is putting on a play and it is recognized that efficient committee work will greatly facilitate progress in the undertaking. With good guidance one of the objectives of this group might well be finding out how to be more effective chairmen or members of a working committee. Desirable outcomes will be listed as the responsibilities and skills required to be effective as a chairman or committee member. Then, as the program is planned and committees are set up to accomplish the main purpose which brought the group together, the situations in which the desirable outcomes might be shown are easily identified. The example should make it plain, however, that the leader who really expects to help adults develop the concepts and attitudes discussed in Chapter 18 must guide those adults to see their needs in relation to this development as these are manifested in the activity that is being carried on. To do this the leader must have insight into the maturational level of each individual and the drives within the individual that are responsible for his behavior in the group. Each individual must be helped to become conscious of his behavior and the reasons for his responses in the group. In this way new understandings of democratic behavior may be gained as well as a clarification of the forces instrumental in modifying the individual's behavior in the direction of the outcomes set up as desirable.

## Deciding Upon Ways To Evaluate

The next step is the selection or development of the instruments or methods to be used in evaluating. Care must be taken in this step to see that the means selected will serve to help the adults and the leader find out what they want to know. Many procedures and instruments have been devised which are listed in a later section of the chapter. New ones are constantly appearing with the rising concern for the area of human relations which teachers and leaders in health education, physical education and recreation will do well to investigate for potential use. Although a developed instrument may not be satisfactory to evaluate in the specific situation, it may lend itself to adaption in the situation or suggest ways to devise an instrument that will provide the desired information. There will be as many procedures and instruments selected as are needed to find out whether the outcomes listed are being attained.

## Interpretation of Findings

The final step in evaluation is the interpretation of results from the use of evaluative procedures and tools. Scores, descriptions, judgments, are valuable only as they are related by the leader and the participants to the objectives to be attained. Evaluation should show in terms of understandings, motivation and satisfaction in what ways the objectives are being attained. Evaluation thus serves as a basis for replanning to achieve the objectives better or to modify them in the light of what has so far been attained. Evaluation is thus a continuous process, an integral part of every aspect of a unified, planned program. It begins when a group decides what it wants to do and ends only when a given project has been completed or a stated problem has been solved. It should and can be a conscious process on the part of every person involved if the leader and the participants together set up the objectives, plan the program and carry it out in a democratic, cooperative pattern.

## Tools and Techniques

The selection or the development of an evaluating device demands further discussion in relation to the particular ways and means we can assess progress in the attainment of the concepts, beliefs and practices suggested in Chapters 18 and 19. The highly controlled test situation will not be very helpful. In dealing with human relations problems in a group, validity will be destroyed by the isolation of too specific reactions. The partly controlled or slightly controlled type of evaluative procedure must suffice. Furthermore, in working with adult groups, evaluation as a part of the on-going process is more in demand than end-product evaluation and the evaluating devices that take a minimum of time will prove most useful.

For use, then, in appraising democratic relations in health education, physical education or recreation experiences for adults selections might be made from the following tools as they are appropriate in a given situation:

A. Response in writing to written or oral questions
   1. Standardized tests
      a. Knowledge, intelligence, achievement
      b. Abilities and aptitudes
      c. Character and personality
      d. Interest and attitudes
      e. Special areas
   2. Rating charts
      a. By self
      b. By others
   3. Check lists and inventories
   4. Questionnaires
B. Observation and review
   1. Rating scales, charts and check lists
   2. Anecdotal records
   3. Longitudinal case studies
   4. Cross-sectional field studies
   5. Guess-who sketches
   6. Sociometric tests
C. Interview and conference
   1. Directed self-appraisal
   2. Directed group appraisal
   3. Historical study—biographical
   4. Attitudes, interests, beliefs
D. Projective techniques
   1. Rorschach method
   2. Thematic apperception test
   3. Role playing or sociodrama

The scores from standardized tests will be helpful in understanding the individual and in appraising change. So many of these tests are available that information regarding the test is necessary for interpretation. The *Mental Measurements Yearbook* edited by Oscar Buros is a ready source book for information regarding various tests as well as a critical review of the test and its uses.[1] If one is working with adults in the college situation, some data regarding test scores will be available at the counseling center which might prove valuable to the leader in understanding the reticence or particular behavior patterns of members in the group. Since many veterans have submitted to batteries of tests at a counseling center a good many adults in the community situation may have valuable data to be released to a group leader with the permission of the veteran.

Even though the standardized tests as such are not useful, a careful study of these evaluative devices will assist in the formation of rating charts, checklists, inventories and questionnaires developed for specific use in the group. This is particularly true of standardized tests of character, personality, interests and attitudes. While the validity may be challenged of such tests as the Allport-Vernon Study of Values, the California Test of Personality, the Guilford-Martin Temperament Profile Chart and the Minnesota Multiphasic Personality Inventory, a careful study of these devices may help to avoid common errors in developing specific rating charts, checklists, inventories and questionnaires.[2] Self-ratings are found to be one of the best ways of evaluating the interests and attitudes of adults and are an important tool to assess progress in developing democratic relations. Self-ratings are often considered invalid because of the difficulty that persons have in accurately assessing their feelings. They may purposely falsify their report in order to make the results more in line with reactions that are socially acceptable. The self-rating checked against similar ratings made by others, however, may be a means of helping the individual face up to realities.

In all appraisal tools involving written questions, ambiguities in definitions must be reckoned with in interpretation. The desire to make ratings, checklists and questionnaires objective, valid and reliable through statistical treatment is one of the dangers that

---

[1] Buros, Oscar, editor. *Educational, Psychological and Personality Tests.* Third Mental Measurements Yearbook. New Brunswick: Rutgers University Press, 1949.
[2] *Ibid.*

should be faced. These tools lose validity in sweeping general interpretations.

The rating chart, the checklist and the rating scale may be the record of observation and conference as well as the record of response to a written question. Observation is a technique used constantly by the leader and the members in a group although it may not be recorded. Observation involves judgments which should be weighed in the light of the value pattern of the judge.

Such judgments recorded over a period of time as brief descriptive phrases of behavior increase the objectivity of the technique. These anecdotal records are valuable in over-all evaluation of progress not only for the individual but for the group planning, thinking and behavior. The complete accumulative record important to the longitudinal case study is more valuable through the developmental years than in the adult situation except as the case study might reveal such problems as prevent an individual from adequately identifying with the group in planning and action. The cross-sectional field study, showing the behavior of an individual in other roles as well as the one of the particular group under consideration, will point to the needs of the individual and may also, in analysis, suggest tensions in the group which prompt behavioral tendencies that are good or bad.

The sociometric test, explained in Chapter 16, has real value for detecting the locus of influence in the group, the ramifications of such influence and a detection of barriers which may well exist in the group preventing real growth in democratic spirit, planning and action.

Any observation of behavior must be carefully planned to reduce the subjectivity of the reactions of the observer and to clearly understand the manifestations of the skills, attitude or concept to be evaluated. Unless a simplified checklist or rating chart is provided the record is apt to be too time consuming to be carefully made and subjectivity replaces objectivity. The data from observation require knowledge, understanding and sensitivity in interpretation.

The interview or group conference as an evaluation medium is useful in the adult situation. It is not a technique easily administered or interpreted by the novice. Individuals may be interviewed at some length only to find that we have a heterogeneous mass of data which tells no coherent story. The interview or conference must be planned and directed toward some goal if an intelligent interpretation is to be made. A record system must be devised that makes later study possible. It is a most valuable device when used by an individual with interview or conference techniques to understand the individual and to appraise change in individual attitudes and beliefs or to appraise group attitudes and progress. It is difficult to use it as a quantitative measure and its value lies in redirecting emphasis which may have been lost in the on-goingness of an experience.

The projective techniques belong in the hands of competently trained psychometricians. While they may be invaluable in understanding an individual or helping the individual to understand himself, their administration and interpretation belong to the specialist. Role playing or the sociodrama, however, may be an excellent medium through which an adult group may become more acutely conscious of the problem it is attacking or the problems which deter its progress. Enacting roles may focus attention on tensions which are not otherwise recognized and give clues needed to resolve them.

On the whole, the readiness of an adult group to use techniques for evaluating in the area of human relations should guide selection. Little is accomplished by recommending procedures which do not seem to the adults concerned to have an integral relation to what they want to do. An adult education class or recreation group in which reading followed by discussion is the usual pattern of work will more quickly see pertinency of instruments to evaluate the discussions than a group whose main goal is to play volleyball or put on a play. However, in any type of group, if group process is the method used, opportunities arise for guiding adults toward concern with *how* they are accomplishing what they set out to do. It is through this concern and the subsequent analyses of group operations that adults may be helped to develop more democratic relations in experiences provided by health education, physical education and recreation.

## Group Evaluation

When a group of adults come together as members of a community tennis club, an adult recreation badminton class, a YWCA square dance group or a workshop, each individual in the group responds through his social behavior to every other member in the group according to his appraisal of these others. Through seeing, the personal appearance of members in the group is apprehended according to the value pattern of the observer. The same is true as he hears the words spoken by another or watches his action patterns. The judgments made design the relations among group members. The entire past experiences of each individual, by which each one's value pattern developed, are a force in the relations developed. However, new experiences are potent to change these value systems. It is change in the direction of democratic relations with which we are concerned.

We know today through experimental research that the attitudes and values of individuals in a group which are basic to their judgments and actions in relation to other members will be modified in expression according to the social climate in which the group is functioning and that this climate is dependent upon the attitudes and methods of the leader. Lieberman reminds us that:

We can, of course, nullify our opportunities if our work is conducted along authoritarian lines and if responsibilities are carried by executive or sponsoring committees so that the individual member's function is limited to attendance, the payment of dues, and an occasional vote. If we wish to perpetuate democracy, we must permit democracy to be experienced. . . . Each group experience leaves its effect. A member may learn either to be submissive to authority or to share authority. He may learn either to evaluate life around him critically, or to accept everything traditional. He may learn to contribute to the development of his group and assume his share of responsibility for its welfare and function, or he may learn to believe that only people with special gifts can assume such responsibility.[3]

In the democratic way the group evaluates itself with the skilled guidance of the leader. Evaluation includes spontaneous appreciations for a contribution made, a job well done, the equally quick

[3] Lieberman, Joshua, editor. *New Trends in Group Work.* New York: Association Press, 1938, p. vi.

response to ineffective action and the carefully planned procedures through which leader and group try to find out what has been accomplished. When there is concern with democratic concepts and attitudes and this concern has been expressed in specific objectives, the evaluation program will include means to find out not only what was done but also how it was done. The process of working together will be given attention along with the end for which the process is functioning.

It should be emphasized here, as it has been pointed out elsewhere, that the development of concepts and attitudes basic to democratic relations will be, in the beginning of a program, the teacher's or leader's objective. Adults participate in health education, physical education and recreation programs for many reasons and seldom among these will there be found any conscious awareness of a need to become more understanding and more skilled in democratic relations. There will be, however, allied purposes, such as to enjoy activities with others, to make friends, to work on a project with others. It becomes a part of the leader's job to help these adults "to live by the way," to do and to see the significance of how they do, to take time to think about and improve the process of working together and the relations that evolve in the process.

## Check Points for a Democratic Adult Program

What are the essential features of an adult program which is democratic in its procedures and in the relations being developed among group members? Answers to this question may provide a good starting point for determining the specifics in any situation to be evaluated. The question may be rephrased. Is there an environmental situation "to live by the way" which provides:

1. *Opportunities for Self or Individual Expression.* Examples of suitable experiences include working with materials such as metal, wood, paint, clay, plastics; communicating through words, movement and sound such as writing, speaking, dance, sports, music; giving some form of volunteer service; using particular competencies to aid others—for example, assisting with instruction or administration, serving as chairman, group representative and the like.

2. *Opportunities for Recognition from the Group.* Examples might include being a chairman of an important on-going com-

mittee; a president of some club, or captain of some team (finance campaign, a folk dance demonstration team, a discussion unit regarding a debate on current legislation). In short, there must be evidence of a process of honest integration of the "I" in the "we" and "we" to "ours" as well as to "theirs." A mutual interdependent, interacting process serves as a bulwark and is essential to the continuance of the democratic way of life. It is based on the satisfactions the individual obtains in the group.

3. *Opportunities for Experience in a Mutually Agreed upon Group Problem-Solving Situation.* This is a must. A mutual problem makes possible a cohesive unit; it also favorably affects both individual and group morale.

Examples include participation in dramatic events or sports. Folk dancing, experience in a glee club, a speaking choir or a discussion group, a workshop, are additional examples.

It is one thing for the program to offer opportunities for individual expression; the way the opportunities are utilized is something else again. It is through evaluating behavior by the leader and participant that the way in which opportunities are being used becomes apparent. The following example describes the use one young woman made of her opportunity and what the leader did about it.

Mary joined an adult class in badminton saying that she wanted to make some new friends and chose a badminton class because of concern for her expanding waistline. These were the reasons she gave the teacher of the group the evening she signed for the course. The teacher noted that Mary came to the first meetings, took little initiative in identifying with the group, waiting for the teacher to arrange her games and her partner in the play. She spent considerable time alone on the sidelines. She was a little late in arriving and one of the first to leave when the class was over. The teacher did what she could, but realized that Mary needed to be made aware of her aloof behavior if she was to move toward her stated objectives.

The teacher prepared two guess-who sketches which were read to the group at the beginning of the fourth lesson. The two sketches were read and discussed. Since they represented two leaders in the group they were easily identified and were fun for everyone. The class asked for more. The teacher prepared several others, including one for Mary prepared with a good deal of care and caution. Its theme centered around aloofness, reticence and a sense of not wanting to be bothered. When Mary was guessed as a possible identification, the leader observed the startled look on her face. She started to defend her behavior then, rather abruptly, stopped and admitted not trying to be a part of the group. Later in the evening Mary asked the teacher for an interview to talk over her participation in the badminton class.

Helping individuals to gain recognition in the group is, of course, closely allied with aiding them to make use of opportunities for self-expression. For instance, Mary's awareness of how others viewed her behavior, and help in the interview with the teacher in seeing ways to change her behavior could very well have led to forms of self-expression which gained her a place in the group and recognition through sharing responsibility for group action. The following paragraphs describe a case in which an individual became increasingly responsible for group success as he gained recognition for his efforts to serve the group.

This group had been in existence for a long time. The leadership was potentially good but dormant. Officers and committee chairmen were voted into their respective positions automatically as being the next in line. Bob was made chairman of the program committee.

The club's advisor complimented the new chairman on receiving the office and Bob expressed some concern about how "he" was going to build the program for "his" club. Following a lead from the adviser Bob contacted an excellent speaker and got his acceptance to speak before the club. Acceptance of responsibility began to show in Bob's behavior. A few days before the meeting he called in at the advisor's office to say he did not think there would be a good turnout for the meeting. Upon inquiry the advisor learned that Bob was the only one "in the know" about the importance of the invited speaker. Bob asked for help. The advisor asked how about his committee providing it. Bob admitted he had not kept his committee informed and had not called a meeting to plan the event. Whatever help could be given had to be given fast because the event was only two days away. The advisor tried to help by writing a memo letter to each member of the club, telling how pleased and impressed he was to know about Bob's program for his first meeting. He added a comment that this was a speaker not to miss and that he had changed his personal plans in order to be present.

The meeting was very successful. The speaker was good—worth coming to hear; Bob was complimented by his clubmates. He responded that this was "only the beginning," and named the members of his committee and said that they had many good ideas for programs still to come. Following the meeting Bob called his committee together. Some real discussing and planning of the program was done, involving each committee member in sharing responsibility. Committee members developed behavior that evidenced that they, too, had a stake in the success of the program.

Bob's story illustrates the frequently repeated adage that success is usually more potent than failure to stimulate further efforts. As Hearn puts it in Chapter 2 of this book, the advisor used augmentation instead of reduction of the means for meeting Bob's needs. Failure of the program might have terminated the existence of that group, since a pattern had developed of expecting a few to do for the group without involvement of the entire membership in group problems. A further spread of responsibility might well follow the program committee's involvement with guidance toward this development on the part of the advisor.

Workshops usually provide good examples of entire groups working together to solve common problems. In most workshops there is direct concern with how the group is operating. An evaluative instrument developed by one such group is presented. It has provision for both staff and group evaluation of individuals' participation in the workshop.

## Staff Evaluation [4]

*Note:* The committee requests the staff to evaluate each individual on the basis of observed behavior in these two areas:

I. Individual growth through contribution

II. Individual growth through understanding

*Instructions:* Check the individual items; from these place a composite for each part at the top. The rating is done on the following basis:

1. Inadequate
2. Below average
3. Average
4. Effective
5. Very effective

---

[4] Health Education Workshop sponsored by the Department of Physical Education, University of California, Los Angeles, Summer Session, 1950. Permission to reprint granted by Dr. Carl Haven Young, Chairman of the Department of Physical Education, University of California, Los Angeles.

PART I                     INDIVIDUAL GROWTH THROUGH CONTRIBUTION

    1 2 3 4 5    To what extent has the student shown consistent interest and earnestness of purpose in the work-shop?

    1 2 3 4 5    To what extent did the individual volunteer to serve in the capacity of:

    (a) recorder, or do a job outside committee project

    (b) chairman or representative for group on work-shop committees (recreation, evaluation, or special)?

    1 2 3 4 5    To what extent did the student do creative work? Creative thinking? Producing results—making things meaningful?

    1 2 3 4 5    To what extent did the student demonstrate growth in:

    (a) Ability to speak in a group

    (b) Learning to do critical listening?


PART II                    INDIVIDUAL GROWTH THROUGH UNDERSTANDING

    1 2 3 4 5    To what extent has the student demonstrated an acceptance of the "group process" and democratic procedure as a technique?

    1 2 3 4 5    To what extent has the student shown willingness to give full support to *group goals*—approve them —clarify them?

    1 2 3 4 5    How effective was the "role" the student played to the "good" of the progress of the group?

    1 2 3 4 5    To what extent did the student fulfill his assign-ment in the group project—did he contribute some research?

    1 2 3 4 5    To what extent did he show willingness to assume the reponsibility that goes with an assignment in the group—written briefs to be reviewed?

# Group Evaluation of Participant

I. PURPOSES OF THE LARGE INTEREST GROUP
   A. Operation
      1. Establish a permissive atmosphere.
      2. Make decisions.
      3. Set goals, and focus purposes.
      4. Re-direct goals.
   B. Productivity
      1. Completion of group purpose or project.
      2. Satisfaction of individual purposes.

II. RATING SCALE
   5 very effective
   4 effective
   3 average
   2 below average
   1 inadequate

III. DIRECTIONS FOR SCORING:

Put a circle around the number which indicates your judgment of each item under parts A, B and C. Next average the scores for all items under A, and mark the average score on the summary scale to the left. Do the same for B and C. For example in Part B if your item scores are:

        1 2 *3* 4 5
        1 2 *3* 4 5    [In this printed form the circled
        1 2 *3* 4 5    numbers have been italicized.]
        1 2 *3* 4 5
      *Summary Score:* 1 2 *3* 4 5

IV. CRITERIA FOR EVALUATING INDIVIDUAL'S CONTRIBUTION TO GROUP.
   A. Communication
          1. Oral
  1 2 3 4 5  a. Did he usually participate in discussions?
  1 2 3 4 5  b. Were his comments clearly stated?
  1 2 3 4 5  c. Were his comments of value in furthering the discussion?
  1 2 3 4 5  d. Did he help to clarify issues?
  1 2 3 4 5  e. Were his statements based upon resource material (reading, experience) rather than personal opinion?
          2. Written
  1 2 3 4 5  a. Did he make written contributions?
  1 2 3 4 5  b. Were they of value to the group project?
  1 2 3 4 5  c. Were they clear and understandable?

*Summary Score:* 1 2 3 4 5

B. Planning

1 2 3 4 5  1. Did he offer specific suggestions to help the group in determining its work to be done? Sacrifice individual purposes for group purposes?

1 2 3 4 5  2. Did he help to keep the group working in line with its goal? (Observations were related to discussion and activities.)

1 2 3 4 5  3. Did he volunteer for tasks to be done: Recorder, representative, chairman, research?

1 2 3 4 5  4. Did he follow thru and accomplish the task for which he volunteered?

*Summary Score:* 1 2 3 4 5

C. Initiative and cooperation

1 2 3 4 5  1. Did he help to develop and maintain the permissive atmosphere? Give others opportunity to speak (not monopolizing)?
Encouraging others to speak (aware that some not participating)?
Enthusiastic?

1 2 3 4 5  2. Did he stimulate the group to see new possibilities in group action, and work being done?

1 2 3 4 5  3. Did he help to keep the group's morale high?
A sense of humor, especially when things bog down?
Encouraging first attempts by other members?

1 2 3 4 5  4. Did he show some originality in interpreting ideas, and handling materials, as contrasted to passive acceptance of "facts," and "authorities"?

1 2 3 4 5  5. Did he make resource materials (written, experience) available to the group?

1 2 3 4 5  6. Did he suggest the need for outside resource help when the group appeared to be at a standstill?

*Summary Score:* 1 2 3 4 5

The instrument presented contains many suggestions regarding breaking down the general goal of "working together productively and democratically" into specific criteria for evaluating. Such criteria may be derived and used without the development of a scale or even a questionnaire. Observation and discussion of participation may be used, supplemented by simple evaluating tools such as an End-of-Meeting evaluation slip covering two or three vital points or two or three questions to direct individual self-appraisal.

It is of the utmost importance for professional leaders to know how to move from their general convictions and belief in democracy toward concrete programs for developing democratic relations. The opportunities to do this evolve as individual and group needs become apparent.

## Individual Evaluation

Here again, the evaluative process, if it is to be effective, must begin with a functional rather than a structural attitude. Each individual should be periodically presented with an opportunity to evaluate himself as well as other individuals in the group. Such evaluation, however, should be "real," not imaginary. Actual behavior rather than just "say so" should be the criterion. The following questions may provide clues to the kinds of attitudes and actions to be considered.

1. *Is there evidence of an insatiable curiosity?* Does he constantly and continually seek answers? Does he continue to raise questions as goals to achieve? Does he "look" and really "see" or is the look a blank stare of oblivion? Is he, like a child, unafraid not to know?

An individual might set up such criteria as these to evaluate himself:

Am I curious enough to want to know what really is happening in the group?

Do I raise $64 questions, not only for others but for myself to answer? Do the questions lead to success in knowing?

Do I employ all my faculties of seeing, feeling, touching, smelling, tasting, to satisfy my curiosity?

Is it embarrassing for me not to know?

Am I an honest doubter as well as an honest believer?

2. *Is there evidence of a balanced attitude between persons and things?* Does he treat others as persons of dignity, seeking cooperative relations regardless of differences? Are things organized for use to enrich life or, as is too often the case, are people organized for expediency and the efficiency of things? Does he endeavor to understand the other person's viewpoint? Does he display an attitude of giving more than receiving?

Democratic persons manipulate and use things for their own benefit and for the benefit of others. Willingness to use other human beings as tools characterizes one type of nondemocratic personality, willingness to be exploited characterizes a counterpart type.

3. *Is there evidence of an attitude of accepting democratically provided responsibilities as challenges rather than chores?* That is, does he enjoy chairing a committee for promoting funds or planning for other people's enjoyment? Does he accept the challenge of raising funds for the Community Chest or some other worthy need in a democracy? Does he grasp at the opportunity to write a skit for radio or stage production for some "Y" or church or school function? Is there a sense of unselfish service, a sense of direction, of perspective which provides for vision?

Does the individual side-step opportunities for personal growth? Does he change the subject when it looks as if he is going to be asked to do a job? Does he let George do it? Is he unwilling to give time or to prepare to render service to the group?

4. *Is there evidence of participation: of doing rather than mere wishing and talking about doing?* Is there joyous effort? That which is constantly used lives and that which is consistently unused deteriorates and eventually dies. Efficient use demands training and the further development of skill and acuity. Has he captured the meaning and essence of putting into personal practice the principle of overload rather than underload? Is there evidence of staying power? Does he seem to get the most out of life's opportunities? Is he riding the crest of the wave on the surfboard of some selected avenue of expression to the shore of fulfilment and satisfaction? Is there evidence of fulfilment by creating new combinations of known skills? Does the traveling rather than or more than the arriving bring the joy of effort and the reward of doing?

Professional leaders and teachers are in a position to help individuals ask and find answers to such questions as have been raised through guidance of group evaluation in ways exemplified in the previous section of this chapter. They must supplement this guidance by helping individuals to solve their problems when opportunities to provide such help arise. The following case illustrates the second type of procedure:

Shirley was elected president of the graduate Women's Physical Education Club. Each week she presided at the meeting of the executive committee planning the details of a recreational program for the women on the campus. Shirley planned her agenda for the meeting very carefully, yet no matter how much time she spent planning, the group neither discussed the problems adequately nor finished the agenda. This left Shirley with a sense that the problems had not been discussed adequately. She was disturbed and went to the faculty sponsor with the problem of "what to do?"

Faculty sponsor: "Perhaps you could change your meeting time so that the group would have a double period?"

Shirley: "We've tried that and from our schedules and the fact that some of the women live off campus, that doesn't seem possible."

Faculty sponsor: "Does the group sense the problem which you suggest?"

Shirley: "I think so, but you know they all know each other so well it's kind of hard to eliminate the sociability. It's hard to keep them talking to the point."

Faculty sponsor: "Perhaps an evaluative discussion of the problem by the group or an evaluation might point out the difficulty."

Shirley: "I don't think we have time for the group to have an evaluative discussion. We can't get through the business we have to attend to as it is."

In further conference, it was agreed that the sponsor would act as a group observer, try to see how the group operated and make a report to the leader after the next meeting. The observer's report included the following facts:

1. The group convened at 2:55. It was 3:06 when the president called the meeting to order.

2. The president reviewed her entire agenda for the meeting and at 3:14 asked for the first report.

3. Following the report of member one, the president repeated the report in brief and asked for discussion. Discussion was generally addressed to the president who made a comment before asking the opinion of another.

4. The meeting was abruptly adjourned in the middle of a discussion of a problem about two-thirds through the agenda.

After Shirley read the summary of the meeting, she came for another interview. She had studied the report carefully and was quite excited about the judgments she had made regarding herself as a leader of the group. Not only had she sensed her shortcomings as a discussion leader but she had a new appreciation for the leader's role in the group process and was eager to have the evaluative discussion so that the entire group might better understand its member roles in making discussion effective.

Evaluation in Shirley's case served not only to help her to understand better her role in the group, but it convinced her that the technique should be used with the entire group, so that each woman might see herself in the group and see the places where group planning and action were not productive.

## Self-Appraisal of the Leader

The professional leader in group situations has need for understanding his own shortcomings as a leader guiding experiences through which maximum growth in democratic relations might result. Below are some suggestions for ways in which teachers and leaders may appraise themselves. After each question is answered the self-appraiser should ask himself another question, namely, how do I know this is an accurate judgment or appraisal?

I. *A Twelve Inch Rule for Appraising Attitudes*
  1. Do I believe in individuals as persons of dignity and respect?
  2. Do I believe in the principle of equality of opportunity for all—all the time?
  3. Do I think and talk democracy, plan democratic opportunities for all individuals and groups under my leadership?
  4. Do I believe in decentralizing all groups to workable units as committees, clubs, interests in natural groups?
  5. Do I believe in creating as well as capitalizing on problem-solving frames of reference in which to guide persons and groups under my leadership?
  6. Do I believe in the process and principle of maturation (organic and social growth and development) and endeavor constantly to apply this to groups and individuals under my guidance?
  7. Do I believe in the oneness of mind, body and spirit and apply this to my professional services?
  8. Do I believe in and understand the importance of forming conceptions of democracy through many perceptions of it gained through experience?
  9. Do I display maturity in using and understanding the different semantic problems inherent within the experiences of persons with whom I am privileged to serve?
  10. Do I believe in adequate planning, searching and researching?

11. Do I believe in the freedom of man to live and to help let live?

12. Do I believe in the "doing" and experience curriculum?

II. *A Twelve Inch Rule for Appraising Personal Skills*

A. *Planning*

1. Do I plan and organize for the many rather than the few?

2. Do I include specific opportunities for instruction, participation and competition for all?

3. Do I know of and employ "up to the minute" methods of individual and group activities?

B. *As a leader*

4. Do I perform to demonstrate essential skills for others rather than play the role of the exhibitionist?

5. Do I look and act the part of a friend and assigned leader with all with whom I come into contact?

6. Do I give recognition for achievement when it is earned?

C. *Guidance*

7. Do I seek and exploit "teachable moments" for the best interest of persons whom I serve?

8. Do I mechanically treat all alike or do I take into account the individual differences in persons under my leadership?

9. Do I seek to guide individuals toward clarifying their own goals and toward setting more socially satisfactory and individually satisfying goals?

D. *Evaluation*

10. Do I constantly and continuously practice high standards of research, but with discernment and understanding wherever persons are involved?

11. Do I suspend judgment until I muster all available facts.

12. Do I make use of all evaluative information?

The final step in evaluation is the use of findings. The interpretations of scores, descriptions or judgments are valuable only as they are conceived in relation to the purpose for which the evaluation was made and then used to redirect planning and action. Such evaluation is never finished. When it is perceived as a continuous process, within an orderly framework, it develops the quality of appraisal bringing about modification of the individual's behavior in the group in the direction of becoming a more democratic human being. In any situation, evaluation of behavior thus becomes the point of departure for developing democratic human relations.

# Bibliography

BARTLETT, ROBERT M. *They Dared to Live.* New York: Association Press, 1937.

BARTLETT, ROBERT M. *They Did Something About It.* New York: Association Press, 1941.

BINGHAM, WALTER V., and MOORE, BRUCE V. *How To Interview.* New York: Harper and Brothers, 1934.

BUROS, OSCAR, editor. *Educational, Psychological and Personality Tests.* Third Mental Measurements Yearbook. New Brunswick: Rutgers University Press, 1949.

CABOT, RICHARD C. *What Men Live By.* Boston: Houghton Mifflin Co., 1914.

CALKINS, EARNEST E. *Care and Feeding of Hobby Horses.* New York: Leisure League of America, 1934.

GREENBIE, SYDNEY. *Leisure for Living.* Toronto: George J. McLeod, 1940.

CHARTERS, WERRETT, W., and FRY, VAUGHN. *The Ohio Study of Recreation Leadership Training.* Columbus: Bureau of Educational Research, The Ohio State University, 1942.

HOPKINS, L. THOMAS. *Interaction—The Democratic Process.* Boston: D. C. Heath and Co., 1941.

JACKS, LAWRENCE P. *Education Through Recreation.* New York: Harper and Brothers, 1932.

LAIRD, DONALD A. *The Technique of Personal Analysis.* New York: McGraw-Hill Book Co., 1945.

LIEBERMAN, JOSHUA, editor. *New Trends in Group Work.* New York: Association Press, 1938.

MIEL, ALICE. "A Group Studies Itself." Teachers College Record. 49: 31-43; October 1947.

MOORE, BERNICE MILBURN, and SUTHERLAND, ROBERT J. *Profiles of Community Action.* Austin, Texas: The Hogg Foundation, 1950.

MILLER, JOHN H. *Take a Look at Yourself.* New York: Abington-Cokesbury Press, 1943.

OVERSTREET, HARRY A. *A Guide to Civilized Leisure.* New York: W. W. Norton and Co., 1934.

PANZAR, MARTIN. *It's Your Future.* New York: Whittlesey House, 1943.

PORTER, EDNA. *Community Wise.* New York: Woman's Press, n.d.

ROMNEY, G. OTT. *Off the Job Living.* New York: A. S. Barnes and Co., 1945.

# Alphabetical Bibliography

ADAMS, JAMES TRUSLOW. *The American.* New York: Charles Scribner's Sons, 1943.

ADAMS, THOMAS R. *Education for International Understanding.* New York: Institute of Adult Education, Teachers College, Columbia University, 1949.

AGAR, HERBERT. *A Time for Greatness.* New York: Little, Brown and Co., 1942.

ALEXANDER, FRANZ *Our Age of Unreason.* Philadelphia: J. P. Lippincott Co., 1942.

ALLEE, CLYDE. *Social Life of Animals.* New York: W. W. Norton and Co., 1938.

ALLEN, FREDERICK LEWIS. *Since Yesterday.* New York: Harper and Brothers, 1940.

AMERICAN ASSOCIATION OF SCHOOL ADMINISTRATORS. *Health in Schools.* Twentieth Yearbook. Washington, D. C.: the Association, a department of the National Education Association, 1942.

AMERICAN COUNCIL ON EDUCATION, COMMISSION ON TEACHER EDUCATION. *Helping Teachers Understand Children.* Washington, D. C.: American Council on Education, 1945.

AMERICAN YOUTH COMMISSION. *Youth and the Future.* Washington, D. C.: American Council on Education, 1942.

ANDERSON, JOHN E. *The Psychology of Development and Personal Adjustment.* New York: Henry Holt and Co., 1949.

ANDERSON, RUTH H. "Skills for Social Living." *Educational Leadership.* 1: 144-47; December 1943.

ANGYAL, ANDRAS. *Foundations for a Science of Personality.* New York: Commonwealth Fund, 1941.

ANSHEN, RUTH N., editor. *The Family: Its Function and Destiny.* New York: Harper and Brothers, 1949.

ARMSTRONG, HERBERT C. "Teacher-Parent Conference." *California Journal of Elementary Education.* 11: 31-45; August 1942.

ASSOCIATION FOR SUPERVISION AND CURRICULUM DEVELOPMENT. *Toward Better Teaching.* 1949 Yearbook. Washington, D. C.: the Association, a department of the National Education Association, 1949.

ASSOCIATION FOR SUPERVISION AND CURRICULUM DEVELOPMENT. *Organizing the Elementary School for Living and Learning.* 1947 Yearbook. Washington, D. C.: the Association, a department of the National Education Association, 1947.

ASSOCIATION FOR SUPERVISION AND CURRICULUM DEVELOPMENT. *Leadership Through Supervision.* 1946 Yearbook. Washington, D. C.: the Association, a department of the National Education Association, 1946.

AUER, J. JEFFRY, and EWBANK, HENRY. *Handbook for Discussion Leaders.* New York: Harper and Brothers, 1947.

BARKER, ROGER; KOUNIN, JACOB; and WRIGHT, HERBERT. *Child Behavior and Development.* New York: McGraw-Hill Book Co., 1943.

BARR, ARVIL S.; BURTON, WILLIAM H.; and BRUECKNER, LEO J. *Supervision.* New York: Appleton-Century-Crofts, Inc., 1947.

BARTLETT, ROBERT M. *They Dared To Live.* New York: Association Press, 1937.

[ 531 ]

BARTLETT, ROBERT M. *They Did Something About It*. New York: Association Press, 1941.

BAXTER, BERNICE. *Teacher-Pupil Relationships*. New York: Macmillan Co., 1941.

BAXTER, BERNICE, and BRADEN, ANNE. *An Overview of Elementary Education*. Boston: D. C. Heath and Co., 1945.

BAXTER, BERNICE, and CASSIDY, ROSALIND. *Group Experience—The Democratic Way*. New York: Harper and Brothers, 1943.

BEARD, CHARLES A., and BEARD, MARY. *America in Mid-Passage*. New York: Macmillan Co., 1939.

BEISE, DOROTHY. "A Comparative Analysis of the Physical Education Background, Interests and Desires of College Students as an Evaluation Procedure." *Research Quarterly*. 11: 120-34; December 1940.

BELL, HOWARD N. *Matching Youth and Jobs*. Washington, D. C.: American Council on Education, 1940.

BENEDICT, RUTH. *Patterns of Culture*. Boston: Houghton Mifflin Co., 1934.

BENNE, KENNETH D. "Leaders Are Made Not Born." *Childhood Education*. 24: 302-8; January 1948.

BENNE, KENNETH D., and SHEATS, PAUL. "Functional Roles of Group Members." *Journal of Social Issues*. 4: 41-49; Spring 1948.

BENNETT, BRUCE L. "Physical Education and Social Learning in the Secondary School." *Journal of the American Association of Health, Physical Education and Recreation*. 20: 452-53; September 1949.

BENNETT, MARGARET E. *College and Life*. New York: McGraw-Hill Book Co., 1941.

BENNETT, MARGARET E., and HAND, HAROLD. *Designs for Personality*. New York: McGraw-Hill Book Co., 1938.

BERNSTEIN, SAUL. *Charting Group Process*. New York: Association Press, 1949.

BETTELHEIM, BRUNO. *Love Is Not Enough—The Treatment of Emotionally Disturbed Children*. Glencoe, Ill.: Free Press, 1950.

BIESTER, LILLIAN L.; GRIFFITHS, WILLIAM; and PEARCE, N. D. *Units in Personal Health and Human Relations*. Minneapolis: University of Minneapolis Press, 1949.

BINGHAM, WALTER V., and MOORE, V. V. *How to Interview*. New York: Harper and Brothers, 1934.

BLOS, PETER. *The Adolescent Personality*. New York: Appleton-Century-Crofts, Inc., 1941.

BONNEY, MERLE E. "Popular and Unpopular Children: A Sociometric Study." *Sociometry Monograph* No. 9. New York: Beacon House, n.d.

BOSSARD, JAMES H. S. *The Sociology of Child Development*. New York: Harper and Brothers, 1948.

BOWMAN, HENRY A. *Marriage for Moderns*. New York: McGraw-Hill Book Co., 1941.

BRADFORD, LELAND P.; BERNE, KENNETH D.; and LIPPITT, RONALD A. "The Promise of Group Dynamics for Education." *National Education Association Journal*. 37: 350-52; September 1948.

BRECKENRIDGE, MARIAN E., and VINCENT, E. LEE. *Child Development*. Revised edition. Philadelphia: W. B. Saunders Co., 1943.

BREEN, MARY J. *Partners in Play*. New York: A. S. Barnes and Co., 1936.

BRIGGS, THOMAS H., and OTHERS. *The Emotionalized Attitudes*. New York: Bureau of Publications, Teachers College, Columbia University, 1940.

BROGAN, DENIS W. *The American Character*. New York: Alfred A. Knopf, 1944.

BROWN, IDA S. *Training in Group Development with University Students—An Experiment*. Unpublished dissertation, University of California, Los Angeles, 1950.

BROWN, JAMES F. *Psychology and the Social Order*. New York: McGraw-Hill Book Co., 1936.

BROWN, MERLE S. "The Role of the Teacher Today." *Childhood Education* 26: 70-73; October 1949.

BROWN, SPENCER. *They See for Themselves*. New York: Harper and Brothers, 1945.

BROUWER, PAUL J. *Student Personnel Services in General Education*. Washington, D. C.: American Council on Education, 1949.

BROWNELL, CLIFFORD L. *Principles of Health Education Applied*. New York: McGraw-Hill Book Co., 1949.

BUCK, PEARL. *Of Men and Women*. New York: John Day Publishing Co., 1941.

BURKLE, LOUISE E. "Planning Recreation Activities for Women." *Industrial Bulletin Service*. New York: National Recreation Association. (Reprint or speech at Industrial Recreation Conference, January 27-28, 1946.)

BULLIS, H. EDMUND, and O'MALLEY, EMILY E. *Human Relations in the Classroom*. Wilmington, Del.: State Society for Mental Hygiene, 1947.

BURNS, CECIL. *Leisure in the Modern World*. New York: Century Co., 1932.

BUROS, OSCAR, editor. *Educational, Psychological and Personality Tests*. Third Mental Measurements Yearbook. New Brunswick: Rutgers University Press, 1949.

BURTON, WILLIAM H. *The Guidance of Learning Activities*. New York: Appleton-Century-Crofts, Inc., 1944.

CABOT, RICHARD C. *What Men Live By*. Boston: Houghton Mifflin Co., 1914.

CALIVER, AMBROSE. "Education of Teachers for Improving Majority-Minority Relationships." *United States Office of Education Bulletin 2*. Washington, D. C.: United States Government Printing Office, 1944.

CALKENS, EARNEST E. *Care and Feeding of Hobby Horses*. New York: Leisure League of America, 1934.

CANNON, WALTER B. *The Wisdom of the Body*. New York: W. W. Norton and Co., 1932.

CARR-SAUNDERS, ALEXANDER M. *World Population; Past Growth and Present Trends*. Toronto: Oxford Press, 1936.

CASSIDY, ROSALIND. "Contributions of Physical Education to Democratic Citizenship." *Journal of the American Association for Health, Physical Education and Recreation* 21: 218-19, April 1950.

CASSIDY, ROSALIND. *New Directions in Physical Education for the Adolescent Girl in High School and College*. New York: A. S. Barnes and Co., 1938.

CASSIDY, ROSALIND, and KOZMAN, HILDA CLUTE. *Counseling Girls in a Changing Society*. New York: McGraw-Hill Book Co., 1947.

CARMICHAEL, LEONARD, editor. *Manual of Child Psychology*. New York: John Wiley and Sons, 1946.

CHAMBERS, MERRITT M. *The Community and Its People.* Washington, D. C.: American Council on Education, 1940.

CHANDLER, ALBERT. *The Clash of Political Ideals.* New York: Appleton-Century-Crofts, Inc., 1940.

CHARTERS, WERRETT W., and FRY, VAUGHN W. *The Ohio Study of Recreation Leadership Training.* Columbus: Bureau of Educational Research, The Ohio State University, 1942.

CHASE, JOHN W., editor. *Years of the Modern.* New York: Longmans, Green and Co., 1949.

CHATTO, CLARENCE I. "Health and Physical Education for Democratic Living." *Journal of Health and Physical Education* 17: 466-67; October 1946.

CHERNE, LEO M. *The Rest of Your Life.* New York: Doubleday and Co., 1944.

CHISHOLM, LESLIE. *Guiding Youth in the Secondary School.* New York: American Book Co., 1945.

CITIZENSHIP EDUCATION STUDY. *Democratic Citizenship and Development of Children.* Detroit: Detroit Public Schools and Wayne University, 1949.

CITIZENSHIP EDUCATION STUDY. *Five Qualities of the Good Citizen.* Detroit: Detroit Public Schools and Wayne University, 1948.

CITIZENSHIP EDUCATION STUDY. *Problem Solving.* Detroit: Detroit Public Schools and Wayne University, 1948.

CLAYTON, ALFRED S. *Emergent Mind and Education.* Teachers College Contribution to Education No. 867. New York: Columbia University Press, 1943.

CLOTHIER, FLORENCE. "The Challenge of a Protracted Adolescence." *Vassar Alumnae Magazine* as reprinted in *Child Family Digest* 1: 3-15; October 1949.

COLE, LUELLA. *Attaining Maturity.* New York: Farrar and Rinehart, 1944.

COLLINS, LAURENTINE B.; CASSIDY, ROSALIND; and OTHERS. *Physical Education in the Secondary School.* New York: A. S. Barnes and Co., 1940.

COMMAGER, HENRY S. *The American Mind.* New Haven: Yale University Press, 1950.

COMPLETE REPORT OF THE AMERICAN PUBLIC HEALTH ASSOCIATION. *Community Organization for Health Education.* New York: American Public Health Association, 1941.

COOK, LLOYD ALLEN. "Educating for Community Action and Unity." *Social Education.* 6: 304-8; November 1942.

COOK, LLOYD ALLEN. "The Frame of Reference in the College Study." *Journal of Educational Sociology.* 21: 31-42; September 1947.

THE COUNCIL ON MEDICAL SERVICE and THE COMMITTEE ON RURAL HEALTH. *The Community Health Council.* Chicago: American Medical Association, 1949.

COWELL, CHARLES C. "Diary Analysis: A Suggested Technique for the Study of Children's Activities and Interests." *Research Quarterly* 8: 158-72; May 1937.

COWELL, CHARLES C. "The Guidance Functions and Possibilities of Physical Education." *Journal of the American Association for Health, Physical Education and Recreation* 20: 238-394; April 1949.

COWELL, CHARLES C. "Mental Hygiene Functions and Possibilities of Play and Physical Education." *Elementary School Journal* 50: 196-203; December 1949.

COWELL, CHARLES C. "Play Behavior and Personality Analysis." *Educational Research Bulletin.* The Ohio State University, October 20, 1937.

COWELL, CHARLES C. "Physical Education as Applied Social Science." *Educational Research Bulletin,* The Ohio State University 16: 147-55; September 1937.

COYLE, GRACE. "Definition of the Functions of the Group Worker." *The Group* 11: 11-12; May 1949.

COYLE, GRACE. *Group Experience and Democratic Values.* New York: Woman's Press, 1947.

COYLE, GRACE. *Group Work with American Youth.* New York: Harper and Brothers, 1948.

CRAMPTON, C. WARD. "Live Long and Like It." *Public Affairs Pamphlets* No. 139. New York: Public Affairs Committee, 1948.

CRAWFORD, JOHN E., and WOODWARD, LUTHER E. *Better Ways of Growing Up.* Philadelphia: Muhlenberg Press, 1948.

CROW, LESTER, and CROW, ALICE. *Our Teen Age Boys and Girls.* New York: McGraw-Hill Book Co., 1945.

CUNNINGHAM, RUTH. *We, the Children.* Washington, D. C.: National Education Association, 1945.

CUNNINGHAM, RUTH, and ASSOCIATES. "Johnny Doesn't Belong." *National Education Association Journal* 37: 578-79; December 1948.

CUNNINGHAM, RUTH, and ASSOCIATES. "Leadership and the Group." *National Education Association Journal* 37: 502-503; November 1948.

DAVIS, W. ALLISON, and HAVIGHURST, ROBERT J. *Father of the Man.* Boston: Houghton Mifflin Co., 1947.

DEAN, VERA MICHELES. "A Strategy for a War of Ideas." *Nation* 171: 185-87; August 26, 1950.

DEERING, IVAH. *Let's Try Thinking: A Handbook of Democratic Action.* Yellow Springs, Ohio: Antioch Press, 1942.

DE HUSZAR, GEORGE G. *Practical Applications of Democracy.* New York: Harper and Brothers, 1945.

DEWEY, JOHN. *Freedom and Culture.* New York: G. P. Putnam's Sons, 1939.

DEWEY, JOHN. *How We Think.* Boston: D. C. Heath and Co., 1933.

DEWEY, JOHN. *Human Nature and Conduct.* New York: Henry Holt and Co., 1922.

DIEDERICH, PAUL B. "Evaluation Records." *Educational Method* 15: 432-40; May 1936.

DIMOCK, HEDLEY, and OTHERS. *Camping in a Democracy.* New York: Association Press, 1946.

DIMOCK, HEDLEY S., and TRECKER, HARLEIGH B. *The Supervision of Group Work and Recreation.* New York: Association Press, 1949.

DOLLARD, JOHN D. *Caste and Class in a Southern Town.* New Haven: Yale University Press, 1937.

DOLLARD, JOHN D., and ASSOCIATES. *Frustration and Aggression.* New Haven: Yale University Press, 1939.

DRISCOLL, GERTRUDE. *How to Study the Behavior of Children.* New York: Bureau of Publications, Teachers College, Columbia University, 1941.

"The Dynamics of the Discussion Group." Entire issue of *Journal of Social Issues,* Spring 1948.

*Educational Leadership.* Journal of the Association for Supervision and Curriculum Development 7: 79-144; November 1949.

ELLIOT, EUGENE B. *Understanding Through Discussion*. Lansing, Mich.: Superintendent of Public Instruction, Bulletin No. 339, 1945.

ELLIOTT, HARRISON S. *The Process of Group Thinking*. New York: Association Press, 1928.

ELLIOTT, MERLE. "Patterns of Friendship in the Classroom." *Progressive Education* 18: 383-90; November 1941.

ENGLISH, O. SPURGEON, and PEARSON, GERALD H. *Emotional Problems of Living*. New York: W. W. Norton and Co., 1945.

ERICKSON, CLIFFORD E., and HAPP, MARION C. *Guidance Practices at Work*. New York: McGraw-Hill Book Co., 1946.

FAEGRE, MARION L. *Child Care and Training*. Minneapolis: University of Minnesota Institute of Child Welfare, 1947.

FAEGRE, MARION L. *Your Child from Six to Twelve*. Children's Bureau Publication No. 324. Washington, D. C.: United States Government Printing Office, 1949.

FANSLER, THOMAS. *Discussion Methods for Adult Groups*. New York: American Association for Adult Education, n.d.

FANSLER, THOMAS. *Teaching Adults by Discussion*. New York: Service Bureau for Adult Education, New York University, 1938.

FENTON, NORMAN. *The Counselor's Interview with the Student*. Palo Alto, Calif.: Stanford University Press, 1943.

FENTON, NORMAN. *Mental Hygiene in School Practice*. Palo Alto, Calif.: Stanford University Press, 1943.

FLEMING, CHARLOTTE M. *Adolescence*. New York: International Universities Press, 1949.

FOLLETT, MARY P. *Creative Experience*. New York: Longmans, Green and Co., 1924.

FOLSOM, JOSEPH K. *The Family and the Democratic Society*. New York: John Wiley and Sons, 1943.

FOSHEY, A. WELLESLEY. "Evaluating Social Learnings." *Childhood Education* 26: 65-69; October 1949.

FOSTER, JOSEPHINE C., and HEADLEY, NEITH E. *Education in the Kindergarten*. Second edition. New York: American Book Co., 1948.

FRANK, LAWRENCE K. *Society as the Patient*. New Brunswick: Rutgers University Press, 1948.

FRANK, LAWRENCE K. "This Is the Adolescent." As reprinted in *Child-Family Digest* 1: 52-59; September 1949.

FROMM, ERICH. *Escape from Freedom*. New York: Farrar and Rinehart, 1941.

FURFEY, PAUL H. "The Group Life of the Adolescent." *Journal of Educational Sociology* 14: 195-204; December 1940.

GESELL, ARNOLD. *The First Five Years of Life*. New York: Harper and Brothers, 1940.

GESELL, ARNOLD, and ILG, FRANCES. *The Child from Five to Ten*. New York: Harper and Brothers, 1947.

GESELL, ARNOLD, and ILG, FRANCES. *Infant and Child in the Culture of Today*. New York: Harper and Brothers, 1943.

GIRL SCOUTS, NATIONAL ORGANIZATION. *Leadership of Girl Scout Troops—Intermediate Program*. New York: Girl Scouts of the United States, 1943.

GILCHRIST, ROBERT S. *Building Friendly Relations.* Columbus: The Ohio State University, 1947.

GILES, HENRY H. *Teacher-Pupil Planning.* New York: Harper and Brothers, 1941.

GOODENOUGH, FLORENCE L. *Developmental Psychology.* New York: Appleton-Century-Crofts, Inc., 1945.

GORDON, THOMAS. "What Is Gained by Group Participation?" *Educational Leadership* 7: 220-26; January 1950.

GREENBIE, SYDNEY. *Leisure for Living.* Toronto: George J. McLeod, 1940.

GROOM, WILLIAM S. "The Health Council." *Journal of Health and Physical Education* 17: 332; June 1946.

GUY, GEORGE V. "Group Study Procedures: A Selected Bibliography." *Educational Leadership* 7: 266-69; January 1950.

GUMPERT, MARTIN. "Our Unknown Aged." *Nation* 171: 182-83; August 26, 1950.

HAAS, ROBERT BARTLETT. *Learning To Read Ourselves and Others: An Approach Through Sociometry and the Psychodrama.* Claremont, Calif.: Claremont Reading Conference, 1948.

HAAS, ROBERT BARTLETT, editor. *Psychodrama and Sociodrama in American Education.* New York: Beacon House, 1949.

HALDANE, JOHN. *Organism and Environment.* New Haven: Yale University Press, 1917.

HARSH, CHARLES M., and SCHRICKEL, HARRY G. *Personality Development and Assessment.* New York: Ronald Press, 1950.

HARSHFIELD, H. W., and SCHMIDT, J. "Playing Out Our Problems in Sociodrama." *Sociatry* 2: 365-67; December-March 1948.

HARTFORD, ELLIS FORD. "Civic Leadership Through Clubs." *Social Education* 2: 91-93; February 1938.

HARTLEY, EUGENE L. *Problems in Prejudice.* New York: King's Crown Press, 1946.

HARTMAN, GEORGE W. *Educational Psychology.* New York: American Book Co., 1941.

HARTSHORNE, HUGH, and MAY, MARK A. *Studies in Deceit.* New York: Macmillan Co., 1928.

HAVIGHURST, ROBERT J. *Developmental Tasks and Education.* Chicago: University of Chicago Press, 1948.

HAVIGHURST, ROBERT J., and TABA, HILDA. *Adolescent Character and Personality.* New York: John Wiley and Sons, 1949.

HEARD, GERALD. *Man the Master.* New York: Harper and Brothers, 1941.

HEFFERNAN, HELEN. *Techniques To Be Used in Solving an Educational Problem by the Discussion Method.* Sacramento, Calif.: State Department of Education, 1944.

HEMPHILL, JOHN K. *Situational Factors in Leadership.* Columbus: Bureau of Educational Research, The Ohio State University Monograph 32, 1949.

HENDRY, CHARLES E. *Decade of Group Work.* New York: Association Press, 1948.

HERRICK, CHARLES J. *The Thinking Machine.* Chicago: University of Chicago Press, 1929.

HERRICK, VIRGIL E. "Workshop Patterns and Processes." *Childhood Education* 24: 426-29; May 1948.

HERRON, JOHN S. "Human Relations, Democracy and Physical Education." *Journal of Health and Physical Education.* 17: 510; November 1946.

HILDRETH, GERTRUDE. *Child Growth Through Education.* New York: Ronald Press, 1948.

HISCOCK, IRA V. *Ways to Community Health Education.* New York: Commonwealth Fund, 1949.

HJELTE, GEORGE. *The Administration of Public Recreation.* New York: Macmillan Co., 1940.

HOLLINGSHEAD, ARTHUR T. *Guidance in Democratic Living.* New York: Appleton-Century-Crofts, Inc., 1941.

HOLLINGSHEAD, AUGUST B. *Elmtown's Youth.* New York: John Wiley and Sons, 1949.

HOPKINS, L. THOMAS. "Atmosphere for Learning." *Teachers College Record* 46: 99-105; November 1944.

HOPKINS, L. THOMAS. *Interaction—The Democratic Process.* Boston: D. C. Heath and Co., 1941.

HORNEY, KAREN. *The Neurotic Personality of Our Time.* New York: W. W. Norton and Co., 1937.

HORNEY, KAREN. *Our Inner Conflicts.* New York: W. W. Norton and Co., 1945.

HOSLETT, SCHUYLER D. *Human Factors in Management.* Parkville, Mo.: Park College Press, 1946.

HOSKING, ELIZABETH. "Developing Good Human Relations." *School Executive* 68: 51-52; December 1948.

HOWARD, PALMER, and LIPPITT, RONALD A. "Training Community Leadership Toward More Effective Group Living." *Adult Education Bulletin* 10: 168-74; August 1946.

HOYT, ELIZABETH. "Freedom from Want: A World Goal." *Public Affairs Pamphlets* No. 80. New York: Public Affairs Committee, 1943.

HUGGETT, ALBERT. *Growth and Learning in the Elementary Schools.* Boston: D. C. Heath and Co., 1946.

HULLFISH, GORDON H. "The Basic American Dilemma." *Journal of Health and Physical Education* 17: 582-84; December 1946.

HUNTER, RUTH A., and MORGAN, DAVID A. "Problems of College Students." *Journal of Educational Psychology* 40: 79-92; February 1949.

HURLOCK, ELIZABETH. *Child Growth and Development.* New York: McGraw-Hill Book Co., 1949.

HUSSEY, DELIA. "The Play Route in Human Relations." *Childhood Education* 25: 157-160; December 1948.

INSTITUTE FOR ADULT EDUCATION. *Handbook of Adult Education in the United States.* Part 4, Section 2, "Media and Methods for Instruction," 1941, p. 253-80.

JACKS, LAWRENCE P. *Education Through Recreation.* New York: Harper and Brothers, 1932.

JENKINS, DAVID H. "Feedback and Group Self-Evaluation." *Journal of Social Issues* 4: 50-60; Spring 1948.

JENKINS, DAVID H. "Research in Group Dynamics." *Social Education* 12: 347-49; December 1948.

JENKINS, GLADYS G.; SHACTER, HELEN; and BAUER, W. E. *These Are Our Children.* Chicago: Scott, Foresman and Co., 1950.

JENNINGS, HELEN H. *Sociometry in Group Relations.* Washington, D. C.: American Council on Education, 1948.

JERSILD, ARTHUR T. *Child Psychology.* Revised edition. New York: Prentice-Hall, 1946.

JERSILD, ARTHUR T., and ASSOCIATES. *Child Development and the Curriculum.* New York: Bureau of Publications, Teachers College, Columbia University, 1946.

JERSILD, ARTHUR T.; TASCH, RUGH J.; and OTHERS. *Children's Interests.* New York: Bureau of Publications, Teachers College, Columbia University, 1949.

JOHNSON, GERALD W. *Incredible Tale.* New York: Harper and Brothers, 1950.

JOHNSON, WENDELL. *People in Quandaries.* New York: Harper and Brothers, 1946.

JONES, EDWINA; MORGAN, EDNA; and LANDIS, PAUL E. *Easy Steps to Health.* Laidlaw Brothers, 1950.

JONES, EDWINA; MORGAN, EDNA; and LANDIS, PAUL E. *Your Health and You.* Chicago: Laidlaw Brothers, 1950.

JONES, EDWINA; MORGAN, EDNA; and STEVENS, GLADYS. *Methods and Materials in Elementary Physical Education.* New York: World Book Co., 1951.

JONES, EDWINA, and STEVENS, GLADYS. "Workshop Practices in Elementary School Physical Education." *Journal of the American Association of Health, Physical Education and Recreation* 20: 366-76; June 1949.

KALLEN, HORACE M. *The Education of Free Men.* New York: Strauss and Co., 1949.

KANT, IMMANUEL. *The Fundamental Principles of the Metaphysics of Ethics.* New York: Appleton-Century-Crofts, Inc., 1938.

KELIHER, ALICE. "The Commission on Human Relations." *Progressive Education* 17: 497-504; November 1940.

KELLEY, EARL. *Education for What Is Real.* New York: Harper and Brothers, 1947.

KELLEY, JANET AGNES. *College Life and the Mores.* New York: Bureau of Publications, Teachers College, Columbia University, 1949.

KILPATRICK, WILLIAM H. *Better Human Relations.* New York: Freedom Pamphlets, Anti-Defamation League of B'nai B'rith, 1949.

KINSEY, ALFRED C.; POMEROY, WARDELL B.; and MARTIN, CLYDE E. *Sexual Behavior in the Human Male.* Philadelphia: W. B. Saunders Co., 1948.

KLEIN, PAUL E., and MOFFITT, RUTH E. *Counseling Techniques in Adult Education.* New York: McGraw-Hill Book Co., 1949.

KLUCKHOHN, CLYDE, and MURRAY, HENRY A. *Personality in Nature, Society and Culture.* Cambridge: Harvard University Press, 1948.

KNICKERBOCKER, IRVING. "Leadership—A Conception and Some Implications." *Journal of Social Issues* 4: 23-40; Summer 1948.

KOZMAN, HILDA CLUTE; CASSIDY, ROSALIND; and JACKSON, CHESTER O. *Methods in Physical Education.* Philadelphia: W. B. Saunders Co., 1947.

KROGMAN, WILTON M. "Physical Anthropology and Race Relations: A Biosocial Evaluation." *Scientific Monthly* 66: 317-21; April 1948.

KUHLEN, RAYMOND, and BRETSCH, HOWARD. "Sociometric Status and Personal Problems of Adolescents." *Sociometry* 10: 122-32; May 1947.

LAIRD, DONALD A. *The Technique of Personal Analysis.* New York: McGraw-Hill Book Co., 1945.

LANDIS, PAUL. *Adolescence and Youth.* New York: McGraw-Hill Book Co., 1945.

LANG, SIDNEY. *Education and Leisure.* London: J. M. Dent and Sons, 1930.

LA SALLE, DOROTHY. *The Guidance of Children Through Physical Education.* New York: A. S. Barnes and Co., 1946.

LASKER, BRUNO. *Race Attitudes in Children.* New York: Henry Holland Co., 1929.

LEE, IRVING J. "Why Discussions Go Astray." *A Review of General Semantics* 4: 81-88; Winter 1947.

LEWIN, KURT. *A Dynamic Theory of Personality.* New York: McGraw-Hill Book Co., 1935.

LEWIN, KURT. "Dynamics of Group Action." *Educational Leadership* 1: 195-200; January 1944.

LEWIN, KURT. "Field Theory and Experiments in Social Psychology." *American Journal of Sociology* 44: 868-96; May 1939.

LEWIN, KURT. "Field Theory and Learning." National Society for the Study of Education. *The Psychology of Learning.* Forty-First Yearbook Part II. Bloomington, Ill.: Public Schools Publishing Co., 1942, Chapter IV.

LEWIN, KURT, and LIPPITT, RONALD A. *A Research Center for Group Dynamics.* New York: Beacon House, 1947.

LEWIN, KURT; LIPPITT, RONALD A.; and WHITE, RALPH K. "Patterns of Aggressive Behavior in Experimentally Created Social 'Climates.'" *Journal of Social Psychology* 10: 271-99; May 1939.

LEVY, RONALD, and OSTEN, RHEA. *Handbook for Group Development.* Chicago: Sociometric Research Associates, 338 Michigan Avenue, Chicago, 1950.

LIE, TRYGVE. "United Nations—A Year of Progress." Introduction to the Fourth Annual Report on the Work of the United Nations, July 7, 1949. *United Nations Bulletin,* August 15, 1949.

LIEBERMAN, JOSHUA, editor. *New Trends in Group Work.* New York: Association Press, 1938.

LIEBMAN, JOSHUA. *Peace of Mind.* New York: Simon and Schuster, 1946.

LIGON, ERNEST M. *A Greater Generation.* New York: Macmillan Co., 1949.

LILIENTHAL, DAVID E. *This I Do Believe.* New York: Harper and Brothers, 1949.

LILIENTHAL, DAVID E. "Youth in the Atomic Age." *National Education Association Journal* 37: 370-71; September 1948.

LINDEMAN, EDUARD C. *The Good of American Education.* New York: Farrar and Rinehart, 1940.

LINDEMAN, EDUARD C. *Leisure—A National Issue.* New York: Association Press, 1939.

LINSTROM, DAVID E. *Democracy in Action.* Springfield: Illinois State Library, 1943.

LIPPITT, RONALD A. "Better Human Relations." *School Executive* 67: 47-49; January 1948.

LIPPITT, RONALD A. *Training in Community Relations Toward New Group Skills.* New York: Harper and Brothers, 1949.

LLOYD-JONES, ESTHER, and FEDDER, RUTH. *Coming of Age.* New York: Whittlesey House, 1941.

LLOYD-JONES, ESTHER, and SMITH, MARGARET R. *A Student Personnel Program for Higher Education.* New York: McGraw-Hill Book Co., 1938.

LOVE, LESTON L., and OTHERS. *Student Planning in College.* Columbus: The Ohio State University Press, 1941.

LUNDBERG, GEORGE A. *Leisure: A Suburban Study.* New York: Columbia University Press, 1934.

LYLE, MARY S. *Adult Education for Democracy and Family Life.* Ames, Iowa: The Collegiate Press, 1944.

LYND, ROBERT S. *Knowledge for What?* Princeton, N. J.: Princeton University Press, 1939.

LYND, ROBERT S., and LYND, HELEN M. *Middletown.* New York: Harcourt, Brace and Co., 1929.

LYND, ROBERT S., and LYND, HELEN M. *Middletown in Transition.* Harcourt, Brace and Co., 1937.

LYSTER, ALVA M. *Social Problems of the High School Boy.* Austin, Texas: Steck Co., 1935.

MAC LEISH, ARCHIBALD. "The Conquest of America." *Atlantic* 184: 17-22; August 1949.

MAYFARTH, FRANCES, editor. *Adventures in Human Relations.* Washington, D. C.: Association for Childhood Education, 1948.

MC CLELLAND, F. M., and RATLIFF, JOHN A. "The Use of Sociometry as an Aid in Promoting Social Adjustment in a Ninth Grade Home Room." *Sociometry* 10: 147-53; May 1947.

MC CLUNG, LEE ALFRED. "Race Riots Aren't Necessary." *Public Affairs Pamphlets* No. 107. New York: Public Affairs Committee, 1945.

MC GREGOR, DOUGLAS, and OTHERS "The Consultant Role and Organizational Leadership." *Journal of Social Issues* 4: 2-53; Summer 1948.

MC KINNEY, FRED. "Case History Norms of Unselected Students with Emotional Problems." *Journal of Consulting Psychology* 11: 258-69; September-October 1947.

MC WILLIAMS, CAREY. *Prejudice.* Boston: Little Brown and Co., 1944.

MEAD, GEORGE H. *Mind, Self and Society.* Chicago: University of Chicago Press, 1934.

MEAD, MARGARET. *And Keep Your Powder Dry.* New York: William Morrow and Co., 1942.

MEAD, MARGARET. *From the South Seas.* New York: William Morrow and Co., 1939.

MEAD, MARGARET. *Male and Female.* New York: William Morrow and Co., 1949.

MEEK, LOIS H., and OTHERS. *The Personal-Social Development of Boys and Girls.* New York: Progressive Education Association, 1940.

MENNINGER, KARL A. *The Human Mind.* New York: Alfred A. Knopf, 1930.

MENNINGER, KARL A. *Love Against Hate.* New York: Harcourt, Brace and Co., 1942.

MENNINGER, WILLIAM C. *Psychiatry in a Troubled World.* New York: Macmillan Co., 1948.

MEYER, HAROLD D., and BRIGHTBILL, CHARLES K. *Community Recreation.* Boston: D. C. Heath and Co., 1948.

MIEL, ALICE. "A Group Studies Itself." *Teachers College Record* 49: 31-44; October 1947.

MIEL, ALICE. "Toward Democratic Socialization." *Childhood Education* 26: 50-51; October 1949.

MILLER, JOHN H. *Take a Look at Yourself.* New York: Abingdon-Cokesbury Press, 1943.

MINNEAPOLIS PUBLIC SCHOOLS. *Living and Learning in the Elementary School.* Minneapolis: Minneapolis Public Schools, 1949.

MITCHELL, ELMER D., and MASON, BERNARD S. *The Theory of Play.* New York: A. S. Barnes and Co., 1939.

MOHR, GEORGE J. "Psychiatric Problems of Adolescence." *Journal of American Medical Association* 137: 1589-92; August 28, 1948.

MOON, BUCKLIN. *The High Cost of Prejudice.* New York: Julian Messner, 1947.

MOONEY, ROSS J. *Manual To Accompany the Problem Check List, College Form.* Columbus: Bureau of Educational Research, The Ohio State University, 1942.

MOONEY, ROSS J. *A Study of Student Needs in Non-Academic Areas.* Columbus: Bureau of Educational Research, The Ohio State University, 1939.

MOORE, BERNICE MELBURN, and SUTHERLAND, ROBERT L. *Profiles of Community Action.* Austin, Texas: The Hogg Foundation, 1950.

MORENO, FLORENCE P. "Combining Role and Sociometric Testing." *Sociometry* 9: 155-61 May-August 1946.

MORENO, JACOB L. *Who Shall Survive?* New York: Beacon House, 1934.

MORGAN, CLIFFORD. *Physiological Psychology.* New York: McGraw-Hill Book Co., 1943.

MUMFORD, LEWIS. *The Condition of Man.* New York: Harcourt, Brace and Co., 1944.

MUMFORD, LEWIS. *The Culture of Cities.* New York: Harcourt, Brace and Co., 1938.

MUMFORD, LEWIS. *Faith for Living.* New York: Harcourt, Brace and Co., 1940.

MURPHY, GARDNER. *Personality—A Biosocial Approach to Origins and Structure.* New York: Harper and Brothers, 1947.

MURPHY, GARDNER; MURPHY, LOIS BARTLAY; and NEWCOMB, THEODORE M. *Experimental Social Psychology.* New York: Harper and Brothers, 1937.

MURRAY, HENRY A. *Explorations in Personality.* New York: Oxford University Press, 1938.

MYRDAL, GUNNAR. *An American Dilemma.* New York: Harper and Brothers, 1944.

NASH, JAY B. *Physical Education: Interpretations and Objectives.* New York: A. S. Barnes and Co., 1948.

NASH, JAY B. *Spectatoritis.* New York: A. S. Barnes and Co., 1934.

NASH, JAY B. *Teachable Moments.* New York: A. S. Barnes and Co., 1938.

NATIONAL ASSOCIATION FOR PHYSICAL EDUCATION OF COLLEGE WOMEN. *Practices of Promise in the Understanding and Use of the Democratic Process.* Supplement to Annual Proceedings, The Association, April 1949.

NATIONAL EDUCATION ASSOCIATION and AMERICAN ASSOCIATION OF SCHOOL AD-
MINISTRATORS, EDUCATIONAL POLICIES COMMISSION. *Learning the Ways of
Democracy.* Washington, D. C.: the Commission, 1940.

NATIONAL EDUCATION ASSOCIATION and AMERICAN ASSOCIATION OF SCHOOL AD-
MINISTRATORS, EDUCATIONAL POLICIES COMMISSION. *The Purposes of Education in American Democracy.* Washington, D. C.: the Commission, 1938.

NATIONAL EDUCATION ASSOCIATION and THE AMERICAN MEDICAL ASSOCIATION,
JOINT COMMITTEE ON HEALTH PROBLEMS IN EDUCATION. *Health Education.*
Washington, D. C.: National Education Association, 1948.

NATIONAL EDUCATION ASSOCIATION, DEPARTMENT OF SUPERVISION AND CURRIC-
ULUM DEVELOPMENT. *Group Planning in Education.* 1945 Yearbook. Washington, D. C.: the Department, 1945.

NATIONAL EDUCATION ASSOCIATION, DEPARTMENT OF SUPERVISORS AND DIREC-
TORS OF INSTRUCTION. *Leadership at Work.* Fifteenth Yearbook. Washington,
D. C.: the Department, 1943.

NATIONAL EDUCATION ASSOCIATION, DEPARTMENT OF SUPERVISORS AND DIREC-
TORS OF INSTRUCTION. *Mental Health in the Classroom.* Thirteenth Yearbook.
Washington, D. C.: the Department, 1940.

NATIONAL INSTITUTE OF SOCIAL RELATIONS. *It Pays to Talk it Over.* Washington, D. C.: National Institute of Social Relations, n.d.

NATIONAL LABORATORY IN GROUP DEVELOPMENT. *Report of the Second Summer
Laboratory Session.* National Education Association and Research Center for
Group Dynamics, University of Michigan Bulletin No. 3, 1948.

NATIONAL SOCIETY FOR THE STUDY OF EDUCATION. *Adolescence.* Forty-Third
Yearbook, Part I. Chicago: University of Chicago Press, 1944.

NATIONAL SOCIETY FOR THE STUDY OF EDUCATION. *Learning and Instruction.*
Forty-Ninth Yearbook, Part I. Chicago: University of Chicago Press, 1950.

NEWCOMB, THEODORE M., and HARTLEY, EUGENE L. *Readings in Social Psychology.* New York: Henry Holt and Co., 1947.

NEWMEYER, MARTIN H., and NEWMEYER, ESTHER S. *Leisure and Recreation.*
Revised edition. New York: A. S. Barnes and Co., 1949.

NYLEN, DONALD, and BRADFORD, LELAND P. "We Can Work Together." *National
Education Association Journal* 37: 463-58; October, 1948.

OBERTEUFFER, DELBERT. *Physical Education.* New York: Harper and Brothers,
1951.

OBERTEUFFER, DELBERT. *School Health Education.* New York: Harper and
Brothers, 1949.

O'KEEFE, PATTRIC RUTH, and FAHEY, HELEN. *Education through Physical
Activities.* St. Louis, Mo.: C. V. Mosby Co., 1949.

OLSON, WILLARD C. *Child Development.* Boston: D. C. Heath and Co., 1949.

OLSON, WILLARD C. "Human Relations in the Classroom." *National Education
Association Journal* 36: 640-41; December, 1947.

OLSON, WILLARD C. "The Improvement of Human Relations in the Classroom."
*Childhood Education* 22: 317-25; March, 1946.

OVERSTREET, HARRY A. *A Guide to Civilized Leisure.* New York: W. W. Norton
and Co., 1934.

OVERSTREET, HARRY A. *The Mature Mind.* New York: W. W. Norton and Co.,
1949.

PANZAR, MARTIN. *It's Your Future.* New York: Whittlesey House, 1943.

PATERSON, ROBERT G. *Foundations of Community Health Education.* New York: McGraw-Hill Book Co., 1950.

PATRICK, GEORGE T. *What Is Mind?* New York: Macmillan Co., 1929.

PIERCE, WELLINGTON C. *Youth Comes of Age.* New York: McGraw-Hill Book Co., 1948.

PITCAIRN-CRABBE FOUNDATION LECTURE SERIES. *Modern Education and Human Values.* Pittsburgh: University of Pittsburgh Press, 1947.

PLANT, JAMES S. *Personality and the Cultural Pattern.* New York: Commonwealth Fund, 1937.

"Portfolio of Teaching Techniques." *Educators Washington Dispatch.* Washington, D. C.: 1950.

PORTER, EDNA. *Community Wise.* New York: Woman's Press, n.d.

POTASHIN, REVA. "A Sociometric Study of Children's Friendships." *Sociometry* 9: 48-70; February 1946.

PRATT, CAROLINE. *I Learn from Children.* New York: Simon and Schuster, 1948.

PRATT, GEORGE K. *Soldier to Civilian.* New York: McGraw-Hill Book Co., 1944.

PRESCOTT, DANIEL A., editor. *Emotion and the Educative Process.* Washington, D. C.: American Council on Education, 1938.

PRESIDENT'S COMMISSION ON HIGHER EDUCATION. *Higher Education for American Democracy.* Washington, D. C.: Superintendent of Documents, 1949.

PRESSEY, LUELLA C. *Some College Students and Their Problems.* Columbus: The Ohio State University Press, 1929.

PRESSEY, SIDNEY L., and ROBINSON, FRANCIS P. *Psychology and the New Education.* New York: Harper and Brothers.

PRESSMAN, FRANK, JR., and MILLER, S. M., editors. "Participation, Culture and Personality." *Journal of Social Issues* 5: 10-11; Winter 1949.

PRICE, RUTH. *Creative Group Work on the Campus.* New York: Bureau of Publications, Teachers College, Columbia University, 1946.

RADIR, RUTH. *Modern Dance for the Youth of America.* New York: A. S. Barnes and Co., 1944.

RAINEY, HOMER P. *How Fare American Youth?* New York: Appleton-Century-Crofts, Inc., 1938.

RATHS, LOUIS E. "Criteria for a Program for Evaluation." *Educational Research Bulletin,* The Ohio State University, 17: 846; March 16, 1938.

RATHS, LOUIS E. "What Is Teaching?" *School Bulletin,* No. 3, Minneapolis Public Schools, September 30, 1948.

RAUTMAN, ARTHUR L. "The Physical Education Teacher as a Personal Model." *Journal of the American Association of Health, Physical Education and Recreation* 21: 10-14; January 1950.

REDL, FRITZ. *The Need Concept and Its Place in Educational Planning.* Washington, D. C.: Division of Child Development and Teacher Personnel, Commission on Teacher Education, American Council on Education, 1940 (mimeo.)

REMMERS, H. H., and SHUMBERG, BENJAMIN. *Examiner Manual for S. R. A. Youth Inventory.* Chicago: Science Research Associates, August 1949.

RESEARCH CENTER FOR GROUP DYNAMICS. *Human Relations,* Vol. I. Ann Arbor, Mich.: University of Michigan, 1947.

*Review of Educational Research.* December 1948

ROETHLISBERGER, FRITZ J. *Management and Morale.* Cambridge: Harvard University Press, 1942.

ROETHLISBERGER, FRITZ J., and DICKSON, WILLIAM J. *Management and the Worker.* Cambridge: Harvard University Press, 1939.

ROMNEY, G. OTT. *Off the Job Living.* New York: A. S. Barnes and Co., 1948.

ROSE, ARNOLD, and ROSE, CAROLINE. *America Divided—Minority Group Relations in the United States.* New York: Alfred A. Knopf, 1948.

RUGG, HAROLD. *Foundations for American Education.* New York: World Book Co., 1947.

RUSSELL, BERTRAND. *Authority and the Individual.* New York: Simon and Schuster, 1949.

SAUL, LEON J. *Emotional Maturity.* Philadelphia: J. P. Lippincott Co., 1947.

SCHNELL, DOROTHY. *Characteristics of Adolescence.* Minneapolis: Burgess Publishing Co., 1946.

SCHUMACHER, HENRY C. "Mental and Emotional Disturbances in Adolescence." *Journal of Child Psychology* as reprinted in *Child-Family Digest* 1: 10-20, July 1949.

"Science Panel Sees Mankind as a Unity." *United Nations Reporter* 22: 3; September 10, 1950.

SEIDENFELD, MORTON A. "The Role of Mental Hygiene in Health." *Journal of Health and Physical Education* 18: 295-96; May 1947.

SHERIF, MUZAFER. *An Outline of Social Psychology.* New York: Harper and Brothers, 1948.

SHEVIAKOV, GEORGE, and REDL, FRITZ. *Discipline for Today's Children and Youth.* Washington, D. C.: National Education Association, 1944.

SIMKHOVITCH, MARY K. *Group Life.* New York: Association Press, 1940.

SIZER, JAMES P. *The Commercialization of Leisure.* Boston: R. G. Badger, 1917.

SKUBIC, ELVERA. "A Study in Acquaintanceship and Social Status in Physical Education Classes." *Research Quarterly* 20: 80-87; March 1949.

SLAVSON, SAMUEL R. *Creative Group Education.* New York: Association Press, 1937.

SLAVSON, SAMUEL R. "Group Work and Mental Health." *The Group* 11: 4-11; May 1949.

SLAVSON, SAMUEL R. *Recreation and the Total Personality.* New York Association Press, 1948.

SMITH, BRADFORD. "In the Town Meeting Tradition." *Adult Education Journal* 8: 18-20; January 1949.

SMITH, EUGENE R., and TYLER, RALPH W. *Appraising and Recording Student Progress.* New York: Harper and Brothers, 1942.

SOROKIN, PETER. *Society, Culture and Personality.* New York: Harper and Brothers, 1947.

STAFF OF THE PHYSICAL EDUCATION DEPARTMENT, UNIVERSITY OF CALIFORNIA, LOS ANGELES. *Group Process in Physical Education.* New York: Harper and Brothers, 1951.

STEINER, JESSE F. *Americans at Play.* New York: McGraw-Hill Book Co., 1933.

STEINZOR, BERNARD. "The Intent Behind Behavior: A Study in Group Dynamics." *Educational Leadership* 5: 301-306; February 1948.

SPITZ, DAVID. *Patterns of Anti-Democratic Thought*. New York: Macmillan Co., 1949.

STOCK, DOROTHY. "An Investigation into the Interrelation Between the Self Concept and Feelings Directed Toward Other Persons and Groups." *Journal of Consulting Psychology* 13: 176-80; June 1949.

STODDARD, GEORGE A. "Patterns of Growth in Human Intelligence." *Proceedings of the National Academy of Sciences*. 27: 13; October 13, 1941.

STOGDILL, RALPH M. "Personal Factors Associated with Leadership." *Journal of Psychology* 25: 35-71; June 1948.

STOGDILL, RALPH M., and SHARTLE, C. L. "Methods for Determining Patterns of Leadership Behavior in Relation to Organization, Structure, and Objectives." *Journal of Applied Psychology* 32: 286-91; June 1948.

STRANG, RUTH. *Behavior and Background of Students in College and Secondary School*. New York: Harper and Brothers, 1937.

STRANG, RUTH. *Counseling Technics in College and Secondary School*. New York: Harper and Brothers, 1941.

STRANG, RUTH. *Group Technics in College and Secondary School*. New York: Harper and Brothers, 1938.

STRANG, RUTH. "Manifestations of Maturity in Adolescents." *Mental Hygiene* 33: 563-69; October, 1949.

STRANG, RUTH. *Reporting to Parents*. Practical Suggestions for Teaching Series No. 10. New York: Columbia University Press, 1947.

STRANG, RUTH. *The Role of the Teacher in Personnel Work*. New York: Bureau of Publications, Teachers College, Columbia University, 1935.

STRATEMEYER, FLORENCE B.; FORNER, HAMDEN L.; and MC KIM, MARGARET G. *Developing a Curriculum for Modern Living*. New York: Bureau of Publications, Teachers College, Columbia University, 1947.

STRODE, JOSEPHINE, and STRODE, PAULINE R. *Social Skills in Case Work*. New York: Harper and Brothers, 1942.

SUERKIN, ERNST R. "Human Relations in the Classroom." *School Executive* 68: 49; October, 1948.

SYMONDS, PERCIVAL M. "Changes in Sex Differences in Problems and Interests of Adolescents with Increasing Age." *Journal of Genetic Psychology* 50: 83-9; March, 1937.

TABA, HILDA. "What Is Evaluation up to and up Against in Inter-Group Education?" *Journal of Educational Sociology* 21: 19-24; September, 1947.

TABA, HILDA, and VAN TIL, WILLIAM, editors. *Democratic Human Relations*. Sixteenth Yearbook. Washington, D. C.: National Council for the Social Studies, a department of the National Education Association, 1945.

TAYLOR, CATHERINE W. *Do Adolescents Need Parents?* New York: Appleton-Century-Crofts, Inc., 1937.

TAYLOR, HAROLD A. "Education and Human Relations." *School and Society* 69: 345-47; May 1949.

TEAD, ORDWAY. *The Art of Leadership*. New York: Whittlesey House, 1935.

TEAD, ORDWAY. *The Case for Democracy and Its Meaning in Modern Life*. New York: Association Press, 1938.

TERMAN, LEWIS M. "A Preliminary Study in the Psychology and Pedagogy of Leadership." *Pedagogical Seminary* 11: 413-51; November 1904.

TERMAN, LEWIS M., and MILES, CATHERINE C. *Sex and Personality.* McGraw-Hill Book Co., 1936.

THELEN, HERBERT A. "Engineering Research in Curriculum Building." *Journal of Educational Research* 41: 577-96; April 1948.

THELEN, HERBERT. "Group Leaders Look at Frustration." *Educational Leadership* 7: 260-66; January 1950.

TOLMAN, EDWARD C. "The Psychology of Social Issues." *Journal of Social Issues,* Supplement Series No. 3, December 1949.

TOOGOOD, RUTH. "A Survey of Recreational Interests and Pursuits of College Women." *Research Quarterly* 10: 90-100; October 1939.

TRAGER, HELEN, and BROWN, SPENCER. *Making Democracy Work in Your Community.* New York: Bureau of International Education for Anti-Defamation League of B'nai B'rith. n.d.

TRAGER, HELEN, and RADKE, MARIAN. "Guidance for Human Relations Education." *Childhood Education* 25: 210-5; January 1949.

TRAGER, HELEN, and RADKE, MARIAN. *Guidance for Human Relations Education.* New York: Bureau for International Education, 1942.

TRAXLER, ARTHUR. *Techniques of Guidance.* New York: Harper and Brothers, 1945.

TRAYER, MAURICE E., and PACE, CHARLES R. *Evaluation in Teacher Education.* Washington, D. C.: American Council on Education, 1944.

TRECKER, HARLEIGH B. *Social Group Work.* New York: Woman's Press, 1948.

TUCKER, EDYTHE. "A Functioning School Health Council." *Journal of Health and Physical Education* 19: 321; May 1948.

"Two Lessons of Group Dynamics." *Educators Washington Dispatch.* Washington, D. C., 1948.

TYLER, RALPH. "Techniques for Evaluating Behavior." *Educational Research Bulletin,* The Ohio State University 13: 1-12; January 17, 1934.

UNITED STATES DEPARTMENT OF AGRICULTURE, BUREAU OF AGRICULTURAL ECONOMICS. *Group Discussion and Its Techniques.* Washington, D. C.: United States Government Printing Office, n.d.

UTTERBACK, WILLIAM E. *Decision Through Discussion.* Columbus: The Ohio State University Press, 1948.

WARNER, W. LLOYD. *Democracy in Jonesville.* New York: Harper and Brothers, 1949.

WARNER, W. LLOYD; HAVIGHURST, ROBERT J.; and LOEB, MARTIN B. *Who Shall Be Educated?* New York: Harper and Brothers, 1944.

WATSON, GOODWIN B. *Action for Unity.* New York: Harper and Brothers, 1947.

WATSON, GOODWIN. "What Are the Effects of a Democratic Atmosphere on Children?" *Progressive Education* 17: 336-42; May 1940.

*What Schools Can Do—101 Patterns of Educational Practice.* New York: Columbia University Press, 1946.

WICKMAN, E. KOESTER. *Children's Behavior and Teacher's Attitudes.* New York: Commonwealth Fund, 1928.

WILLIAMS, JESSE FEIRING. *Principles of Physical Education.* Fifth edition. Philadelphia: W. B. Saunders Co., 1948.

WILLIAMS, JESSE FEIRING, and ABERNATHY, RUTH. *Health Education in Schools.* New York: Ronald Press, 1949.

WILLIAMS, JESSE FEIRING, and BROWNELL, CLIFFORD. *The Administration of Health and Physical Education.* Philadelphia: W. B. Saunders Co., 1947.

WILSON, GERTRUDE, and RYLAND, GLADYS. *Social Group Work Practice.* Boston: Houghton Mifflin Co., 1949.

WINSLOW, C. E. A. *The School Health Program.* New York: McGraw-Hill Book Co., 1938.

WITTY, PAUL. "An Analysis of the Personality Traits of the Effective Teacher." *Journal of Educational Research* 40: 662-71; May 1947.

WRENN, G. GILBERT, and BELL, REGINALD. *Student Personal Problems.* New York: Farrar and Rinehart, 1942.

WRENN, G. GILBERT, and HARLEY, DUDLEY L. *Time on Their Hands.* Washington, D. C.: American Council on Education, 1941.

WRIGHT, HERBERT F. "How the Psychology of Motivation Is Related to Curriculum Development." *Journal of Educational Psychology* 39: 149-56; November 1948.

WRINKLE, WILLIAM L. *Improving Marking and Reporting Practices in Elementary and Secondary Schools.* New York: Rinehart and Co., 1947.

YAEGER, WILLIAM A. *Home, School, Community Relations.* Pittsburgh: University of Pittsburgh Press, 1939.

YOUNG, KIMBALL. *Personality and Problems of Adjustment.* New York: F. S. Crofts and Co., 1941.

YOUNG, KIMBALL. *Sociology, A Study of Society and Culture.* New York: American Book Co., 1949.

YOUNG, L. L. "Sociometric and Related Techniques for Appraising Social Status in an Elementary School." *Sociometry* 10: 168-77; May 1947.

ZACHARY, CAROLINE B. *Emotion and Conduct in Adolescence.* New York: Appleton-Century-Crofts, Inc., 1940.

ZANDER, ALVIN F. "On the Symptoms and Survival of Senile Groups." *Educational Leadership* 5: 319-22; February 1948.

ZANDER, ALVIN F.; LIPPITT, RONALD A.; and HENDRY, CHARLES. "Reality Practice in Education." *Psychodrama Monograph* No. 9. New York: Beacon House, 1948.

ZIRBES, LAURA. "The Workshop Idea." *Childhood Education* 24: 402-403; May 1948.

# INDEX OF PERSONS

# SUBJECT INDEX

[ 553 ]